Everyday Mathematics®

The University of Chicago School Mathematics Project

Math Masters

The McGraw·Hill Companies

The University of Chicago School Mathematics Project (UCSMP)
Max Bell, Director, UCSMP Elementary Materials Component; Director, *Everyday Mathematics* First Edition
James McBride, Director, *Everyday Mathematics* Second Edition
Andy Isaacs, Director, *Everyday Mathematics* Third Edition
Amy Dillard, Associate Director, *Everyday Mathematics* Third Edition

Authors
Max Bell, John Bretzlauf, Amy Dillard, Robert Hartfield, Andy Isaacs, James McBride, Kathleen Pitvorec, Peter Saecker, Robert Balfanz*, William Carroll*, Sheila Sconiers*

**First Edition only*

Technical Art
Diana Barrie

Teachers in Residence
Carla L. LaRochelle
Rebecca W. Maxcy

Editorial Assistant
Laurie K. Thrasher

Contributors
Martha Ayala, Virginia J. Bates, Randee Blair, Donna R. Clay, Vanessa Day, Jean Faszholz, James Flanders, Patti Haney, Margaret Phillips Holm, Nancy Kay Hubert, Sybil Johnson, Judith Kiehm, Deborah Arron Leslie, Laura Ann Luczak, Mary O'Boyle, William D. Pattison, Beverly Pilchman, Denise Porter, Judith Ann Robb, Mary Seymour, Laura A. Sunseri-Driscoll

Photo Credits
©Corbis, p. 114 *top right;* ©Gregory Adams/Getty Images, cover, *top right;* ©Getty Images, cover, *center,* pp. v, 68, 346 *top left, center right, bottom right;* ©Tony Hamblin; Frank Lane Picture Agency/Corbis, cover, *bottom left;* ©Ken O'Donoghue, pp. 57, 293; ©Vladimir Pcholkin/Getty Images, pp. 93 *right,* 101; ©PhotoEdit, Inc., p. 346 top *right;* ©Shutterstock, p. 346 *center left, bottom left;* ©Roger Wood/Corbis, p. 93 *left.*

This material is based upon work supported by the National Science Foundation under Grant No. ESI-9252984. Any opinions, findings, conclusions, or recommendations expressed in this material are those of the authors and do not necessarily reflect the views of the National Science Foundation.

www.WrightGroup.com

Printed in the United States of America.

Send all inquiries to:
Wright Group/McGraw-Hill
P.O. Box 812960
Chicago, IL 60681

ISBN 0-07-604589-7

8 9 QWD 12 11 10 09 08 07

The **McGraw·Hill** *Companies*

Contents

Teaching Masters 

Study Link Masters 

Unit 1

Unit 2

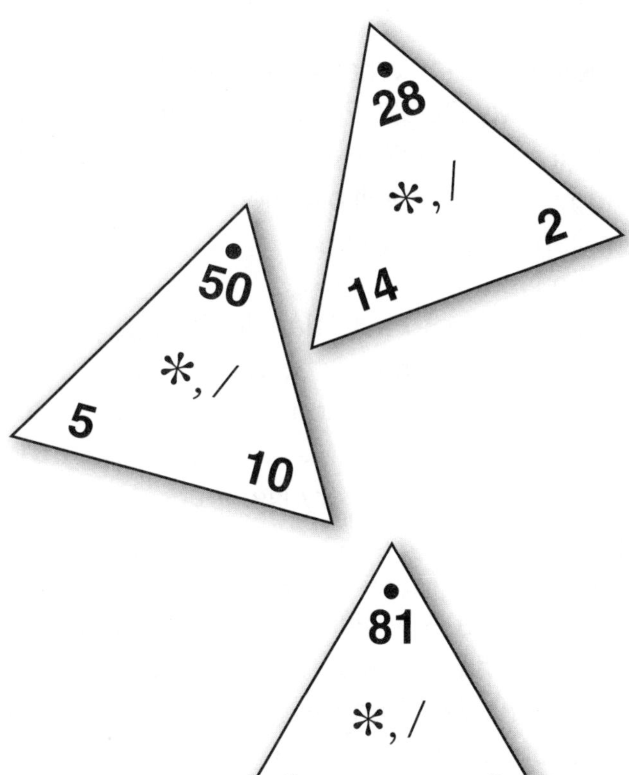

Unit 3

Unit 4

Unit 5

Unit 6

Unit 8

Unit 9

Unit 10

Unit 11

Unit 12

Project Masters

Teaching Aid Masters

Game Masters

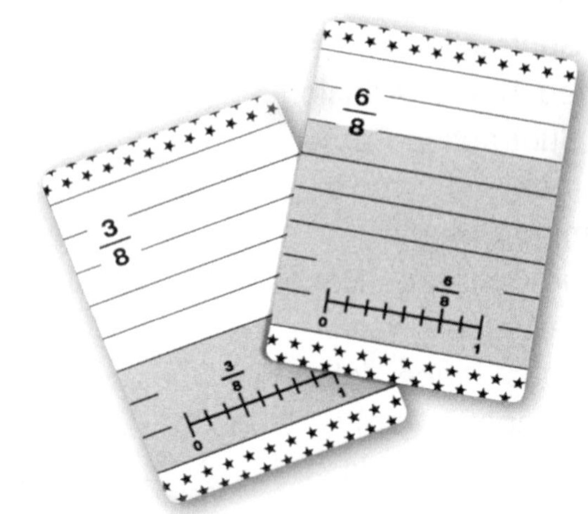

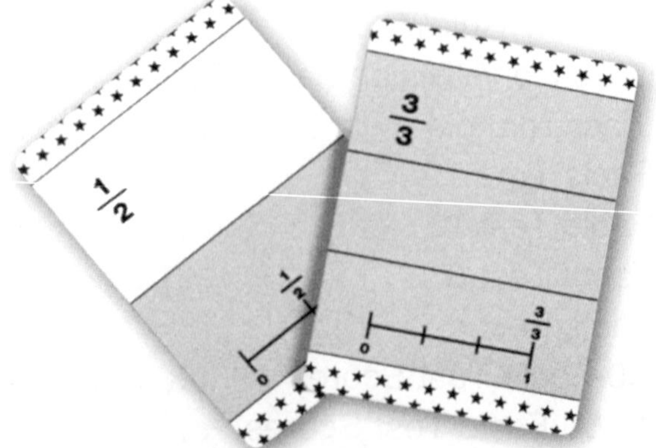

Teaching Masters and Study Link Masters

Name Date Time

LESSON 1·2

Collinear-Points Puzzle

Three or more points on the same line are called **collinear points.**

Example: Points *A, B,* and *C* are collinear points on the line below. *ABC* means that *A, B,* and *C* are collinear points, and point *B* is between points *A* and *C.*

A B C

1. The following are true statements about $\overleftrightarrow{EH}$:
   EFH and *FGH*
   The following are false statements about $\overleftrightarrow{EH}$:
   FEH and *FHG*

   E F G H

   a. Name two more true statements about line *EH.* ______

   b. Name two more false statements about line *EH.* ______

2. Place collinear points *J, K, L, M, N,* and *O* on the line below using these clues:
   - *J* and *O* are not between any points.
   - *MKL*
   - *NLJ*
   - *MKN*

3. Show a different solution to the puzzle in Problem 2.

4. Create a collinear-points puzzle on the back of this page. Be sure to give enough clues. Record your solution on the line below. Ask someone to solve your puzzle. Can the problem solver find more than one solution to your puzzle?

10

Name Date Time

STUDY LINK 1·3

Angles and Quadrangles

SRB 92 99 100

Use a straightedge to draw the geometric figures.

1. Draw 2 examples of a rectangle.

2. Draw 2 examples of a trapezoid.

3. How are the polygons in Problems 1 and 2 similar? How are they different?

4. a. Draw right angle *DEF.*

   b. What is the vertex of the angle? Point ______

   c. What is another name for ∠*DEF*? ∠ ______

5. Draw an angle that is larger than a right angle. Label the vertex *K.*

Practice

6. 9 + 8 = ______
7. 7 + 8 = ______
8. 30 + 80 = ______
9. ______ = 50 + 40
10. ______ = 17 + 94
11. 158 + 93 = ______

11

Name Date Time

Unit 1: Family Letter

Introduction to *Fourth Grade Everyday Mathematics*®

Welcome to *Fourth Grade Everyday Mathematics.* It is part of an elementary school mathematics curriculum developed by the University of Chicago School Mathematics Project (UCSMP).

Everyday Mathematics offers students a broad background in mathematics. Some approaches may differ from those you used as a student, but the approaches used are based on research, field test results, and the mathematics students will need in this century.

Fourth Grade Everyday Mathematics emphasizes the following content:

Algebra and Uses of Variables Reading, writing, and solving number sentences

Algorithms and Procedures Exploring addition, subtraction, multiplication, and division methods; inventing individual procedures and algorithms; and experimenting with calculator procedures

Coordinate Systems and Other Reference Frames Using numbers in reference frames: number lines, coordinates, times, dates, and latitude and longitude

Exploring Data Collecting, organizing, displaying, and interpreting numerical data

Functions, Patterns, and Sequences Designing, exploring, and using geometric and number patterns

Geometry and Spatial Sense Developing an intuitive sense about 2- and 3-dimensional objects, their properties, uses, and relationships

Measures and Measurement Exploring metric and U.S. customary measures: linear, area, volume, weight; and exploring geographical measures

Numbers, Numeration, and Order Relations Reading, writing, and using whole numbers, fractions, decimals, percents, negative numbers; and exploring scientific notation

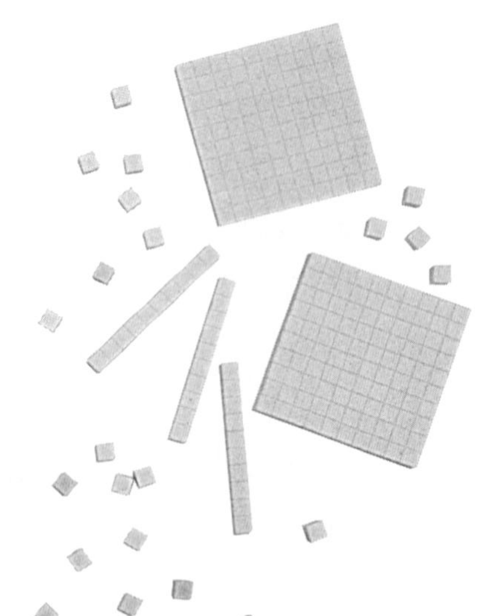

Operations, Number Facts, and Number Systems Practicing addition and subtraction to proficiency; and developing multiplication and division skills

Problem Solving and Mathematical Modeling Investigating methods for solving problems using mathematics in everyday situations

Naming and Constructing Geometric Figures

During the next few weeks, the class will study the geometry of 2-dimensional shapes. Students will examine definitions and properties of shapes and the relationships among them. Students will use compasses to construct shapes and to create their own geometric designs.

Please keep this Family Letter for reference as your child works through Unit 1.

Vocabulary

Important terms in Unit 1:

concave (nonconvex) polygon A polygon in which at least one vertex is "pushed in."

concave polygon

convex polygon A polygon in which all vertices are "pushed outward."

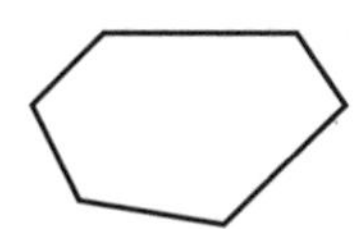

convex polygon

endpoint A point at the end of a line segment or a ray.

line Informally, a straight path that extends infinitely in opposite directions.

line segment A straight path joining two points. The two points are called the endpoints of the segment.

parallelogram A quadrilateral that has two pairs of parallel sides. Opposite sides of a parallelogram have equal lengths. Opposite angles of a parallelogram have the same measure.

polygon A 2-dimensional figure that is made up of three or more line segments joined end to end to make one closed path. The line segments of a polygon may not cross.

quadrangle (quadrilateral) A polygon that has four sides and four angles.

ray A straight path that extends infinitely from a point called its endpoint.

rhombus A quadrilateral whose sides are all the same length. All rhombuses are parallelograms. Every square is a rhombus, but not all rhombuses are squares.

trapezoid In *Everyday Mathematics,* a quadrilateral that has exactly one pair of parallel sides.

vertex The point where the rays of an angle, the sides of a polygon, or the edges of a polyhedron meet.

Do-Anytime Activities

To work with your child on concepts taught in this unit, try these interesting and rewarding activities:

1. Help your child discover everyday uses of geometry as found in art, architecture, jewelry, toys, and so on.
2. See how many words your child can think of that have Greek/Latin prefixes such as *tri-, quad-, penta-, hexa-,* and *octa-*.
3. Help your child think of different ways to draw or make figures without the use of a compass, protractor, or straightedge. For example, you can trace the bottom of a can to make a circle, bend a straw to form a triangle, or make different shapes with toothpicks.
4. Challenge your child to draw or build something, such as a toothpick bridge, using triangular and square shapes. Or show pictures of bridges and point out the triangles used in bridges to provide support.

Building Skills through Games

In Unit 1, your child will play the following games.

Addition Top-It See *Student Reference Book,* page 263. This game provides practice with addition facts.

Polygon Pair-Up See *Student Reference Book,* page 258. This game provides practice identifying properties of polygons.

Sprouts See *Student Reference Book,* page 313. This game provides practice with simple vertex-edge graphs and developing game strategies.

Subtraction Top-It See *Student Reference Book,* pages 263 and 264. This is a variation of *Addition Top-It* and provides practice with subtraction facts.

Sz'kwa See *Student Reference Book,* page 310. This game provides practice with intersecting line segments and developing game strategies.

As You Help Your Child with Homework

As your child brings assignments home, you may want to go over the instructions together, clarifying them as necessary. The answers listed below will guide you through this unit's Study Links.

Study Link 1•2

2. a. 

b. 

c. The line has arrows on both ends, but the line segment does not.

3. a. D C

b. No. A ray's endpoint must be listed first when naming a ray.

4. A ruler has markings on it, so it can be used to measure.

Study Link 1•3

Sample answers:

1. 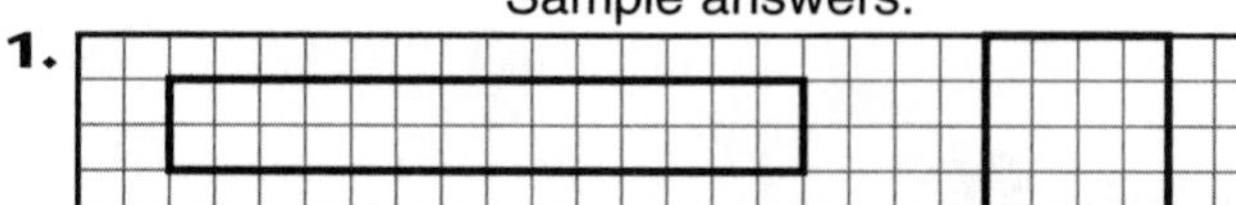

2. 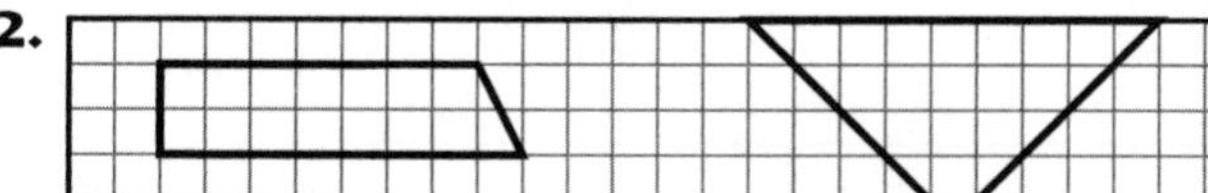

3. The polygons in Problems 1 and 2 have 4 sides and at least 1 pair of parallel sides. The Problem 1 polygons have 2 pairs of equal, parallel sides and all right angles.

4. a. 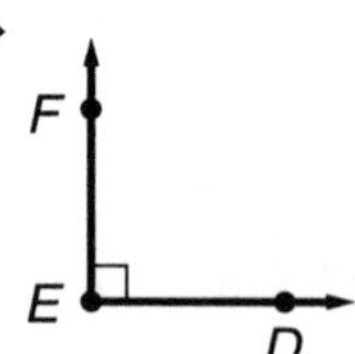

b. *E* **c.** *FED*

5. 

Study Link 1•4

1. Sample answer:

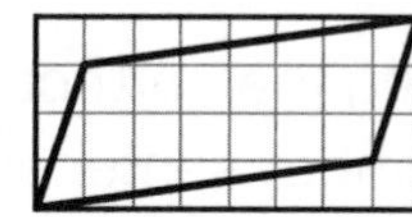

2. a. yes **b.** yes **c.** yes **d.** no

3. Sample answer:

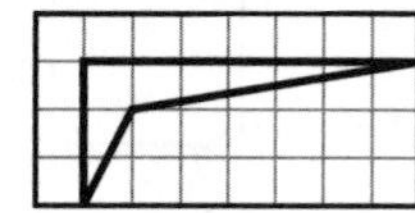

4. kite

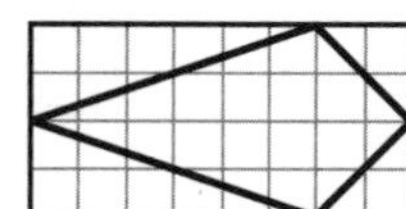

Study Link 1•5

1. rectangle **2.** Equilateral triangle

3. rhombus

Study Link 1•6

1. A, B, C, E, F, G, I **2.** B, C

3. C, E, F, I **4.** A

5. A, B, D, F, G, H, I **6.** D, G, H

7. 2

Study Link 1•8

1. Sample answers:

a. square

c. hexagon

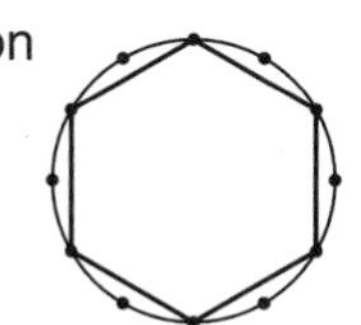

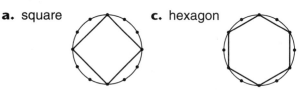

2. Sample answer: Sides are all the same length, and interior angles are all the same measure.

Name Date Time

Relation-Symbol *Top-It*

1. Cut out the relation symbol cards at the bottom of the page.

2. Shuffle 4 each of the number cards 0–9 and place the deck facedown on the table.

3. Each student turns over 2 cards and makes the largest 2-digit number possible.

4. Students take turns placing the correct relation symbol (>, <, or =) between the cards and reading the number sentence.

Example:

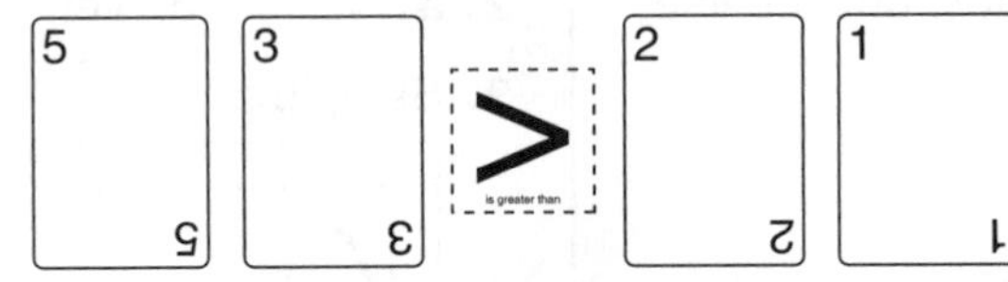

53 is greater than 21.

5. The student with the larger number takes the cards.

6. Play ends when not enough cards are left for each student to have another turn. The student with the most cards wins.

7. Record number sentences for several rounds of play.

53 > 21

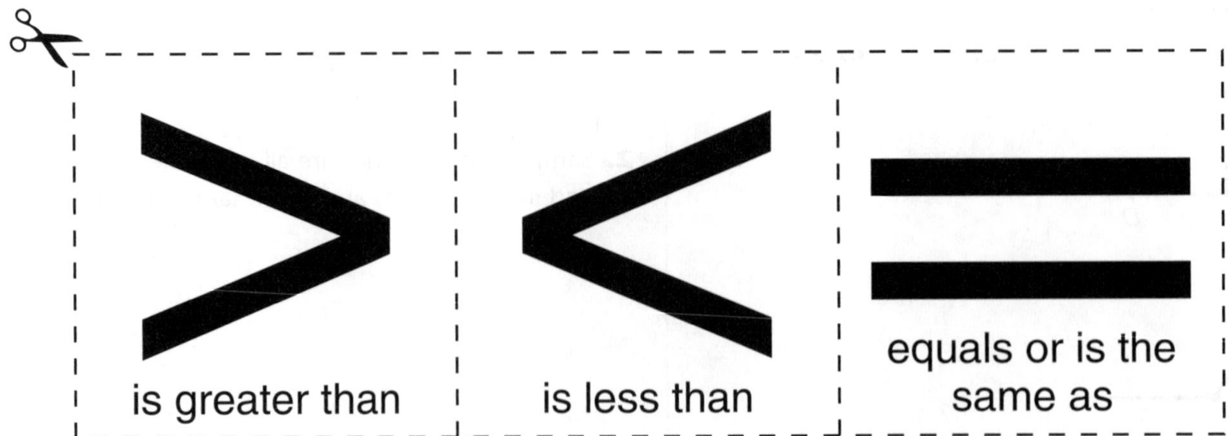

Name Date Time

Symbols Scavenger Hunt

Mathematicians use symbols instead of writing out words such as *is greater than, is less than,* and *equals.* Search the *Student Reference Book* to find as many symbols as you can. Record the symbols and the words they stand for in the table below.

Symbol	Meaning
$>$	*is greater than*

Name Date Time

Symbols Scavenger Hunt

Mathematicians use symbols instead of writing out words such as *is greater than, is less than,* and *equals.* Search the *Student Reference Book* to find as many symbols as you can. Record the symbols and the words they stand for in the table below.

Symbol	Meaning
$>$	*is greater than*

Name ________________ Date ________________ Time ________________

STUDY LINK 1·2

Line Segments, Lines, and Rays

1. List at least 5 things in your home that remind you of line segments.

____

____

____

Use a straightedge to complete Problems 2 and 3.

2. **a.** Draw and label line *AB*.

b. Draw and label line segment *AB*.

c. Explain how your drawings of $\overleftrightarrow{AB}$ and $\overline{AB}$ are different.

____

____

3. **a.** Draw and label ray *CD*.

b. Anita says $\overrightarrow{CD}$ can also be called $\overrightarrow{DC}$. Do you agree? Explain.

____

____

4. Explain how a ruler is different from a straightedge.

____

____

Practice

5. 13 − 7 = ______ **6.** 15 − 8 = ______ **7.** ______ = 90 − 50

8. 140 − 60 = ______ **9.** ______ = 57 − 39 **10.** 115 − 86 = ______

Name Date Time

Geoboard Line Segments

A **line segment** is made up of 2 points and the straight path between them. Rubber bands can be used to represent line segments on a geoboard.

Example:

This line segment touches 5 pins.

Practice making line segments, and then follow the directions below.

Record your work.

1. Make a line segment that touches 4 pins.

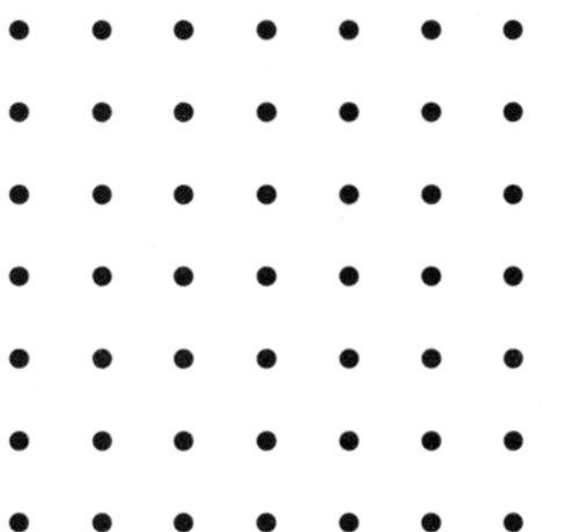

2. Make a line segment that touches 4 different pins.

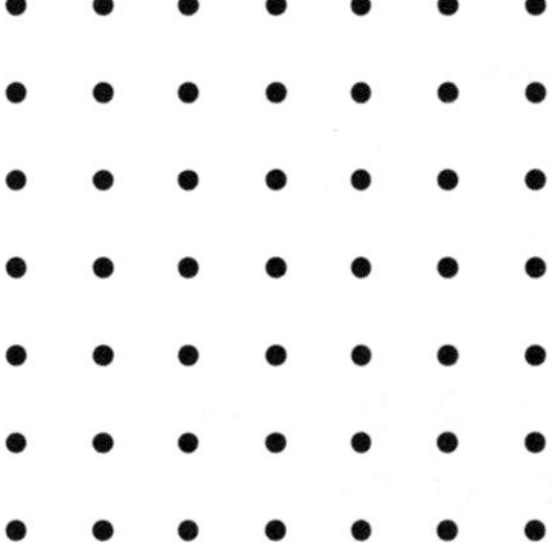

3. Make the shortest line segment possible.

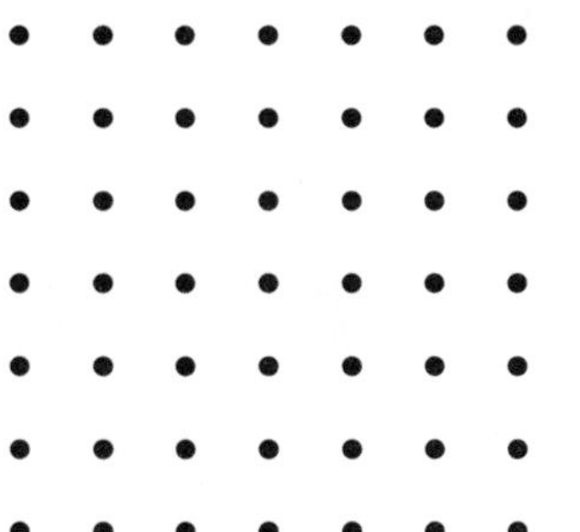

4. Make the longest line segment possible.

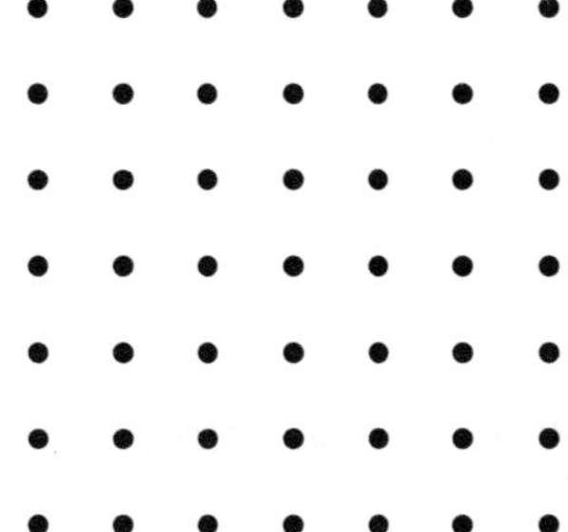

5. Cami says she cannot make a **line** on her geoboard. Do you agree? Explain why or why not. (*Hint:* Look up **line** in the glossary of your *Student Reference Book.*)

____

____

Name Date Time

LESSON 1•2

Collinear-Points Puzzle

Three or more points on the same line are called **collinear points.**

Example: Points *A, B,* and *C* are collinear points on the line below. *ABC* means that *A, B,* and *C* are collinear points, and point *B* is between points *A* and *C.*

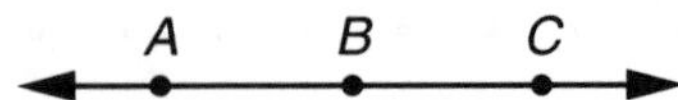

1. The following are true statements about $\overleftrightarrow{EH}$:
EFH and *FGH*
The following are false statements about $\overleftrightarrow{EH}$:
FEH and *FHG*

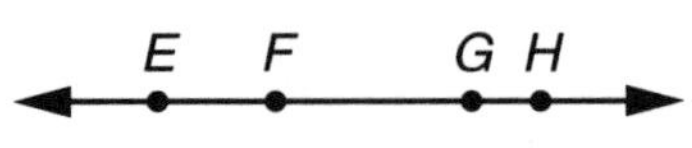

a. Name two more true statements about line *EH.* ____________________

____

b. Name two more false statements about line *EH.* ____________________

____

2. Place collinear points *J, K, L, M, N,* and *O* on the line below using these clues:

- *J* and *O* are not between any points.
- *MKL*
- *NLJ*
- *MKN*

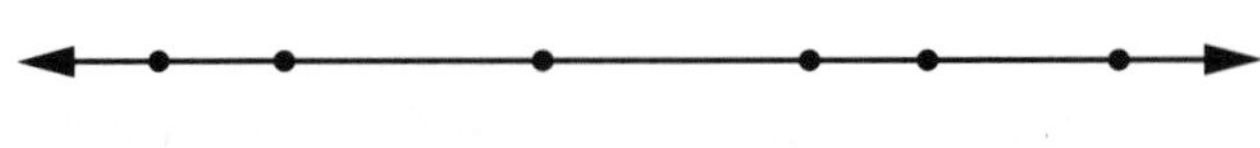

3. Show a different solution to the puzzle in Problem 2.

4. Create a collinear-points puzzle on the back of this page. Be sure to give enough clues. Record your solution on the line below. Ask someone to solve your puzzle. Can the problem solver find more than one solution to your puzzle?

Name Date Time

Angles and Quadrangles

Use a straightedge to draw the geometric figures.

1. Draw 2 examples of a rectangle.

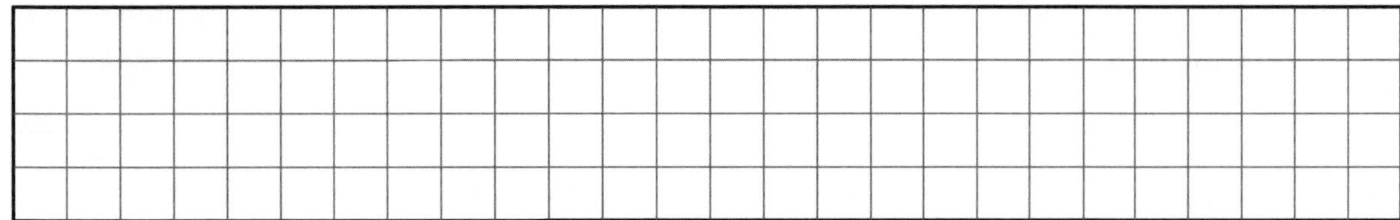

2. Draw 2 examples of a trapezoid.

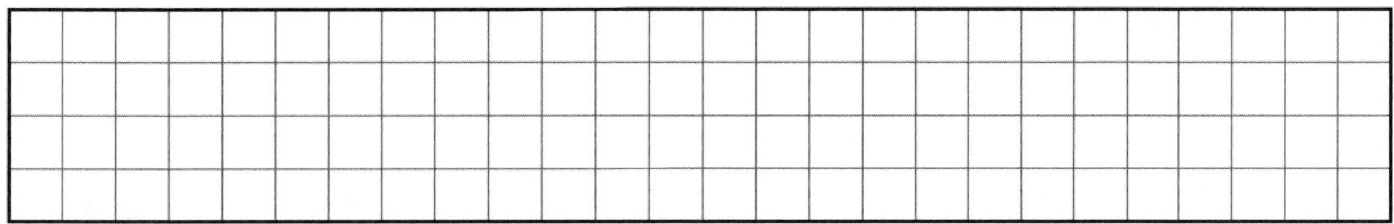

3. How are the polygons in Problems 1 and 2 similar? How are they different?

____

____

____

4. **a.** Draw right angle *DEF*.

b. What is the vertex of the angle? Point ________

c. What is another name for $\angle DEF$? $\angle$ ________

5. Draw an angle that is larger than a right angle. Label the vertex *K*.

Practice

6. $9 + 8 =$ ________

7. $7 + 8 =$ ________

8. $30 + 80 =$ ________

9. ________ $= 50 + 40$

10. ________ $= 17 + 94$

11. $158 + 93 =$ ________

Name Date Time

LESSON 1·3

Pattern-Block Sort

Label one sheet of paper: **These fit the rule.**
Label another sheet of paper: **These do NOT fit the rule.**

Sort the pattern blocks (hexagon, trapezoid, square, triangle, 2 rhombuses) according to the rules given below. Then use the shapes marked "PB" on your Geometry Template to record the results of your sort.

1. Exactly 4 sides

These fit the rule.	These do NOT fit the rule.

2. All sides the same length

These fit the rule.	These do NOT fit the rule.

3. 4 sides *and* all sides the same length

These fit the rule.	These do NOT fit the rule.

4. All angles the same measure, *and* all sides the same length

These fit the rule.	These do NOT fit the rule.

5. Make up your own rule. Sort the pattern blocks according to your rule. Record your rule and the pattern blocks that fit your rule on the back of this page.

Name Date Time

Polygon Search

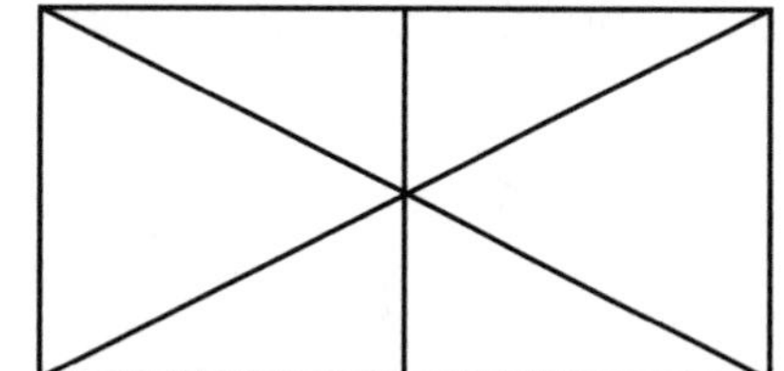

1. Study the figure at the right.

a. How many triangles do you see?

______

b. How many triangles have a right angle?

______

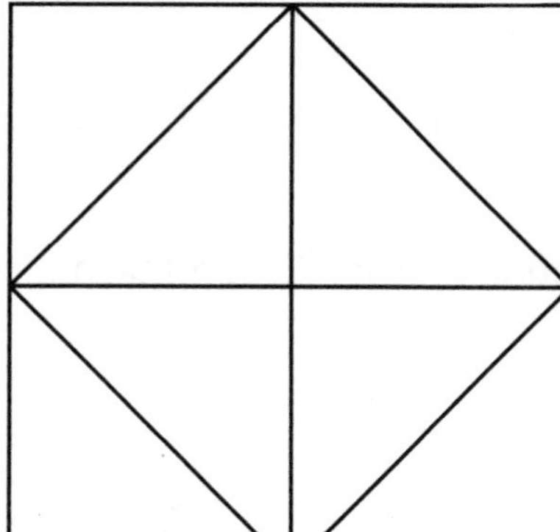

2. Study the figure at the right.

a. How many squares do you see?

______

b. How many triangles?

______

c. How many rectangles that are *not* squares?

______

3. Make up a geometry puzzle like the one in Problem 2. Use a straightedge to draw line segments to connect some of the dots in the array. Write the answers on the back of this page. Then ask someone to count the number of different polygons in your puzzle.

Name Date Time

Math Message: Properties of Polygons

All of these have something in common.

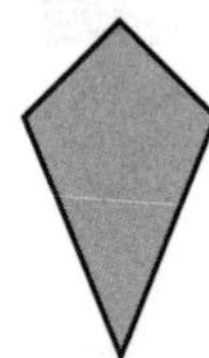   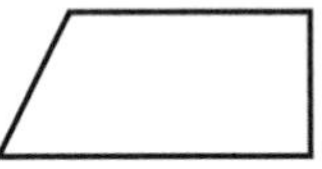 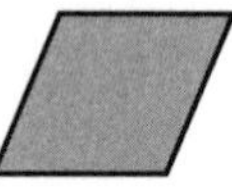

None of these has it.

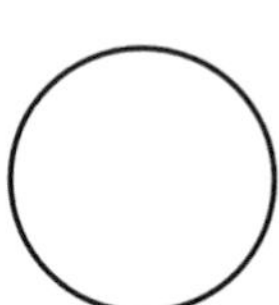 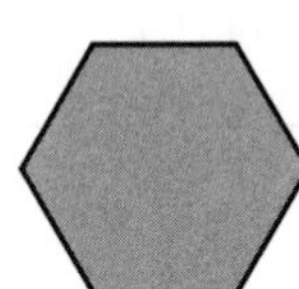   

1. Which of these has it? Circle them.

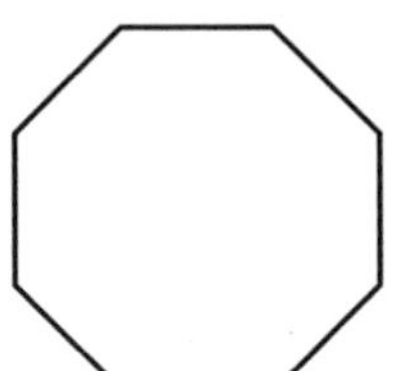 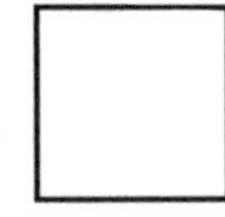 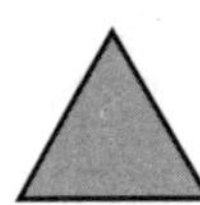 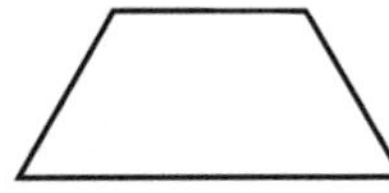  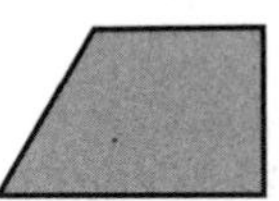

2. What property do the circled polygons have in common? ______________________

____

____

3. Use your straightedge to draw a polygon that has this property.

Name Date Time

Classifying Quadrangles

1. A parallelogram is a quadrangle (quadrilateral) that has 2 pairs of parallel sides.

Draw a parallelogram.

2. Answer *yes* or *no*. Explain your answer.

a. Is a rectangle a parallelogram? ____________

____

b. Is a square a parallelogram? ____________

____

c. Is a square a rhombus? ____________

____

d. Is a trapezoid a parallelogram? ____________

____

3. Draw a quadrangle that has at least 1 right angle.

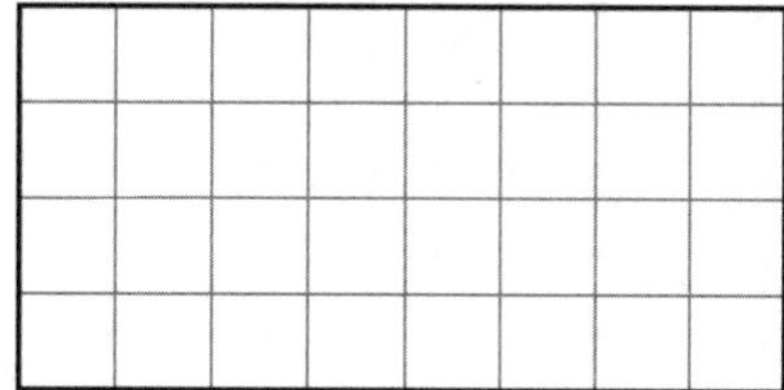

4. Draw a quadrangle that has 2 pairs of equal sides but is NOT a parallelogram.

This is called a ____________.

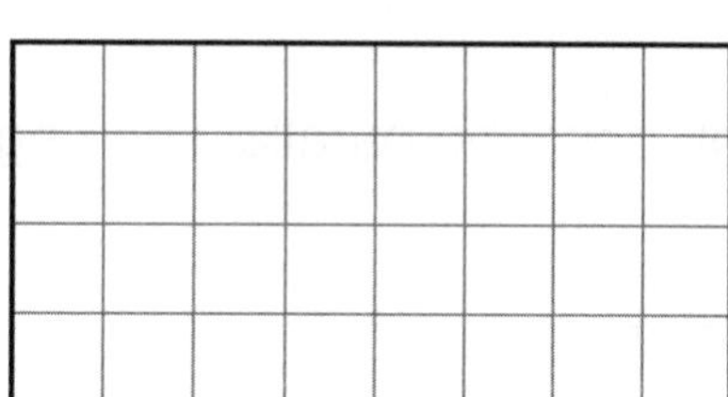

Practice

5. 12 − 6 = _______ **6.** 16 − 7 = _______ **7.** 210 − 150 = _______

8. _______ = 140 − 80 **9.** _______ = 93 − 58 **10.** 123 − 76 = _______

Name Date Time

Parallel Line Segments

1. All of these are **parallel** line segments. Make each pair on your geoboard.

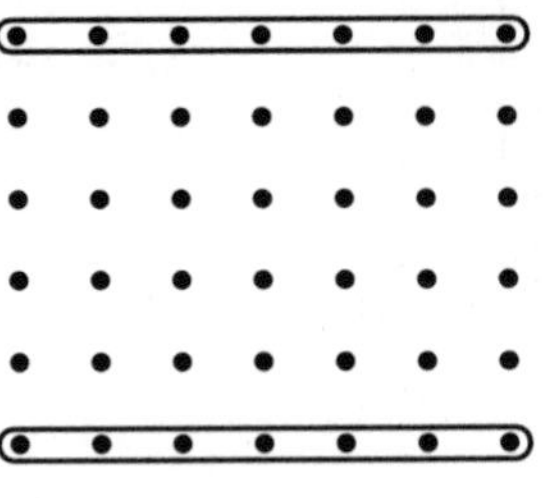
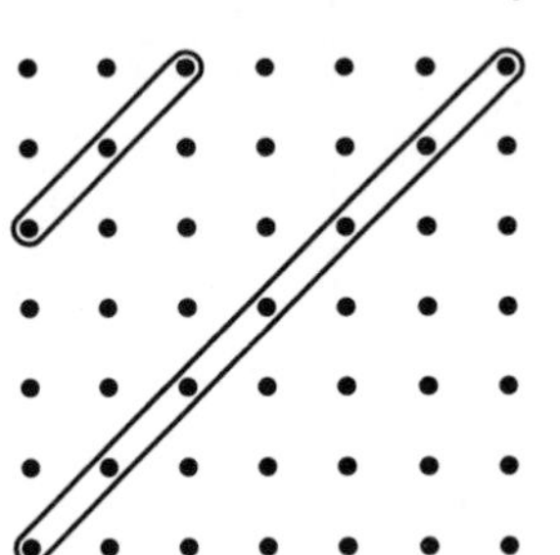
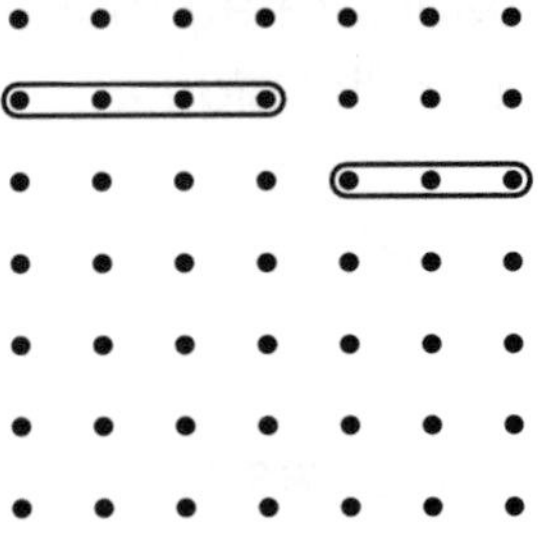

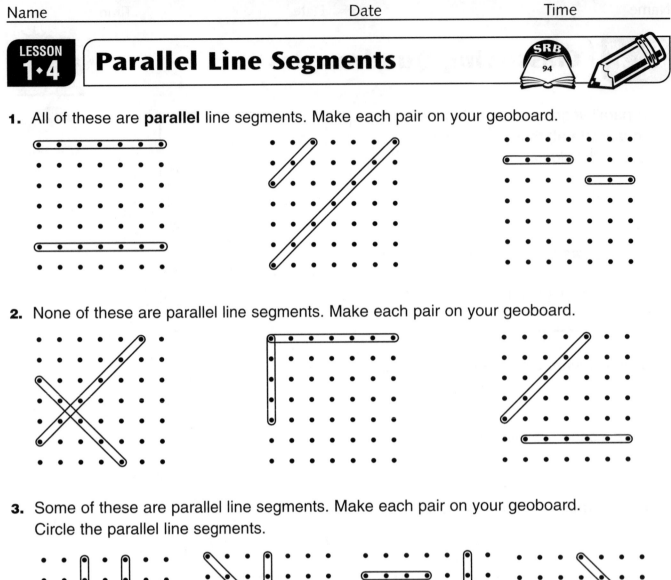

2. None of these are parallel line segments. Make each pair on your geoboard.

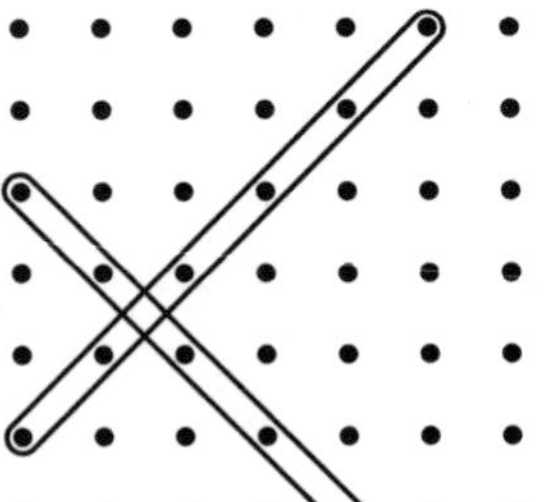
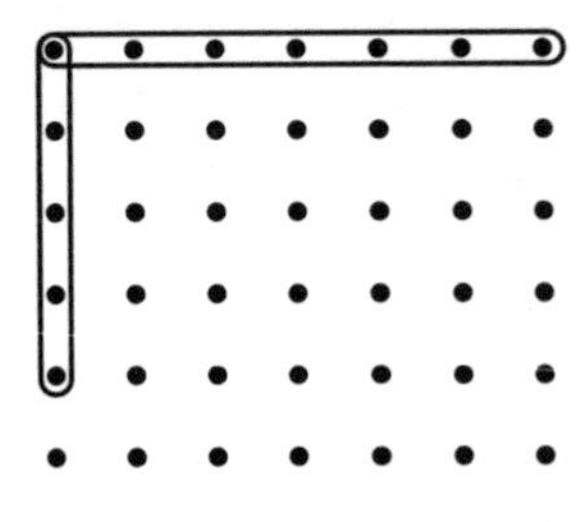
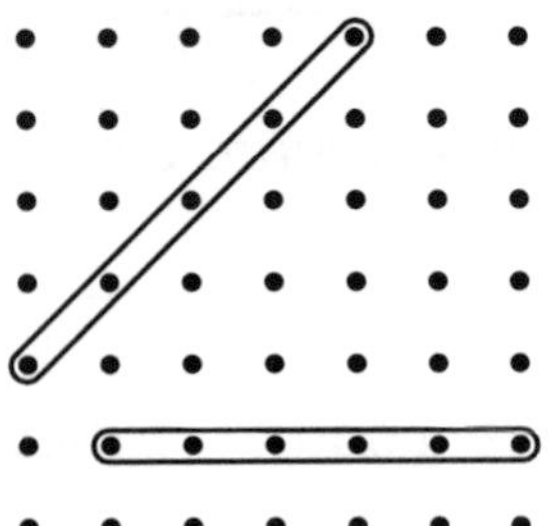

3. Some of these are parallel line segments. Make each pair on your geoboard. Circle the parallel line segments.

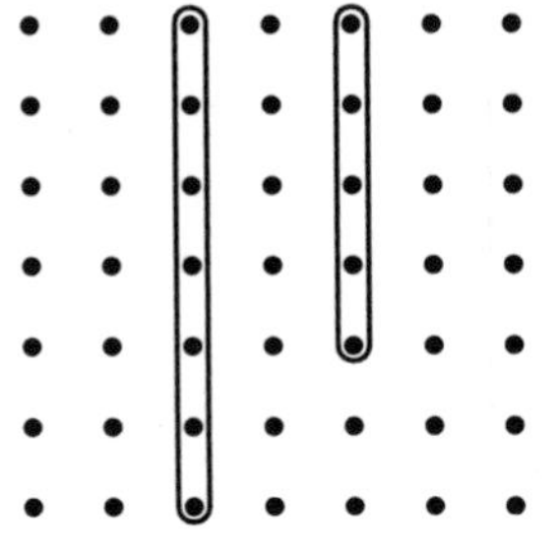
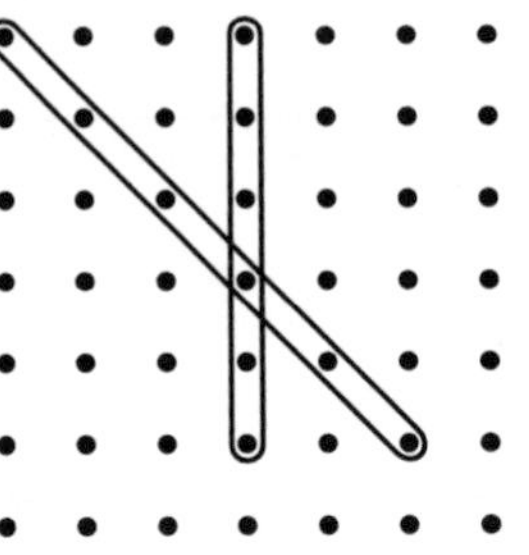
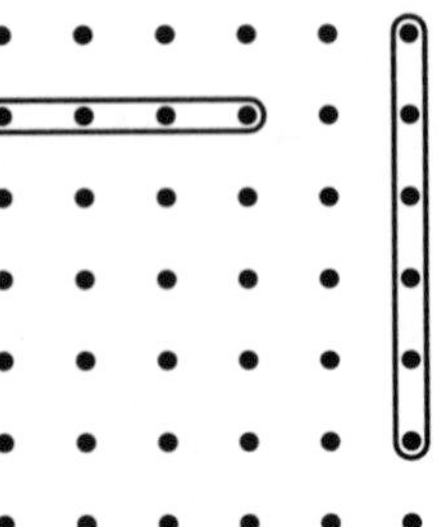
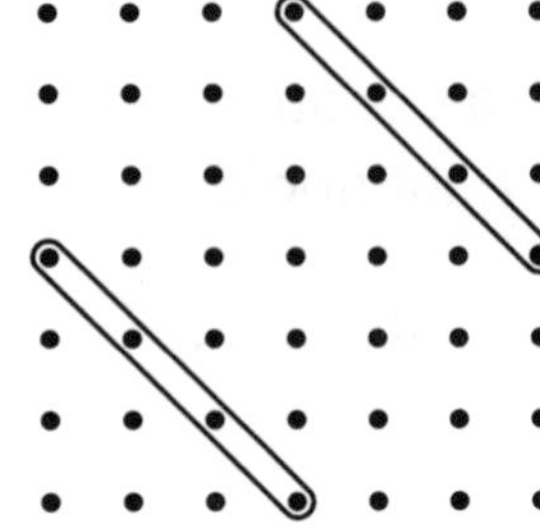

4. How would you describe parallel line segments to a friend?

____

____

____

____

5. Practice making other parallel line segments on your geoboard.

Name Date Time

Straw-Squares Puzzle

1. Gather 17 straws of the same length. Arrange them as shown to the right.

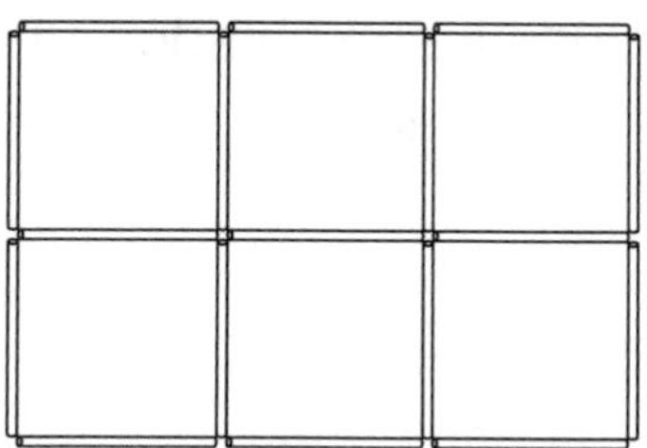

The arrangement of straws forms a rectangle. The object of this puzzle is to remove straws from the arrangement so that only 2 squares remain.

- You must remove *exactly 6* straws from the arrangement.
- You may not move any of the other straws.

2. Record your work on the picture above by marking an X on the straws you removed. Trace over the remaining straws that form the 2 squares.

Name Date Time

Straw-Squares Puzzle

1. Gather 17 straws of the same length. Arrange them as shown to the right.

The arrangement of straws forms a rectangle. The object of this puzzle is to remove straws from the arrangement so that only 2 squares remain.

- You must remove *exactly 6* straws from the arrangement.
- You may not move any of the other straws.

2. Record your work on the picture above by marking an X on the straws you removed. Trace over the remaining straws that form the 2 squares.

Name Date Time

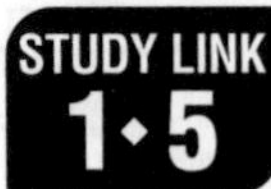

Polygon Riddles

Answer each riddle. Then use a straightedge to draw a picture of the shape in the space to the right.

1. I am a quadrangle.
I have 2 pairs of parallel sides.
All of my angles are right angles.
I am not a square.

What am I? ______________________

2. I am a polygon.
All of my sides have the same measure.
All of my angles have the same measure.
I have 3 sides.

What am I? ______________________

3. I am a polygon.
I am a quadrangle.
All of my sides are the same length.
None of my angles are right angles.

What am I? ______________________

Try This

4. On the back of this page, make up your own polygon riddle using 4 clues. Make 2 of the clues hard and 2 of the clues easy. Check your riddle by using a straightedge to draw a picture of the polygon. Ask a friend or someone at home to solve your polygon riddle.

Practice

5. $8 + 9 =$ ______ **6.** $7 + 8 =$ ______ **7.** $90 + 70 =$ ______

8. ______ $= 60 + 50$ **9.** ______ $= 54 + 59$ **10.** $185 + 366 =$ ______

Name Date Time

Polygons on a Geoboard

Practice using rubber bands to make polygons on a geoboard, then follow the directions below. Use a straightedge to record your work.

1. Make a triangle in which each side touches at least 4 pins.

2. Make a square in which each side touches at least 3 pins.

3. Make a trapezoid.

4. Make a hexagon that only touches 8 pins.

5. Compare your polygons with those of a partner. In the space below, make a list of how the polygons are alike and how they are different.

Name Date Time

LESSON 1•5

The Greedy Triangle

1. Make an equilateral triangle using your straws. Use a straightedge to draw the shape you made in the table below.

2. With the straws, continue adding one side and one angle to show all the changes that the triangle went through.

3. Complete the table below while making the shapes.

Shape	Drawing of Shape	Number of Sides	Number of Angles
equilateral triangle		3	3
quadrilateral		4	
pentagon		5	
hexagon		6	
heptagon		7	
octagon		8	
nonagon		9	
decagon		10	

Name Date Time

What Is a Kite?

These are kites.

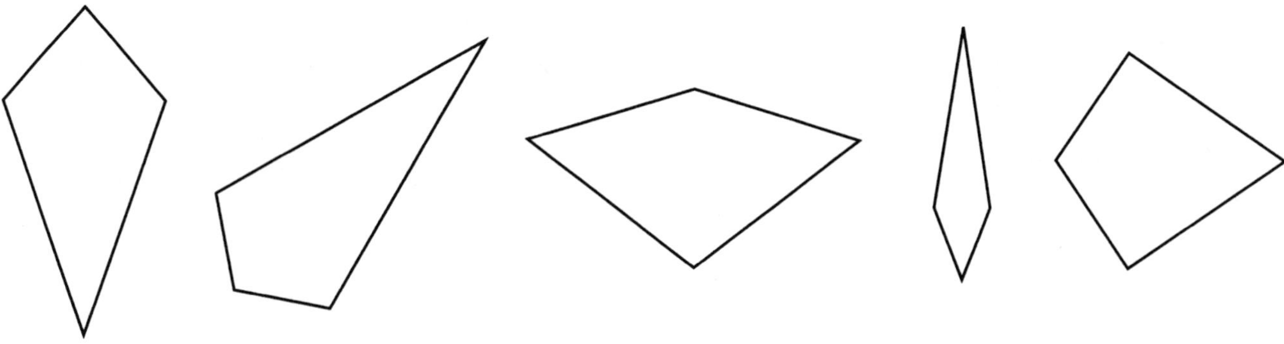

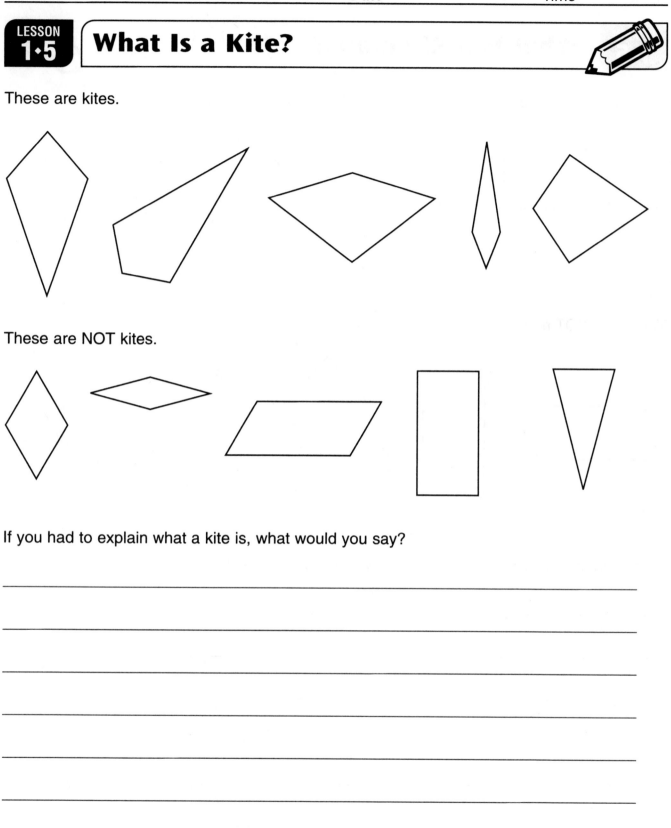

These are NOT kites.

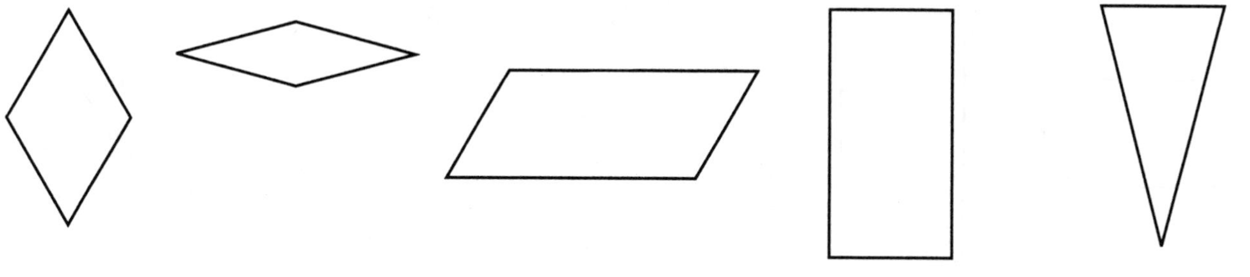

If you had to explain what a kite is, what would you say?

____

____

____

____

____

____

____

Name Date Time

What Is a Rhombus?

These are rhombuses.

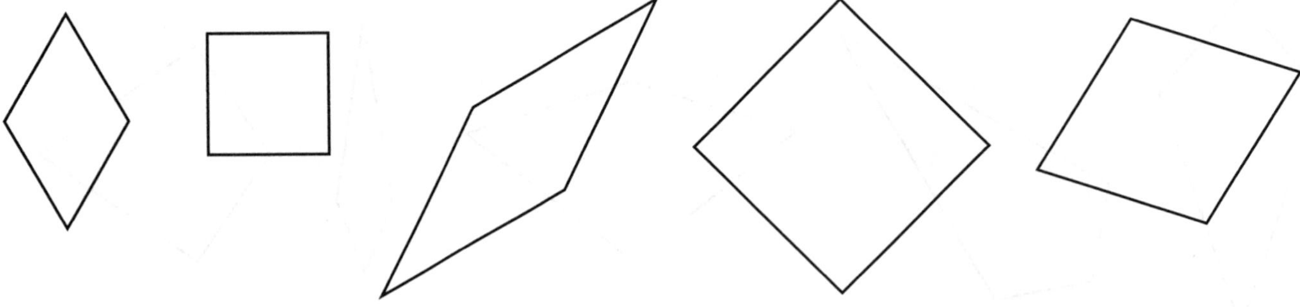

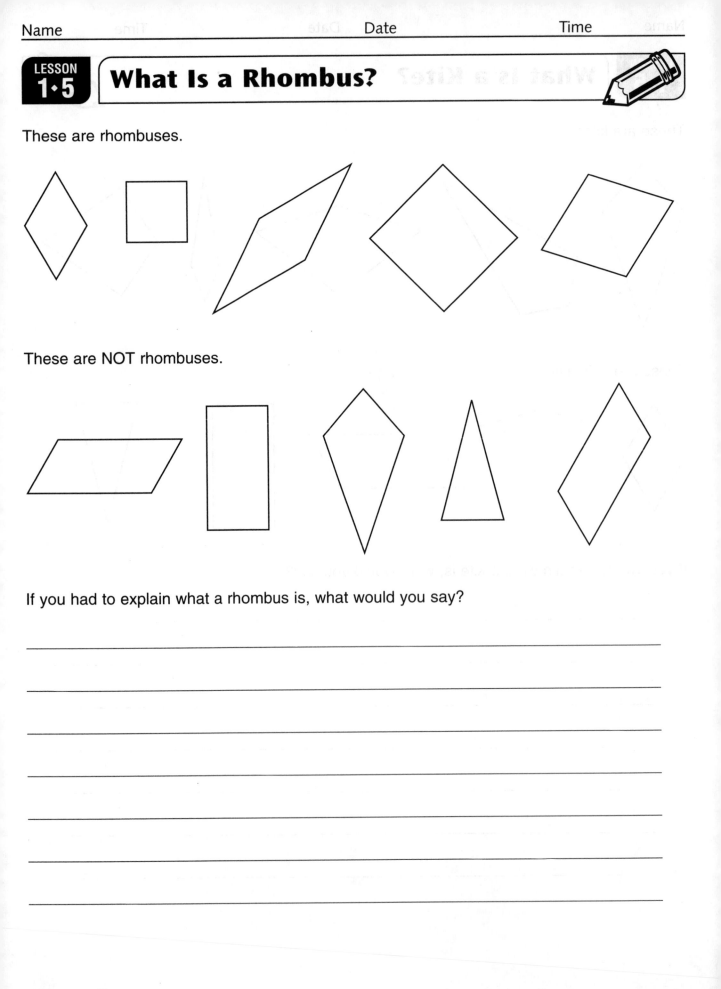

These are NOT rhombuses.

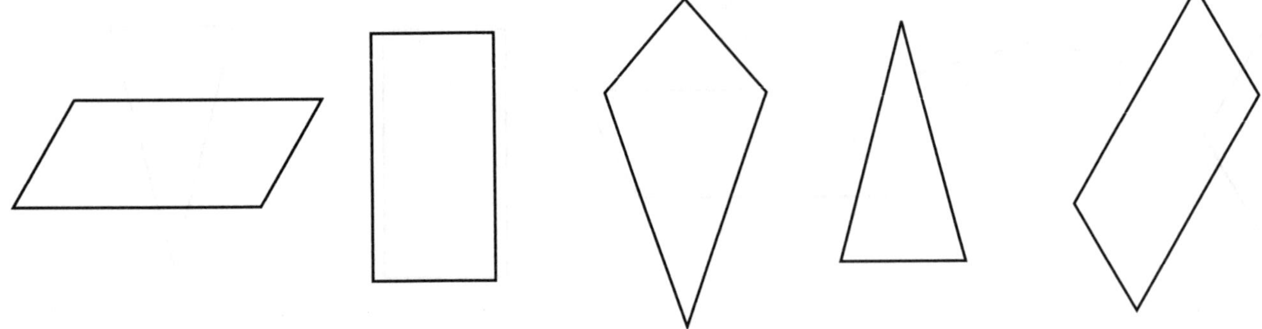

If you had to explain what a rhombus is, what would you say?

____

____

____

____

____

____

____

Name Date Time

Properties of Geometric Figures

A	B	C
D	E	F
G	H	I

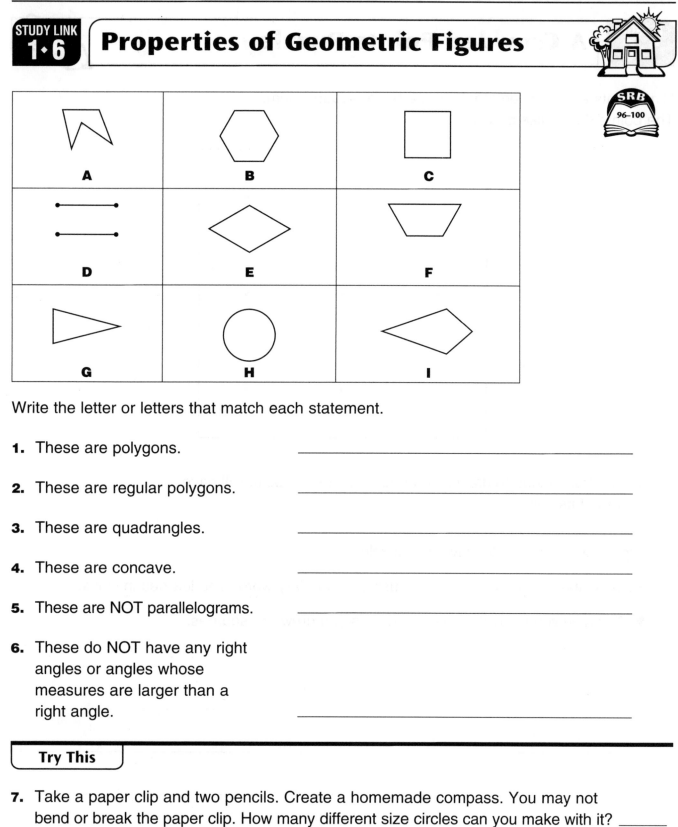

Write the letter or letters that match each statement.

1. These are polygons. ______________________
2. These are regular polygons. ______________________
3. These are quadrangles. ______________________
4. These are concave. ______________________
5. These are NOT parallelograms. ______________________
6. These do NOT have any right angles or angles whose measures are larger than a right angle. ______________________

Try This

7. Take a paper clip and two pencils. Create a homemade compass. You may not bend or break the paper clip. How many different size circles can you make with it? ______

Practice

8. 30 + 50 = ______
9. 40 + 60 = ______
10. 250 + 140 = ______
11. ______ = 80 − 20
12. ______ = 120 − 70
13. 460 − 230 = ______

Name Date Time

A Crowded-Points Puzzle

Nine points are crowded together in a large, square room.
The points do not like crowds.

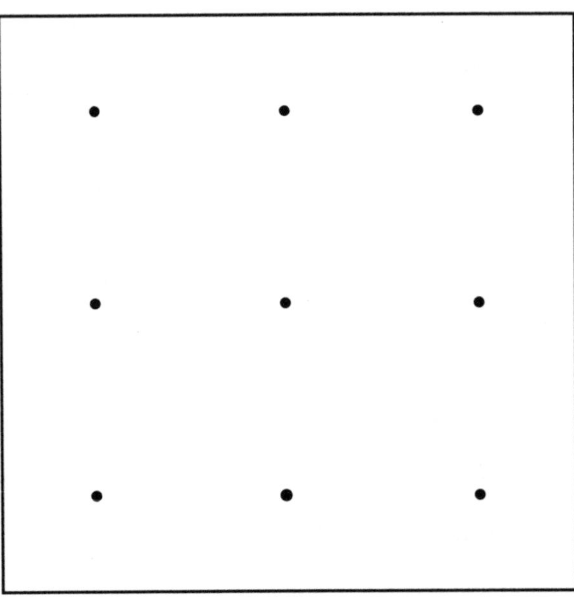

1. Use a straightedge to draw 2 squares so that each point will have a room of its own.

2. Explain what you did to solve this puzzle.

   - Describe the squares you drew using vocabulary words you learned in class.
   - Tell how you know that the 2 polygons you drew are squares.

____

____

____

____

____

Name Date Time

Math Message

Name ______________________

Date ____________

Point *B* is about 2 centimeters from point *A*. Point *C* is about 2 centimeters from point *A*.

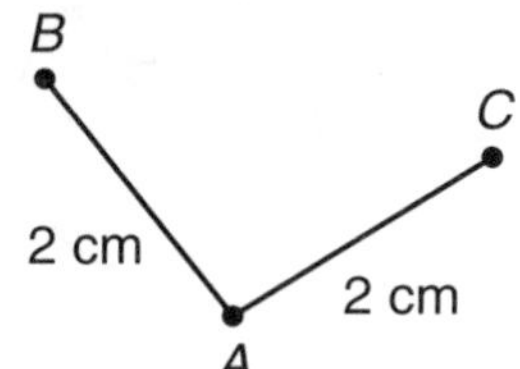

1. Draw 20 more points. Each must be about 2 centimeters from point *A*.
2. What did you draw? ____________

Name ______________________

Date ____________

Point *B* is about 2 centimeters from point *A*. Point *C* is about 2 centimeters from point *A*.

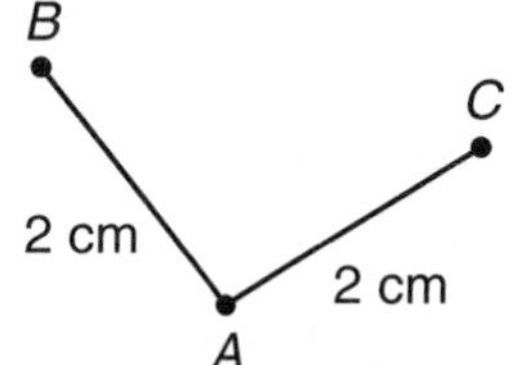

1. Draw 20 more points. Each must be about 2 centimeters from point *A*.
2. What did you draw? ____________

Name ______________________

Date ____________

Point *B* is about 2 centimeters from point *A*. Point *C* is about 2 centimeters from point *A*.

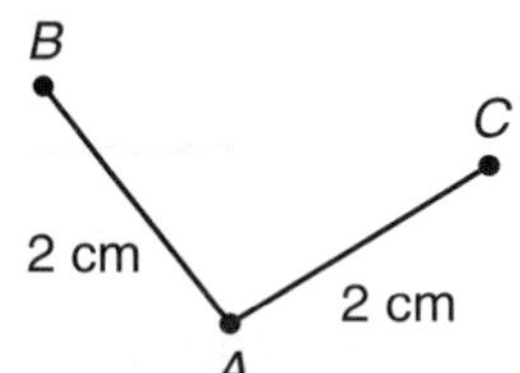

1. Draw 20 more points. Each must be about 2 centimeters from point *A*.
2. What did you draw? ____________

Name ______________________

Date ____________

Point *B* is about 2 centimeters from point *A*. Point *C* is about 2 centimeters from point *A*.

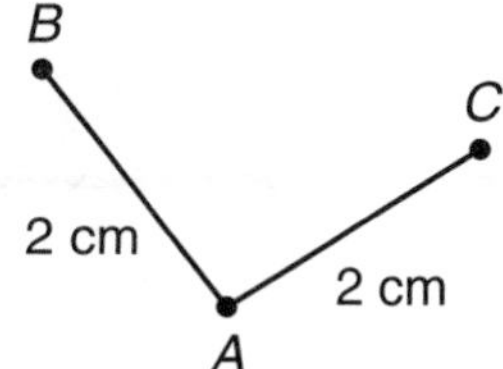

1. Draw 20 more points. Each must be about 2 centimeters from point *A*.
2. What did you draw? ____________

Name Date Time

STUDY LINK 1•7 The Radius of a Circle

1. Find 3 circular objects. Trace around them to make 3 circles in the space below or on the back of this page. For each circle, do the following:

   a. Draw a point to mark the approximate center of the circle. Then draw a point on the circle.

   b. Use a straightedge to connect these points. This line segment is a **radius** of the circle.

   c. Use a ruler to measure the radius to the nearest centimeter. If you do not have a ruler at home, cut out the one at the bottom of this page.

   d. Record the measure of the radius next to the circle.

Example:

Practice

2. ______ = 80 + 20
3. ______ = 30 + 90
4. 580 + 370 = ______
5. 120 − 30 = ______
6. 160 − 70 = ______
7. 650 − 280 = ______

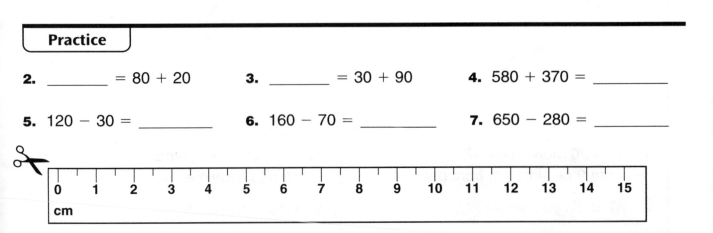

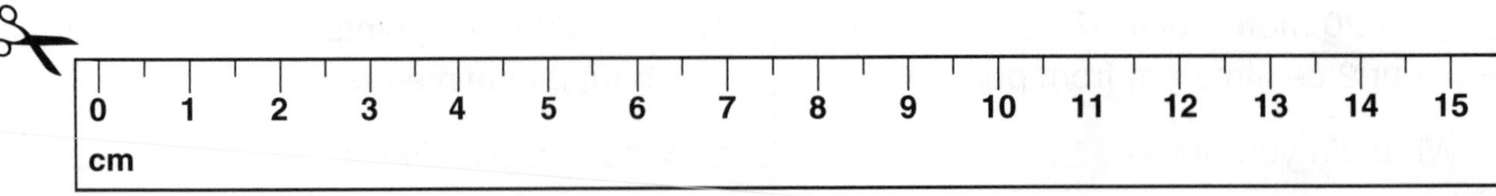

Name Date Time

LESSON 1•7

Tangent Circles

Two circles that "barely touch" (touch at just one point) are said to be **tangent** to each other.

On a separate sheet of paper, draw two congruent circles that are tangent to each other. Then draw a third congruent circle that is tangent to each of the other two circles.

Here is one way.

1. Draw a circle. Afterward, do not change the opening of the compass.

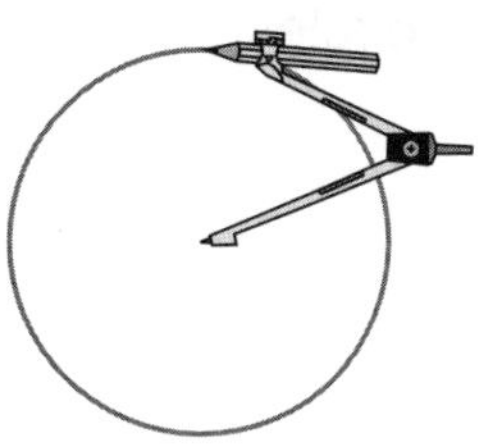

2. Use a straightedge to draw a line segment from the center of the circle. Make the segment at least twice as long as the radius of the circle.

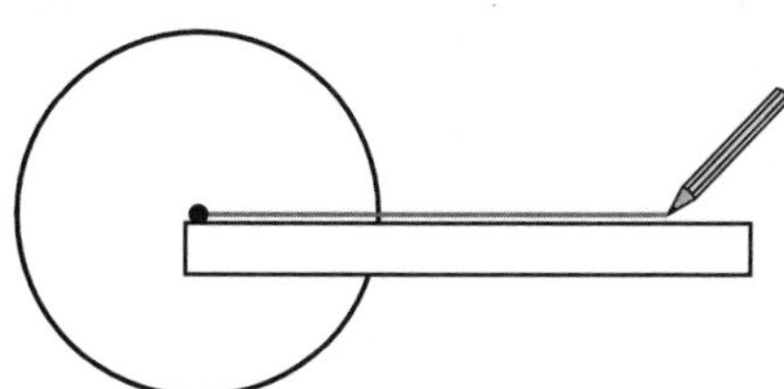

3. On this segment, mark a point that is outside of the circle. Make the distance from the circle to the point equal to the radius of the circle. Use your compass.

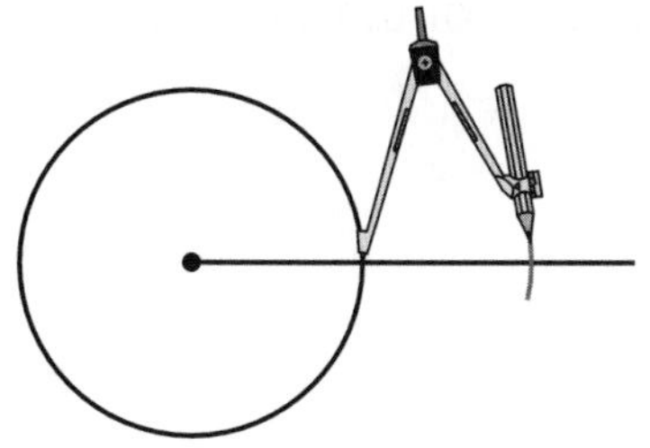

4. Draw a second circle, using the point you marked for the center of the circle.

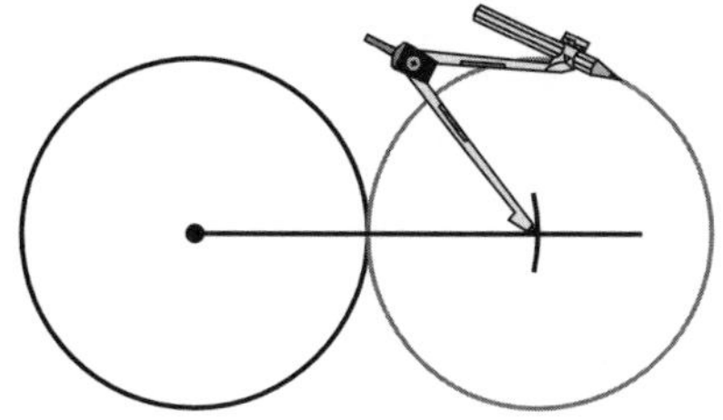

Directions continue on *Math Masters,* page 28.

LESSON 1•7 Tangent Circles *continued*

5. Open the compass so that the anchor is on the center of one circle and the pencil point is on the center of the other circle.

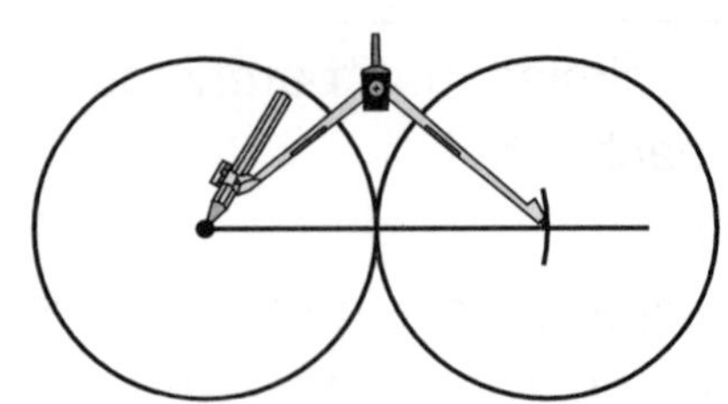

6. Swing the compass and make a mark (an arc) above the two circles.

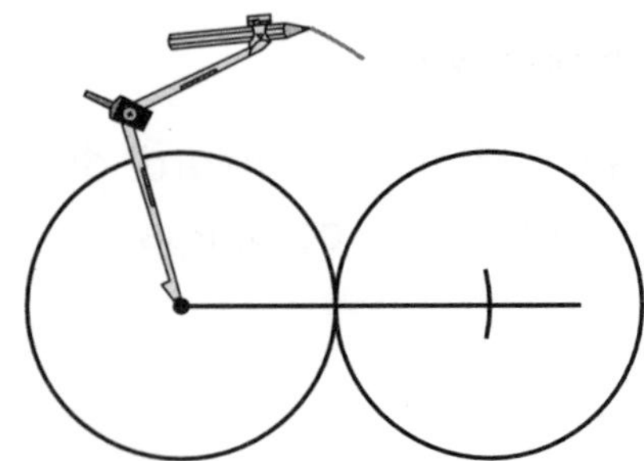

7. Move the anchor to the center of the other circle and make an arc through the first arc.

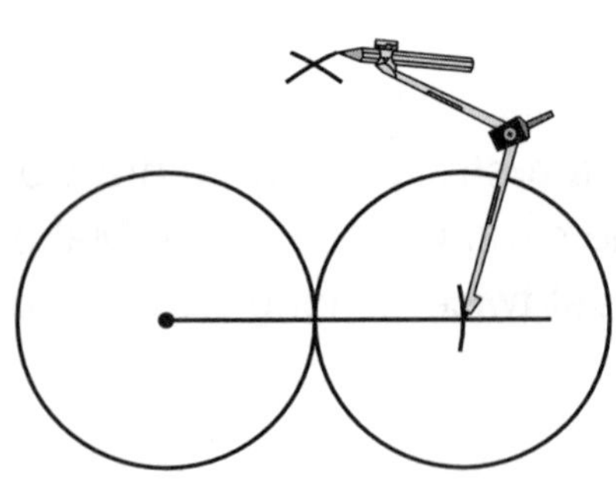

8. Close the compass to the original opening (the radius of the original circles).

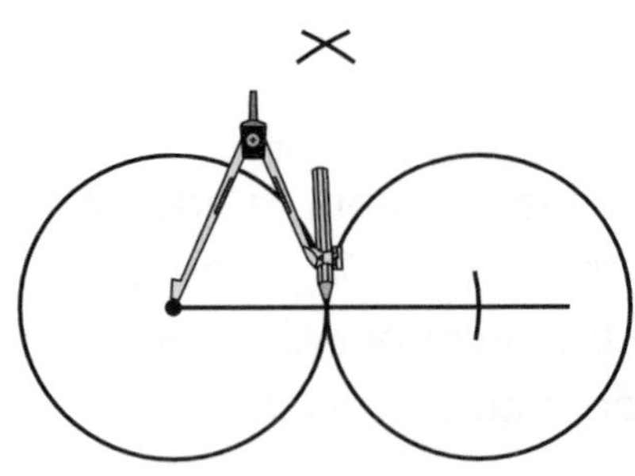

9. Put the anchor on the point where the two arcs intersect. Draw a third circle.

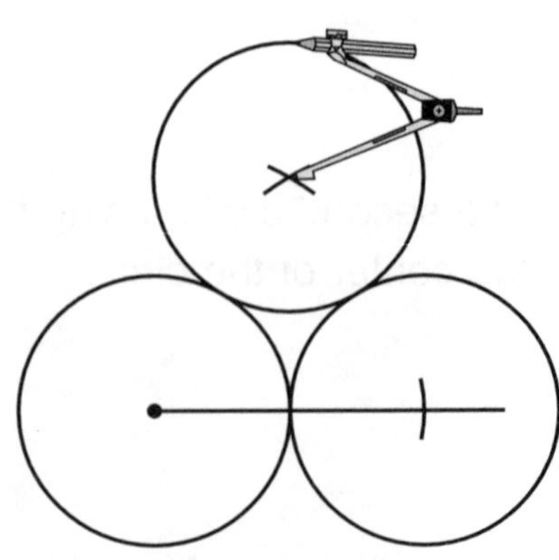

Name Date Time

Radius, Chord, and Diameter

A **radius** is a line segment that connects the center of a circle with any point on the circle.

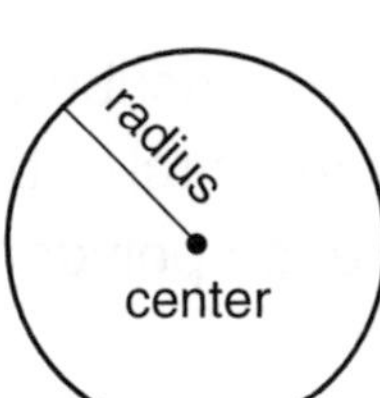

A **chord** is a line segment that connects 2 points on a circle.

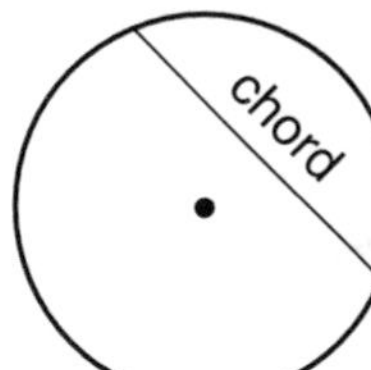

A **diameter** is a special chord. It is special because it is the chord with the largest possible length for that circle.

Use your straightedge to inscribe the polygons described in Problems 1–4.

1. Draw 4 chords to make a rectangle.

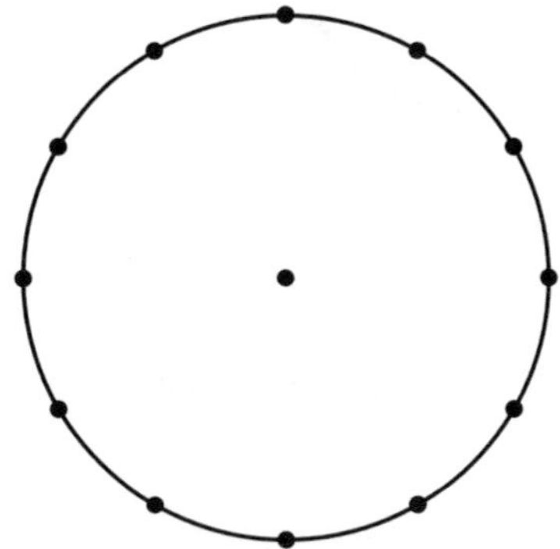

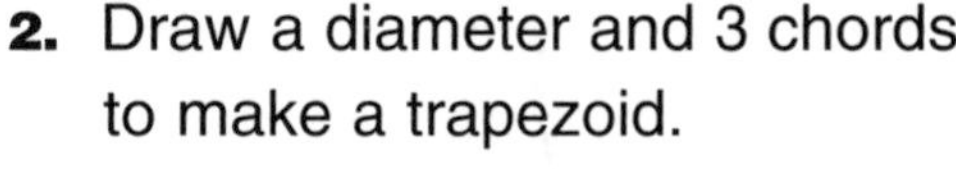

2. Draw a diameter and 3 chords to make a trapezoid.

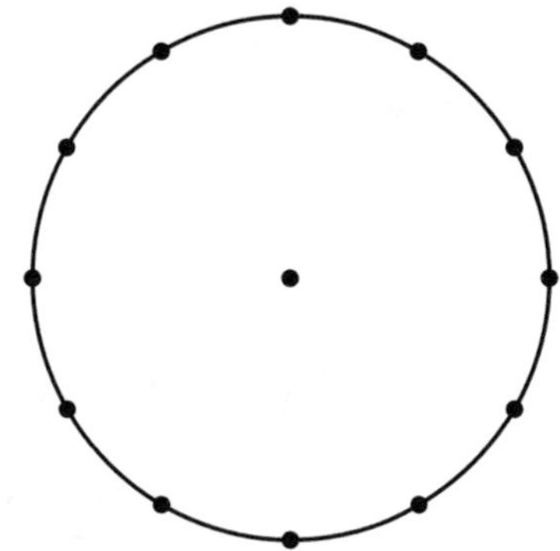

3. Draw 3 chords to make an isosceles triangle.

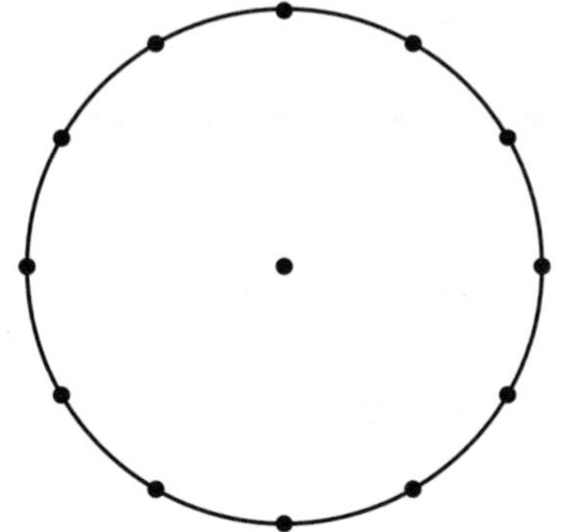

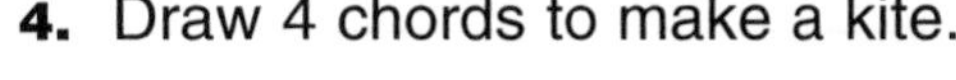

4. Draw 4 chords to make a kite.

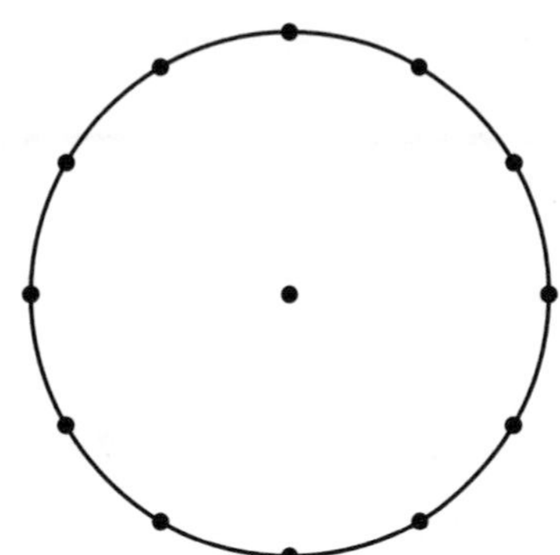

Name Date Time

Inscribed Polygons

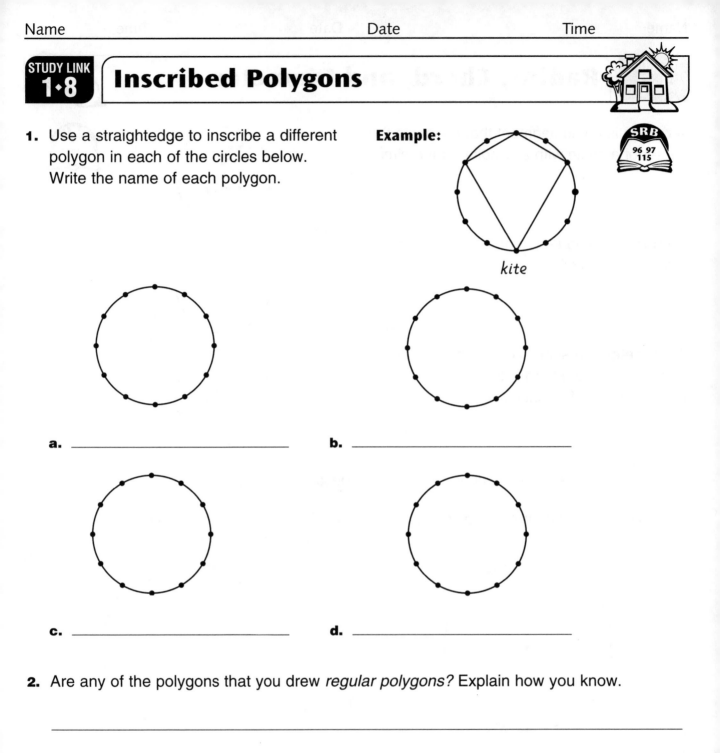

1. Use a straightedge to inscribe a different polygon in each of the circles below. Write the name of each polygon.

Example:

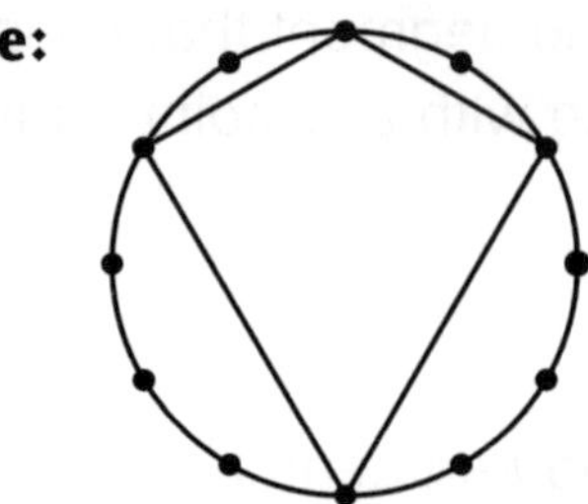

kite

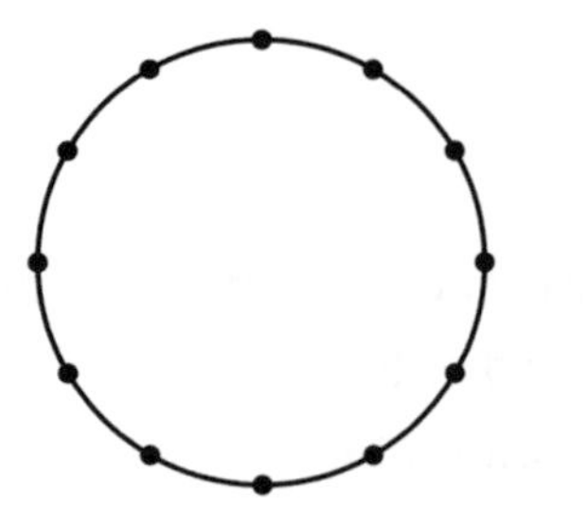

a. ______________________ b. ______________________

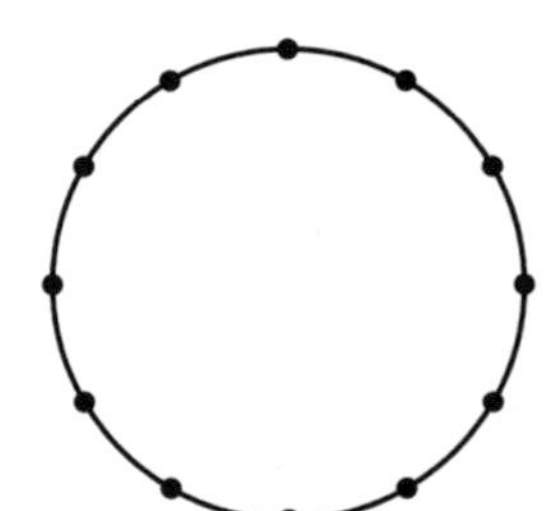

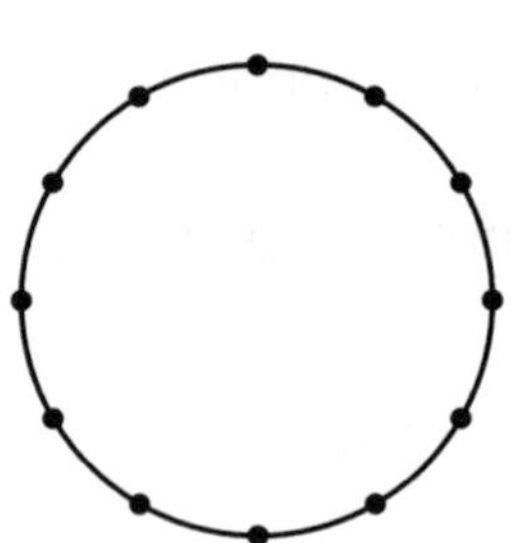

c. ______________________ d. ______________________

2. Are any of the polygons that you drew *regular polygons?* Explain how you know.

____

____

____

Practice

3. 41 + 27 = ________

4. ________ = 263 + 59

5. 461 + 398 = ________

6. ________ = 72 − 36

7. 158 − 71 = ________

8. 742 − 349 = ________

Name Date Time

A Hexagon Design

1. Outline the regular hexagon in the design to the right using a red crayon or pencil. Use your crayons or pencils to color the design in an interesting way.

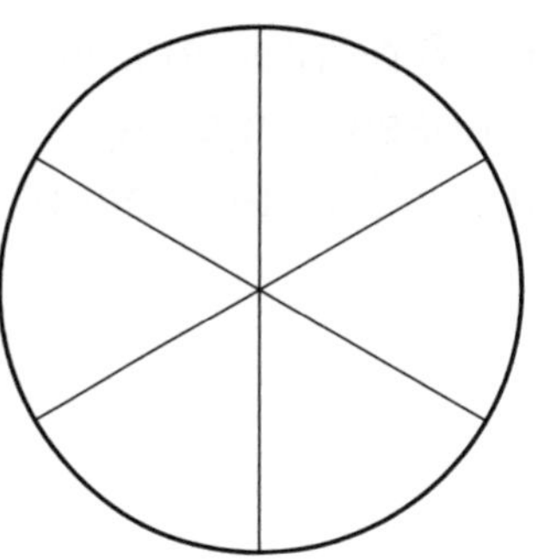

2. How do you know the polygon you outlined is a regular hexagon? ______________________

____

____

____

Name Date Time

A Hexagon Design

1. Outline the regular hexagon in the design to the right using a red crayon or pencil. Use your crayons or pencils to color the design in an interesting way.

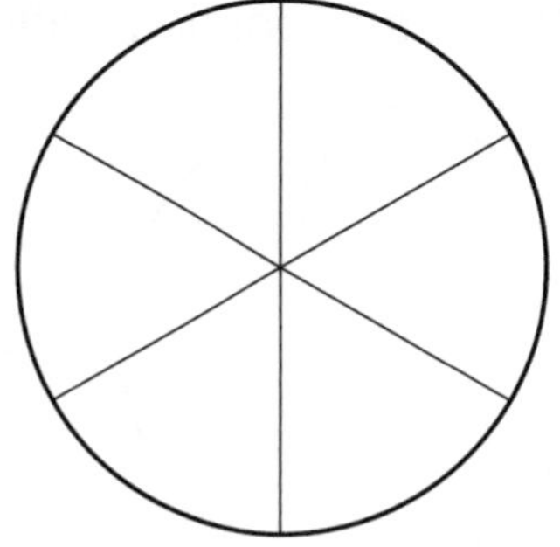

2. How do you know the polygon you outlined is a regular hexagon? ______________________

____

____

____

Name Date Time

Creating 6-Point Designs

1. This 6-pointed star is called a **hexagram.** Use your compass and straightedge to construct a hexagram on a separate sheet of paper.

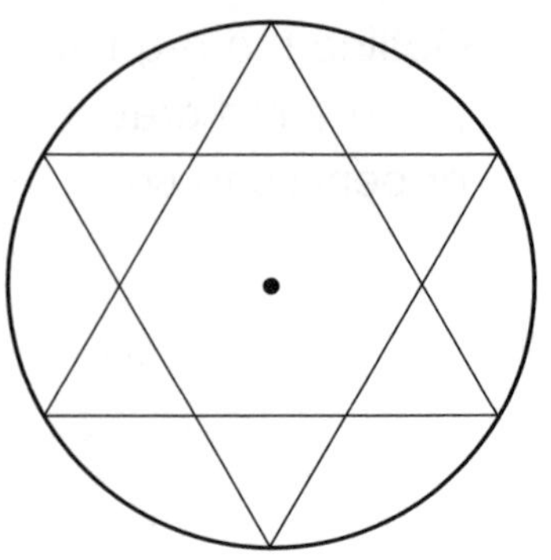

2. Construct another large hexagram on a separate sheet of paper. Draw a second hexagram inside the first, and then a third hexagram inside the second. Make a hexagram design by coloring your construction.

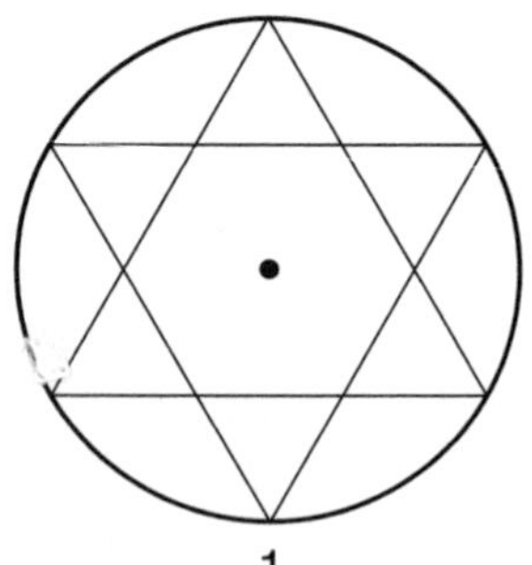
1

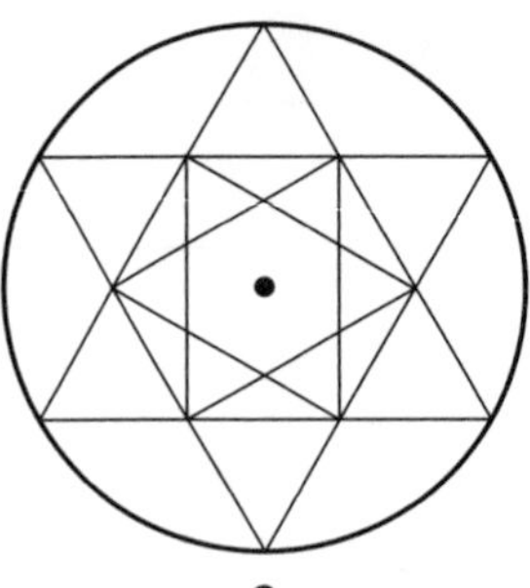
2

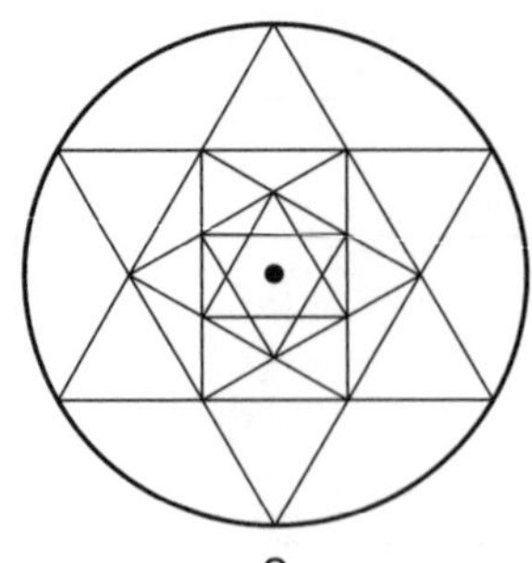
3

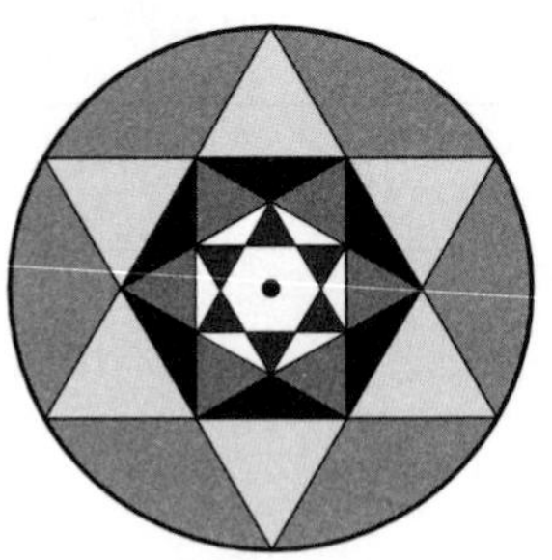
Sample design

3. Construct the hexagram pattern several more times. Color each one in a different way to create a new design.

4. Construct the following pattern several times on separate sheets of paper. Color each one in a different way.

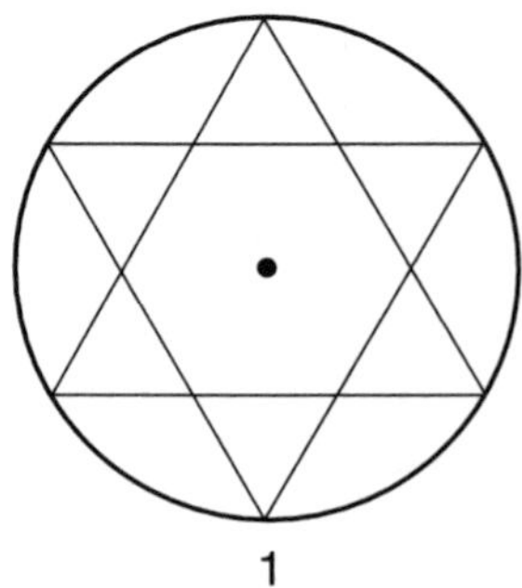
1

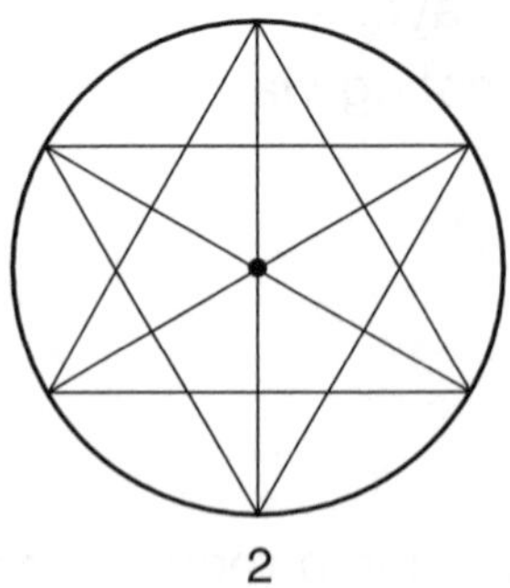
2

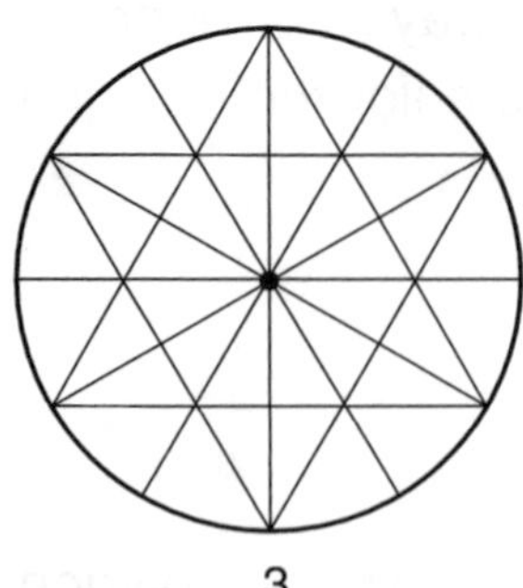
3

Try This

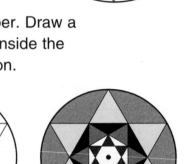

5. Create and color your own 6-point designs on separate sheets of paper.

Name Date Time

An Inscribed Equilateral Triangle

Follow each step below. Draw on a separate sheet of paper. Repeat these steps several times. Then cut out your best work and tape it to the bottom of this page.

Step 1 Draw a circle. (Keep the same compass opening for Steps 2 and 3.) Draw a dot on the circle. Place the anchor of your compass on the dot and draw a mark on the circle.

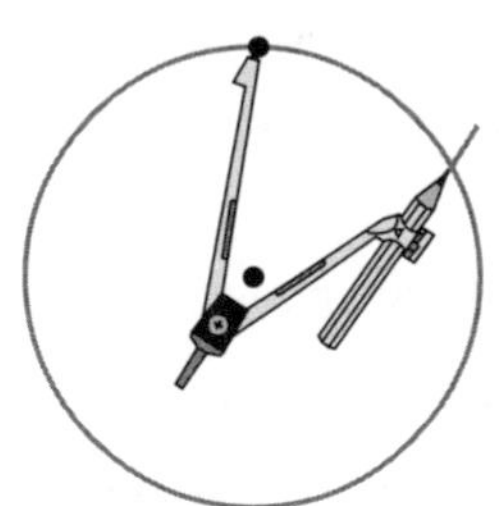

Step 2 Place the anchor of your compass on the mark you just made and draw another mark on the circle.

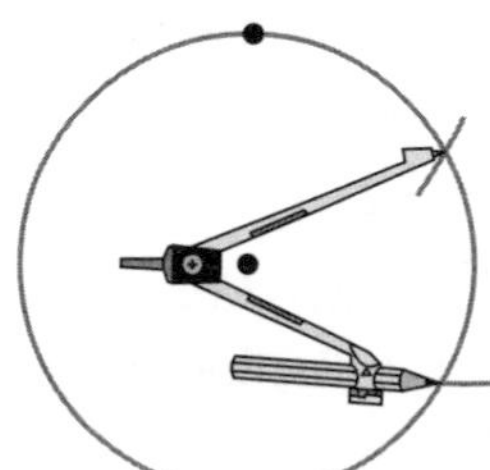

Step 3 Do this 4 more times to divide the circle into 6 equal parts. The 6th mark should be on the dot you started with or very close to it.

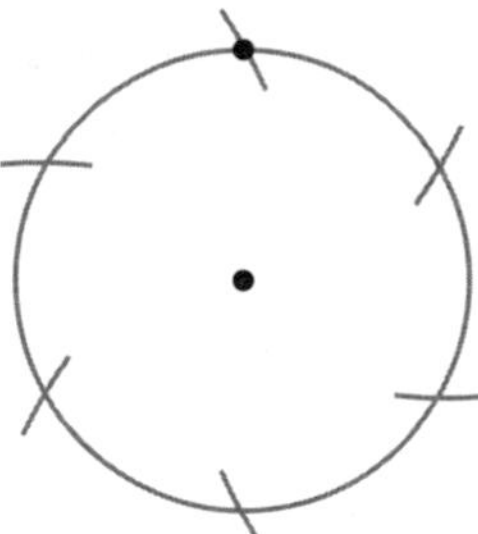

Step 4 With your straightedge, connect 3 alternating marks (every other mark) on the circle to form an equilateral triangle. Use your compass to check that the sides of the equilateral triangle are about the same length.

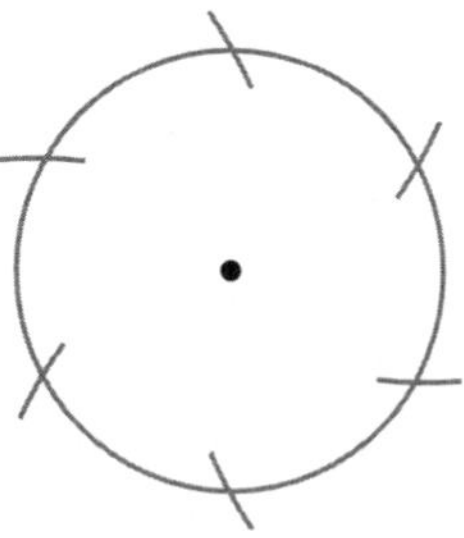

Name Date Time

Unit 2: Family Letter

Using Numbers and Organizing Data

Your child is about to begin this year's work with numbers. The class will examine what numbers mean and how they are used in everyday life.

In today's world, numbers are all around us—in newspapers and magazines and on TV. We use them

- to count things *(How many people are in the room?)*
- to measure things *(How tall are you?)*
- to create codes *(What is your Social Security number?)*
- to locate things in reference frames *(What time is it?)*
- to express rates, scales, and percents *(How many miles per gallon does your car get? What percent voted for Jamie?)*

Sometimes students will need to interpret a collection of numbers. The class will learn to organize such collections of numbers in tables and graphs and to draw conclusions about them.

Computation is an important part of problem solving. Fortunately, we are no longer restricted to paper-and-pencil methods of computation. We can use calculators or computer programs to solve lengthy or complex problems. Your child will practice mental and paper-and-pencil methods of computation, use a calculator, and have opportunities to decide which is most appropriate for solving a particular problem.

Many of us were taught that there is just one way to do computations. For example, we may have learned to subtract by "borrowing." We may not have realized that there are other ways of subtracting numbers. While students will not be expected to learn more than one method, they will examine several different methods and realize that there are often several ways to arrive at the same result. They will have the option of using the methods with which they are comfortable or even inventing one of their own.

Mathematics games will be used throughout the school year to practice various arithmetic skills. Through games, practice becomes a thinking activity to be enjoyed. The games your child will play in this unit will provide practice with renaming numbers, with addition, and with subtraction. They require very little in the way of materials, so you may play them at home as well.

Please keep this Family Letter for reference as your child works through Unit 2.

Name Date Time

Unit 2: Family Letter *cont.*

Vocabulary

Important terms in Unit 2:

algorithm A set of step-by-step instructions for doing something, such as carrying out a computation or solving a problem.

base 10 Our number system in which each place in a number has a value 10 times the place to its right and $\frac{1}{10}$ the place to its left.

column-addition A method for adding numbers in which the addends' digits are first added in each place-value column separately, and then 10-for-1 trades are made until each column has only one digit. Lines are drawn to separate the place-value columns.

	100s	10s	1s
	2	4	8
+	1	8	7
Add the columns:	3	12	15
Adjust the 1s and 10s:	3	13	5
Adjust the 10s and 100s:	4	3	5

equivalent names Different names for the same number. For example, 2 + 6, 4 + 4, 12 − 4, 18 − 10, 100 − 92, 5 + 1 + 2, eight, VIII, and ~~////~~ /// are equivalent names for 8.

line plot A sketch of data in which check marks, Xs, or other marks above a labeled line show the frequency of each value.

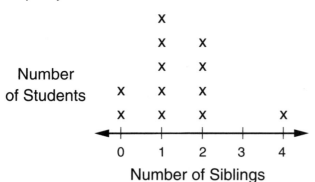

Number of Siblings	0	1	2	3	4
Number of Students	X X	X X X X X	X X X X		X

mean The sum of a set of numbers divided by the number of numbers in the set. The mean is often referred to simply as the "average."

median The middle value in a set of data when the data are listed in order from least to greatest. If there is an even number of data points, the median is the *mean* of the two middle values.

mode The value or values that occur most often in a set of data.

name-collection box A diagram that is used for writing *equivalent names* for a number. The box to the right shows names for 8.

8
2 + 6
4 + 4
VIII
eight

partial-differences subtraction A way to subtract in which differences are computed separately for each place (ones, tens, hundreds, and so on). The partial differences are then added to give the final answer.

		932
		− 356
Subtract the hundreds:	900 − 300 →	600
Subtract the tens:	30 − 50 →	− 20
Subtract the ones:	2 − 6 →	− 4
Find the total:	600 − 20 − 4 →	576

partial-sums addition A way to add in which sums are computed for each place (ones, tens, hundreds, and so on) separately. The partial sums are then added to give the final answer.

		496
		229
		+ 347
Add the hundreds:	400 + 200 + 300 →	900
Add the tens:	90 + 20 + 40 →	150
Add the ones:	6 + 9 + 7 →	+ 22
Find the total:	900 + 150 + 22 →	1,072

range The difference between the maximum and the minimum in a set of data.

trade-first subtraction A subtraction method in which all trades are done before any subtractions are carried out.

whole numbers The numbers 0, 1, 2, 3, 4, and so on.

Do-Anytime Activities

To work with your child on the concepts taught in this unit, try these interesting and rewarding activities:

1. Have your child see how many numbers he or she can identify in newspapers, magazines, advertisements, or news broadcasts.
2. Have your child collect and compare the measurements (height and weight) or accomplishments of favorite professional athletes.
3. Look up the different time zones of the United States and the world, quizzing your child on what time it would be at that moment at a particular location.
4. Have your child look for different representations of the same number. For example, he or she may see the same money amounts expressed in different ways, such as 50¢, $0.50, or 50 cents.

Building Skills through Games

In Unit 2, your child will play the following games. For detailed instructions, see the *Student Reference Book.*

Addition Top-It See *Student Reference Book,* page 263. This game provides practice with addition facts.

Fishing for Digits See *Student Reference Book,* page 242. This game provides practice identifying digits and the values of the digits, and adding and subtracting.

High-Number Toss See *Student Reference Book,* page 252. This game provides practice reading, writing, and comparing numbers.

Name That Number See *Student Reference Book,* page 254. This game reinforces skills in using all four operations.

Polygon Pair-Up See *Student Reference Book,* page 258. This game provides practice identifying properties of polygons.

Subtraction Target Practice See *Student Reference Book,* page 262. This game provides practice with subtraction and estimation.

Subtraction Top-It See *Student Reference Book,* pages 263 and 264. This is a variation of *Addition Top-It* and provides practice with subtraction facts.

STUDY LINK 1•9 **Unit 2: Family Letter** *cont.*

As You Help Your Child with Homework

As your child brings assignments home, you may want to go over the instructions together, clarifying them as necessary. The answers listed below will guide you through this unit's Study Links.

Study Link 2•2

1. Sample answers: 8 × 8; 32 × 2; 10 + 54

2. Sample answers: 2 × 66; 11 × 12; 66 + 66; 30 + 30 + 30 + 30 + 12; (50 × 2) + 32

3. Sample answers: 20 + 20; 80 ÷ 2; $\frac{1}{2}$ × 80

4. Sample answers: 9 × 4; 72 ÷ 2; (12 × 4) – 12

Study Link 2•3

1. 876,504,000 **2.** 23,170,080

3. 876,504,000

4. **a.** thousand; 400,000

b. million; 80,000,000

c. million; 500,000,000

d. thousand; 30,000

5. **b.** 596,708 **d.** 1,045,620

6. **b.** 13,877,000 **d.** 150,691,688

Study Link 2•4

2. 581,970,000 **3.** 97,654,320

5. **a.** 487,000,063 **b.** 15,000,297

6. 97,308,080

Study Link 2•5

2. 27 **3.** 8 **4.** 2 **5.** 6 **6.** 5

Study Link 2•6

1.

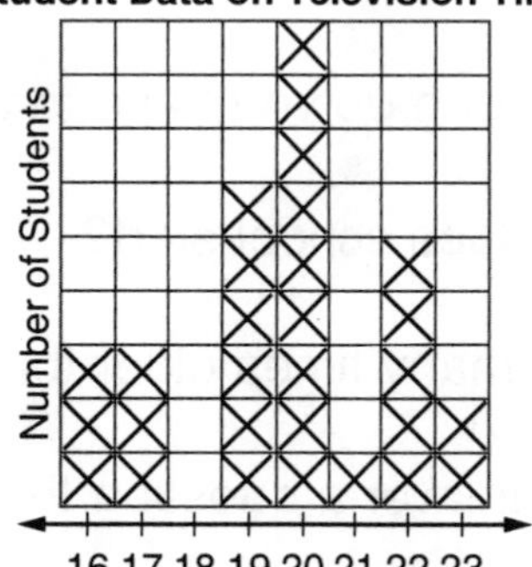

2. **a.** 23 **b.** 16 **c.** 7 **d.** 20 **e.** 20

4. 19.7

Study Link 2•7

1. 152 **2.** 510 **3.** 613

4. 1,432 **5.** 2,520 **6.** 5,747

11. 136 **12.** 720 **13.** 225

14. 720 **15.** 1,573 **16.** 2,356

Study Link 2•8

1. **a.** 645 **b.** 19 **c.** 626 **d.** 151

2. Giraffe, Asian elephant, and rhinoceros

3. 90 **4.** dog **5.** mouse

Study Link 2•9

1. 68 **11.** 29

2. 382 **12.** 57

3. 367 **13.** 406

4. 3,746 **14.** 224

5. 2,889 **15.** 4,479

6. 2,322 **16.** 2,538

Name Date Time

Uses of Numbers

Answer the following questions:

1. How many students are in your class? ______________ students
2. What is your mailing address? ______________
3. In what year were you born? ______________
4. About how long do you have to eat lunch at school? ______________ minutes
5. What time does school start? ______________
6. About how many times older than you is your principal? ______________
7. Write and answer a question that has a number for an answer.

____

____

Name Date Time

Uses of Numbers

Answer the following questions:

1. How many students are in your class? ______________ students
2. What is your mailing address? ______________
3. In what year were you born? ______________
4. About how long do you have to eat lunch at school? ______________ minutes
5. What time does school start? ______________
6. About how many times older than you is your principal? ______________
7. Write and answer a question that has a number for an answer.

____

____

Name Date Time

Numbers Everywhere

Find examples of numbers—all kinds of numbers. Look in newspapers and magazines. Look in books. Look on food packages. Ask people in your family for examples.

Write your numbers below. If an adult says you may, cut out the numbers and tape them onto the back of this page.

Be sure you write what the numbers mean.

Example: Mount Everest is 29,028 feet high. It is the world's tallest mountain.

____

____

____

____

____

____

____

____

____

____

____

____

____

____

____

____

____

Practice

1. $5 \times 3 =$ ______ **2.** ______ $= 4 \times 3$ **3.** ______ $= 10 \div 2$ **4.** $8 \div 4 =$ ______

Name Date Time

Solving Frames-and-Arrows Problems

1. On the number line below, count by 3s starting with 0. Circle every number that is part of the count.

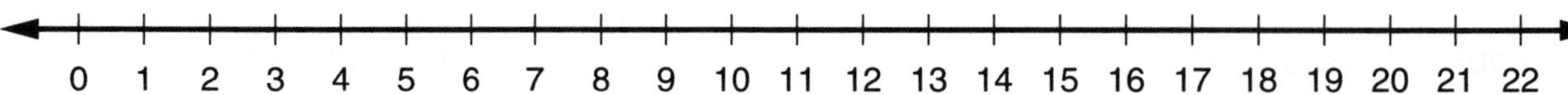

2. Use the rule to fill in the missing numbers.

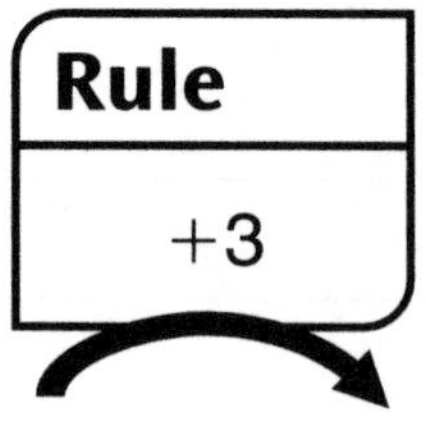

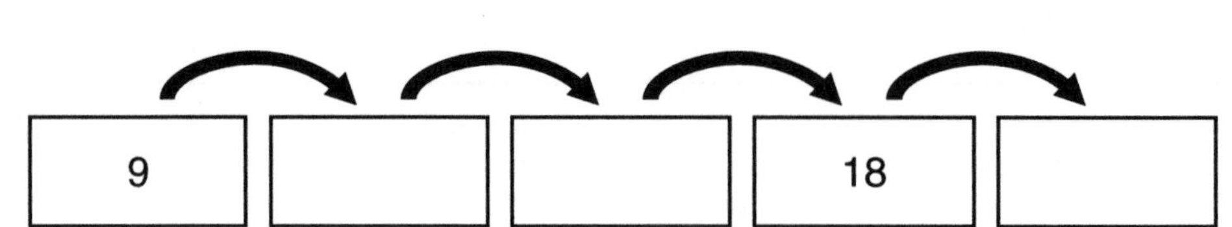

3. Find the rule and fill in the missing numbers.

a.

b.

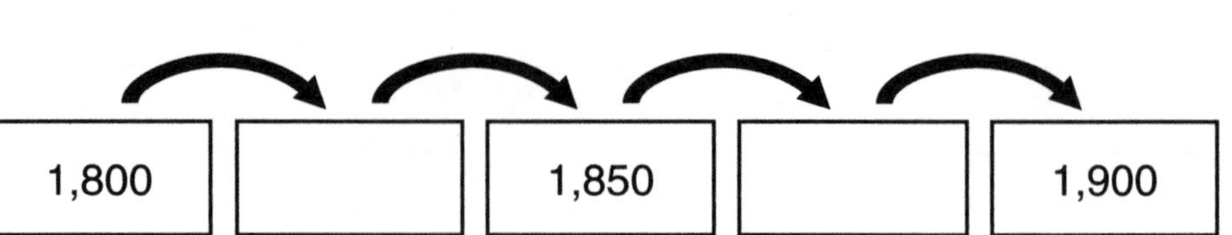

4. Explain how you figured out the rule for Problem 3b.

____

____

Try This

5. Find the missing numbers.

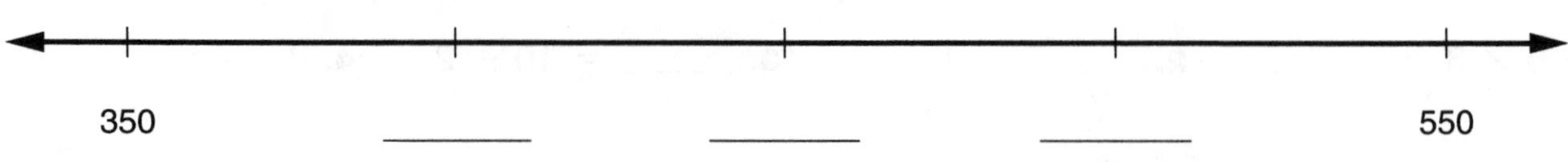

Name Date Time

Missing Numbers on a Number Line

Mrs. Gonzalez told her students that there is a strategy they can always use to find missing numbers on a number line when the missing numbers are the same distance apart.

Solve the problems.

1. 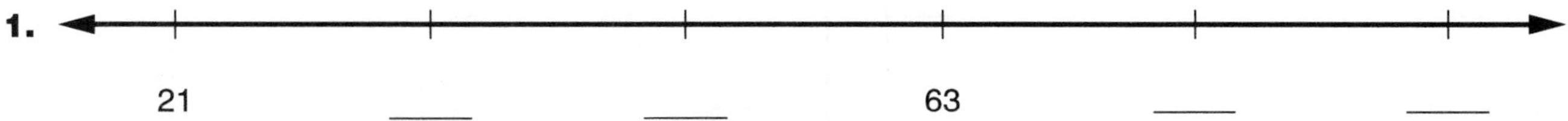

2. 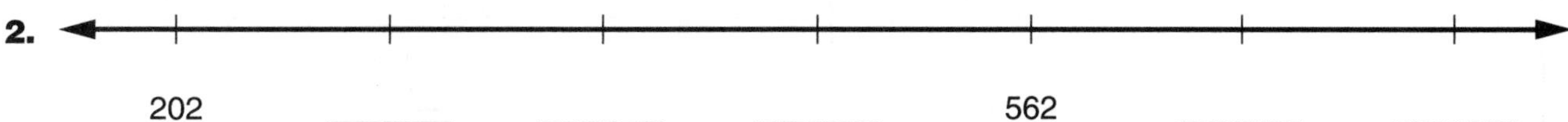

3. 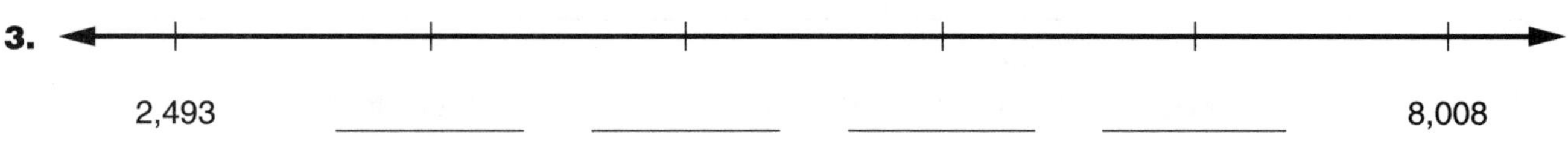

4. 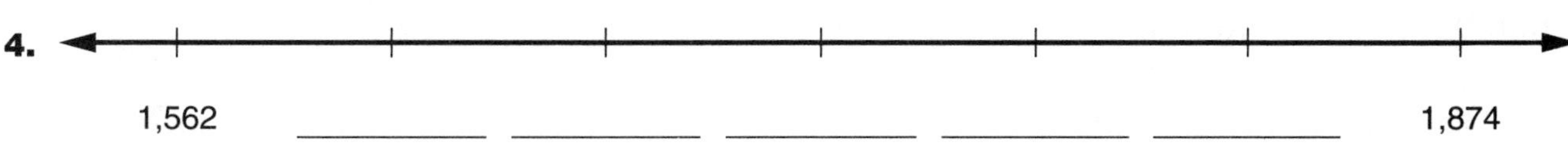

5. Describe a strategy that the students in Mrs. Gonzalez's class might have used to solve all of the problems on this page.

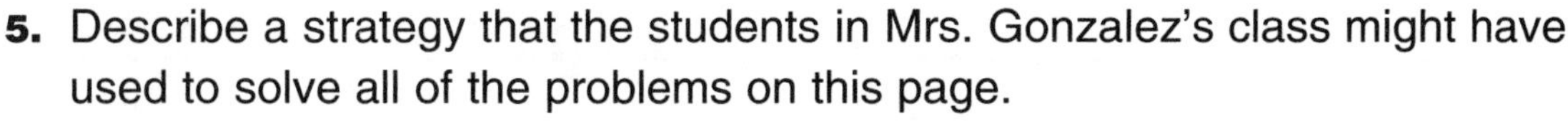

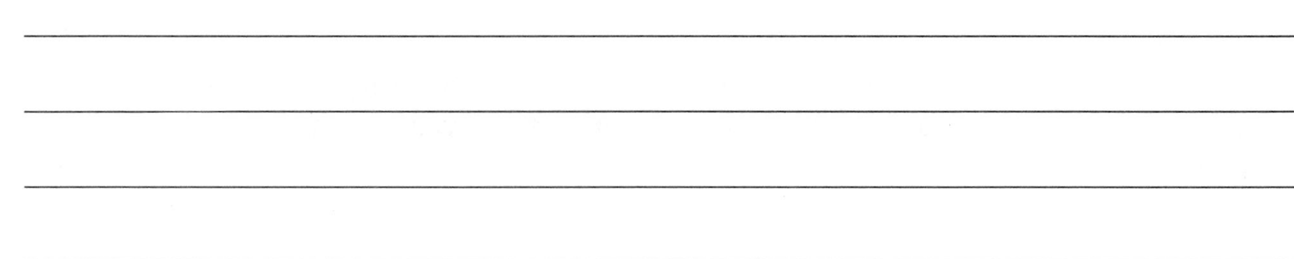

6. Create a number-line problem like the ones above. Ask a partner to solve it.

Name Date Time

STUDY LINK 2·2

Many Names for Numbers

1. Write five names for 64.

64

2. Write five names for 132.

132

3. Pretend that the 4-key on your calculator is broken. Write six ways to display the number 40 on the calculator without using the 4-key. Try to use different numbers and operations.

Example: $2 \times 2 \times 10$

__________ __________ __________

__________ __________ __________

Try This

4. Now pretend that all the keys on your calculator work except for the 3-key and the 6-key. Write six ways to display the number 36 without using these keys.

__________ __________ __________

__________ __________ __________

Practice

5. $20 + 60 =$ ________

6. ________ $= 60 + 90$

7. ________ $= 80 - 30$

8. $110 - 40 =$ ________

Name Date Time

Domino Sums

Materials ☐ 1 or 2 sets of double-9 dominoes or *Math Masters,* pages 394–396

☐ number cards 0–18 (1 each; from the Everything Math Deck, if available)

Directions

1. Lay out the number cards in order from 0 through 18.

2. Place each domino above the number card that shows the sum of the domino's dots. In the example below, the sum of 4 and 1 is 5, and the sum of 2 and 3 is 5.

   2 + 3 and 4 + 1 are **equivalent names** for the number 5.

Example:

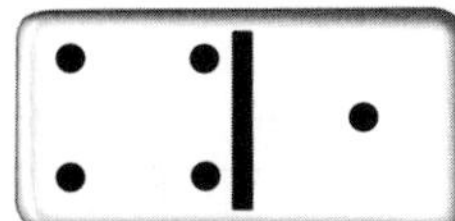

3. In the space below, list the addition facts shown by the dominoes. Before you begin, decide how you will organize the facts.

Name Date Time

LESSON 2•2

Pan-Balance Problems

A **pan balance** is used to weigh objects. When the weight of the objects in one pan is the same as the weight of the objects in the other pan, the pans are in perfect balance.

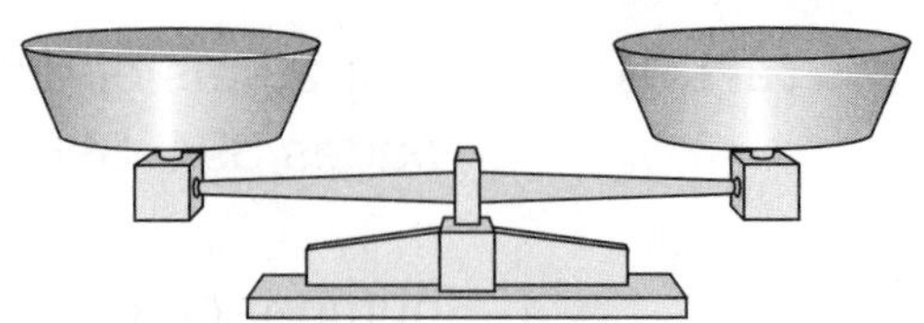

In each figure below, the pans hold **equivalent names** for a number. The pans are in perfect balance. Fill in the missing numbers. Write the name for the pan balance.

Example:

5 + 5 + [5] | 3 × [5]

a. □ = 5

b. Pan-balance name 15

1. 13 + ○ | 27 − ○

a. ○ = ________

b. Pan-balance name ________

2. 96 − ⬡ | ⬡ + 66

a. ⬡ = ________

b. Pan-balance name ________

3. ⬠ × 7 | 63 ÷ ⬠

a. ⬠ = ________

b. Pan-balance name ________

4. 36 − ⏢ | (60 ÷ 4) × (⏢ ÷ 3)

a. ⏢ = ________

b. Pan-balance name ________

Place Value in Whole Numbers

1. Write the number that has

   6 in the millions place,
   4 in the thousands place,
   7 in the ten-millions place,
   5 in the hundred-thousands place,
   8 in the hundred-millions place, and
   0 in the remaining places.

   ___ ___ 6, ___ ___ ___, ___ ___ ___

2. Write the number that has

   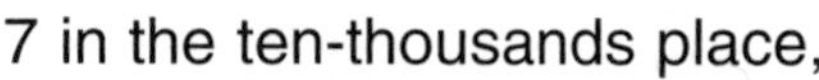

   7 in the ten-thousands place,
   3 in the millions place,
   1 in the hundred-thousands place,
   8 in the tens place,
   2 in the ten-millions place, and
   0 in the remaining places.

   ___ ___, ___ ___ ___, ___ ___ ___

3. Compare the two numbers you wrote in Problems 1 and 2.

   Which is greater? ____________________

4. The 6 in 46,711,304 stands for 6 million, or 6,000,000.

   a. The 4 in 508,433,529 stands for 400 ______________, or ______________.

   b. The 8 in 182,945,777 stands for 80 ______________, or ______________.

   c. The 5 in 509,822,119 stands for 500 ______________, or ______________.

   d. The 3 in 450,037,111 stands for 30 ______________, or ______________.

Try This

5. Write the number that is 1 hundred thousand more.

   a. 210,366 310,366
   b. 496,708 ______________
   c. 321,589 ______________
   d. 945,620 ______________

6. Write the number that is 1 million more.

   a. 3,499,702 4,499,702
   b. 12,877,000 ______________
   c. 29,457,300 ______________
   d. 149,691,688 ______________

Practice

7. 32, 45, 58, _____, _____, _____

   Rule: ________

8. _____, _____, _____, 89, 115, 141

   Rule: ________

Name Date Time

LESSON 2•3

Number-Grid Puzzles

1. Find the missing numbers.

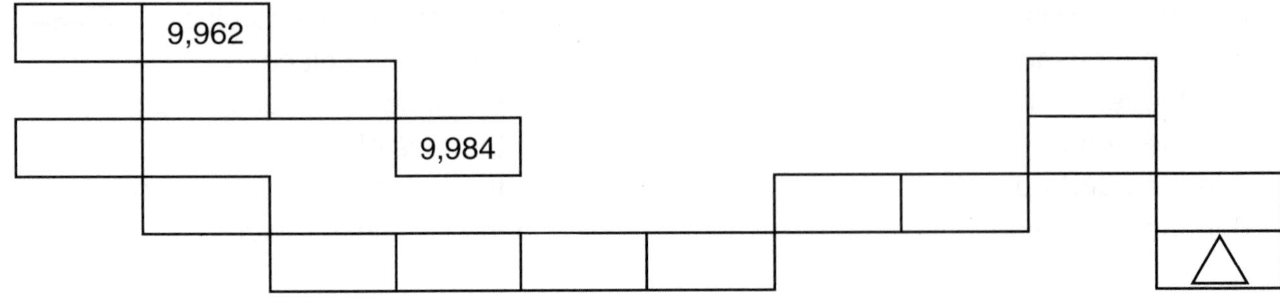

a. △ = ______________ **b.** Explain how you found △.

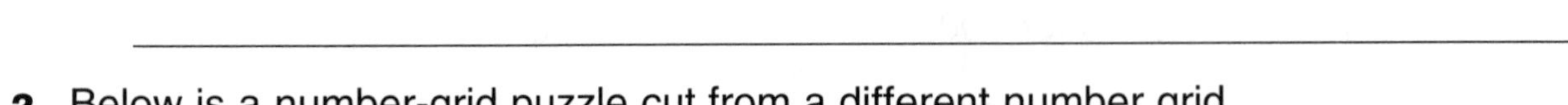

2. Below is a number-grid puzzle cut from a different number grid. Figure out the pattern, and use it to fill in the missing numbers.

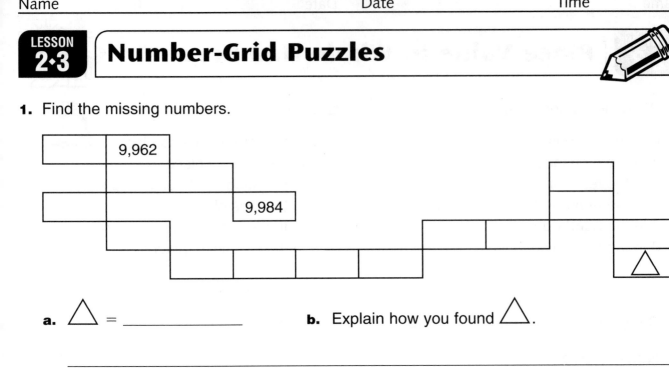

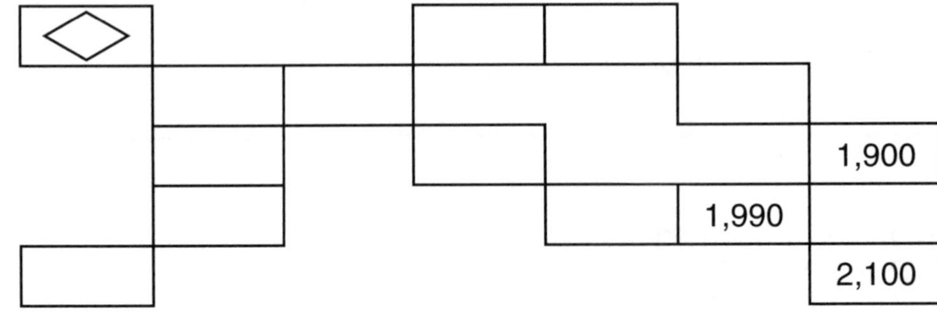

a. ◇ = ______________ **b.** Explain how you found ◇.

c. Describe how this number grid is different from number grids you have used before.

Name Date Time

Calculator "Change" Problems

Use this page with *Math Journal 1,* page 36, Problem 1.

	Start with	Place of Digit	Change to	Operation	New Number
a.	570	Tens			
b.	409	Hundreds			
c.	54,463	Thousands			
d.	760,837	Tens			
e.	52,036,458	Ones			
f.		Ten Thousands			
g.		Millions			

Make up your own calculator "change" problems.

	Start with	Place of Digit	Change to	Operation	New Number
a.					
b.					
c.					
d.					
e.					
f.					
g.					
h.					
i.					

Name Date Time

Place Values in Whole Numbers

1. Write the numbers in order from smallest to largest.

15,964 1,509,460 150,094,400
1,400,960 15,094,600

____

____

____

____

____

2. Write the number that has

5 in the hundred-millions place,
7 in the ten-thousands place,
1 in the millions place,
9 in the hundred-thousands place,
8 in the ten-millions place, and
0 in all other places.

___ ___ ___, ___ ___ ___, ___ ___ ___

3. Write the largest number you can. Use each digit just once.

3 5 0 7 9 2 6 4 ______________________

4. Write the value of the digit 8 in each numeral below.

a. **8**0,007,941 ______________________ **b.** **8**35,099,714 ______________________

c. **8**,714,366 ______________________ **d.** **8**60,490 ______________________

5. Write each number using digits.

a. four hundred eighty-seven million, sixty-three ______________________

b. fifteen million, two hundred ninety-seven ______________________

Try This

6. I am an 8-digit number.

- The digit in the thousands place is the result of dividing 64 by 8.
- The digit in the millions place is the result of dividing 63 by 9.
- The digit in the ten-millions place is the result of dividing 54 by 6.
- The digit in the tens place is the result of dividing 40 by 5.
- The digit in the hundred-thousands place is the result of dividing 33 by 11.
- All the other digits are the result of subtracting any number from itself.

What number am I? ___ ___, ___ ___ ___, ___ ___ ___

Name Date Time

Use a Place-Value Tool

1. Display each number below in your place-value flip book. Then display, read, and record the numbers that are 10 more, 100 more, and 1,000 more. Circle the digit that changed.

Number	10 more	100 more	1,000 more
146	1⑤6	②46	①,146
508			
2,368			
4,571			
15,682			

2. Display each number below in your place-value flip book. Then display, read, and record the numbers that are 10 less, 100 less, and 1,000 less. Circle the digit that changed.

Number	10 less	100 less	1,000 less
2,345	2,3③5	2,②45	①,345
3,491			
6,839			
12,367			
45,130			

3. Use your place-value flip book to help you answer the following questions.

a. What number is 50 more than 329? ________

b. What number is 300 more than 517? ________

c. What number is 60 less than 685? ________

d. What number is 400 less than 932? ________

Name Date Time

LESSON 2•4

Crack the Muffin Code

Daniel takes orders at the Marvelous Muffin Bakery. The muffins are packed into boxes that hold 1, 3, 9, or 27 muffins. When a customer asks for muffins, Daniel fills out an order slip.

- If a customer orders 5 muffins, Daniel writes CODE 12 on the order slip.
- If a customer orders 19 muffins, Daniel writes CODE 201 on the order slip.
- If a customer orders 34 muffins, Daniel writes CODE 1021 on the order slip.

1. What would Daniel write on the order slip if a customer asked for 47 muffins? Explain.

CODE ______________________

____

____

____

____

2. If the Marvelous Muffin Bakery always packs its muffins into the fewest number of boxes possible, what is a code Daniel would never write on an order slip? Explain.

CODE ______________________

____

____

____

____

3. The largest box used by the bakery holds 27 muffins. Daniel thinks the bakery should have a box one size larger. How many muffins would the new box hold? Explain.

________ muffins

____

____

____

____

Name Date Time

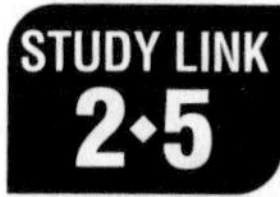

Collecting Data

1. Make a list of all the people in your family. Include all the people living at home now. Also include any brothers or sisters who live somewhere else. The people who live at home do not have to be related to you. Do not forget to write your name in the list.

You will need this information to learn about the sizes of families in your class.

__________ __________ __________

__________ __________ __________

__________ __________ __________

How many people are in your family? ________ people

The tally chart at the right shows the number of books that some students read over the summer. Use the information to answer the questions below.

Number of Books Reported	Number of Students
2	///
3	𝍸
4	
5	𝍸 //
6	𝍸 /
7	//
8	////

2. How many students reported the number of books they read? ______

3. What is the **maximum** (the largest number of books reported)? ______

4. What is the **minimum** (the smallest number of books reported)? ______

5. What is the **range?** ______

6. What is the **mode** (the most frequent number of books reported)? ______

Practice

7. 30 + 50 = ______

8. ______ = 70 + 70 + 70

9. ______ = 90 + 80 + 60

10. 100 + 40 + 70 = ______

Name Date Time

Dice-Roll Tally Chart

Tally marks are vertical marks used to keep track of a count.
The fifth tally mark crosses the first four.

SRB 71

Examples:

/ one	// two	/// three	//// four	𝍸 five
𝍸 / six	𝍸 // seven	𝍸 /// eight	𝍸 //// nine	𝍸 𝍸 ten

1. Roll a pair of dice and find the sum.
2. Make a tally mark next to the sum in the chart below.
3. Set a timer for 3 minutes. Roll the dice and make a tally mark for each sum until the timer goes off.

Sum	Tallies
2	
3	
4	
5	
6	
7	
8	
9	
10	
11	
12	

4. Answer the questions below.
   - **a.** How many times did you roll a sum of

     4? _____ times

     7? _____ times

     11? _____ times
   - **b.** Which sum was rolled the most number of times? _____
   - **c.** Which sum was rolled the least number of times? _____
   - **d.** How many times did you roll the dice in all?

     _____ times
   - **e.** On the back of this page, write two more things that you notice about the data you collected.

Name Date Time

Making a Prediction Based on a Sample

Sometimes large numbers of people or things are impossible to count or take too much time to count. A smaller **sample** of data is often used to make predictions about a larger group or **population.**

You and your class collected, recorded, and analyzed data about the number of raisins found in $\frac{1}{2}$-ounce boxes of raisins.

Use the raisin data you collected on journal page 38 to answer the following questions.

1. Without opening it, how many raisins do you think are in a large box (12 or 15 ounces) of raisins?

   About ______ raisins are in a ______-ounce box.

2. Explain the strategy you used to make your prediction.

   ____

   ____

   ____

3. Suppose you only knew the number of raisins in a single $\frac{1}{2}$-ounce box of raisins. Would that affect your prediction about the number of raisins in the large box? Why or why not?

   ____

   ____

   ____

   ____

Name Date Time

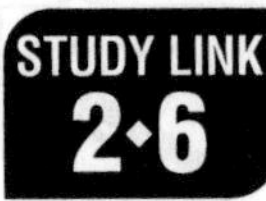

Line Plots

The students in Sylvia's class estimated how much time they spend watching television each week. The tally chart below shows the data they collected.

Number of Hours per Week Spent Watching TV	Number of Students
16	///
17	///
18	
19	~~////~~ /
20	~~////~~ ////
21	/
22	~~////~~
23	//

1. Construct a line plot for the data.

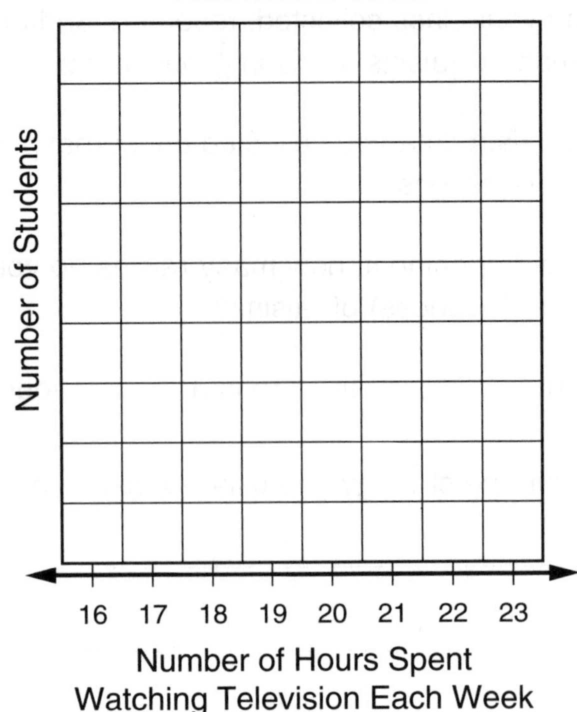

2. Find the following landmarks for the data:

a. The maximum number of hours spent watching television each week. _______ hours

b. minimum _______ hours

c. range _______ hours

d. mode _______ hours

e. median _______ hours

3. Estimate the amount of time that you watch television each week. _______ hours

Try This

4. Calculate the mean number of hours Sylvia and her classmates spent watching TV each week. _______ hours

Practice

5. 80 + 30 = _______

6. _______ = 90 + 90

7. _______ = 70 + 60

8. 120 + 30 = _______

Name Date Time

LESSON 2·6

Find the Median Number

The number in the middle of an ordered set of data is called the **middle value,** or **median.**

For Problems 1–3,

- Draw nine cards from a deck of number cards.
- Arrange the cards in order from smallest to largest.
- Record the numbers in the boxes below.
- Circle the number in the middle.

Example: 0 2 5 5 (7) 8 9 13 18

smallest largest

1. | | | | | | | | | |

smallest largest

The median of my nine cards is ______.

2. | | | | | | | | | |

smallest largest

The median of my nine cards is ______.

3. | | | | | | | | | |

smallest largest

The median of my nine cards is ______.

4. Describe how you found the middle number in the problems above.

____

____

____

5. If you arranged the cards in Problem 1 in order from *largest* to *smallest,* would the middle number stay the same? ______ Explain.

____

____

____

Name Date Time

Comparing Family-Size Data

1. Create a display that compares the family-size data from your class with those of other fourth-grade classes.

2. Compare the maximum, minimum, range, mode, and median for family size for each class. Write about the similarities and differences. Use the back of this page if you need more space.

____

____

____

____

____

____

____

Combine and organize the data from all of the classes. Then answer the following questions.

3. What is the *median* family size for all of the classes? ________ people

4. How does your class median compare with the larger sample?

____

____

5. What is the *mean* family size for all of the classes? ________ people

6. If you had to predict the family size of a student from your school that you did not know, what would you predict? Explain your answer.

____

____

____

Name Date Time

Multidigit Addition

Make a ballpark estimate. Use the **partial-sums method** to add. Compare your answer with your estimate to see if your answer makes sense.

1. $67 + 85$

Ballpark estimate: ____________

2. $439 + 71$

Ballpark estimate: ____________

3. $227 + 386$

Ballpark estimate: ____________

4. $493 + 939$

Ballpark estimate: ____________

5. $732 + 1,788$

Ballpark estimate: ____________

6. $4,239 + 1,508$

Ballpark estimate: ____________

Practice

7. $8 \times 7 =$ ______ **8.** $9 \times 9 =$ ______ **9.** ______ $\div 6 = 9$ **10.** ______ $\div 4 = 8$

Name Date Time

Multidigit Addition *continued*

Make a ballpark estimate. Use the **column-addition method** to add.
Compare your answer with your estimate to see if your answer makes sense.

11. $\begin{array}{r} 89 \\ +\ 47 \\ \hline \end{array}$

Ballpark estimate: ______

12. $\begin{array}{r} 634 \\ +\ 86 \\ \hline \end{array}$

Ballpark estimate: ______

13. $\begin{array}{r} 148 \\ +\ 77 \\ \hline \end{array}$

Ballpark estimate: ______

14. $\begin{array}{r} 481 \\ +\ 239 \\ \hline \end{array}$

Ballpark estimate: ______

15. $\begin{array}{r} 746 \\ +\ 827 \\ \hline \end{array}$

Ballpark estimate: ______

16. $\begin{array}{r} 508 \\ +\ 1{,}848 \\ \hline \end{array}$

Ballpark estimate: ______

Practice

17. 16, 21, 26, ______, ______, ______ Rule: ______

18. ______, 52, ______, 104, 130, ______ Rule: ______

Name ____________________ Date ____________ Time ____________

Addition Number Stories

Use *Math Masters,* page 405 and base-10 blocks to solve the number stories.
Record what you did in the parts-and-total diagrams.

Example:

The class had 43 blue crayons and 15 red crayons.

How many crayons did they have in all?

58 crayons

Total	
58	
Part	**Part**
43	15

1. Auntie May had 24 fish and 11 hamsters. How many pets did she have altogether?

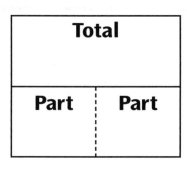

   ________ pets

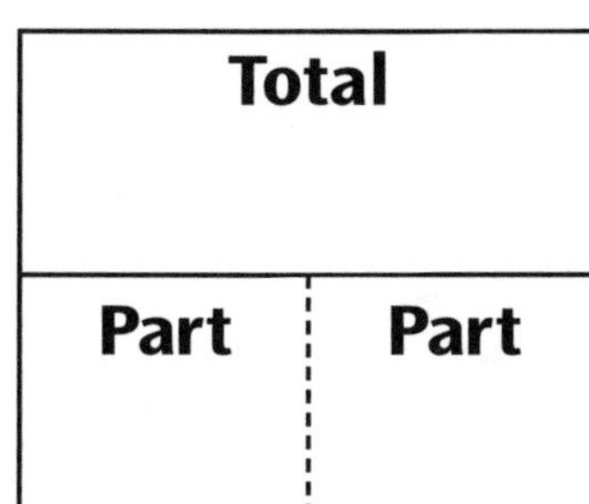

2. Jordan made a flower basket for his mother that had 23 daisies and 8 roses. How many flowers were in the basket?

   ________ flowers

Total	
Part	**Part**

3. Lucia had 38 cents and Madison had 29 cents. If they put their money together, how much money would they have?

   ________ cents

Total	
Part	**Part**

4. Miguel has 54 baseball cards. Janet gave him 47 more baseball cards. How many baseball cards does he have now?

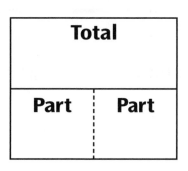

   ________ baseball cards

Total	
Part	**Part**

Name Date Time

LESSON 2·8

Measuring and Drawing Line Segments

Measure the following line segments to the nearest $\frac{1}{2}$ centimeter.

1. ______________________________

About _______ cm

2. ______________________________________

About _______ cm

3. ________________________________

About _______ cm

4. ____

About ________ cm

Draw line segments having the following lengths:

5. 8 centimeters

6. 10 centimeters

7. 3.5 centimeters

Try This

8. Draw a line segment having the following length: 46 millimeters

Name Date Time

STUDY LINK 2•8

Gestation Period

The period between the time an animal becomes pregnant and the time its baby is born is called the **gestation period.** The table below shows the number of days in the average gestation period for some animals.

1. For the gestation periods listed in the table ...

a. what is the maximum number of days?

_______ days

b. what is the minimum number of days?

_______ days

c. what is the range (the difference between the maximum and the minimum)?

_______ days

d. what is the median (middle) number of days?

_______ days

Average Gestation Period (in days)	
Animal	**Number of Days**
dog	61
giraffe	457
goat	151
human	266
Asian elephant	645
mouse	19
squirrel	44
rhinoceros	480
rabbit	31

Source: World Almanac

2. Which animals have an average gestation period that is longer than 1 year?

____

3. How much longer is the average gestation period for a goat than for a dog? _______ days

4. Which animal has an average gestation period that is about twice as long as a rabbit's? _______________

5. Which animal has an average gestation period that is about half as long as a squirrel's? _______________

Practice

6. 56 + 33 = _______

7. _______ = 167 + 96

8. _______ = 78 − 32

9. 271 − 89 = _______

Name Date Time

Construct a "Real" Graph

Do this activity with a partner.

Materials ☐ set of pattern blocks from your teacher

☐ graph mat (4 copies of *Math Masters,* page 406 taped together)

1. Display the pattern blocks on the graph mat so that you can easily count and compare the number of hexagons, trapezoids, triangles, squares, blue rhombi, and tan rhombi.

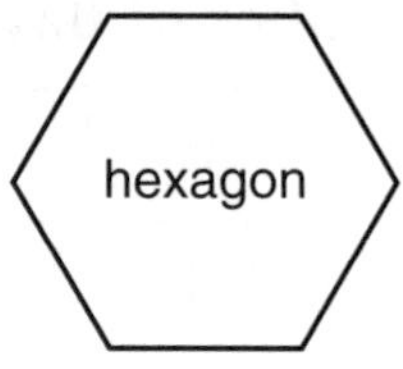

trapezoid

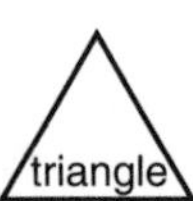

square

2. Use your display to answer the following questions.

a. Which pattern block appears the most? ______________ The least? ______________

b. How many hexagons and triangles are there altogether? ________

c. How many more trapezoids are there than squares? ________

3. Use your display to complete the following statements.

a. There are fewer ______________ than ______________.

b. There are more ______________ than ______________.

c. There is the same number of ______________ as ______________.

4. Write a question that can be answered by looking at your display. Answer your question.

a. Question ____

____

b. Answer ________

Try This

5. How many more quadrangles are there than nonquadrangles? ________

Name Date Time

"One Size Fits All" Claim

Makers of adjustable baseball caps claim that "one size fits all." Do you think this is a true statement? Use the head-size data you collected on journal pages 46 and 47 to help you decide.

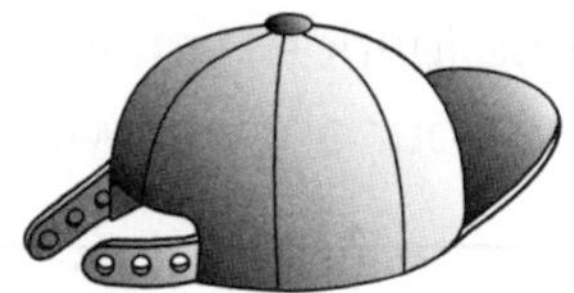

1. Select a baseball cap and adjust the headband to the smallest size. Measure and record the distance around the inside of the baseball cap to the nearest half centimeter.

   Smallest size: ________ cm

2. Now adjust the headband to the largest size. Measure and record.

   Largest size: ________ cm

3. Compare the measurements above with the head-size data you and your class collected. Could this baseball cap be worn by everyone in the class? Explain your answer.

   ____

   ____

   ____

   ____

   ____

4. Do you think you have enough information to decide whether or not the claim "one size fits all" is true? ________ Explain.

   ____

   ____

   ____

   ____

   ____

Name Date Time

Multidigit Subtraction

Make a ballpark estimate. Use the **trade-first subtraction method** to subtract. Compare your answer with your estimate to see if your answer makes sense.

1. $\begin{array}{r} 96 \\ -\ 28 \\ \hline \end{array}$

Ballpark estimate: ______

2. $\begin{array}{r} 469 \\ -\ 87 \\ \hline \end{array}$

Ballpark estimate: ______

3. $\begin{array}{r} 732 \\ -\ 365 \\ \hline \end{array}$

Ballpark estimate: ______

4. $\begin{array}{r} 4{,}321 \\ -\ 575 \\ \hline \end{array}$

Ballpark estimate: ______

5. $\begin{array}{r} 5{,}613 \\ -\ 2{,}724 \\ \hline \end{array}$

Ballpark estimate: ______

6. $\begin{array}{r} 6{,}600 \\ -\ 4{,}278 \\ \hline \end{array}$

Ballpark estimate: ______

Practice

7. 8 × ______ = 64 **8.** 9 × ______ = 72 **9.** 56 = ______ × 8 **10.** 42 = ______ × 7

Name Date Time

Multidigit Subtraction *continued*

Make a ballpark estimate. Use the **partial-differences method** to subtract. Compare your answer with your estimate to see if your answer makes sense.

11.

$$\begin{array}{r} 84 \\ -\ 55 \\ \hline \end{array}$$

Ballpark estimate:

____

12.

$$\begin{array}{r} 136 \\ -\ 79 \\ \hline \end{array}$$

Ballpark estimate:

____

13.

$$\begin{array}{r} 573 \\ -\ 167 \\ \hline \end{array}$$

Ballpark estimate:

____

14.

$$\begin{array}{r} 506 \\ -\ 282 \\ \hline \end{array}$$

Ballpark estimate:

____

15.

$$\begin{array}{r} 5{,}673 \\ -\ 1{,}194 \\ \hline \end{array}$$

Ballpark estimate:

____

16.

$$\begin{array}{r} 3{,}601 \\ -\ 1{,}063 \\ \hline \end{array}$$

Ballpark estimate:

____

Practice

17. ________, ________, 55, 44, ________, 22 Rule: ________

18. ________, ________, ________, ________, 72, 81 Rule: ________

Name Date Time

Subtraction by Counting Up

Use the **counting-up method** to solve these problems. Use the number lines if they are helpful.

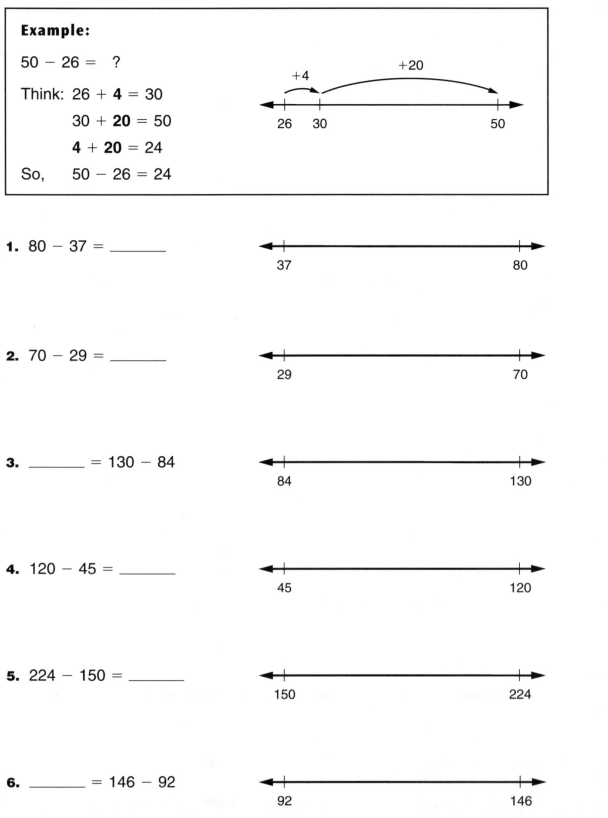

Example:

50 − 26 = ?

Think: 26 + **4** = 30

30 + **20** = 50

4 + **20** = 24

So, 50 − 26 = 24

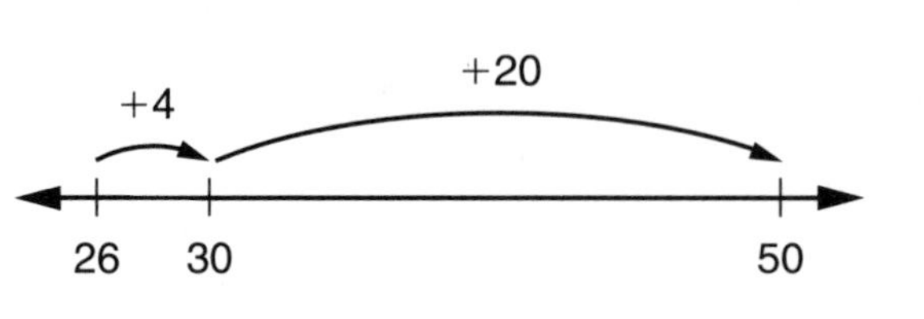

1. 80 − 37 = _______

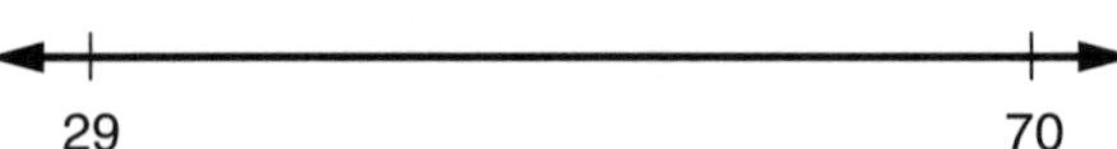

2. 70 − 29 = _______

3. _______ = 130 − 84

4. 120 − 45 = _______

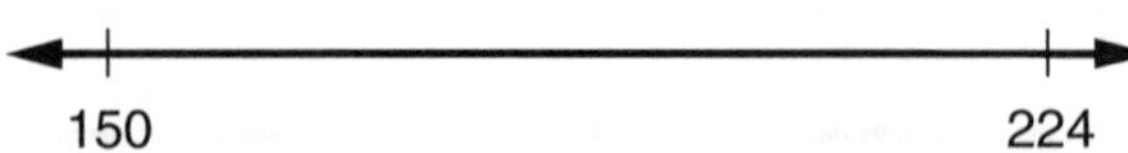

5. 224 − 150 = _______

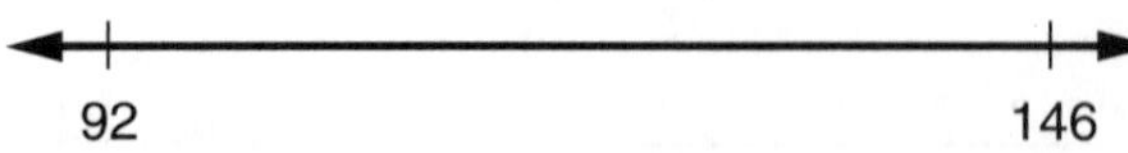

6. _______ = 146 − 92

92 146

Name Date Time

LESSON 2•9 Number-Tile Problems

Cut out the 20 number tiles at the bottom of the page. Use them to help you solve the problems.

1. Use five odd-numbered tiles to make the smallest possible difference.

$$\begin{array}{r} \square\,\square\,\square \\ -\quad \square\,\square \\ \hline \end{array}$$

2. Use five even-numbered tiles (that includes 0) to make the largest possible difference. Do not use 0 as the first digit.

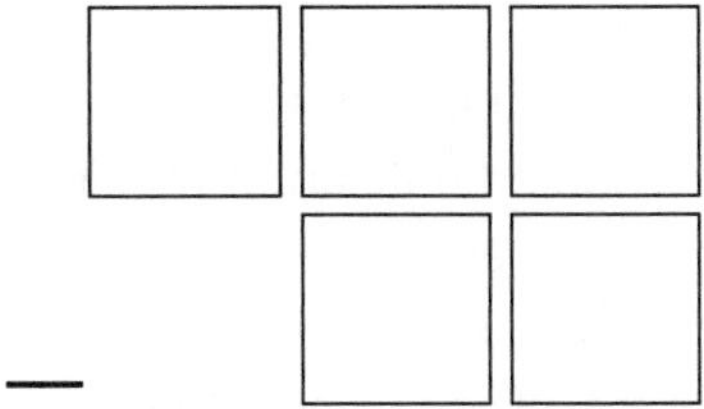

3. Use one set of the number tiles 0–9. Find the missing digits in these addition and subtraction problems.

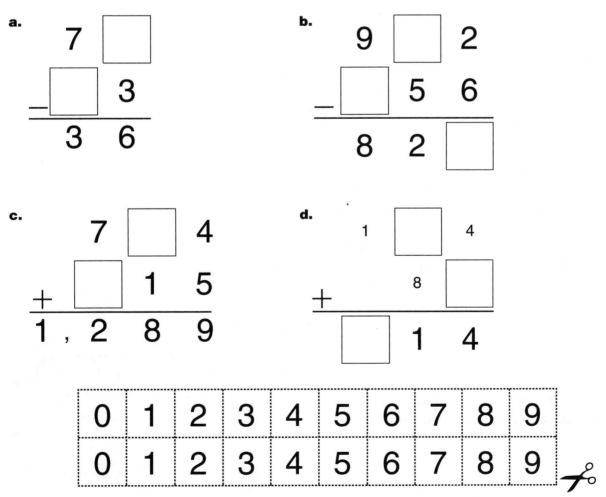

a.

$$\begin{array}{r} 7\ \square \\ -\ \square\ 3 \\ \hline 3\ 6 \end{array}$$

b.

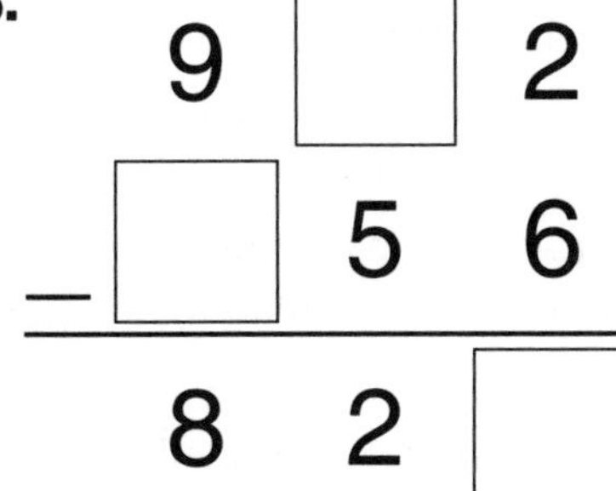

c.

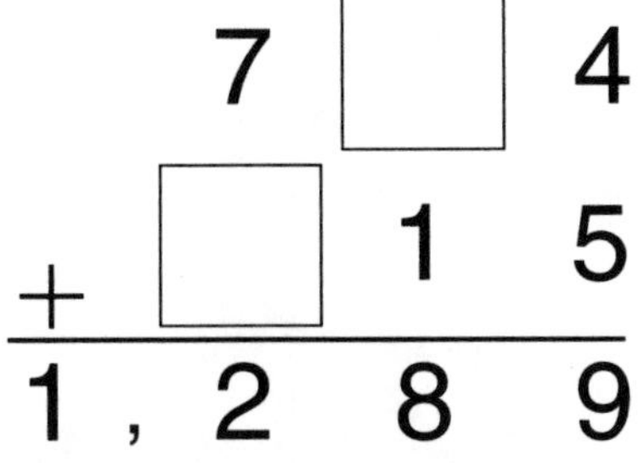

d.

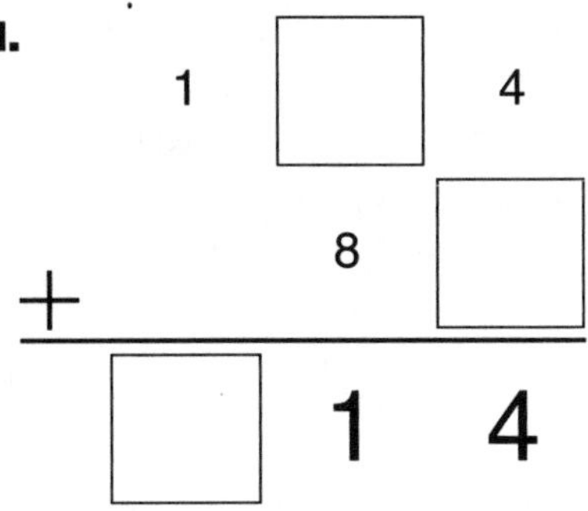

0	1	2	3	4	5	6	7	8	9
0	1	2	3	4	5	6	7	8	9

Name Date Time

Unit 3: Family Letter

Multiplication and Division; Number Sentences and Algebra

20
*, /
4 5

One of our goals in the coming weeks is to finish memorizing the multiplication facts for single-digit numbers. To help students master the facts, they will play several math games. Ask your child to teach you one of the games described in the *Student Reference Book,* and play a few rounds together.

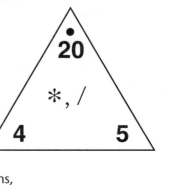

The class will also take a series of 50-facts tests for multiplication. Because correct answers are counted only up to the first mistake (and not counted thereafter), your child may at first receive a low score. If this happens, don't be alarmed. Before long, scores will improve dramatically. Help your child set a realistic goal for the next test, and discuss what can be done to meet that goal.

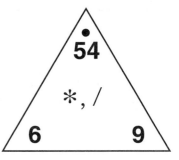

54
*, /
6 9

Your child will use Multiplication/Division Fact Triangles to review the relationship between multiplication and division. (For example, $4 \times 5 = 20$, so $20 \div 5 = 4$ and $20 \div 4 = 5$.) You can use the triangles to quiz your child on the basic facts and test your child's progress.

In this unit, alternative symbols for multiplication and division are introduced. An asterisk (*) may be substituted for the traditional × symbol, as in $4 * 5 = 20$. A slash (/) may be used in place of the traditional ÷ symbol, as in $20/4 = 5$.

In Unit 3, the class will continue the World Tour, a yearlong project in which the students travel to a number of different countries. Their first flight will take them to Cairo, Egypt. These travels serve as background for many interesting activities in which students look up numerical information, analyze this information, and solve problems.

Finally, the class will have its first formal introduction to solving equations in algebra. (Informal activities with missing numbers in number stories have been built into the program since first grade.) Formal introduction to algebra in fourth grade may surprise you, because algebra is usually regarded as a high school subject. However, an early start in algebra is integral to the *Everyday Mathematics* philosophy.

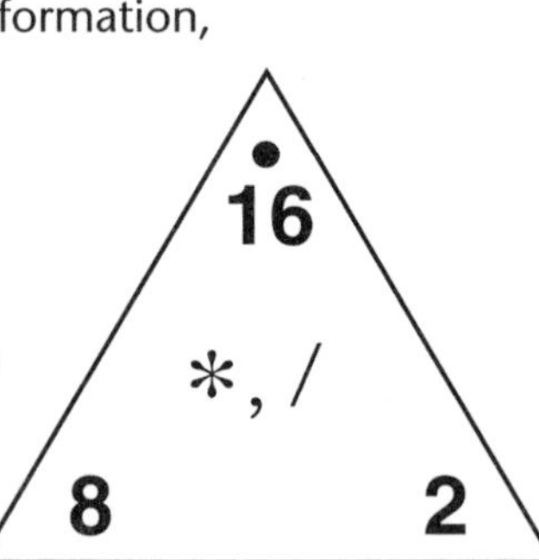

Please keep this Family Letter for reference as your child works through Unit 3.

Vocabulary

Important terms in Unit 3:

dividend In division, the number that is being divided. For example, in 35 ÷ 5 = 7, the dividend is 35.

divisor In division, the number that divides another number. For example, in 35 ÷ 5 = 7, the divisor is 5.

Fact family A set of related arithmetic facts linking two inverse operations. For example, 4 + 8 = 12, 8 + 4 = 12, 12 − 4 = 8, and 12 − 8 = 4 is an addition/subtraction fact family, and 4 ∗ 8 = 32, 8 ∗ 4 = 32, 32/4 = 8, and 32/8 = 4 is a multiplication/division fact family.

Fact Triangle A triangular flash card labeled with the numbers of a *fact family* that students can use to practice addition/subtraction or multiplication/division facts.

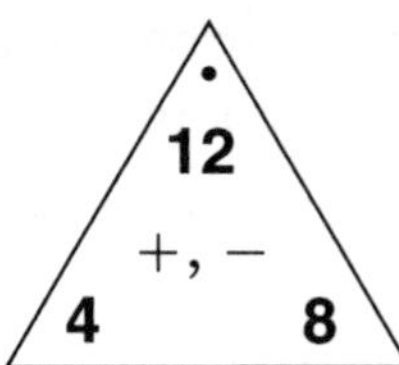

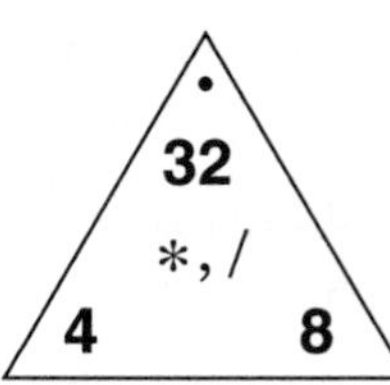

factor One of two or more numbers that are multiplied to give a product. For example, 4 ∗ 1.5 = 6; so 6 is the product, and 4 and 1.5 are the factors. See also *factor of a counting number* n.

factor of a counting number *n* A counting number whose product with some other counting number equals *n*. For example, 2 and 3 are factors of 6 because 2 ∗ 3 = 6. But 4 is not a factor of 6 because 4 ∗ 1.5 = 6 and 1.5 is not a counting number.

multiple of a number *n* A product of *n* and a counting number. The multiples of 7, for example, are 7, 14, 21, 28, and so on.

number sentence Two numbers or expressions separated by a relation symbol (=, >, <, ≥, ≤, or ≠). Most number sentences also contain at least one operation symbol (+, −, ×, ∗, ·, ÷, /). Number sentences may also have grouping symbols, such as parentheses.

open sentence A *number sentence* in which one or more *variables* hold the places of missing numbers. For example, 5 + *x* = 13 is an open sentence.

percent (%) Per hundred, or out of a hundred. For example, "48% of the students in the school are boys" means that, on average, 48 out of every 100 students in the school are boys; $48\% = \frac{48}{100} = 0.48$

product The result of multiplying two numbers called *factors*. For example, in 4 ∗ 3 = 12, the product is 12.

quotient The result of dividing one number by another number. For example, in 35 ÷ 5 = 7, the quotient is 7.

square number A number that is the product of a counting number and itself. For example, 25 is a square number because 25 = 5 ∗ 5. The square numbers are 1, 4, 9, 16, 25, and so on.

variable A letter or other symbol that represents a number. A variable can represent one specific number. For example, in the number sentence 5 + *n* = 9, only *n* makes the sentence true. A variable may also stand for many different numbers. For example, *x* + 2 < 10 is true if *x* is any number less than 8. And in the equation *a* + 3 = 3 + *a*, *a* stands for all numbers.

"What's My Rule?" problem A type of problem that asks for a rule for relating two sets of numbers. Also, a type of problem that asks for one of the sets of numbers, given a rule and the other set of numbers.

Rule
×8

in	out
6	48
10	80
3	
	56
	64

Do-Anytime Activities

To work with your child on the concepts taught in this unit, try these interesting and rewarding activities:

1. Continue to work on multiplication and division facts by using Fact Triangles and fact families and by playing games described in the *Student Reference Book.*
2. As the class proceeds through the unit, give your child multidigit addition and subtraction problems related to the lessons covered, such as 348 + 29, 427 + 234, 72 − 35, and 815 − 377.
3. Help your child recognize and identify real-world examples of right angles, such as the corner of a book, and examples of parallel lines, such as railroad tracks.

Building Skills through Games

In Unit 3, your child will play the following games.

Baseball Multiplication See *Student Reference Book,* pages 231 and 232.

Two players will need 4 regular dice, 4 pennies, and a calculator to play this game. Practicing the multiplication facts for 1–12 and strengthening mental arithmetic skills are the goals of *Baseball Multiplication.*

Beat the Calculator See *Student Reference Book,* page 233.

This game involves 3 players and requires a calculator and a deck of number cards, four each of the numbers 1 through 10. Playing *Beat the Calculator* helps your child review basic multiplication facts.

Division Arrays See *Student Reference Book,* page 240.

Materials for this game include number cards, 1 each of the numbers 6 through 18; a regular (6-sided) die; 18 counters; and paper and pencil. This game, involving 2 to 4 players, reinforces the idea of dividing objects into equal groups.

Multiplication Top-It See *Student Reference Book,* page 264.

The game can be played with 2 to 4 players and requires a deck of cards, four each of the numbers 1 through 10. This game helps your child review basic multiplication facts.

Name That Number See *Student Reference Book,* page 254.

Played with 2 or 3 players, this game requires a complete deck of number cards and paper and pencil. Your child tries to name a target number by adding, subtracting, multiplying, and dividing the numbers on as many of the cards as possible.

As You Help Your Child with Homework

As your child brings assignments home, you may want to go over the instructions together, clarifying them as necessary. The answers listed below will guide you through some of the Study Links in this unit.

Study Link 3•1

1. 60, 230, 110, 280, 370

2. 110, 80, 310, 240, 390

3. 34, 675, 54; +46 **4.** 9, 50, 420; ×7

5. 2, 400, 2,000 **6.** Answers vary.

7. 115 **8.** 612 **9.** 1,440

Study Link 3•2

2. 1, 2, 3, 4, 6, 9, 12, 18, 36 **3.** 1, 16; 2, 8; 4, 4

4. 56 **5.** Sample answer: 4, 8, 12, 16 **6.** 53

7. 388 **8.** 765

Study Link 3•3

1. 24 **2.** 54 **3.** 28 **4.** 16

5. 45 **6.** 18 **7.** 40 **8.** 25

9. 48 **11.** 1, 2, 3, 6, 9, 18

Study Link 3•4

1. 6 **2.** 8 **3.** 6 **4.** 3

6. 20; 5 **7.** 18; 6 **8.** 49; 7 **9.** 9; 2

10. 7; 5 **11.** 7; 4

12. Sample answer: 10, 15, 20, 25

13. 1, 2, 3, 4, 6, 8, 12, 24

Study Link 3•5

1. 5 **2.** 7 **3.** 72 **4.** 10

5. 32 **15.** 1,646 **16.** 5,033

17. 289 **18.** 1,288

Study Link 3•6

3. a. T

4. about 128,921 miles;
132,000 − 3,079 = 128,921

5. a. 4

6. 1, 2, 3, 4, 6, 12

7. Sample answers: 16, 24, 32, 40

Study Link 3•7

	Cities	Measurement on Map (inches)	Real Distance (miles)
1.	Cape Town and Durban	4	800
2.	Durban and Pretoria	$1\frac{3}{4}$	350
3.	Cape Town and Johannesburg	4	800
4.	Johannesburg and Queenstown	2	400
5.	East London and Upington	$2\frac{1}{2}$	500
6.	____ and ____	Answers vary.	

Study Link 3•8

1. 659 − 457 = 202; 202

2. 1,545 + 2,489 = 4,034; 4034

3. 700 − 227 = 473; 473

4. 1,552 − 1,018 = 534; 534

5. 624 + 470 + 336 = 1,430; 1,430 **6.** 9

7. 6, 12, 18, 24, 30, 36, 42, 48, 54, 60

Study Link 3•9

1. F **2.** F **3.** T **4.** T

5. F **6.** T **7.** T **8.** ?

11. b. 7 * 8 = 56 **12.** 36, 60, 84; +12

13. 54, 216, 324; +54

Study Link 3•10

1. 27 **2.** 33 **3.** 1 **4.** 24

5. 37 **6.** 8 **7.** 3 * (6 + 4) = 30

8. 15 = (20/4) + 10 **9.** 7 + (7 * 3) = 4 * 7

10. 9 * 6 = (20 + 7) * 2

11. 72 ÷ 9 = (2 * 3) + (18 ÷ 9)

12. 35 ÷ (42 ÷ 6) = (10 − 6) + 1 **13.** ?

14. ? **15.** F **16.** T **17.** F **18.** T

Name Date Time

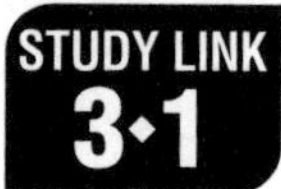

"What's My Rule?"

Complete the "What's My Rule?" tables and state the rules.

1. in → Rule: Add 40 → out

in	out
20	
190	
70	
240	
330	

2. in → Rule: −60 → out

in	out
	50
	20
	250
	180
	330

3. Rule: ________

in	out
131	177
	80
104	150
629	
	100

4. Rule: ________

in	out
70	490
	63
	350
20	140
60	

Try This

5. Rule: There are 20 nickels in $1.00.

dollars	nickels
3	60
	40
5	100
20	
100	

6. Create your own.

Rule: ________

in	out

Practice

7. ________ = 47 + 68

8. 359 + 253 = ________

9. 787 + 653 = ________

Name Date Time

"What's My Rule?" Polygon Sides

1. Use square pattern blocks to help you complete the table.

SRB 162–166

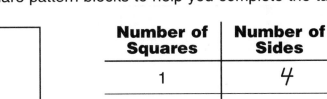

Number of Squares	Number of Sides
1	4
2	8
3	
5	
7	
8	

2. Suppose there are 12 squares. Explain how to find the number of sides without counting.

____

____

3. Use triangle pattern blocks to help you complete the table.

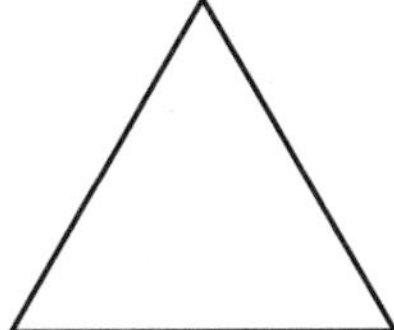

Number of Triangles	Number of Sides
1	3
2	6
	15
	12
	9
	18

4. Suppose there are 30 sides. Explain how to find the number of triangles without counting.

____

____

Name _______________ Date _______________ Time _______________

"What's My Rule?" Perimeter

The distance around a shape is called its **perimeter.** The perimeter of a square pattern block is 4 inches.

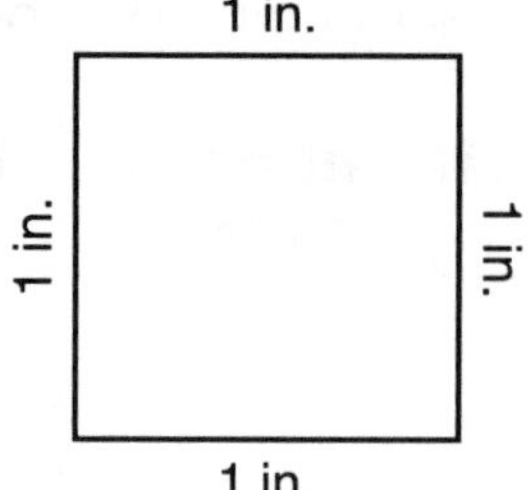

$1 + 1 + 1 + 1 = 4$

1. Place 2 square pattern blocks side by side. What is the perimeter of the shape?

_________ inches

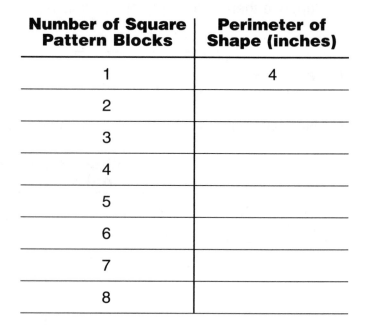

2. Complete the "What's My Rule?" table. Use square pattern blocks to create the shapes.

Number of Square Pattern Blocks	Perimeter of Shape (inches)
1	4
2	
3	
4	
5	
6	
7	
8	

3. Explain the rule for finding the perimeter of the shapes.

____

____

____

4. Use your rule to complete the following: 214 square pattern blocks are placed side by side. What is the perimeter of the shape? _________ inches

Try This

5. Use words or symbols to explain the rule for finding the perimeter of shapes made by placing hexagon pattern blocks side by side.

____

____

Name Date Time

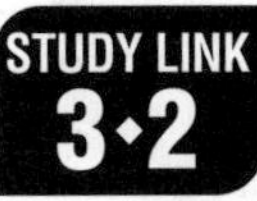

Multiplication Facts

1. Complete the Multiplication/Division Facts Table below.

*,/	1	2	3	4	5	6	7	8	9	10
1						6				
2										
3	3		9							
4		8								
5										
6										
7		14								
8										
9										
10										

2. List all the *factors* of 36. ______

3. List the *factor pairs* of 16. ______ and ______, ______ and ______, ______ and ______

4. Name the *product* of 8 and 7. ______

5. Name four *multiples* of 4. ______, ______, ______, ______

Practice

6. ______ = 91 − 38 7. ______ = 630 − 242 8. 1,462 − 697 = ______

Name Date Time

Rectangular Arrays

Rectangular arrays can be used to model multiplication facts.
Follow these steps to build arrays with centimeter cubes.

1. Place a deck of number cards (1–10) facedown on the table. Turn over 2 cards.
   - Use one card for the number of rows in the array.
   - Use the other card for the number of cubes in each row.

2. Use centimeter cubes to build the array.

Example:

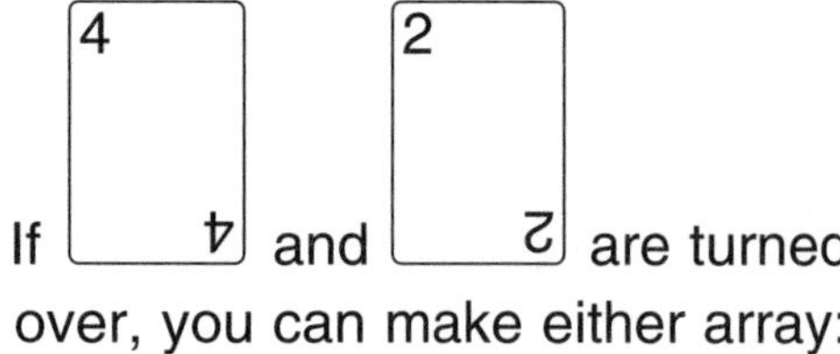

If [4] and [2] are turned over, you can make either array:

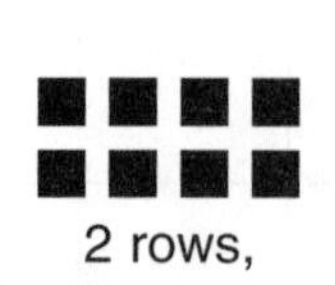

2 rows,
4 cubes per row

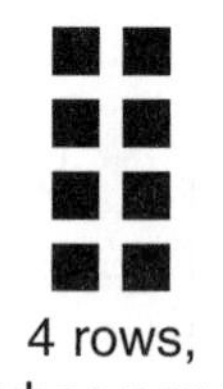

4 rows,
2 cubes per row

3. Record some of the arrays you made in the table below.

How many rows?	How many cubes in each row?	How many cubes in all?	Number model
4	2	8	4 * 2 = 8

Name Date Time

Prime Numbers

A rectangular array shows two factors of a number.

1. On centimeter grid paper, draw as many arrays as you can for each of the following numbers:

   2, 3, 4, 5, 6, 7, 11, 12, 15, 16

   Example: Two different arrays can be made for 8.

   1, 2, 4, and 8 are factors of 8.

2. Write a number model for each array and its turn-around fact.

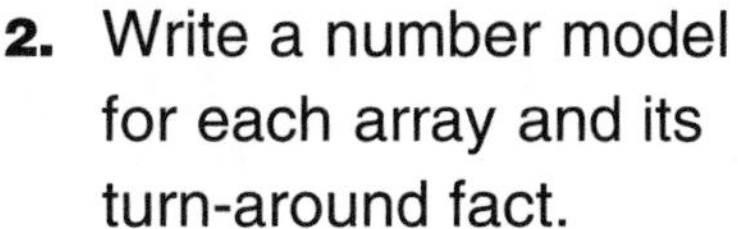

$1 * 8 = 8$ $8 * 1 = 8$

$4 * 2 = 8$

$2 * 4 = 8$

3. Record your results in the table.

Numbers with Only 1 Array	Numbers with More than 1 Array
	8

4. The numbers you listed in the left-hand column are called **prime numbers.** Use the data you collected to write a definition for prime numbers.

____

____

____

____

Try This

5. There are 20 other prime numbers that are less than 100. List them below.

____

____

Name Date Time

STUDY LINK 3·3

Fact Triangles

Complete these Multiplication/Division Fact Triangles.

1. 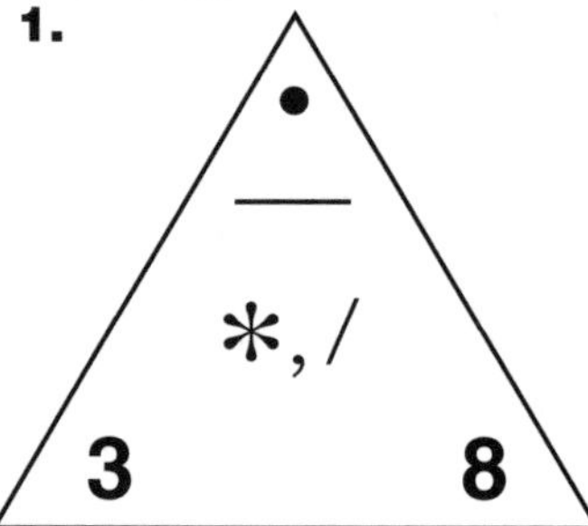

2. 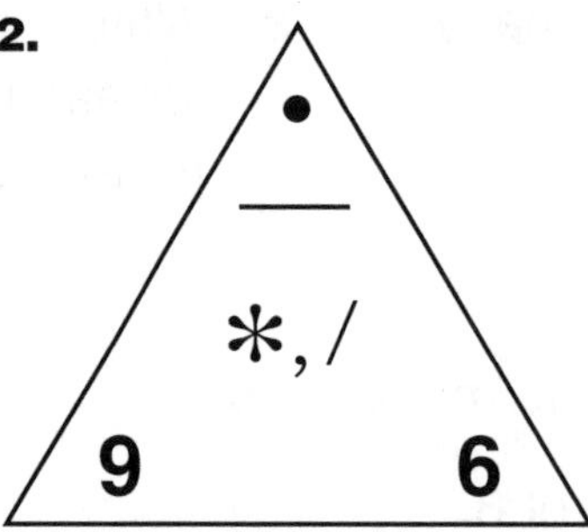

3. 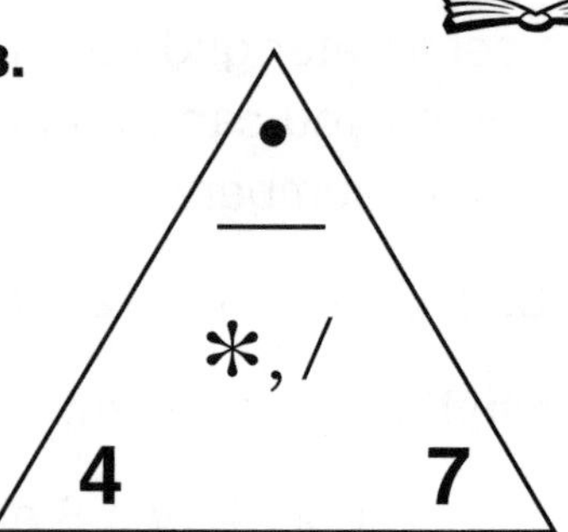

4. 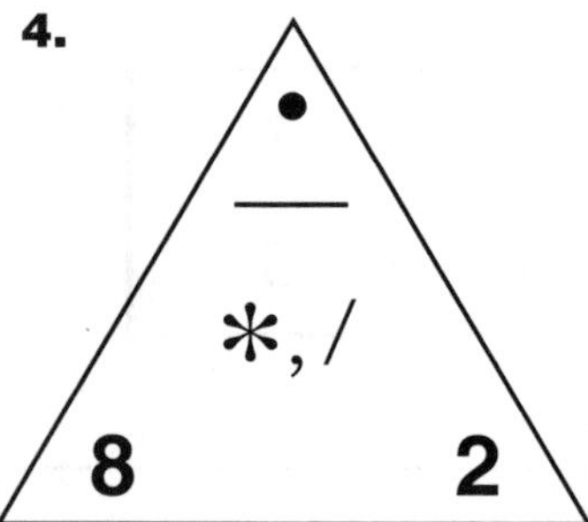

5. 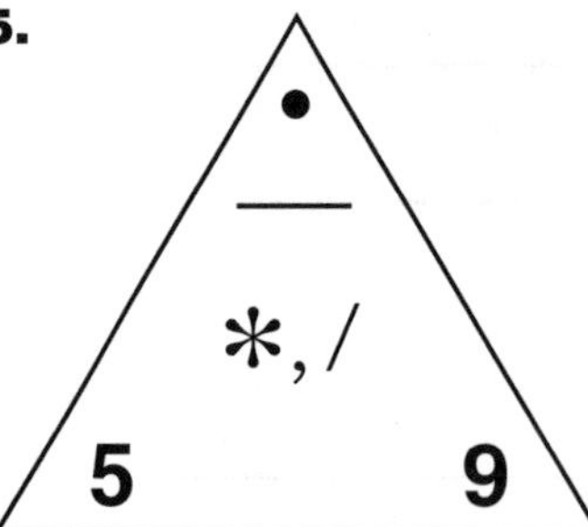

6. 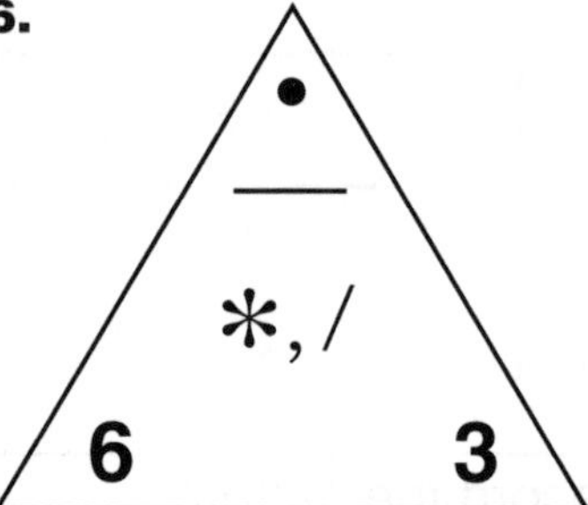

7. 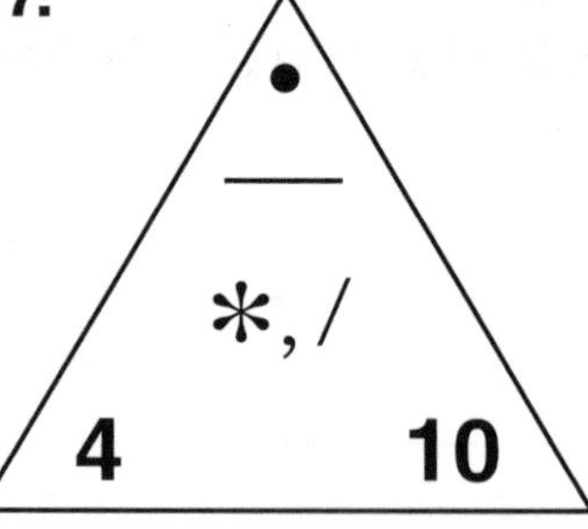

8. 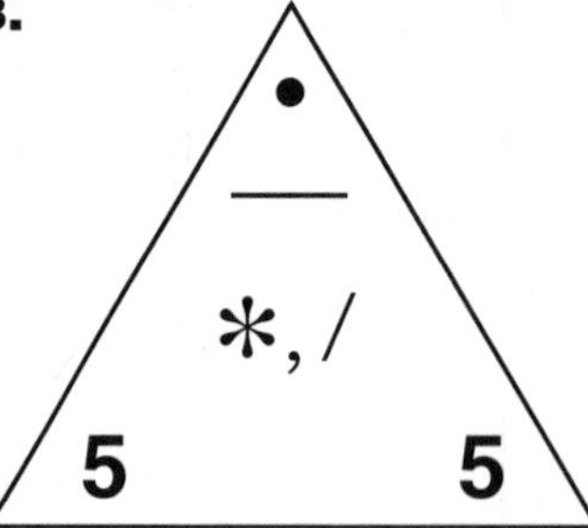

9. 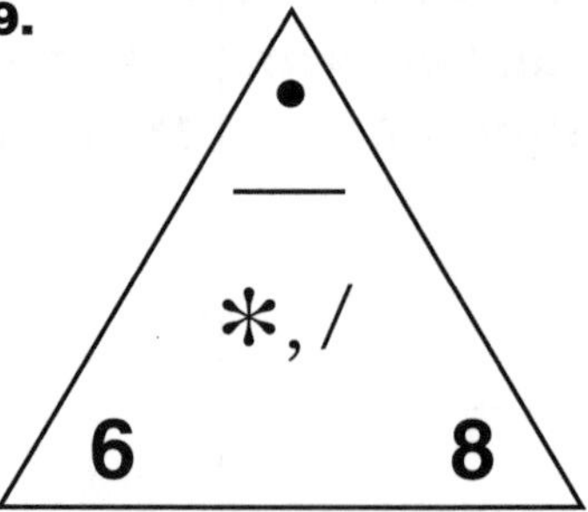

Practice

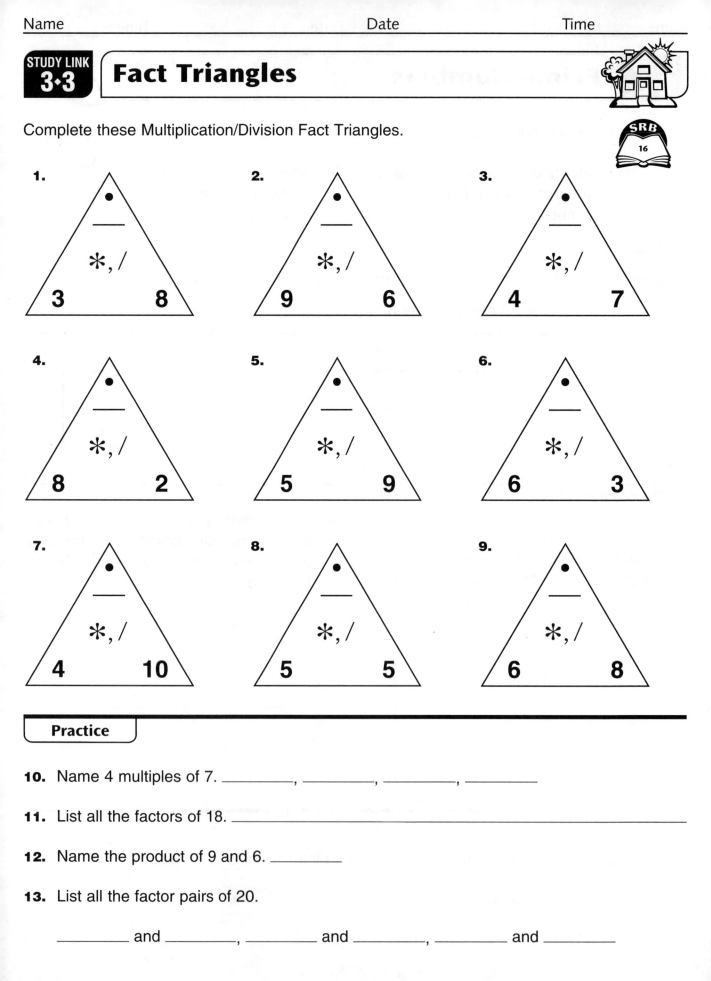

10. Name 4 multiples of 7. ________, ________, ________, ________

11. List all the factors of 18. ____________________

12. Name the product of 9 and 6. ________

13. List all the factor pairs of 20.

________ and ________, ________ and ________, ________ and ________

Name Date Time

Skip-Count Patterns

1. Start at 0. Skip count by 2s.
Record the pattern.

									0
1	2	3	4	5	6	7	8	9	10
11	12	13	14	15	16	17	18	19	20
21	22	23	24	25	26	27	28	29	30
31	32	33	34	35	36	37	38	39	40
41	42	43	44	45	46	47	48	49	50
51	52	53	54	55	56	57	58	59	60
61	62	63	64	65	66	67	68	69	70
71	72	73	74	75	76	77	78	79	80
81	82	83	84	85	86	87	88	89	90
91	92	93	94	95	96	97	98	99	100

2. Start at 0. Skip count by 3s.
Record the pattern.

									0
1	2	3	4	5	6	7	8	9	10
11	12	13	14	15	16	17	18	19	20
21	22	23	24	25	26	27	28	29	30
31	32	33	34	35	36	37	38	39	40
41	42	43	44	45	46	47	48	49	50
51	52	53	54	55	56	57	58	59	60
61	62	63	64	65	66	67	68	69	70
71	72	73	74	75	76	77	78	79	80
81	82	83	84	85	86	87	88	89	90
91	92	93	94	95	96	97	98	99	100

3. Start at 0. Skip count by 4s.
Record the pattern.

									0
1	2	3	4	5	6	7	8	9	10
11	12	13	14	15	16	17	18	19	20
21	22	23	24	25	26	27	28	29	30
31	32	33	34	35	36	37	38	39	40
41	42	43	44	45	46	47	48	49	50
51	52	53	54	55	56	57	58	59	60
61	62	63	64	65	66	67	68	69	70
71	72	73	74	75	76	77	78	79	80
81	82	83	84	85	86	87	88	89	90
91	92	93	94	95	96	97	98	99	100

4. Start at 0. Skip count by 6s.
Record the pattern.

									0
1	2	3	4	5	6	7	8	9	10
11	12	13	14	15	16	17	18	19	20
21	22	23	24	25	26	27	28	29	30
31	32	33	34	35	36	37	38	39	40
41	42	43	44	45	46	47	48	49	50
51	52	53	54	55	56	57	58	59	60
61	62	63	64	65	66	67	68	69	70
71	72	73	74	75	76	77	78	79	80
81	82	83	84	85	86	87	88	89	90
91	92	93	94	95	96	97	98	99	100

5. On the back of this page, write about the skip-count patterns you see in each grid.

Name Date Time

Calculating Combinations

Super Sweet sells ice-cream sundaes. Each sundae comes with one scoop of ice cream and one topping.

Ice-Cream Flavors	Toppings
chocolate	hot fudge
vanilla	whipped cream
strawberry	sprinkles
cookie dough	nuts
fudge swirl	

1. How many *different* sundaes that have one scoop of ice cream and one topping can Super Sweet sell? ______ sundaes

   Use an organized list, table, or picture to solve the problem. Show your work.

2. Super Sweet has decided to add butterscotch to the list of available toppings. How many *different* sundaes can Super Sweet sell now? ______ sundaes

   Explain how you found your answer.

   ____

   ____

3. Explain how you might use multiplication to solve a problem like this.

   ____

   ____

Name Date Time

Math Message

Name ______________________

Date ____________

Ms. Chen's students took their first 50-facts test. These are their scores for the first minute of the test.

26%, 8%, 36%, 18%, 18%, 20%, 40%, 10%, 22%

1. What is the median score? _____%

2. What is the mean score? _____%

Name ______________________

Date ____________

Ms. Chen's students took their first 50-facts test. These are their scores for the first minute of the test.

26%, 8%, 36%, 18%, 18%, 20%, 40%, 10%, 22%

1. What is the median score? _____%

2. What is the mean score? _____%

Name ______________________

Date ____________

Ms. Chen's students took their first 50-facts test. These are their scores for the first minute of the test.

26%, 8%, 36%, 18%, 18%, 20%, 40%, 10%, 22%

1. What is the median score? _____%

2. What is the mean score? _____%

Name ______________________

Date ____________

Ms. Chen's students took their first 50-facts test. These are their scores for the first minute of the test.

26%, 8%, 36%, 18%, 18%, 20%, 40%, 10%, 22%

1. What is the median score? _____%

2. What is the mean score? _____%

Name ______ Date ______ Time ______

STUDY LINK 3•4

Mystery Numbers

Find the mystery numbers.

1. I am thinking of a mystery number. If I multiply it by 4, the answer is 24. What is the number? ______

2. I am thinking of another number. If I multiply it by 3, the answer is 24. What is the number? ______

3. I multiplied a number by itself and got 36. What is the number? ______

4. If I multiply 7 by a number, I get 21. What is the number? ______

5. Write your own mystery number problem.

______

______

Fill in the missing numbers.

6.	4 * 5 = ______	______ * 4 = 20
7.	______ = 6 * 3	18 = ______ * 3
8.	7 * 7 = ______	______ * 7 = 49
9.	______ * 2 = 18	18 = ______ * 9
10.	35 = ______ * 5	______ * 7 = 35
11.	28 = ______ * 4	______ * 7 = 28

Practice

12. Name 4 multiples of 5. ______, ______, ______, ______

13. List all the factors of 24. ______

Name Date Time

Find the Mean

The table shows the number of books in several students' backpacks.

SRB 75

Student	John	Mito	Kate	Ezra	Lina	Luz	Nick
Number of Books	5	2	6	4	0	1	3

1. Place centimeter cubes on the bar graph below to show the number of books in each student's backpack.

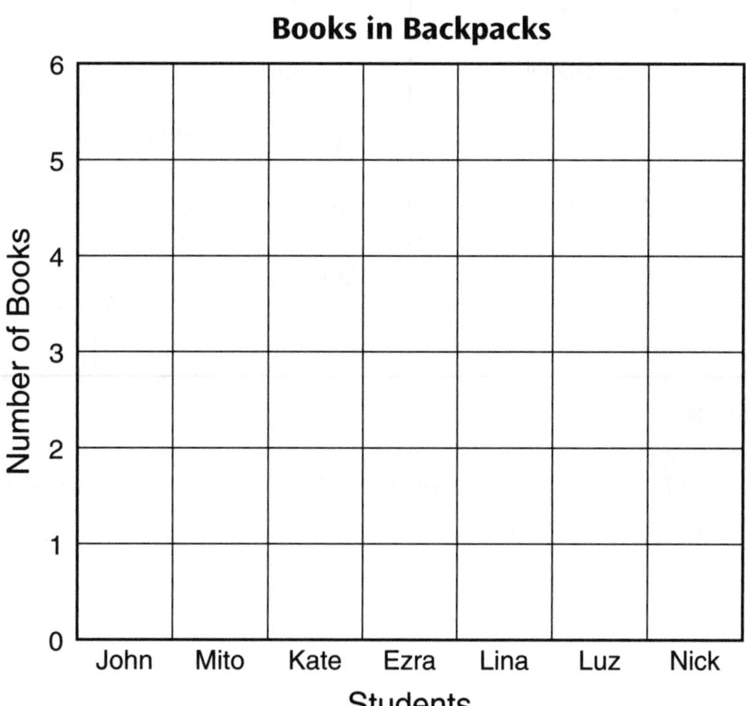

2. Now move the cubes around so that all of the students have the same number of books.

How many books are in each student's backpack now? ________ books

When you "even out" the number of books so that each student's backpack has the same number of books, you are finding the **mean** or the **average** of the data set.

3. Complete the statement.

The mean, or average, number of books in the students' backpacks is ________.

Name Date Time

Compare the Mean and Median

Imagine that you are given a chance to play for a professional baseball team. Before you meet the owner, you will need to think about your salary demands.

Below is a list of some 2004 New York Yankees players' salaries.

Player	Salary	Player	Salary
Brown, Kevin	\$15,714,286	Lofton, Kenny	\$3,100,000
Cairo, Miguel	\$900,000	Matsui, Hideki	\$7,000,000
Clark, Tony	\$750,000	Posada, Jorge	\$9,000,000
Flaherty, John	\$775,000	Rodriguez, Alex	\$22,000,000
Giambi, Jason	\$12,428,571	Sierra, Ruben	\$1,000,000
Gordon, Tom	\$3,500,000	Wilson, Enrique	\$700,000
Jeter, Derek	\$18,600,000		

Source: USA Today Salary Database

1. Would you want your salary to be based on the mean or the median of these players' salaries? Explain your answer.

____

____

2. When news organizations report the salaries of professional teams, they usually use the median. Why do you think they report the median instead of the mean?

____

____

3. If you were an owner of a team, would you rather report your players' mean or median salaries? Explain your answer.

____

____

____

Name Date Time

STUDY LINK 3·5

Missing Numbers

Complete each fact by filling in the missing numbers.
Use the Multiplication/Division Facts Table to help you.

1. 30 / 6 = ________

2. 21 / ________ = 3

3. 9 = ________ ÷ 8

4. 100 / ________ = 10

5. ________ / 4 = 8

6. 25 ÷ ________ = ________

7. ________ = 42 / ________

8. 8 / ________ = ________

9. 4 = ________ / ________

10. ________ ÷ ________ = 1

11. ________ / 2 = ________

12. 10 * ________ = ________

Try This

13. 5 * ________ * ________ = 30

14. 54 = ________ * ________ * ________

*,/	1	2	3	4	5	6	7	8	9	10
1	1	2	3	4	5	6	7	8	9	10
2	2	4	6	8	10	12	14	16	18	20
3	3	6	9	12	15	18	21	24	27	30
4	4	8	12	16	20	24	28	32	36	40
5	5	10	15	20	25	30	35	40	45	50
6	6	12	18	24	30	36	42	48	54	60
7	7	14	21	28	35	42	49	56	63	70
8	8	16	24	32	40	48	56	64	72	80
9	9	18	27	36	45	54	63	72	81	90
10	10	20	30	40	50	60	70	80	90	100

Practice

15. ________ = 989 + 657

16. 314 + 4,719 = ________

17. 887 − 598 = ________

18. ________ = 2,004 − 716

Name Date Time

Fractions and Division

Four friends want to share 3 pizzas evenly. Each person cannot have a whole pizza, so the pizzas need to be divided.

1. How many slices of pizza should each person get? ______ slices. Use a drawing to explain your answer.

2. Marisa says these expressions all mean the same thing:

$\frac{1}{4}$ of 3 $\qquad \frac{3}{4} \qquad 3 \div 4 \qquad 4\overline{)3}$

Do you agree or disagree? Explain your answer.

____

____

____

Name Date Time

Fractions and Division

Four friends want to share 3 pizzas evenly. Each person cannot have a whole pizza, so the pizzas need to be divided.

1. How many slices of pizza should each person get? ______ slices. Use a drawing to explain your answer.

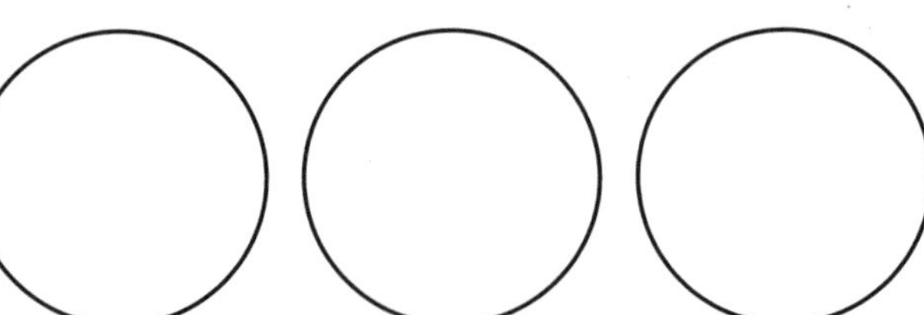

2. Marisa says these expressions all mean the same thing:

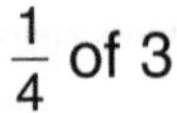

$\frac{1}{4}$ of 3 $\qquad \frac{3}{4} \qquad 3 \div 4 \qquad 4\overline{)3}$

Do you agree or disagree? Explain your answer.

____

____

____

Name Date Time

Number Stories about Egypt

1. The Nile in Africa is about 4,160 miles long. The Huang River in Asia is about 800 miles shorter than the Nile. How long is the Huang River?

   Number model: ______________________ About ________ miles

2. The Suez Canal links the Mediterranean and Red Seas. It is 103 miles long and was opened in 1869. For how many years has the Suez Canal been open?

   Number model: ______________________ ________ years

3. Egypt has about 3,079 miles of railroad. The United States has about 132,000 miles of railroad. How many fewer miles of railroad does Egypt have than the United States?

   Number model: ______________________ About ________ miles

4. The population of Cairo, the capital of Egypt, is about 10,834,000. The population of Washington, D.C., is about 563,000.

   a. True or false? About $10\frac{1}{2}$ million more people live in Cairo than in Washington, D.C. ________

   b. Explain how you solved the problem.

   ____

   ____

Try This

5. The area of Egypt is about 386,700 square miles. The area of Wyoming is about 97,818 square miles.

   a. Egypt is about how many times as large as Wyoming? ________

   b. Explain how you solved the problem.

   ____

   ____

Practice

6. List all the factors of 12. ______________________

7. Name 4 multiples of 8. ________, ________, ________, ________

Name Date Time

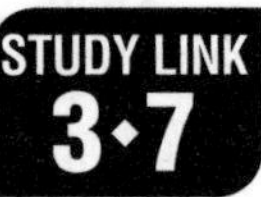

Map Scale

Here is a map of South Africa. Use a ruler to measure the shortest distance between cities. Measure to the nearest $\frac{1}{4}$ inch. Use the map scale to convert these measurements to real distances.

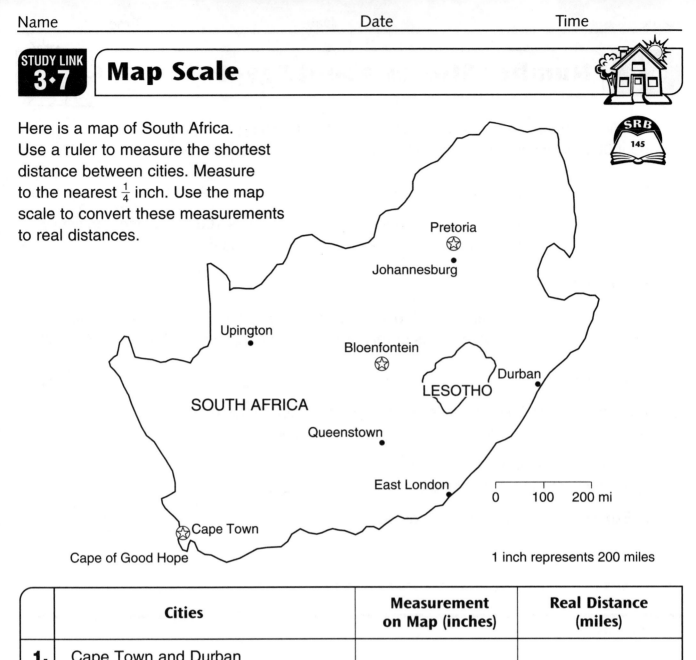

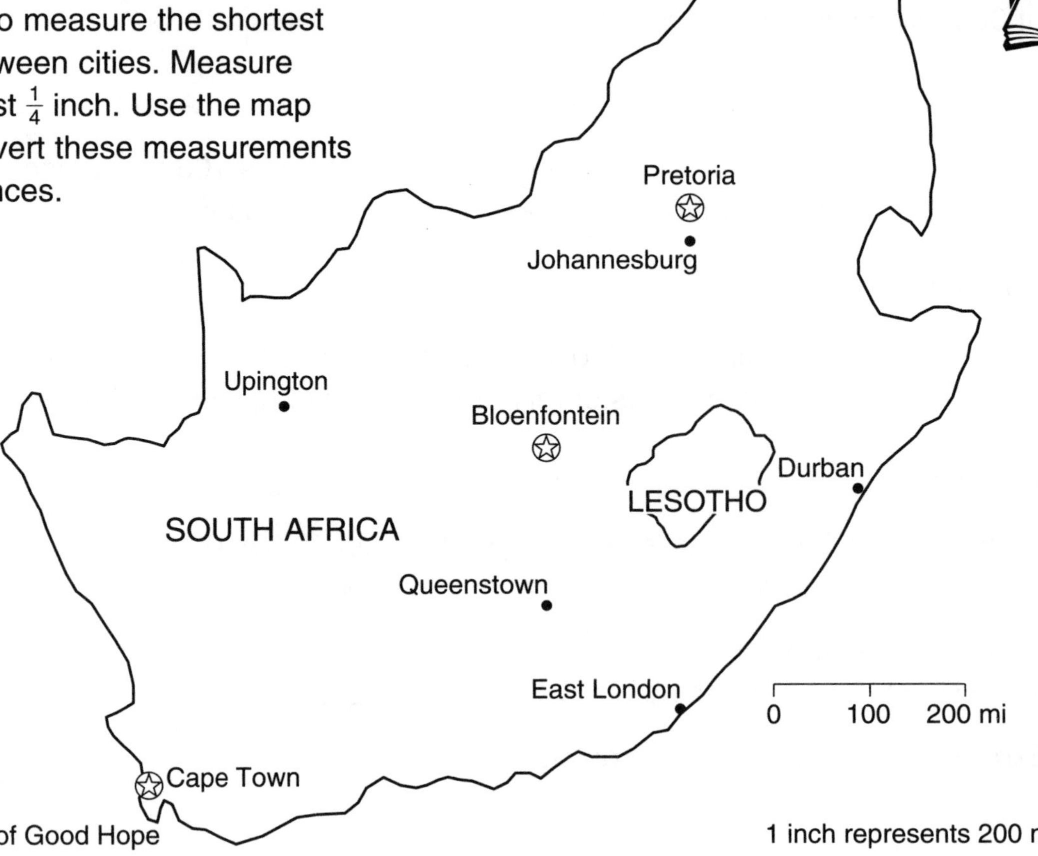

	Cities	Measurement on Map (inches)	Real Distance (miles)
1.	Cape Town and Durban		
2.	Durban and Pretoria		
3.	Cape Town and Johannesburg		
4.	Johannesburg and Queenstown		
5.	East London and Upington		
6.	____________ and ____________		

Practice

7. ____________ = 767 + 254

8. 193 + 6,978 = ____________

9. 562 − 388 = ____________

10. ____________ = 4,273 − 678

Name Date Time

Measure Line Segments

Sometimes you do not need an exact measurement. Measuring to the nearest $\frac{1}{2}$ inch might be good enough.

Cut out the ruler at the bottom of the page. Use it to measure the line segments to the nearest $\frac{1}{2}$ inch. Record your measurements.

1. ____

Think: Is the measure of the line segment closer to 4 inches or $4\frac{1}{2}$ inches?

About ________ in.

2. ____________________

Think: Is the measure of the line segment closer to 2 inches or $2\frac{1}{2}$ inches?

About ________ in.

3. ___________________________________

Think: Is the measure of the line segment closer to $3\frac{1}{2}$ inches or 4 inches?

About ________ in.

4. Allison and Marta measured the line segment below to the nearest $\frac{1}{2}$ inch. Allison said, "The line segment measures about $5\frac{1}{2}$ inches." Marta said, "I think it measures about 6 inches." Who do you agree with? Explain your answer.

____

____

____

____

5. On the back of this page, draw several line segments. Use your ruler to measure them to the nearest $\frac{1}{2}$ inch. Record your measurements.

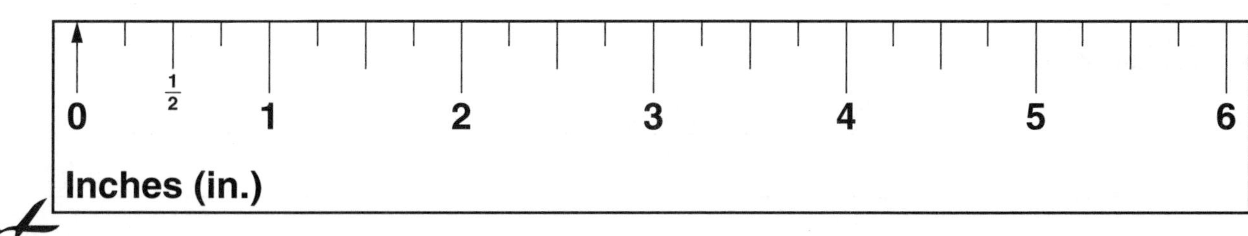

Name Date Time

Compare Map Scales

Different maps use different scales. On one map, 1 inch might represent 10 actual miles, but on another map, 1 inch might represent 100 miles.

1. Record the globe scale you used in Lesson 3-7. 1 inch → _______ miles

2. Locate the maps on pages *282–293* in your *Student Reference Book*. Record the map scale for each region.

a. Region 1: Africa 1 in. → ________ miles

b. Region 2: Europe 1 in. → ________ miles

c. Region 3: South America 1 in. → ________ miles

d. Region 4: Asia 1 in. → ________ miles

3. Do you think changing a map scale changes actual distances? Explain your answer.

____

____

4. Complete the table below to justify your answer to Problem 3. Measure to the nearest $\frac{1}{2}$ inch.

Distance Between	Measurement on Globe (inches)	Air Distance (miles)	Measurement on Region 3 Map (inches)	Air Distance (miles)
Bogotá, Colombia, and Brasilia, Brazil				
Quito, Ecuador, and Sucre, Bolivia				

Try This

5. A **cartographer** is a person who makes maps.

a. Give an example of a map scale that would show very little detail. __________ → ______________

b. Explain your answer.

____

____

Name ______________________ Date ______________ Time ______________

Addition and Subtraction Number Stories

SRB 153

1. In 1896, the United Kingdom had the largest navy in the world with 659 ships. France had the second-largest navy with 457 ships. The United States was tenth with only 95 ships. How many more ships did the United Kingdom have than France?

____________________ **Answer:** __________ more ships
(number model)

2. Rhode Island, the smallest state in the United States, has an area of 1,545 square miles. The area of the second-smallest state, Delaware, is 2,489 square miles. What is the combined area of these two states?

____________________ **Answer:** __________ square miles
(number model)

3. A polar bear can weigh as much as 700 kilograms. An American black bear can weigh as much as 227 kilograms. How much more can a polar bear weigh than an American black bear?

____________________ **Answer:** __________ kilograms more
(number model)

4. The Pacific leatherback turtle's maximum weight is about 1,552 pounds. The Atlantic leatherback turtle's maximum weight is about 1,018 pounds. What is the difference between the turtles' weights?

____________________ **Answer:** __________ pounds
(number model)

5. According to the National Register of Historic Places, New York City has the most historic places in the United States with 624 sites. Philadelphia is second with 470 sites, and Washington, D.C., is third with 336 sites. How many historic sites are there in these three cities?

____________________ **Answer:** __________ historic sites
(number model)

Practice

6. The numbers 81, 27, and 45 are multiples of __________.

7. List the first ten multiples of 6.

______, ______, ______, ______, ______, ______, ______, ______, ______, ______

Name Date Time

Situation Diagrams

Situation diagrams can help you organize the information in a number story and can help you decide what to do to solve the problem.

Decide which diagram to use for each problem. Complete the diagram. Then solve the problem.

1. 283 students attended the football game. 371 students attended the soccer game. How many more students attended the soccer game? _______ students

Total
Part Part

Start
Change
End

Quantity
Quantity
Difference

2. Shawn had $145.00 in his bank account. He took out some money to buy a new bike. Now he has $85.00 in his account. How much did his bike cost? __________

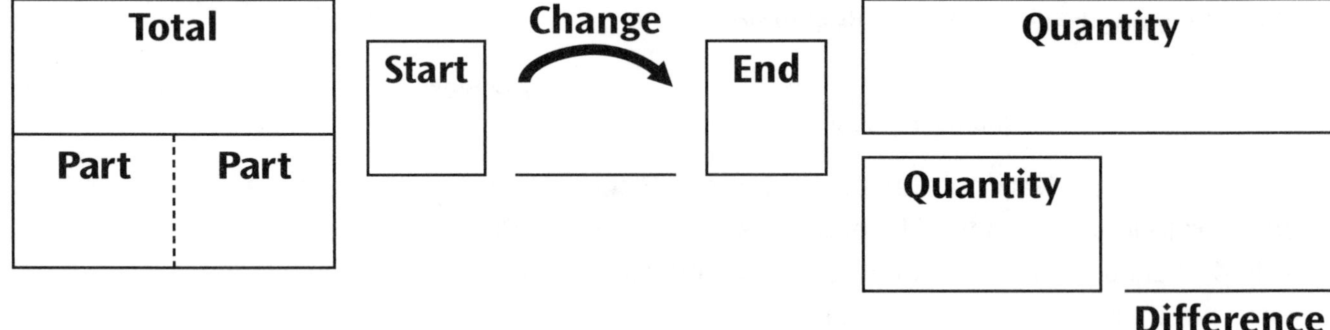

3. Aldo bought milk for 55 cents and a peanut butter and jelly sandwich for $1.25. How much money did he spend? __________

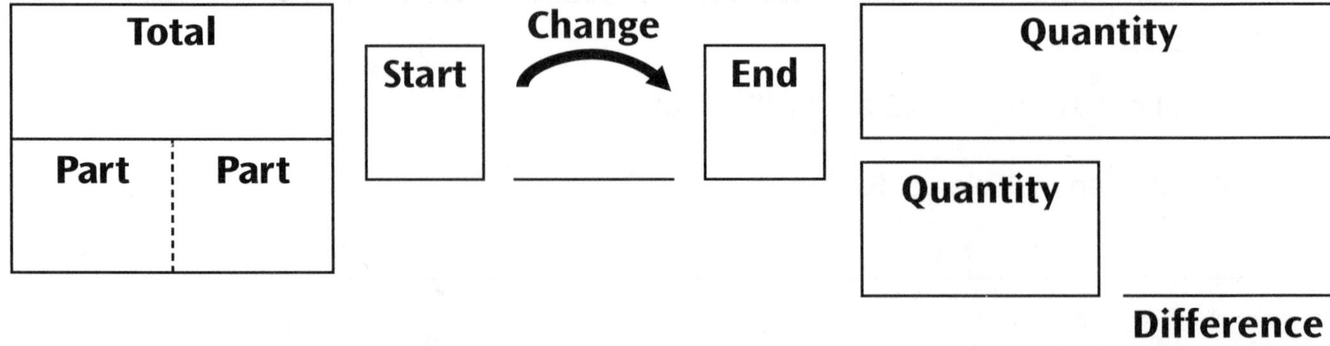

Name Date Time

LESSON 3•8 The Great Pyramid and the Gateway Arch

Great Pyramid of Giza

Gateway Arch

The Great Pyramid of Giza is perhaps the greatest structure ever built by humans. It stands in the desert near Cairo, Egypt. Completed about 2580 B.C., it was the tomb of Pharaoh (king) Khufu. It is estimated that 100,000 workers labored more than 20 years to build the Great Pyramid. It contains more than 2 million stone blocks with an average weight of about $2\frac{1}{2}$ tons each.

Originally the Great Pyramid was about 147 meters tall. Over the years, stones were removed from its surface, reducing its height by about 9 meters. The Great Pyramid was the tallest structure in the world for 44 centuries, until the Eiffel Tower was built in Paris in 1889.

Today the tallest monument in the United States is the Gateway Arch, also known as the Jefferson National Expansion Memorial, in St. Louis, Missouri. The Gateway Arch was completed in 1965 and is about 192 meters tall.

1. How much taller is the Gateway Arch than the Great Pyramid?

   About ____________ meters

2. Underline the information in the essay that you used to solve Problem 1.

3. Use data from the essay above to write your own problem. Ask a partner to solve it.

   ____

   ____

   ____

   ____

   ____

Name Date Time

Number Sentences

Next to each number sentence, write T if it is true, F if it is false, or ? if you can't tell.

1. $20 - 12 = 8 * 3$ ______

2. $7 = 14 * 2$ ______

3. $497 < 500$ ______

4. $16 / 4 = 4$ ______

5. $15 + 10 = 5$ ______

6. $24 > 11 + 11$ ______

7. $100 - 5 = 95$ ______

8. $33 - 4$ ______

9. Write two true number sentences. ______________________

____

10. Write two false number sentences. ______________________

____

11. a. Explain why $7 * 8$ is not a number sentence.

____

____

b. How could you change $7 * 8$ to make a true number sentence?

____

____

c. How could you change $7 * 8$ to make a false number sentence?

____

____

Practice

12. 24, ______, 48, ______, 72, ______ Rule: ______

13. ______, 108, 162, ______, 270, ______ Rule: ______

Name Date Time

> and < Symbols

Different symbols are used to show that numbers and amounts are not equal.

Example:

> means "is greater than"   < means "is less than"

Below are some ways to help you remember these symbols. Try each one.

The alligator eats the bigger number.

1. 3,568 ____ 3,896

2. 7 + 6 ____ 9 + 8

3. 600 + 900 ____ 700 + 300

4. 7 ∗ 6 ____ 5 ∗ 8

The less-than symbol looks like the fingers and thumb on your left hand. The words *left* and *less* start with the same letter. The less-than symbol points to the lesser number.

5. 13,009 ____ 13,053

6. 8 + 8 ____ 9 + 6

7. 500 + 800 ____ 700 + 700

8. 5 ∗ 10 ____ 9 ∗ 7

---

2 < 5   5 > 2

Mark two dots next to the greater number. Mark one dot next to the lesser number. Connect each of the two dots to the single dot, and the symbol will be correct.

9. 34,783 ____ 34,239

10. 11 − 6 ____ 12 − 8

11. 12,000 − 7,000 ____ 18,000 − 9,000

12. 36 / 9 ____ 25 / 5

13. What is your favorite way to remember the > and < symbols? Pick one from above, or tell about your own idea.

____

____

Name Date Time

A Number-Sentence Puzzle

1. Cut out the number tiles at the bottom of the page. Tape them in the number sentences below so that

- each number sentence is true,
- the same digit appears only one time in each row, and
- the same digit appears only one time in each column.

	*		=		*	
	*		>		*	
	*		<		*	

2. Explain the strategy you used to solve this problem.

2	2	2	3	3	3
4	4	4	6	6	6

Name Date Time

STUDY LINK 3·10

Parentheses in Number Sentences

Write the missing number to make each number sentence true.

1. (45 / 5) ∗ 3 = ______

2. 9 + (4 ∗ 6) = ______

3. (20 ÷ 4) ÷ 5 = ______

4. ______ = (33 − 25) ∗ 3

5. ______ = (25 / 5) + (8 ∗ 4)

6. (33 + 7) / (3 + 2) = ______

Insert parentheses ( ) to make each number sentence true.

7. 3 ∗ 6 + 4 = 30

8. 15 = 20 / 4 + 10

9. 7 + 7 ∗ 3 = 4 ∗ 7

10. 9 ∗ 6 = 20 + 7 ∗ 2

Try This

Insert two sets of parentheses to make each number sentence true.

11. 72 ÷ 9 = 2 ∗ 3 + 18 ÷ 9

12. 35 ÷ 42 ÷ 6 = 10 − 6 + 1

Write T if it is true, F if it is false, or ? if you can't tell.

13. (6 ∗ 5) / 3 ______

14. (3 ∗ 7) / (15 − 12) ______

15. 30 = 1 + (4 ∗ 6) ______

16. (4 ∗ 6) + 13 = 47 − 10 ______

17. 15 > (7 ∗ 6) ∗ (10 − 9) ______

18. 20 < (64 ÷ 8) ∗ (12 ÷ 4) ______

Practice

19. __________ = 494 + 3,769

20. 5,853 + 4,268 = __________

21. __________ = 8,210 − 654

22. 7,235 − 906 = __________

Name Date Time

Number Models with Parentheses

Joel and his parents were buying treats for his birthday party. He asked his mother and father, "How much is 6 plus 6 times 3?" His mother said "36," and his father said "24."

1. How did his mother get 36? ______________________

____

2. How did his father get 24? ______________________

____

Joel's parents both thought their answers were correct. Finally Joel said, "I want to buy 1 six-pack of vanilla cupcakes and 3 six-packs of chocolate cupcakes." Then Joel's parents knew whose answer made more sense.

3. Which answer, 36 or 24, makes more sense in this situation? Explain.

____

Name Date Time

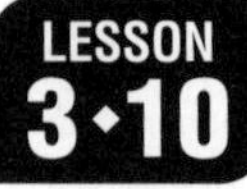

Number Models with Parentheses

Joel and his parents were buying treats for his birthday party. He asked his mother and father, "How much is 6 plus 6 times 3?" His mother said "36," and his father said "24."

1. How did his mother get 36? ______________________

____

2. How did his father get 24? ______________________

____

Joel's parents both thought their answers were correct. Finally Joel said, "I want to buy 1 six-pack of vanilla cupcakes and 3 six-packs of chocolate cupcakes." Then Joel's parents knew whose answer made more sense.

3. Which answer, 36 or 24, makes more sense in this situation? Explain.

____

Name Date Time

STUDY LINK 3·11

Open Sentences

Write T if the number sentence is true and F if the number sentence is false.

1. $35 = 7 * 5$ ______

2. $43 > 34$ ______

3. $25 + 25 < 50$ ______

4. $49 - (7 \times 7) = 0$ ______

Make a true number sentence by filling in the missing number.

5. ______ $= 12 / (3 + 3)$

6. $(60 - 28) / 4 =$ ______

7. $(3 \times 8) \div 6 =$ ______

8. $30 - (4 + 6) =$ ______

Make a true number sentence by inserting parentheses.

9. $4 * 2 + 10 = 18$

10. $16 = 16 - 8 * 2$

11. $27 / 9 / 3 = 1$

12. $27 / 9 / 3 = 9$

Find the solution of each open sentence below. Write a number sentence with the solution in place of the variable. Check to see whether the number sentence is true.

Example: $6 + x = 14$ **Solution:** 8 **Number sentence:** $6 + 8 = 14$

	Open sentence	Solution	Number sentence
13.	$12 + x = 32$	______	______________________
14.	$s = 200 - 3$	______	______________________
15.	$5 * y = 40$	______	______________________
16.	$7 = x / 4$	______	______________________

Practice

17. $366 + 7,565 =$ ________

18. $3,238 + 9,784 =$ ________

19. $9,325 - 756 =$ ________

20. $4,805 - 2,927 =$ ________

Name Date Time

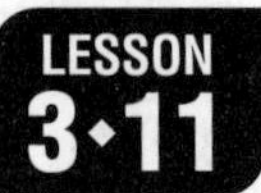

Solve Open Sentences

Rami picked up a Fact Triangle and asked,
"6 times 7 equals what number?"

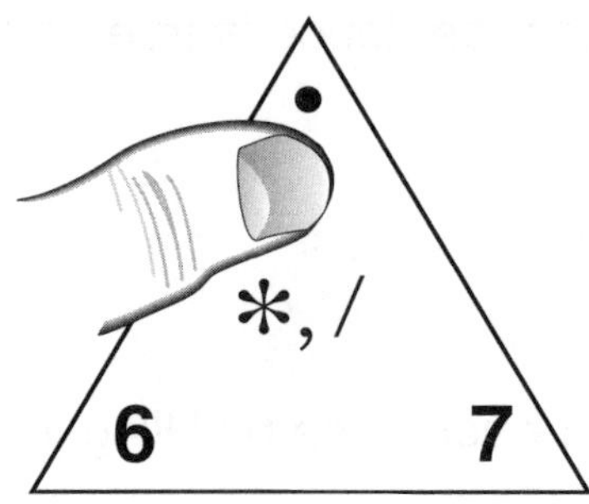

Number sentence: *6 * 7 = ?*

Solution: *? = 42*

Cole picked up a different Fact Triangle and asked,
"3 times what number equals 15?"

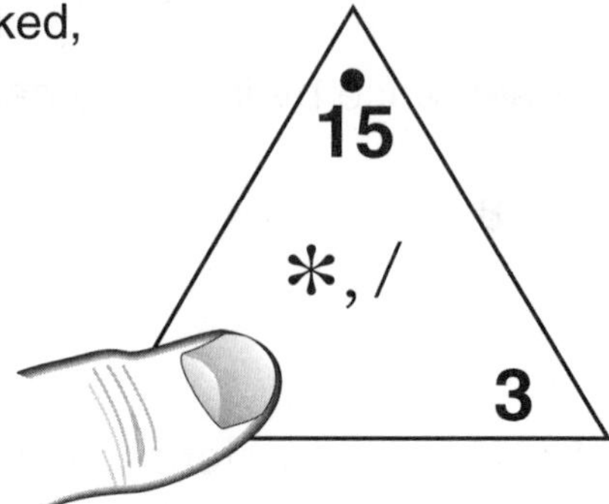

Number sentence: *3 * ? = 15*

Solution: *? = 5*

Choose six Multiplication/Division Fact Triangles. Cover one corner with your thumb. Write the number sentence and the solution.

1. Number sentence: ______________________ Solution: ____________________

2. Number sentence: ______________________ Solution: ____________________

3. Number sentence: ______________________ Solution: ____________________

4. Number sentence: ______________________ Solution: ____________________

5. Number sentence: ______________________ Solution: ____________________

6. Number sentence: ______________________ Solution: ____________________

Name Date Time

Solve Open Sentences

Each letter in the animal names on this page has a value.

C	E	I	L	M	W	Y
8	17	2	12	9	10	4

A	D	K	N	O	P

Some of the values of the letters are known. Some of the values of the letters are unknown.

Use the information below to find the unknown values.

COW is worth 23.

KOALA is worth 46.

DONKEY is worth 66.

MONKEY is worth 54.

LION is worth 35.

PANDA is worth 83.

Name Date Time

Solve Open Sentences

Each letter in the animal names on this page has a value.

C	E	I	L	M	W	Y
8	17	2	12	9	10	4

A	D	K	N	O	P

Some of the values of the letters are known. Some of the values of the letters are unknown.

Use the information below to find the unknown values.

COW is worth 23.

KOALA is worth 46.

DONKEY is worth 66.

MONKEY is worth 54.

LION is worth 35.

PANDA is worth 83.

Name Date Time

Unit 4: Family Letter

Decimals and Their Uses

In previous grades, your child had many experiences with money written in decimal notation. In the next unit, the class will learn about other uses of decimals.

The class will focus on examples of decimals in everyday life. For example, some thermometers have marks that are spaced $\frac{2}{10}$ of a degree apart. These marks give a fairly precise measurement of body temperature, such as 98.6 °F.

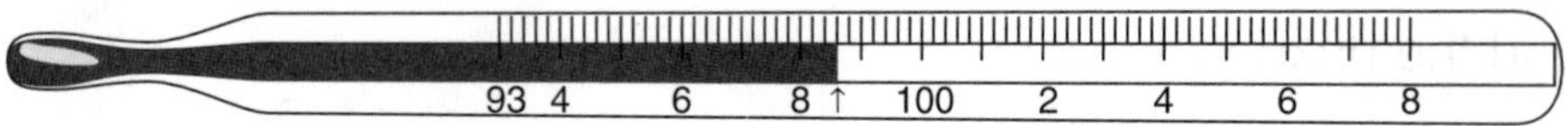

Normal body temperature is about 98.6 °F.

Students will explore how decimals are used in measuring distances, times, and gasoline mileage.

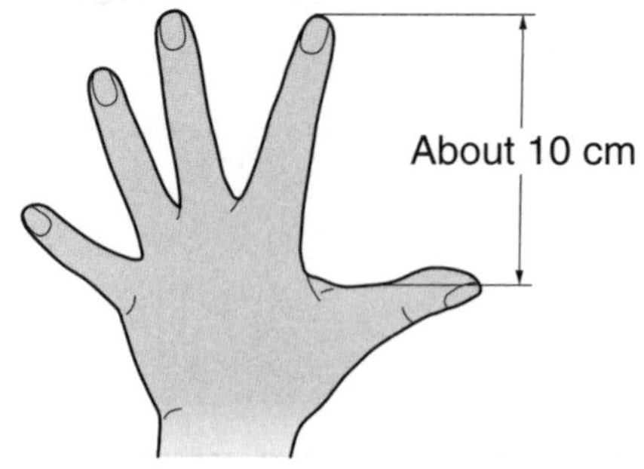

We will also begin a yearlong measurement routine. Students will find their own "personal references," which they will use to estimate lengths, heights, and distances in metric units. For example, your child might discover that the distance from the base of his or her thumb to the tip of his or her index finger is about 10 centimeters and then use this fact to estimate other distances.

The World Tour will continue. In small groups, students will gather information about different countries in Africa and then share what they have learned with the class. Students can then compare and interpret data for a large number of countries from the same region.

Please keep this Family Letter for reference as your child works through Unit 4.

Vocabulary

Important terms in Unit 4:

centimeter (cm) In the metric system, a unit of length equivalent to $\frac{1}{100}$ of a meter; 10 millimeters; $\frac{1}{10}$ of a decimeter.

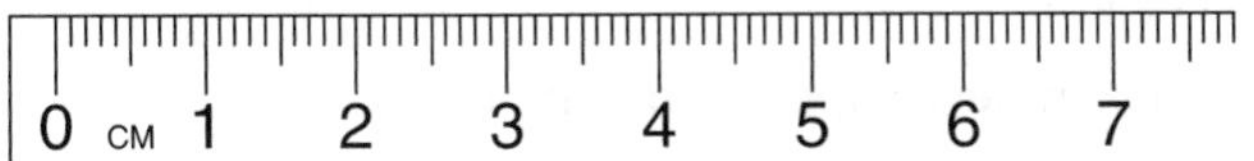

decimeter (dm) In the metric system, a unit of length equivalent to $\frac{1}{10}$ of a meter; 10 centimeters.

hundredths In base-10 *place-value* notation, the place in which a digit has a value equal to $\frac{1}{100}$ of itself; the second digit to the right of the decimal point.

meter (m) In the metric system, the unit of length from which other units of length are derived. One meter is the distance light will travel in a vacuum (empty space) in $\frac{1}{299,792,458}$ second; 100 centimeters; 10 decimeters.

millimeter (mm) A metric unit of length equivalent to $\frac{1}{1,000}$ of a meter; $\frac{1}{10}$ of a centimeter.

ONE Same as *whole.*

ones The place-value position in which a digit has a value equal to the digit itself.

personal measurement reference
A convenient approximation for a standard unit of measurement. For example, many people have thumbs that are approximately one inch wide.

place value A number writing system that gives a digit a value according to its position, or place, in the number. In our standard, base-10 system, each place has a value ten times that of the place to its right and 1 tenth the value of the place to its left.

1,000s	100s	10s	1s		0.1s	0.01s	0.001s
Thousands	Hundreds	Tens	Ones	.	Tenths	Hundredths	Thousandths

tens The place-value position in which a digit has a value equal to 10 times itself.

tenths In base-10 *place-value* notation, the place in which a digit has a value equal to $\frac{1}{10}$ of itself; the first digit to the right of the decimal point.

thousandths In base-10 *place-value* notation, the place in which a digit has a value equal to $\frac{1}{1,000}$ of itself; the third digit to the right of the decimal point.

whole (or ONE, or unit) In *Everyday Mathematics,* an entire object, collection of objects, or quantity being considered; 100%. Same as the ONE or unit whole.

Do-Anytime Activities

To work with your child on the concepts taught in this unit, try the interesting activities listed below. For each activity, discuss the use of decimals and the meanings of place values.

1. Have your child track the sports statistics of a favorite athlete.
2. Have your child compare prices of items in the supermarket.
3. Help your child create and use new personal reference measures.
4. Together, find statistics about countries in the World Tour. Look in newspapers and almanacs.

Building Skills through Games

In Unit 4, your child will play the following games.

Baseball Multiplication See *Student Reference Book,* pages 231 and 232. The game provides practice with multiplication facts.

Fishing for Digits See *Student Reference Book,* page 242. The game provides practice in identifying digits, the values of the digits, adding, and subtracting.

Name That Number See *Student Reference Book,* page 254. The game provides practice with using operations to represent numbers in different ways.

***Number Top-It* (Decimals)** See *Student Reference Book,* page 256. The game provides practice with comparing, ordering, reading, and identifying the value of digits in decimal numbers.

Polygon Pair-Up See *Student Reference Book,* page 258. The game provides practice in identifying properties of polygons.

Product Pile-Up See *Student Reference Book,* page 259. The game provides practice with multiplication facts.

As You Help Your Child with Homework

As your child brings assignments home, you may want to go over the instructions together, clarifying them as necessary. The answers listed below will guide you through some of the Study Links in this unit.

Study Link 4•1

1.

1,000s	100s	10s	1s
6	8	5	4

3.

10s	1s		0.1s	0.01s	0.001s
7	3	.	0	0	4

Study Link 4•3

Sample answers:

3. 5.05, 5.25, 5.95

4. 4.15, 4.55, 4.99

5. 21.4, 21.98, 21.57

6. 0.89, 0.85, 0.82

7. 2.155, 2.16, 2.159

8. 0.84, 0.88, 0.87

Study Link 4•4

1. Seikan and Channel Tunnel

2. Between 90 and 130 miles

3. Sample answer: I rounded the tunnel lengths to "close-but-easier" numbers and added $35 + 30 + 20 + 15 + 15 = 115$ to find the total length.

4. 12 miles **5.** 8 miles

Study Link 4•5

1. 120.41 **2.** 1.46 **3.** 5.18 **4.** 0.03

5. $>$ **6.** $<$ **7.** $>$ **8.** $>$

9. Sample answer: $2.33 + 4.21$

10. Sample answer: $6.83 - 5.31$

Study Link 4•6

1. a. \$0.76 **b.** \$2.43 **c.** \$4.64 **d.** \$2.95

2. \$16.40 **3.** \$2.57 **4.** \$7.32 **5.** \$18.10

6. \$10.78

7. Loaf of bread; Sample answer: The price of a loaf of bread in 2000 was \$0.88. The expected price of a loaf of bread in 2025 is \$3.31. This was almost 4 times its cost in 2000.

Study Link 4•7

1. $\frac{335}{1,000}$; 0.335 **2.** $\frac{301}{1,000}$; 0.301

3. $\frac{7}{100}$; 0.07 **4.** $1\frac{5}{100}$; 1.05

5. 0.346 **6.** 0.092 **7.** 0.003 **8.** 2.7

9. 0.536 **10.** 0.23 **11.** 7.008 **12.** 0.4

13. $>$ **14.** $>$ **15.** $<$ **16.** $<$

Study Link 4•8

1. a. 7 cm **b.** 0.07 m **2. a.** 12 cm **b.** 0.12 m

3. a. 4 cm **b.** 0.04 m **4. a.** 6 cm **b.** 0.06 m

5. a. 2 cm **b.** 0.02 m **6. a.** 14 cm **b.** 0.14 m

Study Link 4•9

2. 180 mm **3.** 4 cm **4.** 3,000 mm

5. 400 cm **6.** 7 m **7.** 460 cm

8. 794 cm **9.** 4.5 m **10.** 0.23 m

11. 60 cm **12.** 8 cm **13.** 7 cm

Study Link 4•10

2. a. 65 mm **b.** 2.6 cm **c.** 610 cm

3. a. 50 mm **b.** 3 cm **c.** 300 cm

4. a. 800 mm **b.** 11 cm **c.** 5 m

5. a. 430 mm **b.** 9.8 cm **c.** 0.34 m

6. a. 6 mm **b.** 0.4 cm **c.** 5,200 mm

Name Date Time

LESSON 4·1

Place-Value Number Lines

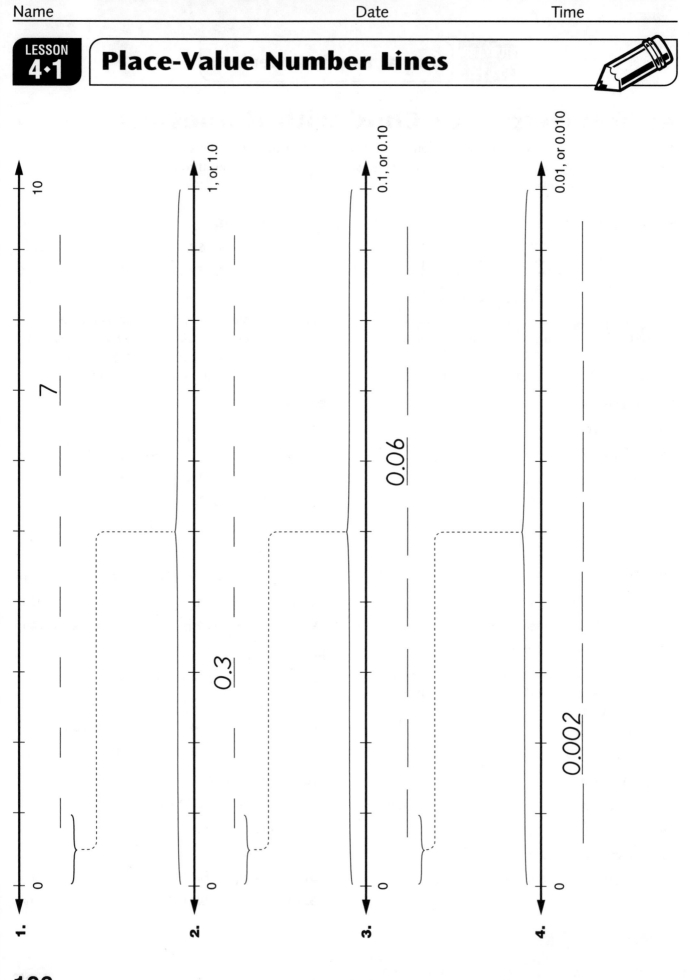

1. 0 ... 7 ... 10

2. 0 ... 0.3 ... 1, or 1.0

3. 0 ... 0.06 ... 0.1, or 0.10

4. 0 ... 0.002 ... 0.01, or 0.010

Name Date Time

LESSON 4•1 Place-Value Chart

1,000s	100s	10s	1s				
Thousands	Hundreds	Tens	Ones	.			

Name Date Time

Place-Value Puzzles

Use the clues to write the digits in the boxes and find each number.

1.
- Write 5 in the tens place.
- Find $\frac{1}{2}$ of 24. Subtract 4. Write the result in the hundreds place.
- Add 7 to the digit in the tens place. Divide by 2. Write the result in the thousands place.
- In the ones place, write an even number greater than 2 that has not been used yet.

1,000s	100s	10s	1s

2.
- Divide 15 by 3. Write the result in the hundredths place.
- Multiply 2 by 10. Divide by 10. Write the result in the ones place.
- Write a digit in the tenths place that is 4 more than the digit in the hundredths place.
- Add 7 to the digit in the ones place. Write the result in the thousandths place.

100s	10s	1s		0.1s	0.01s	0.001s
			.			

3.
- Write the result of 6 ∗ 9 divided by 18 in the ones place.
- Double 8. Divide by 4. Write the result in the thousandths place.
- Add 3 to the digit in the thousandths place. Write the result in the tens place.
- Write the same digit in the tenths and hundredths place so that the sum of all the digits is 14.

10s	1s		0.1s	0.01s	0.001s
		.			

Practice

Write true or false.

4. 6 ∗ 5 = 15 + 15 ________ **5.** 15 + 7 < 13 − 8 ________ **6.** 72 / 9 > 9 ________

Name Date Time

Money and Decimals

Use only $1 bills , dimes , and pennies .

1. Use as few bills and coins as possible to show each amount below. Record your work.

Amount	$1 bills	Dimes	Pennies
$1.26	1	2	6
$1.11			
$2.35			
$3.40			
$2.06			
$0.96			
$0.70			
$0.03			

2. Describe any patterns you see in the table.

____

____

____

____

3. You can use $1 bills, dimes, and pennies to make any amount of money. Why do you think we have nickels, quarters, and half-dollars?

____

____

____

Name Date Time

Decimals All Around

Find examples of decimals in newspapers, in magazines, in books, or on food packages. Ask people in your family for examples.

Write your numbers below or, if an adult says you may, cut them out and tape them on this page. Be sure to write what the numbers mean. For example, "The body temperature of a hibernating dormouse may go down to 35.6°F."

____

____

____

____

____

____

____

____

____

____

____

____

____

Practice

Write true or false.

1. 286 + 286 = 462 ________

2. 907 − 709 = 200 ________

3. 641 + 359 = 359 + 641 ________

4. 2,345 − 198 = 2,969 − 822 ________

Name Date Time

LESSON 4•2 The ONE

Use base-10 blocks to help you solve the following problems.

1. If [long] is ONE, then what is [cube]? ________ What is [flat]? ________

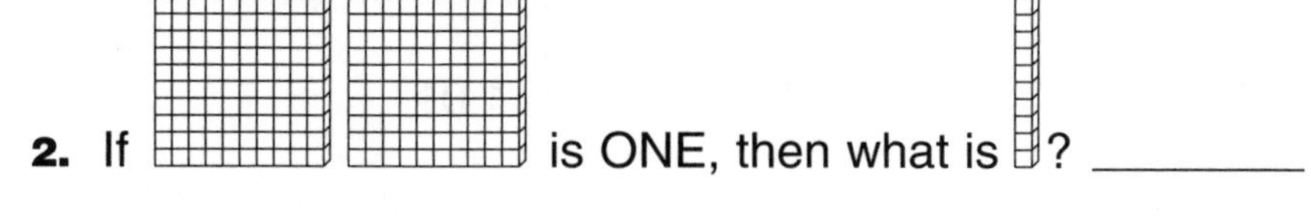

2. If [2 flats] is ONE, then what is [long]? ________ What is [cube]? ________

3. If [5 longs] is ONE, then what is [cube]? ________ What is [flat]? ________

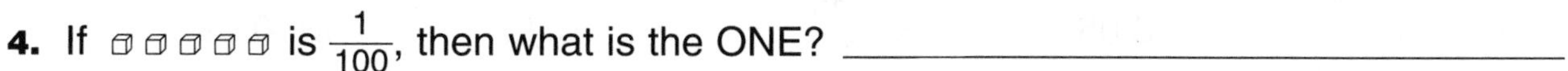

4. If [5 cubes] is $\frac{1}{100}$, then what is the ONE? ____________________

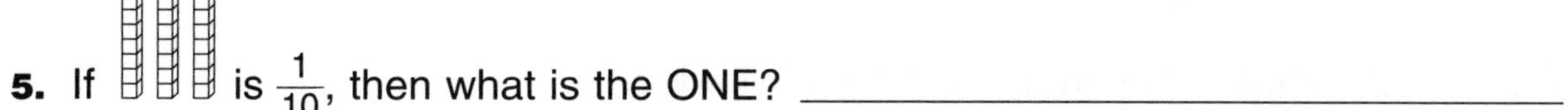

5. If [3 longs] is $\frac{1}{10}$, then what is the ONE? ____________________

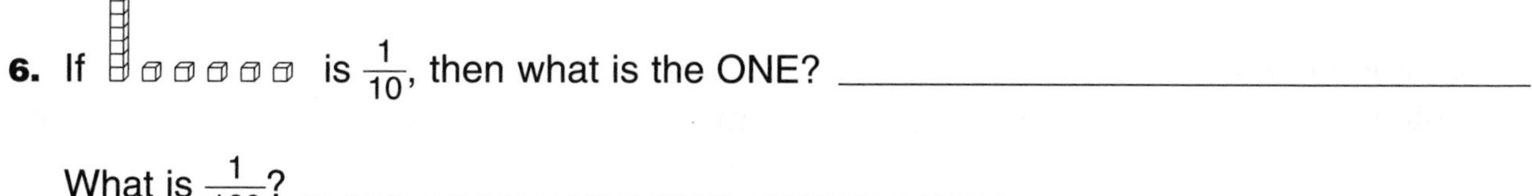

6. If [1 long and 5 cubes] is $\frac{1}{10}$, then what is the ONE? ____________________

What is $\frac{1}{100}$? ____________________

7. Explain how you solved Problem 6.

____

____

____

____

Name Date Time

STUDY LINK 4•3

Ordering Decimals

Mark the approximate locations of the decimals and fractions on the number lines below. Rename fractions as decimals as necessary.

1.

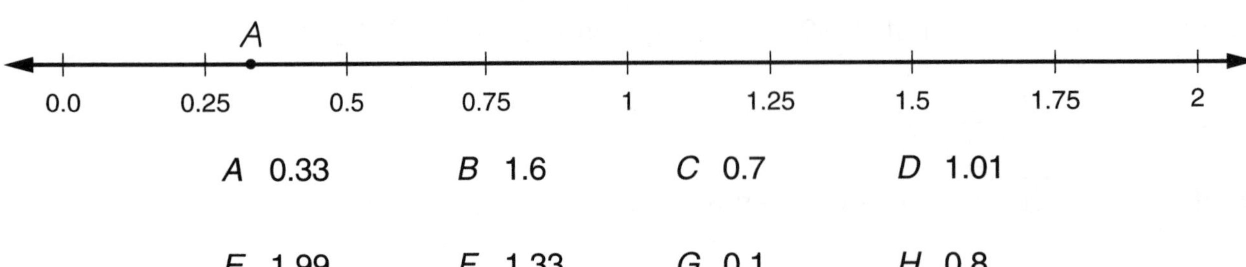

A 0.33 *B* 1.6 *C* 0.7 *D* 1.01

E 1.99 *F* 1.33 *G* 0.1 *H* 0.8

2.

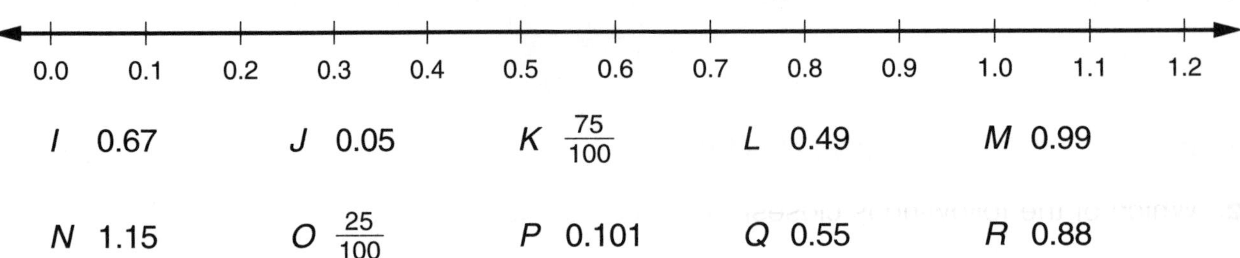

I 0.67 *J* 0.05 *K* $\frac{75}{100}$ *L* 0.49 *M* 0.99

N 1.15 *O* $\frac{25}{100}$ *P* 0.101 *Q* 0.55 *R* 0.88

Use decimals. Write 3 numbers that are between the following:

3. \$5 and \$6 \$________ \$________ \$________

4. 4 centimeters and 5 centimeters ________ cm ________ cm ________ cm

5. 21 seconds and 22 seconds ________ sec ________ sec ________ sec

6. 8 dimes and 9 dimes \$________ \$________ \$________

7. 2.15 meters and 2.17 meters ________ m ________ m ________ m

8. 0.8 meter and 0.9 meter ________ m ________ m ________ m

Practice

9. $x + 17 = 23$ $x =$ _____ **10.** $5 * n = 35$ $n =$ _____ **11.** $32 / b = 4$ $b =$ _____

Name Date Time

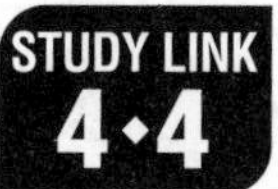

Railroad Tunnel Lengths

The table below shows the five longest railroad tunnels in the world.

Tunnel	Location	Year Completed	Length in Miles
Seikan	Japan	1988	33.46
Channel	France/England	1994	31.35
Moscow Metro	Russia	1979	19.07
London Underground	United Kingdom	1939	17.30
Dai-Shimizu	Japan	1982	13.98

Use estimation to answer the following questions.

1. Which two tunnels have a combined length of about 60 miles?

____________________ and ____________________

2. Which of the following is closest to the combined length of all five tunnels? Choose the best answer.

- ⬭ Less than 90 miles
- ⬭ Between 90 and 130 miles
- ⬭ Between 130 and 160 miles
- ⬭ More than 160 miles

3. Explain how you solved Problem 2.

____

____

4. About how many miles longer is the Channel Tunnel than the Moscow Metro Tunnel?

About ______ miles

Try This

5. The Cascade Tunnel in Washington State is the longest railroad tunnel in the United States. It is about $\frac{1}{4}$ the length of the Seikan. About how long is the Cascade Tunnel?

About ______ miles

Practice

6. $190 + b = 200$ $b =$ ______

7. $g - 500 = 225$ $g =$ ______

Name Date Time

Items to Purchase

light bulbs

4-pack

$1.09

VCR tape

$3.25

tissues

$0.73

transparent tape

$0.84

batteries

4-pack

$3.59

toothpaste

$1.39

ballpoint pen

$0.39

tennis balls

can of 3

$2.59

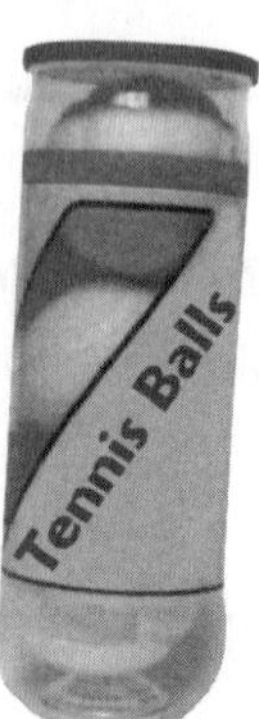

paperback book

$2.99

Name Date Time

Estimate Purchase Cost

Cost of Item 1	Cost of Item 2	Cost of Item 3	Number Model I Used to Estimate
$1.09	$1.39	$0.84	$1.00 + $1.40 + $1.00 = $3.40

Name Date Time

Estimate Purchase Cost

Cost of Item 1	Cost of Item 2	Cost of Item 3	Number Model I Used to Estimate
$1.09	$1.39	$0.84	$1.00 + $1.40 + $1.00 = $3.40

Name Date Time

Will I Run Out of Gas?

You are driving with your family from Denver, Colorado, to Des Moines, Iowa. You know the following:

- Your car's gasoline tank holds about 12.1 gallons.
- Your car uses about 1 gallon of gasoline for every 30 miles on the highway.
- You start your trip with a full tank.

Here is a map of the route you follow.

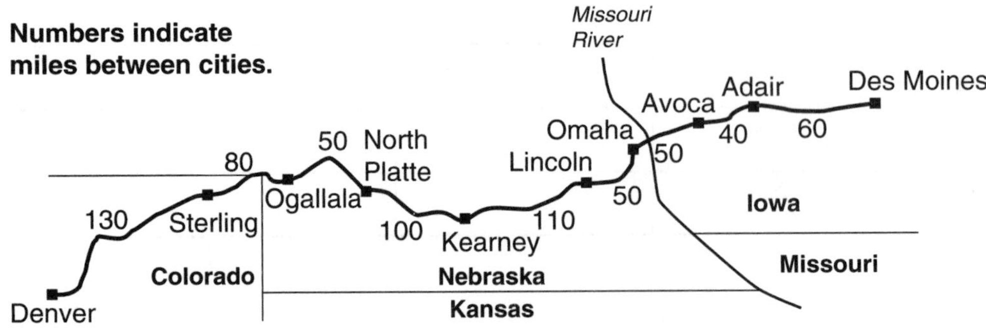

1. About how many gallons of gasoline would your car use traveling from Denver to Sterling? About ________ gallons

2. When you get to Ogallala, you would expect your gas tank to be

a. almost empty. **b.** about $\frac{1}{4}$ full. **c.** about $\frac{1}{2}$ full. **d.** about $\frac{3}{4}$ full.

3. Is it OK to wait until you get to Kearney to buy more gas? Explain.

____

____

____

4. You stop at North Platte to buy more gasoline. If you buy 7.6 gallons, about how many gallons are there in your tank now? About ________ gallons

5. Could you get to Des Moines from North Platte without running out of gas if you filled your gasoline tank just one more time? ______________

If so, where would you stop? ______________________________

Name Date Time

Decimal Magic Square

Insert decimal points so that the sum of the numbers in each row, column, and diagonal is equal to 6.5.

3 0	1 6	9 0	2 2	1 5 0
2 0	8 0	2 1	1 4	2 0
7 0	2 5	1 3 0	1 0	1 9 0
2 4	1 2	5 0	1 8	6 0
1 1	4 0	1 7	1 0 0	2 3

Name Date Time

Decimal Magic Square

Insert decimal points so that the sum of the numbers in each row, column, and diagonal is equal to 6.5.

3 0	1 6	9 0	2 2	1 5 0
2 0	8 0	2 1	1 4	2 0
7 0	2 5	1 3 0	1 0	1 9 0
2 4	1 2	5 0	1 8	6 0
1 1	4 0	1 7	1 0 0	2 3

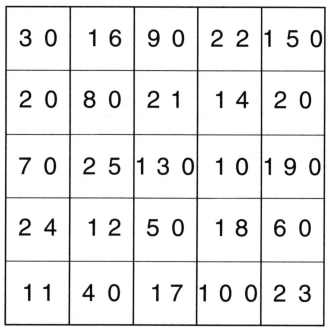

Name Date Time

Math Message

What's wrong with this problem?
What is the correct answer?

$$\begin{array}{r} 0.76 \\ +\ 0.2 \\ \hline 0.78 \end{array}$$

Name Date Time

Math Message

What's wrong with this problem?
What is the correct answer?

$$\begin{array}{r} 0.76 \\ +\ 0.2 \\ \hline 0.78 \end{array}$$

Name Date Time

Math Message

What's wrong with this problem?
What is the correct answer?

$$\begin{array}{r} 0.76 \\ +\ 0.2 \\ \hline 0.78 \end{array}$$

Name Date Time

Math Message

What's wrong with this problem?
What is the correct answer?

$$\begin{array}{r} 0.76 \\ +\ 0.2 \\ \hline 0.78 \end{array}$$

Name Date Time

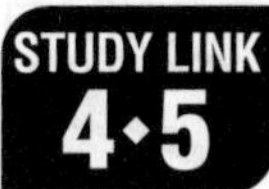

Addition and Subtraction of Decimals

Add or subtract. Show your work.

1. 96.45 + 23.96 = ________

2. 1.06 + 0.4 = ________

3. 9.87 − 4.69 = ________

4. 0.4 − 0.37 = ________

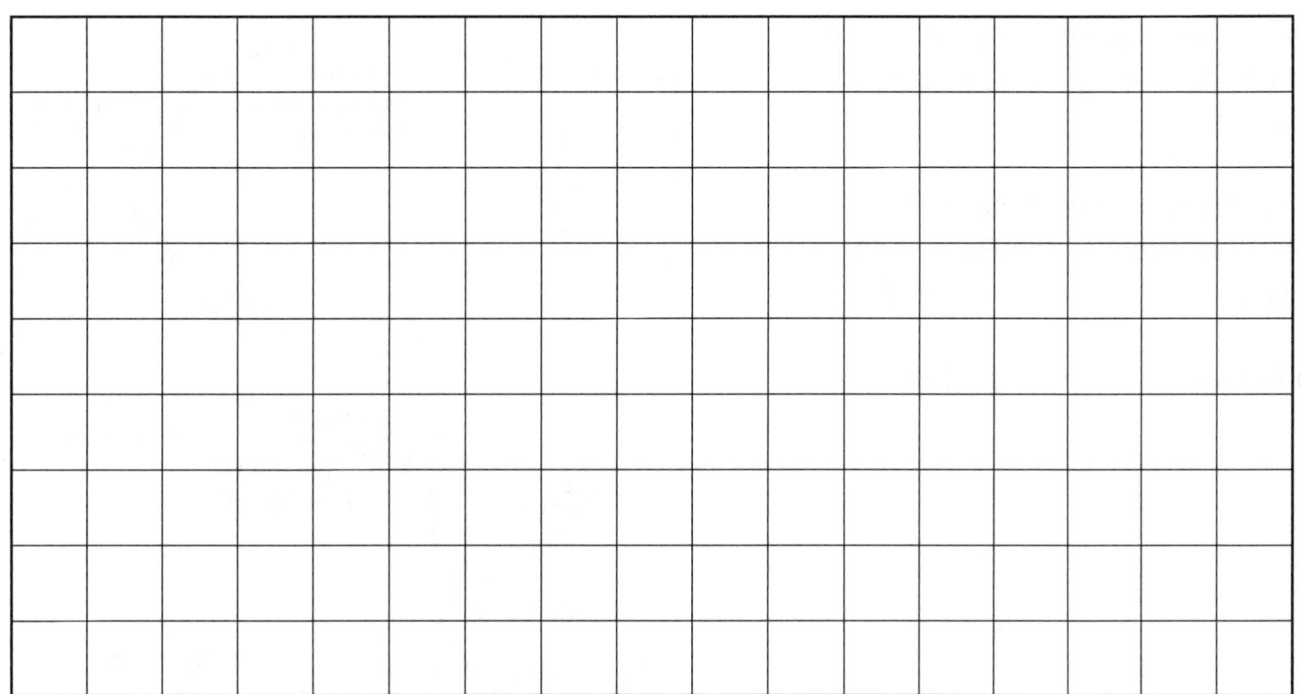

Write $<$, $>$, or $=$ to make each statement true.

5. 2.78 + 9.1 ______ 3.36 + 8.49

6. 0.08 + 0.97 ______ 1.04 + 0.03

7. 13.62 − 4.9 ______ 9.4 − 1.33

8. 9.4 − 5.6 ______ 8.3 − 4.7

9. Name two 3-digit numbers whose sum is 6.54. ________ + ________ = 6.54

10. Name two 3-digit numbers whose difference is 1.52. ________ − ________ = 1.52

Practice

11. 13 = 7 + *s* *s* = ______

12. 8 ∗ *g* = 24 *g* = ______

13. 36 / *p* = 6 *p* = ______

14. *m* / 9 = 8 *m* = ______

Name Date Time

A Hiking Trail

The Batona Trail is a hiking trail in southern New Jersey. The Batona Hiking Club measured the trail very carefully and found that it is about 47.60 kilometers long.

The trail crosses several roads, so it can be reached by car at a number of places.

Carpenter Spring is at the north end of the trail. Washington Road, near Batsto, is at the trail's south end.

Go to *Math Masters,* page 121.

Map of Batona Trail

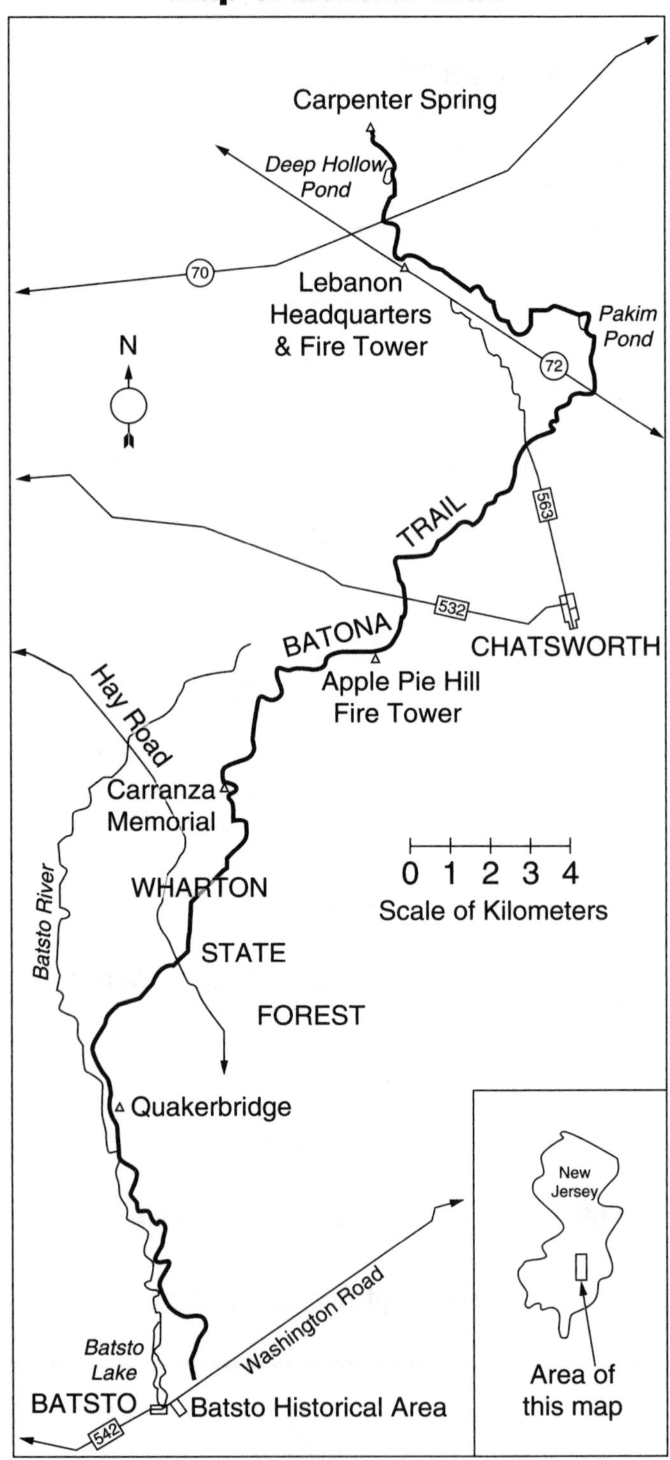

Source: Batona Hiking Club of Philadelphia

Name Date Time

A Hiking Trail *continued*

The following table shows distances from several points of interest from the north to the south end of the trail. Fill in the missing distances.

Batona Trail

Point of Interest	Distance from Carpenter Spring (km)	Distance from Washington Road (km)
Carpenter Spring	0	47.60
Deep Hollow Pond	1.91	45.69
Route 70	3.37	
Lebanon Headquarters	4.66	
Pakim Pond	9.91	
Route 72	12.10	
Route 563		33.56
Route 532	19.53	
Apple Pie Hill Fire Tower	21.31	
Carranza Memorial		19.80
Hay Road	33.05	
Quakerbridge	37.92	9.68
Washington Road	47.60	0

How can you check your answers?

Name Date Time

Keeping a Bank Balance

Date	Transaction		Current Balance
January 2	Deposit	$100.00	$ 100.00
January 14	Deposit	$14.23	+ $ 14.23 $ 114.23
February 4	Withdrawal	$16.50	$ ______ $ ______
February 11	Deposit	$33.75	$ ______ $ ______
February 14	Withdrawal	$16.50	$ ______ $ ______
March 19	Deposit	$62.00	$ ______ $ ______
March 30	Withdrawal	$104.26	$ ______ $ ______
March 31	Interest	$0.78	$ ______ $ ______
April 1	Deposit	$70.60	$ ______ $ ______
April 3	Withdrawal	$45.52	$ ______ $ ______
April 28	Withdrawal	$27.91	$ ______ $ ______

Name Date Time

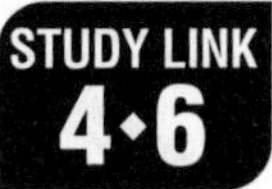

Rising Grocery Prices

The table below shows some USDA grocery prices for the year 2000 and estimates of grocery prices for the year 2025.

Grocery Item	Price in 2000	Estimated Price in 2025
dozen eggs	$1.02	$1.78
loaf of white bread	$0.88	$3.31
pound of butter	$2.72	$7.36
gallon of milk	$2.70	$5.65

1. How much more is each item predicted to cost in 2025?

a. eggs ________ **b.** bread ________ **c.** butter ________ **d.** milk ________

2. The year is 2000. You buy bread and butter. You hand the cashier a $20 bill. How much change should you receive? ________

3. The year is 2025. You buy eggs and milk. You hand the cashier a $10 bill. How much change should you receive? ________

4. The year is 2000. You buy all 4 items. What is the total cost? ________

5. The year is 2025. You buy all 4 items. What is the total cost? ________

6. If the predictions are correct, how much more will you pay in 2025 for the 4 items than you paid in 2000? ________

7. Which item is expected to have the greatest price increase? ________

Explain your answer. ________________________________

____

____

Practice

8. List the first ten multiples of 3. ____, ____, ____, ____, ____, ____, ____, ____, ____, ____

9. List the first ten multiples of 7. ____, ____, ____, ____, ____, ____, ____, ____, ____, ____

Name Date Time

"Goodie Bags"

The table at the right shows different items that the party store sells to make goodie bags. Use the information in the table to answer the questions below. Show or write what you did to solve each problem.

Item	Price
erasers	$0.16 each
clay	2 cans for $1.22
key chains	$0.59 each
rubber balls	3 for $0.51
markers	4 packs for $5.60
stickers	$1.39 per pack
whistles	$0.18 each
marbles	$1.41 per bag
gum	3 packs for $1.86

1. Kareem put a pack of stickers, a rubber ball, and a pack of gum in each of his goodie bags. What is the cost of each bag? ____________

2. Ella created a bag that cost the same amount as Kareem's bag but was not filled with the same things. What did Ella put in her bag?

____

3. Create your own goodie bag. You must place 5 different items in your bag and the total cost must be between $3.25 and $3.50. Tell what is in your bag and how much you spent.

____

____

Name Date Time

Modeling Decimals

Base-10 Blocks					Fraction	Decimal
Total Cubes	Big Cubes	Flats	Longs	Cubes		
235	0	2	3	5	$\frac{235}{1,000}$	0.235
832						
408						
790						
64						
8						
200						
20						
2						
1,843						
27,051						

Name Date Time

STUDY LINK 4•7

Tenths, Hundredths, Thousandths

Complete the table. The big cube is the ONE.

Base-10 Blocks	Fraction Notation	Decimal Notation
1.		
2.		
3.		
4.		

Write each number in decimal notation.

5. $\frac{346}{1,000}$ ____________

6. $\frac{92}{1,000}$ ____________

7. $\frac{3}{1,000}$ ____________

8. $2\frac{7}{10}$ ____________

Write each of the following in decimal notation.

9. 536 thousandths ____________

10. 23 hundredths ____________

11. 7 and 8 thousandths ____________

12. 4 tenths ____________

Write $<$ or $>$.

13. 0.407 ______ 0.074

14. 0.65 ______ 0.437

15. 0.672 ______ 0.7

16. 2.38 ______ 2.4

Practice

17. 6.05 + 1.24 = ____________

18. ____________ = 47.90 + 0.76

19. ____________ = 8.71 − 2.78

20. 46.8 − 3.77 = ____________

Name Date Time

Batting Averages

The women listed in this table were members of the 2004 U.S. Olympic Softball Team. These are their batting statistics after the 2004 Olympics in Athens, Greece.

Player	At Bats (AB)	Hits (H)	Batting Average $\left(\frac{H}{AB}\right)$
Berg, Laura	19	7	0.368
Bustos, Crystl	26	9	0.346
Fernandez, Lisa	22	12	0.545
Freed, Amanda	6	1	0.167
Jung, Lovieanne	20	6	0.300
Mendoza, Jessica	20	5	0.250
Nuveman, Stacey	16	5	0.313
O'Brien Amico, Leah	25	5	0.200
Topping, Jenny	6	4	0.667
Watley, Natasha	30	12	0.400

Source: U.S. Softball Official Web site

1. Which players have a better batting average than Crystl Bustos?

____

2. If the coaches need a strong hitter to bat first, which player should they choose? Why?

____

____

3. Some players were up at bat more times than others. If a player is up at bat more times, does this mean she will have a higher batting average? Explain.

____

____

____

4. a. Based on her batting average, if Mendoza went to bat 1,000 times, about how many hits should she get? __________ hits

b. 100 times? __________ hits **c.** 10 times? __________ hits

Name Date Time

STUDY LINK 4•8

Measuring in Centimeters

Measure each line segment to the nearest centimeter. Record the measurement in centimeters and meters.

Example: ____________________

a. About 5 centimeters **b.** About 0.05 meter

1. ______________________________

a. About ________ centimeters **b.** About ________ meter

2. ____

a. About ________ centimeters **b.** About ________ meter

3. ________________

a. About ________ centimeters **b.** About ________ meter

4. _________________________

a. About ________ centimeters **b.** About ________ meter

5. _______

a. About ________ centimeters **b.** About ________ meter

6. ____

a. About ________ centimeters **b.** About ________ meter

Practice

7. ____________ = 10.06 + 10.04

8. 38.93 + 92.4 = ____________

9. 16.85 − 14.23 = ____________

10. ____________ = 20.9 − 8.57

0 1 2 3 4 5 6 7 8 9 10 11 12 13 14 15

Centimeters

Name Date Time

Metric Units of Linear Measure

Use a meterstick and base-10 cubes and longs to answer the following questions.

SRB 128

1. What is the length of a base-10 cube? ________ cm

?

2. What is the length of a base-10 long? ________ cm

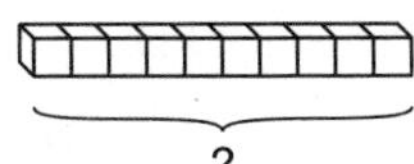

?

3. a. If you placed base-10 cubes side by side along a meterstick, how many cubes would you need to equal the length of 1 meter?

________ cubes

b. How many centimeters are in 1 meter? ________ cm

4. a. If you placed base-10 longs side by side along a meterstick, how many longs would you need to equal the length of 1 meter?

________ longs

b. A length of 10 centimeters is called a **decimeter.** How many decimeters are in 1 meter?

________ decimeters

Name Date Time

Metric Prefixes

1. Research metric units of length and record your results in the table below.

Unit	Prefix	Number of Meters
terameter	*tera-*	1,000,000,000,000
meter		1
millimeter	*milli-*	$\frac{1}{1{,}000}$

2. Describe any patterns you see in the table.

Name Date Time

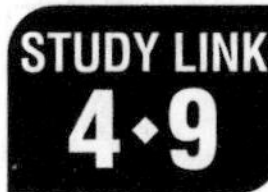

Metric Measurements

1. Use your personal references to estimate the lengths of 4 objects in metric units. Then measure each object. Record your estimates and measurements.

Object	Estimated Length	Actual Length

Complete.

2. 18 cm = ____________ mm
3. ____________ cm = 40 mm
4. 3 m = ____________ mm
5. 4 m = ____________ cm
6. ____________ m = 700 cm
7. 4.6 m = ____________ cm
8. 7.94 m = ____________ cm
9. ____________ m = 450 cm
10. ____________ m = 23 cm
11. 0.6 m = ____________ cm

Measure each line segment to the nearest $\frac{1}{2}$ cm.

12. ______________________________________

About ______ centimeters

13. ______________________________

About ______ centimeters

Practice

Insert < or >.

14. 0.68 _____ 0.32
15. 9.13 _____ 9.03
16. 0.65 _____ 0.6

Name Date Time

Matching Metric Units

Metric Units of Linear Measure	
millimeter (mm)	decimeter (dm)
centimeter (cm)	meter (m)

1. Write the abbreviation for the correct unit after each measurement below.

a. A crayon is about 85 _______ long.

b. A thumb is about 2 _______ across.

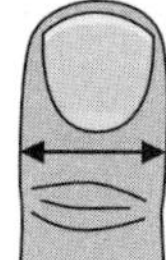

c. An arm span is about 110 _______.

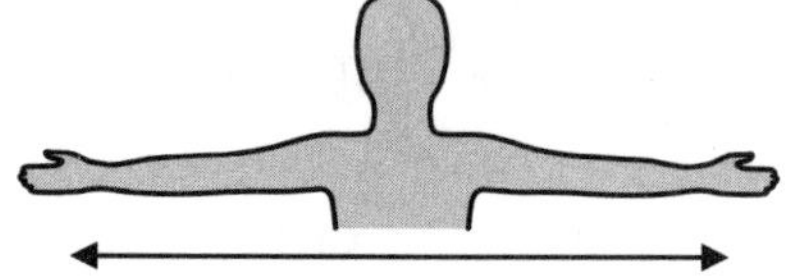

d. A journal is about 280 _______ long.

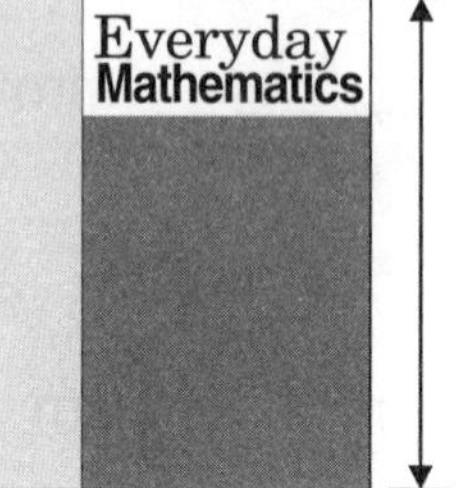

e. The height of your table or desk is about 7 _______.

f. A door opening is about 1 _______ wide.

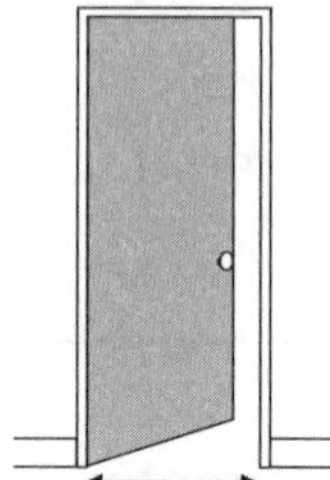

2. Describe any patterns you see in the measurements and units above.

____

____

____

3. Make up 2 examples of your own. Measure the objects in a unit of your choice.

____

____

Name Date Time

Decimals and Metric Units

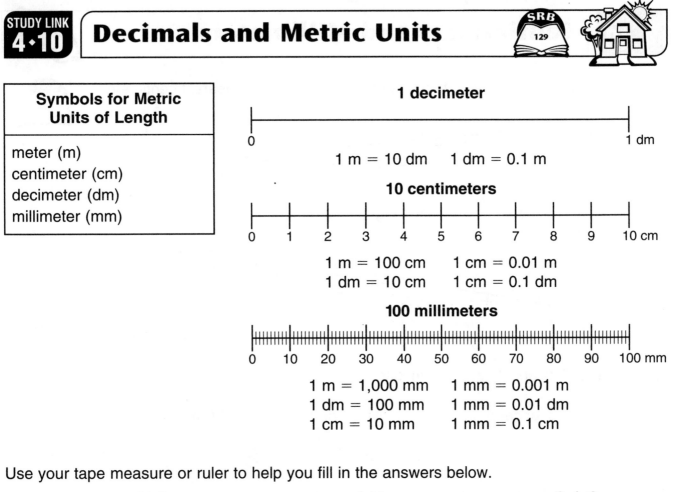

Symbols for Metric Units of Length
meter (m) centimeter (cm) decimeter (dm) millimeter (mm)

1 decimeter

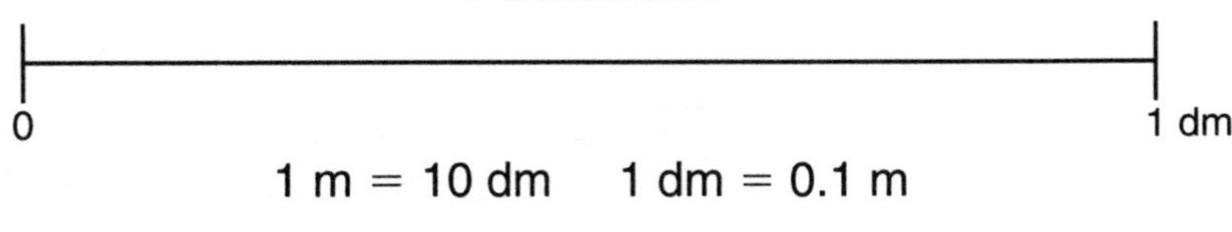

1 m = 10 dm   1 dm = 0.1 m

10 centimeters

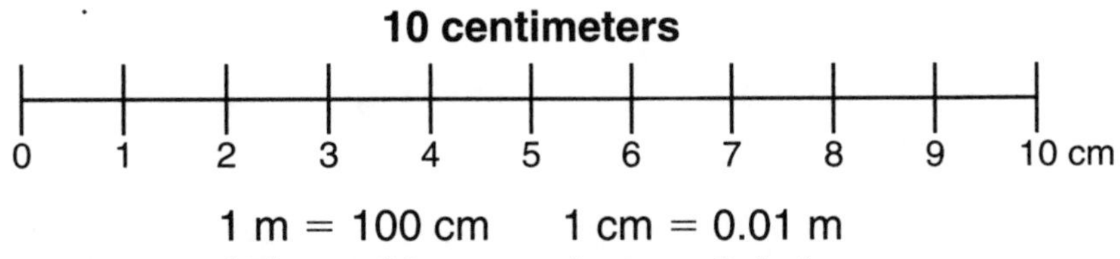

1 m = 100 cm   1 cm = 0.01 m
1 dm = 10 cm   1 cm = 0.1 dm

100 millimeters

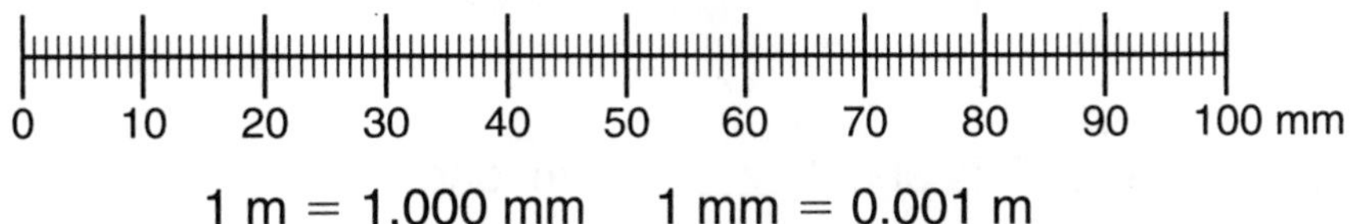

1 m = 1,000 mm   1 mm = 0.001 m
1 dm = 100 mm   1 mm = 0.01 dm
1 cm = 10 mm   1 mm = 0.1 cm

Use your tape measure or ruler to help you fill in the answers below.

1. a. 4.2 cm = 42 mm **b.** 64 mm = 6.4 cm **c.** 2.6 m = 260 cm

2. a. 6.5 cm = _______ mm **b.** 26 mm = _______ cm **c.** 6.1 m = _______ cm

3. a. 5 cm = _______ mm **b.** 30 mm = _______ cm **c.** 3 m = _______ cm

4. a. 80 cm = _______ mm **b.** 110 mm = _______ cm **c.** _______ m = 500 cm

5. a. 43 cm = _______ mm **b.** 98 mm = _______ cm **c.** _______ m = 34 cm

6. a. 0.6 cm = _______ mm **b.** 4 mm = _______ cm **c.** 5.2 m = _________ mm

Practice

7. 21, 49, and 56 are multiples of ______________.

8. 45, 63, and 18 are multiples of ______________.

Name Date Time

Centimeters and Millimeters

Cut out the ruler below. Use it to measure the pencils to the nearest centimeter.

1. a.

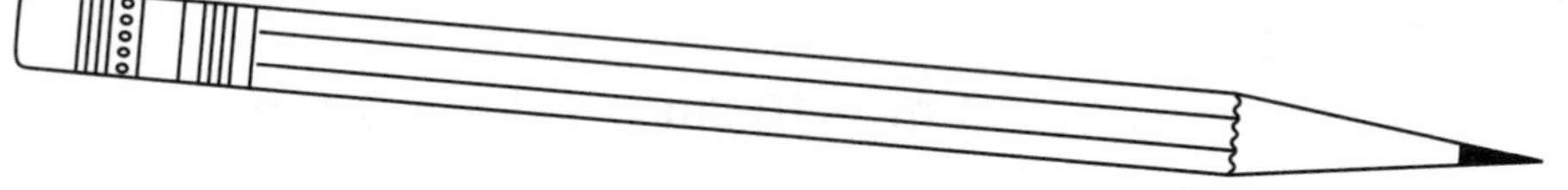

Pencil A is about _______ cm long.

b.

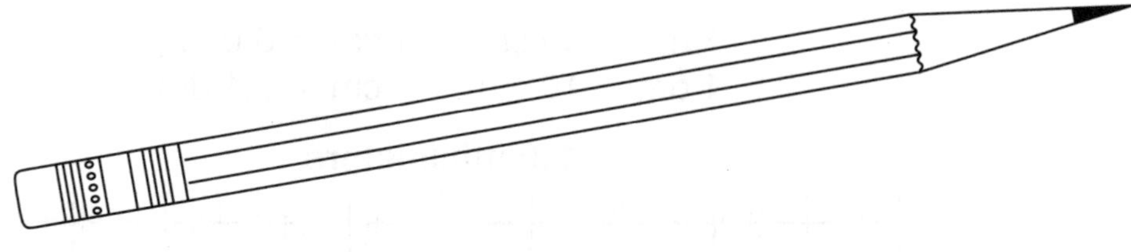

Pencil B is about _______ cm long.

2. One pencil is longer than the other. Which pencil is longer? Circle your answer.

Pencil A Pencil B

3. How did you figure out which pencil is longer?

____

____

____

4. Marco wants to know the difference in length between the two pencils. Can you tell him? Why or why not?

____

____

____

0 1 2 3 4 5 6 7 8 9 10 11 12 13 14 15

Centimeters

Name Date Time

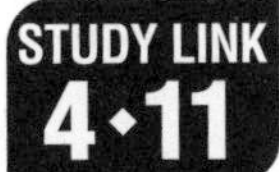

Unit 5: Family Letter

Big Numbers, Estimation, and Computation

In this unit, your child will begin to multiply 1- and 2-digit numbers using what we call the **partial-products method.** In preparation for this, students will learn to play the game *Multiplication Wrestling.* Ask your child to explain the rules to you and play an occasional game together. While students are expected to learn the partial-products method, they will also investigate the **lattice multiplication method,** which students have often enjoyed in the past.

If your child is having trouble with multiplication facts, give short (five-minute) reviews at home, concentrating on the facts he or she finds difficult.

Another important focus in this unit is on reading and writing big numbers. Students will use big numbers to solve problems and make reasonable estimates. Help your child locate big numbers in newspapers and other sources, and ask your child to read them to you. Or, you can read the numbers and have your child write them.

Sometimes it is helpful to write big numbers in an abbreviated form so that they are easier to work with. One way is to use **exponents,** which tell how many times a number, called the base, is used as a factor. For example, 100,000 is equal to $10 * 10 * 10 * 10 * 10$. So 100,000 can be written as 10^5. The small raised 5 is called an exponent, and 10^5 is read as "10 to the fifth power." This will be most students' first experience with exponents, which will be studied in depth during fifth and sixth grades.

The class is well into the World Tour. Students are beginning to see how numerical information about a country helps them get a better understanding of the country—its size, climate, location, and population distribution—and how these characteristics affect the way people live. The next stop on the World Tour will be Budapest, Hungary, the starting point for an exploration of European countries. Encourage your child to bring to school materials about Europe, such as articles in the travel section of your newspaper, magazine articles, and travel brochures.

Please keep this Family Letter for reference as your child works through Unit 5.

Vocabulary

Important terms in Unit 5:

billion 1,000,000,000, or 10^9; 1,000 million.

estimate A close, rather than exact, answer; an approximate answer to a computation; a number close to another number.

exponent See *exponential notation.*

exponential notation A way to show repeated multiplication by the same factor. For example, 2^3 is exponential notation for $2 * 2 * 2$. The small, raised 3 is the exponent. It tells how many times the number 2, called the base, is used as a factor.

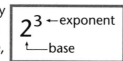

2^3 ← exponent; 2 ← base

extended multiplication fact A multiplication fact involving multiples of 10, 100, and so on. In an extended multiplication fact, each factor has only one digit that is not 0. For example, $400 * 6 = 2{,}400$ and $20 * 30 = 600$ are extended multiplication facts.

lattice multiplication A very old way to multiply multidigit numbers. The steps below show how to find the product 46 ∗ 73 using lattice multiplication.

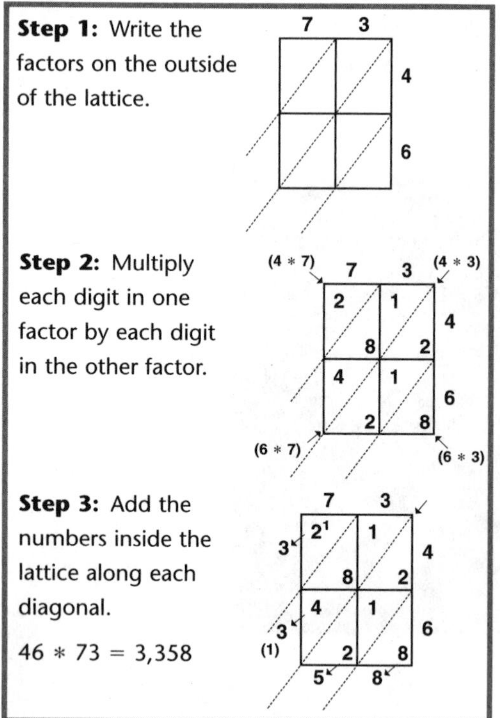
Step 1: Write the factors on the outside of the lattice.
7 3
4
6
Step 2: Multiply each digit in one factor by each digit in the other factor.
(4 ∗ 7)
(4 ∗ 3)
(6 ∗ 7)
(6 ∗ 3)
Step 3: Add the numbers inside the lattice along each diagonal.
46 ∗ 73 = 3,358

magnitude estimate A rough estimate of whether a number is in the 1s, 10s, 100s, 1,000s, and so on.

million 1,000,000, or 10^6; 1,000 thousand.

partial-products multiplication A way to multiply in which the value of each digit in one factor is multiplied by the value of each digit in the other factor. The final product is the sum of the partial products. The example shows how to use the method to find 73 ∗ 46.

Partial-Products Multiplication
Multiply each part of one factor by each part of the other factor. Then add the partial products.

	73
	∗ 46
40 ∗ 70 →	2,800
40 ∗ 3 →	120
6 ∗ 70 →	420
6 ∗ 3 →	+ 18
	3,358

power of 10 A whole number that can be written as a product using only 10s as factors. For example, 100 is equal to $10 * 10$, or 10^2. 100 is 10 to the second power or the second power of 10 or 10 squared.

round a number To approximate a number to make it easier to work with or to make it better reflect the precision of data. Often, numbers are rounded to a nearest *power of 10*. For example, 12,964 rounded to the nearest thousand is 13,000.

Do-Anytime Activities

To work with your child on concepts taught in this unit, try these interesting and rewarding activities:

1. To help your child practice handling big numbers, have him or her look up the distances from Earth to some of the planets in the solar system, such as the distance from Earth to Mars, to Jupiter, to Saturn, and so on.
2. Have your child look up the box-office gross of one or more favorite movies.
3. Help your child look up the populations and land areas of the state and city in which you live and compare them with the populations and areas of other states and cities.
4. Have your child locate big numbers in newspapers and other sources and ask him or her to read them to you. Or, you can read the numbers and have your child write them.

Building Skills through Games

In Unit 5, your child will practice multiplication skills and build his or her understanding of multidigit numbers by playing the following games. For detailed instructions, see the *Student Reference Book.*

Beat the Calculator See *Student Reference Book* page 233.
This game develops automaticity with extended multiplication facts.

High-Number Toss See *Student Reference Book* page 252.
This game reinforces understanding of place value.

Multiplication Wrestling See *Student Reference Book* page 253.
This game reinforces understanding of the partial-products method for multiplication.

Number Top-It See *Student Reference Book* page 255.
This game strengthens understanding of place value.

Product Pile Up See *Student Reference Book* page 259.
This game develops automaticity with multiplication facts.

STUDY LINK 4•11

Unit 5: Family Letter *cont.*

As You Help Your Child with Homework

As your child brings assignments home, you may want to go over the instructions together, clarifying them as necessary. The answers listed below will guide you through some of the Study Links in this unit.

Study Link 5•1

9. 1.48 **10.** 1.13 **11.** 8.17

Study Link 5•2

1. 42; 420; 420; 4,200; 4,200; 42,000

2. 27; 270; 270; 2,700; 2,700; 27,000

3. 32; 320; 320; 3,200; 3,200; 32,000

4. 3; 5; 50; 3; 3; 500

5. 6; 6; 60; 9; 900; 9,000

6. 5; 500; 50; 8; 80; 800

7. 15 **8.** 9.5 **9.** 4.26

Study Link 5•3

Sample answers:

1. 850 + 750 = 1,600; 1,601

2. 400 + 1,000 + 500 = 1,900; 1,824

3. 400 + 750 = 1,150

4. 600 + 650 + 350 = 1,600; 1,595

5. 300 + 300 + 500 = 1,100

6. 800 + 700 = 1,500; 1,547

7. 700 + 200 + 400 = 1,300

8. 100 + 700 + 800 = 1,600; 1,627

9. 750 + 400 + 200 = 1,350

10. 600 + 800 = 1,400

11. 4,800 **12.** 2,100 **13.** 45,000

Study Link 5•4

Sample answers:

1. 20 * 400 = 8,000; 1,000s

2. 10 * 20 = 200; 100s

3. 5 * 400 = 2,000; 1,000s

4. 2 * 20 * 10,000 = 400,000; 100,000s

5. Either 3 or 4 digits; 10 * 10 = 100 and 90 * 90 = 8,100

Study Link 5•5

1. 392 **2.** 2,200 **3.** 11,916

4. a. 7 * 200 = 1,400; 1,000s **b.** 1,267 hours

5. less **6.** 7,884 **7.** 11,436

8. 1,258 **9.** 4,689

Study Link 5•6

1. 4,074 **2.** 1,680 **3.** 2,100 **4.** 486

5. 3,266 **6.** 17,000 **7.** 7,471 **8.** 37,632

9. 5,722 **10.** 10,751 **11.** 916 **12.** 2,769

Study Link 5•7

7. 6,552

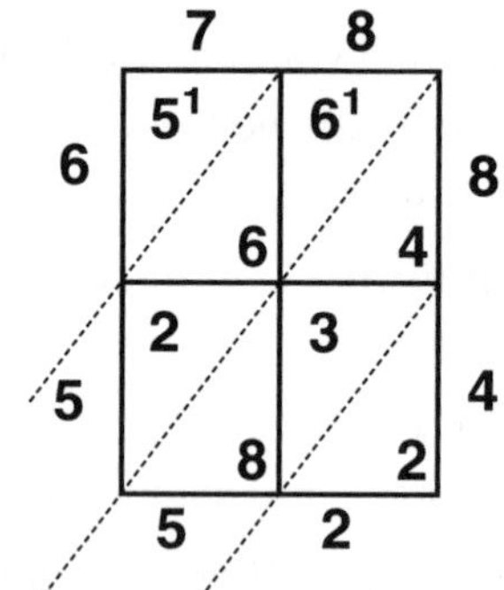

$$
\begin{array}{r}
84 \\
*\ 78 \\ \hline
5{,}600 \\
280 \\
640 \\
+\ \ 32 \\ \hline
6{,}552
\end{array}
$$

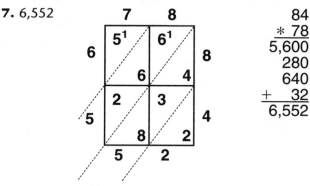

9. 39.57 **10.** 74.22 **11.** 33.77 **12.** 71.15

Study Link 5•8

92,106,954,873

12. 92 billion, 106 million, 954 thousand, 873

13. 370 **14.** 3,168 **15.** 1,656 **16.** 2,632

Study Link 5•9

7. 441 **8.** 2,970 **9.** 5,141

Study Link 5•10

2. Phoenix Mercury and San Antonio Stars; Sacramento Monarchs and Seattle Storm

4. 4,152 **5.** 798 **6.** 3,212

Study Link 5•11

1. China **2.** France **4.** Italy and the United States

Name Date Time

Multiplication/Division Puzzles

Solve the multiplication/division puzzles mentally. Fill in the blank boxes.

SRB 17

Examples:

*, /	300	2,000
2	600	4,000
3	900	6,000

*, /	80	50
4	320	200
8	640	400

1.

*, /	70	400
8		
9		

2.

*, /	5	7
80		
600		

3.

*, /	9	4
50		
7,000		

4.

*, /		600
7	3,500	
		2,400

5.

*, /		80
30	2,700	
		56,000

6.

*, /	4,000	
	36,000	
20		10,000

Make up and solve some puzzles of your own.

7.

*, /		

8.

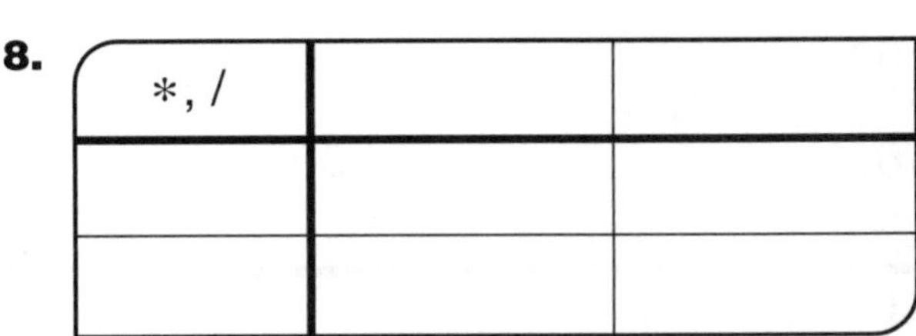

*, /		

Practice

9. ________ = 0.56 + 0.92

10. ________ = 2.86 − 1.73

11. 19.11 − 10.94 = ________

12. ________ = 0.52 + 0.25

Name Date Time

STUDY LINK 5·2

Extended Multiplication Facts

SRB 17

Solve mentally.

1. 6 * 7 = ____________

6 * 70 = ____________

60 * 7 = ____________

60 * 70 = ____________

600 * 7 = ____________

60 * 700 = ____________

2. 9 * 3 = ____________

9 * 30 = ____________

90 * 3 = ____________

90 * 30 = ____________

900 * 3 = ____________

90 * 300 = ____________

3. 4 * 8 = ____________

4 * 80 = ____________

40 * 8 = ____________

40 * 80 = ____________

400 * 8 = ____________

40 * 800 = ____________

4. 5 * ____________ = 15

30 * ____________ = 150

30 * ____________ = 1,500

____________ * 50 = 150

____________ * 500 = 1,500

30 * ____________ = 15,000

5. ____________ * 9 = 54

____________ * 90 = 540

____________ * 90 = 5,400

60 * ____________ = 540

6 * ____________ = 5,400

6 * ____________ = 54,000

6. 8 * ____________ = 40

8 * ____________ = 4,000

80 * ____________ = 4,000

____________ * 50 = 400

____________ * 5 = 400

____________ * 500 = 400,000

Practice

7. ________ = 6.3 + 8.7

8. 7.36 + 2.14 = ________

9. ________ = 9.74 − 5.48

10. ________ = 4.6 − 2.8

Name Date Time

LESSON 5·2

Partial-Sums Addition

SRB 10

Example: 2,000 + 280 + 300 + 42 = ?

	2,000	
	280	
	300	
	+ 42	
Add the thousands:	2,000	
Add the hundreds:	500	(200 + 300)
Add the tens:	120	(80 + 40)
Add the ones:	+ 2	
Find the total:	2,622	

Solve each problem.

1. 800 + 120 + 160 + 24 = ___________

2. 700 + 420 + 50 + 30 = ___________

3. ___________ = 600 + 180 + 40 + 12

4. ___________ = 2,400 + 160 + 420 + 28

5. ___________ = 1,500 + 90 + 240 + 24

6. 5,600 + 420 + 400 + 30 = ___________

Name Date Time

A *Multiplication Wrestling* Competition

1. Twelve players entered a *Multiplication Wrestling* competition. The numbers they chose are shown in the following table. The score of each player is the product of the two numbers. For example, Aidan's score is 741, because 13 ∗ 57 = 741. Which of the 12 players do you think has the highest score? ________________

Group A	Group B	Group C
Aidan: 13 ∗ 57	Indira: 15 ∗ 73	Miguel: 17 ∗ 35
Colette: 13 ∗ 75	Jelani: 15 ∗ 37	Rex: 17 ∗ 53
Emily: 31 ∗ 75	Kuniko: 51 ∗ 37	Sarah: 71 ∗ 53
Gunnar: 31 ∗ 57	Liza: 51 ∗ 73	Tanisha: 71 ∗ 35

Check your guess with the following procedure. *Do not do any arithmetic for Steps 2 and 3.*

2. In each pair below, cross out the player with the lower score. Find that player's name in the table above and cross it out as well.

Aidan; Colette	Indira; Jelani	Miguel; Rex
Emily; Gunnar	Kuniko; Liza	Sarah; Tanisha

3. Two players are left in Group A. Cross out the one with the lower score.
Two players are left in Group B. Cross out the one with the lower score.
Two players are left in Group C. Cross out the one with the lower score.

Which 3 players are still left?

____

4. Of the 3 players who are left, which player has the lowest score? ________________
Cross out that player's name.

5. There are 2 players left. What are their scores? ________________

____

6. Who won the competition? ________________

Name Date Time

LESSON 5·3

Flight Coupons

The airline you are using on the World Tour will give you a $200 discount coupon for every 15,000 miles you fly. Suppose you have flown the distances shown in the table below.

Route	Distance
Washington, D.C. → Cairo	5,980 mi
Cairo → Accra	2,420 mi
Accra → Cairo	2,420 mi
Cairo → Budapest	1,380 mi
Budapest → London	1,040 mi

1. Have you flown enough miles to get a discount coupon? ___________
2. Describe the strategy you used to solve the problem.

____

____

____

✂- -

Name Date Time

LESSON 5·3

Flight Coupons

The airline you are using on the World Tour will give you a $200 discount coupon for every 15,000 miles you fly. Suppose you have flown the distances shown in the table below.

Route	Distance
Washington, D.C. → Cairo	5,980 mi
Cairo → Accra	2,420 mi
Accra → Cairo	2,420 mi
Cairo → Budapest	1,380 mi
Budapest → London	1,040 mi

1. Have you flown enough miles to get a discount coupon? ___________
2. Describe the strategy you used to solve the problem.

____

____

____

Name Date Time

STUDY LINK 5·3

Estimating Sums

SRB 181

For all problems, write a number model to estimate the sum.

- If the estimate is greater than or equal to 1,500, find the exact sum.
- If the estimate is less than 1,500, **do not** solve the problem.

1. 867 + 734 = ______

Number model: ______

2. 374 + 962 + 488 = ______

Number model: ______

3. 382 + 744 = ______

Number model: ______

4. 581 + 648 + 366 = ______

Number model: ______

5. 318 + 295 + 493 = ______

Number model: ______

6. 845 + 702 = ______

Number model: ______

7. 694 + 210 + 386 = ______

Number model: ______

8. 132 + 692 + 803 = ______

Number model: ______

9. 756 + 381 + 201 = ______

Number model: ______

10. 575 + 832 = ______

Number model: ______

Practice

11. 60 * 80 = ______

12. 30 * 70 = ______

13. 50 * 900 = ______

14. 40 * 800 = ______

Name Date Time

"Closer To" with Base-10 Blocks

You can use base-10 blocks to help you **round** numbers.

Example: Round 64 to the nearest ten.

- Build a model for 64 with base-10 blocks.
- *Think:* What **multiples of 10** are nearest to 64?
  If I take the ones (cubes) away, I would have **60.**
  If I add more ones to make the next ten, I would have **70.**
- Build models for 60 and 70.

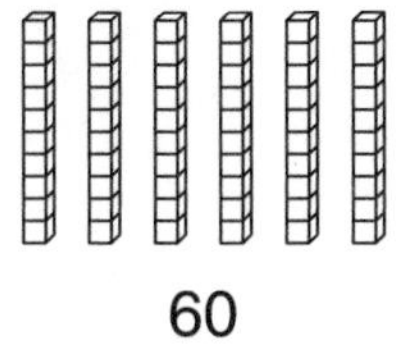

60

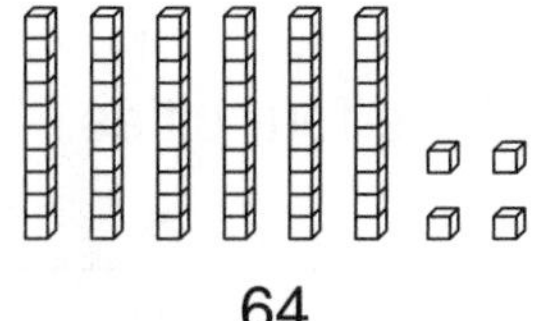

64

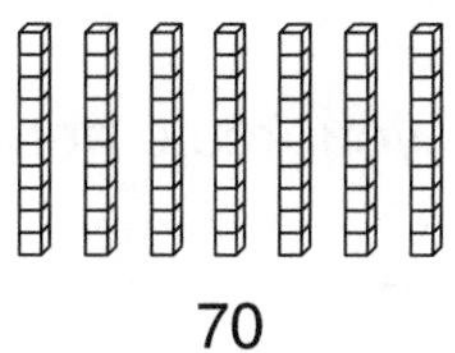

70

Think: Is 64 closer to 60 or 70? 64 is closer to 60. So, 64 rounded to the nearest ten is 60.

Build models to help you choose the closer number.

1. Round 87 to the nearest ten.

List the three numbers you will build models for: _______, _______, _______

87 is closer to _______. So, 87 rounded to the nearest ten is _______.

2. Round 43 to the nearest ten.

List the three numbers you will build models for: _______, _______, _______

43 is closer to _______. So, 43 rounded to the nearest ten is _______.

3. Round 138 to the nearest ten.

List the three numbers you will build models for: _______, _______, _______

138 is closer to _______. So, 138 rounded to the nearest ten is _______.

4. Round 138 to the nearest *hundred.*

List the three numbers you will build models for: _______, _______, _______

138 is closer to _______. So, 138 rounded to the nearest hundred is _______.

Name Date Time

A Traveling Salesperson Problem

A salesperson plans to visit several cities. To save time and money, the trip should be as short as possible. If the salesperson were visiting only a few cities, it would be possible to figure the shortest route in a reasonable time. But what if the trip includes 10 cities? There would be 3,628,800 possible routes! Computer scientists are trying to find ways to solve this problem on the computer without having to do an impossible number of calculations.

Think like a computer. Imagine that you begin a trip in Seattle and have to visit Denver, Birmingham, and Bangor for business.

1. Estimate to find the shortest *route* that would include each city. Use the map on journal page 112.

2. Describe your route between each of the four cities.

____

____

____

____

____

Try This

3. Describe a route that includes each city that would take the shortest amount of *time*.

____

____

____

Name Date Time

What Do Americans Eat?

Answer the following questions:

1. How many eggs did you eat in the last 7 days? ____________

2. How many cups of milk did you drink in the last 7 days? ____________

3. How many cups of yogurt did you eat in the last 7 days? ____________

Name Date Time

LESSON 5•4

What Do Americans Eat?

Answer the following questions:

1. How many eggs did you eat in the last 7 days? ____________

2. How many cups of milk did you drink in the last 7 days? ____________

3. How many cups of yogurt did you eat in the last 7 days? ____________

Name Date Time

What Do Americans Eat?

Answer the following questions:

1. How many eggs did you eat in the last 7 days? ____________

2. How many cups of milk did you drink in the last 7 days? ____________

3. How many cups of yogurt did you eat in the last 7 days? ____________

Name Date Time

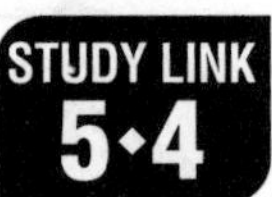

Estimating Products

Estimate whether the answer will be in the tens, hundreds, thousands, or more. Write a number model to show how you estimated. Then circle the box that shows your estimate.

1. A koala sleeps an average of 22 hours each day. About how many hours does a koala sleep in a year?

Number model: ____________________

10s	100s	1,000s	10,000s	100,000s	1,000,000s

2. A prairie vole (a mouselike rodent) has an average of 9 babies per litter. If it has 17 litters in a season, about how many babies are produced?

Number model: ____________________

10s	100s	1,000s	10,000s	100,000s	1,000,000s

3. Golfers lose, on average, about 5 golf balls per round of play. About how many golf balls will an average golfer lose playing one round every day for one year?

Number model: ____________________

10s	100s	1,000s	10,000s	100,000s	1,000,000s

4. In the next hour, the people in France will save 12,000 trees by recycling paper. About how many trees will they save in two days?

Number model: ____________________

10s	100s	1,000s	10,000s	100,000s	1,000,000s

Try This

5. How many digits can the product of two 2-digit numbers have? Give examples to support your answer.

____

Practice

6. 60 * 7 = ________ **7.** 4 * 80 = ________ **8.** ________ = 200 * 9

Name Date Time

A Curved Number Line

The number lines below are curved like hills. Use them to help you **round** numbers.

Example 1:

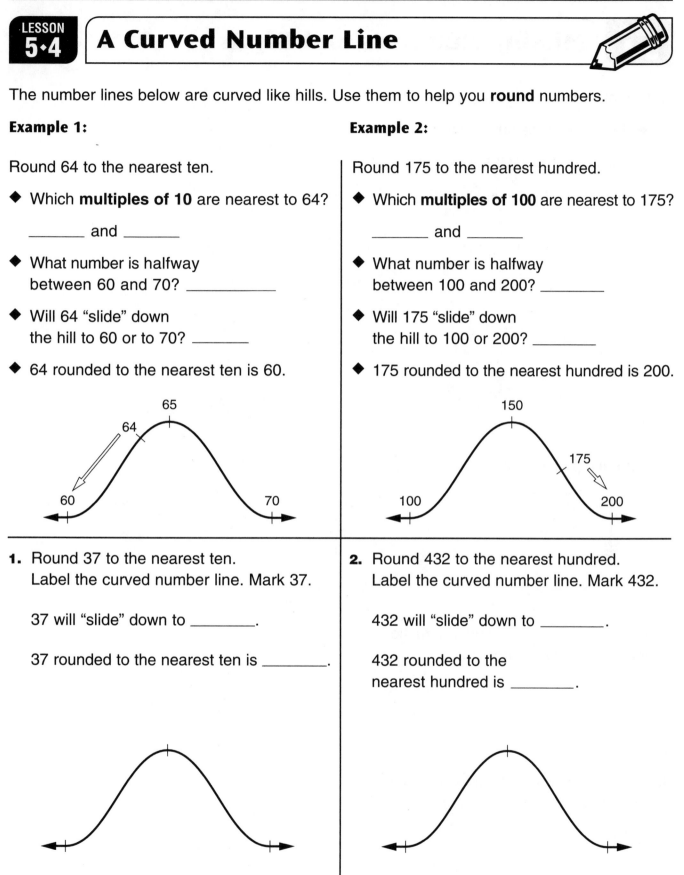

Round 64 to the nearest ten.

- Which **multiples of 10** are nearest to 64?

  _______ and _______

- What number is halfway between 60 and 70? __________
- Will 64 "slide" down the hill to 60 or to 70? _______
- 64 rounded to the nearest ten is 60.

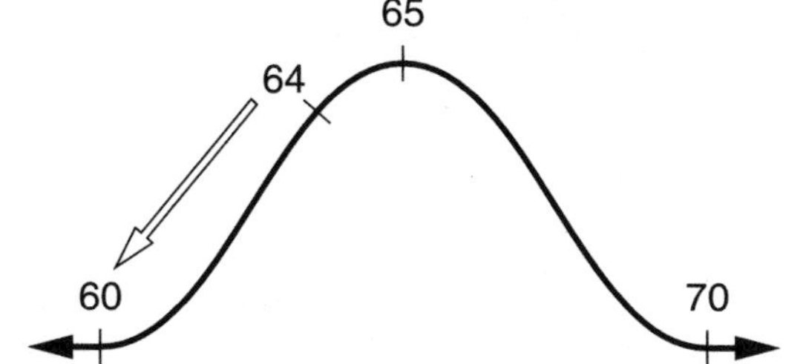

Example 2:

Round 175 to the nearest hundred.

- Which **multiples of 100** are nearest to 175?

  _______ and _______

- What number is halfway between 100 and 200? ________
- Will 175 "slide" down the hill to 100 or 200? ________
- 175 rounded to the nearest hundred is 200.

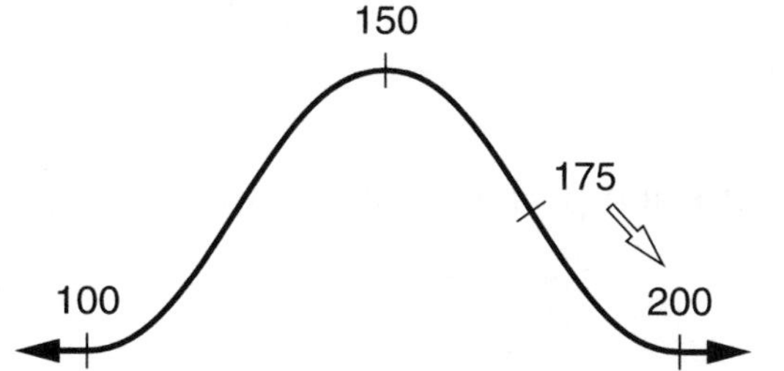

1. Round 37 to the nearest ten.
Label the curved number line. Mark 37.

37 will "slide" down to ________.

37 rounded to the nearest ten is ________.

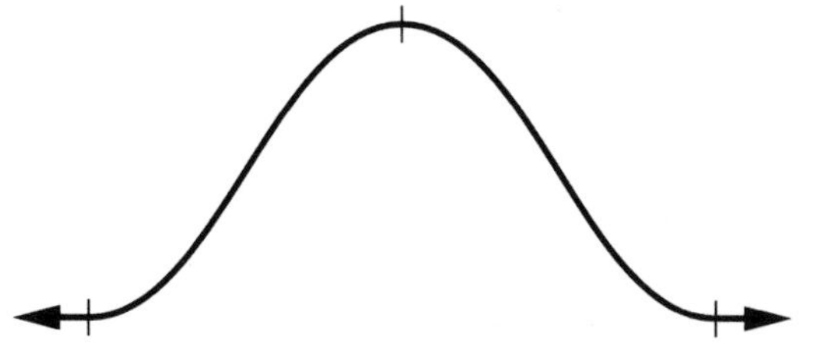

2. Round 432 to the nearest hundred.
Label the curved number line. Mark 432.

432 will "slide" down to ________.

432 rounded to the nearest hundred is ________.

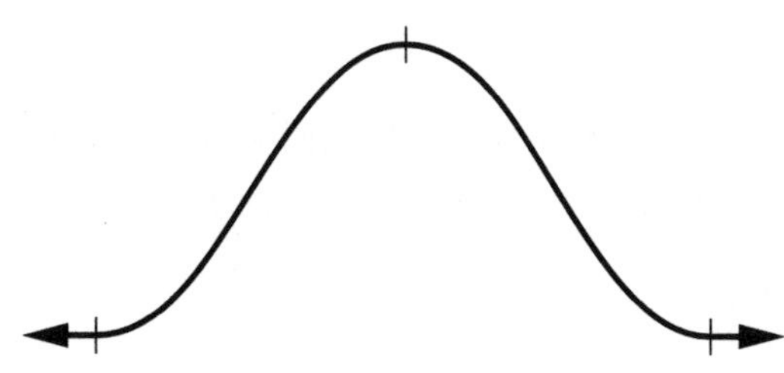

Name Date Time

Missing Numbers and Digits

1. Complete the number sentences.

- Fill in the circles using the numbers 3, 4, 6, or 7.
- Fill in the rectangles using the numbers 47, 62, 74, or 86.
- Some numbers will be used more than once.

a. ◯ × ▭ = 329

b. ◯ × ▭ = 258

c. ◯ × ▭ = 372

d. ◯ × ▭ = 248

e. ◯ × ▭ = 444

f. ◯ × ▭ = 296

2. For each problem, fill in the squares using the digits 4, 6, and 7.

a.

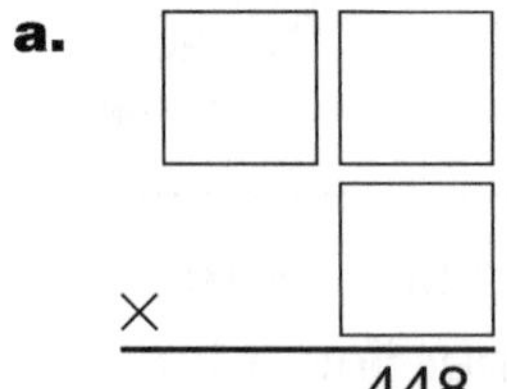

448

b.

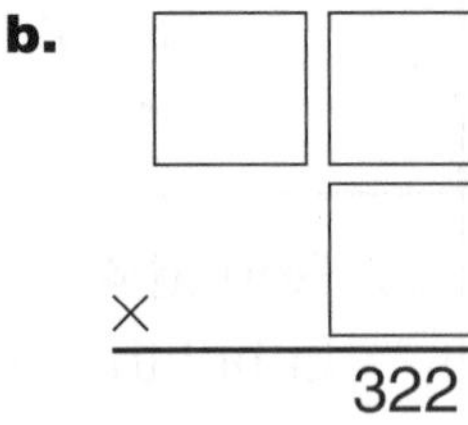

322

c.

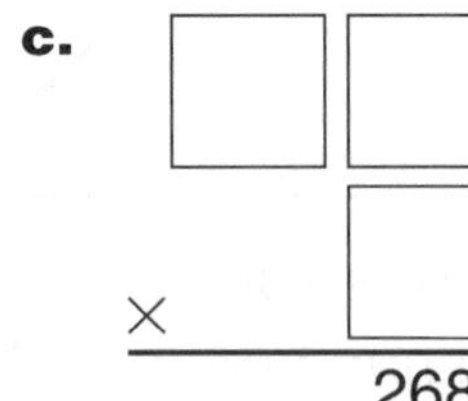

268

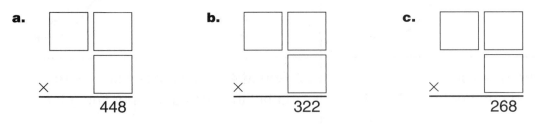

3. Use the digits 6, 7, 8, and 9 to make the largest product possible.

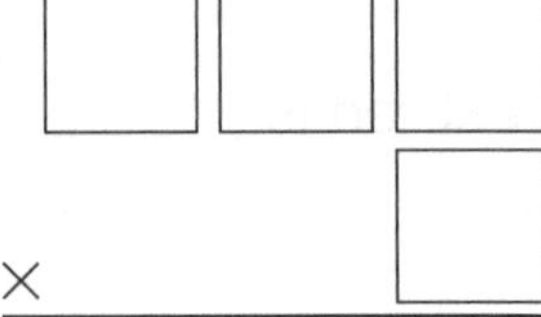

4. Use the digits 6, 7, 8, and 9 to make the smallest product possible.

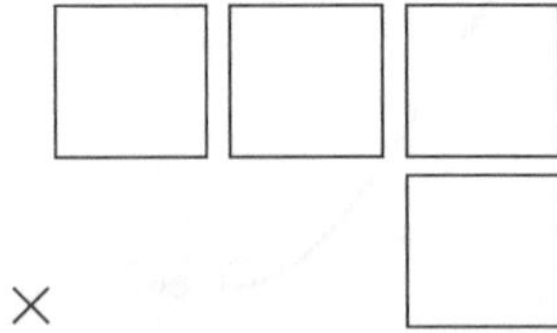

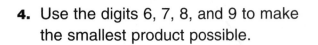

Name Date Time

STUDY LINK 5•5

Multiplication

Multiply using the partial-product method. Show your work in the grid below.

1. 56 ∗ 7 = ____________ **2.** 8 ∗ 275 = ____________ **3.** ____________ = 1,324 ∗ 9

4. Maya goes to school for 7 hours each day. If she does not miss any of the 181 school days, how many hours will Maya spend in school this year?

a. Estimate whether the answer will be in the tens, hundreds, thousands, or more. Write a number model to show how you estimated. Circle the box that shows your estimate.

Number model: ____________________

10s	100s	1,000s	10,000s	100,000s	1,000,000s

b. Exact answer: ____________ hours

5. The average eye blinks once every 5 seconds. Is that more than or less than a hundred thousand times per day? Explain your answer.

____

____

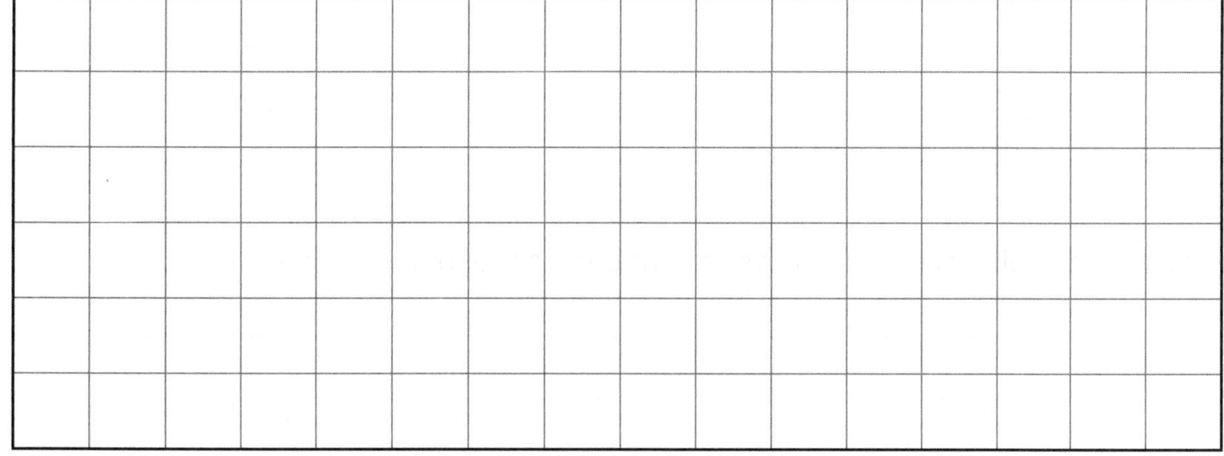

Practice

6. ____________ = 495 + 7,389 **7.** 5,638 + 5,798 = ____________

8. 3,007 − 1,749 = ____________ **9.** ____________ = 8,561 − 3,872

Name Date Time

Patterns in Extended Facts

1. Use base-10 blocks to help you solve the problems in the first 2 columns. Use the patterns to help you solve the problems in the third column. Use a calculator to check your work.

2 * 1 =	20 * 1 =	200 * 1 =
2 * 10 =	20 * 10 =	200 * 10 =
2 * 100 =	20 * 100 =	200 * 100 =

2. Use what you learned in Problem 1 to help you solve the problems in the table below. Use a calculator to check your work.

2 * 4 =	20 * 4 =	200 * 4 =
2 * 40 =	20 * 40 =	200 * 40 =
2 * 400 =	20 * 400 =	200 * 400 =

3. Explain how knowing 2 * 4 can help you find the answer to 20 * 40.

____

____

____

____

4. Make up and solve some problems of your own that use this pattern.

______________ ______________

______________ ______________

______________ ______________

Name Date Time

An Old Puzzle

An old puzzle begins like this: "A man has 6 houses. In each house, he keeps 6 cats. Each cat has 6 whiskers. On each whisker sit 6 fleas."

1. Answer the last line of the puzzle: "Houses, cats, whiskers, fleas—how many are there in all?"

____

2. Use number models or illustrations to explain how you solved the puzzle.

Name Date Time

An Old Puzzle

An old puzzle begins like this: "A man has 6 houses. In each house, he keeps 6 cats. Each cat has 6 whiskers. On each whisker sit 6 fleas."

1. Answer the last line of the puzzle: "Houses, cats, whiskers, fleas—how many are there in all?"

____

2. Use number models or illustrations to explain how you solved the puzzle.

Name Date Time

STUDY LINK 5·6

More Multiplication

Multiply using the partial-products algorithm. Show your work.

SRB 18

1. 582 * 7 = ____________
2. 56 * 30 = ____________
3. 42 * 50 = ____________
4. ____________ = 27 * 18
5. ____________ = 46 * 71
6. 340 * 50 = ____________

Try This

7. ____________ = 241 * 31
8. ____________ = 768 * 49

Practice

9. ____________ = 283 + 5,439
10. 6,473 + 4,278 = ____________
11. 5,583 − 4,667 = ____________
12. ____________ = 9,141 − 6,372

Name Date Time

A Dart Game

Vanessa played a game of darts. She threw 9 darts. Each dart hit the target. She scored 550 points.

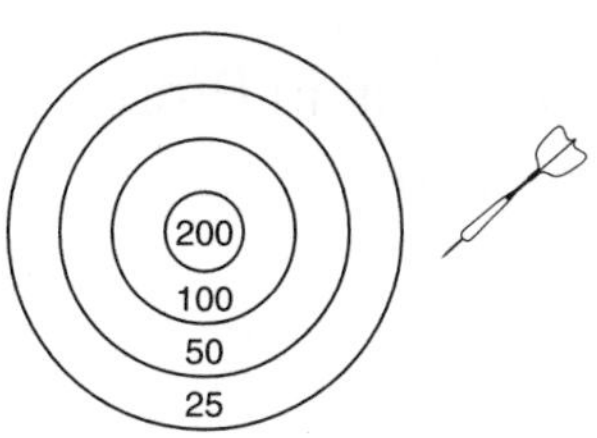

Where might each of her 9 darts have hit? Use the table to show all possible solutions.

200	100	50	25

Name Date Time

A Dart Game

Vanessa played a game of darts. She threw 9 darts. Each dart hit the target. She scored 550 points.

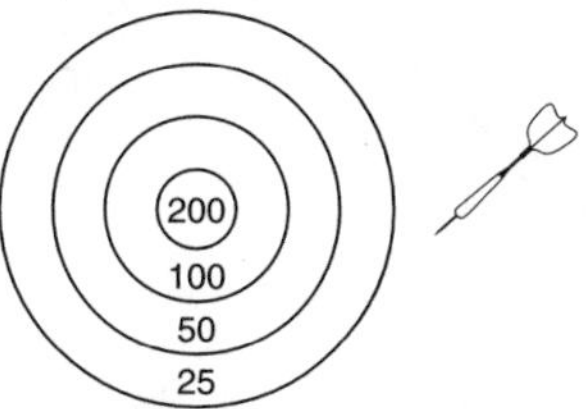

Where might each of her 9 darts have hit? Use the table to show all possible solutions.

200	100	50	25

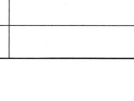

Name Date Time

Sorting Numbers

Study the Venn diagrams in Problems 1 and 2. Label each circle and add at least one number to each section.

1.

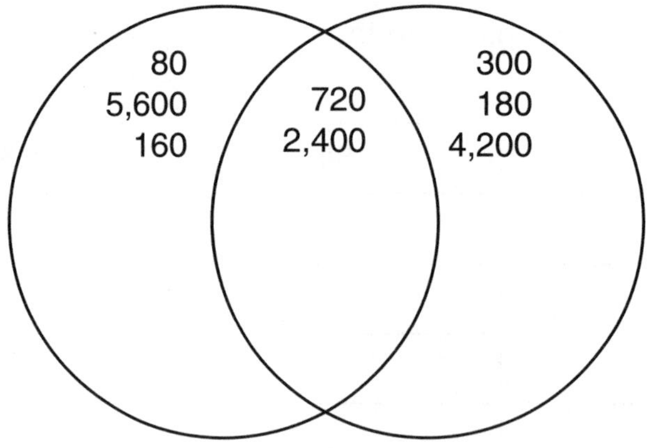

_______________ _______________

Try This

2.

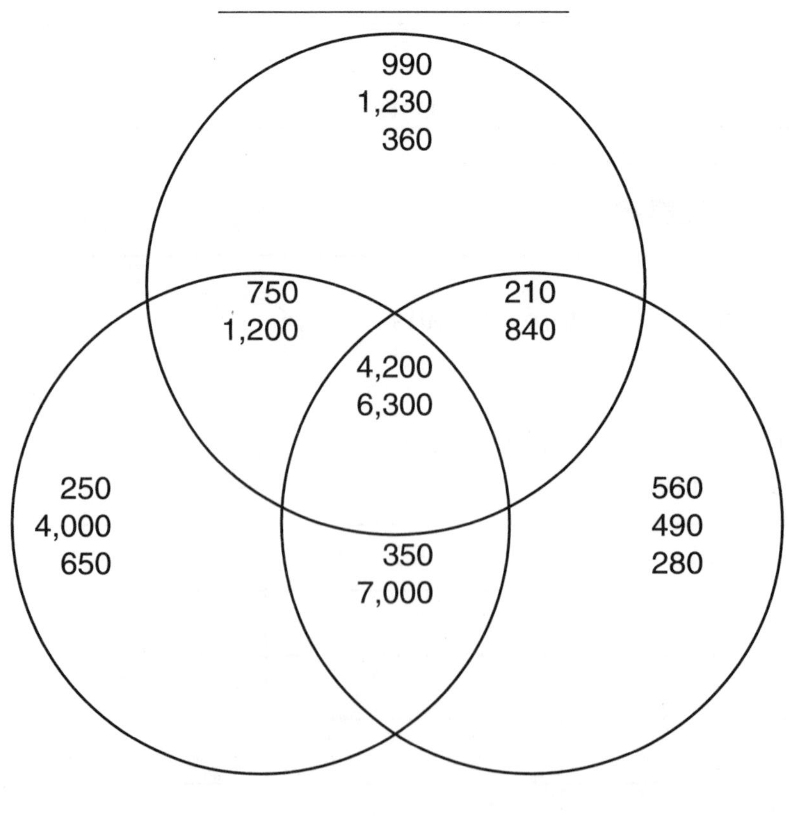

_______________ _______________

Name Date Time

STUDY LINK 5•7

Lattice Multiplication

Use the lattice method to find the following products.

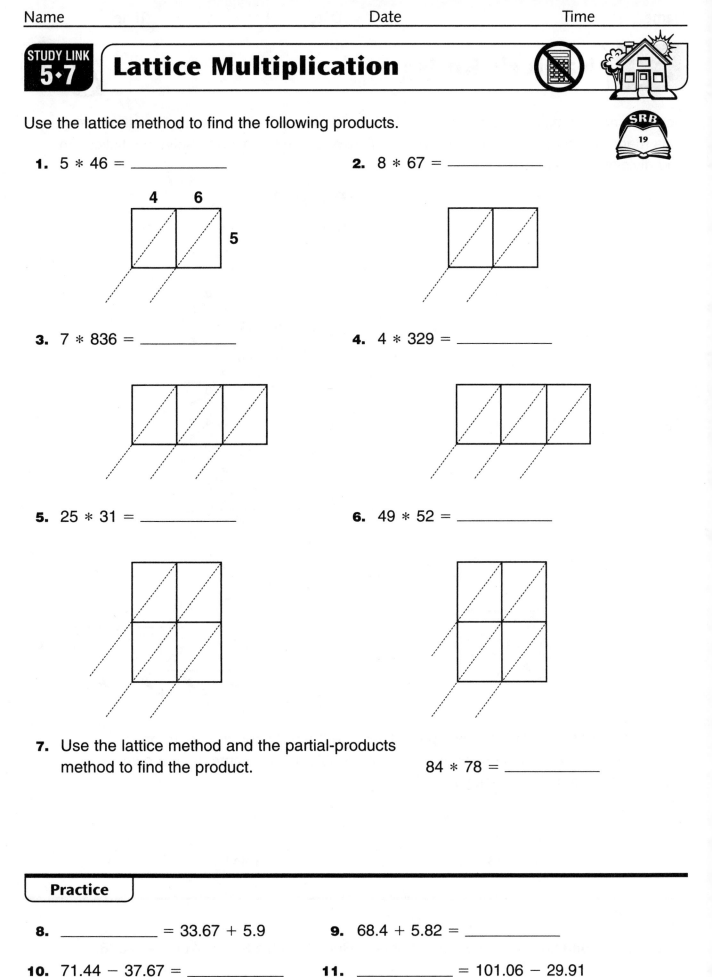

1. 5 * 46 = ___________

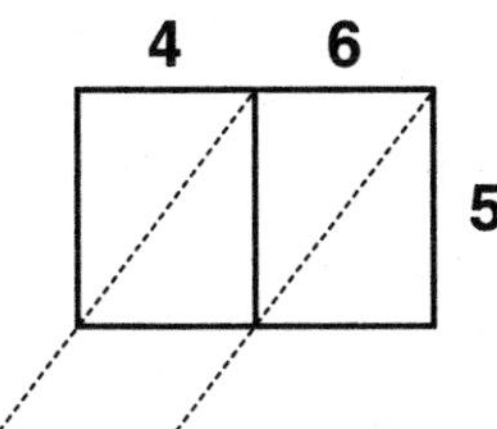

2. 8 * 67 = ___________

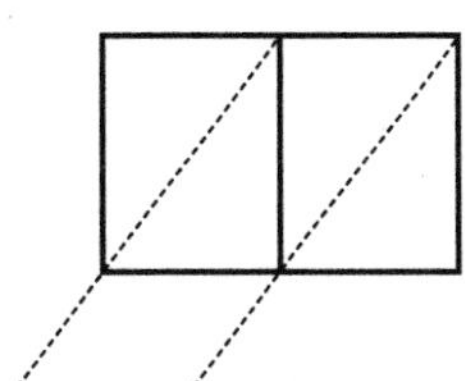

3. 7 * 836 = ___________

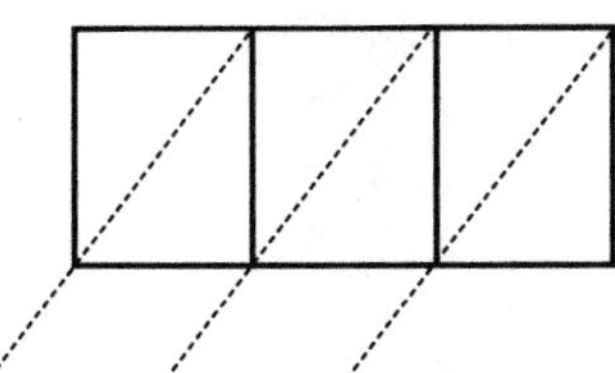

4. 4 * 329 = ___________

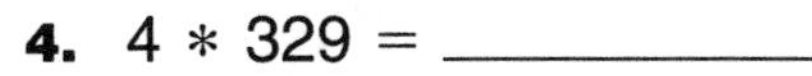

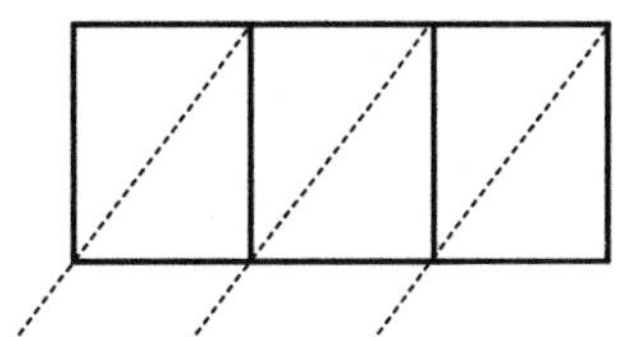

5. 25 * 31 = ___________

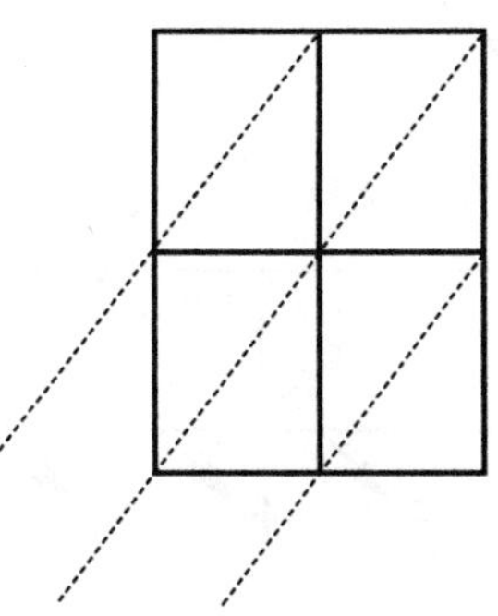

6. 49 * 52 = ___________

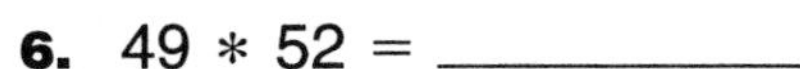

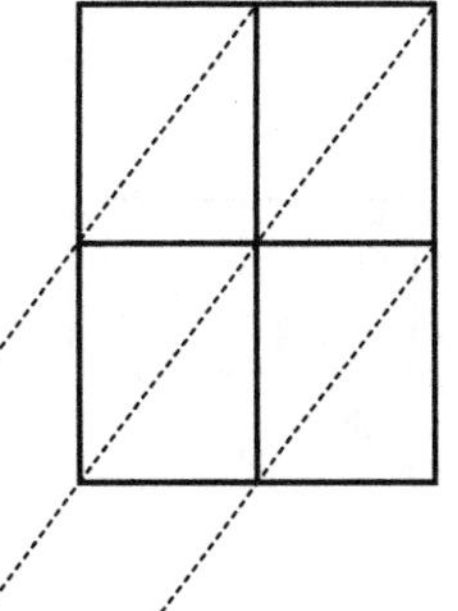

7. Use the lattice method and the partial-products method to find the product.

84 * 78 = ___________

Practice

8. ___________ = 33.67 + 5.9

9. 68.4 + 5.82 = ___________

10. 71.44 − 37.67 = ___________

11. ___________ = 101.06 − 29.91

Name Date Time

Napier's Rods

Scottish mathematician John Napier (1550–1617) devised a multiplication method using rods made of bone, wood, or heavy paper. These rods were used to solve multiplication and division problems.

Example 1:

4 ∗ 67 = 268

	6	7
1	0/6	0/7
2	1/2	1/4
3	1/8	2/1
4	2/4	2/8
5	3/0	3/5
6	3/6	4/2
7	4/2	4/9
8	4/8	5/6
9	5/4	6/3

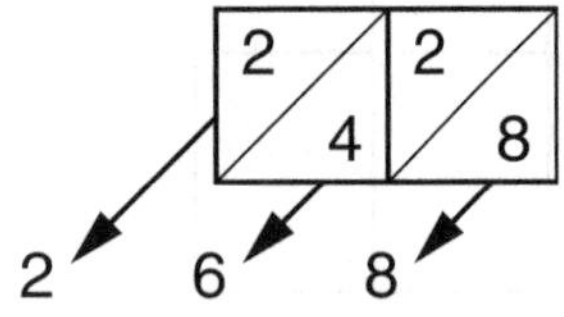

Example 2:

8 ∗ 5,239 = 41,912

	5	2	3	9
1	0/5	0/2	0/3	0/9
2	1/0	0/4	0/6	1/8
3	1/5	0/6	0/9	2/7
4	2/0	0/8	1/2	3/6
5	2/5	1/0	1/5	4/5
6	3/0	1/2	1/8	5/4
7	3/5	1/4	2/1	6/3
8	4/0	1/6	2/4	7/2
9	4/5	1/8	2/7	8/1

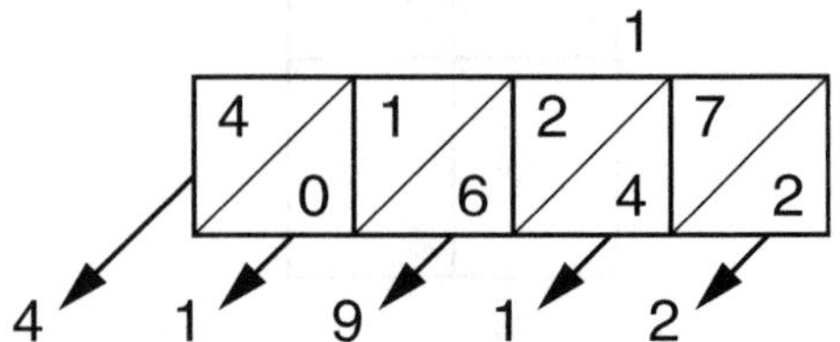

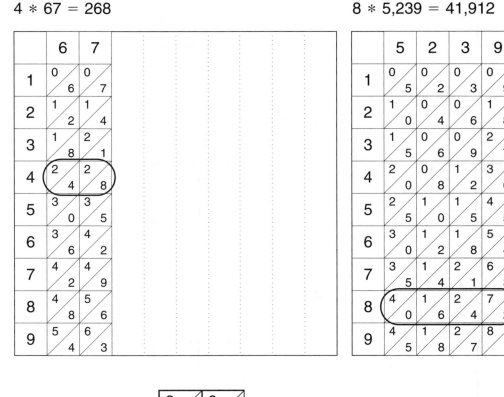

Cut out the rods on *Math Masters,* page 159. Use the rods and the board on *Math Masters,* page 160 to solve the following problems and some of your own. Use another method to check your answers.

1. 5 ∗ 79 = ____________

2. 7 ∗ 92 = ____________

3. ____________ = 6 ∗ 236

4. ____________ = 9 ∗ 5,841

Try This

5. Show a friend how you would use Napier's Rods to solve 3 ∗ 407 or 9 ∗ 5,038.

Name Date Time

Napier's Rods *continued*

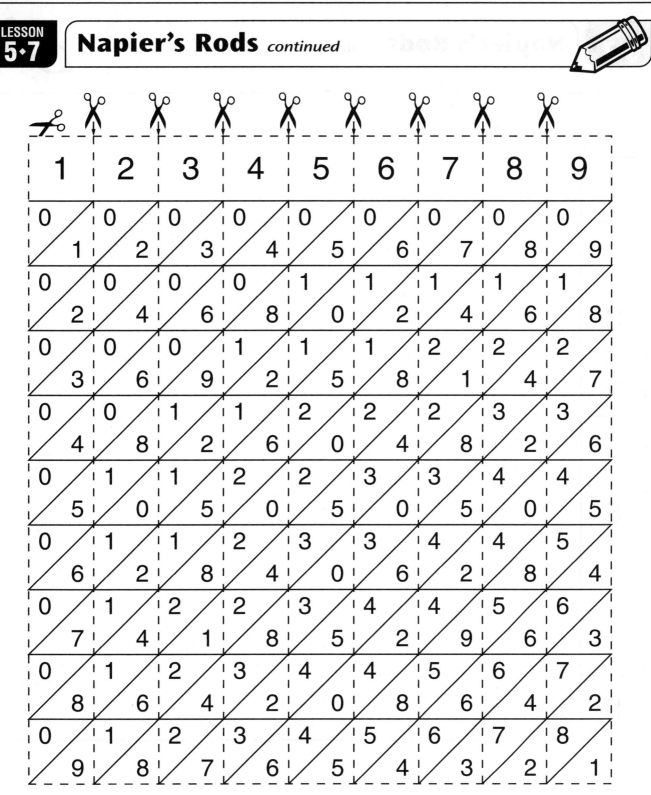

1	2	3	4	5	6	7	8	9
0/1	0/2	0/3	0/4	0/5	0/6	0/7	0/8	0/9
0/2	0/4	0/6	0/8	1/0	1/2	1/4	1/6	1/8
0/3	0/6	0/9	1/2	1/5	1/8	2/1	2/4	2/7
0/4	0/8	1/2	1/6	2/0	2/4	2/8	3/2	3/6
0/5	1/0	1/5	2/0	2/5	3/0	3/5	4/0	4/5
0/6	1/2	1/8	2/4	3/0	3/6	4/2	4/8	5/4
0/7	1/4	2/1	2/8	3/5	4/2	4/9	5/6	6/3
0/8	1/6	2/4	3/2	4/0	4/8	5/6	6/4	7/2
0/9	1/8	2/7	3/6	4/5	5/4	6/3	7/2	8/1

Name Date Time

Napier's Rods *continued*

1
2
3
4
5
6
7
8
9

Name Date Time

Fact Lattice Patterns

1. Look at a Multiplication/Division Facts Table. Find the shaded diagonal showing the doubles facts.

2. Find the doubles facts on the Fact Lattice on *Math Masters,* page 435. Shade the doubles facts lightly with a colored pencil.

3. Compare the two fact tables.

   a. List 3 things the tables have in common.

   ____

   ____

   ____

   ____

   b. List 3 things that are different on the Fact Lattice.

   ____

   ____

   ____

   ____

4. Describe 2 patterns that you see on the Fact Lattice.

   a. ______________________________

   ____

   ____

   b. ______________________________

   ____

   ____

5. Which of your Fact Lattice patterns is also in the Multiplication/Division Facts Table in your journal?

   ____

Name Date Time

A 50-by-40 Array

Name Date Time

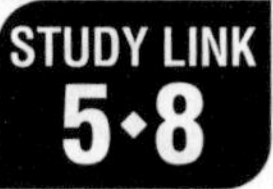

Place-Value Puzzle

Use the clues below to fill in the place-value chart.

Billions				Millions				Thousands				Ones		
100B	10B	1B	,	100M	10M	1M	,	100Th	10Th	1Th	,	100	10	1

1. Find $\frac{1}{2}$ of 24. Subtract 4. Write the result in the hundreds place.
2. Find $\frac{1}{2}$ of 30. Divide the result by 3. Write the answer in the ten-thousands place.
3. Find 30 ÷ 10. Double the result. Write it in the one-millions place.
4. Divide 12 by 4. Write the answer in the ones place.
5. Find 9 * 8. Reverse the digits in the result. Divide by 3.
   Write the answer in the hundred-thousands place.
6. Double 8. Divide the result by 4. Write the answer in the one-thousands place.
7. In the one-billions place, write the even number greater than 0
   that has not been used yet.
8. Write the answer to 5 ÷ 5 in the hundred-millions place.
9. In the tens place, write the odd number that has not been used yet.
10. Find the sum of all the digits in the chart so far.
    Divide the result by 5, and write it in the ten-billions place.
11. Write 0 in the empty column whose place value is less than billions.
12. Write the number in words. For example, 17,450,206 could be written as
    "17 million, 450 thousand, 206."

    ____

Practice

13. 74 * 5 = __________
14. __________ = 396 * 8
15. __________ = 92 * 18
16. 56 * 47 = __________

Name Date Time

A Roomful of Dots

Suppose you filled your classroom from floor to ceiling with dot paper (2,000 dots per sheet).

1. About how many dots do you think there would be on all the paper needed to fill your classroom? Make a check mark next to your guess.

   _________ less than a million

   _________ between a million and a half billion

   _________ between half a billion and a billion

   _________ more than a billion

2. One ream of paper weighs about 5 pounds and has 500 sheets of paper. About how many pounds would the paper needed to fill your classroom weigh? Make a check mark next to your guess.

   _________ less than 100,000 pounds

   _________ between 100,000 pounds and 500,000 pounds

   _________ between 500,000 pounds and a million pounds

   _________ more than a million pounds

3. Now, work with your group to make more accurate estimates for Problems 1 and 2. Explain what you did.

   My group's estimates:

   Number of dots: ______________________

   Weight of the paper: ______________________

Name Date Time

LESSON 5•8

How Much Is a Million?

David M. Schwartz, the author of *How Much Is a Million?,* used 7 pages of his book to show approximately 100,000 tiny stars.

He wrote, "If this book had a million tiny stars, they would fill seventy pages.... If this book had a billion tiny stars, its pages spread side by side would stretch almost ten miles.... If you put a trillion of our stars onto a gigantic roll of paper, it would stretch all the way from New York to New Zealand."

1. About how many pages would be needed to show a trillion tiny stars? Explain.

2. Describe a strategy you could use, other than counting each star, to find the number of tiny stars on one page of *How Much Is a Million?*

Name Date Time

LESSON 5•8

How Much Is a Million?

David M. Schwartz, the author of *How Much Is a Million?,* used 7 pages of his book to show approximately 100,000 tiny stars.

He wrote, "If this book had a million tiny stars, they would fill seventy pages.... If this book had a billion tiny stars, its pages spread side by side would stretch almost ten miles.... If you put a trillion of our stars onto a gigantic roll of paper, it would stretch all the way from New York to New Zealand."

1. About how many pages would be needed to show a trillion tiny stars? Explain.

2. Describe a strategy you could use, other than counting each star, to find the number of tiny stars on one page of *How Much Is a Million?*

Name Date Time

Place Value and Powers of 10

Millions	Hundred Thousands	Ten Thousands	Thousands	Hundreds	Tens	Ones
1,000,000			1,000	100		1
10 [100,000s]			10 [100s]	10 [10s]		10 [tenths]
		10 ∗ 10 ∗ 10 ∗ 10		10 ∗ 10		
	10^5		10^3	10^2		10^0

Fill in this place-value chart as follows:

1. Write standard numbers in Row 1.
2. In Row 2, write the value of each place to show that it is 10 times the value of the place to its right.
3. In Row 3, write the place values as products of 10s.
4. In Row 4, show the values as powers of 10. Use exponents. The exponent shows how many times 10 is used as a factor. It also shows how many zeros are in the standard number.

Name Date Time

Many Names for Powers of 10

Below are different names for powers of 10. Write the names in the appropriate name-collection boxes. Circle the names that do not fit in any of the boxes.

1,000,000	10,000	1,000
100	10	10 [100,000s]
10 [10,000s]	10^6	10 [1,000s]
10^3	10 ∗ 10 ∗ 10 ∗ 10	one thousand
10^5	10 ∗ 10 ∗ 10 ∗ 10 ∗ 10	10 [10s]
10 ∗ 10	ten	10^1
10 [tenths]	10^0	1

1. **100,000**

2. **10^2**

3. **1 million**

4. **one**

5. **10 ∗ 10 ∗ 10**

6. **10^4**

Practice

7. 63 ∗ 7 = ________

8. ________ = 495 ∗ 6

9. ________ = 97 ∗ 53

Name Date Time

Powers of 10 on a Calculator

Experiment to see what happens when your calculator can no longer display all of the digits in a power of 10.

Clear your calculator's memory, then program it to multiply over and over by 10 as follows:

Calculator	Key Sequence
Calculator A	(On/Off) and (Clear) together
	(Op1) (×) 10 (Op1) 10 (Op1) (Op1) (Op1) ...
Calculator B	(AC)
	10 (×) (×) (=) (=) (=) ...

1. What is the largest power of 10 that your calculator can display before it switches from decimal notation to exponential notation?

____

2. Write what the calculator displays after it switches from decimal notation to exponential notation.

____

3. If there are different kinds of calculators in your classroom, is the largest power of 10 that they can display the same or different from your calculator? If it is different, tell how. Write your answer on the back of this page.

Try This

4. What is the smallest power of 10 that your calculator can display before it switches from decimal notation to exponential notation?

____

Explain what you did to find out.

____

____

Name Date Time

Rounding

1. Round the seating capacities in the table below to the nearest thousand.

Women's National Basketball Association Seating Capacity of Home Courts		
Team	**Seating Capacity**	**Rounded to the Nearest 1,000**
Charlotte Sting	24,042	
Cleveland Rockers	20,562	
Detroit Shock	22,076	
New York Liberty	19,763	
Phoenix Mercury	19,023	
Sacramento Monarchs	17,317	
San Antonio Stars	18,500	
Seattle Storm	17,072	

2. Look at your rounded numbers. Which stadiums have about the same capacity?

____

3. Round the population figures in the table below to the nearest million.

U.S. Population by Official Census from 1940 to 2000		
Year	**Population**	**Rounded to the Nearest Million**
1940	132,164,569	
1960	179,323,175	
1980	226,542,203	
2000	281,421,906	

Source for both tables: The World Almanac and Book of Facts 2004

Practice

4. ______ = 692 ∗ 6 5. ______ = 38 ∗ 21 6. 44 ∗ 73 = ______

Name Date Time

Number Lines

1. For each number line, record the number that is halfway between the lower and higher number. Then plot a number that is *less* than the halfway number.

a.

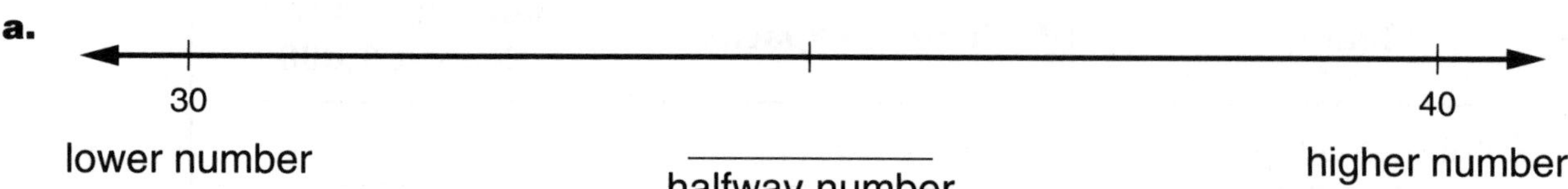

lower number ____ halfway number higher number

b.

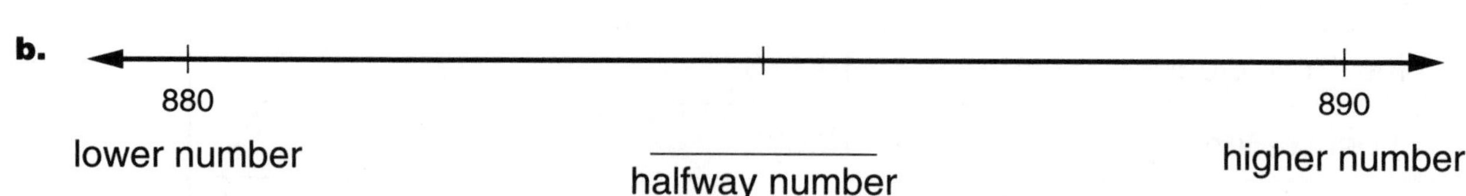

lower number ____ halfway number higher number

2. For each number line, record the number that is halfway between the lower and higher number. Then plot a number that is *greater* than the halfway number.

a.

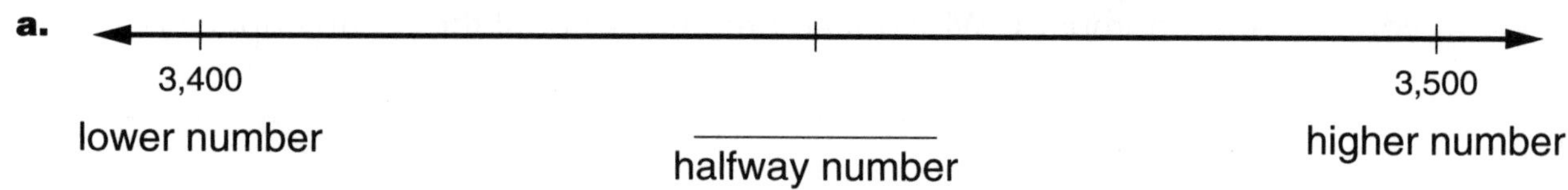

lower number ____ halfway number higher number

b.

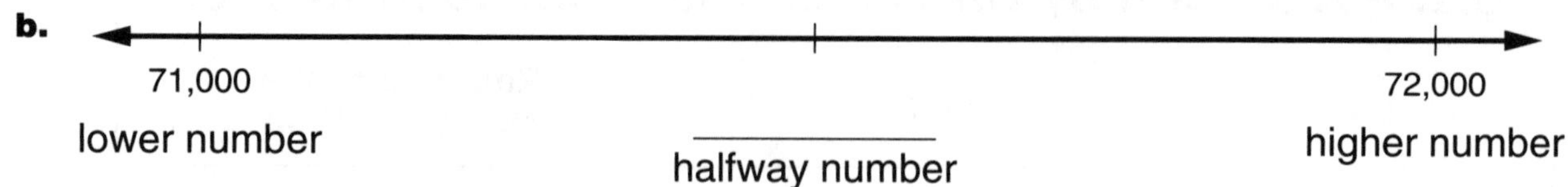

lower number ____ halfway number higher number

3. Make up a problem of your own.

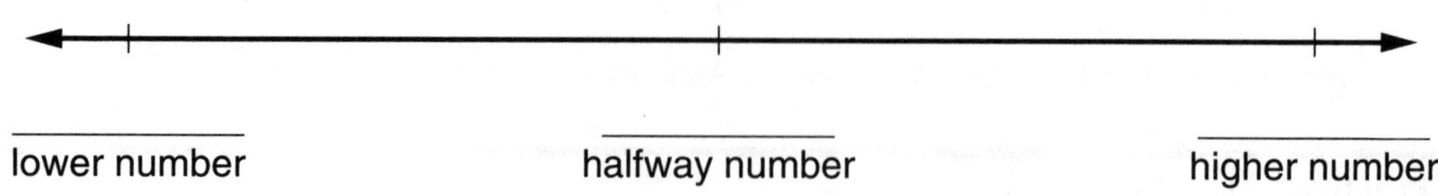

____ lower number ____ halfway number ____ higher number

Name Date Time

Rounding Bar Graph Data

Each bar represents the 2003 population of a country.

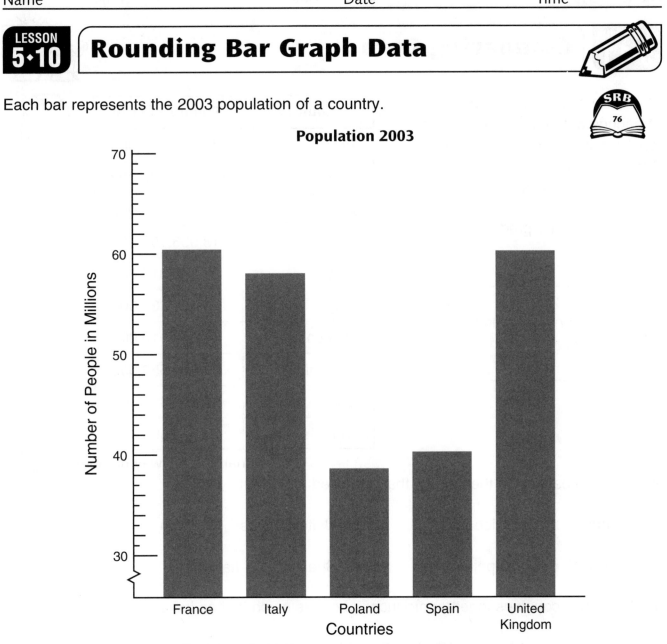

Population 2003

Source: *The World Factbook*

1. Estimate the population of each country to the nearest 10 million, to the nearest 5 million, and to the nearest 1 million. Organize your information in a table on the back of this sheet.

2. Describe the strategy you used to round to the nearest million.

Name Date Time

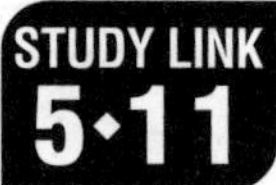

Comparing Data

SRB 4

This table shows the number of pounds of fruit produced by the top 10 fruit-producing countries in 2001. Read each of these numbers to a friend or a family member.

Country	Pounds of Fruit
Brazil	77,268,294,000
China	167,046,420,000
France	26,823,740,000
India	118,036,194,000
Iran	28,599,912,000
Italy	44,410,538,000
Mexico	34,549,912,000
Philippines	27,028,556,000
Spain	36,260,392,000
United States	73,148,598,000

1. Which country produced the most fruit?

____

2. Which country produced the least fruit?

____

3. For each pair, circle the country that produced more fruit.

a. India Mexico

b. United States Iran

c. Brazil Philippines

d. Spain Italy

4. Which two countries together produced about as much fruit as India?

____

Practice

Estimate the sum. Write a number model.

5. 687 + 935 _______________

6. 2,409 + 1,196 + 1,327 _______________

7. 11,899 + 35,201 _______________

Name Date Time

Unit 6: Family Letter

Division; Map Reference Frames; Measures of Angles

The first four lessons and the last lesson of Unit 6 focus on understanding the division operation, developing a method for dividing whole numbers, and solving division number stories.

Though most adults reach for a calculator to do a long-division problem, it is useful to know a paper-and-pencil procedure for computations such as $567 \div 6$ and $15\overline{)235}$. Fortunately, there is a method that is similar to the one most of us learned in school but is much easier to understand and use. This method is called the **partial-quotients method.**

Students have had considerable practice with extended division facts, such as $420 \div 7 = 60$, and questions, such as "About how many 12s are in 150?" Using the partial-quotients method, your child will apply these skills to build partial quotients until the exact quotient and remainder are determined.

Full-circle (360°) protractor

This unit also focuses on numbers in map coordinate systems. For maps of relatively small areas, rectangular coordinate grids are used. For world maps and the world globe, the system of latitude and longitude is used to locate places.

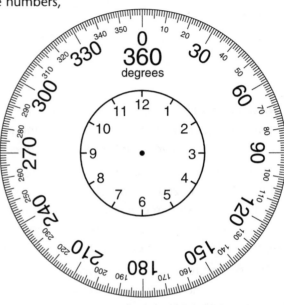

Because this global system is based on angle measures, the class will practice measuring and drawing angles with full-circle (360°) and half-circle (180°) protractors. If you have a protractor, ask your child to show you how to use this tool.

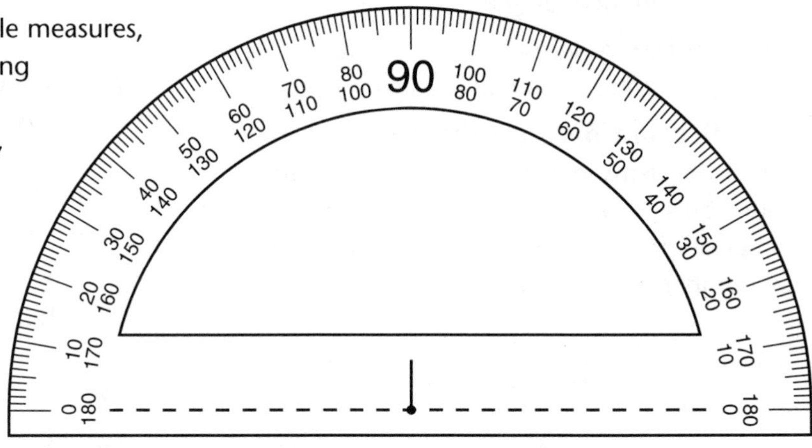

Half-circle (180°) protractor

The class is well into the World Tour. Students have visited Africa and are now traveling in Europe. They are beginning to see how numerical information about a country helps them get a better understanding of the country—its size, climate, location, and population distribution—and how these characteristics affect the way people live. Your child may want to share with you information about some of the countries the class has visited. Encourage your child to take materials about Europe to school, such as magazine articles, travel brochures, and articles in the travel section of your newspaper.

Please keep this Family Letter for reference as your child works through Unit 6.

Vocabulary

Important terms in Unit 6:

acute angle An angle with a measure greater than 0° and less than 90°.

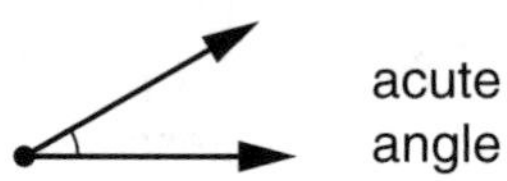

coordinate grid (also called a *rectangular coordinate grid*) A reference frame for locating points in a plane using *ordered number pairs,* or *coordinates.*

equal-groups notation A way to denote a number of equal-sized groups. The size of the groups is written inside square brackets and the number of groups is written in front of the brackets. For example, 3 [6s] means 3 groups with 6 in each group.

index of locations A list of places together with a reference frame for locating them on a map. For example, "Billings D3," indicates that Billings can be found within the rectangle where column 3 and row D of a grid meet on the map.

meridian bar A device on a globe that shows degrees of latitude north and south of the equator.

multiplication/division diagram A diagram used for problems in which a total is made up of several equal groups. The diagram has three parts: a number of groups, a number in each group, and a total number.

rows	chairs per row	chairs in all
6	4	24

obtuse angle An angle with a measure greater than 90° and less than 180°.

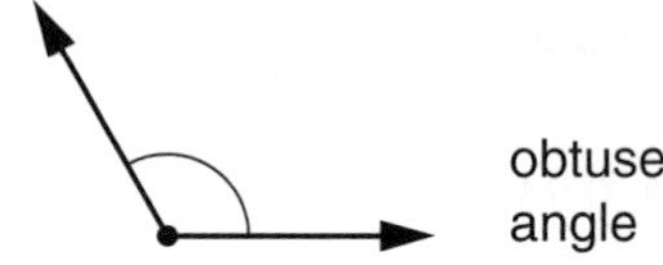

ordered number pair Two numbers that are used to locate a point on a *coordinate grid.* The first number gives the position along the horizontal axis, and the second number gives the position along the vertical axis. The numbers in an ordered pair are called *coordinates.* Ordered pairs are usually written inside parentheses: (2,3).

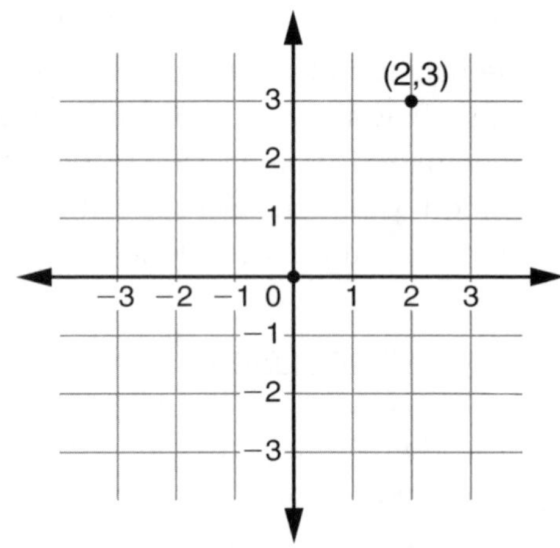

protractor A tool used for measuring or drawing angles. A half-circle protractor can be used to measure and draw angles up to 180°. A full-circle protractor can be used to measure and draw angles up to 360°. One of each type is on the Geometry Template.

quotient The result of dividing one number by another number. For example, in 35 ÷ 5 = 7, the quotient is 7.

reflex angle An angle with a measure greater than 180° and less than 360°.

straight angle An angle with a measure of 180°.

vertex The point at which the rays of an angle, the sides of a polygon, or the edges of a polyhedron meet. Plural is vertexes or vertices.

Do-Anytime Activities

To work with your child on concepts taught in this unit, try these interesting and rewarding activities:

1. Help your child practice division by solving problems for everyday situations.
2. Name places on the world globe and ask your child to give the latitude and longitude for each.
3. Encourage your child to identify and classify acute, right, obtuse, straight, and reflex angles in buildings, bridges, and other structures.
4. Work together with your child to construct a map, coordinate system, and index of locations for your neighborhood.

Building Skills through Games

In Unit 6, your child will practice using division and reference frames and measuring angles by playing the following games. For detailed instructions, see the *Student Reference Book.*

Angle Tangle See *Student Reference Book,* page 230.

This is a game for two players and will require a protractor. The game helps students practice drawing, estimating the measure of, and measuring angles.

Division Dash See *Student Reference Book,* page 241.

This is a game for one or two players. Each player will need a calculator. The game helps students practice division and mental calculation.

Grid Search See *Student Reference Book,* pages 250 and 251.

This is a game for two players, and each player will require *two* playing grids. The game helps students practice using a letter-number coordinate system and developing a search strategy.

Over and Up Squares See *Student Reference Book,* page 257.

This is a game for two players and will require a playing grid. The game helps students practice using ordered pairs of numbers to locate points on a rectangular grid.

As You Help Your Child with Homework

As your child brings assignments home, you may want to go over the instructions together, clarifying them as necessary. The answers listed below will guide you through some of the Study Links in this unit.

Study Link 6•1

1. 8 rows **2.** 120,000 quills **3.** 21 boxes

Study Link 6•2

1. 38 **2.** 23 **3.** 47

Study Link 6•3

1. 13 marbles; 5 left **2.** 72 prizes, 0 left

3. 22 R3 **4.** 53 R3

Study Link 6•4

1. $15\frac{4}{8}$ or $15\frac{1}{2}$; Reported it as a fraction or decimal; Sample answer: You can cut the remaining strawberries into halves to divide them evenly among 8 students.

2. 21; Ignored it; Sample answer: There are not enough remaining pens to form another group of 16.

Study Link 6•5

1–7.

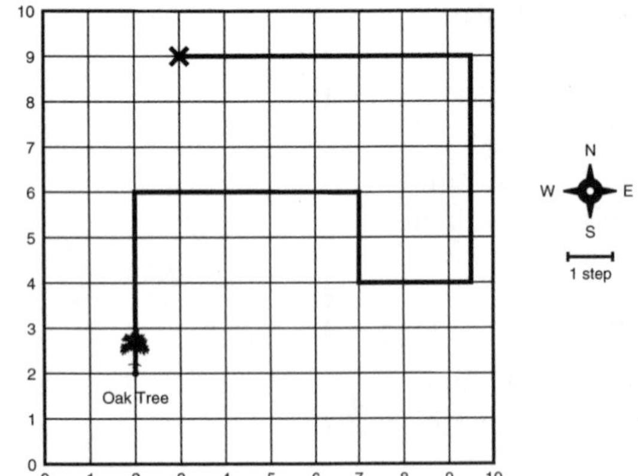

Study Link 6•6

1. >; 101° **2.** <; 52°

3. >; 144° **4.** <; 137°

6. 24 **7.** 8 R2 **8.** 157 **9.** 185 R3

Study Link 6•7

1. 60° **2.** 150° **3.** 84° **4.** 105°

5. 32° **6.** 300°

Study Link 6•8

1.

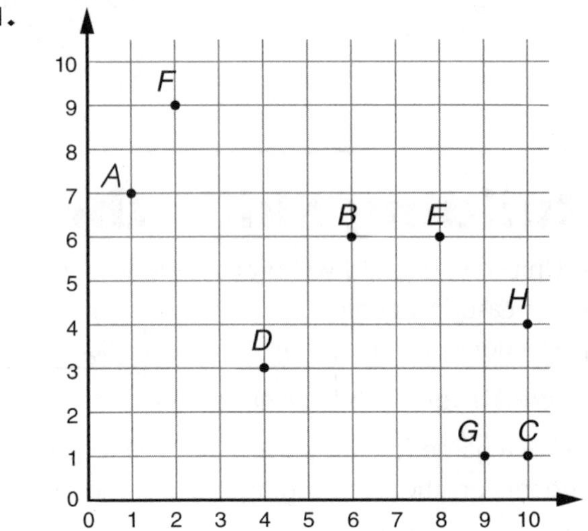

2. *K* (4,8); *L* (7,7); *M* (10,5); *N* (1,8); *O* (6,2); *P* (8,4); *Q* (10,2); *R* (3,10)

Study Link 6•9

1.

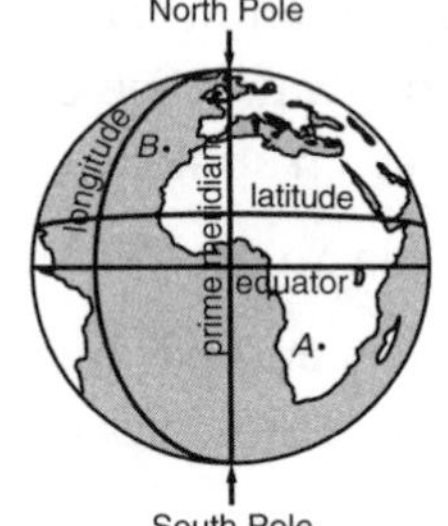

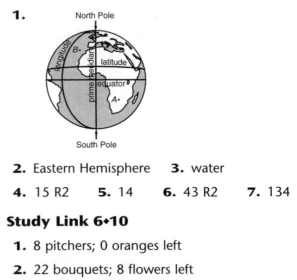

2. Eastern Hemisphere **3.** water

4. 15 R2 **5.** 14 **6.** 43 R2 **7.** 134

Study Link 6•10

1. 8 pitchers; 0 oranges left

2. 22 bouquets; 8 flowers left

3. 45 R6 **4.** 69 **5.** 180

6. 2,233 **7.** 1,827 **8.** 16,287

Name Date Time

Multiplication/Division Number Stories

Fill in each Multiplication/Division Diagram. Then write a number model.
Be sure to include a unit with your answer.

1. Trung wants to rearrange his collection of 72 animals on a shelf in his room. How many equal rows of 9 animals can he make?

rows	animals per row	animals in all

Number model: ______________________

Answer: ______________________

2. An average porcupine has about 30,000 quills. About how many quills would 4 porcupines have?

porcupines	quills per porcupine	quills in all

Number model: ______________________

Answer: ______________________

3. There are 168 calculators for the students at Madison School. A box holds 8 calculators. How many boxes are needed to hold all of the calculators?

boxes	calculators per box	calculators in all

Number model: ______________________

Answer: ______________________

Practice

4. ____________ = 6.17 + 8.77

5. ____________ = 12.13 − 4.44

Name _______________ Date _______________ Time _______________

STUDY LINK 6·2

Equal-Grouping Division Problems

For Problems 1–3, fill in the multiples-of-10 list if it is helpful. If you prefer to solve the division problems in another way, show your work.

1. The community center bought 228 juice boxes for a picnic. How many 6-packs is that?

10 [6s] = ____________

20 [6s] = ____________

30 [6s] = ____________

40 [6s] = ____________

50 [6s] = ____________

Number model: ________________________

Answer: ____________ 6-packs

2. There are 8 girls on each basketball team. There are 184 girls in the league. How many teams are there?

10 [8s] = ____________

20 [8s] = ____________

30 [8s] = ____________

40 [8s] = ____________

50 [8s] = ____________

Number model: ________________________

Answer: ____________ teams

3. How many 3s are in 142?

10 [3s] = ____________

20 [3s] = ____________

30 [3s] = ____________

40 [3s] = ____________

50 [3s] = ____________

Number model: ________________________

Answer: ____________

Practice

4. ____________ = 661 * 4 **5.** 13 * 96 = ____________ **6.** ____________ = 59 * 82

Name Date Time

Multiples of 10 and 100

Fill in the missing numbers in the problems below.

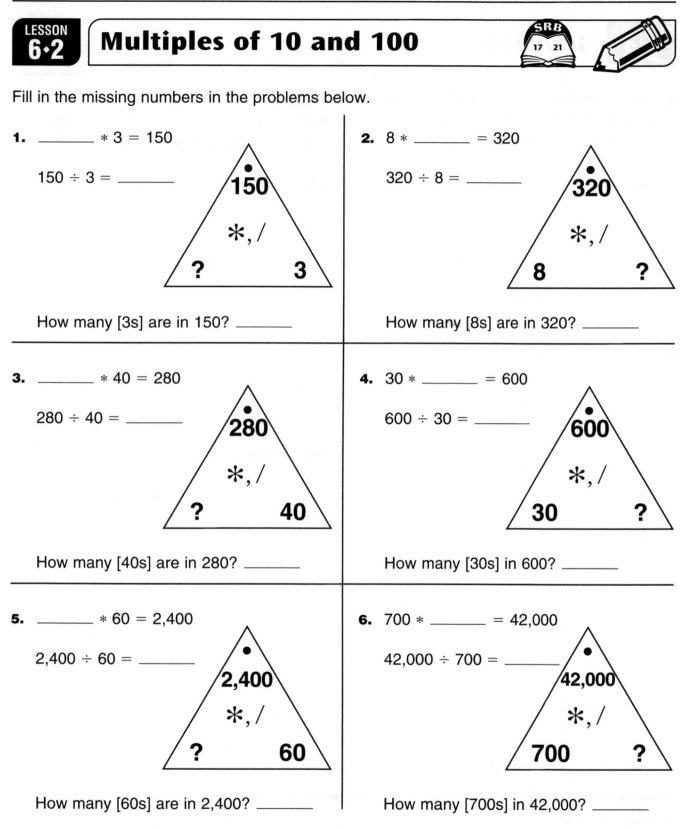

1. _______ ∗ 3 = 150

150 ÷ 3 = _______

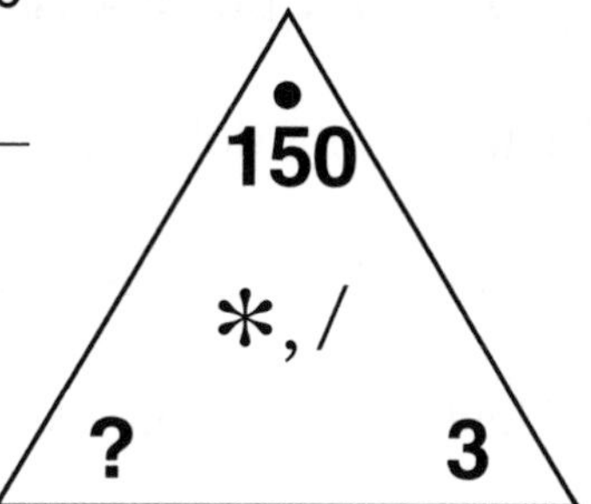

How many [3s] are in 150? _______

2. 8 ∗ _______ = 320

320 ÷ 8 = _______

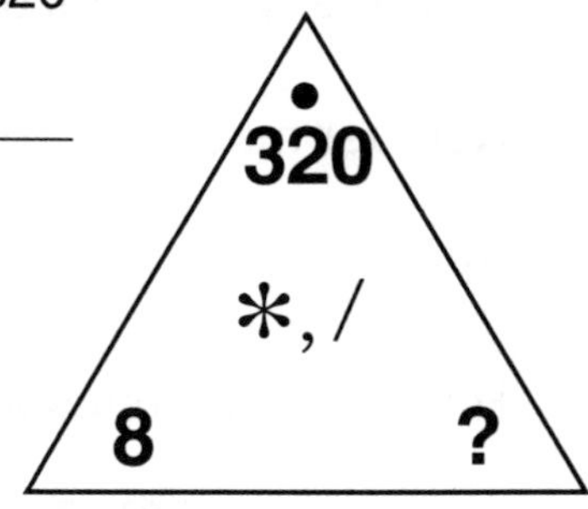

How many [8s] are in 320? _______

3. _______ ∗ 40 = 280

280 ÷ 40 = _______

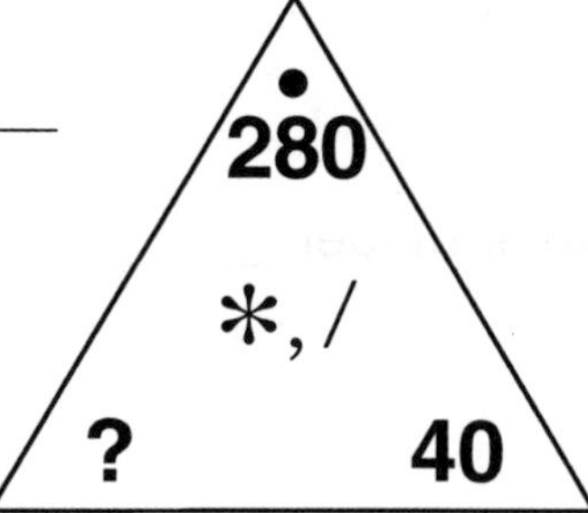

How many [40s] are in 280? _______

4. 30 ∗ _______ = 600

600 ÷ 30 = _______

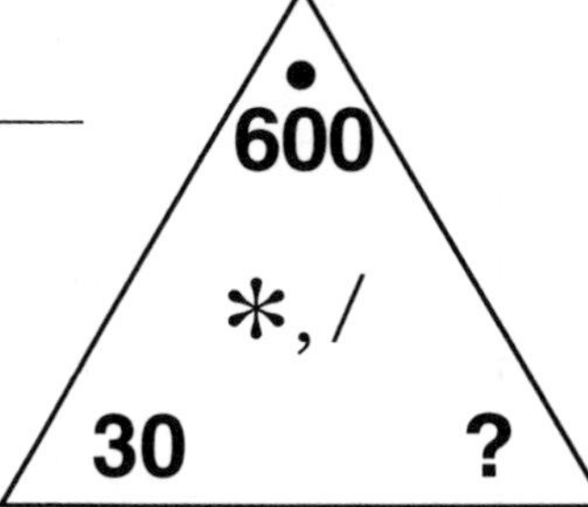

How many [30s] in 600? _______

5. _______ ∗ 60 = 2,400

2,400 ÷ 60 = _______

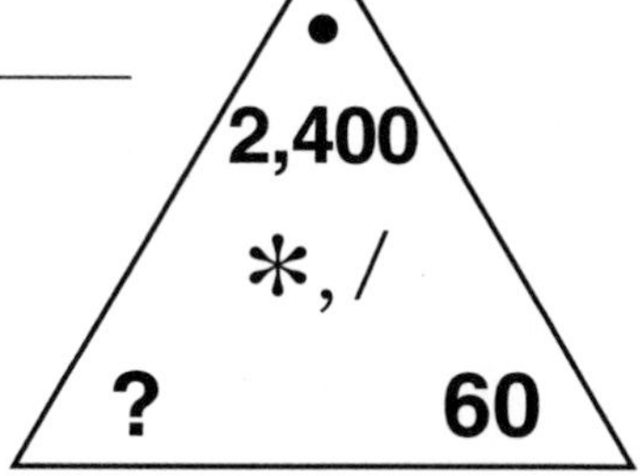

How many [60s] are in 2,400? _______

6. 700 ∗ _______ = 42,000

42,000 ÷ 700 = _______

42,000

∗, /

700 ?

How many [700s] in 42,000? _______

7. Explain how solving one problem in each set helps you solve the other two problems.

____

____

Name Date Time

STUDY LINK 6•3

Division

1. Bernardo divided a bag of 83 marbles evenly among five friends and himself. How many marbles did each get?

   Number model: ____________________

   Answer: ________ marbles

   How many marbles are left over?

   ________ marbles

2. The carnival committee has 360 small prizes to share equally with 5 carnival booths. How many prizes will each booth get?

   Number model: ____________________

   Answer: ________ prizes

   How many prizes are left over?

   ________ prizes

3. $4\overline{)91}$ Answer: ____________

4. 427 / 8 Answer: ____________

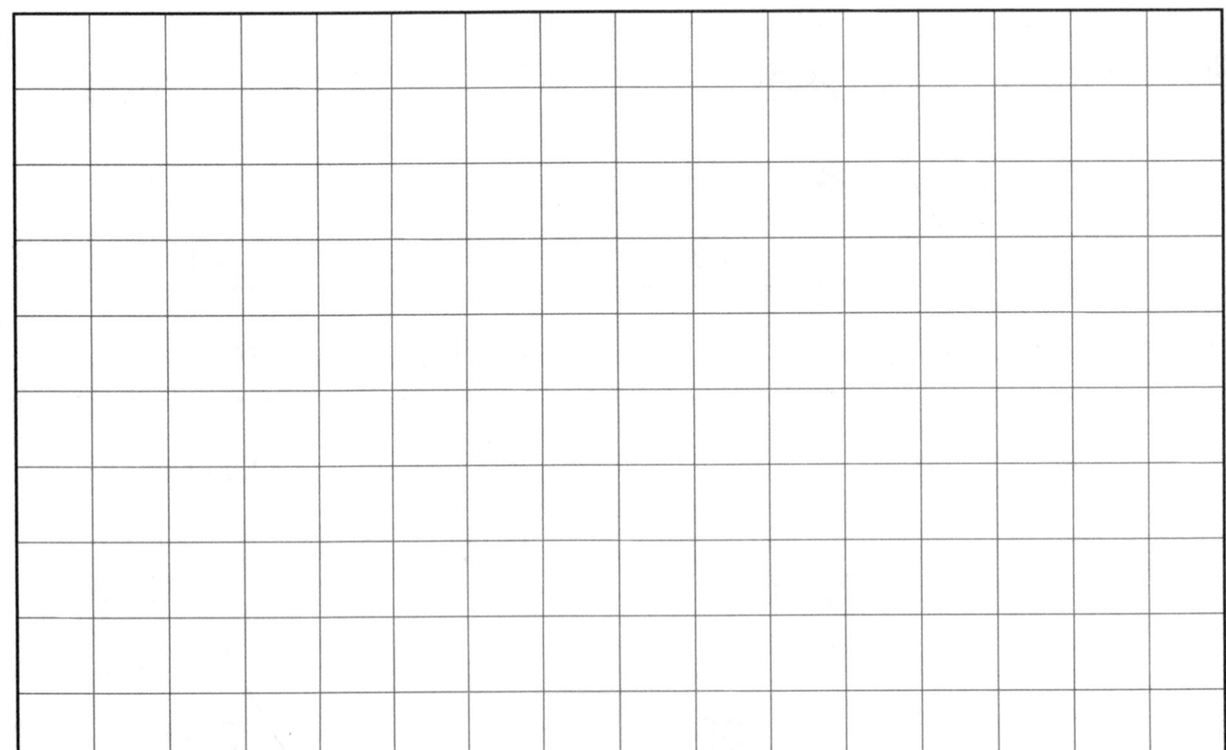

Practice

5. ____________ = 34.96 + 1.58

6. ____________ = 300.2 + 2.378

7. 43.27 − 12.67 = ____________

8. 74.6 − 31.055 = ____________

Name Date Time

A Pen Riddle

Mrs. Swenson bought 2 pens for each of her 3 daughters.

- She gave the clerk a $10 bill.
- Her change was all in nickels.
- Her change was less than 50 cents.
- Each pen cost the same amount.
- No sales tax was charged.

1. What was the cost of each pen? ______________

2. Show or explain how you got your answer.

Name Date Time

A Pen Riddle

Mrs. Swenson bought 2 pens for each of her 3 daughters.

- She gave the clerk a $10 bill.
- Her change was all in nickels.
- Her change was less than 50 cents.
- Each pen cost the same amount.
- No sales tax was charged.

1. What was the cost of each pen? ______________

2. Show or explain how you got your answer.

Name Date Time

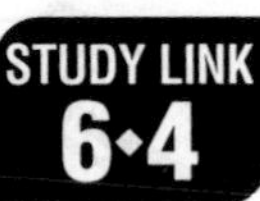

Interpreting Remainders

1. Mrs. Patel brought a box of 124 strawberries to the party. She wants to divide the strawberries evenly among 8 people. How many strawberries will each person get?

Picture:

Number model: ____________________

Answer: ______________ strawberries

What did you do about the remainder? Circle the answer.

A. Ignored it

B. Reported it as a fraction or decimal

C. Rounded the answer up

Why? ______________________________

____

____

2. Mr. Chew has a box of 348 pens. He asks Maurice to divide the pens into groups of 16. How many groups can Maurice make?

Picture:

Number model: ____________________

Answer: ______________ groups

What did you do about the remainder? Circle the answer.

A. Ignored it

B. Reported it as a fraction or decimal

C. Rounded the answer up

Why? ______________________________

____

____

Practice

3. $68 \div 7 =$ ______________

4. ______________ $= 74 \div 4$

5. $\frac{468}{9} =$ ______________

6. $3\overline{)95} =$ ______________

Name Date Time

A Remainder of One

Use 25 centimeter cubes to represent the 25 ants in the story *A Remainder of One.*

1. Divide the cubes into 2 equal rows.
Draw what you did.

How many cubes are in each row?

________ cubes

How many cubes are left over?

________ cube(s)

2. Divide the cubes into 3 equal rows.
Draw what you did.

How many cubes are in each row?

________ cubes

How many cubes are left over?

________ cube(s)

3. Divide the cubes into 4 equal rows.
Draw what you did.

How many cubes are in each row?

________ cubes

How many cubes are left over?

________ cube(s)

4. Divide the cubes into 5 equal rows.
Draw what you did.

How many cubes are in each row?

________ cubes

How many cubes are left over?

________ cube(s)

Name Date Time

Multiples Number Story

Paolo has fewer than 40 marbles in a bag. If he splits up the marbles among his 4 friends, he'll have 3 left over.

If he divides them among his 7 friends, he'll have 2 left over.

1. How many marbles are in the bag? _______ marbles

2. Show or explain how you got your answer.

Name Date Time

Multiples Number Story

Paolo has fewer than 40 marbles in a bag. If he splits up the marbles among his 4 friends, he'll have 3 left over.

If he divides them among his 7 friends, he'll have 2 left over.

1. How many marbles are in the bag? _______ marbles

2. Show or explain how you got your answer.

Name Date Time

Treasure Hunt

Marge and her friends are playing Treasure Hunt. Help them find the treasure. Follow the directions. Draw the path from the oak tree to the treasure. Mark the spot where the treasure is buried.

1. Start at the dot under the oak tree; face north. Walk 4 steps.
2. Make a quarter turn, clockwise. Walk 5 steps.
3. Face south. Walk 2 steps.
4. Face east. Walk $2\frac{1}{2}$ steps.
5. Make a $\frac{3}{4}$ turn, clockwise. Walk 5 steps.
6. Make a $\frac{3}{4}$ turn, clockwise. Walk $6\frac{1}{2}$ steps.
7. Make an X to mark the spot where you end.

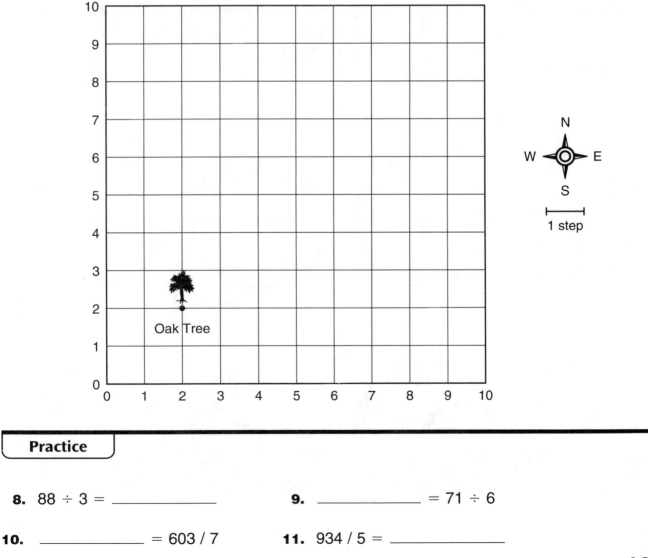

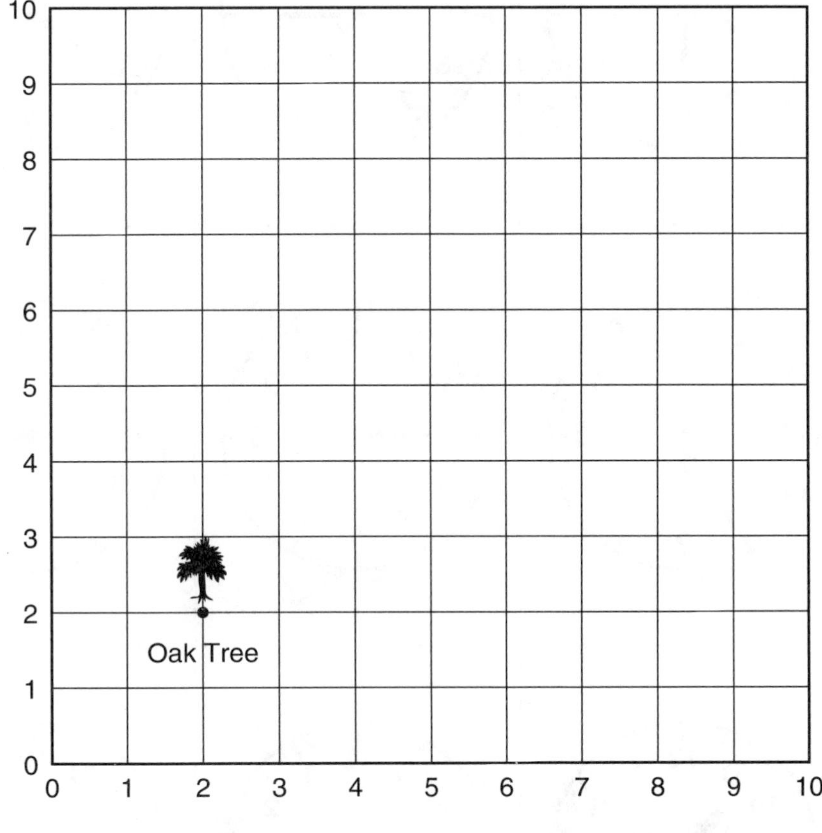

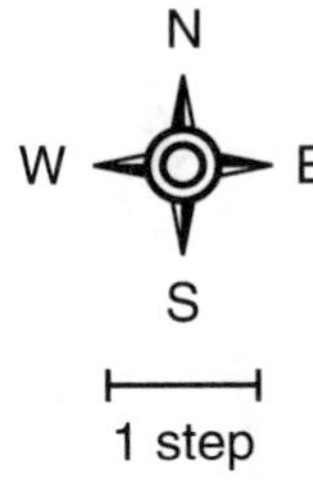

Practice

8. 88 ÷ 3 = ____________

9. ____________ = 71 ÷ 6

10. ____________ = 603 / 7

11. 934 / 5 = ____________

Name Date Time

LESSON 6•5

Time (Analog)

Name Date Time

LESSON 6•5

Time (Digital)

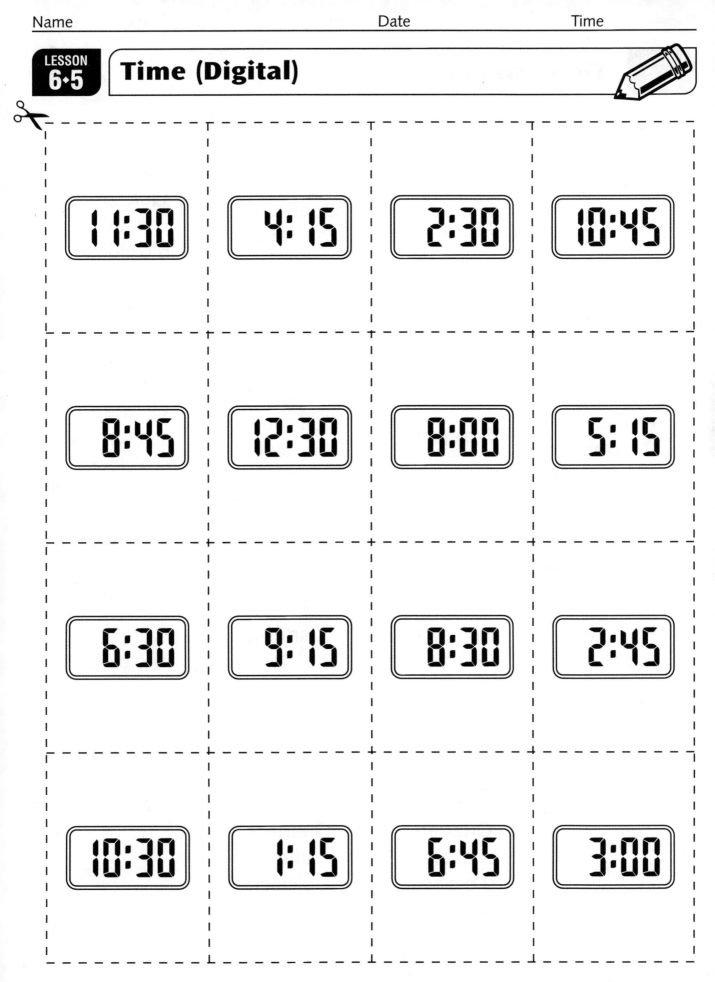

11:30	4:15	2:30	10:45
8:45	12:30	8:00	5:15
6:30	9:15	8:30	2:45
10:30	1:15	6:45	3:00

Name Date Time

Time (Words)

8 o'clock	Half-past 2 o'clock	Quarter-to 7 o'clock	Quarter-past 5 o'clock
Half-past 8 o'clock	3 o'clock	Quarter-to 11 o'clock	Quarter-after 4 o'clock
Half-past 6 o'clock	Half-past 12 o'clock	Quarter-to 3 o'clock	Half-past 10 o'clock
Quarter-to 9 o'clock	Quarter-after 9 o'clock	Quarter-after 1 o'clock	Half-past 11 o'clock

Name Date Time

Clock Angle Challenge

Use the full-circle protractor and the clock from journal pages 152 and 153 to help you solve the problems below.

1. How long does it take the *hour hand* to move 1°? ______

Explain. ______

______

2. How long does it take the *minute hand* to move 1°? ______

Explain. ______

______

______

Name Date Time

Clock Angle Challenge

Use the full-circle protractor and the clock from journal pages 152 and 153 to help you solve the problems below.

1. How long does it take the *hour hand* to move 1°? ______

Explain. ______

______

2. How long does it take the *minute hand* to move 1°? ______

Explain. ______

______

______

Name Date Time

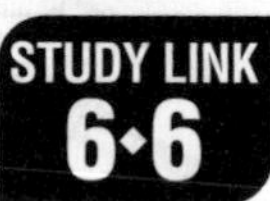

Measuring Angles

First estimate and then use your full-circle protractor to measure each angle.

1. This angle is ____________ (>, <) 90°.

∠G: ____________°

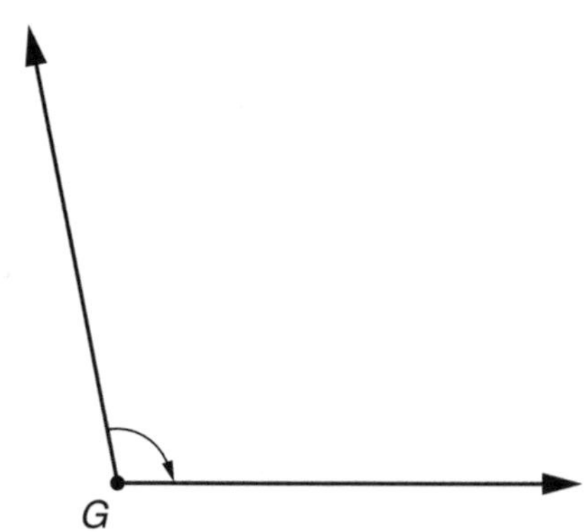

2. This angle is ____________ (>, <) 90°.

∠H: ____________°

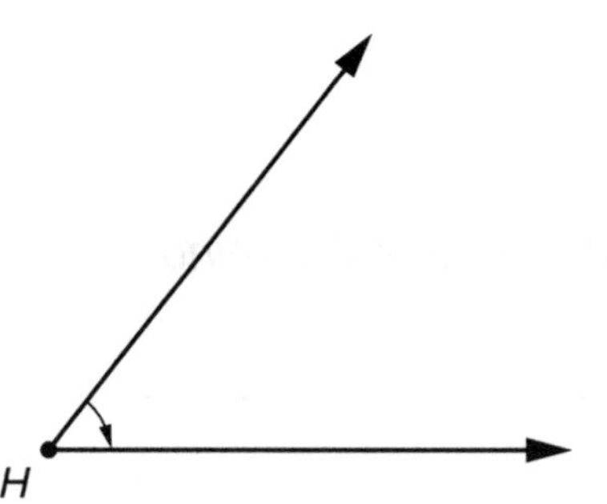

3. This angle is ____________ (>, <) 90°.

∠I: ____________°

4. This angle is ____________ (>, <) 90°.

∠J: ____________°

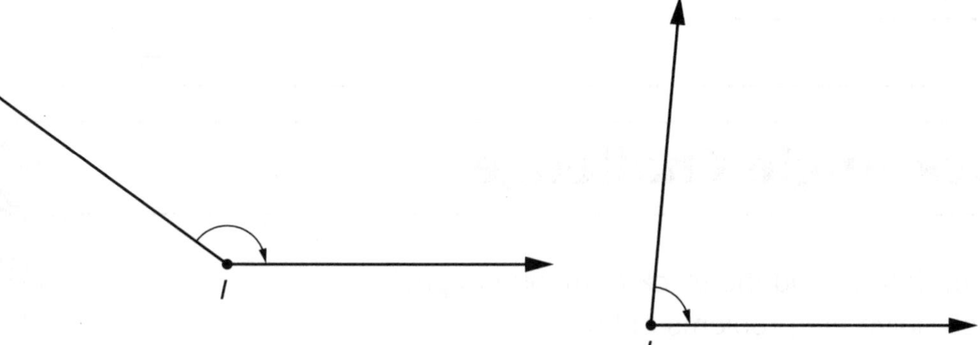

Try This

5. On the back of this page, draw and label angles with the following degree measures:

∠ABC 78° ∠DEF 145° ∠GHI 213° ∠JKL 331°

Practice

6. ____________ = 96 ÷ 4

7. 66 ÷ 8 = ____________

8. ____________ = 314 ÷ 2

9. 928 ÷ 5 = ____________

Name Date Time

A Waxed-Paper Protractor

1. Follow the steps below to make a waxed-paper protractor.

Step 1: Take a sheet of waxed paper.

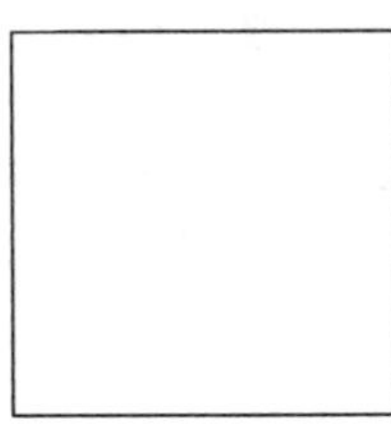

Step 2: Fold the paper in half. Be sure to crease it tightly.

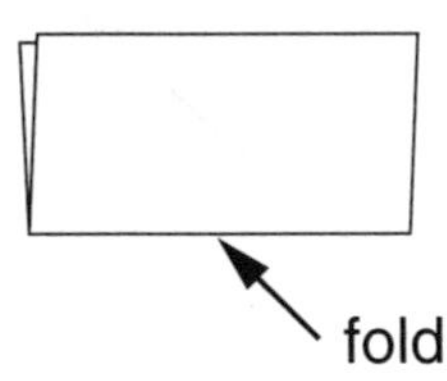

Step 3: Fold it in half again.

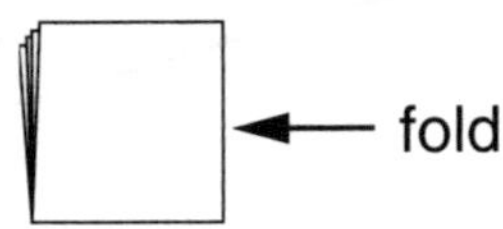

Step 4: Bring the folded edges together and fold it in half. Repeat this step again.

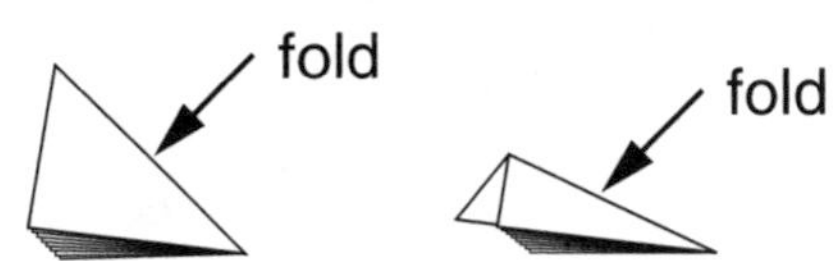

Step 5: Cut off the top.

Step 6: Unfold.

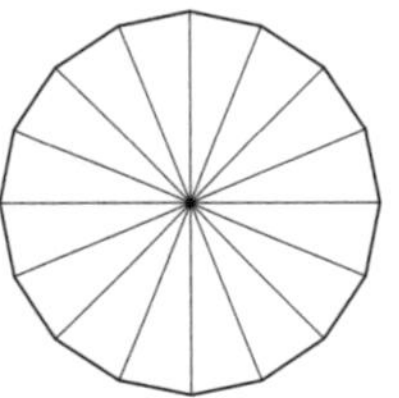

2. Use your waxed-paper protractor to measure the angles below.

a.

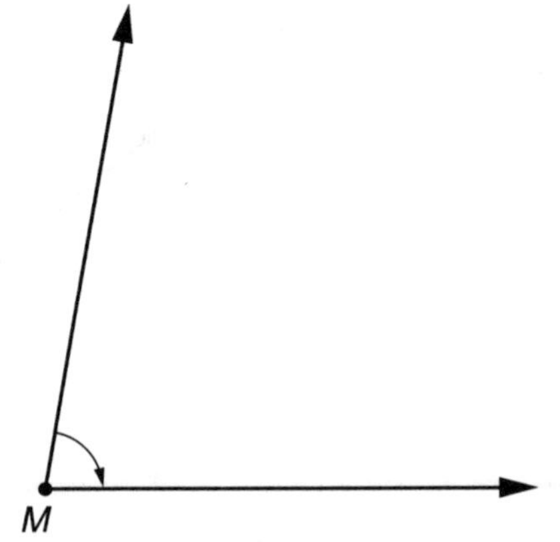

b.

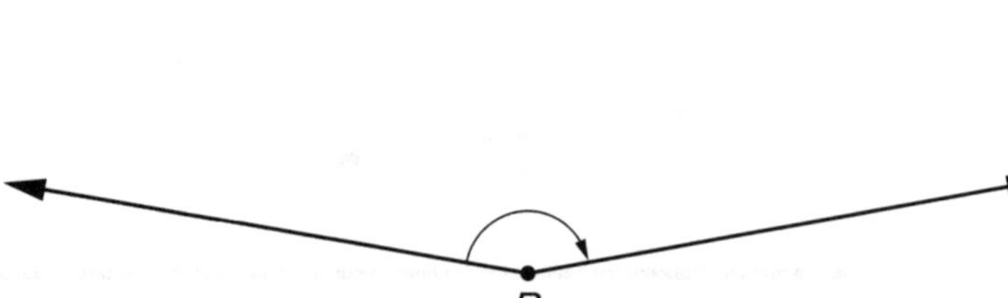

Angle *M* measures about ______ wedges.

Angle *R* measures about ______ wedges.

3. Use a straightedge to draw more angles on the back of this sheet.
Measure the angles and record the numbers of wedges.

Name Date Time

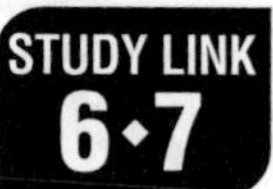

Measuring Angles with a Protractor

First estimate whether the angles measure more or less than 90°. Then use a half-circle protractor to measure them.

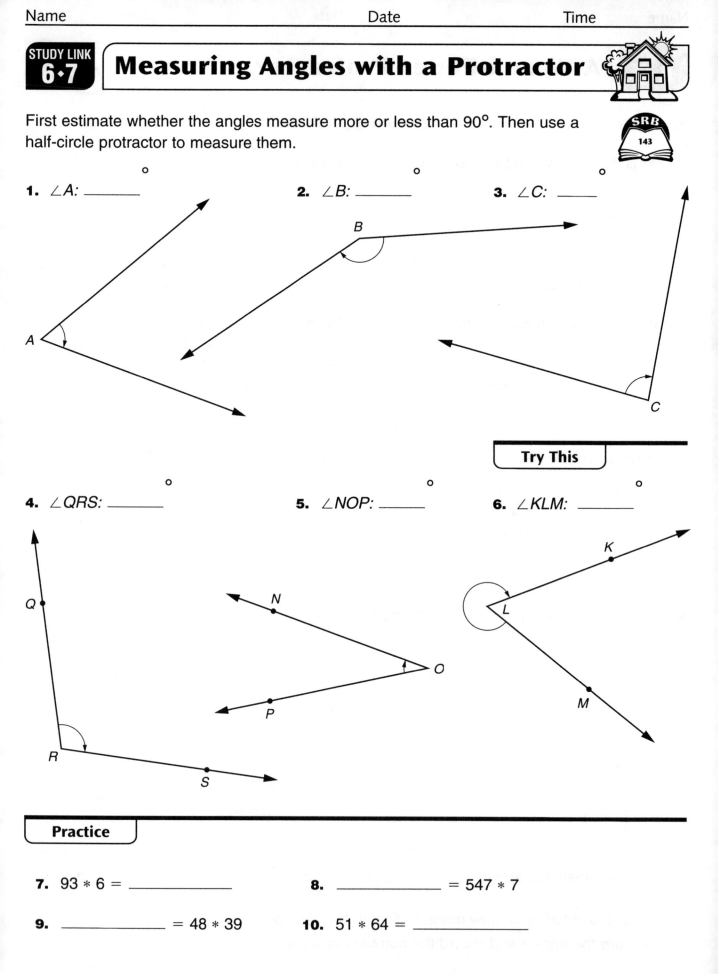

1. ∠A: ______°

2. ∠B: ______°

3. ∠C: ______°

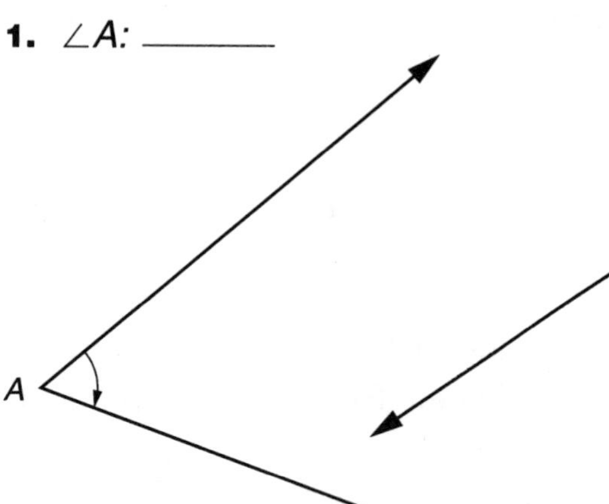

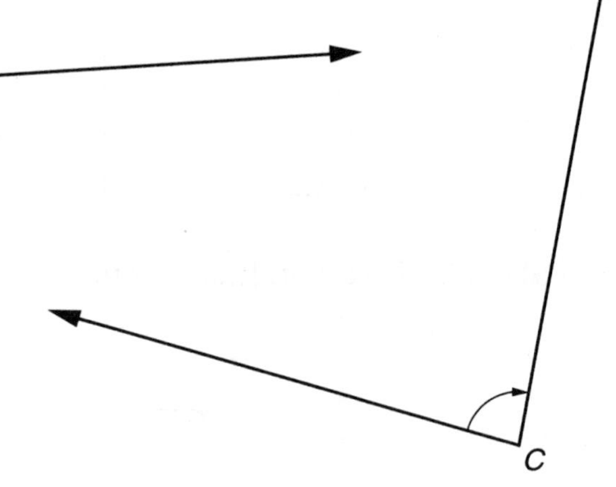

4. ∠QRS: ______°

5. ∠NOP: ______°

6. ∠KLM: ______°

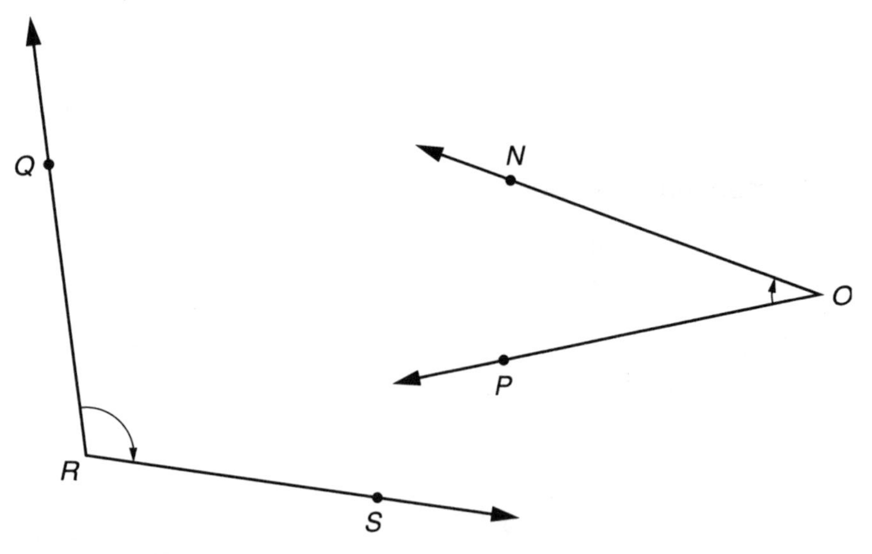

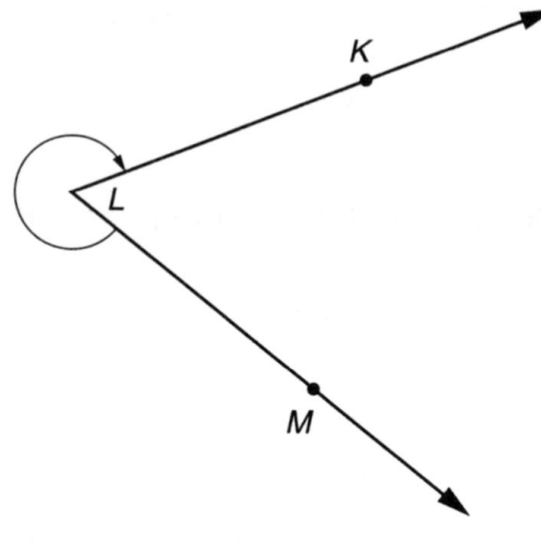

Practice

7. 93 * 6 = ____________

8. ____________ = 547 * 7

9. ____________ = 48 * 39

10. 51 * 64 = ____________

Name Date Time

LESSON 6•7 Exploring Triangle Measures

You need 2 sheets of paper, a straightedge, and a protractor.

1. Draw a large triangle on each sheet of paper. The 2 triangles should not look the same.

2. Label the vertices of one triangle *A, B,* and *C*. Label the vertices of the other triangle *D, E,* and *F*. Be sure to write the labels inside the triangles.

3. Using your protractor, measure each angle as accurately as you can. Record the degree measures in the tables below.

4. Find the sum of the degree measures in triangle *ABC* and in triangle *DEF*.

Angle	Degree Measure
$\angle A$	About ______°
$\angle B$	About ______°
$\angle C$	About ______°
Sum	About ______°

Angle	Degree Measure
$\angle D$	About ______°
$\angle E$	About ______°
$\angle F$	About ______°
Sum	About ______°

5. Write a true statement about the sum of the measures of the 3 angles of a triangle.

____

____

Name Date Time

STUDY LINK 6•8

Coordinate Grids

1. Plot and label each point on the coordinate grid.

SRB 144

A (1,7)

B (6,6)

C (10,1)

D (4,3)

E (8,6)

F (2,9)

G (9,1)

H (10,4)

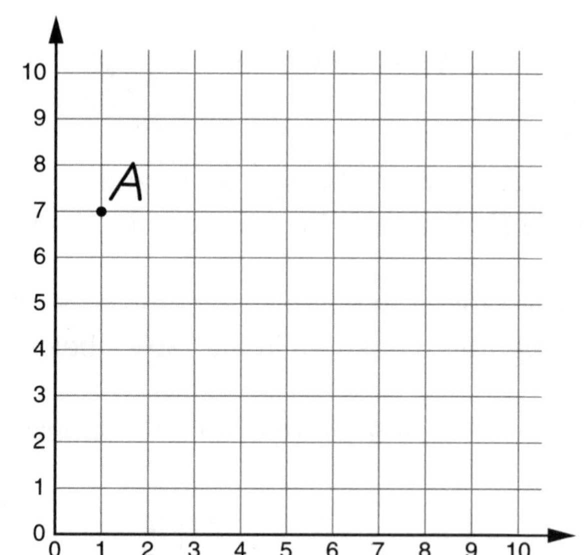

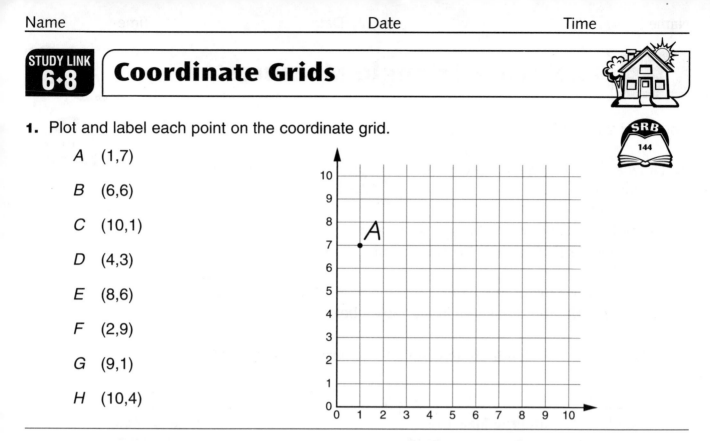

2. Write the ordered number pair for each point plotted on the coordinate grid.

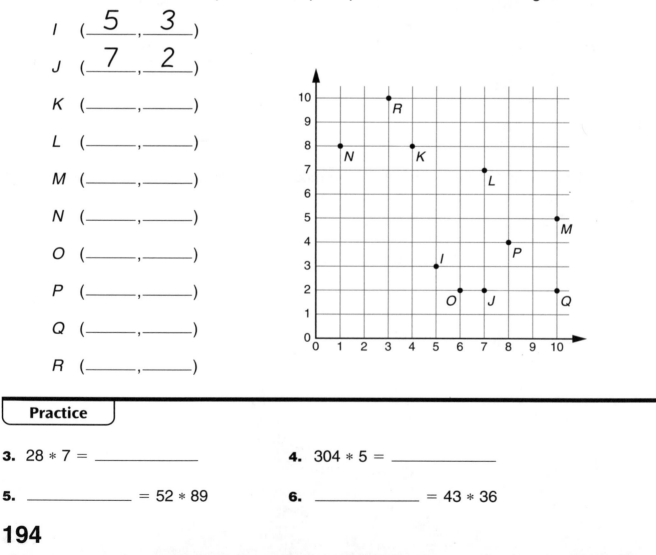

I (5, 3)

J (7, 2)

K (____, ____)

L (____, ____)

M (____, ____)

N (____, ____)

O (____, ____)

P (____, ____)

Q (____, ____)

R (____, ____)

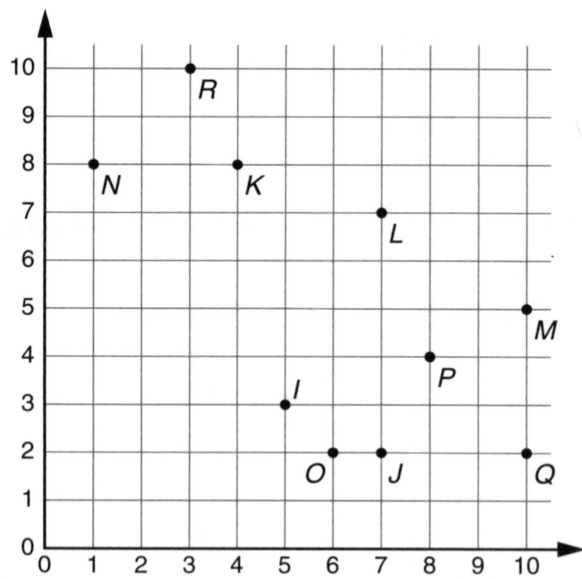

Practice

3. 28 * 7 = ________

4. 304 * 5 = ________

5. ________ = 52 * 89

6. ________ = 43 * 36

Name Date Time

Latitude and Longitude

Use your *Student Reference Book* to help you complete this Study Link. Read the examples and study the figures on pages 272 and 273.

1. Do the following on the picture of the world globe.

a. Label the North and South Poles.

b. Draw and label the equator.

c. Label the prime meridian.

d. Draw and label a line of latitude that is north of the equator.

e. Draw and label a line of longitude that is west of the prime meridian.

f. Mark a point that is in the Southern Hemisphere and also in the Eastern Hemisphere. Label the point *A*.

g. Mark a point that is in the Northern Hemisphere and also in the Western Hemisphere. Label the point *B*.

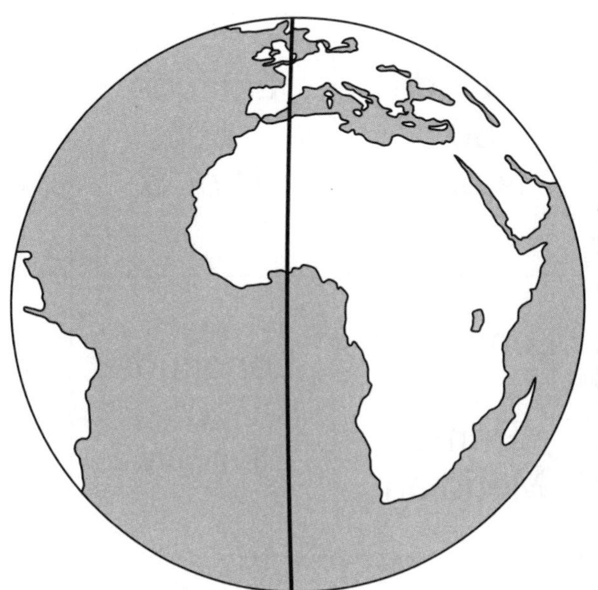

2. The entire continent of Africa is shown in the figure above. Is Africa mostly in the Western Hemisphere or in the Eastern Hemisphere?

____

3. Do the equator and prime meridian meet over water or over land? _______________

Practice

4. _______________ = 47 / 3

5. $7\overline{)98}$ _______________

6. 217 ÷ 5 = _______________

7. _______________ = 804 / 6

Name Date Time

Latitude and Longitude Cards

Latitude 0° Equator	Latitude 10° N or S	Latitude 20° N or S	Latitude 30° N or S	Latitude 40° N or S
Latitude 50° N or S	Latitude 60° N or S	Latitude 70° N or S	Latitude 80° N or S	Latitude 90° N or S
Longitude 0° Prime Meridian	Longitude 10° E or W	Longitude 20° E or W	Longitude 30° E or W	Longitude 40° E or W
Longitude 50° E or W	Longitude 60° E or W	Longitude 70° E or W	Longitude 80° E or W	Longitude 90° E or W
Longitude 100° E or W	Longitude 110° E or W	Longitude 120° E or W	Longitude 130° E or W	Longitude 140° E or W
Longitude 150° E or W	Longitude 160° E or W	Longitude 170° E or W	Longitude 180° International Date Line	Longitude PLAYER'S CHOICE

Name Date Time

Division

1. It takes 14 oranges to make a small pitcher of juice. Annette has 112 oranges. How many pitchers of juice can she make?

Number model: ______________________

Answer: __________ pitchers of juice

How many oranges are left over? __________ oranges

2. Each bouquet needs 17 flowers. The florist has 382 flowers in his store. How many bouquets can the florist make?

Number model: ______________________

Answer: __________ bouquets

How many flowers are left over? __________ flowers

3. $726 \div 16 =$ __________

4. $4\overline{)276}$ __________

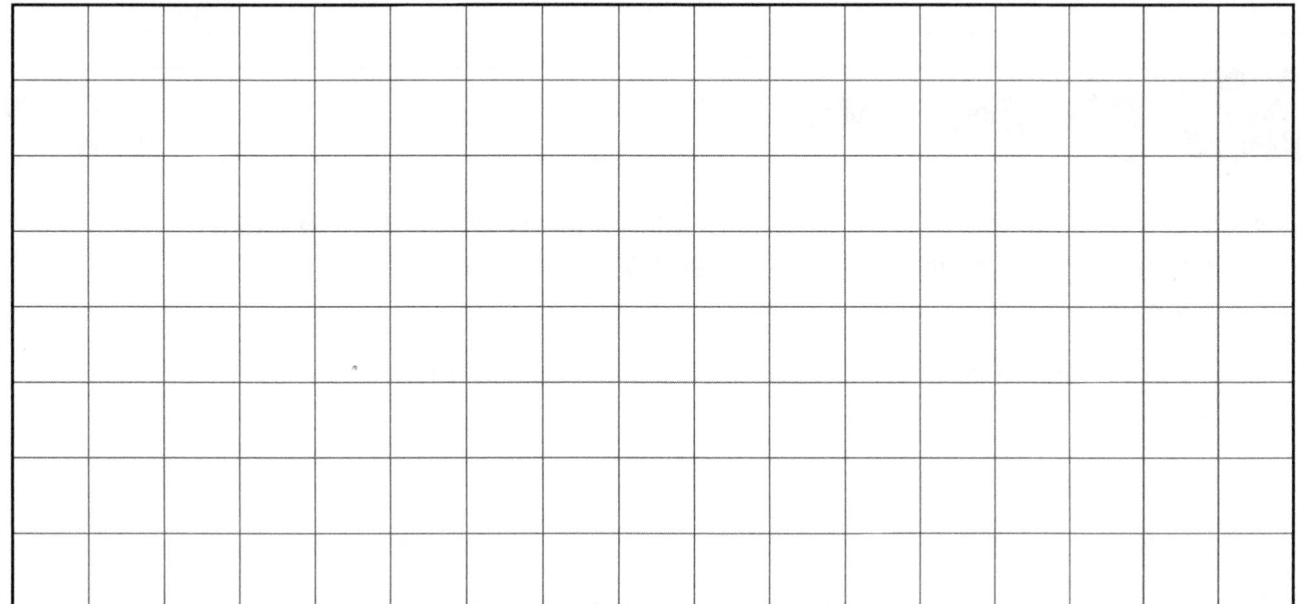

Practice

5. $45 * 4 =$ __________

6. __________ $= 319 * 7$

7. __________ $= 29 * 63$

8. $89 * 183 =$ __________

Name Date Time

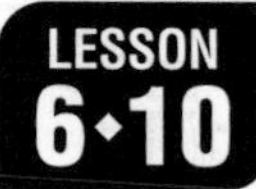

Division "Magic"

1. Write a 3-digit number. _______ Enter it into your calculator twice to make a 6-digit number. For example, if you picked 259, then you would enter 259259 in your calculator.

2. Divide the 6-digit number by 7. Then divide the result by 11. Finally, divide that result by 13.

3. What is the final quotient? _______

4. Repeat Steps 1 and 2. New number: _______ Final quotient: _______

5. Do you think this trick works with *any* three-digit number? Explain.

____

____

____

Name Date Time

LESSON 6•10

Division "Magic"

1. Write a 3-digit number. _______ Enter it into your calculator twice to make a 6-digit number. For example, if you picked 259, then you would enter 259259 in your calculator.

2. Divide the 6-digit number by 7. Then divide the result by 11. Finally, divide that result by 13.

3. What is the final quotient? _______

4. Repeat Steps 1 and 2. New number: _______ Final quotient: _______

5. Do you think this trick works with *any* three-digit number? Explain.

____

____

____

Name Date Time

Unit 7: Family Letter

Fractions and Their Uses; Chance and Probability

One of the most important ideas in mathematics is the concept that a number can be named in many different ways. For example, a store might advertise an item at $\frac{1}{2}$ off its original price or at a 50% discount—both mean the same thing. Much of the mathematics your child will learn involves finding equivalent names for numbers.

A few weeks ago, the class studied decimals as a way of naming numbers between whole numbers. Fractions serve the same purpose. After reviewing the meaning and uses of fractions, students will explore equivalent fractions—fractions that have the same value, such as $\frac{1}{2}$, $\frac{2}{4}$, $\frac{3}{6}$, and so on. As in past work with fractions, students will handle concrete objects and look at pictures, because they first need to "see" fractions in order to understand what fractions mean.

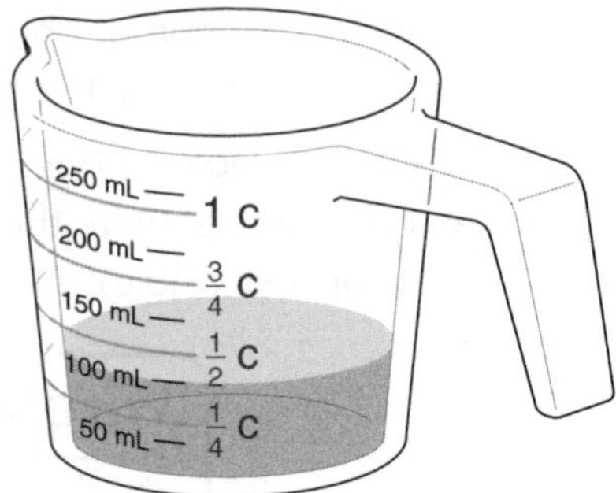

A measuring cup showing fractional increments

Fractions are also used to express the chance that an event will occur. For example, if we flip a coin, we say that it will land heads-up about $\frac{1}{2}$ of the time. The branch of mathematics that deals with chance events is called **probability.** Your child will begin to study probability by performing simple experiments.

Please keep this Family Letter for reference as your child works through Unit 7.

Vocabulary

Important terms in Unit 7:

denominator The number below the line in a fraction. In a fraction where the whole is divided into equal parts, the denominator represents the number of equal parts into which the whole (or ONE or unit whole) is divided. In the fraction $\frac{a}{b}$, b is the denominator.

equal chance outcomes or **equally likely outcomes** If each of the possible outcomes for a chance experiment or situation has the same chance of occurring, the outcomes are said to have an equal chance or to be equally likely. For example, there is an equal chance of getting heads or tails when flipping a coin, so heads and tails are equally likely outcomes.

equivalent fractions Fractions with different denominators that name the same number. For example, $\frac{1}{2}$ and $\frac{4}{8}$ are equivalent fractions.

fair (coin, die, or spinner) A device that is free from bias. Each side of a fair die or coin will come up about equally often. Each section of a fair spinner will come up in proportion to its area.

A die has six faces. If the die is fair, each face has the same chance of coming up.

fair game A game in which every player has the same chance of winning.

mixed number A number that is written using both a whole number and a fraction. For example, $2\frac{1}{4}$ is a mixed number equal to $2 + \frac{1}{4}$.

numerator The number above the line in a fraction. In a fraction where the whole (or ONE or unit whole) is divided into a number of equal parts, the numerator represents the number of equal parts being considered. In the fraction $\frac{a}{b}$, a is the numerator.

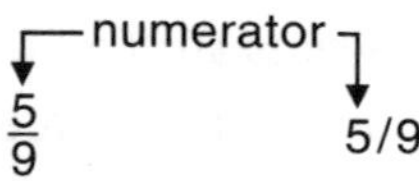

probability A number from 0 through 1 that tells the chance that an event will happen. The closer a probability is to 1, the more likely the event is to happen.

whole (or ONE or unit whole) The entire object, collection of objects, or quantity being considered; the ONE; the unit whole; 100%.

"whole" box In *Everyday Mathematics,* a box in which students write the name of the whole (or ONE or unit whole).

Whole
24 pennies

Do-Anytime Activities

To work with your child on concepts taught in this unit, try these interesting and rewarding activities:

1. Have your child look for everyday uses of fractions in grocery items, clothing sizes, cookbooks, measuring cups and spoons, and statistics in newspapers and on television.
2. Encourage your child to express numbers, quantities, and measures, such as a quarter of an hour, a quart of orange juice, a dozen eggs, and a pint of milk.
3. While grocery shopping, help your child compare prices by looking at shelf labels or calculating unit prices. Help your child make decisions about the "better buy." If a calculator is available, have your child take it to the store.
4. Have your child look for everyday uses of probabilities in games, sports, and weather reports. Ask your child to make a list of events that could never happen, might happen, and are sure to happen.

Building Skills through Games

In this unit, your child will work on his or her understanding of fractions and probability by playing the following games. For detailed instructions, see the *Student Reference Book.*

Chances Are See *Student Reference Book,* pages 236 and 237.
This game is for 2 players and requires one deck of *Chances Are* Event Cards and one deck of *Chances Are* Probability Cards. The game develops skill in using probability terms to describe the likelihood of events.

Fraction Match See *Student Reference Book,* page 243.
This game is for 2 to 4 players and requires one deck of *Fraction Match* cards. The game develops skill in naming equivalent fractions.

Fraction Of See *Student Reference Book,* pages 244 and 245.
This game is for 2 players and requires one deck of *Fraction Of* Fraction Cards and one deck of *Fraction Of* Set Cards. The game develops skill in finding the fraction of a number.

Fraction Top-It See *Student Reference Book,* page 247.
This is a game for 2 to 4 players and requires one set of 32 Fraction Cards. The game develops skill in comparing fractions.

Getting to One See *Student Reference Book,* page 248.
This is a game for 2 players and requires one calculator. The game develops skill in estimation.

Grab Bag See *Student Reference Book,* page 249.
This game is for 2 players or two teams of 2 and requires one deck of *Grab Bag* cards. The game develops skill in calculating the probability of an event.

STUDY LINK 6•11

Unit 7: Family Letter *cont.*

As You Help Your Child with Homework

As your child brings assignments home, you may want to go over the instructions together, clarifying them as necessary. The answers listed below will guide you through some of the Study Links in this unit.

Study Link 7•2

1. **b.** 4 **c.** 12 **d.** 8 **2.** 6
3. 12 **4.** 7 **5.** 28
6. 10 **7.** 30 **8.** 10
9. 12 **10.** 12 **11.** $2\frac{1}{2}$
12. 23 **13.** $19\frac{2}{3}$ **14.** 13
15. $41\frac{7}{9}$

Study Link 7•3

1. 50-50 chance **2.** very unlikely
4. 5 **5.** 592 **6.** 3,948
7. 1,690 **8.** 16,170

Study Link 7•4

3. 8 **4.** 0.881 **5.** 9.845
6. 1.59 **7.** 0.028

Study Link 7•5

1. Less than \$1.00; 0.75 + 0.10 = 0.85
2. $3\frac{3}{4}$ **3.** $\frac{1}{6}$ **4.** $2\frac{3}{8}$
5. Sample answers:

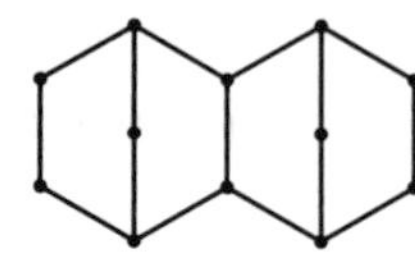

$\frac{1}{4} + \frac{1}{4} + \frac{1}{4} + \frac{1}{4} = 1$

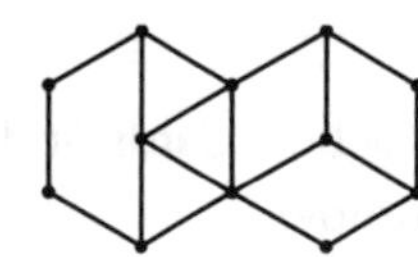

$\frac{1}{4} + \frac{3}{12} + \frac{3}{6} = 1$

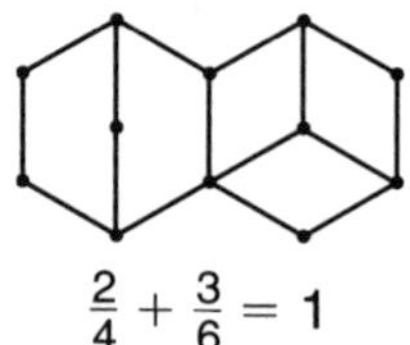

$\frac{2}{4} + \frac{3}{6} = 1$

6. 8 **7.** 45 **8.** 49 **9.** 22

Study Link 7•6

1. C, F, I **2.** B, D **3.** E, H **4.** A, G
5. $\frac{2}{3}$ **7.** $\frac{5}{6}$ **9.** $\frac{1}{2}$ **10.** $\frac{1}{6}$

Study Link 7•7

5. $23\frac{3}{4}$ **6.** 19 **7.** 42

Study Link 7•8

Sample answers for 1–10:

1. $\frac{2}{10}, \frac{1}{5}, \frac{20}{100}$ **2.** $\frac{6}{10}, \frac{3}{5}, \frac{60}{100}$
3. $\frac{5}{10}, \frac{1}{2}, \frac{50}{100}$ **4.** $\frac{3}{4}, \frac{30}{40}, \frac{75}{100}$
5. 0.3 **6.** 0.63 **7.** 0.7 **8.** 0.4
9. 0.70; $\frac{70}{100}$ **10.** 0.2; $\frac{2}{10}$ **11.** 702 **12.** 3,227
13. 975

Study Link 7•9

1. $>$ **2.** $<$ **3.** $=$
4. $=$ **5.** $<$ **6.** $>$
7. Answers vary. **8.** Answers vary.
9. $\frac{1}{4}, \frac{4}{10}, \frac{3}{7}, \frac{24}{50}$ **10.** $\frac{1}{12}, \frac{3}{12}, \frac{7}{12}, \frac{8}{12}, \frac{11}{12}$
11. $\frac{1}{50}, \frac{1}{20}, \frac{1}{5}, \frac{1}{3}, \frac{1}{2}$ **12.** $\frac{4}{100}, \frac{4}{12}, \frac{4}{8}, \frac{4}{5}, \frac{4}{4}$
13. 5 **14.** 100 **15.** 36

Study Link 7•10

3. 28 **4.** 27 **5.** 30 **6.** 36

Study Link 7•11

3. 29 **4.** $16\frac{1}{2}$ **5.** 105 **6.** $141\frac{1}{5}$

Study Link 7•12

1. Answers vary.
2. Answers vary.
3. Answers vary.
4. **a.** $\frac{1}{4}$ **b.** $\frac{1}{4}$ **c.** $\frac{1}{2}$
5. Sample answer: I think it will be about the same fraction for 1000 times as it was for 20.
6. 336 **7.** 7,866 **8.** 3,870 **9.** 4,828

Name Date Time

Fractions

1. Divide the circle into 6 equal parts.
Color $\frac{5}{6}$ of the circle.

Whole
circle

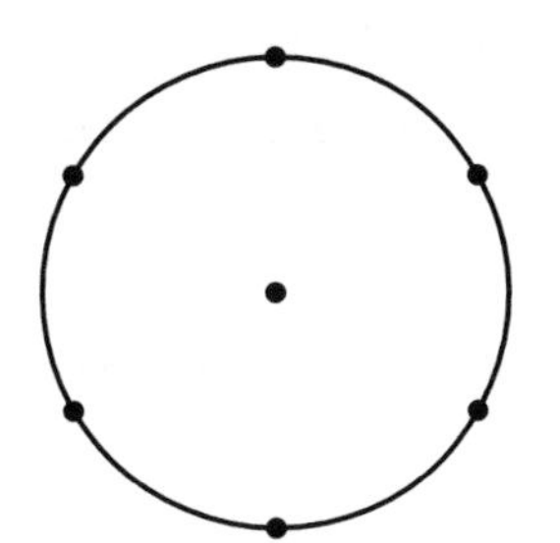

2. Divide the rectangle into 3 equal parts.
Shade $\frac{2}{3}$ of the rectangle.

Whole
rectangle

3. Divide each square into fourths.
Color $1\frac{3}{4}$ of the squares.

Whole
square

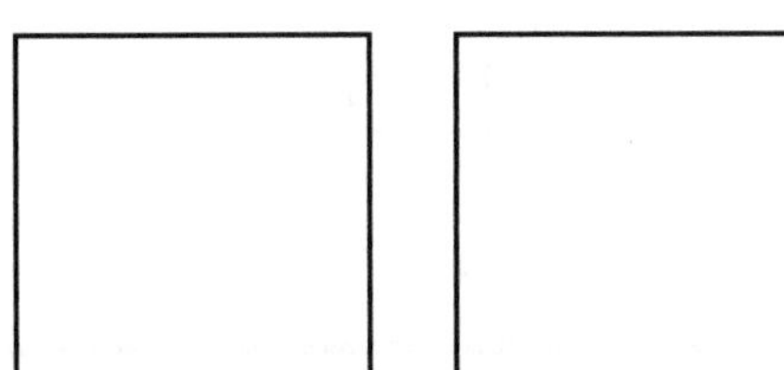

Fill in the missing fractions and mixed numbers on the number lines.

4.

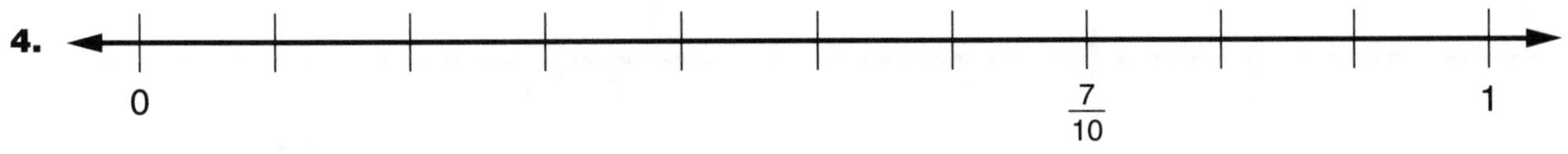

5.

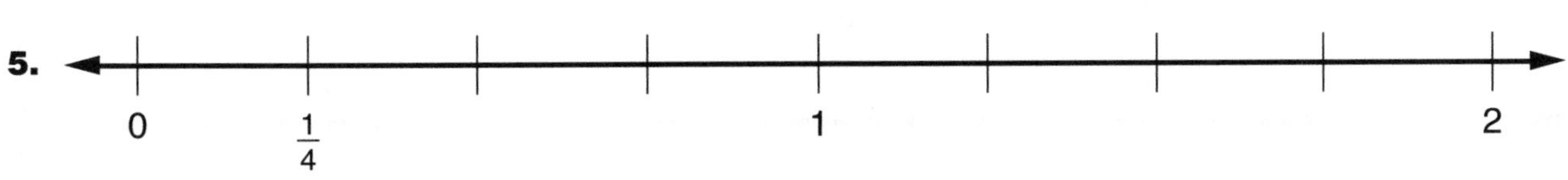

Practice

6. 854 + 267 = ________

7. ________ = 3,398 + 2,635

8. ________ = 6,374 − 755

9. 5,947 − 3,972 = ________

Name Date Time

LESSON 7•1

Fraction Strips

Cut along the dashed lines.

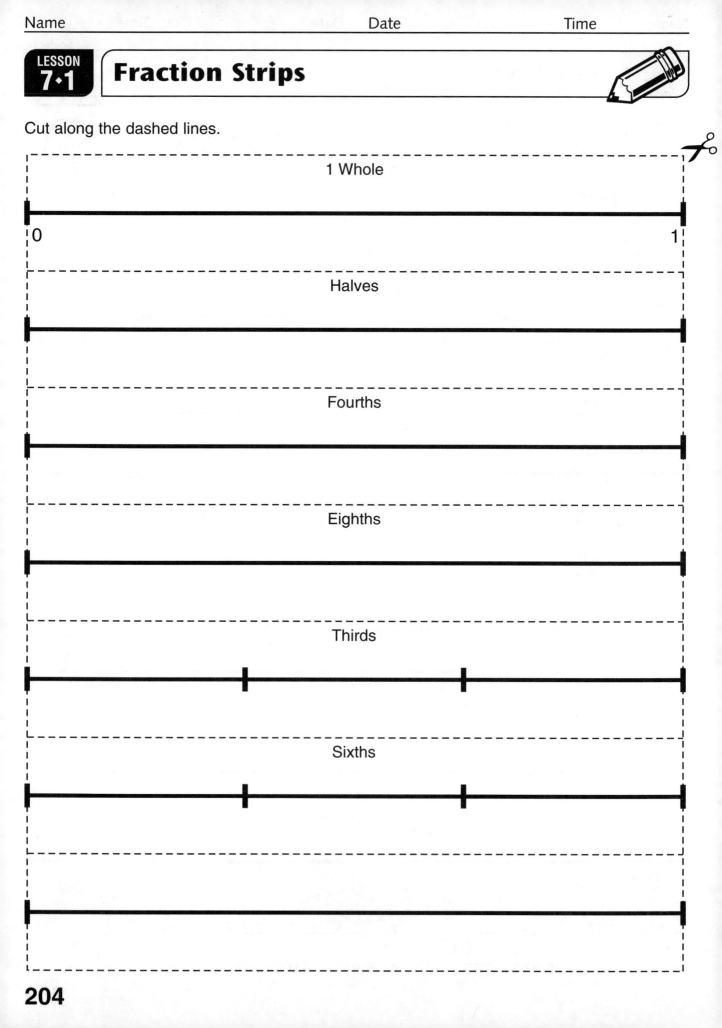

1 Whole

0 1

Halves

Fourths

Eighths

Thirds

Sixths

Name Date Time

Fraction Number-Line Poster

1 Whole
Halves
Fourths
Eighths
Thirds
Sixths

Name Date Time

Constructing an Equilateral Triangle

An **equilateral triangle** is a triangle in which all 3 sides are the same length. Here is one way to construct an equilateral triangle using a compass and straightedge.

Step 1: Draw line segment *AB*.

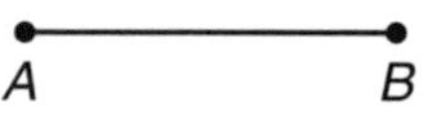

Step 2: Place the anchor of the compass on *A* and the pencil on *B*. Without changing the compass opening, make an arc above the line segment.

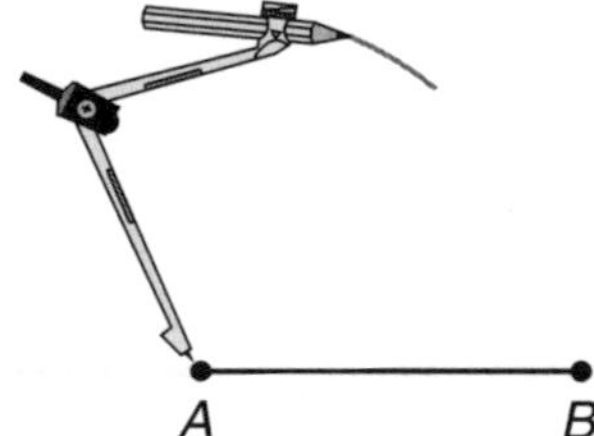

Step 3: Place the anchor on *B*. Keeping the same compass opening, make a second arc that crosses the first arc. Label the point where the two arcs cross as *C*.

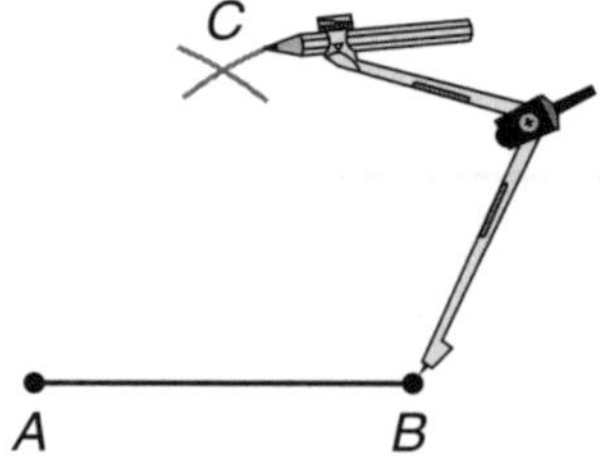

Step 4: Draw line segments *AC* and *BC*.

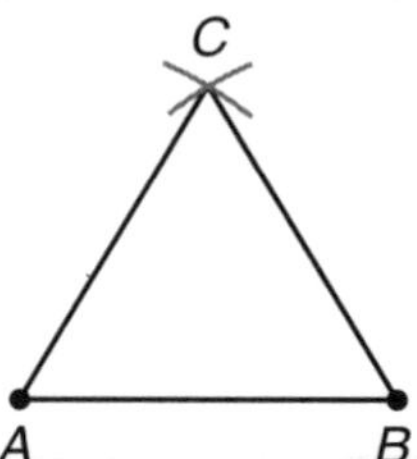

Use your compass and straightedge to construct a very large equilateral triangle on a separate sheet of paper. Cut out your triangle. Divide it into 6 equal parts. Color $\frac{1}{6}$ of it. Tape your triangle on the back of this sheet.

Name Date Time

STUDY LINK 7·2

"Fraction-of" Problems

1. Theresa had 24 cookies. She gave $\frac{1}{6}$ to her sister and $\frac{3}{6}$ to her mother.

Whole

a. Fill in the "whole" box.

b. How many cookies did she give to her sister? ________ cookies

c. How many did she give to her mother? ________ cookies

d. How many did she have left? ________ cookies

Solve.

2. $\frac{1}{3}$ of 18 = ________
3. $\frac{2}{3}$ of 18 = ________
4. $\frac{1}{5}$ of 35 = ________
5. $\frac{4}{5}$ of 35 = ________
6. $\frac{1}{4}$ of 40 = ________
7. $\frac{3}{4}$ of 40 = ________

Try This

8. $\frac{5}{8}$ of 16 = ________
9. $\frac{4}{9}$ of 27 = ________
10. $\frac{3}{5}$ of 20 = ________
11. What is $\frac{1}{4}$ of 10? ________ Explain. ____

____

____

Practice

12. 92 ÷ 4 = ________
13. 59 / 3 = ________
14. ________ = 104 / 8
15. $9\overline{)376}$ = ________

Name Date Time

LESSON 7•2

Hiking Trails

Luis is staying in a large state park that has 8 hiking trails. In the table at the right, each trail is labeled *easy, moderate,* or *rugged,* depending on how difficult that trail is for hiking.

State Park Trails

Trail	Miles	Type
Ice Age	$1\frac{1}{4}$	easy
Kettle	2	moderate
Pine	$\frac{3}{4}$	moderate
Bluff	$1\frac{3}{4}$	rugged
Cliff	$\frac{3}{4}$	rugged
Oak	$1\frac{1}{2}$	easy
Sky	$1\frac{1}{2}$	moderate
Badger	$3\frac{1}{2}$	moderate

Luis figures that it would take him about 20 minutes to walk 1 mile on an easy trail, about 30 minutes on a moderate trail, and about 40 minutes on a rugged trail.

1. About how long will it take Luis to walk the following trails?

a. Kettle Trail: About _______ minutes

b. Cliff Trail: About _______ minutes

c. Oak Trail: About _______ minutes

d. Bluff Trail: About _______ minutes

2. If Luis wants to hike for about $\frac{3}{4}$ of an hour, which trail should he choose? _______________

3. If he wants to hike for about 25 minutes, which trail should he choose? _______________

4. About how long would it take him to complete Pine Trail? About _______ minutes

5. Do you think Luis could walk Badger Trail in less than 2 hours? _______________

Explain. ____

____

____

____

____

Name Date Time

STUDY LINK 7·3

Color Tiles

SRB 45 80

There are 5 blue, 2 red, 1 yellow, and 2 green tiles in a bag.

1. Without looking, Maren picks a tile from the bag. Which of these best describes her chances of picking a blue tile?

Ⓐ likely

Ⓑ 50-50 chance

Ⓒ unlikely

Ⓓ very unlikely

2. Which of these best describes her chances of picking a yellow tile?

Ⓐ certain

Ⓑ likely

Ⓒ 50-50 chance

Ⓓ very unlikely

3. Find the probability of each event. Then make up an event and find the probability.

Event	Favorable Outcomes	Possible Outcomes	Probability
Pick a blue tile	5	10	$\frac{5}{10}$
Pick a red tile		10	$\frac{\square}{10}$
Pick a yellow tile		10	$\frac{\square}{10}$
Pick a green tile		10	$\frac{\square}{10}$
Pick a blue, red, or green tile		10	$\frac{\square}{10}$
		10	$\frac{\square}{10}$

4. Suppose you picked a color tile from the bag 10 times. After each pick, you put the tile back in the bag. How many times would you expect to pick a blue tile? _____ times

Try the experiment. Compare your prediction with the actual results.

Practice

5. 74 ∗ 8 = ____________

6. ____________ = 4 ∗ 987

7. ____________ = 65 ∗ 26

8. 35 ∗ 462 = ____________

Name Date Time

A Deck of Regular Playing Cards

1. How many cards, not including jokers, are in a deck of regular playing cards? ______ cards

2. Use the cards to help you fill in the chart.

Type of Card	Number of Cards in Deck	Type of Card	Number of Cards in Deck
Red		Spade ♠	
Black		Face card (jack, queen, king)	
Diamond ♦		Heart face card	
Heart ♥		9	
Club ♣		4	

Name Date Time

A Deck of Regular Playing Cards

1. How many cards, not including jokers, are in a deck of regular playing cards? ______ cards

2. Use the cards to help you fill in the chart.

Type of Card	Number of Cards in Deck	Type of Card	Number of Cards in Deck
Red		Spade ♠	
Black		Face card (jack, queen, king)	
Diamond ♦		Heart face card	
Heart ♥		9	
Club ♣		4	

Name Date Time

A Playing-Card Experiment

1. Place 52 playing cards in a bag. Shake the bag.

2. Before you begin the experiment, predict the results for each event.

Event	Predicted Results for 52 Picks	Tallies	Actual Results for 52 Picks
Pick a black card	$\frac{\square}{52}$		$\frac{\square}{52}$
Pick a red card			
Pick a face card			
Pick a heart			
Pick an Ace			
Pick an Ace of spades			

3. Now do the experiment.

Step 1: Pick a card from the bag.

Step 2: Record a tally for each event that applies. For example, for the king of clubs put a tally mark next to *black card* and *face card.*

Step 3: Mark an X in the grid to record the number of picks.

Step 4: Return the card to the bag and shake it.

Repeat Steps 1–4 until all 52 boxes in the grid have been filled in.

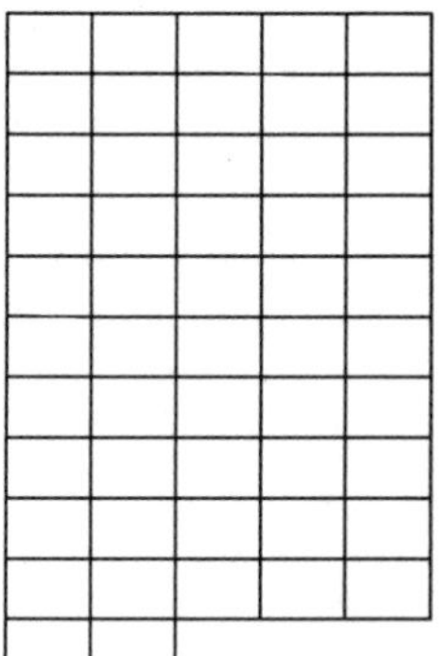

4. Describe how your actual results compare with your predicted results. Be sure to include anything that surprised you.

Name Date Time

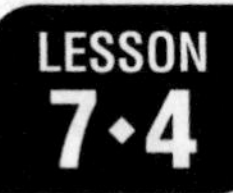

Polygons

Shape A

Shape B

Shape C

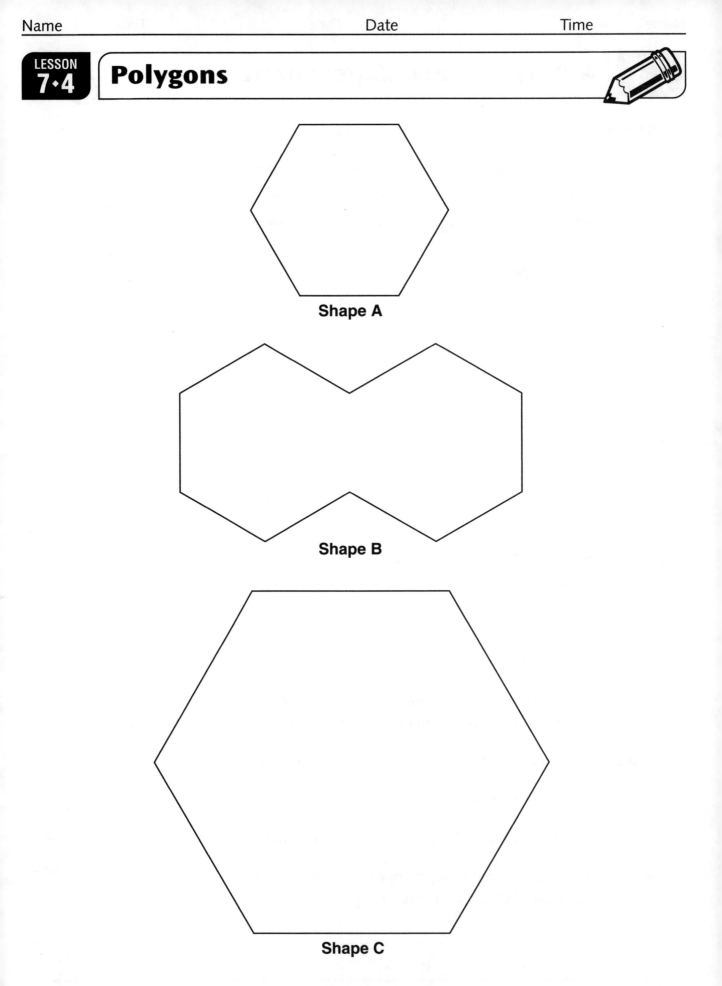

Name Date Time

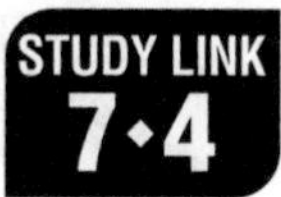

Dividing Squares

Use a straightedge and the dots below to help you divide each of the squares into equal parts.

Example: Squares A, B, C, and D are each divided in half in a different way.

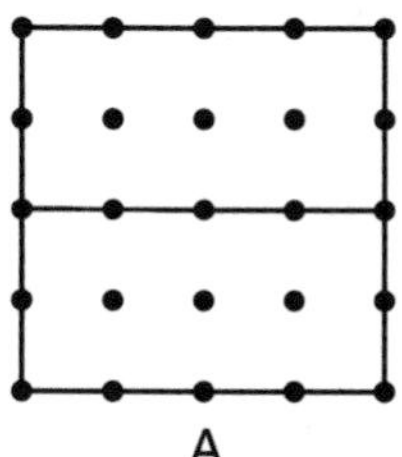
A

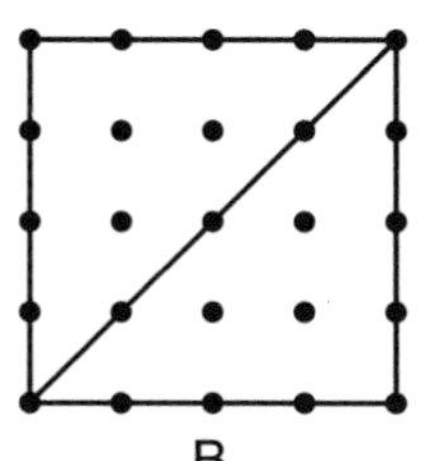
B

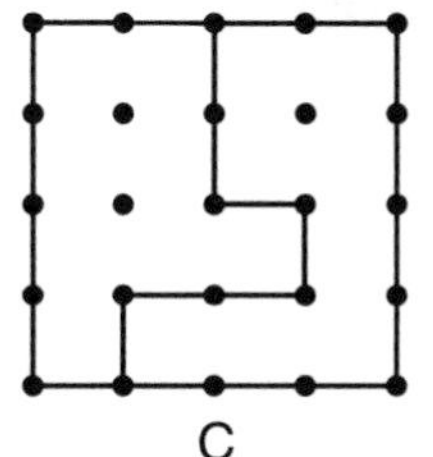
C

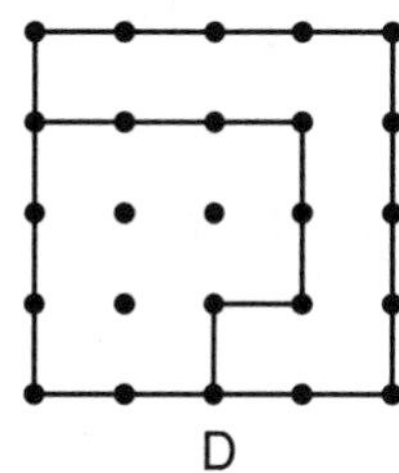
D

1. Square E is divided into fourths. Divide squares F, G, and H into fourths, each in a different way.

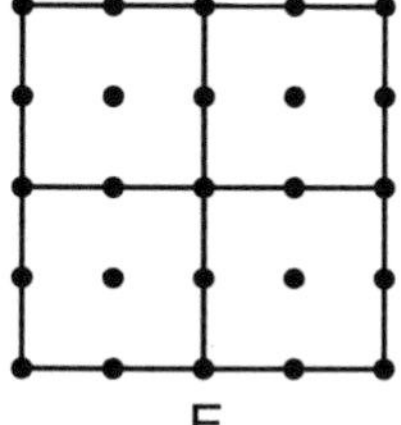
E

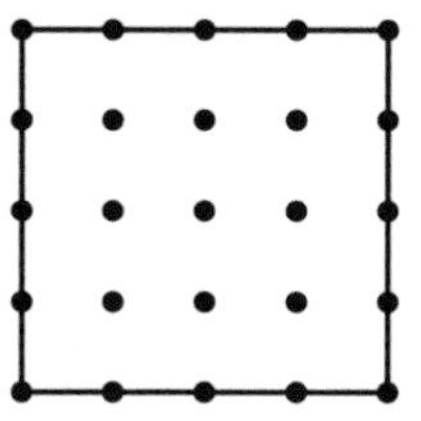
F

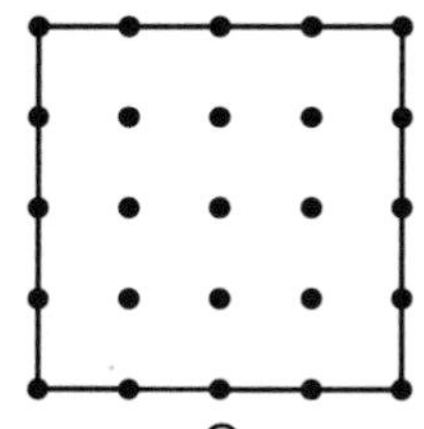
G

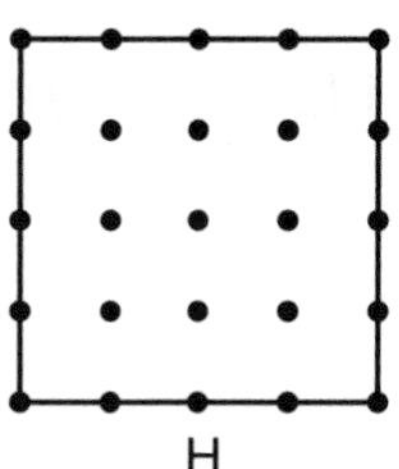
H

2. Square I is divided into eighths. Divide squares J, K, and L into eighths, each in a different way.

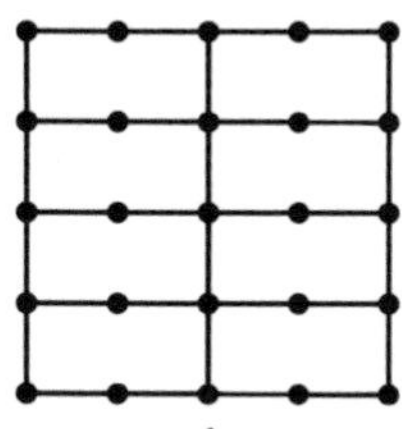
I

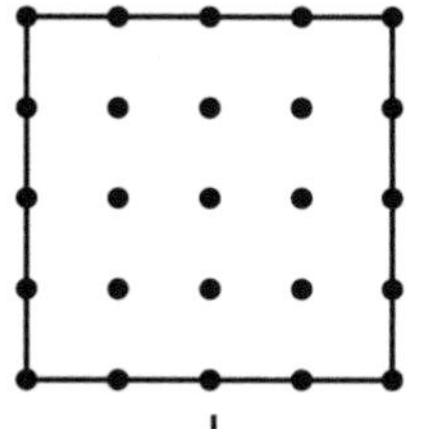
J

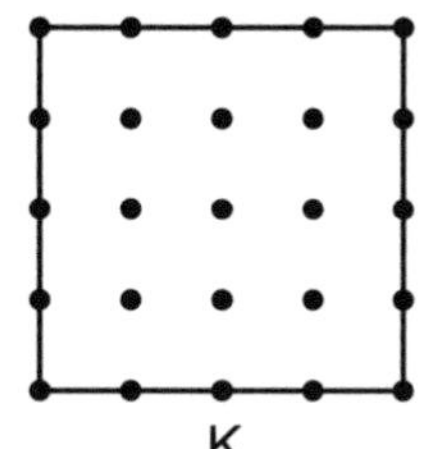
K

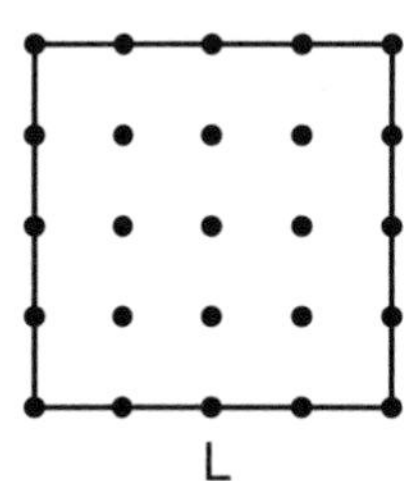
L

3. Rosa has 15 quarters and 10 nickels. She buys juice from a store for herself and her friends. The juice costs 35 cents per can. She gives the cashier $\frac{2}{3}$ of the quarters and $\frac{3}{5}$ of the nickels. The cashier does not give her any change.

How many cans of juice did she buy? ______ cans

Show your work on the back of this paper.

Practice

4. $0.636 + 0.245 =$ ____________

5. ____________ $= 9.085 + 0.76$

6. ____________ $= 1.73 - 0.14$

7. $0.325 - 0.297 =$ ____________

Fractions of Rectangles

Use red, blue, and green crayons to color the squares at the bottom of the page. Cut out the squares. If your teacher has colored tiles, use those instead.

Use your colored squares to build the following rectangles in at least two *different* ways. Record your work.

1. $\frac{1}{2}$ red and $\frac{1}{2}$ blue

2. $\frac{1}{3}$ red, $\frac{1}{3}$ blue, $\frac{1}{3}$ green

3. $\frac{1}{4}$ red, $\frac{1}{2}$ blue, $\frac{1}{4}$ green

4. Make up a problem of your own.

_____ red, _____ blue, _____ green

red	red	red	red	red	red	red	red	red	red
blue	blue	blue	blue	blue	blue	blue	blue	blue	blue
green	green	green	green	green	green	green	green	green	green

Name Date Time

Exploring Tangrams

1. Cut out the tangram pieces at the top of *Math Masters,* page 441, and use all 7 pieces to create the large square at the bottom of the page.

2. If the large square is the whole, or the ONE, find the value of each of the tangram pieces.

Small Square	Large Triangle	Medium Triangle	Small Triangle	Parallelogram

3. Describe the strategy you used to find the value of the small triangle.

____

____

____

____

____

4. Describe how you can prove that you found the correct value of the small triangle.

____

____

____

____

____

Try This

5. Use several tangram pieces to create a polygon for which the small square is worth $\frac{2}{9}$. Trace the polygon on the back of this page. Give the value of each tangram piece in the polygon.

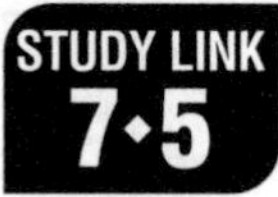

Fractions

1. Jake has $\frac{3}{4}$ of a dollar. Maxwell has $\frac{1}{10}$ of a dollar.
Do they have more or less than $1.00 in all? ____________

Number model: ____________

2. Jillian draws a line segment $2\frac{1}{4}$ inches long. Then she makes the line segment $1\frac{1}{2}$ inches longer. How long is the line segment now? ________ inches

3. A pizza was cut into 6 slices. Benjamin ate $\frac{1}{3}$ of the pizza and Dana ate $\frac{1}{2}$. What fraction of the pizza was left? ________

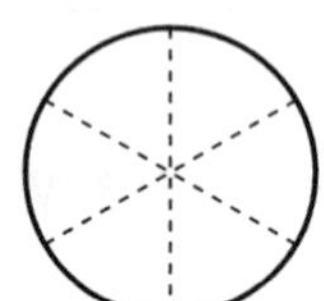

4. Rafael drew a line segment $2\frac{7}{8}$ inches long. Then he erased $\frac{1}{2}$ inch. How long is the line segment now? ________ inches

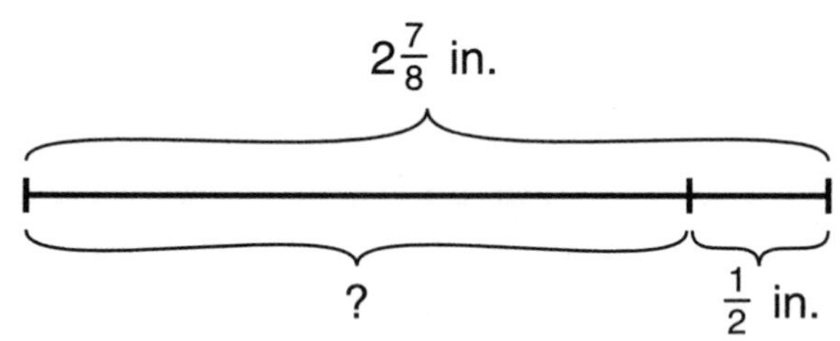

5. Two hexagons together are one whole. Draw line segments to divide each whole into trapezoids, rhombuses, and triangles. Write a number model to show how the parts add up to the whole.

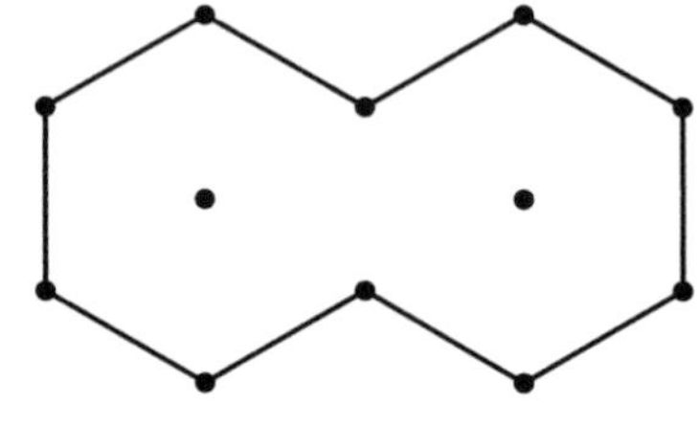
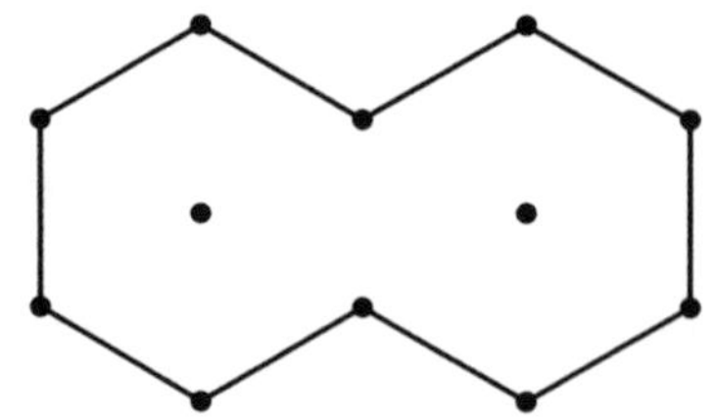
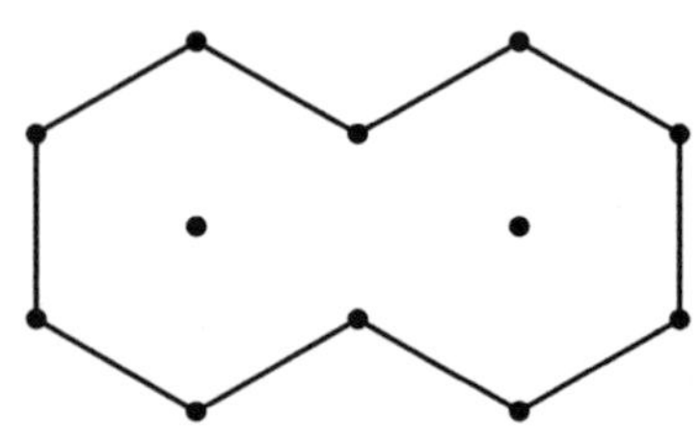

____________ ____________ ____________

Practice

6. $\frac{1}{4}$ of 32 = ______

7. ______ = $\frac{9}{10}$ of 50

8. $\frac{7}{8}$ of 56 = ______

9. ______ = $\frac{11}{12}$ of 24

Name Date Time

Divide *Gator Pie*

Use a straightedge to divide the pies below as Alvin and Alice did in *Gator Pie*. Make sure each gator gets an equal share. Write a number model to show what you did.

1. Two gators

Number model:

_____ + _____ = 1

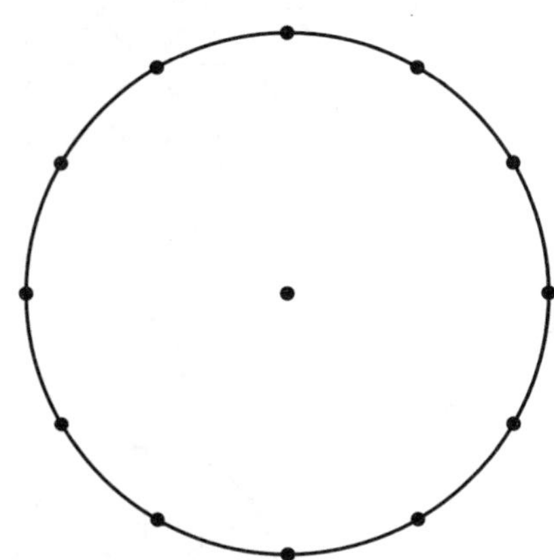

2. Three gators

Number model:

_____ + _____ + _____ = 1

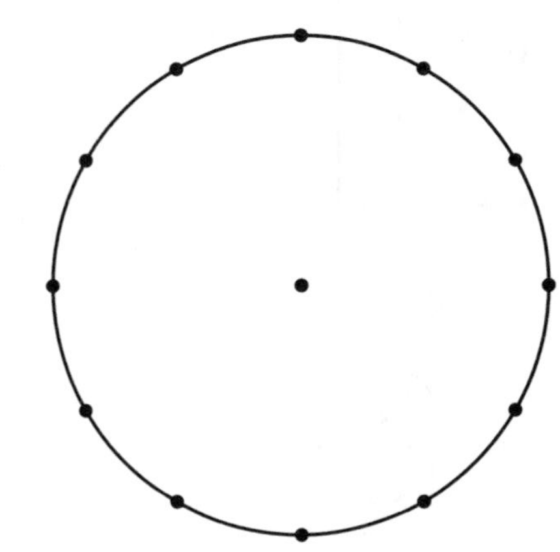

3. Four gators

Number model:

____

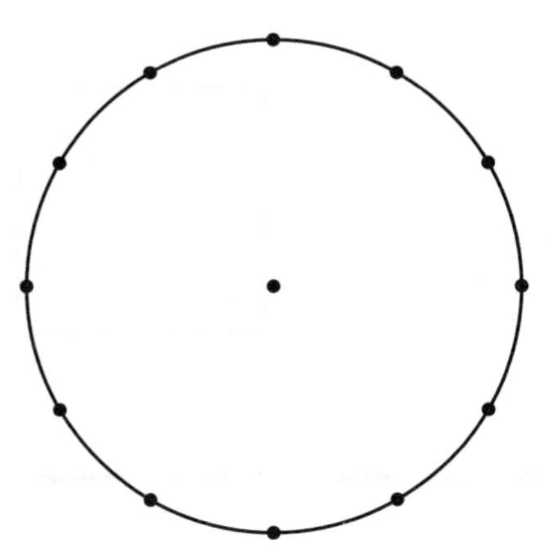

4. Eight gators

Number model:

____

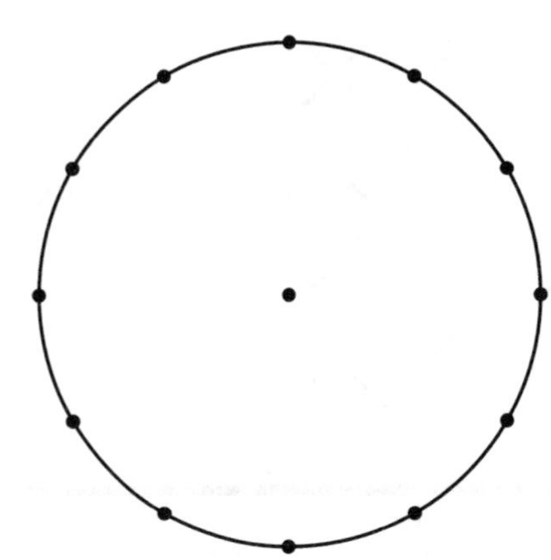

Name Date Time

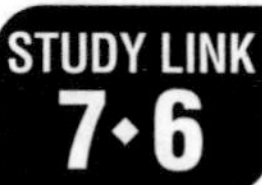

Many Names for Fractions

Write the letters of the pictures that represent each fraction.

1. $\frac{1}{2}$ C, ____________

2. $\frac{3}{4}$ ____________

3. $\frac{4}{5}$ ____________

4. $\frac{2}{3}$ ____________

A

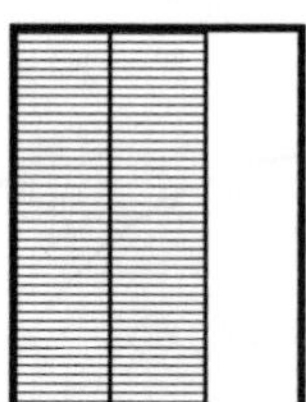

B

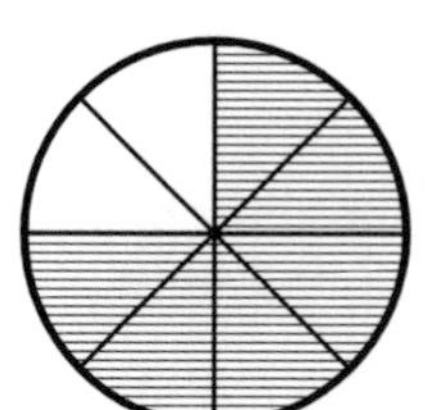

C

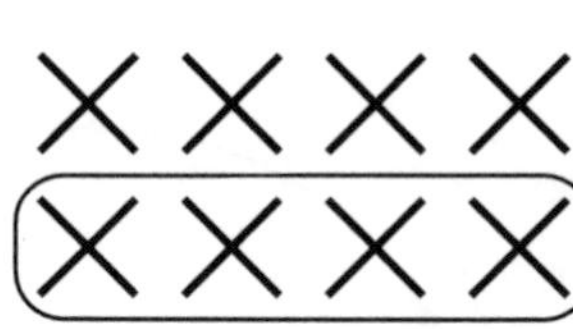

D

E

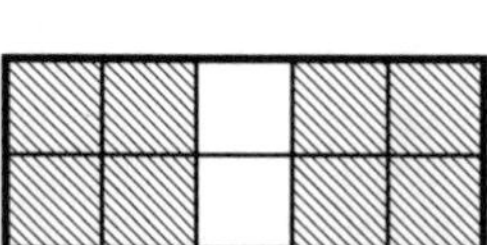

F

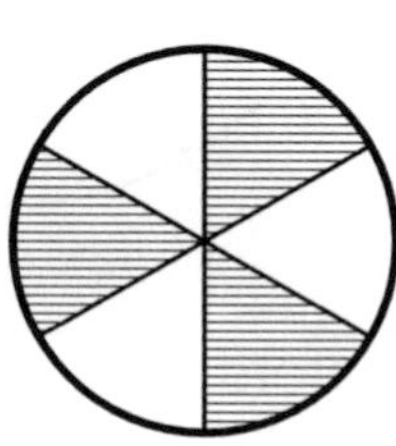

G

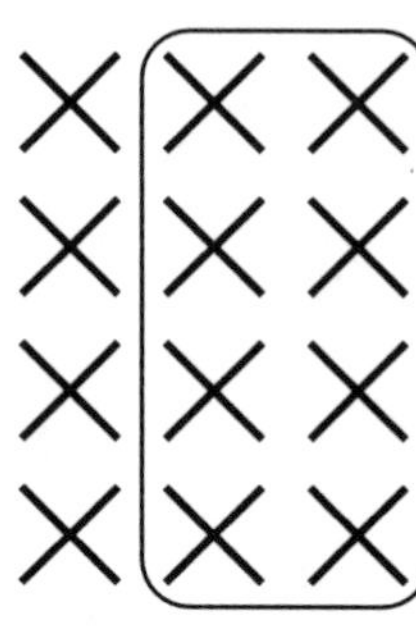

H

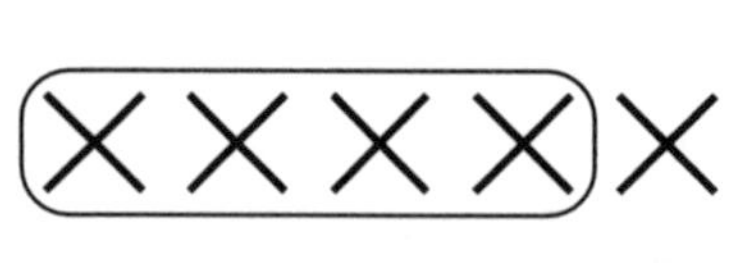

I

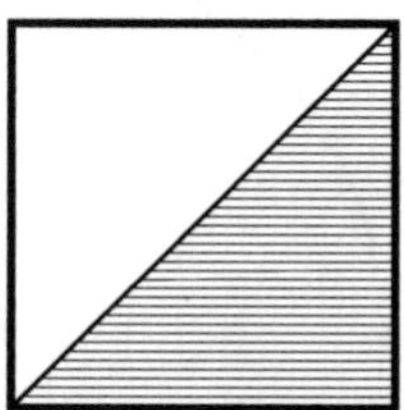

Practice

5. ____________ $= \frac{1}{6} + \frac{3}{6}$

6. $\frac{2}{4} + \frac{1}{4} =$ ____________

7. $\frac{1}{2} + \frac{2}{6} =$ ____________

8. $\frac{5}{6} - \frac{2}{6} =$ ____________

9. $\frac{3}{4} - \frac{1}{4} =$ ____________

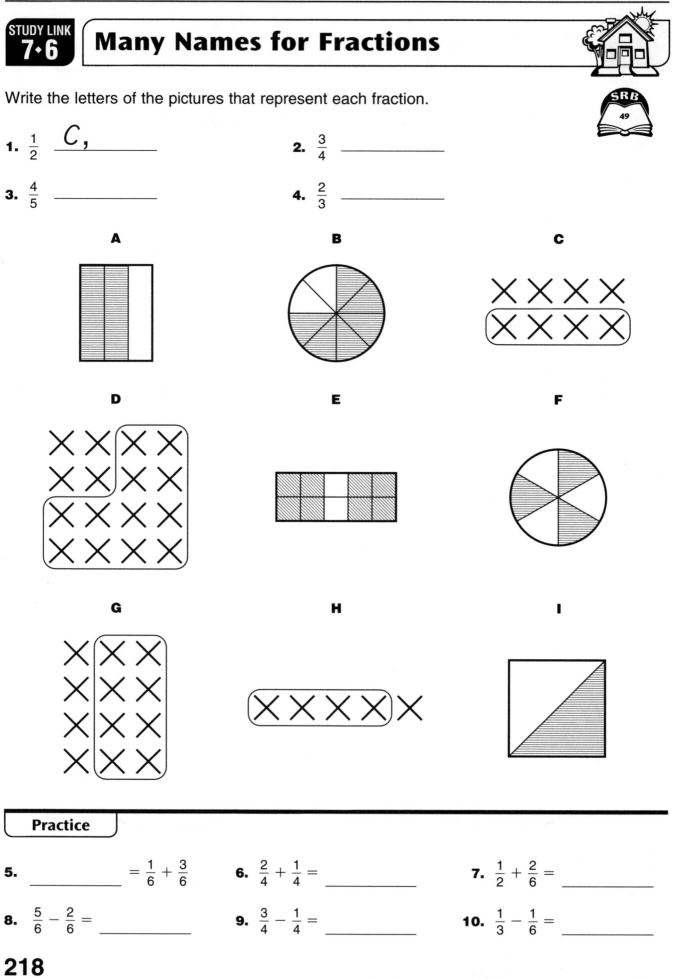

10. $\frac{1}{3} - \frac{1}{6} =$ ____________

Name Date Time

LESSON 7•6

Equivalent Fractions *continued*

3. Cover $\frac{2}{4}$ of the circle with eighths.

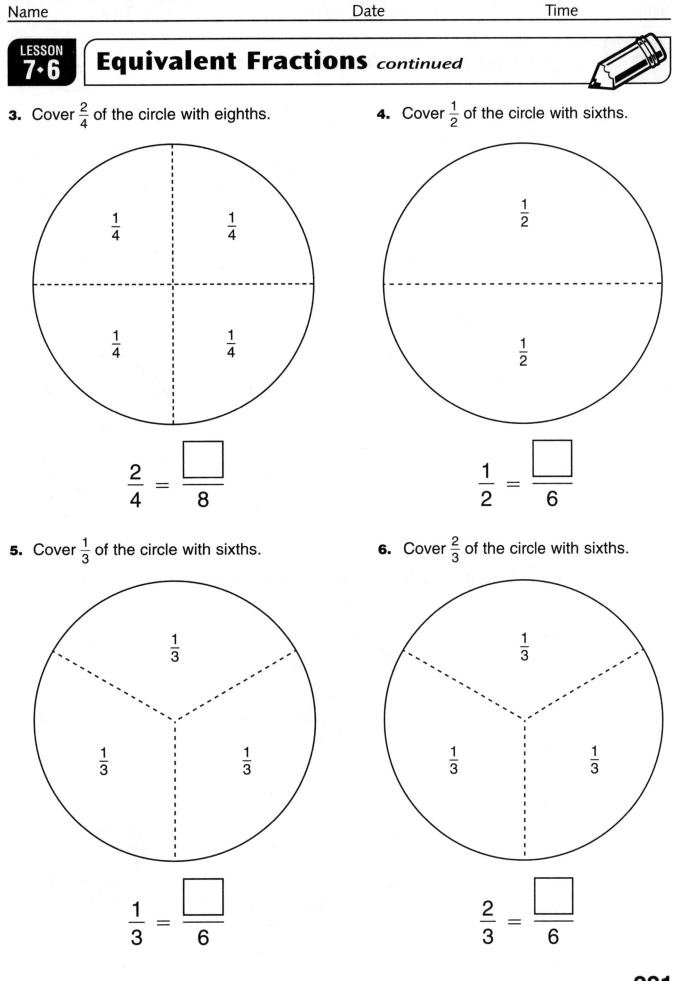

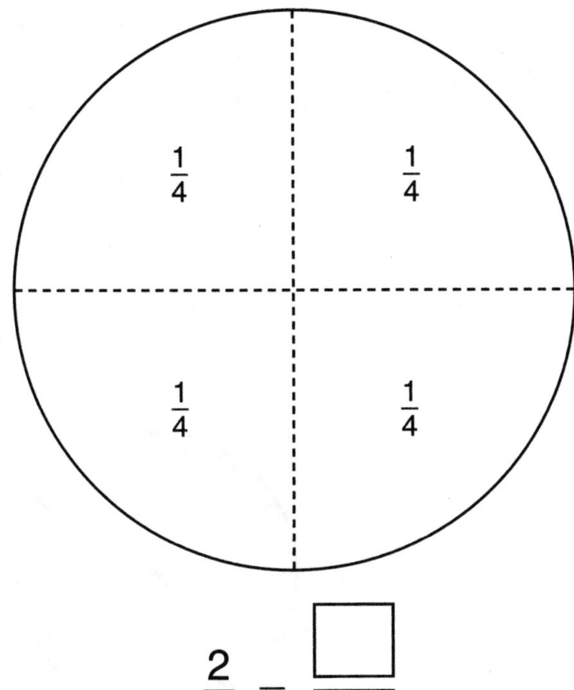

$\frac{2}{4} = \frac{\square}{8}$

4. Cover $\frac{1}{2}$ of the circle with sixths.

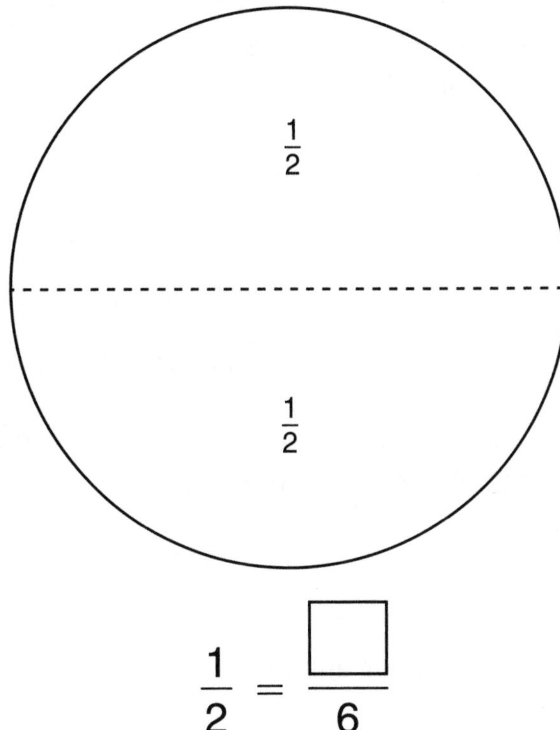

$\frac{1}{2} = \frac{\square}{6}$

5. Cover $\frac{1}{3}$ of the circle with sixths.

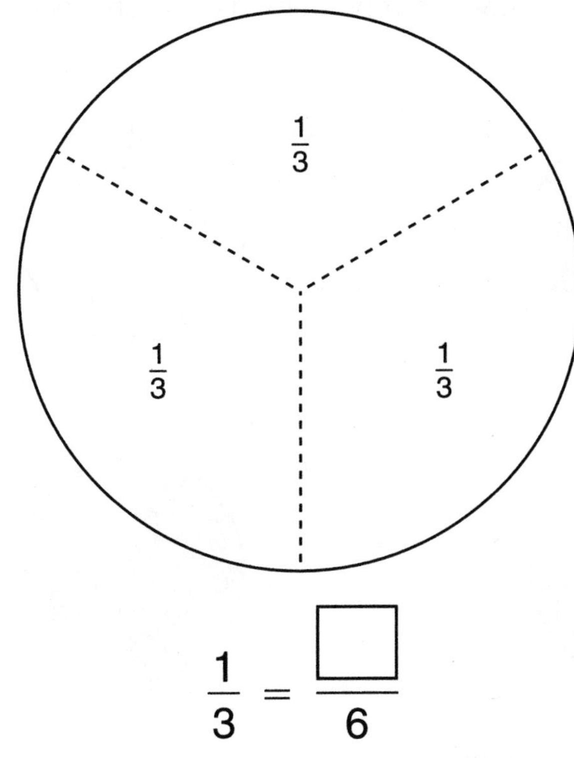

$\frac{1}{3} = \frac{\square}{6}$

6. Cover $\frac{2}{3}$ of the circle with sixths.

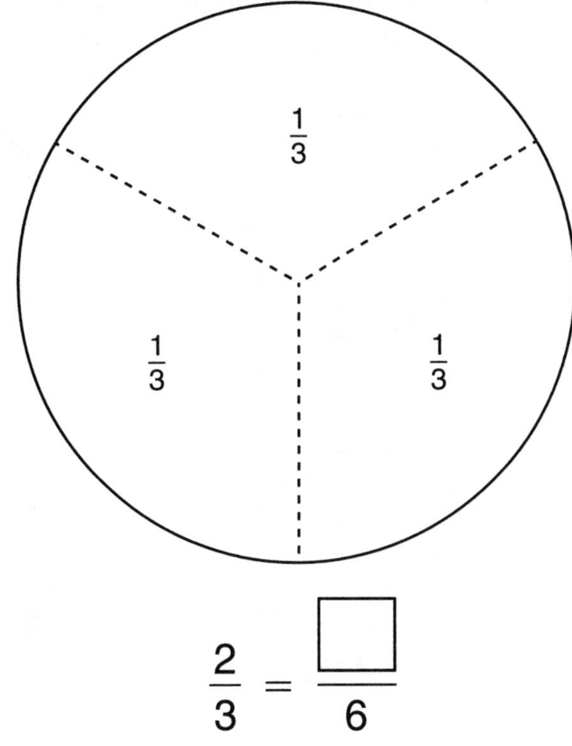

$\frac{2}{3} = \frac{\square}{6}$

Name Date Time

Equivalent Clock Fractions

1. Explain why a hexagon pattern block is useful for modeling equivalencies of fractions with denominators of 2, 3, and 6.

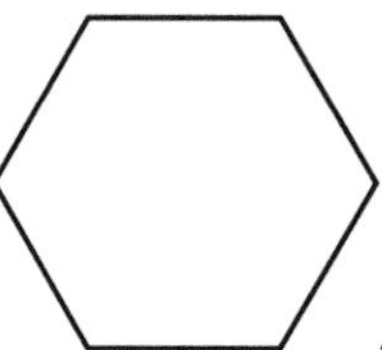
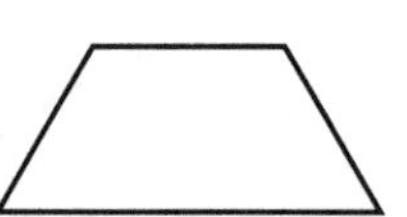
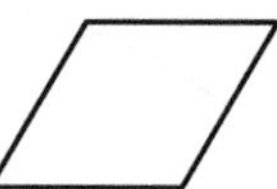
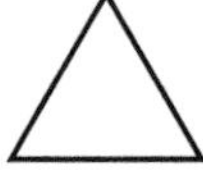

2. Study the clock face. Which denominators can be modeled on the clock face?

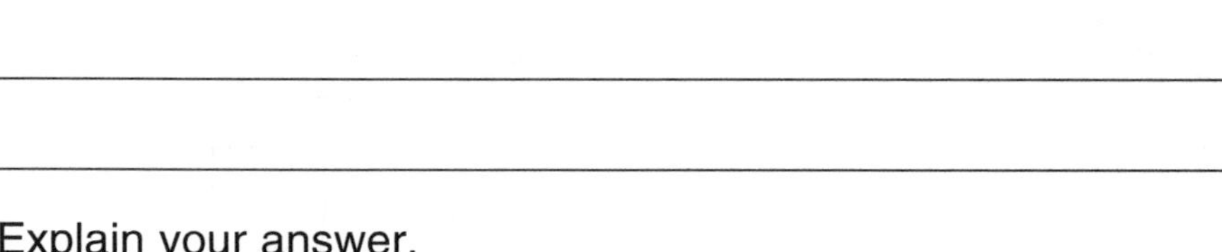

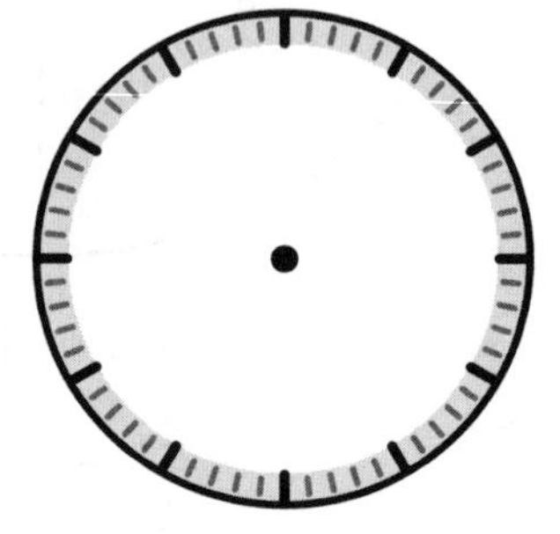

Explain your answer.

3. Using the denominators from Problem 2, name the fraction represented on each clock face in as many different ways as you can.

a.

b.

c.

d.

e.

f.

Name Date Time

Fraction Name-Collection Boxes

In each name-collection box:

Write the missing number in each fraction so that the fraction belongs in the box. Write one more fraction that can go in the box.

1.

$\frac{1}{2}$
$\frac{\square}{4}$
$\frac{5}{\square}$
$\frac{10}{\square}$
$\frac{\square}{18}$

2.

$\frac{2}{3}$
$\frac{\square}{9}$
$\frac{12}{\square}$
$\frac{20}{\square}$
$\frac{\square}{12}$

3.

$\frac{1}{4}$
$\frac{\square}{12}$
$\frac{5}{\square}$
$\frac{10}{\square}$
$\frac{\square}{100}$

4. Make up your own name-collection box problems like the ones above. Ask a friend to solve your problems. Check your friend's work.

a.

b.

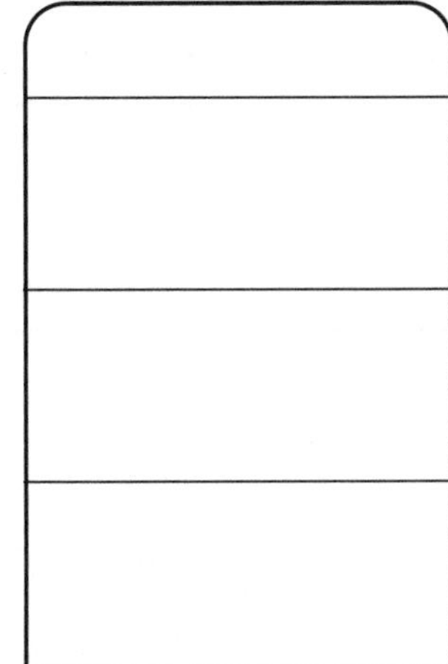

Practice

5. ______ = 95 / 4 **6.** 57 ÷ 3 = ______ **7.** ______ = 882 / 21

Name Date Time

Egyptian Fractions

Ancient Egyptians only used fractions with 1 in the numerator. These are called **unit fractions.** They wrote non-unit fractions, such as $\frac{3}{4}$ and $\frac{4}{9}$, as sums of unit fractions. They did not use the same unit fraction more than once in a sum.

Examples:

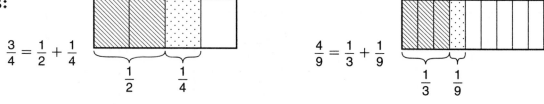

$\frac{3}{4} = \frac{1}{2} + \frac{1}{4}$ $\frac{1}{2}$ $\frac{1}{4}$

$\frac{4}{9} = \frac{1}{3} + \frac{1}{9}$

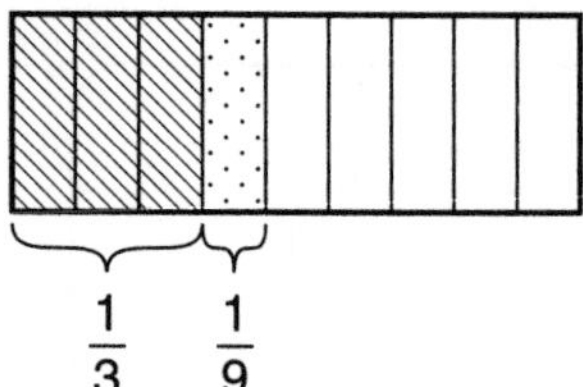

Use drawings and what you know about equivalent fractions to help you find the Egyptian form of each fraction.

1. $\frac{3}{8}$ = ____________

2. $\frac{5}{12}$ = ____________

3. $\frac{7}{10}$ = ____________

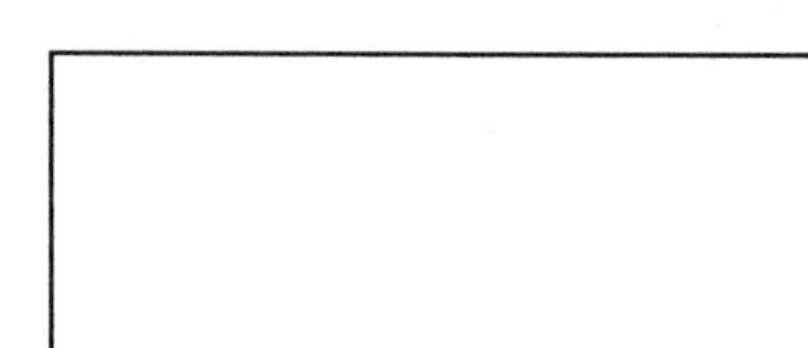

4. $\frac{5}{6}$ = ____________

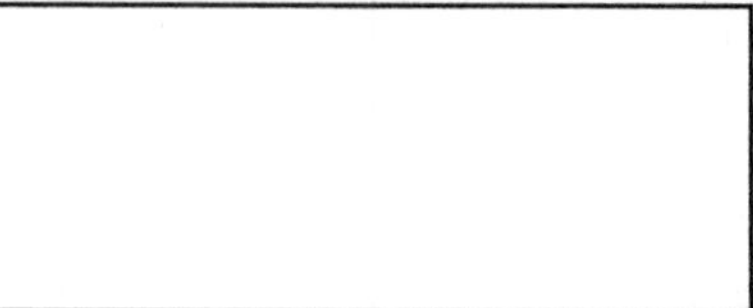

5. $\frac{3}{5}$ = ____________

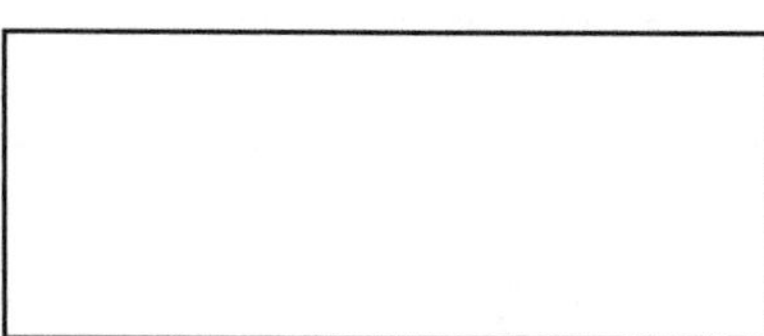

6. $\frac{4}{7}$ = ____________

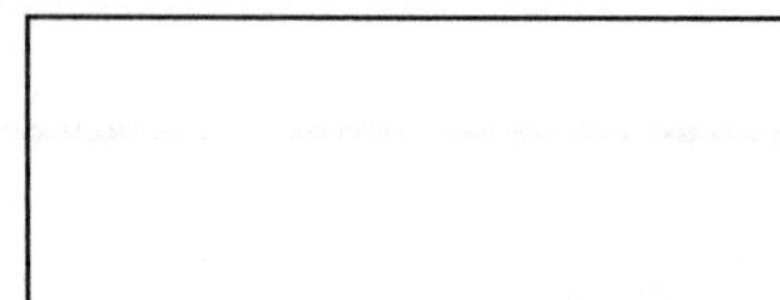

Name Date Time

An Equivalent Fractions Rule

Margot says the value of a fraction does not change if you do the same thing to the numerator and denominator. Margot says that she added 2 to the numerator and the denominator in $\frac{1}{4}$ and got $\frac{3}{6}$.

$$\frac{1 + 2}{4 + 2} = \frac{3}{6}$$

Therefore, she says that $\frac{1}{4} = \frac{3}{6}$. How could you explain or show Margot that she is wrong?

Name Date Time

An Equivalent Fractions Rule

Margot says the value of a fraction does not change if you do the same thing to the numerator and denominator. Margot says that she added 2 to the numerator and the denominator in $\frac{1}{4}$ and got $\frac{3}{6}$.

$$\frac{1 + 2}{4 + 2} = \frac{3}{6}$$

Therefore, she says that $\frac{1}{4} = \frac{3}{6}$. How could you explain or show Margot that she is wrong?

Name Date Time

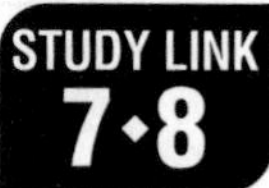

Fractions and Decimals

Write 3 equivalent fractions for each decimal.

SRB 61

Example:

0.8 $\frac{8}{10}$ $\frac{4}{5}$ $\frac{80}{100}$

1. 0.20 ________ ________ ________

2. 0.6 ________ ________ ________

3. 0.50 ________ ________ ________

4. 0.75 ________ ________ ________

Write an equivalent decimal for each fraction.

5. $\frac{3}{10}$ ________ **6.** $\frac{63}{100}$ ________ **7.** $\frac{7}{10}$ ________ **8.** $\frac{2}{5}$ ________

9. Shade more than $\frac{53}{100}$ of the square and less than $\frac{8}{10}$ of the square. Write the value of the shaded part as a decimal and a fraction.

Decimal: ________

Fraction: ________

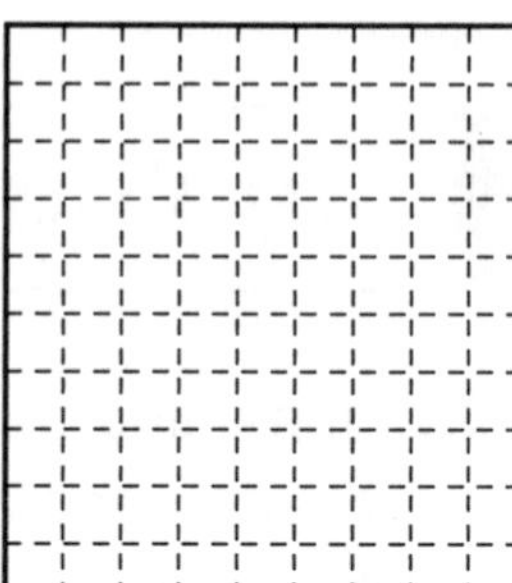

10. Shade more than $\frac{11}{100}$ of the square and less than $\frac{1}{4}$ of the square. Write the value of the shaded part as a decimal and a fraction.

Decimal: ________

Fraction: ________

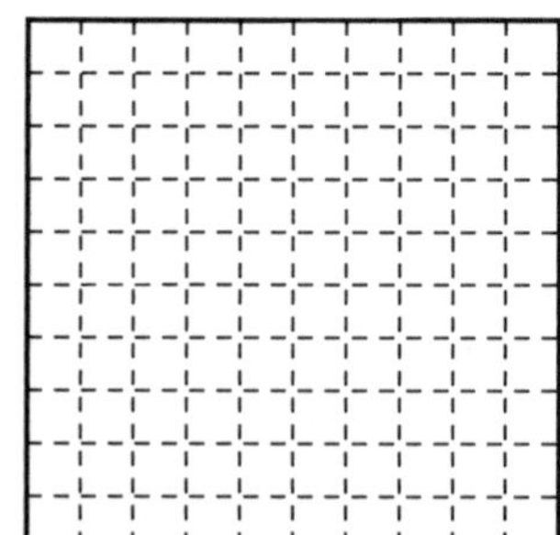

Practice

11. ________ = 78 ∗ 9 **12.** 461 ∗ 7 = ________ **13.** ________ = 39 ∗ 25

Name Date Time

Fraction, Decimal, and Percent Grids

Fill in the missing numbers. Shade the grids.

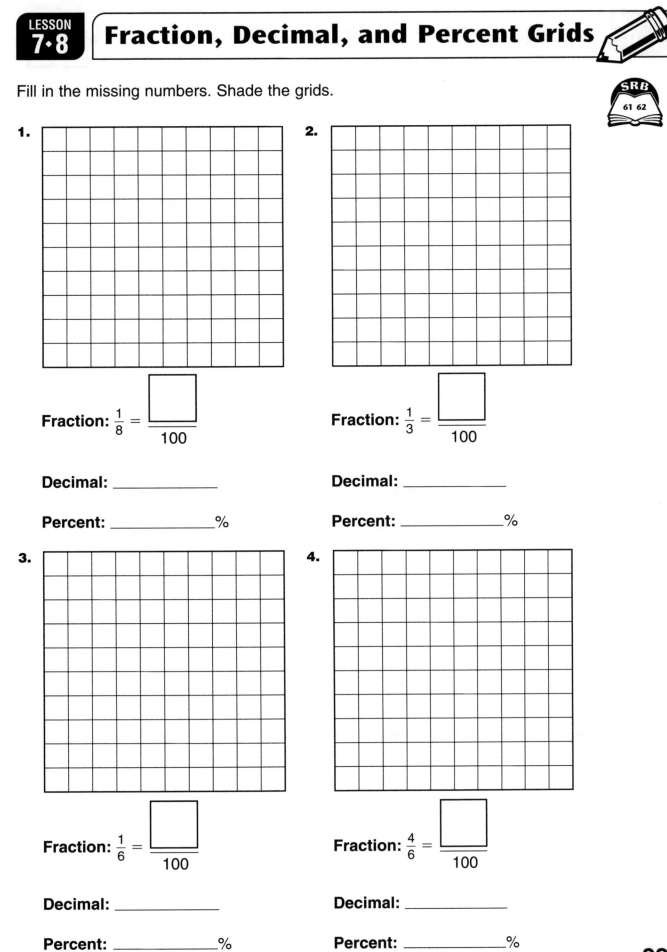

1.

Fraction: $\frac{1}{8} = \frac{\square}{100}$

Decimal: ____________

Percent: ____________%

2.

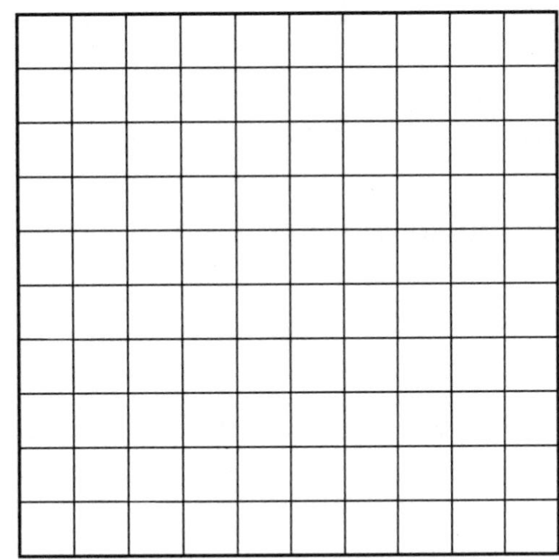

Fraction: $\frac{1}{3} = \frac{\square}{100}$

Decimal: ____________

Percent: ____________%

3.

Fraction: $\frac{1}{6} = \frac{\square}{100}$

Decimal: ____________

Percent: ____________%

4.

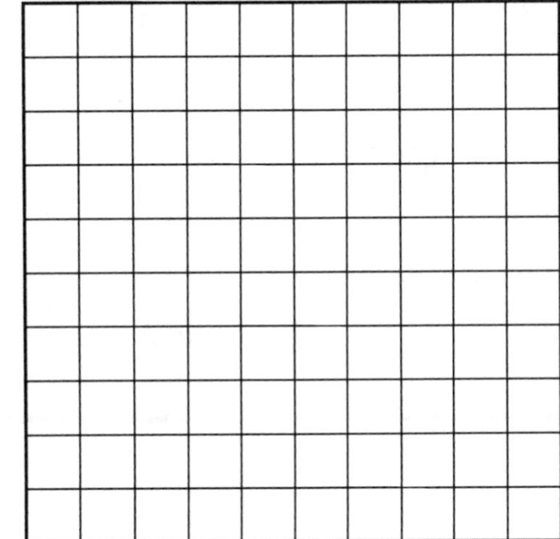

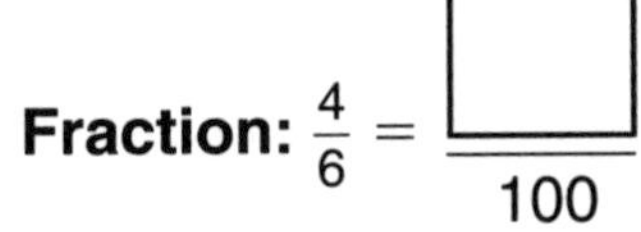

Fraction: $\frac{4}{6} = \frac{\square}{100}$

Decimal: ____________

Percent: ____________%

Name Date Time

Compare and Order Fractions

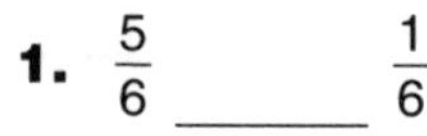

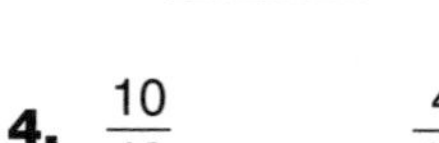

Write $<$, $>$, or $=$ to make each number sentence true.

1. $\frac{5}{6}$ ______ $\frac{1}{6}$
2. $\frac{3}{10}$ ______ $\frac{3}{4}$
3. $\frac{2}{3}$ ______ $\frac{10}{15}$
4. $\frac{10}{40}$ ______ $\frac{4}{16}$
5. $\frac{4}{9}$ ______ $\frac{7}{9}$
6. $\frac{5}{6}$ ______ $\frac{5}{8}$
7. Explain how you solved Problem 1. ______________________________

____

8. Explain how you solved Problem 2. ______________________________

____

9. Circle each fraction that is less than $\frac{1}{2}$.

$\frac{7}{8}$ $\frac{1}{4}$ $\frac{4}{10}$ $\frac{7}{12}$ $\frac{5}{9}$ $\frac{3}{7}$ $\frac{24}{50}$ $\frac{67}{100}$

Write the fractions in order from smallest to largest.

10. $\frac{3}{12}$, $\frac{7}{12}$, $\frac{1}{12}$, $\frac{11}{12}$, $\frac{8}{12}$ ______ ______ ______ ______ ______
    smallest largest

11. $\frac{1}{5}$, $\frac{1}{3}$, $\frac{1}{20}$, $\frac{1}{2}$, $\frac{1}{50}$ ______ ______ ______ ______ ______
    smallest largest

12. $\frac{4}{5}$, $\frac{4}{100}$, $\frac{4}{4}$, $\frac{4}{8}$, $\frac{4}{12}$ ______ ______ ______ ______ ______
    smallest largest

Practice

13. $\frac{1}{6}$ of 30 = ______
14. $\frac{3}{4}$ of ______ = 75
15. $\frac{4}{5}$ of 45 = ______

Name Date Time

Sort Fractions

Cut out the cards. Sort the cards into groups according to the fractions shown on them, and tape them onto a separate sheet of paper. Next to each group, write why you chose to put the cards into the group.

?
0 1

?
0 1

?
0 1

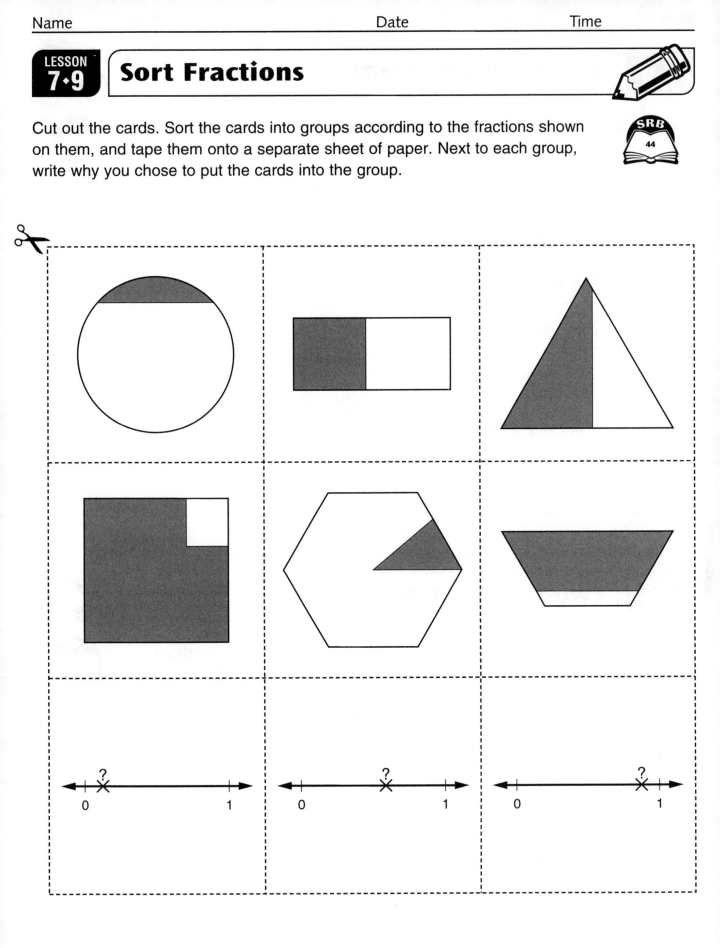

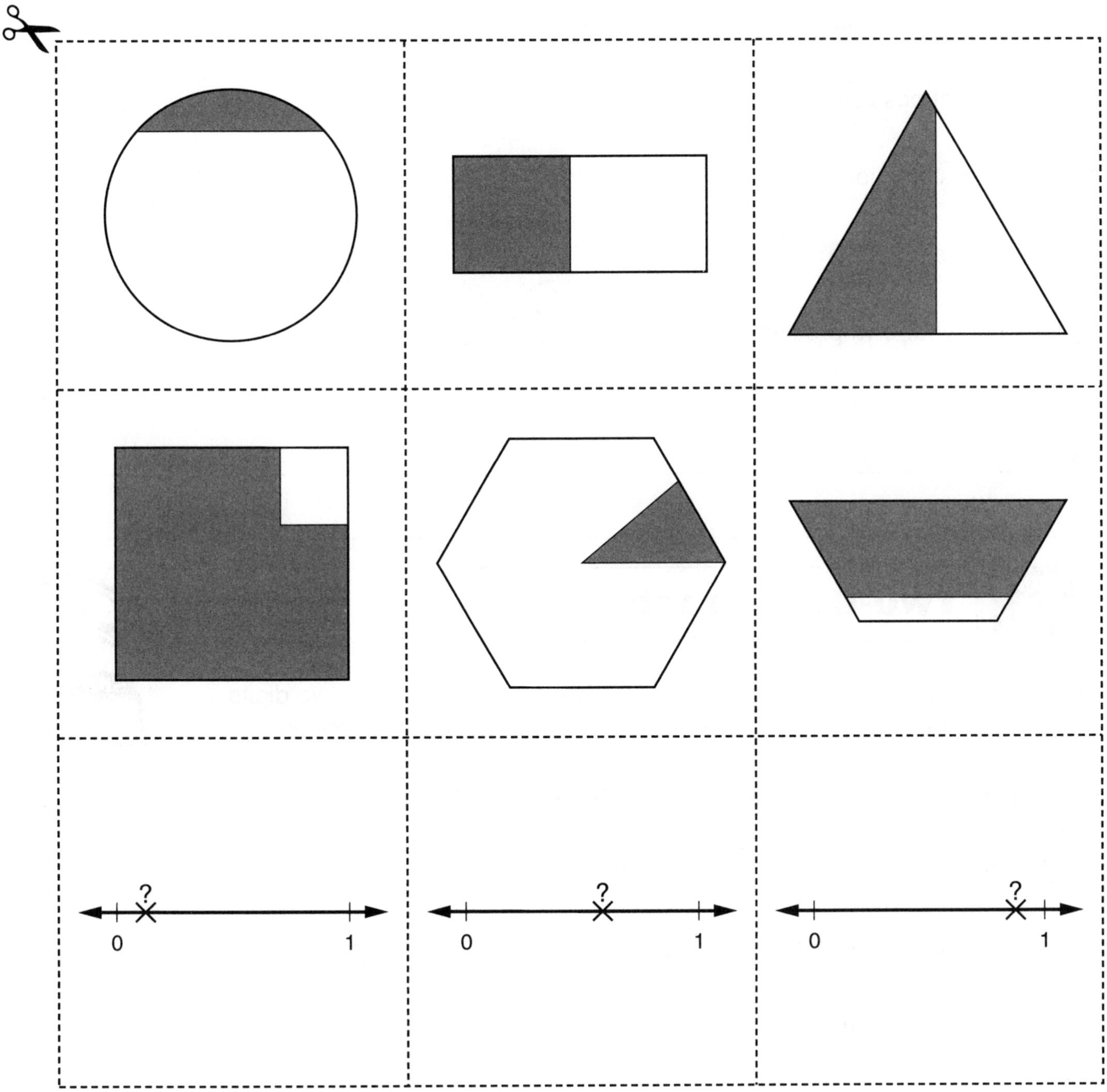

Name Date Time

Two-Digit Fractions

Any fraction can be made from the digits 0–9. A fraction can have two digits like $\frac{3}{4}$ or $\frac{8}{7}$ or many digits like $\frac{347}{983}$. A fraction may not have a denominator of 0.

Use any two digits to make each of the following fractions.

1. The smallest possible fraction greater than 0 ________
2. The largest possible fraction ________
3. The largest fraction less than 1 ________
4. The smallest fraction greater than $\frac{1}{2}$ ________
5. Make up your own problem. ______________________________

Name Date Time

Two-Digit Fractions

Any fraction can be made from the digits 0–9. A fraction can have two digits like $\frac{3}{4}$ or $\frac{8}{7}$ or many digits like $\frac{347}{983}$. A fraction may not have a denominator of 0.

Use any two digits to make each of the following fractions.

1. The smallest possible fraction greater than 0 ________
2. The largest possible fraction ________
3. The largest fraction less than 1 ________
4. The smallest fraction greater than $\frac{1}{2}$ ________
5. Make up your own problem. ______________________________

Name Date Time

What Is the ONE?

For Problems 1 and 2, use your Geometry Template or sketch the shapes.

1. Suppose □ is $\frac{1}{4}$. Draw each of the following:

Example: $\frac{3}{4}$ **a.** 1 **b.** $1\frac{1}{2}$ **c.** 2

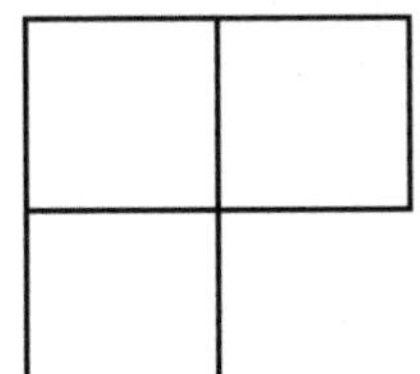

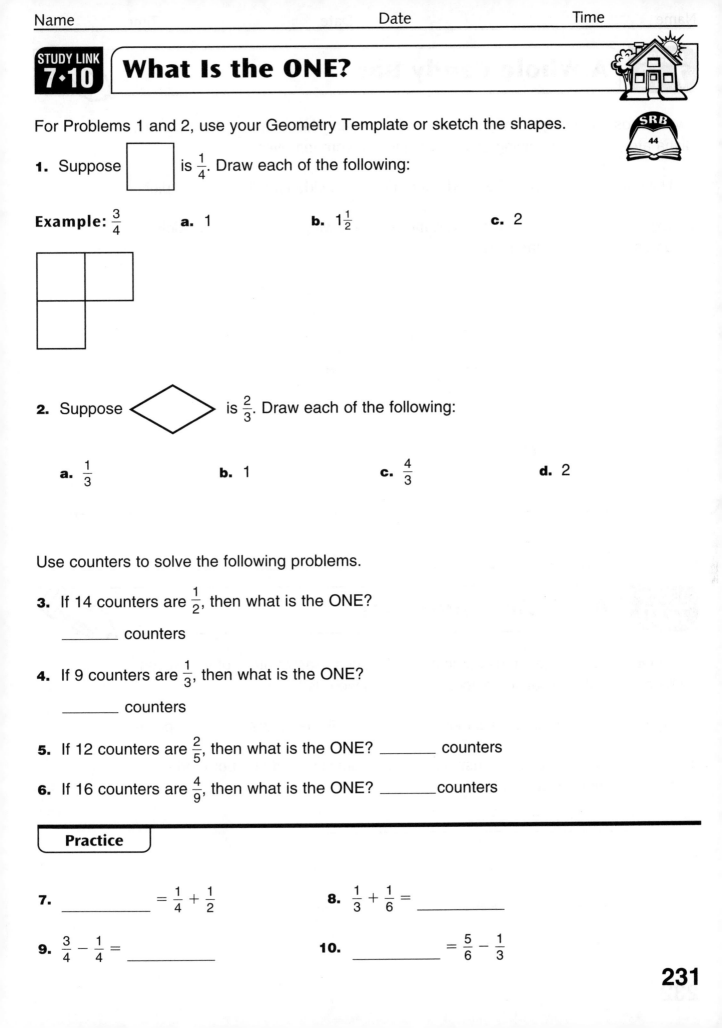

2. Suppose ◇ is $\frac{2}{3}$. Draw each of the following:

a. $\frac{1}{3}$ **b.** 1 **c.** $\frac{4}{3}$ **d.** 2

Use counters to solve the following problems.

3. If 14 counters are $\frac{1}{2}$, then what is the ONE?

_______ counters

4. If 9 counters are $\frac{1}{3}$, then what is the ONE?

_______ counters

5. If 12 counters are $\frac{2}{5}$, then what is the ONE? _______ counters

6. If 16 counters are $\frac{4}{9}$, then what is the ONE? _______ counters

Practice

7. __________ $= \frac{1}{4} + \frac{1}{2}$

8. $\frac{1}{3} + \frac{1}{6} =$ __________

9. $\frac{3}{4} - \frac{1}{4} =$ __________

10. __________ $= \frac{5}{6} - \frac{1}{3}$

Name Date Time

A Whole Candy Bar

Two friends cut a large candy bar into equal pieces. Harriet ate $\frac{1}{4}$ of the pieces. Nisha ate $\frac{1}{2}$ of the remaining pieces. Six pieces were left over.

1. How many pieces was the candy bar originally divided into? _______ pieces

2. Explain how you got your answer. Include a drawing and number models as part of your explanation.

____

____

____

____

Name Date Time

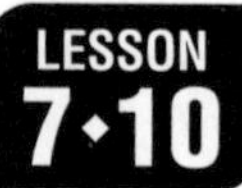

A Whole Candy Bar

Two friends cut a large candy bar into equal pieces. Harriet ate $\frac{1}{4}$ of the pieces. Nisha ate $\frac{1}{2}$ of the remaining pieces. Six pieces were left over.

1. How many pieces was the candy bar originally divided into? _______ pieces

2. Explain how you got your answer. Include a drawing and number models as part of your explanation.

____

____

____

____

Name Date Time

Spinner Experiments

1. Use a paper clip and pencil to make a spinner.

SRB 80 84

a. Spin the paper clip 4 times. Record the number of times it lands on the shaded part and on the white part.

shaded	white

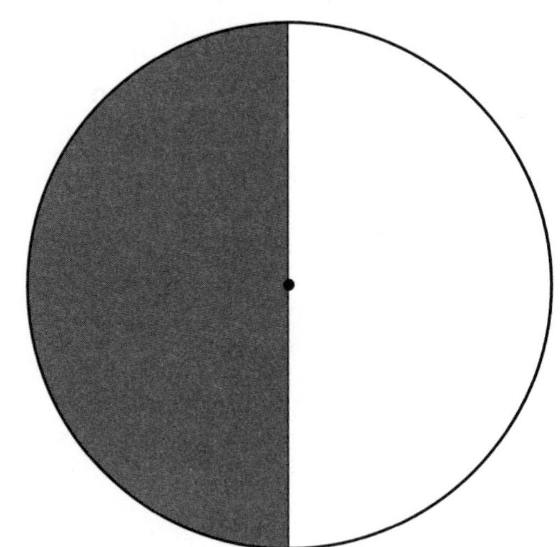

b. Record the number of times the paper clip lands on the shaded part and on the white part **for the whole class.**

shaded	white

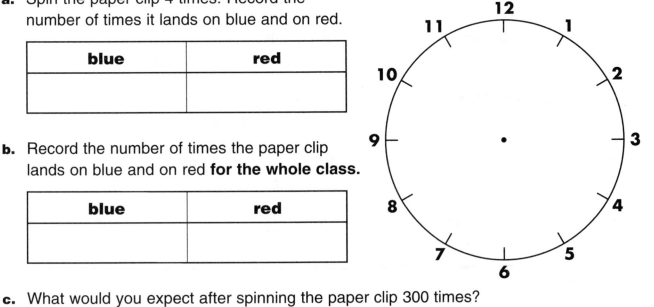

2. Make another spinner. Color the circle blue and red so that the paper clip is **twice as likely** to land on blue as on red.

a. Spin the paper clip 4 times. Record the number of times it lands on blue and on red.

blue	red

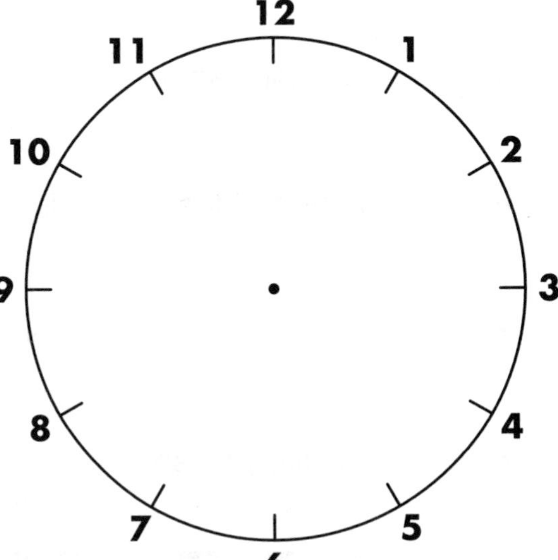

b. Record the number of times the paper clip lands on blue and on red **for the whole class.**

blue	red

c. What would you expect after spinning the paper clip 300 times?

blue	red

Name Date Time

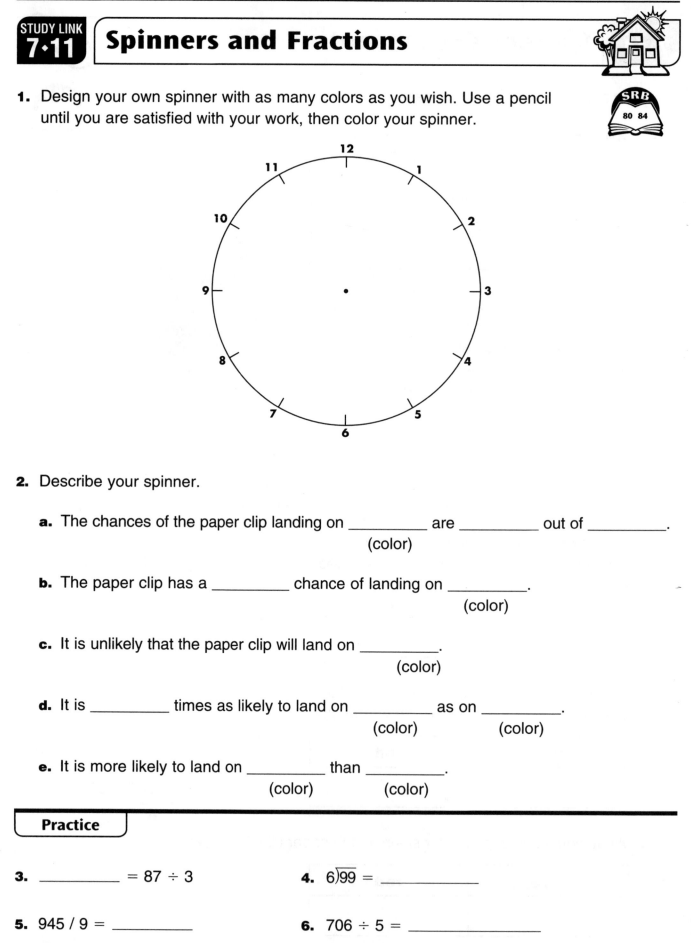

STUDY LINK 7•11

Spinners and Fractions

1. Design your own spinner with as many colors as you wish. Use a pencil until you are satisfied with your work, then color your spinner.

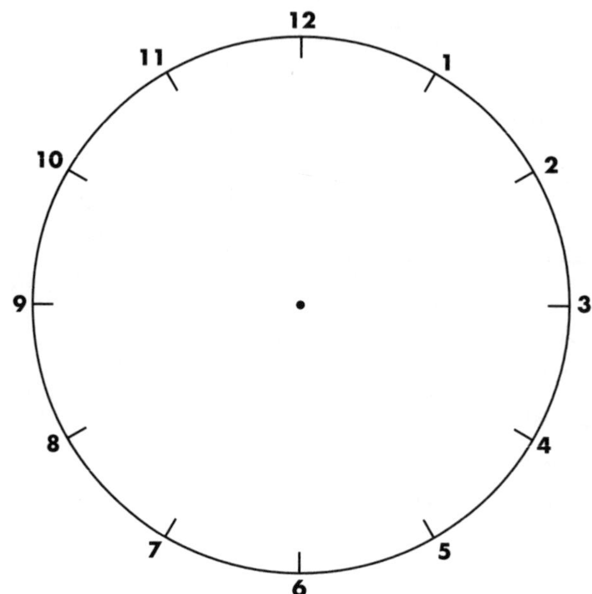

2. Describe your spinner.

   a. The chances of the paper clip landing on ________ (color) are ________ out of ________.

   b. The paper clip has a ________ chance of landing on ________ (color).

   c. It is unlikely that the paper clip will land on ________ (color).

   d. It is ________ times as likely to land on ________ (color) as on ________ (color).

   e. It is more likely to land on ________ (color) than ________ (color).

Practice

3. ________ = 87 ÷ 3

4. $6\overline{)99}$ = ________

5. 945 / 9 = ________

6. 706 ÷ 5 = ________

Name Date Time

Layout of a Kitchen

Pages 235 and 236 will be needed to do Lesson 8-1 in the next unit. Please complete the pages and return them to class.

Every kitchen needs a stove, a sink, and a refrigerator. Notice how the stove, sink, and refrigerator are arranged in the kitchen below. The triangle shows the work path in the kitchen. Walking from the stove to the sink and to the refrigerator forms an invisible "triangle" on the floor.

Front View of Kitchen

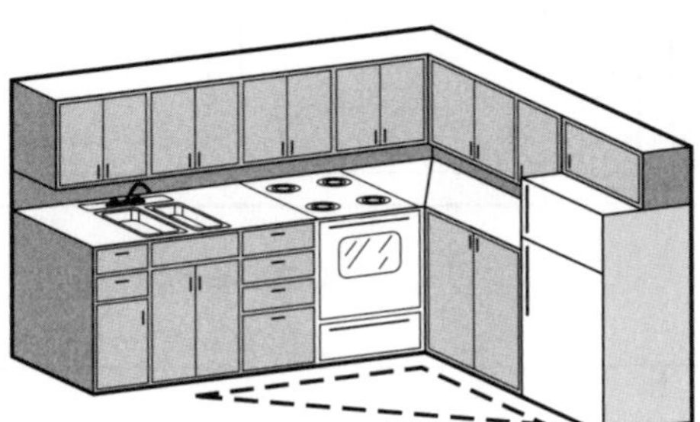

Bird's-Eye View of Kitchen
(looking down at appliances and countertops)

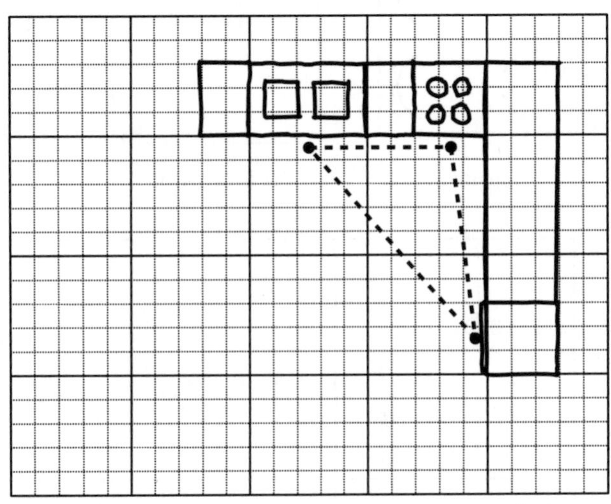

The side of a grid square represents 1 foot.

1. Put one coin or other marker on the floor in front of your sink, one in front of your stove, and one in front of your refrigerator.

2. Measure the distance between each pair of markers. Use feet and inches, and record your measurements below.

Distance between

a. stove and refrigerator About ________ feet ________ inches

b. refrigerator and sink About ________ feet ________ inches

c. sink and stove About ________ feet ________ inches

Name Date Time

Layout of a Kitchen *continued*

3. On the grid below, make a sketch that shows how the stove, sink, and refrigerator are arranged in your kitchen.

Your sketch should show a bird's-eye view of these 3 appliances (including all countertops).

If your oven is separate from your stove, sketch the stove top only.

Use the following symbols in your sketch:

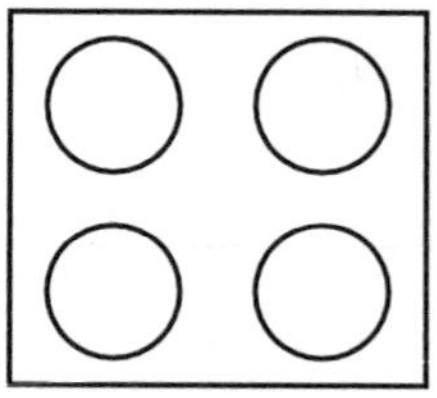

stove 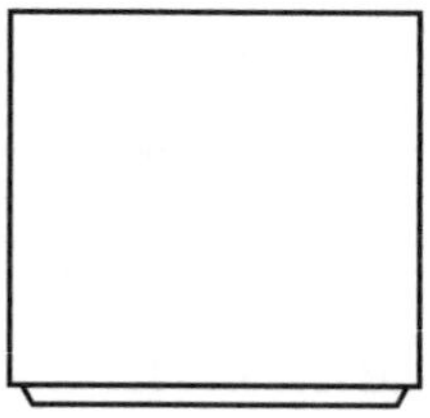 refrigerator 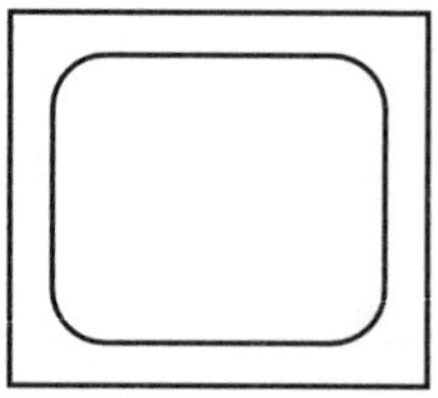 sink 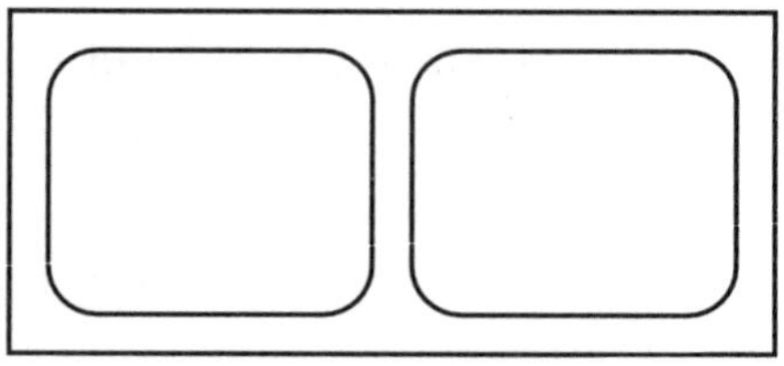 double sink

Name Date Time

Fractions of Circles

Divide each circle into equal parts and color as directed.

SRB 44

1. Divide into 2 equal parts.
Color $\frac{1}{2}$ yellow.

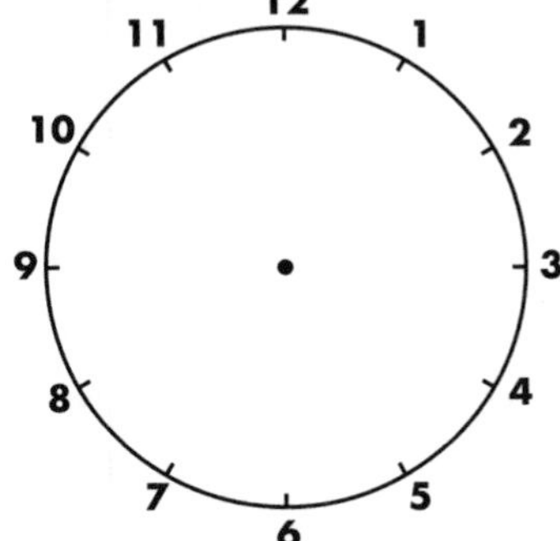

2. Divide into 3 equal parts.
Color $\frac{1}{3}$ red and $\frac{1}{3}$ blue.

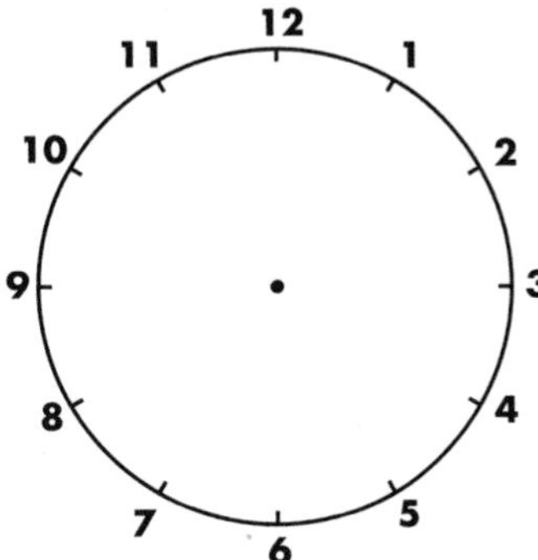

3. Divide into 6 equal parts.
Color $\frac{1}{6}$ green and $\frac{2}{6}$ orange.

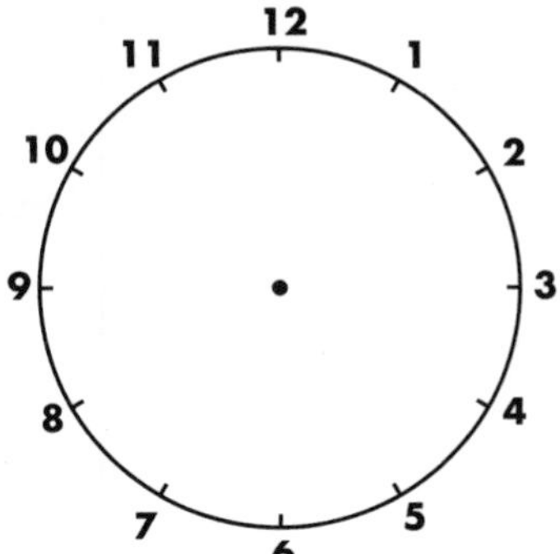

4. Divide into 6 equal parts.
Color $\frac{1}{6}$ green and $\frac{1}{3}$ orange.

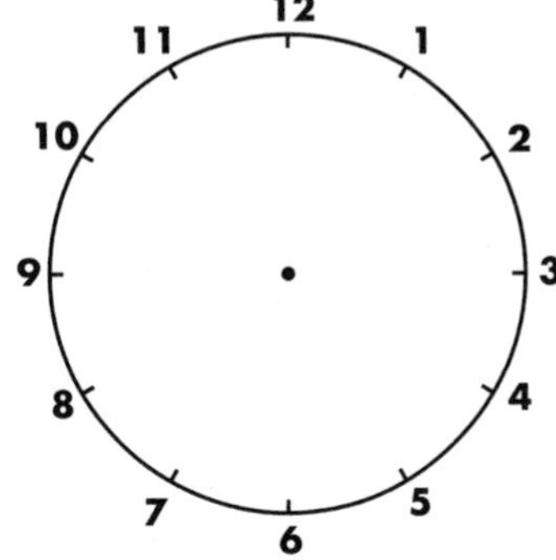

5. Divide into 12 equal parts.
Color $\frac{1}{3}$ red.

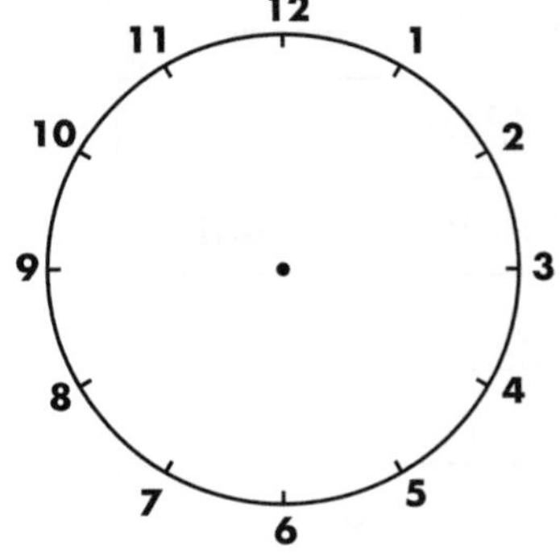

6. Divide into 12 equal parts.
Color $\frac{1}{3}$ red in a different way.

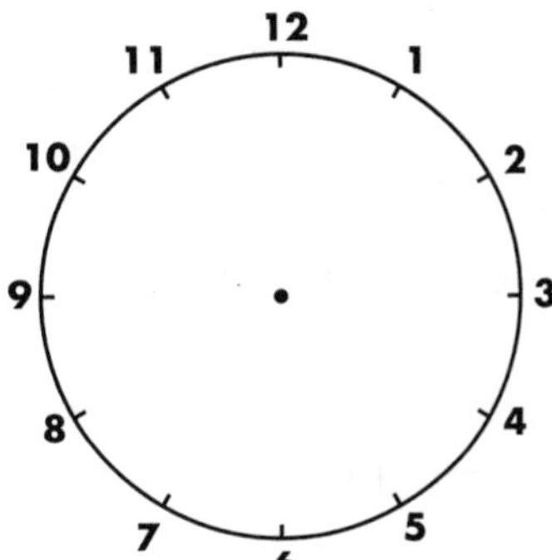

Name Date Time

LESSON 7·12

A Cube-Drop Experiment

Color the squares in the grid above.

The table at the right shows the number of squares you must use for each color.

How to Color the Grid

Color	Number of Squares
yellow	1
red	4
green	10
blue	35
white	50
Total	**100**

Name Date Time

STUDY LINK 7•12

What Are the Chances?

1. You are going to toss 2 pennies 20 times. How many times do you expect the 2 pennies will come up as

   a. 2 heads? ________ times b. 2 tails? ________ times

   c. 1 head and 1 tail? ________ times

2. Now toss 2 pennies together 20 times. Record the results in the table.

A Penny Toss

Results	Number of Times
2 heads	
2 tails	
1 head and 1 tail	

3. What fraction of the tosses came up as

   a. 2 heads? ________ b. 2 tails? ________ c. 1 head and 1 tail? ________

4. Suppose you were to flip the coins 1,000 times. What fraction do you expect would come up as

   a. 2 heads? ______________ b. 2 tails? ______________

   c. 1 head and 1 tail? ______________

5. Explain how you got your answers for Problem 4.

____

____

____

Practice

6. 7 ∗ 48 = ______________ 7. 874 ∗ 9 = ______________

8. ______________ = 45 ∗ 86 9. ______________ = 34 ∗ 142

Name Date Time

Fractions and Percents on Grids

Fractions and percents can be modeled with base-10 blocks.

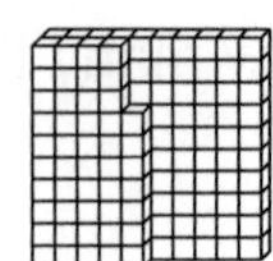

$\frac{47}{100}$ = 47 out of 100 = 47%

Build each fraction with base-10 blocks. Shade the grid, and fill in the missing numbers.

1.

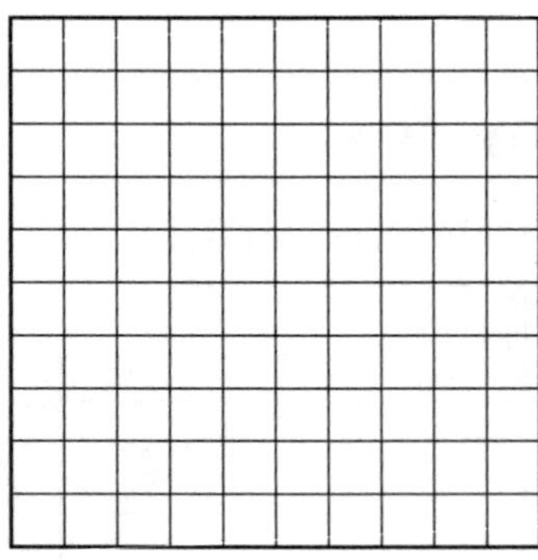

$\frac{30}{100}$ = ______ out of 100 = ______%

2.

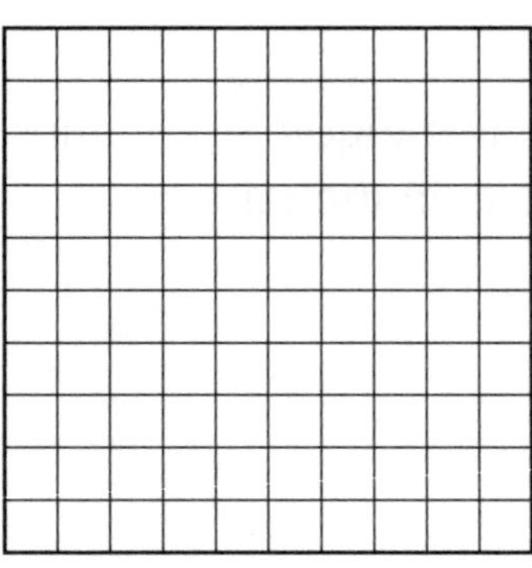

$\frac{76}{100}$ = ______ out of 100 = ______%

3.

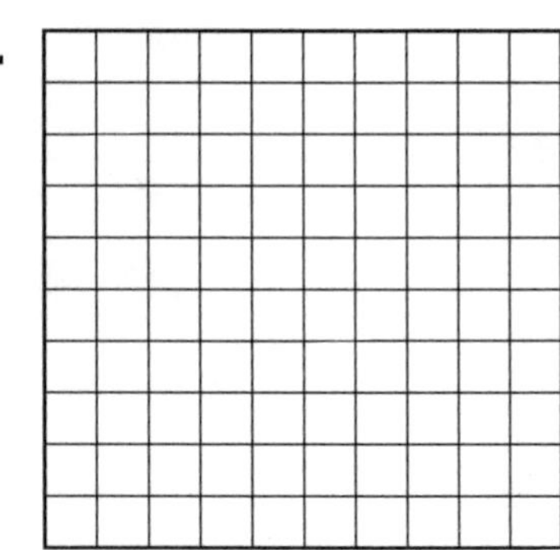

$\frac{4}{100}$ = ______ out of 100 = ______%

4. Create your own.

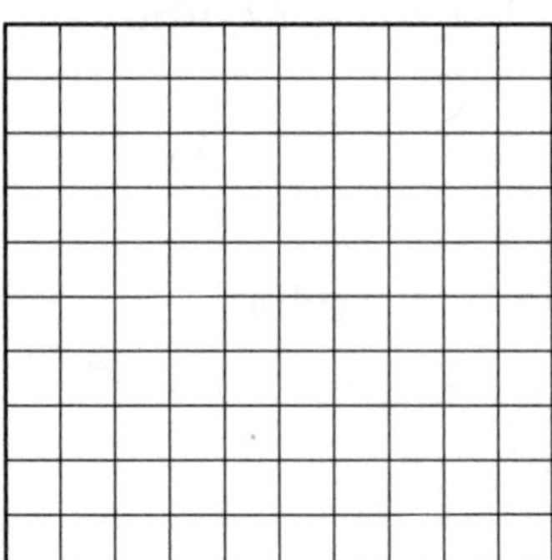

$\frac{\square}{100}$ = ______ out of 100 = ______%

These grids are the whole. Find the percent of each grid that is shaded.

5.

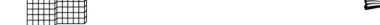

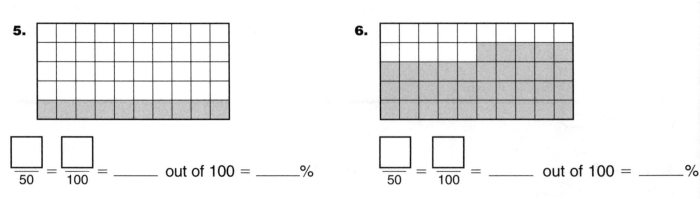

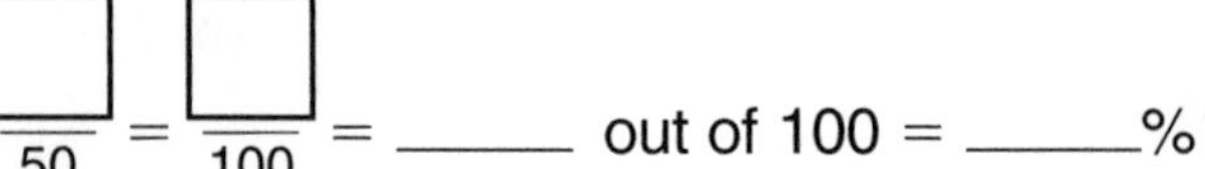

$\frac{\square}{50} = \frac{\square}{100}$ = ______ out of 100 = ______%

6.

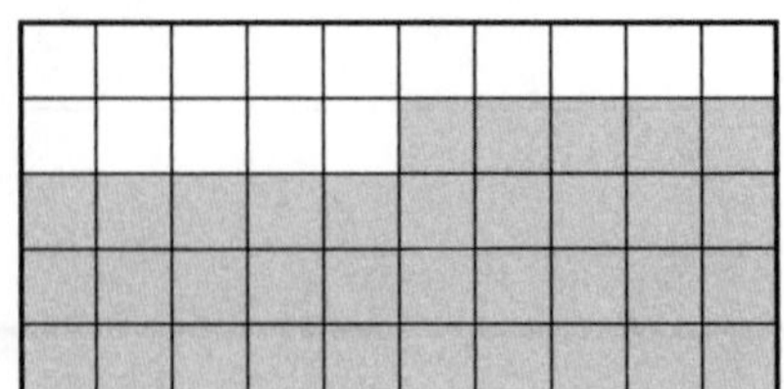

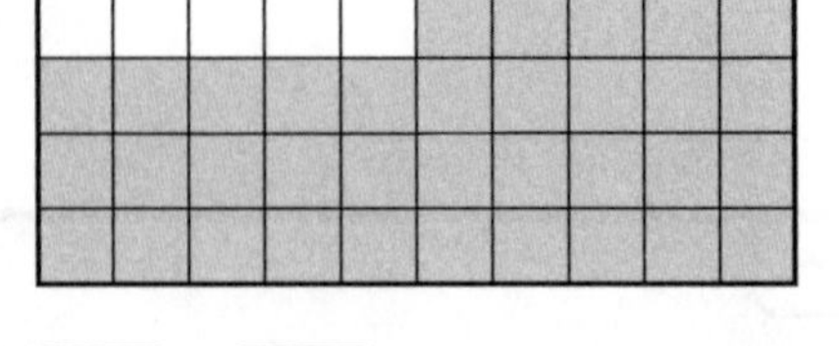

$\frac{\square}{50} = \frac{\square}{100}$ = ______ out of 100 = ______%

Name Date Time

Results for 50 Cube Drops

Results for 50 Cube Drops	
Color	**Number of Drops**
yellow	
red	
green	
blue	
white	
Total	**50**

Results for 50 Cube Drops	
Color	**Number of Drops**
yellow	
red	
green	
blue	
white	
Total	**50**

Results for 50 Cube Drops	
Color	**Number of Drops**
yellow	
red	
green	
blue	
white	
Total	**50**

Results for 50 Cube Drops	
Color	**Number of Drops**
yellow	
red	
green	
blue	
white	
Total	**50**

Results for 50 Cube Drops	
Color	**Number of Drops**
yellow	
red	
green	
blue	
white	
Total	**50**

Results for 50 Cube Drops	
Color	**Number of Drops**
yellow	
red	
green	
blue	
white	
Total	**50**

Name Date Time

LESSON 7•12

Class Results for 1,000 Cube Drops

Color	Students S1	S2	S3	S4	S5	S6	S7	S8	S9	S10	S11	S12	S13	S14	S15	S16	S17	S18	S19	S20	Number of drops	Percent
yellow																						
red																						
green																						
blue																						
white																						
Total	50	50	50	50	50	50	50	50	50	50	50	50	50	50	50	50	50	50	50	50	1,000	100%

Most of the percents you calculate will not be whole-number percents. You can record them as percents in tenths or round them to the nearest whole percent. For example, 96 out of 1,000 is equivalent to 9.6 out of 100. This could be recorded either as 9.6% or 10%. If the answers are rounded, the total might not add up to 100%.

Name Date Time

Unit 8: Family Letter

Perimeter and Area

In previous grades, your child studied the *perimeter* (distance around) and the *area* (amount of surface) of various geometric figures. This next unit will extend your child's understanding of geometry by developing and applying formulas for the areas of figures such as rectangles, parallelograms, and triangles.

Area of a Rectangle

Area = base * height (or length * width)

$A = b * h$ (or $l * w$)

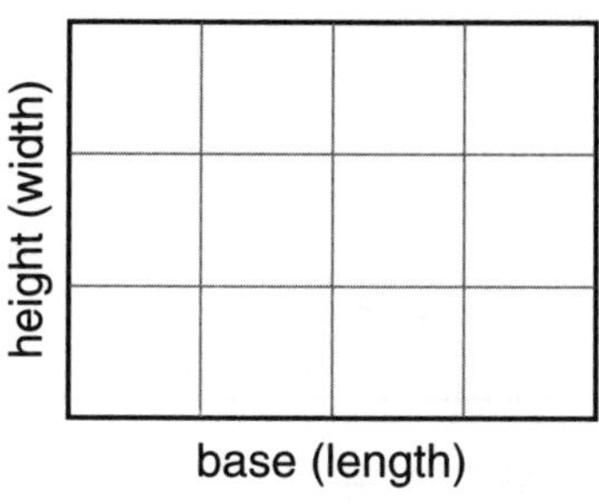

Area of a Parallelogram

Area = base * height

$A = b * h$

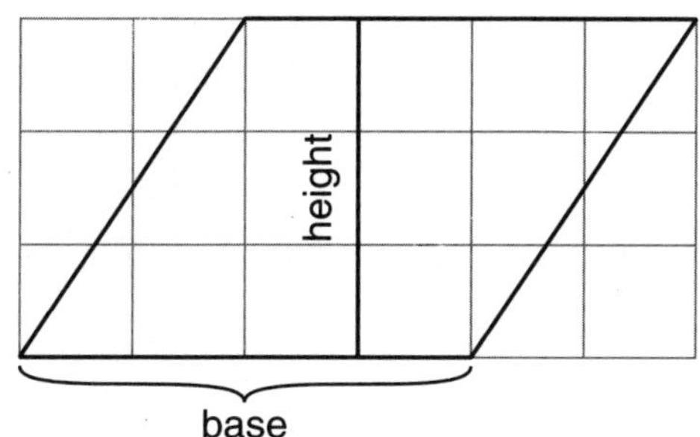

Area of a Triangle

Area = $\frac{1}{2}$ of (base * height)

$A = \frac{1}{2} * b * h$

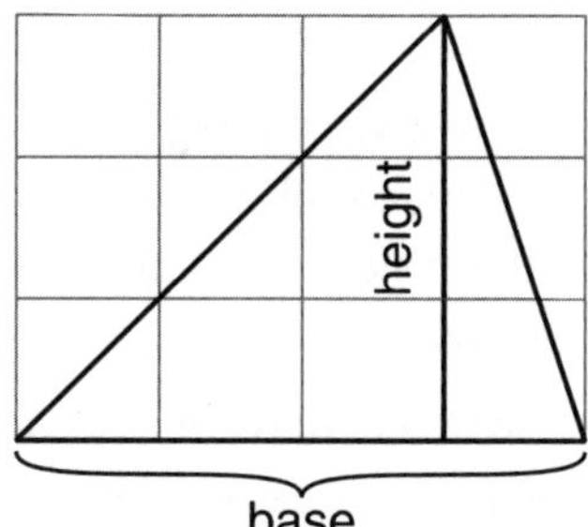

Students will learn how to make scale drawings and apply their knowledge of perimeter, area, and scale drawing by analyzing the arrangement of the appliances in their kitchens and the furniture in their bedrooms.

Students will also calculate the area of the skin that covers their entire body. A rule of thumb is that the area of a person's skin is about 100 times the area of one side of that person's hand. Ask your child to show you how to calculate the area of your own skin.

The World Tour will continue. Students will examine how geographical areas are measured and the difficulties in making accurate measurements. They will compare areas for South American countries by using division to calculate the ratio of areas.

Please keep this Family Letter for reference as your child works through Unit 8.

Vocabulary

Important terms in Unit 8:

area The amount of surface inside a closed 2-dimensional (flat) boundary. Area is measured in *square units,* such as square inches or square centimeters.

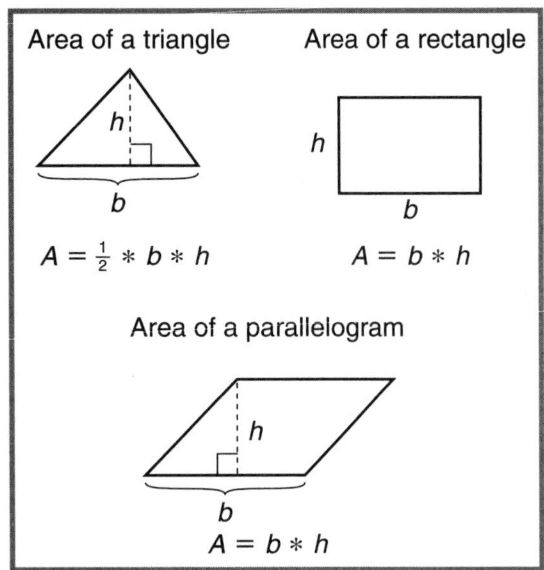

formula A general rule for finding the value of something. A formula is often written using letter *variables,* which stand for the quantities involved.

length The distance between two points on a 1-dimensional figure. Length is measured in units such as inches, meters, and miles.

perimeter The distance around a 2-dimensional shape along the boundary of the shape. The perimeter of a circle is called its circumference. The perimeter of a polygon is the sum of the lengths of its sides.

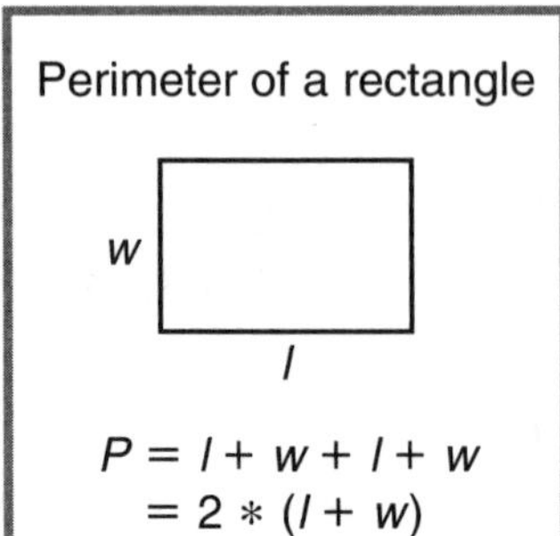

perpendicular Crossing or meeting at right angles. Lines, rays, line segments, and planes that cross or meet at right angles are perpendicular. The symbol ⊥ means "is perpendicular to," as in "line *CD* ⊥ line *AB*." The symbol ⊾ indicates a right angle.

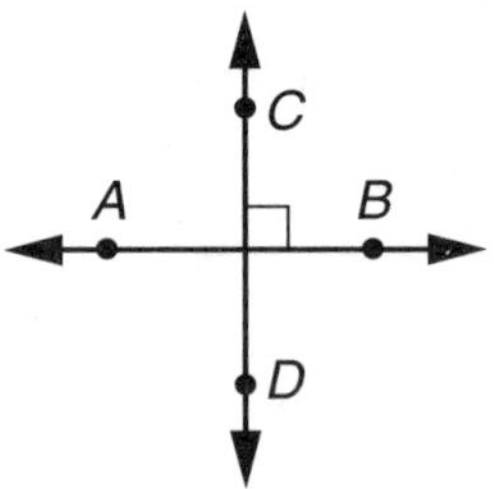

Perpendicular lines

scale The ratio of the distance on a map, globe, drawing, or model to an actual distance.

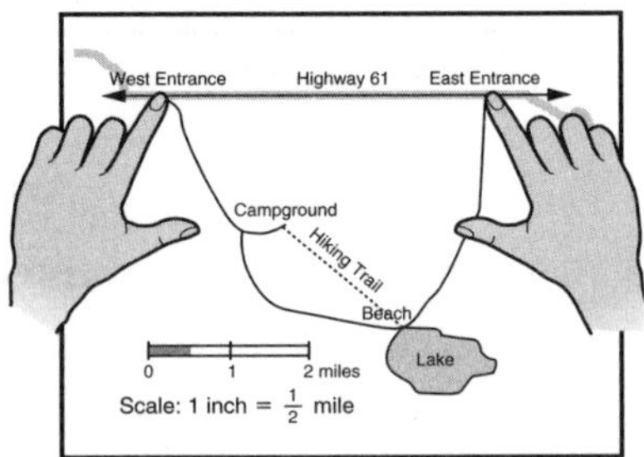

scale drawing A drawing of an object or a region in which all parts are drawn to the same scale as the object. Architects and builders often use scale drawings.

square unit A unit used to measure area. For example, a square that measures one inch on each side has an area of one square inch.

variable A letter or other symbol that represents a number. A variable can represent one specific number, or it can stand for many different numbers.

width The length of one side of a rectangle or rectangular object, typically the shorter side.

Do-Anytime Activities

To work with your child on concepts taught in this unit, try these interesting and engaging activities:

1. Have your child pretend that he or she is a carpenter whose job is to redesign a room—for example, a bedroom, the kitchen, or the living room. Have him or her make a rough estimate of the area of the room. Then help your child check the estimate by finding the actual area using a tape measure or, if possible, blueprints.
2. Have your child pretend that he or she is an architect. Give him or her some dimensions and space requirements to work with. Then have your child design a "dream house," "dream bedroom," or sports stadium, and make a scale drawing for that design.
3. Work with your child to make a scale drawing of your neighborhood. Or have your child make a scale drawing of the floor plan of your house or apartment.
4. Have your child compare the areas of continents, countries, states, or major cities.

Building Skills through Games

In this unit, your child will calculate perimeter and area, compare fractions, identify equivalent fractions, find fractions of collections, and calculate expected probabilities by playing the following games. For detailed instructions, see the *Student Reference Book.*

Fraction Match See *Student Reference Book,* page 243.
This is a game for 2 to 4 players and requires a deck of *Fraction Match* Cards. The game provides practice recognizing equivalent fractions.

Fraction Of See *Student Reference Book,* pages 244 and 245.
This is a game for 2 players and requires 1 deck of *Fraction Of* Fraction Cards, 1 deck of *Fraction Of* Set Cards, and 1 *Fraction Of* Gameboard and Record Sheet. The game provides practice finding fractions of collections.

Fraction Top-It See *Student Reference Book,* page 247.
This is a game for 2 to 4 players and requires a set of Fraction Cards 1 and 2. The game provides practice comparing fractions.

Grab Bag See *Student Reference Book,* page 249.
This is a game for 2 players or two teams of 2 players. It requires 1 deck of *Grab Bag* Cards, 2 *Grab Bag* Record Sheets, and 3 six-sided dice. The game provides practice with variable substitution and calculating probabilities of events.

Rugs and Fences See *Student Reference Book,* pages 260 and 261.
This is a game for 2 players and requires a *Rugs and Fences* Polygon Deck and an Area and Perimeter Deck. The game provides practice finding and comparing the area and perimeter of polygons.

As You Help Your Child with Homework

As your child brings assignments home, you may want to go over the instructions together, clarifying them as necessary. The answers listed below will guide you through some of the Study Links in this unit.

Study Link 8•1

1. 17 feet **2.** 54 inches

3. Sample answer:

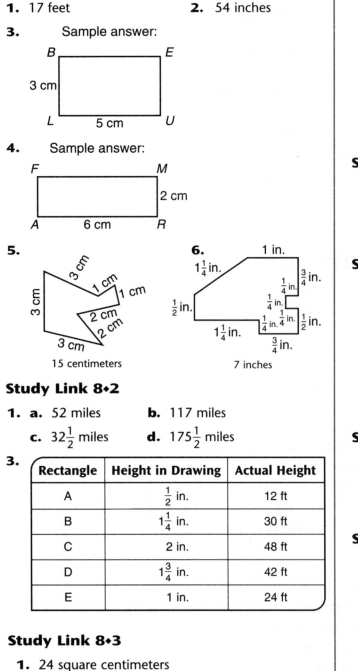

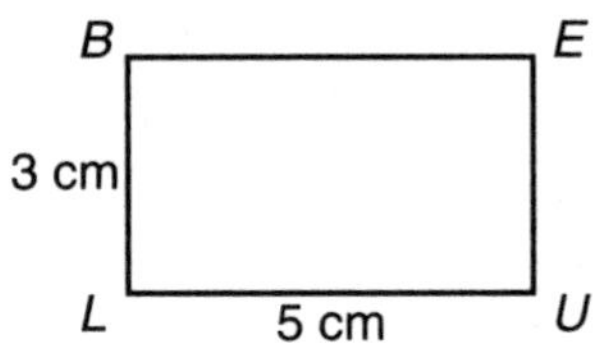

4. Sample answer:

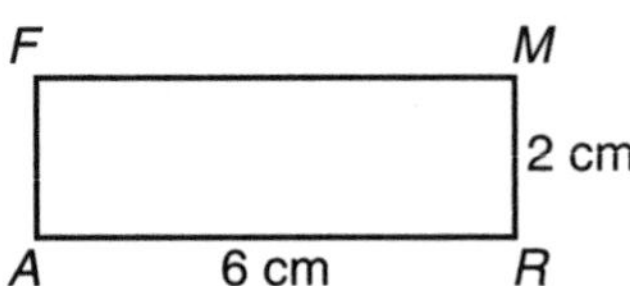

5.

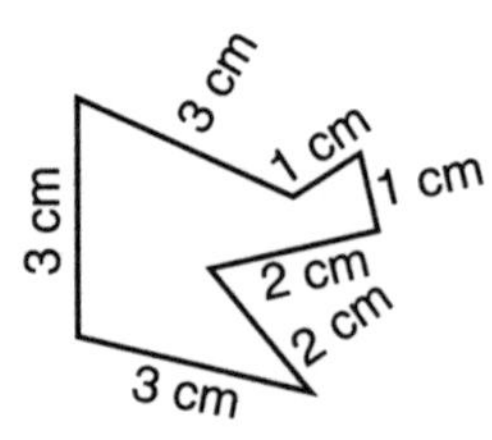

15 centimeters

6.

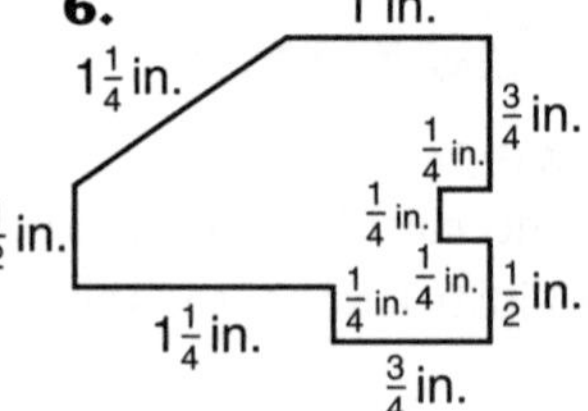

7 inches

Study Link 8•2

1. a. 52 miles **b.** 117 miles

c. $32\frac{1}{2}$ miles **d.** $175\frac{1}{2}$ miles

3.

Rectangle	Height in Drawing	Actual Height
A	$\frac{1}{2}$ in.	12 ft
B	$1\frac{1}{4}$ in.	30 ft
C	2 in.	48 ft
D	$1\frac{3}{4}$ in.	42 ft
E	1 in.	24 ft

Study Link 8•3

1. 24 square centimeters

2. 24 square centimeters

2., continued Sample answer:

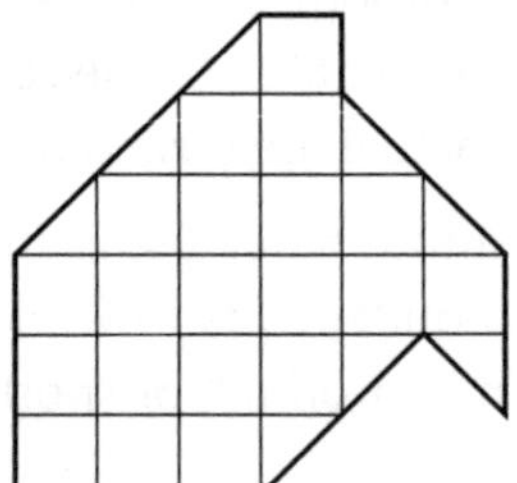

3. 2,072 **4.** 11,740 **5.** 3,593 **6.** 2,848

Study Link 8•4

1. 87,500; 35 grid squares

2. 17,500; 7 grid squares

3. 88.71 **4.** 58.08 **5.** 386.174 **6.** 18.098

Study Link 8•5

1. 48 square feet **2.** 21 square inches

3. 864 square centimeters

4. 300 square meters

5. 9 inches **6.** 10 centimeters

7. 9, 15, 18, 21 **8.** 28, 35, 49, 56

9. 36, 54, 60, 66 **10.** 24, 48, 72, 84

Study Link 8•6

1. $9 * 4 = 36$ **2.** $3 * 8 = 24$

3. $4 * 6 = 24$ **4.** $65 * 72 = 4{,}680$

5. 13 inches **6.** 85 meters

Study Link 8•7

1. $\frac{1}{2} * (8 * 4) = 16$ **2.** $\frac{1}{2} * (12 * 5) = 30$

3. $\frac{1}{2} * (10 * 2) = 10$

4. $\frac{1}{2} * (34 * 75) = 1{,}275$

5. 3 inches **6.** 6 meters

7. 27, 36, 54, 72 **8.** 8, 24, 40, 48

Name Date Time

STUDY LINK 8·1

Perimeter

1. Perimeter = _______ feet

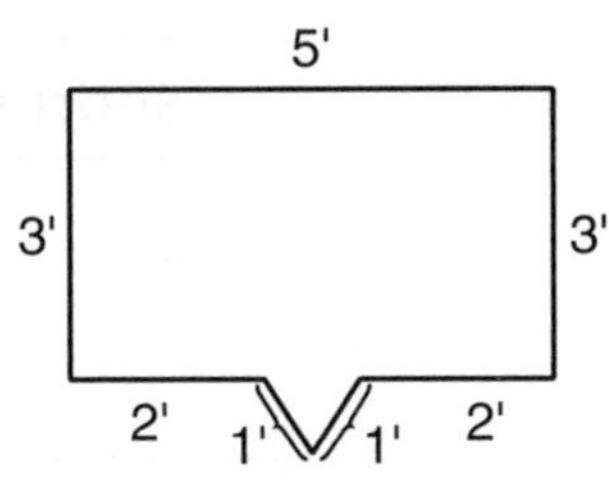

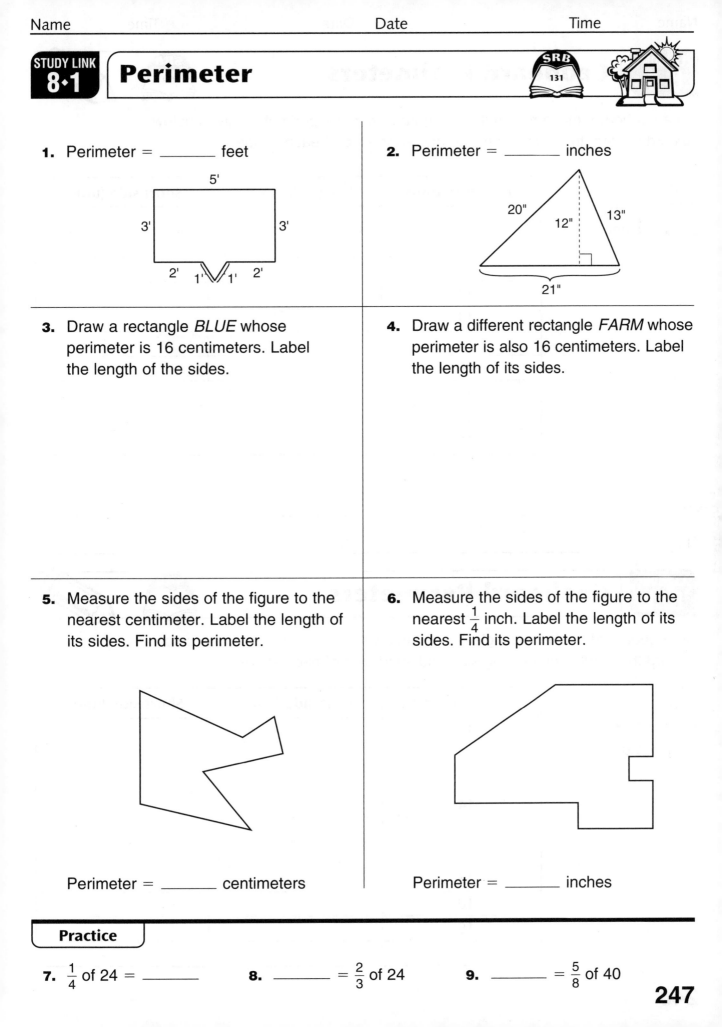

2. Perimeter = _______ inches

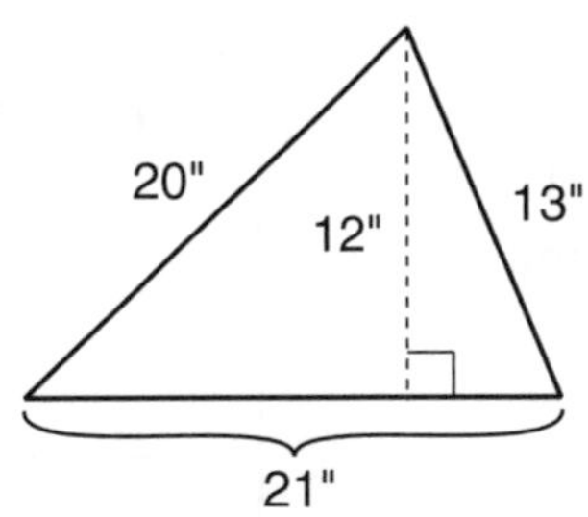

3. Draw a rectangle *BLUE* whose perimeter is 16 centimeters. Label the length of the sides.

4. Draw a different rectangle *FARM* whose perimeter is also 16 centimeters. Label the length of its sides.

5. Measure the sides of the figure to the nearest centimeter. Label the length of its sides. Find its perimeter.

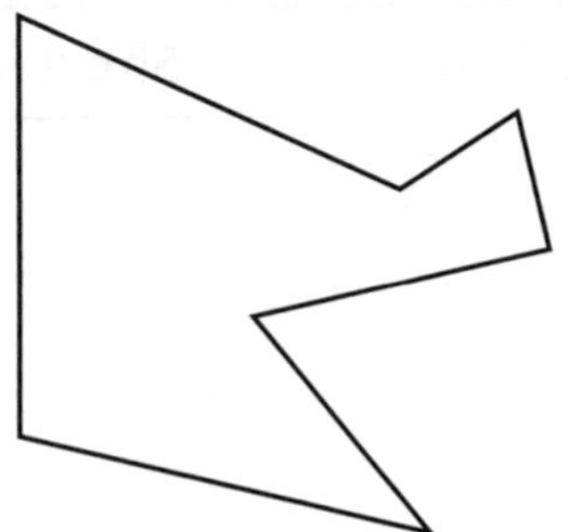

Perimeter = _______ centimeters

6. Measure the sides of the figure to the nearest $\frac{1}{4}$ inch. Label the length of its sides. Find its perimeter.

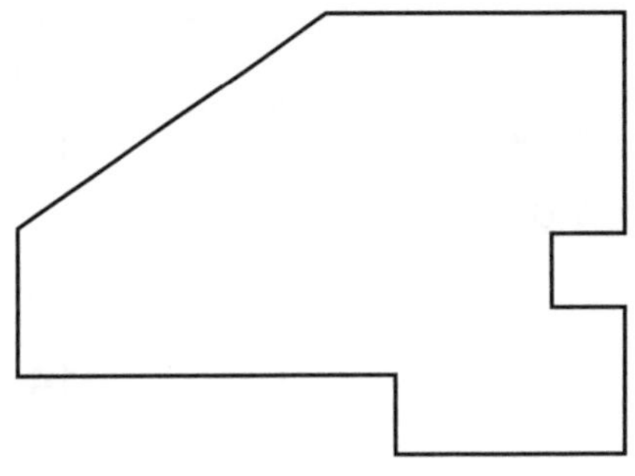

Perimeter = _______ inches

Practice

7. $\frac{1}{4}$ of 24 = _______

8. _______ = $\frac{2}{3}$ of 24

9. _______ = $\frac{5}{8}$ of 40

Name Date Time

Geoboard Perimeters

On a geoboard, make rectangles or squares with the perimeters given below.
Record the lengths of the long side and short side of each shape.

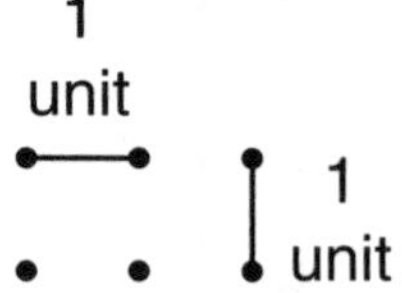

Perimeter (units)	Long side (units)	Short side (units)
12		
12		
12		
14		
14		
14		
16		
16		
16		
16		

Name Date Time

Geoboard Perimeters

On a geoboard, make rectangles or squares with the perimeters given below.
Record the lengths of the long side and short side of each shape.

1
unit
1
unit

Perimeter (units)	Long side (units)	Short side (units)
12		
12		
12		
14		
14		
14		
16		
16		
16		
16		

Name Date Time

Pattern-Block Perimeters

1. Use the following pattern blocks to create shapes with as many *different* perimeters as you can: 1 hexagon, 3 trapezoids, 3 blue rhombi, and 3 triangles.

   - Every shape must include all 10 pattern blocks.
   - Each side of a pattern block measures 1 unit. The long side of a trapezoid pattern block measures 2 units.
   - At least one side of every pattern block must *line up exactly* with a side of another pattern block. See figures.

yes

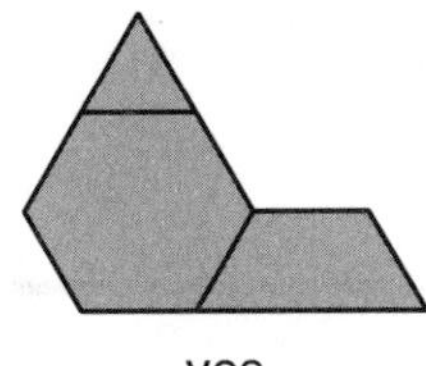
yes

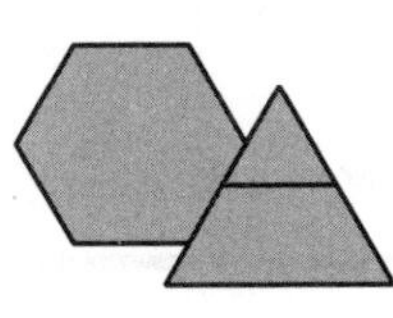
no

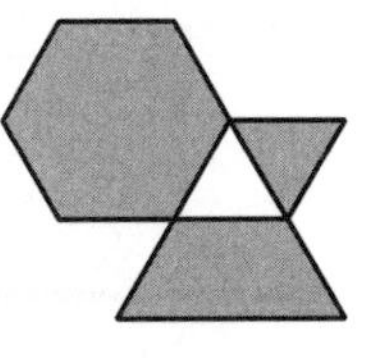
no

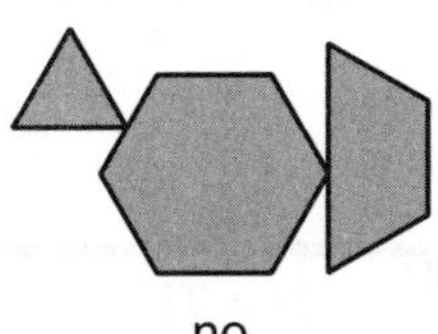
no

2. Use your Geometry Template to record your shapes on a separate sheet of paper. The polygons should all have different perimeters. Write the perimeter next to each shape.

3. What was the smallest perimeter you were able to make? ________ units
   Describe the strategy you used to find this perimeter.

   ____

   ____

   ____

4. What was the largest perimeter you were able to make? ________ units
   Describe the strategy you used to find this perimeter.

   ____

   ____

   ____

Name Date Time

STUDY LINK 8·2

Scale

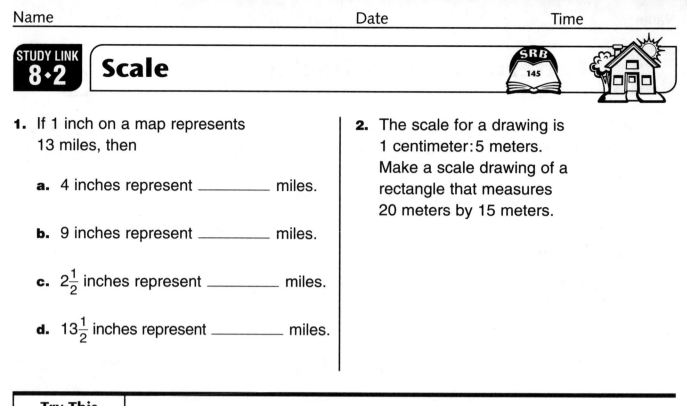

1. If 1 inch on a map represents 13 miles, then

   a. 4 inches represent ________ miles.

   b. 9 inches represent ________ miles.

   c. $2\frac{1}{2}$ inches represent ________ miles.

   d. $13\frac{1}{2}$ inches represent ________ miles.

2. The scale for a drawing is 1 centimeter:5 meters. Make a scale drawing of a rectangle that measures 20 meters by 15 meters.

Try This

3. Scale: $\frac{1}{4}$ inch represents 6 feet. Measure the height of each rectangle to the nearest $\frac{1}{4}$ inch. Complete the table.

A

B

C

D

E

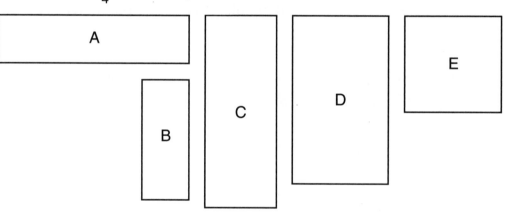

Rectangle	Height in Drawing	Actual Height
A		
B		
C		
D		
E		

Name Date

LESSON 8•2

Foot-Long Foot

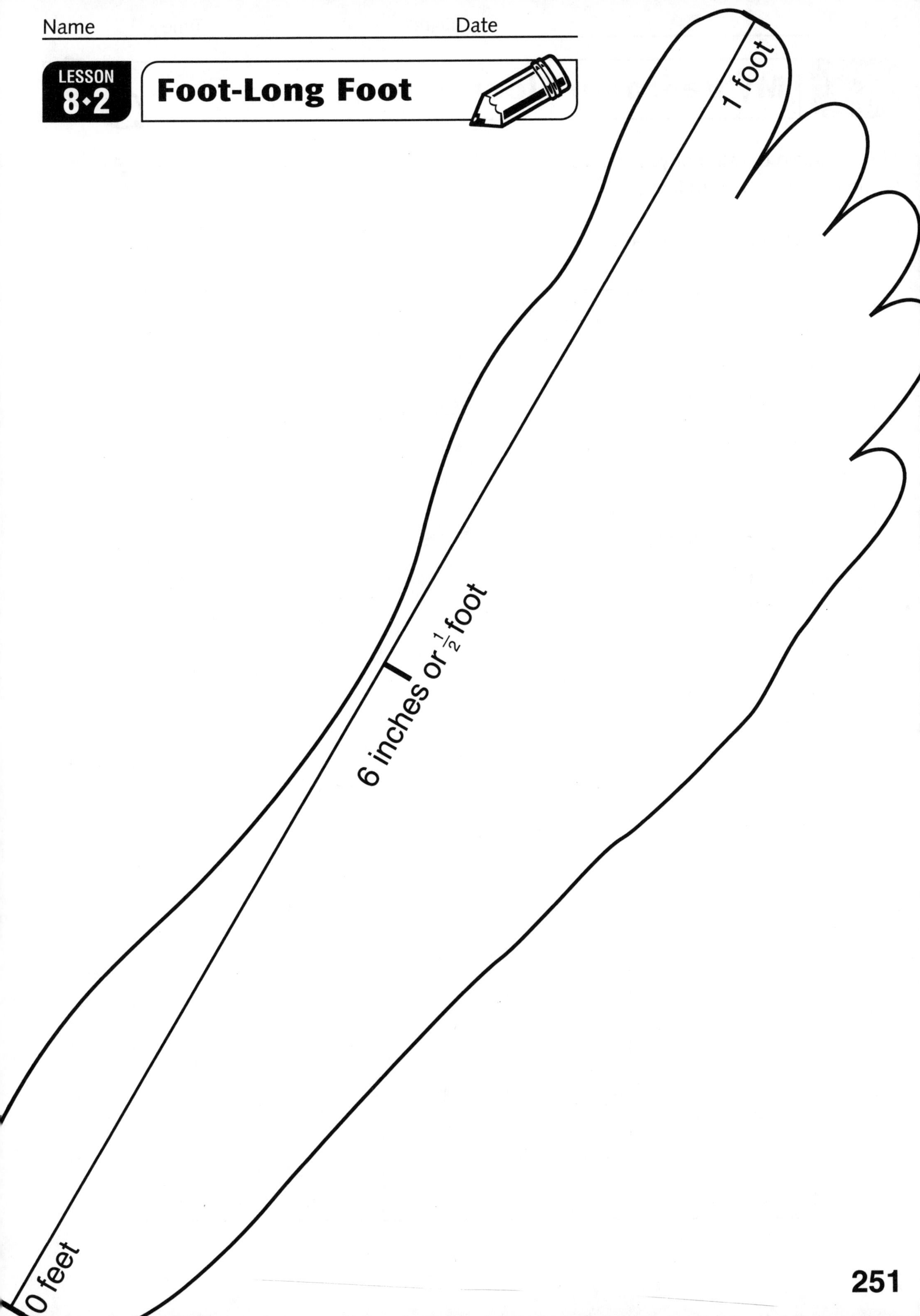

Name Date Time

LESSON 8•2

My Bedroom Floor Plan

Make a scale drawing of your bedroom floor. Round your measurements to the nearest $\frac{1}{4}$ foot (3 inches).

Scale: $\frac{1}{2}$ inch represents 1 foot.

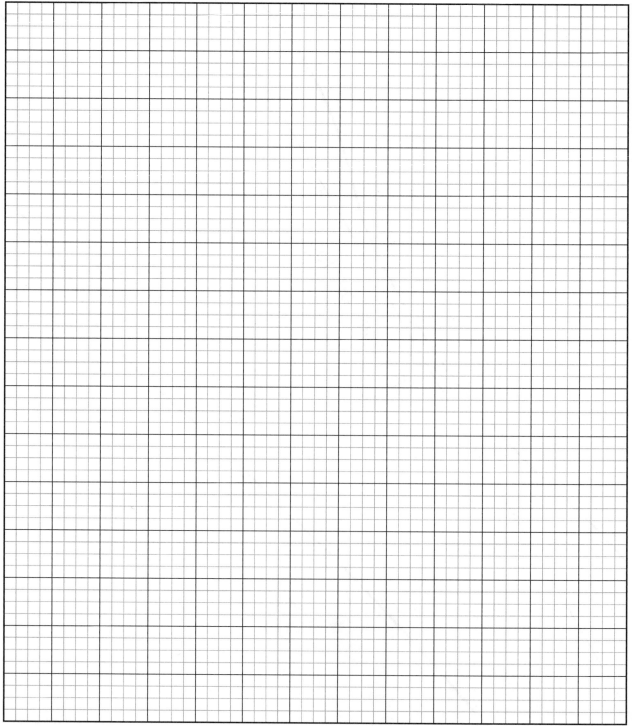

Name Date Time

My Bedroom Floor Plan *continued*

Make a scale drawing of each piece of furniture in your bedroom. Round your measurements to the nearest $\frac{1}{4}$ foot (3 inches). Cut out the scale drawings and tape them in place on your scale drawing of your bedroom floor.

Scale: $\frac{1}{2}$ inch represents 1 foot.

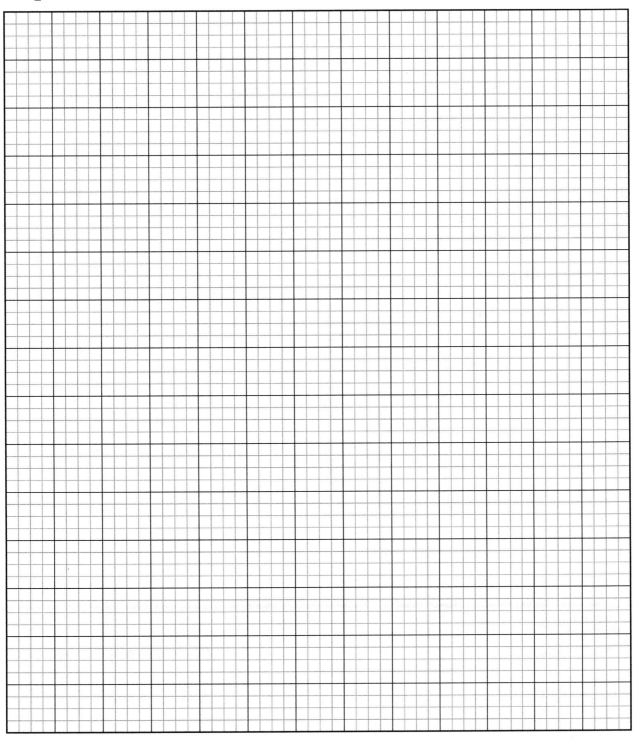

Name Date Time

Exploring Area

1. Rectangle A at the right is drawn on a 1-centimeter grid. Find its area.

   Area = ________ cm^2

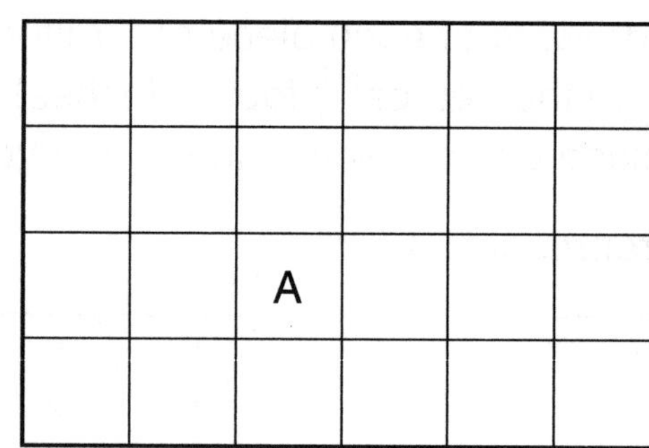

2. Rectangle B has the same area as Rectangle A. Cut out Rectangle B. Then cut it into 5 pieces any way you want.

   Rearrange the pieces into a new shape that is not a rectangle. Then tape the pieces together in the space below. What is the area of the new shape?

   Area of new shape = ________ cm^2

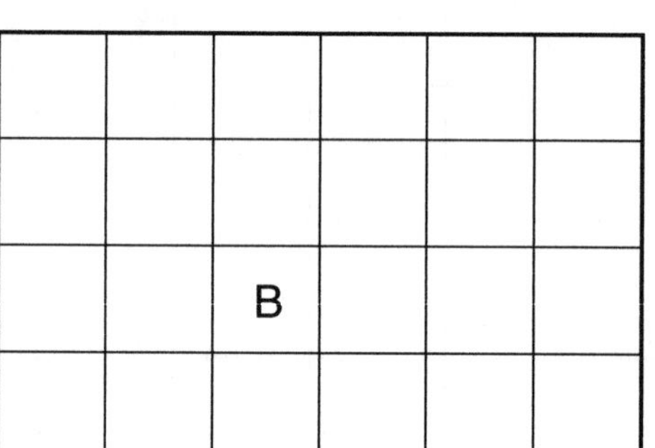

Practice

3. 1,778 + 294 = ____________
4. ____________ = 6,096 + 5,644
5. 4,007 − 414 = ____________
6. ____________ = 8,030 − 5,182

Name Date Time

Areas of Irregular Figures

1. Below is a map of São Paulo State in Brazil. Each grid square represents 2,500 square miles. Estimate the area of São Paulo State.

   I counted about _______ grid squares.

   The area is about ______________ square miles.

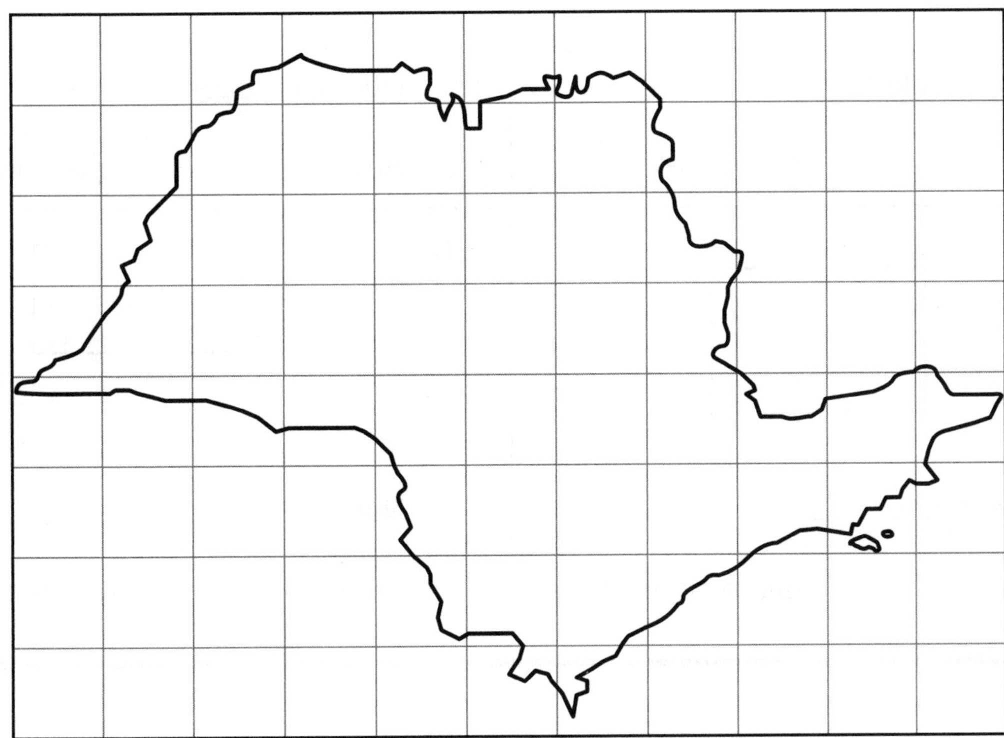

2. To the right is a map of Rio de Janeiro State in Brazil. Each grid square represents 2,500 square miles. Estimate the area of Rio de Janeiro State.

   I counted about _______ grid squares.

   The area is about ______________ square miles.

Practice

3. ____________ = 73.04 + 15.67

4. 86.05 − 27.97 = ____________

5. ____________ = 312.11 + 74.064

6. 57.1 − 39.002 = ____________

Name Date Time

Areas of Rectangles

Find the area of each rectangle.

1.

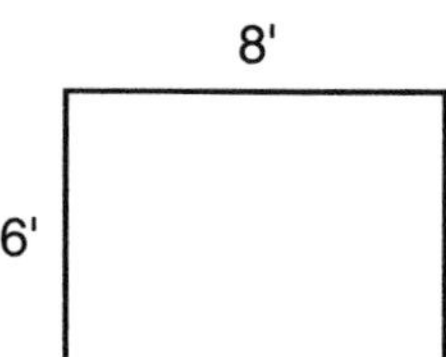

Number model: ____________

Area = ________ square feet

2.

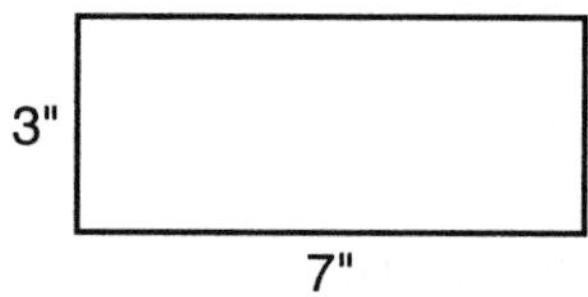

Number model: ____________

Area = ________ square inches

3.

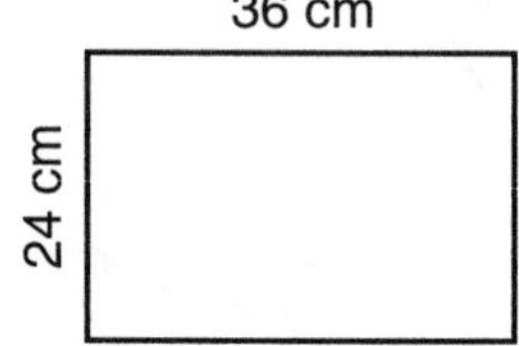

Number model: ____________

Area = ________ square centimeters

4.

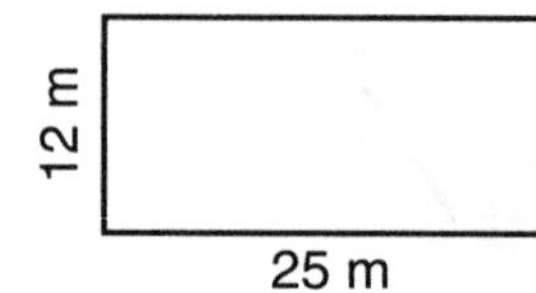

Number model: ____________

Area = ________ square meters

Try This

The area of each rectangle is given. Find the missing length.

5.

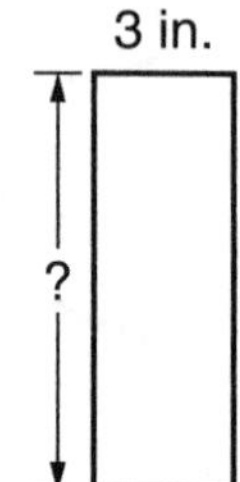

Area = 27 in^2

height = ________ in.

6.

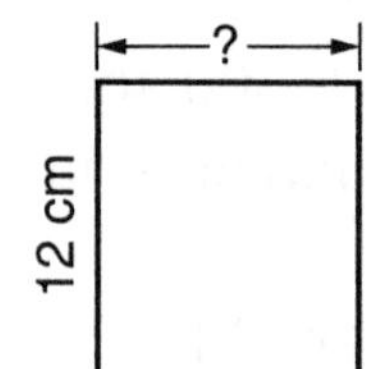

Area = 120 cm^2

base = ________ cm

Practice

7. 3, 6, ______, 12, ______, ______, ______

8. 14, 21, ______, ______, 42, ______, ______

9. 30, ______, 42, 48, ______, ______, ______

10. 12, ______, 36, ______, 60, ______, ______

Name Date Time

Area of a Rectangle

1. Take turns rolling a die. The first roll represents the length of the base of a rectangle. The second roll represents the height of the rectangle.

2. Use square pattern blocks to build the rectangle. Count squares to find the area.

Example:

First roll 4, second roll 3

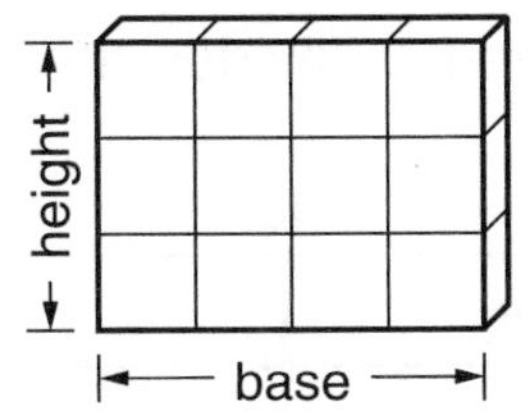

Area: 12 square units

3. Record your results in the table.

First Roll (length of base)	Second Roll (height)	Area (square units)
4	3	12

4. Describe a pattern in your table.

____

____

5. Without building the rectangle, can you use this pattern to find the area of a rectangle with a base of 8 units and a height of 7 units? Explain your answer.

____

____

Name Date Time

The Tennis Court

Area of rectangle = length $*$ width

Tennis can be played either by 2 people or by 4 people. When 2 people play, it is called a game of singles. When 4 people play, it is called a game of doubles.

Here is a diagram of a tennis court. The net divides the court in half.

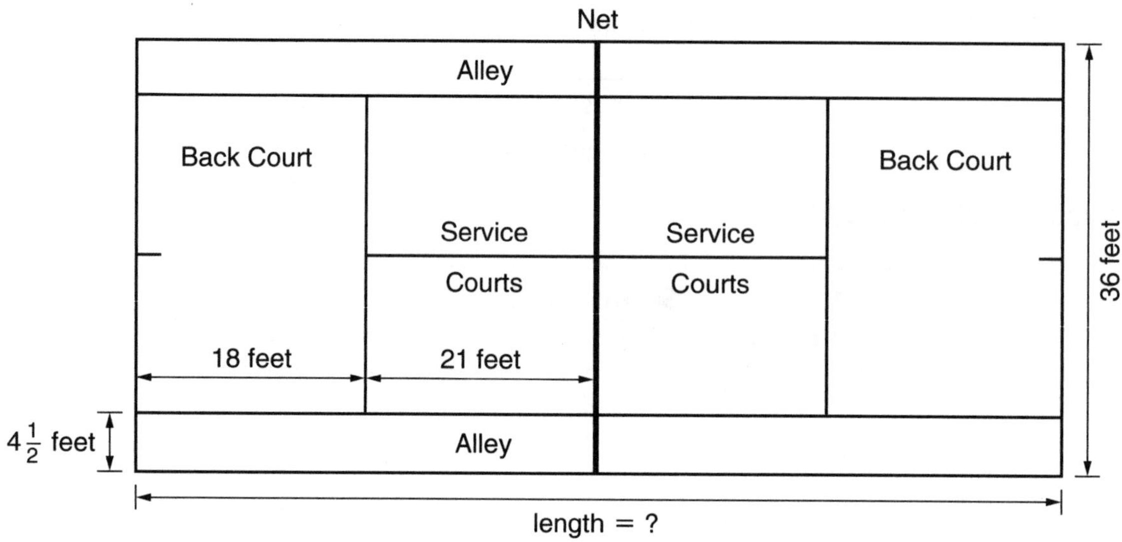

The two *alleys* are used only in doubles. They are never used in singles.

1. What is the total length of a tennis court? ______________

2. The court used in a game of doubles is 36 feet wide. Each alley is $4\frac{1}{2}$ feet wide. What is the width of the court used in a game of singles? ______________

3. What is the **area** of a singles court? ______________

4. What is the **area** of a doubles court? ______________

5. Do you think a player needs to cover more court in a game of singles or in a game of doubles? Explain.

____

____

____

____

Name Date Time

Perimeter and Area

1. Tape together two copies of 1-inch grid paper (*Math Masters,* page 444).

2. Use a 24-inch string loop to find as many different rectangles as possible that have a perimeter of 24 inches.

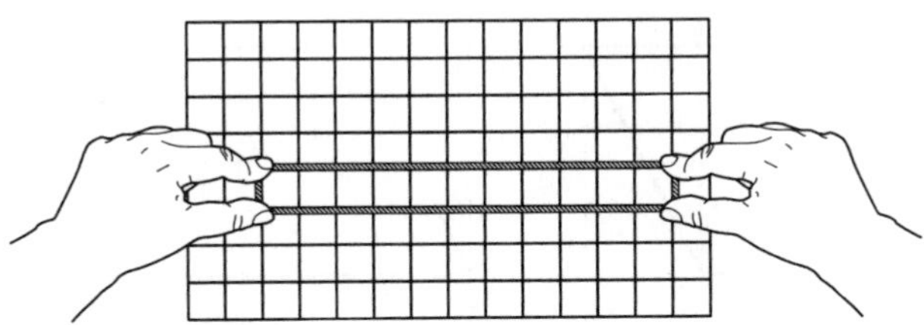

3. Record your results in the table.

Length of Base (in.)	Height (in.)	Perimeter (in.)	Area (in^2)
11	1	24	
		24	
		24	
		24	
		24	
		24	
$10\frac{1}{2}$		24	
	$4\frac{1}{2}$	24	

4. Use your results to describe a relationship between the lengths of sides and areas of rectangles that have the same perimeter.

____

____

____

5. What is another name for the rectangle with the largest area? ____________________

Name Date Time

Areas of Parallelograms

Cut out Parallelogram A. (Use the second Parallelogram A if you make a mistake.) Cut it into 2 pieces so that it can be made into a rectangle. Tape the rectangle onto page 236 in your journal.

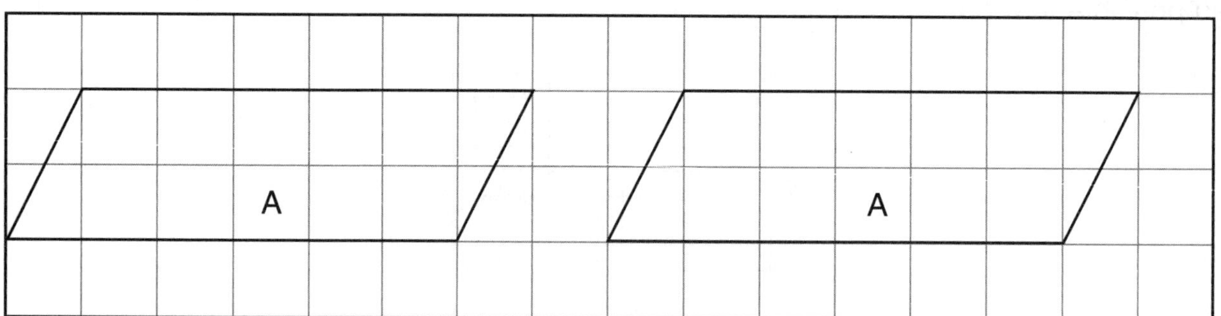

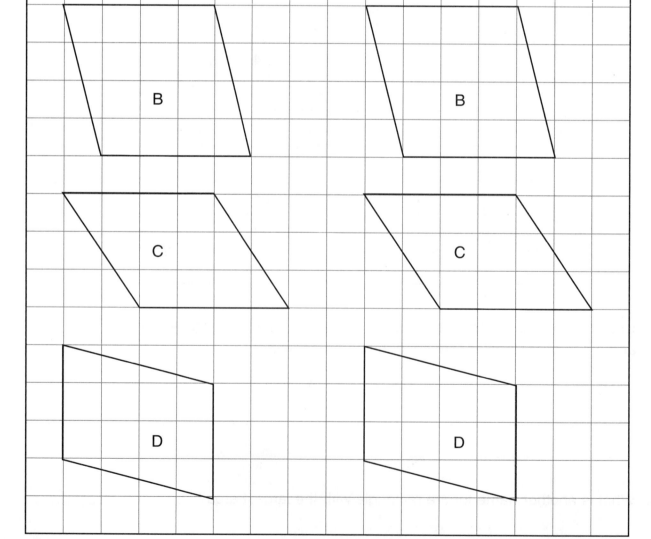

Do the same with Parallelograms B, C, and D.

B B

C C

D D

Name Date Time

Areas of Parallelograms

Find the area of each parallelogram.

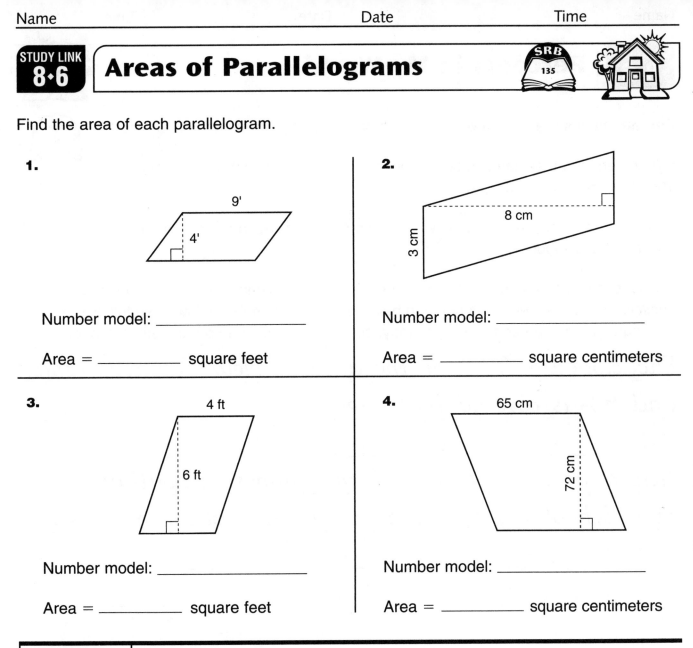

1.

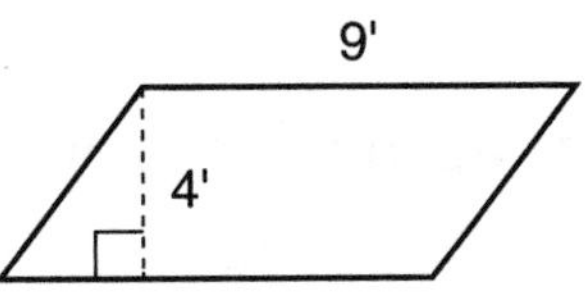

Number model: ______________

Area = __________ square feet

2.

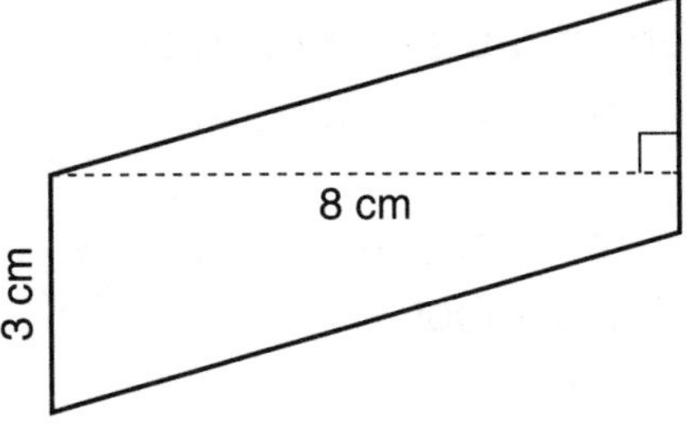

Number model: ______________

Area = __________ square centimeters

3.

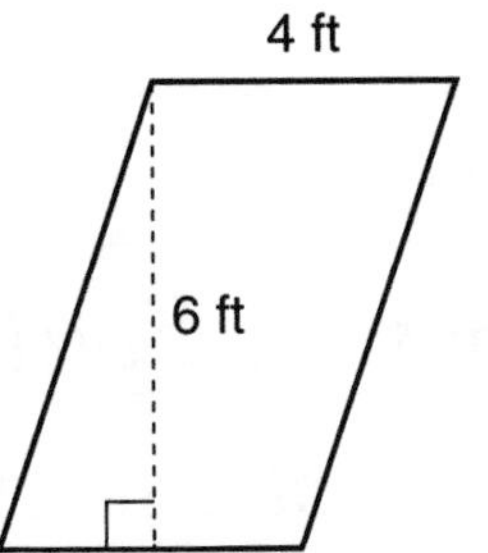

Number model: ______________

Area = __________ square feet

4.

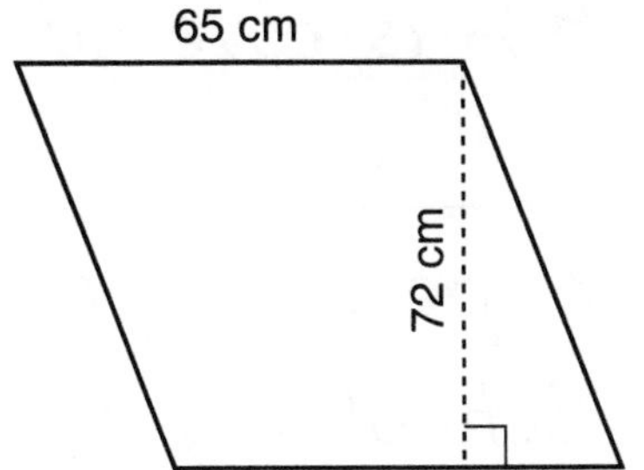

Number model: ______________

Area = __________ square centimeters

Try This

The area of each parallelogram is given. Find the length of the base.

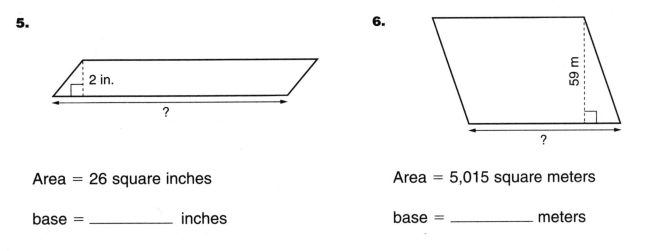

5.

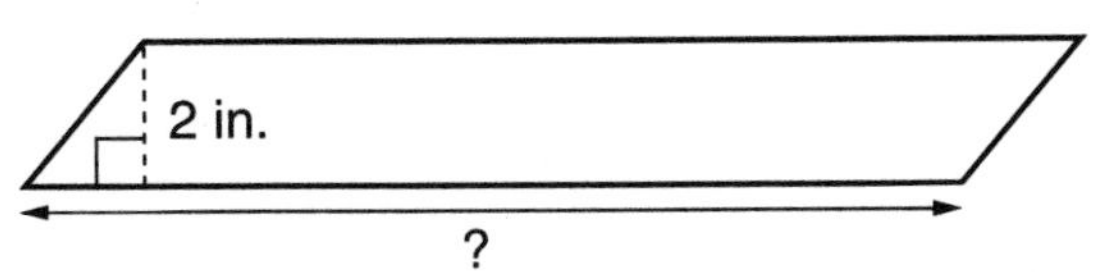

Area = 26 square inches

base = __________ inches

6.

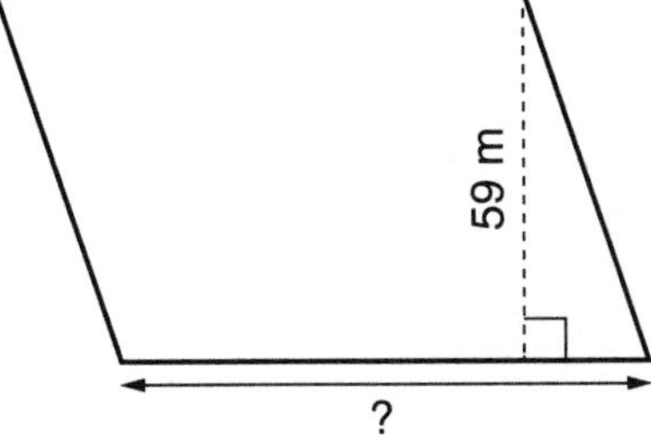

Area = 5,015 square meters

base = __________ meters

Name Date Time

Percents in My World

Percent means "per hundred" or "out of a hundred." *1 percent* means $\frac{1}{100}$ or 0.01.

"48 percent of the students in our school are boys" means that out of every 100 students in the school, 48 are boys.

Percents are written in two ways: with the word *percent,* as in the sentence above, and with the symbol %.

Collect examples of percents. Look in newspapers, magazines, books, almanacs, and encyclopedias. Ask people at home to help. Write the examples below. Also tell where you found them. If an adult says you may, cut out examples and bring them to school.

Encyclopedia: 91% of the area of New Jersey is land, and 9% is covered by water.

Newspaper: 76 percent of the seniors in Southport High School say they plan to attend college next year.

Name Date Time

Perimeter and Area

SRB 150

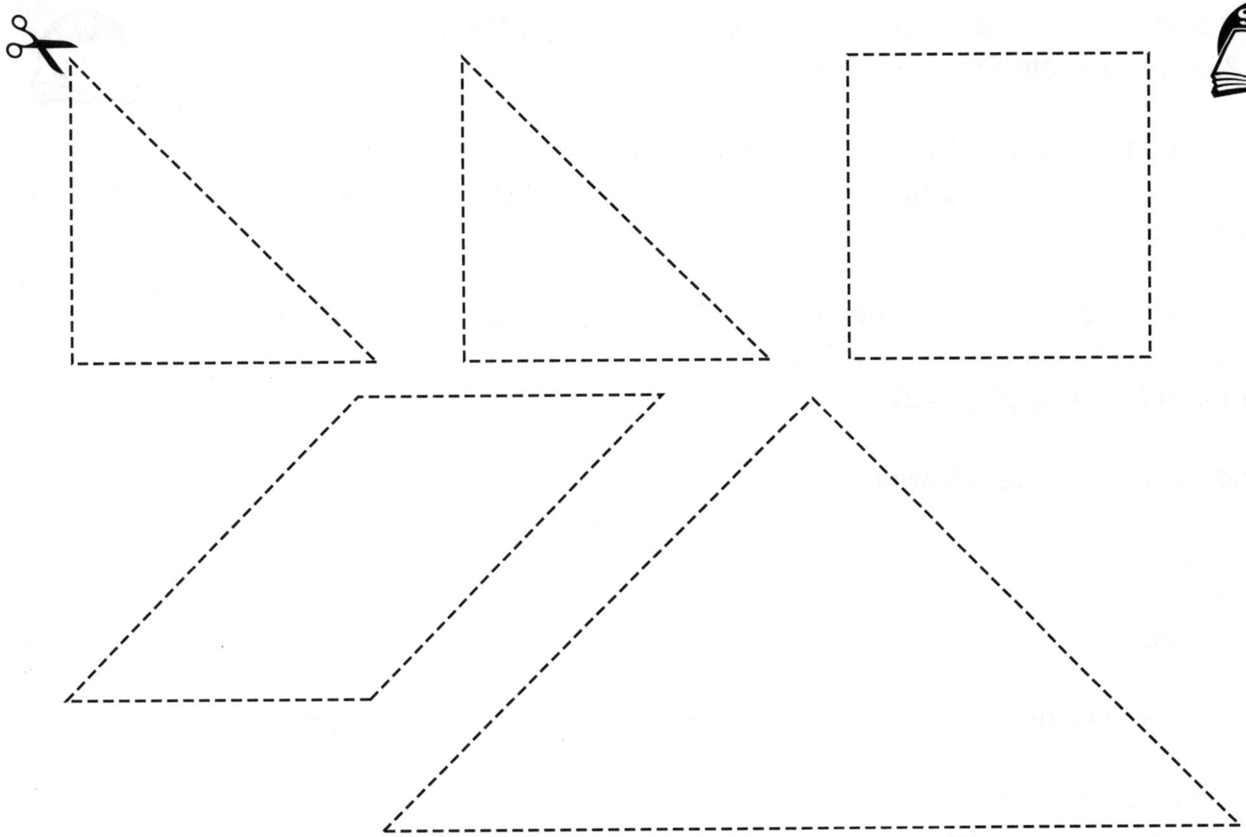

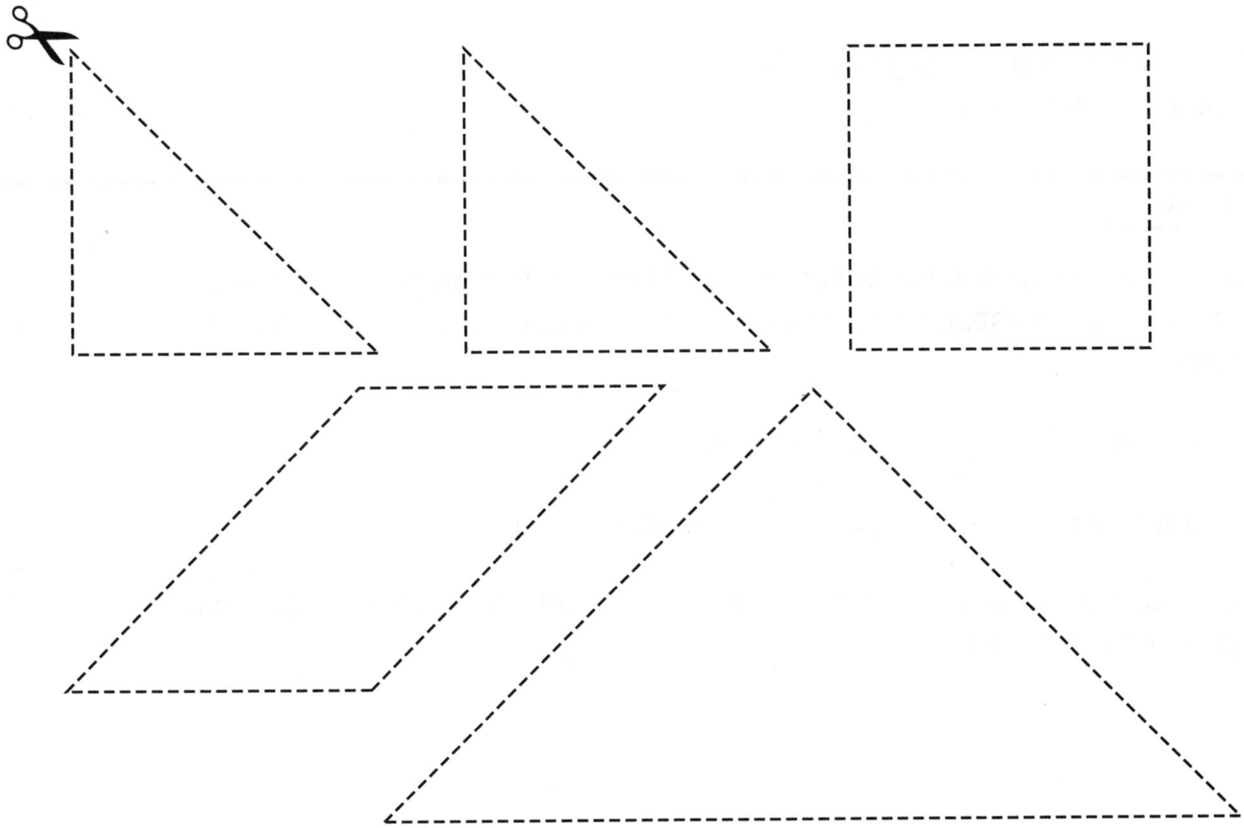

Name Date Time

Perimeter and Area *continued*

Cut out and use only the shapes in the *top half* of *Math Masters,* page 263 to complete Problems 1–5.

1. Make a square out of 4 of the shapes. Draw the square on the centimeter dot grid on *Math Masters,* page 437. Your picture should show how you put the square together.

2. Make a triangle out of 3 of the shapes. One of the shapes should be the shape you did not use to make the square in Problem 1. Draw the triangle on *Math Masters,* page 437.

3. Find the area of the following:

   a. the small triangle ______ cm^2

   b. the square ______ cm^2

   c. the parallelogram ______ cm^2

4. a. What is the perimeter of the large square you made in Problem 1? ______ cm

   b. What is the area of that square? ______ cm^2

5. What is the area of the large triangle you made in Problem 2? ______ cm^2

Try This

6. Cut out the 5 shapes in the bottom half of *Math Masters,* page 263 and add them to the other shapes. Use at least 6 pieces each to make the following shapes.

   a. a square

   b. a rectangle

   c. a trapezoid

   d. any shape you choose

   Tape your favorite shape onto the back of this sheet. Next to the shape, write its perimeter and area.

Name Date Time

LESSON 8•7

Areas of Triangles

Cut out Triangles A and B. Tape them together at the shaded corners to form a parallelogram. Tape the parallelogram in the space next to Triangle A on page 240 in your journal.

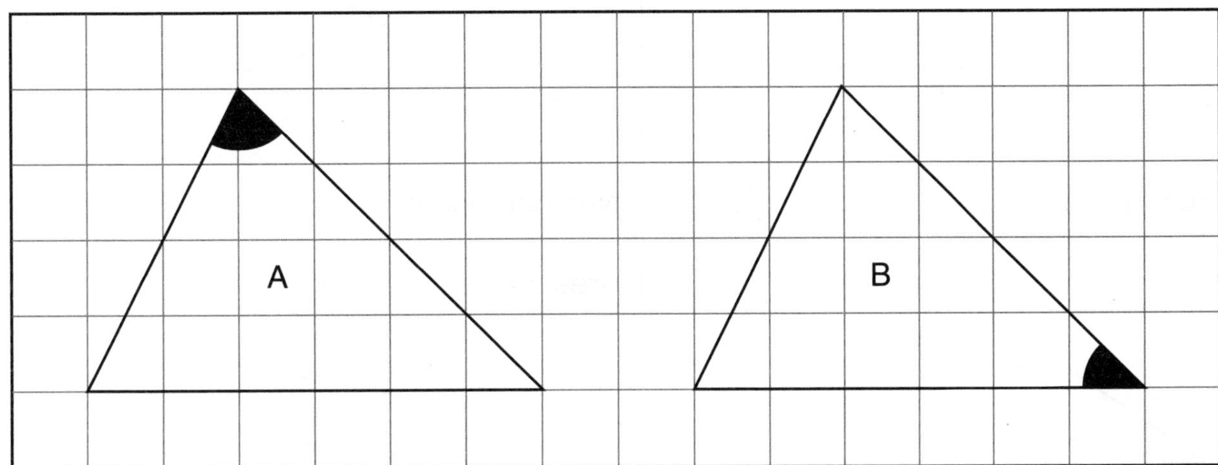

Do the same with the other 3 pairs of triangles.

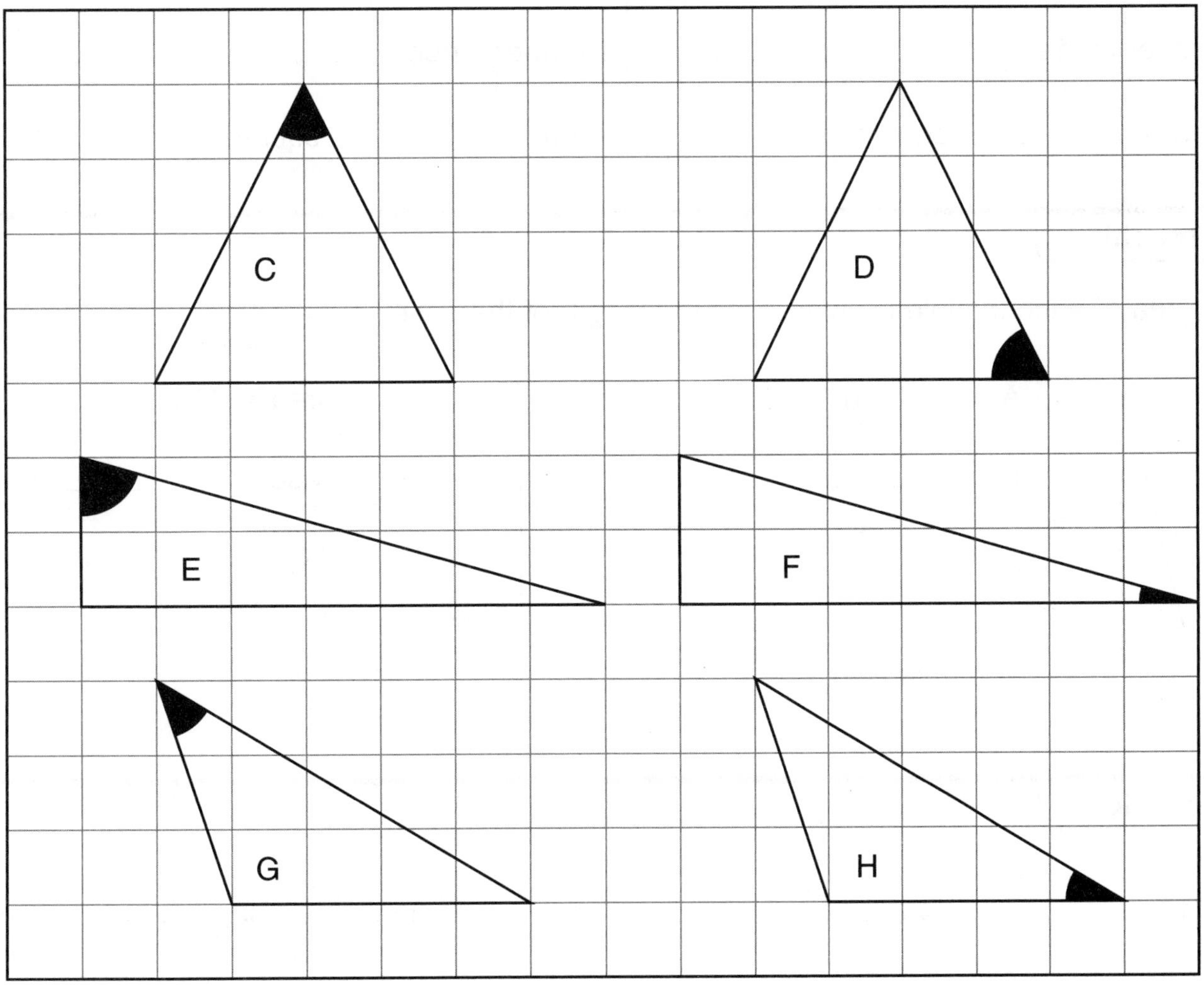

C

D

E

F

G

H

Name Date Time

STUDY LINK 8•7

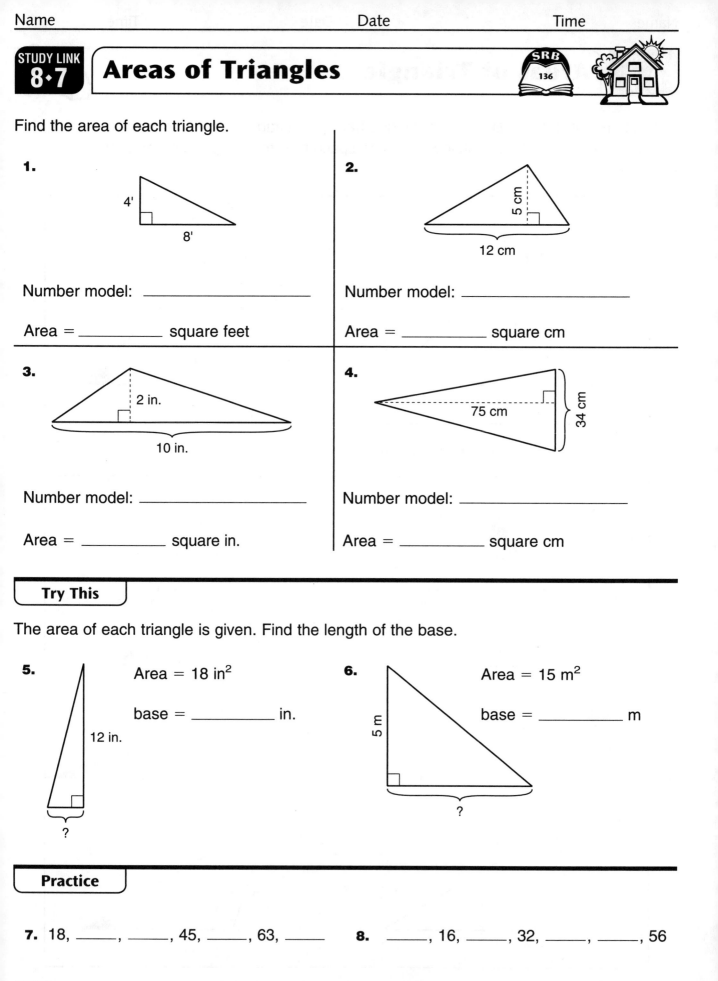

Areas of Triangles

Find the area of each triangle.

1.

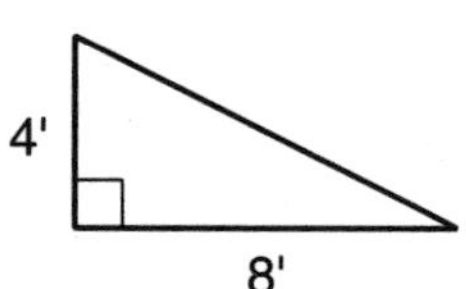

Number model: ____________________

Area = __________ square feet

2.

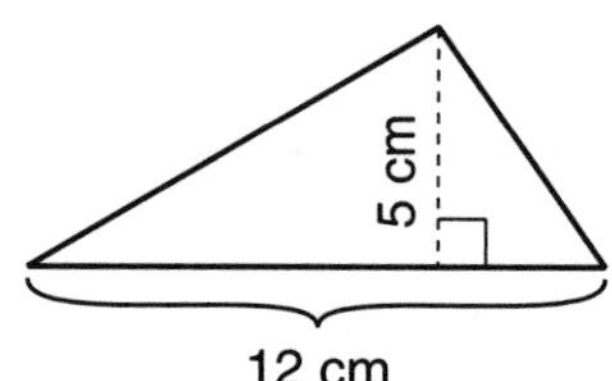

Number model: ____________________

Area = __________ square cm

3.

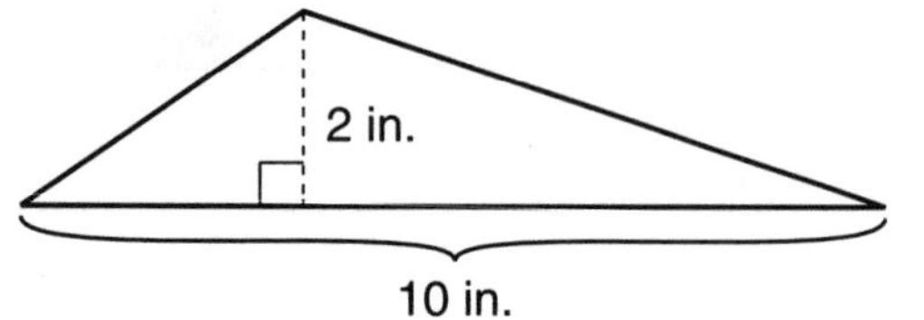

Number model: ____________________

Area = __________ square in.

4.

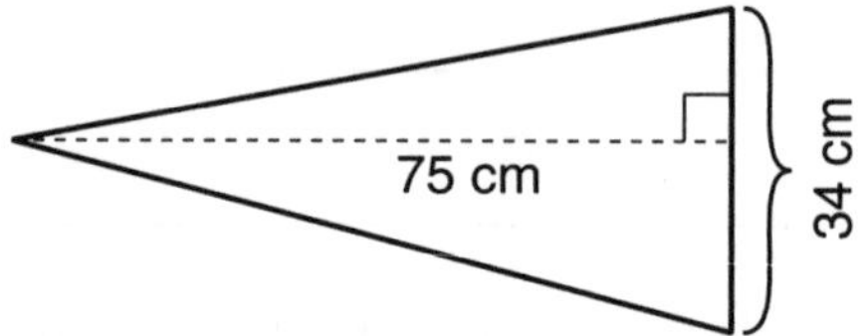

Number model: ____________________

Area = __________ square cm

Try This

The area of each triangle is given. Find the length of the base.

5.

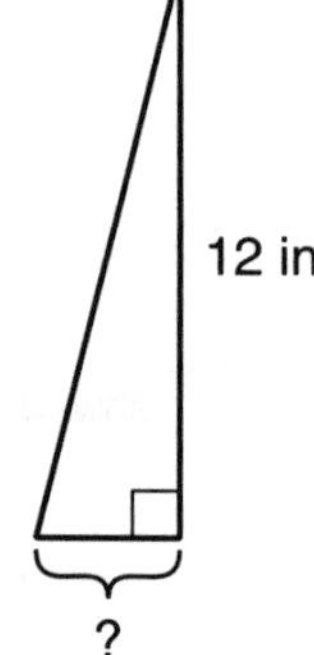

Area = 18 in^2

base = __________ in.

6.

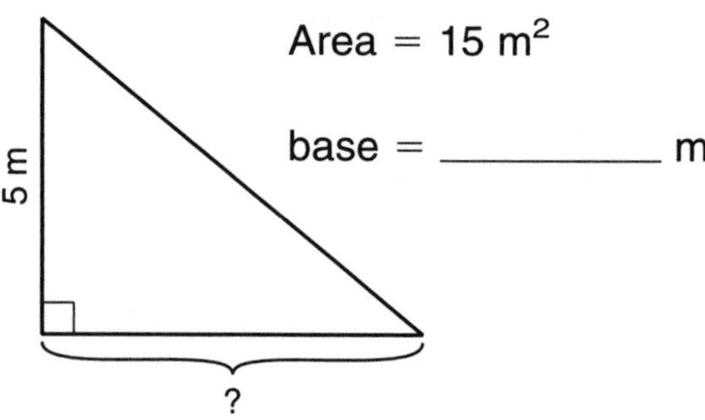

Area = 15 m^2

base = __________ m

Practice

7. 18, _____, _____, 45, _____, 63, _____

8. _____, 16, _____, 32, _____, _____, 56

Name Date Time

Comparing Areas

1. Cut out the hexagon below. Then cut out the large equilateral triangle. You should end up with one large triangle and three smaller triangles.

2. Use the large triangle and the three smaller triangles to form a rhombus.

   a. Sketch the rhombus in the space to the right.

   b. Is the area of the rhombus the same as the area of the hexagon? ________

   c. Is it possible for two different shapes to have the same area? ________

3. Put all the pieces back together to form a hexagon with an equilateral triangle inside.

   How can you show that the area of the hexagon is twice the area of the large triangle?

   ____

   ____

   ____

There are 4 triangles in the hexagon.

- The large triangle is called an **equilateral triangle.** All 3 sides are the same length.
- The smaller triangles are called **isosceles triangles.** Each of these triangles has 2 sides that are the same length.

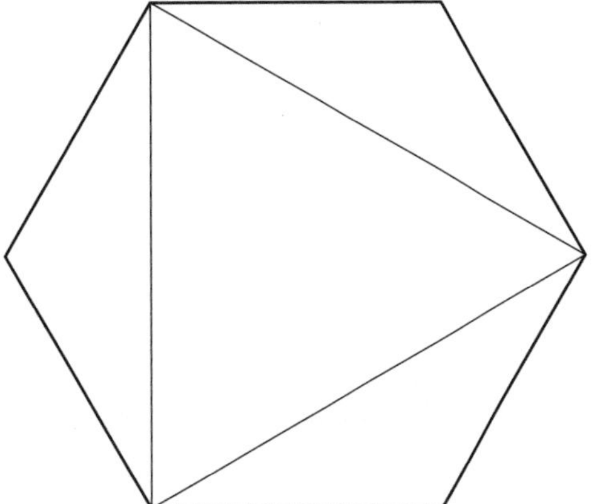

Name Date Time

Area and Perimeter

1. Find the area of the hexagon below *without* counting squares. *Hint:* Divide the hexagon into figures for which you can calculate the areas: rectangles, parallelograms, and triangles. Use a formula to find the area of each of the figures. Record your work.

Total area of hexagon = _______ cm^2

2. Find the perimeter of the hexagon. Use a centimeter ruler.

Perimeter = _______ cm

1 cm

Name Date Time

Turtle Weights

Turtle	Weight (pounds)
Pacific leatherback	1,552
Atlantic leatherback	1,018
Green sea	783
Loggerhead	568
Alligator snapping	220
Flatback sea	171
Hawksbill sea	138
Kemps Ridley	133
Olive Ridley	110
Common snapping	85

Source: The Top 10 of Everything 2004

1. The Atlantic leatherback is about 10 times heavier than the ______________ turtle.

2. The loggerhead is about __________ times the weight of the common snapping turtle.

3. Which turtle weighs about 3 times as much as the loggerhead? ______________

4. The flatback sea turtle and the alligator snapping turtle together weigh about half as much as the ______________ turtle.

5. About how many common snapping turtles would equal the weight of two alligator snapping turtles? __________

6. The Atlantic leatherback is about $\frac{\square}{\square}$ the weight of the Pacific leatherback.

Practice

Name the factors.

7. 50 ______________

8. 63 ______________

9. 90 ______________

Name Date Time

Compare Area

1. Cut out the shapes below and combine them with the shapes cut out by the other members of your group.

2. On a separate sheet of paper, use "times as many" and "fraction-of" language to compare the areas of different pairs of shapes.

Examples:

- The area of Shape B is about 4 times the area of Shape A.
- The area of Shape D is about $\frac{2}{3}$ the area of Shape C.

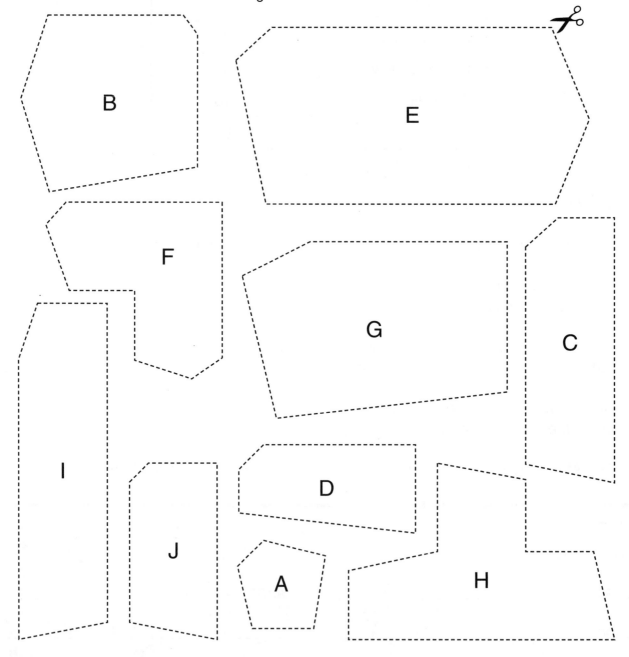

B

E

F

G

C

I

D

J

A

H

Name Date Time

Weight on Different Planets

Mercury has about $\frac{1}{3}$ the gravitational pull on your body mass as does Earth—about 0.37 to be more precise. You would weigh about $\frac{1}{3}$ as much on Mercury as you do on Earth.

The table below shows how much Rich, his brother Jean-Claude, and his sister Gayle would weigh on each planet.

1. Use your calculator to find each planet's gravitational pull relative to Earth's.

		Weight in Pounds			
Planet	**Gravitational Pull Relative to Earth's**	**Rich**	**Jean-Claude**	**Gayle**	**Me**
Earth	1	86	75	50	
Mercury	0.37	31.82	27.75	18.5	
Venus		77.4	67.5	45	
Mars		31.82	27.75	18.5	
Jupiter		202.1	176.25	117.5	
Saturn		78.26	68.25	45.5	
Uranus		75.68	66	44	
Neptune		96.32	84	56	
Pluto		5.16	4.5	3	

Source: NASA Kids, www.nasakids.com/Puzzles/Weight.asp

2. Explain the strategy you used to determine the gravitational pulls.

____

____

Try This

3. Use the information in the table to calculate your own weight on each planet and record it in the "Me" column in the table above.

Name Date Time

Similar Figures

Imagine that you used a copying machine to enlarge the original figures below and on *Math Masters,* page 273 to get **similar** figures. Find the perimeter of each original shape and of its enlargement.

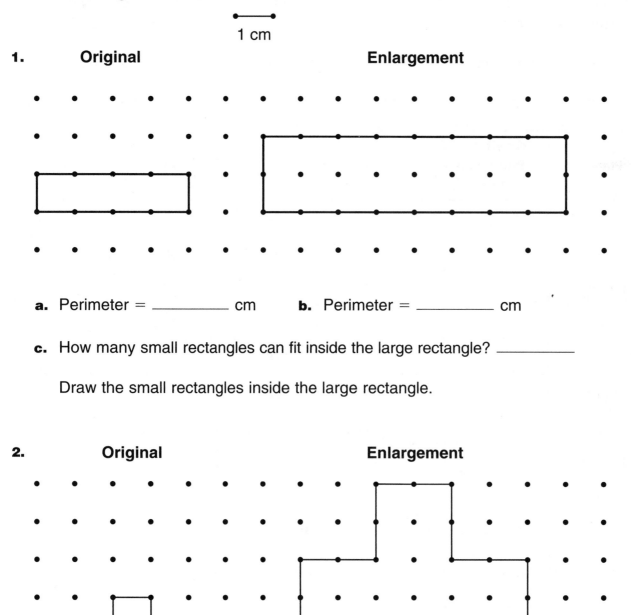

1.

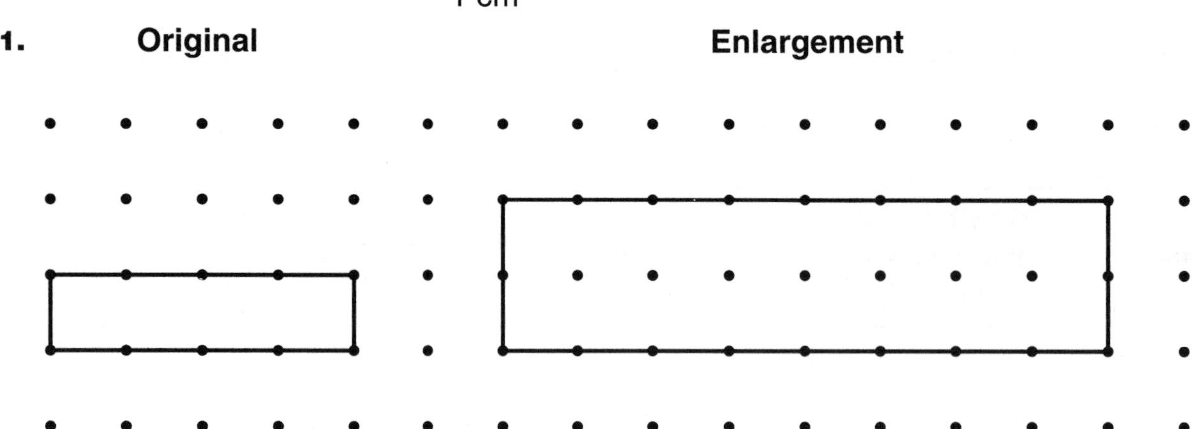

a. Perimeter = ________ cm **b.** Perimeter = ________ cm

c. How many small rectangles can fit inside the large rectangle? ________

Draw the small rectangles inside the large rectangle.

2.

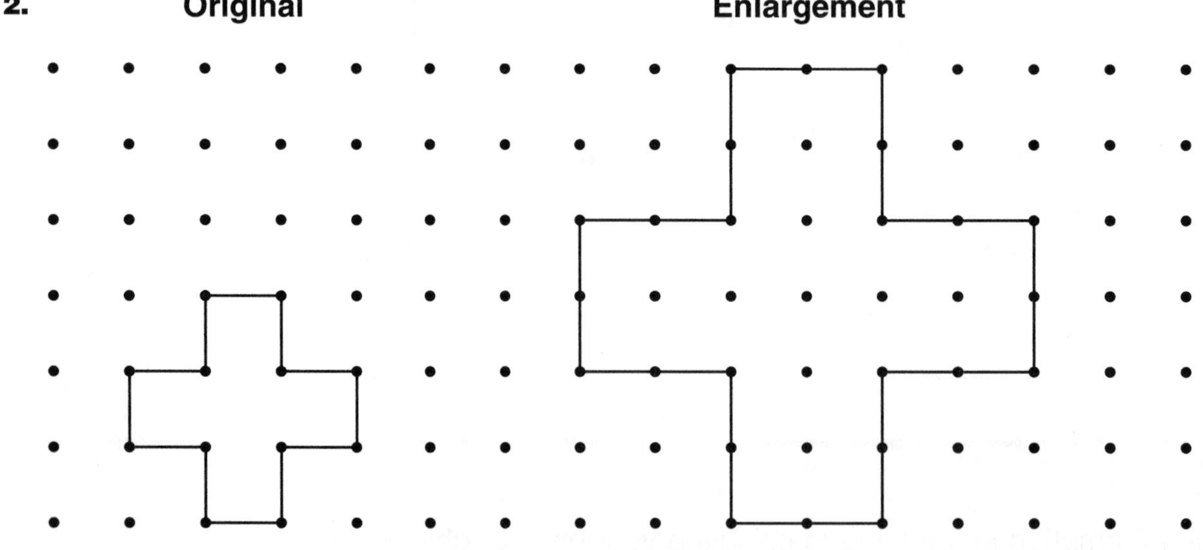

Perimeter = ________ cm Perimeter = ________ cm

Area = ________ cm^2 Area = ________ cm^2

Name Date Time

Similar Figures *continued*

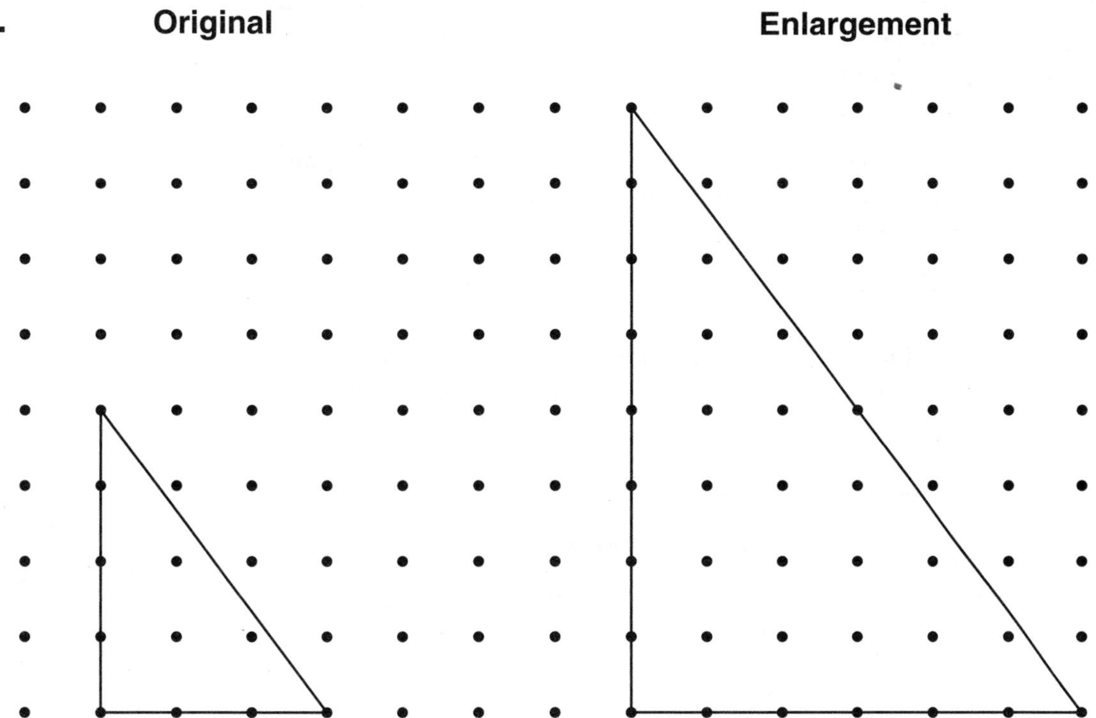

3. Use a centimeter ruler to measure the longest side of each triangle.

a. Perimeter of original = ________ cm

b. Perimeter of enlargement = ________ cm

c. How many small triangles can fit inside the large triangle? ________

d. Draw the small triangles inside the large triangle.

4. Complete the statements.

a. When you enlarge the sides of a shape to twice their original size, the perimeter of the enlargement is ________ times as large as the perimeter of the original shape.

b. When you enlarge the sides of a shape to twice their original size, the area of the enlargement is ________ times as large as the area of the original shape.

Name Date Time

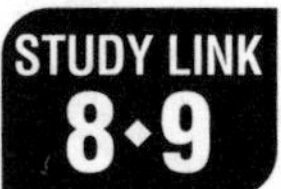

Unit 9: Family Letter

Fractions, Decimals, and Percents

In Unit 9, we will be studying percents and their uses in everyday situations. Your child should begin finding examples of percents in newspapers and magazines, on food packages, on clothing labels, and so on, and bring them to class. They will be used to illustrate a variety of percent applications.

As we study percents, your child will learn equivalent values for percents, fractions, and decimals. For example, 50% is equivalent to the fraction $\frac{1}{2}$ and to the decimal 0.5. The class will develop the understanding that **percent** always refers to a **part out of 100.**

Converting "easy" fractions, such as $\frac{1}{2}$, $\frac{1}{5}$, $\frac{1}{10}$, and $\frac{3}{4}$, to decimal and percent equivalents should become automatic for your child. Such fractions are common in percent situations and are helpful with more difficult fractions, decimals, and percents. To help memorize the "easy" fraction/percent equivalencies, your child will play *Fraction/Percent Concentration.*

"Easy" Fractions	Decimals	Percents
$\frac{1}{2}$	0.50	50%
$\frac{1}{4}$	0.25	25%
$\frac{3}{4}$	0.75	75%
$\frac{2}{5}$	0.40	40%
$\frac{7}{10}$	0.70	70%
$\frac{2}{2}$	1.00	100%

Throughout the unit, your child will use a calculator to convert fractions to percents and will learn how to use the percent key (%) to calculate discounts, sale prices, and percents of discount.

As part of the World Tour, your child will explore population data, such as literacy rates and percents of people who live in rural and urban areas.

Finally, the class will begin to apply the multiplication and division algorithms to problems that contain decimals. The approach used in *Everyday Mathematics* is straightforward: Students solve the problems as if the numbers were whole numbers. Then they estimate the answers to help them locate the decimal point in the exact answer. In this unit, we begin with fairly simple problems. Your child will solve more difficult problems in *Fifth* and *Sixth Grade Everyday Mathematics.*

Please keep this Family Letter for reference as your child works through Unit 9.

Vocabulary

Important terms in Unit 9:

discount The amount by which the regular price of an item is reduced in a sale, usually given as a fraction or percent of the original price, or as a "percent off."

illiterate An illiterate person cannot read or write.

life expectancy The average number of years a person may be expected to live.

literate A literate person can read and write.

100% box The entire object, the entire collection of objects, or the entire quantity being considered.

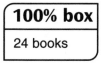

100% box
24 books

percent (%) Per hundred or out of a hundred. For example, "48% of the students in the school are boys" means that, on average, 48 out of 100 students in the school are boys; $48\% = \frac{48}{100} = 0.48$

percent of literacy The percent of the total population that is literate; the number of people out of 100 who are able to read and write. For example, 92% of the population in Mexico is literate—this means that, on average, 92 out of 100 people can read and write.

percent or fraction discount The percent or fraction of the regular price that you save in a "percent off" sale. See example under *regular price.*

rank To put in order by size; to sort from smallest to largest or vice versa.

Countries Ranked from Smallest to Largest Percent of Population, Rural

1	Australia	8%
2	Japan	21%
3	Russia	27%
4	Iran	33%
5	Turkey	34%
6	China	61%
7	Thailand	68%
8	India	72%
9	Vietnam	74%
10	Bangladesh	76%

regular price or list price The price of an item without a discount.

Regular Price	Sale!	Sale Price	You Saved
\$19.95	25% OFF	\$14.96	\$4.99

rural In the country

sale price The amount you pay after subtracting the discount from the regular price. See example under *regular price.*

urban In the city

Do-Anytime Activities

To work with your child on the concepts taught in this unit, try these interesting and rewarding activities:

1. Help your child compile a percent portfolio that includes examples of the many ways percents are used in everyday life.
2. Encourage your child to incorporate such terms as "whole," "halves," "thirds," and "fourths" into his or her everyday vocabulary.
3. Practice renaming fractions as percents, and vice versa, in everyday situations. For example, when preparing a meal, quiz your child on what percent $\frac{3}{4}$ of a cup would be.
4. Look through advertisements of sales and discounts. If the original price of an item and the percent of discount are given, have your child calculate the amount of discount and the sale price. If the original price and sale price are given, have your child calculate the amount and percent of discount.

Building Skills through Games

In this unit, your child will play the following games:

Fraction Match See *Student Reference Book,* page 243.
This game is for 2 to 4 players and requires one deck of *Fraction Match* cards. The game develops skill in naming equivalent fractions.

Fraction/Percent Concentration See *Student Reference Book,* page 246.
Two or three players need 1 set of Fraction/Percent Tiles and a calculator to play this game. Playing *Fraction/Percent Concentration* helps students recognize fractions and percents that are equivalent.

Over and Up Squares See *Student Reference Book,* page 257.
This is a game for 2 players and will require a playing grid. The game helps students practice using ordered pairs of numbers to locate points on a rectangular grid.

Polygon Pair-Up See *Student Reference Book,* page 258.
This game provides practice in identifying properties of polygons. It requires a *Polygon Pair-Up* Property Deck and Polygon Deck.

Rugs and Fences See *Student Reference Book,* pages 260 and 261.
This is a game for 2 players and requires a *Rugs and Fences* Polygon Deck, Area and Perimeter Deck, and Record Sheet. The game helps students practice computing the area and perimeter of polygons.

As You Help Your Child with Homework

As your child brings assignments home, you may want to go over the instructions together, clarifying them as necessary. The answers listed below will guide you through this unit's Study Links.

Study Link 9•1

1. $\frac{90}{100}$; 90% **2.** $\frac{53}{100}$; 53% **3.** $\frac{4}{100}$; 4%
4. $\frac{60}{100}$; 0.60 **5.** $\frac{25}{100}$; 0.25 **6.** $\frac{7}{100}$; 0.07
7. 0.50; 50% **8.** 0.75; 75% **9.** 0.06; 6%

Study Link 9•2

1. 100; $\frac{1}{100}$; 0.01; 1% **2.** 20; $\frac{1}{20}$; 0.05; 5%
3. 10; $\frac{1}{10}$; 0.10; 10% **4.** 4; $\frac{1}{4}$; 0.25; 25%
5. 2; $\frac{1}{2}$; 0.50; 50% **6.** 0.75; 75%
7. 0.20; 20%

Study Link 9•3

1.

$\frac{1}{2}$	0	.	5					
$\frac{1}{3}$	0	.	3	3	3	3	3	3
$\frac{1}{4}$	0	.	2	5				
$\frac{1}{5}$	0	.	2					
$\frac{1}{6}$	0	.	1	6	6	6	6	6
$\frac{1}{7}$	0	.	1	4	2	8	5	7
$\frac{1}{8}$	0	.	1	2	5			
$\frac{1}{9}$	0	.	1	1	1	1	1	1
$\frac{1}{10}$	0	.	1					
$\frac{1}{11}$	0	.	0	9	0	9	0	9
$\frac{1}{12}$	0	.	0	8	3	3	3	3
$\frac{1}{13}$	0	.	0	7	6	9	2	3
$\frac{1}{14}$	0	.	0	7	1	4	2	8
$\frac{1}{15}$	0	.	0	6	6	6	6	6
$\frac{1}{16}$	0	.	0	6	2	5		
$\frac{1}{17}$	0	.	0	5	8	8	2	3
$\frac{1}{18}$	0	.	0	5	5	5	5	5
$\frac{1}{19}$	0	.	0	5	2	6	3	1
$\frac{1}{20}$	0	.	0	5				
$\frac{1}{21}$	0	.	0	4	7	6	1	9
$\frac{1}{22}$	0	.	0	4	5	4	5	4
$\frac{1}{23}$	0	.	0	4	3	4	7	8
$\frac{1}{24}$	0	.	0	4	1	6	6	6
$\frac{1}{25}$	0	.	0	4				

Study Link 9•4

1. 34% **2.** 67% **3.** 84% **4.** 52%
5. 85% **6.** 20% **7.** 25% **8.** 30%
9. 62.5% **10.** 70% **11.** 15% **12.** 37.5%

13. Sample answer: I divided the numerator by the denominator and then multiplied by 100.

14. 86% **15.** 3% **16.** 14% **17.** 83.5%

Study Link 9•5

1. 7%; 7%; 7%; 8%; 10%; 11%; 10%; 10%; 9%; 8%; 7%

3. Sample answer: I divided the number of marriages for each month by the total number of marriages, then multiplied by 100 and rounded to the nearest whole number.

Study Link 9•6

1. The varsity team. They won $\frac{8}{10}$ or 80% of their games. The junior varsity team only won $\frac{6}{8}$ or 75% of their games.

2. 2: 11; $\frac{5}{11}$; 45% 3: 3; $\frac{3}{3}$; 100%
4: 11; $\frac{9}{11}$; 82% 5: 7; $\frac{4}{7}$; 57%
6: 16; $\frac{11}{16}$; 69% 7: 10; $\frac{6}{10}$; 60%
8: 2; $\frac{1}{2}$; 50%

Study Link 9•7

1. 50% **2.** Tuvalu **3.** 5%

4. Dominica; Antigua and Barbuda; and Palau

5. 300%

Study Link 9•8

1. 25.8 **2.** 489.6 **3.** 45.12 **4.** 112.64

7. Sample answer: I estimated that the answer should be about 5 ∗ 20 = 100.

8. 212.4 **9.** 38.64 **10.** 382.13

Study Link 9•9

1. 14.8 **2.** 0.2700 **3.** 24.96 **4.** 0.860
5. 23.4 **6.** 58.32

7. Sample answer: I estimated that the answer should be about $\frac{100}{4} = 25$.

8. 4.2 **9.** 38.7 **10.** 0.65

Name Date Time

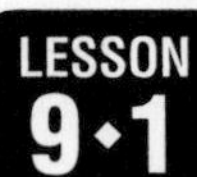

Playing *Fraction Match*

1. Katrina is playing *Fraction Match.* The target card is $\frac{3}{4}$. She has the following cards in her hand. Circle the card she may play.

$\frac{1}{2}$	$\frac{2}{3}$	$\frac{4}{5}$	$\frac{6}{8}$	$\frac{3}{9}$

2. Suppose she had a WILD card in her hand. Write a different fraction, equivalent to $\frac{3}{4}$, that she could name. ______

WILD WILD
WILD
Name an equivalent fraction with a denominator of 2, 3, 4, 5, 6, 8, 9, 10, or 12.

3. Imagine that a WILD card allowed Katrina to name *any* fraction equivalent to $\frac{3}{4}$. Write two fractions that she could name.

______ ______

Name Date Time

Playing *Fraction Match*

1. Katrina is playing *Fraction Match.* The target card is $\frac{3}{4}$. She has the following cards in her hand. Circle the card she may play.

$\frac{1}{2}$	$\frac{2}{3}$	$\frac{4}{5}$	$\frac{6}{8}$	$\frac{3}{9}$

2. Suppose she had a WILD card in her hand. Write a different fraction, equivalent to $\frac{3}{4}$, that she could name. ______

WILD WILD
WILD
Name an equivalent fraction with a denominator of 2, 3, 4, 5, 6, 8, 9, 10, or 12.

3. Imagine that a WILD card allowed Katrina to name *any* fraction equivalent to $\frac{3}{4}$. Write two fractions that she could name.

______ ______

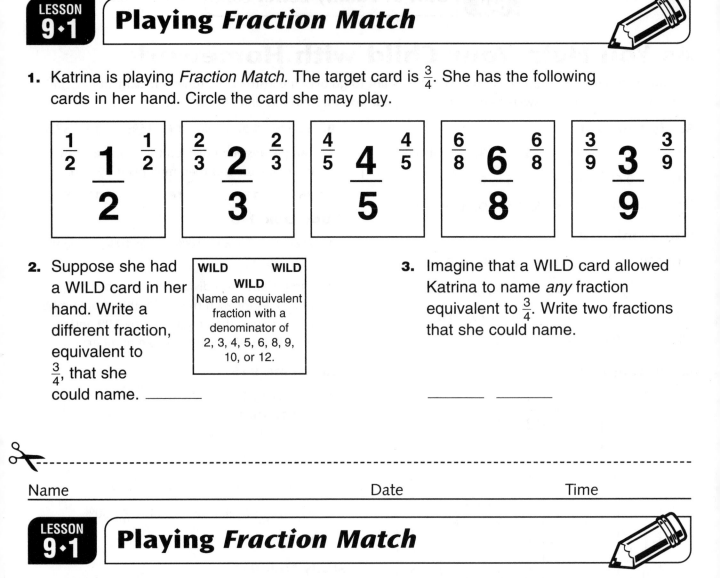

Name Date Time

STUDY LINK 9•1

Fractions, Decimals, and Percents

SRB 61 62

Rename each decimal as a fraction and a percent.

1. $0.90 = \frac{\square}{100} = $ ____% **2.** $0.53 = \frac{\square}{100} = $ ____% **3.** $0.04 = \frac{\square}{100} = $ ____%

Rename each percent as a fraction and a decimal.

4. $60\% = \frac{\square}{100} = $ __.____ **5.** $25\% = \frac{\square}{100} = $ __.____ **6.** $7\% = \frac{\square}{100} = $ __.____

Rename each fraction as a decimal and a percent.

7. $\frac{50}{100} = $ __.____ = ____% **8.** $\frac{75}{100} = $ __.____ = ____% **9.** $\frac{6}{100} = $ __.____ = __%

10. Shade more than $\frac{10}{100}$ and less than $\frac{30}{100}$ of the grid.
Write the value of the shaded part as a decimal and a percent.

Decimal: ________

Percent: ________

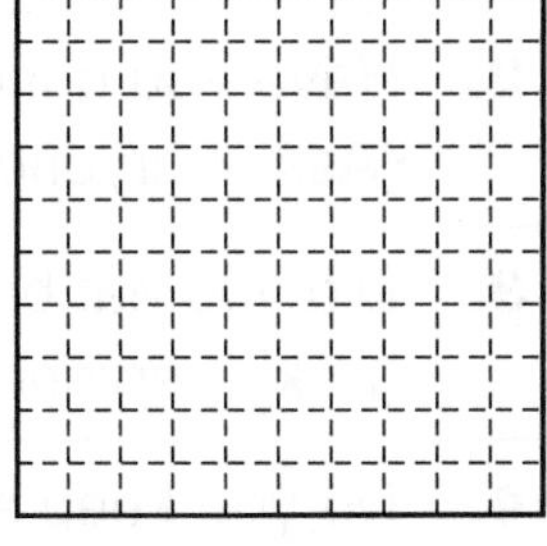

11. Shade more than 25% and less than 60% of the grid.
Write the value of the shaded part as a decimal and a percent.

Decimal: ________

Percent: ________

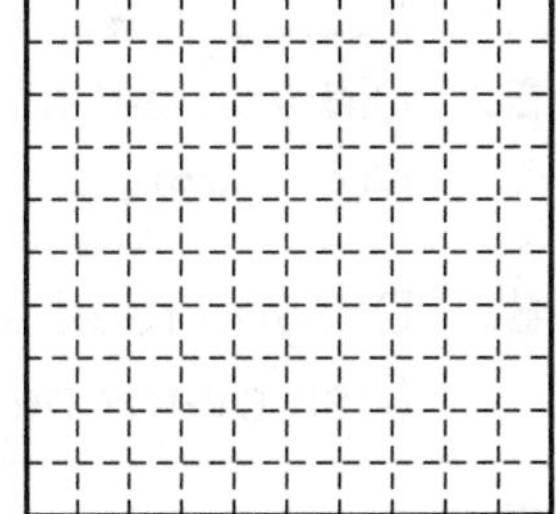

12. Shade more than 0.65 and less than 0.85 of the grid.
Write the value of the shaded part as a decimal and a percent.

Decimal: ________

Percent: ________

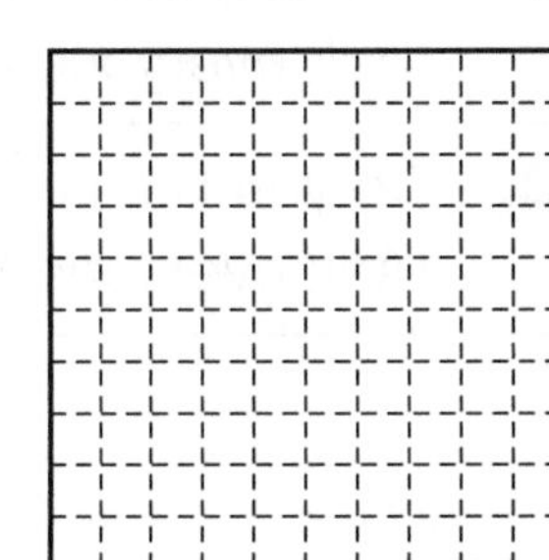

Practice

Order the fractions from smallest to largest.

13. $\frac{3}{6}, \frac{3}{3}, \frac{3}{5}, \frac{3}{7}$ ____________________

14. $\frac{2}{3}, \frac{6}{7}, \frac{1}{2}, \frac{19}{20}$ ____________________

Name Date Time

Trivia Survey

Conduct the survey below. The results will be used in Lesson 9-6.

Find at least five people to answer the following survey questions. You can ask family members, relatives, neighbors, and friends.

BE CAREFUL! You will not ask every person every question. Pay attention to the instructions that go with each question.

Record each answer with a tally mark in the Yes or No column.

Question	Yes	No
1. Is Monday your favorite day? (Ask everyone younger than 20.)		
2. Have you gone to the movies in the last month? (Ask everyone older than 8.)		
3. Did you eat breakfast today? (Ask everyone over 25.)		
4. Do you keep a map in your car? (Ask everyone who owns a car.)		
5. Did you eat at a fast-food restaurant yesterday? (Ask everyone.)		
6. Did you read a book during the last month? (Ask everyone over 20.)		
7. Are you more than 1 meter tall? (Ask everyone over 20.)		
8. Do you like liver? (Ask everyone.)		

Name Date Time

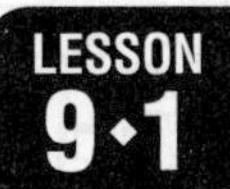

50% of a Square

Benito and Silvia each shaded 50% of a grid.

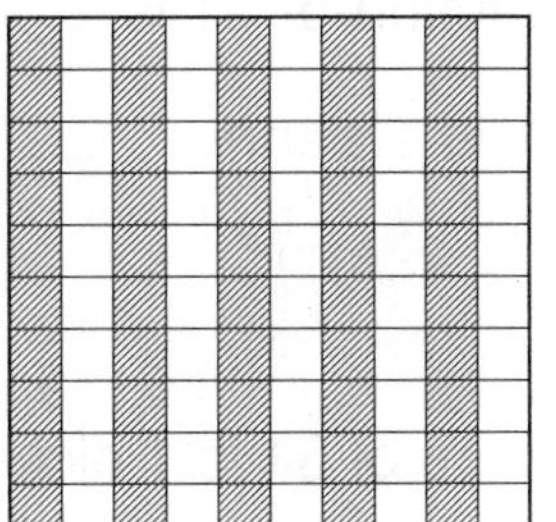

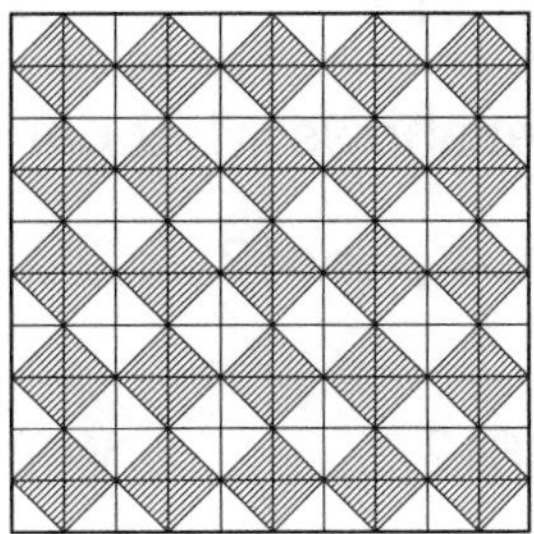

1. Do you think they shaded the grids correctly? Explain your reasoning.

____

____

2. Shade 50% of the grids below in different ways. Explain how you know you have shaded 50%.

a. 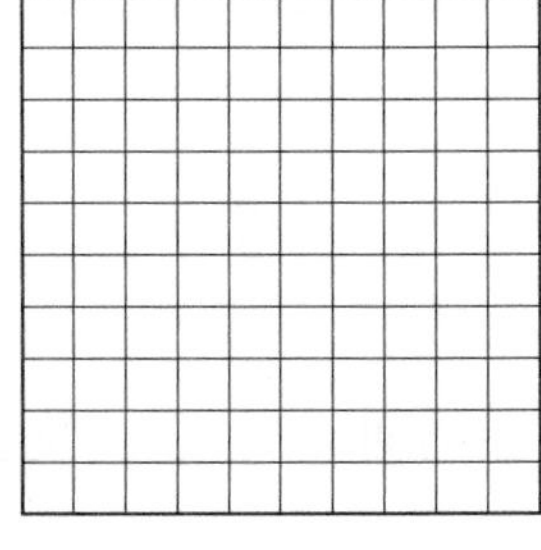

b. 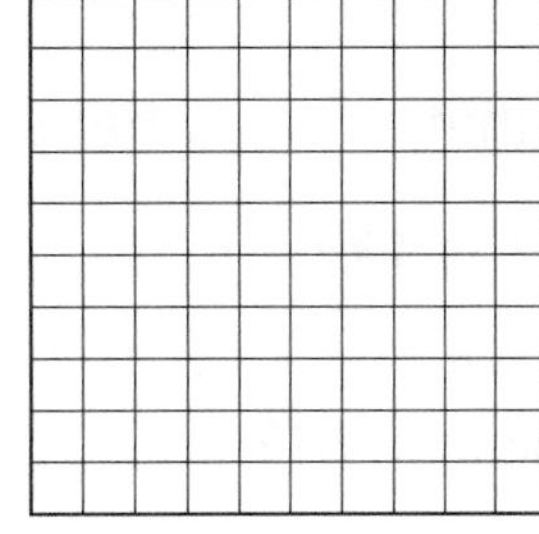

____

____

____

____

Try This

3. Shade 50% of the grid. Explain how you know you have shaded 50%.

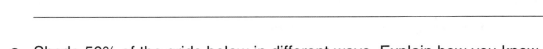

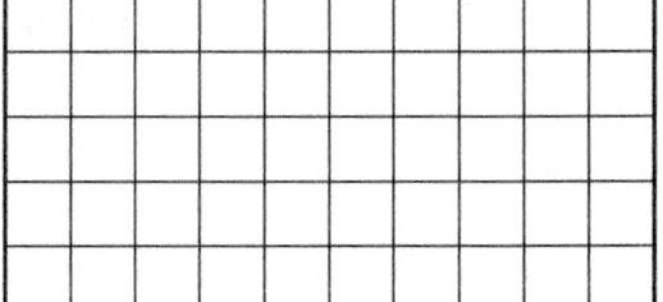

____

____

Name Date Time

STUDY LINK 9•2

Coins as Percents of $1

1. How many pennies in $1? ________ What fraction of $1 is 1 penny? ______________

   Write the decimal that shows what part of $1 is 1 penny. ________

   What percent of $1 is 1 penny? ________%

2. How many nickels in $1? ________ What fraction of $1 is 1 nickel? ______________

   Write the decimal that shows what part of $1 is 1 nickel. ________

   What percent of $1 is 1 nickel? ________%

3. How many dimes in $1? ________ What fraction of $1 is 1 dime? ______________

   Write the decimal that shows what part of $1 is 1 dime. ________

   What percent of $1 is 1 dime? ________%

4. How many quarters in $1? ________ What fraction of $1 is 1 quarter? ______________

   Write the decimal that shows what part of $1 is 1 quarter. ________

   What percent of $1 is 1 quarter? ________%

5. How many half-dollars in $1? ________ What fraction of $1 is 1 half-dollar? ______________

   Write the decimal that shows what part of $1 is 1 half-dollar. ________

   What percent of $1 is 1 half-dollar? ________%

6. Three quarters (75¢) is $\frac{3}{4}$ of $1.

   Write the decimal. ________

   What percent of $1 is

   3 quarters? ________%

7. Two dimes (20¢) is $\frac{2}{10}$ of $1.

   Write the decimal. ________

   What percent of $1 is

   2 dimes? ________%

Practice

8. ____________ = 748 ∗ 6

9. 51 ∗ 90 = ____________

10. ____________ = 28 ∗ 903

Name Date Time

LESSON 9•2

Percent Patterns

Complete each set of statements. Use grids or base-10 blocks, or draw pictures to help you. Look for patterns in your answers.

Example:

50% is the same as 50 per 100.

If there are 50 per 100, then there are

5 per 10. 500 per 1,000.

10 per 20. 100 per 200.

1. 20% is the same as 20 per 100.

If there are 20 per 100, then there are

_____ per 10. _____ per 1,000.

_____ per 20. _____ per 200.

2. 30% is the same as 30 per 100.

If there are 30 per 100, then there are

_____ per 10. _____ per 1,000.

_____ per 20. _____ per 200.

3. 80% is the same as 80 per 100.

If there are 80 per 100, then there are

_____ per 10. _____ per 1,000.

_____ per 20. _____ per 200.

4. 60% is the same as 60 per 100.

If there are 60 per 100, then there are

_____ per 10. _____ per 1,000.

_____ per 20. _____ per 200.

Try This

5. 75% is the same as 75 per 100.

If there are 75 per 100, then there are

_____ per 10. _____ per 1,000.

_____ per 20. _____ per 200.

6. 120% is the same as 120 per 100.

If there are 120 per 100, then there are

_____ per 10. _____ per 1,000.

_____ per 20. _____ per 200.

Name Date Time

Calculator Decimals

1. Use your calculator to rename each fraction below as a decimal.

$\frac{1}{2}$	0	.	5					
$\frac{1}{3}$	0	.	3	3	3	3	3	3
$\frac{1}{4}$								
$\frac{1}{5}$								
$\frac{1}{6}$								
$\frac{1}{7}$								
$\frac{1}{8}$								
$\frac{1}{9}$								
$\frac{1}{10}$								
$\frac{1}{11}$								
$\frac{1}{12}$								
$\frac{1}{13}$								

$\frac{1}{14}$								
$\frac{1}{15}$								
$\frac{1}{16}$								
$\frac{1}{17}$								
$\frac{1}{18}$								
$\frac{1}{19}$								
$\frac{1}{20}$								
$\frac{1}{21}$								
$\frac{1}{22}$								
$\frac{1}{23}$								
$\frac{1}{24}$								
$\frac{1}{25}$								

2. Make up some of your own.

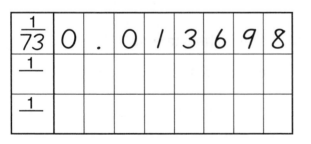

$\frac{1}{73}$	0	.	0	1	3	6	9	8
$\frac{1}{\_\_}$								
$\frac{1}{\_\_}$								

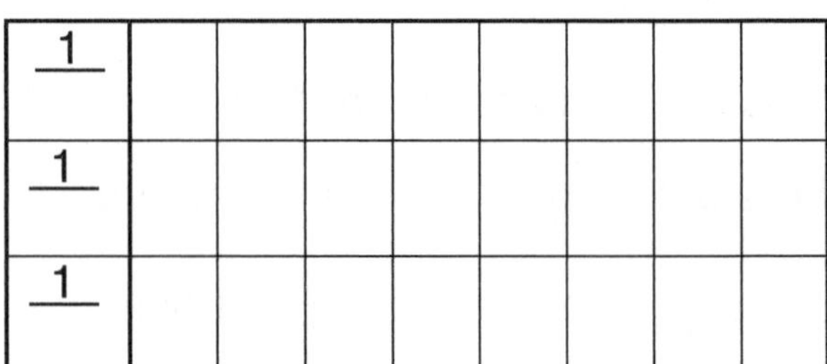

$\frac{1}{\_\_}$								
$\frac{1}{\_\_}$								
$\frac{1}{\_\_}$								

Practice

3. $6\overline{)96}$ = _______

4. 91 / 5 = _______

5. _______ = 864 ÷ 8

6. 575 ÷ 7 = _______

Name Date Time

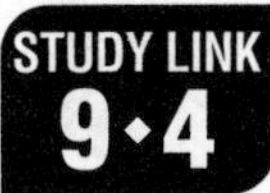

Fractions and Decimals to Percents

Do NOT use a calculator to convert these fractions to percents.
On the back of this page, show your work for Problems 3–6.

1. $\frac{34}{100}$ = ________%

2. $\frac{67}{100}$ = ________%

3. $\frac{42}{50}$ = ________%

4. $\frac{13}{25}$ = ________%

5. $\frac{17}{20}$ = ________%

6. $\frac{25}{125}$ = ________%

Use a calculator to convert these fractions to percents.

7. $\frac{23}{92}$ = ________%

8. $\frac{12}{40}$ = ________%

9. $\frac{20}{32}$ = ________%

10. $\frac{49}{70}$ = ________%

11. $\frac{60}{400}$ = ________%

12. $\frac{21}{56}$ = ________%

13. Describe how you used your calculator to convert the fractions in Problems 7–12 to percents.

____

____

____

Do NOT use a calculator to convert these decimals to percents.

14. 0.86 = ________%

15. 0.03 = ________%

16. 0.140 = ________%

17. 0.835 = ________%

Practice

Order the fractions from smallest to largest.

18. $\frac{7}{16}, \frac{7}{8}, \frac{7}{12}, \frac{7}{9}$ ______________________

19. $\frac{7}{15}, \frac{3}{15}, \frac{8}{15}, \frac{4}{15}$ ______________________

20. $\frac{5}{9}, \frac{15}{16}, \frac{1}{4}, \frac{9}{10}$ ______________________

Name Date Time

LESSON 9•4

"Percent-of" Problems

Use counters to solve the problems on this page.

1. If ○○○○○ ○○○○○ is 100%, draw 50%.

50% of 10 = _____

2. If ○○○○ ○○○○ ○○○○ ○○○○ is 100%, draw 25%.

25% of 16 = _____

3. If ○○○○○ ○○○○○ ○○○○○ ○○○○○ is 100%, draw 10%.

10% of 20 = _____

4. If ○○○ ○○○ is 50%, draw 100%.

50% of _____ = 6

5. If ○○○ ○○○ ○○○ is 75%, draw 100%.

75% of _____ = 9

6. If ○○○○ ○○○○ is 40%, draw 100%.

40% of _____ = 8

7. Pick one of the problems from above and explain how you got your answer.

Problem _____

_____

_____

_____

Name Date Time

LESSON 9•4

Discount Number Stories

1. A store is having a sale on gym shoes.

   - The regular price of the High Flyers is $50. Now they are on sale for $38.
   - The Zingers are $15 off the regular price. When not on sale, the Zingers cost $75 a pair.

   Which pair has the greater "percent-of" discount? Explain your answer.

   ____

   ____

   ____

   ____

   ____

2. The same store is also having a sale on tennis rackets.

   - The regular price of the Smasher is $54.00. It is on sale for 25% off the regular price.
   - The regular price of the Fast Flight is $75.00. It is on sale for 20% off the regular price.

   For which tennis racket are you getting more money taken off the regular price? Explain your answer.

   ____

   ____

   ____

   ____

   ____

Name Date Time

Renaming Fractions as Percents

In 2001, there were about 2,317,000 marriages in the United States. The table below shows the approximate number of marriages each month.

1. Use a calculator to find the percent of the total number of marriages that occurred each month. Round the answers to the nearest whole-number percent.

Month	Approximate Number of Marriages	Approximate Percent of Total Marriages
January	147,000	6%
February	159,000	
March	166,000	
April	166,000	
May	189,000	
June	237,000	
July	244,000	
August	225,000	
September	224,000	
October	217,000	
November	191,000	
December	152,000	

Source: U.S. Department of Health and Human Services

2. According to the table, what is the most popular month for a wedding? ______________

What is the least popular month for a wedding? ______________

3. Describe how you used your calculator to find the percent for each month.

____

____

Practice

Name all the factors of each number.

4. 63 ______________________

5. 28 ______________________

Name Date Time

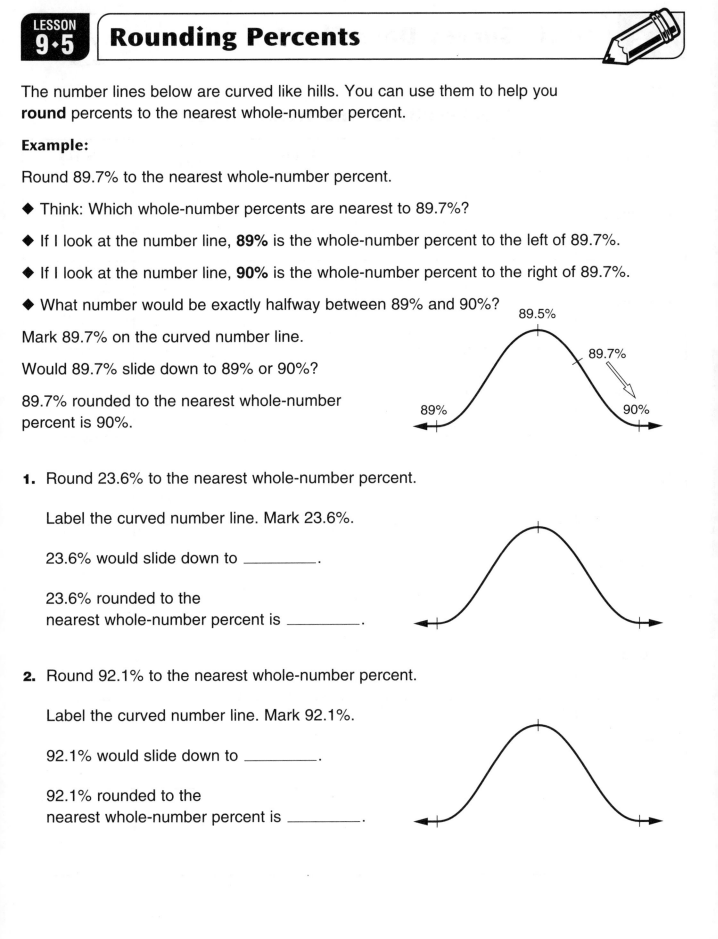

Rounding Percents

The number lines below are curved like hills. You can use them to help you **round** percents to the nearest whole-number percent.

Example:

Round 89.7% to the nearest whole-number percent.

- Think: Which whole-number percents are nearest to 89.7%?
- If I look at the number line, **89%** is the whole-number percent to the left of 89.7%.
- If I look at the number line, **90%** is the whole-number percent to the right of 89.7%.
- What number would be exactly halfway between 89% and 90%?

Mark 89.7% on the curved number line.

Would 89.7% slide down to 89% or 90%?

89.7% rounded to the nearest whole-number percent is 90%.

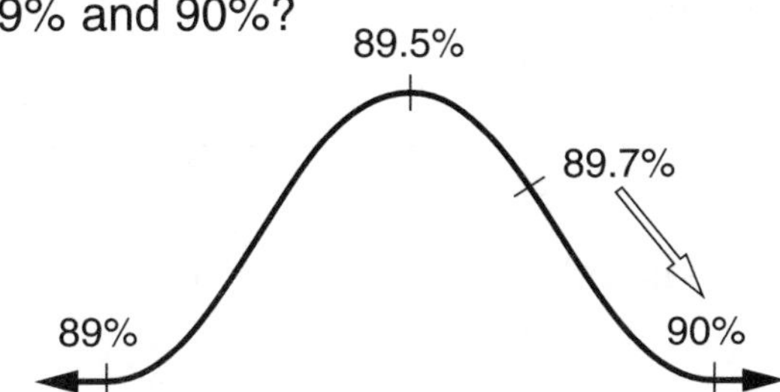

1. Round 23.6% to the nearest whole-number percent.

   Label the curved number line. Mark 23.6%.

   23.6% would slide down to ________.

   23.6% rounded to the nearest whole-number percent is ________.

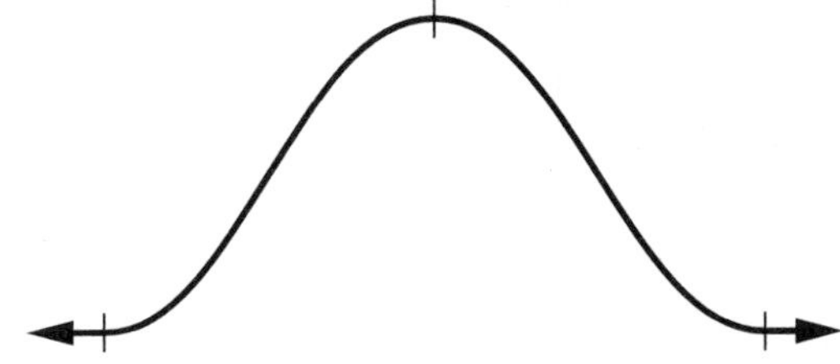

2. Round 92.1% to the nearest whole-number percent.

   Label the curved number line. Mark 92.1%.

   92.1% would slide down to ________.

   92.1% rounded to the nearest whole-number percent is ________.

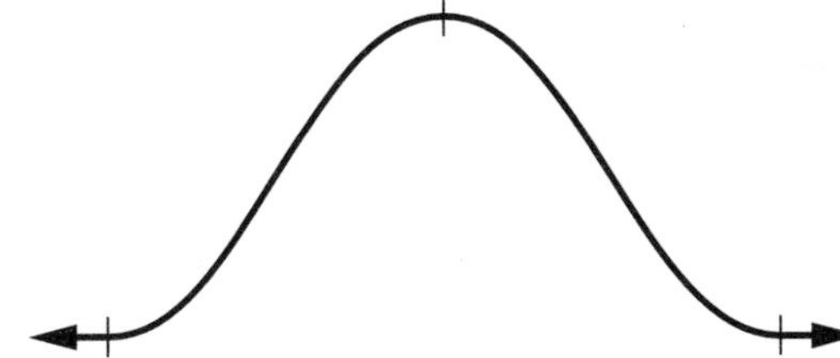

Name Date Time

Trivia Survey Data Chart

Class Results for the Trivia Survey

Question	Yes	No	Total	$\frac{\text{Yes}}{\text{Total}}$	% Yes
1. Monday					
2. movies					
3. breakfast					
4. map					
5. fast food					
6. read					
7. meter					
8. liver					

Name Date Time

Use Percents to Compare Fractions

1. The girls' varsity basketball team won 8 of the 10 games it played. The junior varsity team won 6 of 8 games. Which team has the better record? Explain your reasoning.

____

____

2. Complete the table of shots taken (not including free throws) during a game. Calculate the percent of shots made to the nearest whole percent.

Player	Shots Made	Shots Missed	Total Shots	$\frac{\text{Shots Made}}{\text{Total Shots}}$	% of Shots Made
1	5	12	17	$\frac{5}{17}$	29%
2	5	6			
3	3	0			
4	9	2			
5	4	3			
6	11	5			
7	6	4			
8	1	1			

3. The basketball game is tied. Your team has the ball. There is only enough time for one more shot. Based only on the information in the table, which player would you choose to take the shot? Why?

____

____

____

____

Practice

4. $\frac{1}{3} + \frac{1}{6} =$ ______

5. ______ $= \frac{3}{4} - \frac{1}{2}$

6. ______ $= \frac{7}{10} + \frac{1}{5}$

7. $\frac{5}{8} - \frac{1}{4} =$ ______

Name Date Time

"Fraction-of" a Collection

Part One

1. Estimate the total number of pattern blocks in the jar given to you by your teacher. ________ pattern blocks

2. Estimate the total number of red trapezoids in the jar.

   ________ red trapezoids

3. Write your estimates as a fraction.

   $\frac{\text{total number of red trapezoids}}{\text{total number of pattern blocks}} = \frac{\square}{\square}$

4. Record the estimates made by the members of your group.

   ________ ________ ________ ________

Part Two

5. Count the number of pattern blocks in the jar. ________ pattern blocks

6. Count the number of red trapezoids in the jar. ________ red trapezoids

7. Record the counts as a fraction.

   $\frac{\text{total number of red trapezoids}}{\text{total number of pattern blocks}} = \frac{\square}{\square}$

Part Three

8. Which of your group members' estimates do you think was closest to the actual fraction of trapezoids in the jar? ____________________

   Explain why you think so.

   ____

   ____

   ____

   ____

Name Date Time

Map of Region 4

SRB
301

Title: ______________________________

Russia
Turkey
Iran
China
Japan
India
Bangladesh
Vietnam
Thailand
Australia

Name Date Time

Least-Populated Countries

The table below shows the approximate population for the 10 least-populated countries in the world. Use the data to estimate answers to the problems.

Country	Population
Vatican City	900
Tuvalu	11,000
Nauru	13,000
Palau	20,000
San Marino	28,000
Monaco	32,000
Liechtenstein	33,000
St. Kitts and Nevis	39,000
Antigua and Barbuda	68,000
Dominica	69,000

Source: Top Ten of Everything 2004

1. The population of Liechtenstein is about _______% of the population of Dominica.
2. What country's population is about 33% of Liechtenstein's population? ____________
3. The population of Vatican City is about _______% of the population of Palau.
4. The population of the 10 countries listed is 314,900. What 3 country populations together equal about 50% of that total?

   ____
5. The population of St. Kitts and Nevis is about _______% of Nauru's population.

Practice

6. 27 ∗ 4 = ____________
7. ____________ = 508 ∗ 8
8. ____________ = 63 ∗ 86
9. 849 ∗ 52 = ____________

Name Date Time

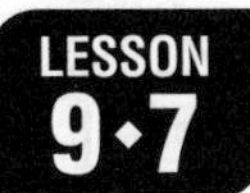

Color-Coded Map for Percent of Literacy

A **literate** person is a person who can read and write. People who cannot read and write are said to be **illiterate.**

Percent of literacy is the fraction of the total population that is literate—the number of people out of 100 who are literate. Young children are not counted until they reach an age at which they are expected to read and write.

1. Make a prediction: Do you think there is a relationship among population statistics on literacy, age, and rural or urban living? ____________

2. In the table below, list the countries in Region 4 from *greatest* to *least* according to the percent of the population that is literate. (See *Student Reference Book,* page 299.)

Rank	Country	Percent of Literacy	Color Code
1	Australia	100%	blue
2			blue
3			blue
4			green
5			green
6			green
7			green
8			red
9			red
10			red

3. Color these countries on the map on *Math Masters,* page 293 according to the color code in the table.

4. Compare this map with the population ages 0–14 and percent rural maps. Do the data support the prediction you made in Problem 1? ____________

   Explain your answer on the back of this page. Include reasons why you think a country might be colored red or blue on all three maps.

Name Date Time

STUDY LINK 9•8

Multiplying Decimals

For each problem below, the multiplication has been done correctly, but the decimal point is missing in the answer. Correctly place the decimal point in the answer.

1. 6 * 4.3 = 2 5 8

2. 72 * 6.8 = 4 8 9 6

3. 0.96 * 47 = 4 5 1 2

4. 5.12 * 22 = 1 1 2 6 4

5. 8,457 * 9.8 = 8 2 8 7 8 6

6. 0.04 * 140 = 5 6

7. Explain how you decided where to place the decimal point in Problem 4.

____

____

____

Try This

Multiply. Show your work.

8. 5.9 * 36 = ________	**9.** 0.46 * 84 = ________	**10.** ________ = 7.21 * 53

Practice

11. ________ = 96 ÷ 6

12. $4\overline{)67}$ = ________

13. ________ = 411 / 3

14. $9\overline{)903}$ = ________

Name Date Time

Multiplying Whole Numbers

Write a number model to estimate each product. Then multiply with a paper-and-pencil algorithm. Show your work.

1. 7 * 68 = ____________
Number model:
____

2. 534 * 6 = ____________
Number model:
____

3. ____________ = 58 * 67
Number model:
____

4. 33 * 275 = ____________
Number model:
____

Try This

5. Margo's favorite socks are on sale for $2.89 per pair.
She has $25. Can she buy 6 pairs? ____________

Explain how to solve this problem without using a paper-and-pencil algorithm.

____

____

____

Name Date Time

STUDY LINK 9·9

Dividing Decimals

For each problem below, the division has been done correctly, but the decimal point is missing in the answer. Correctly place the decimal point in the answer.

1. 88.8 / 6 = 1 4 8
2. 1.35 / 5 = 2 7 0 0
3. 99.84 / 4 = 2 4 9 6
4. 2.58 / 3 = 8 6 0
5. 163.8 / 7 = 2 3 4
6. 233.28 / 4 = 5 8 3 2
7. Explain how you decided where to place the decimal point in Problem 3.

____

____

____

Try This

Divide. Show your work.

8. $6\overline{)25.2}$	9. $4\overline{)154.8}$	10. $9\overline{)5.85}$
Answer: ________	Answer: ________	Answer: ________

Practice

11. _____ $= \frac{5}{8} + \frac{2}{8}$
12. $\frac{5}{9} - \frac{1}{3} =$ _____
13. _____ $= \frac{7}{10} + \frac{2}{10}$
14. $\frac{9}{10} - \frac{1}{2} =$ _____

Name Date Time

LESSON 9·9

Dividing Whole Numbers

Write a number model to estimate each quotient. Then divide with a paper-and-pencil algorithm. Show your work.

1. 79 / 6 = ______________
Number model:
____

2. 92 / 3 = ______________
Number model:
____

3. ______________ = 573 / 4
Number model:
____

4. 945 / 18 = ______________
Number model:
____

Try This

5. The school has $357 to spend on new science books.
If the books cost $9 each, how many books can they buy? ________ books

Explain how to solve this problem without using a paper-and-pencil algorithm.

____

____

____

Name Date Time

Unit 10: Family Letter

Reflections and Symmetry

In this unit, your child will take another look at geometry, with an emphasis on symmetry. Many objects in nature are symmetrical: flowers, insects, and the human body, to name just a few. Symmetry is all around—in buildings, furniture, clothing, and paintings.

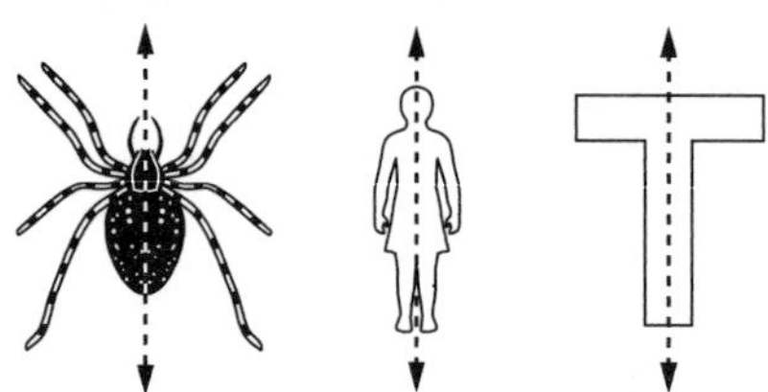

The class will focus on **reflectional symmetry,** also called **line symmetry** or **mirror symmetry,** in which half of a figure is the mirror image of the other half. Encourage your child to look for symmetrical objects, and if possible, to collect pictures of symmetrical objects from magazines and newspapers. For example, the right half of the printed letter T is the mirror image of the left half. If you have a small hand mirror, have your child check letters, numbers, and other objects to see whether they have line symmetry. The class will use a device called a **transparent mirror,** which is pictured below. Students will use it to see and trace the mirror image of an object.

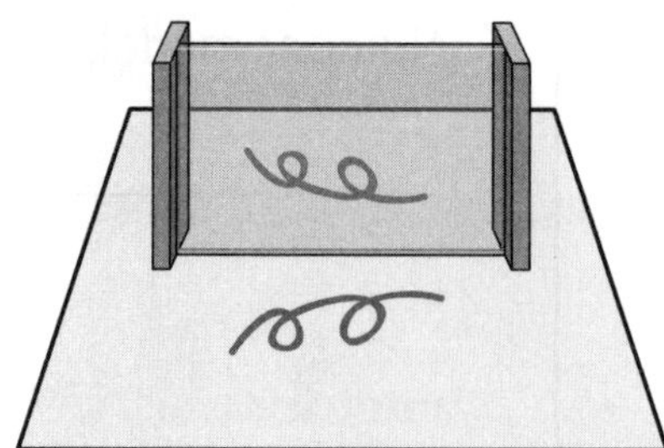

Geometry is not only the study of figures (such as lines, rectangles, and circles), but also the study of transformations or "motions" of figures. These motions include **reflections** (flips), **rotations** (turns), and **translations** (slides). Your child will use these motions to create pictures like the ones below, called **frieze patterns.**

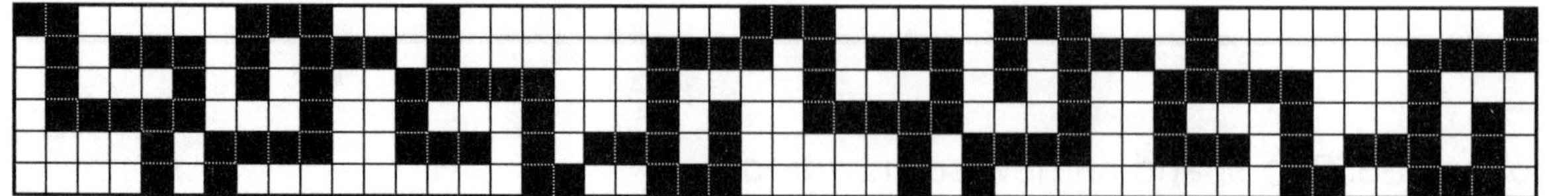

Students will also work with positive and negative numbers, looking at them as reflections of each other across zero on a number line. They will develop skills of adding positive and negative numbers by thinking in terms of credits and debits for a new company, and they will practice these skills in the *Credits/Debits Game.*

Please keep this Family Letter for reference as your child works through Unit 10.

Vocabulary

Important terms in Unit 10:

frieze pattern A geometric design in a long strip in which an element is repeated over and over. The element may be rotated, translated, and reflected. Frieze patterns are often found on the walls of buildings, on the borders of rugs and tiled floors, and on clothing.

image The reflection of an object that you see when you look in the mirror. Also a figure that is produced by a transformation (reflection, translation, or rotation) of another figure. See *preimage*.

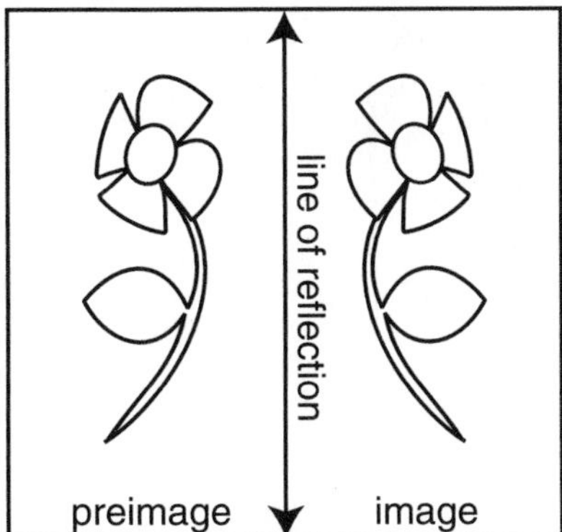

line of reflection A line halfway between a figure (preimage) and its reflected image. In a reflection, a figure is "flipped over" the line of reflection.

line of symmetry A line drawn through a figure that divides the figure into two parts that are mirror images of each other. The two parts look alike, but face in opposite directions.

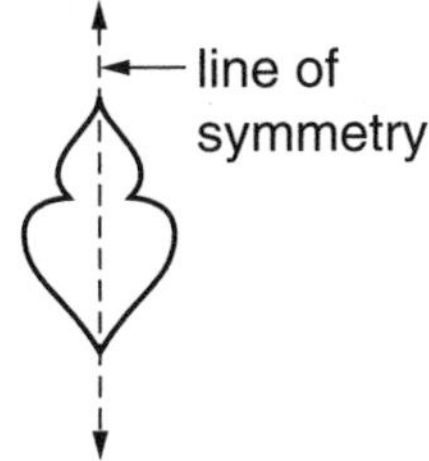

negative number A number that is less than zero; a number to the left of zero on a horizontal number line or below zero on a vertical number line. The symbol "−" may be used to write a negative number. For example, "negative 5" is usually written as −5.

preimage A geometric figure that is somehow changed (by a *reflection,* a *rotation,* or a *translation,* for example) to produce another figure. See *image.*

reflection (flip) The "flipping" of a figure over a line (the *line of reflection*) so that its image is the mirror image of the original (preimage).

reflection

rotation (turn) A movement of a figure around a fixed point, or axis; a "turn."

symmetric Having the same size and shape on either side of a line, or looking the same when turned by some amount less than 360°.

transformation Something done to a geometric figure that produces a new figure. The most common transformations are translations (slides), reflections (flips), and rotations (turns).

translation A movement of a figure along a straight line; a "slide." In a translation, each point of the figure slides the same distance in the same direction.

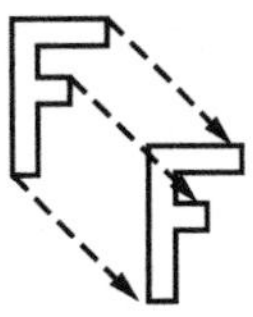

translation

Do-Anytime Activities

To work with your child on concepts taught in this unit, try these interesting and rewarding activities:

1. Have your child look for frieze patterns on buildings, rugs, floors, and clothing. If possible, have your child bring pictures to school or make sketches of friezes that he or she sees.
2. Encourage your child to study the mathematical qualities of the patterns of musical notes and rhythms. Composers of even the simplest of tunes use reflections and translations of notes and chords (groups of notes).
3. Encourage your child to incorporate transformation vocabulary—**symmetric, reflected, rotated,** and **translated**—into his or her everyday vocabulary.

Building Skills through Games

In this unit, your child will play the following games to develop his or her understanding of addition and subtraction of positive and negative numbers, practice estimating and measuring angles, practice plotting ordered pairs in the first quadrant of a coordinate grid, and identify properties of polygons. For detailed instructions, see the *Student Reference Book.*

Angle Tangle See *Student Reference Book,* page 230. Two players need a protactor, straightedge, and several sheets of blank paper to play this game. This game provides practice estimating and measuring angle sizes.

Credits/Debits Game See *Student Reference Book,* page 238. Playing the *Credits/Debits Game* offers students practice adding and subtracting positive and negative numbers.

Over and Up Squares See *Student Reference Book,* page 257. Two players need a gameboard and record sheet, 2 different-colored pencils, and 2 six-sided dice to play this game. Playing this game provides practice plotting ordered pairs and developing a winning game strategy.

Polygon Pair-Up See *Student Reference Book,* page 258. To play this game, two players need a deck of polygon cards, a deck of property cards, and paper and pencils for sketching. Playing this game provides students with practice identifying properties of polygons.

As You Help Your Child with Homework

As your child brings assignments home, you may want to go over the instructions together, clarifying them as necessary. The answers listed below will guide you through some of the Study Links in this unit.

Study Link 10•2

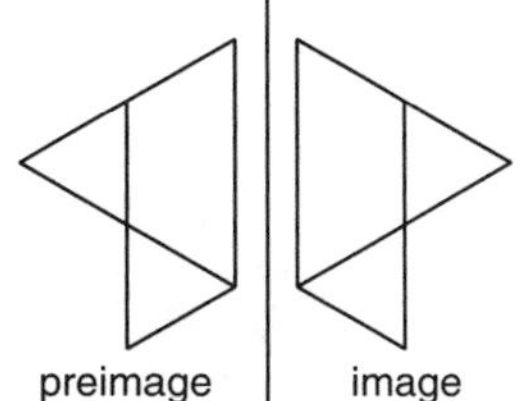

3.

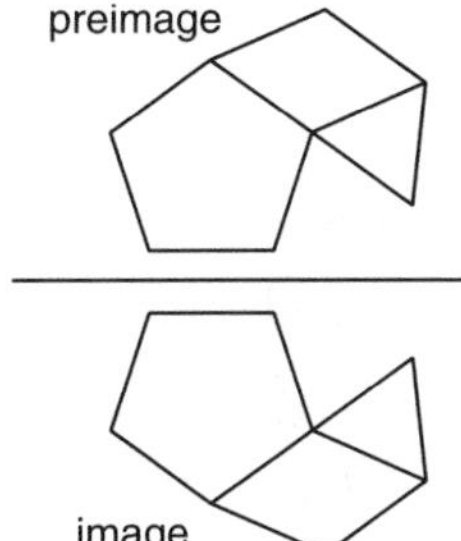

5.

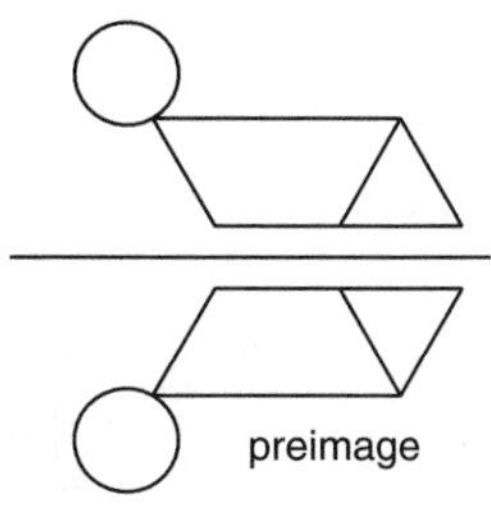

Study Link 10•3

1.

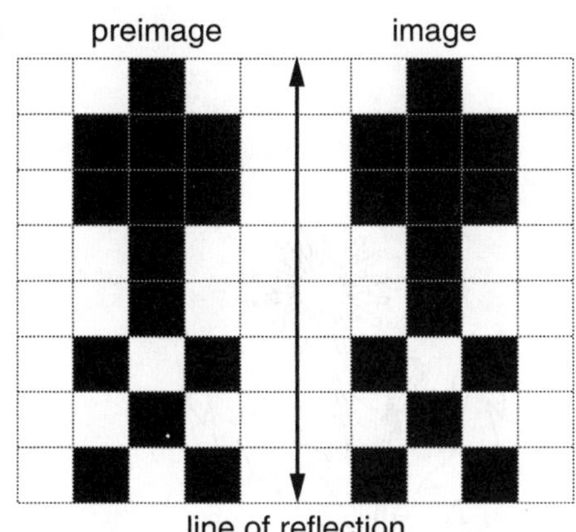

3.

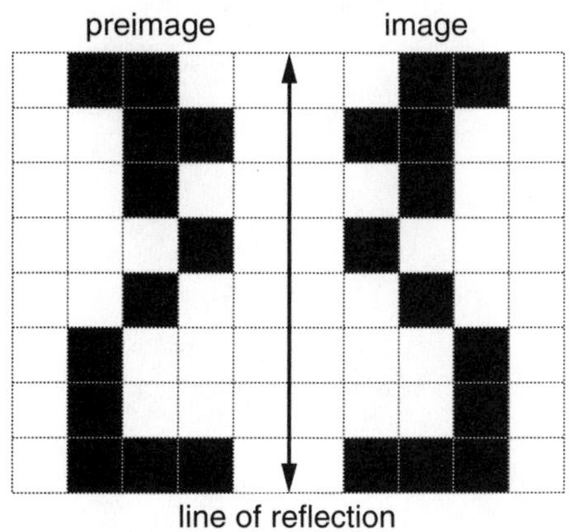

Study Link 10•4

2.

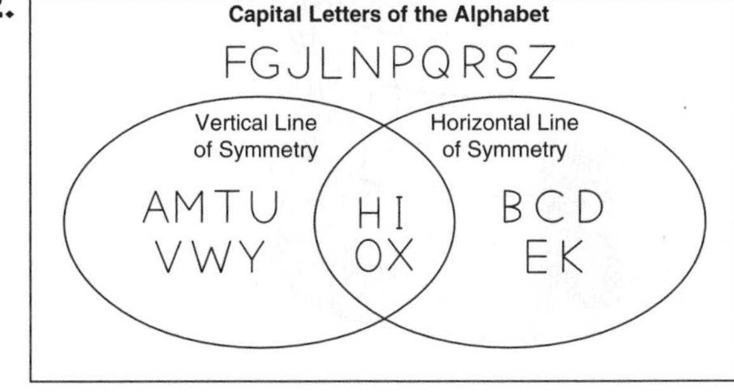

3. Sample answers:

horizontal	**vertical**
BOX	TAX
KID	YOU
BOOK	MAT
KICK	HIM

Study Link 10•5

1. a. reflection **b.** translation **c.** rotation

Study Link 10•6

1. $<$ **2.** $<$ **3.** $<$ **4.** $>$

5. $-8, -3.4, -\frac{1}{4}, \frac{1}{2}, 1.7, 5$

6. $-43, -3, 0, \frac{14}{7}, 5, 22$

7. Sample answers: $\frac{1}{4}, \frac{1}{2}, \frac{3}{4}, 1$

8. Sample answers: $-2, -1, -\frac{1}{2}, -\frac{1}{4}$

9. a. 13 **b.** -5 **c.** -13

10. a. 8 **b.** -2 **c.** -8

11. a. 15 **b.** 11 **c.** -15

Name Date Time

Buzz....

Beetrice, the bee, wants to gather pollen from each flower and then return to her hive. Use your transparent mirror to help Beetrice fly around.

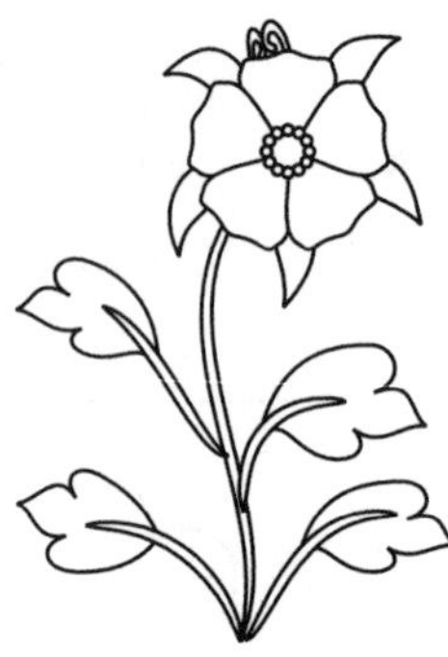

Name Date Time

Build a Clown

Use a transparent mirror to put a hat on the clown's head. When the hat is where you want it, draw the hat. Do the same thing with the other missing parts to complete the clown picture. Then color the picture and cut it out.

Name Date Time

STUDY LINK 10•1 A Reflected Image

There is a simple design in the box in the middle of this page. It is the **preimage.**

Hold this page in front of a mirror, with the printed side facing the mirror. On a blank piece of paper, sketch what the design looks like in the mirror—the **image.**

Compare your sketch (image) with the design on the Study Link page (preimage). Bring both the preimage and image to school tomorrow.

SRB 106

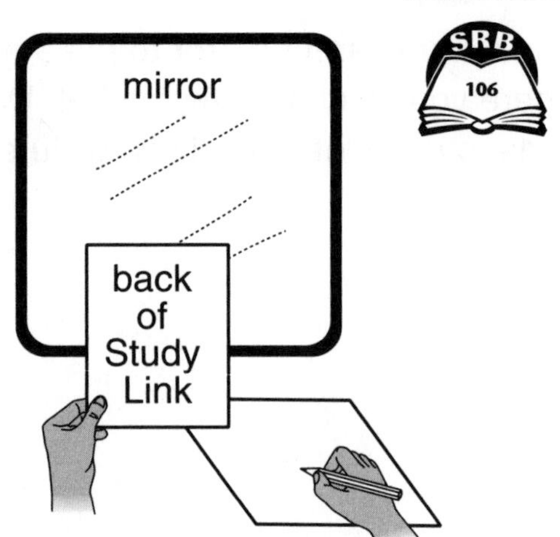

Sketch the design as it looks in the mirror.

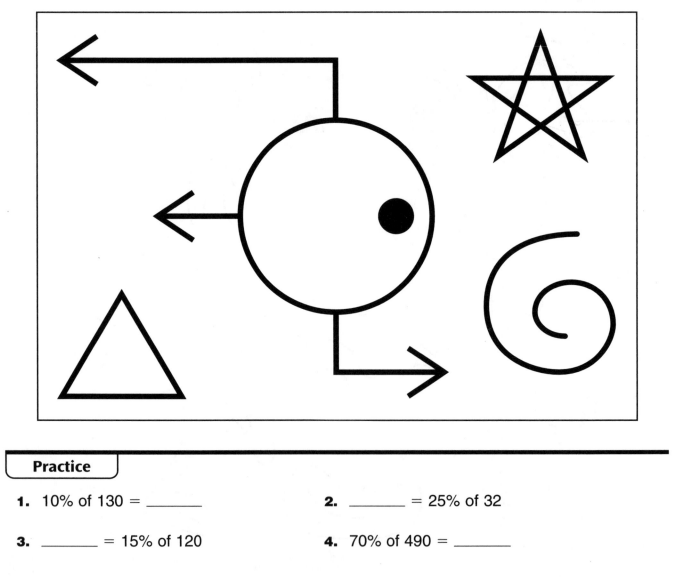

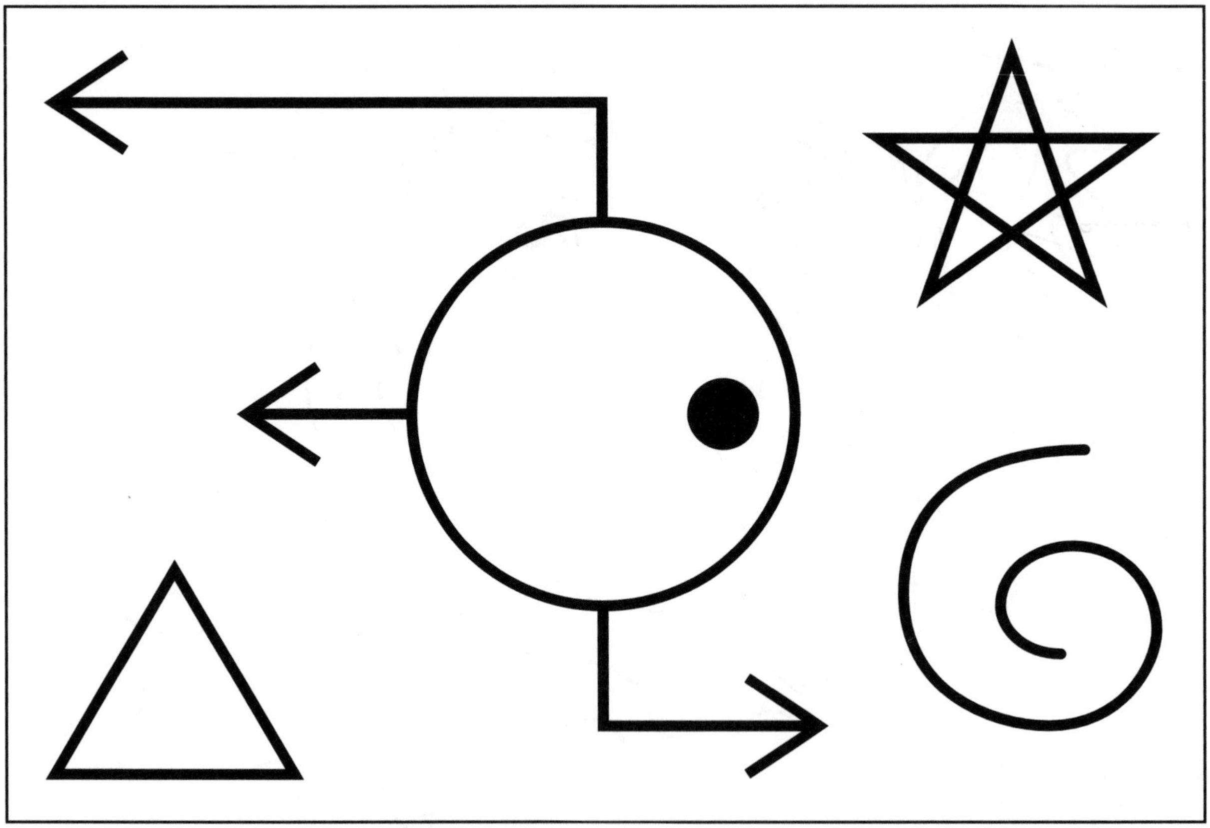

Practice

1. 10% of 130 = ______

2. ______ = 25% of 32

3. ______ = 15% of 120

4. 70% of 490 = ______

Name Date Time

Lines of Reflection

For each preimage and image, draw the line of reflection.

1.

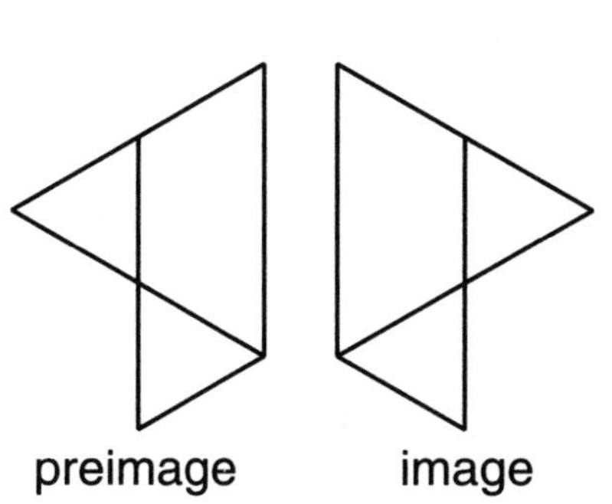

2.

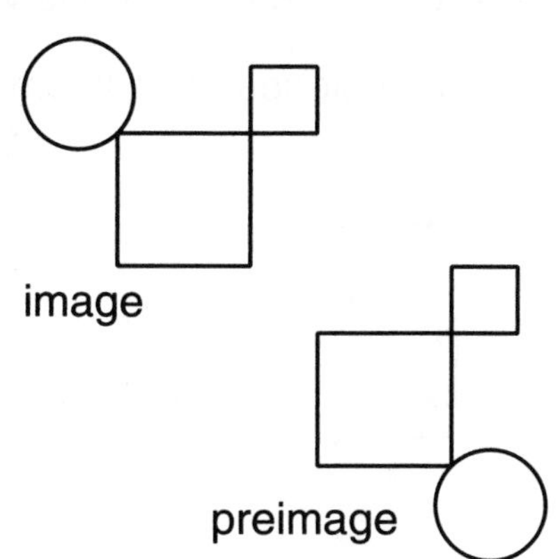

3.

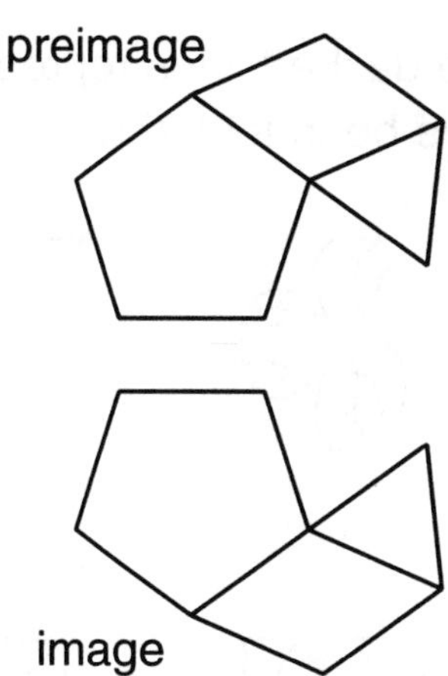

For each preimage, use your Geometry Template to draw the image on the other side of the line of reflection.

4.

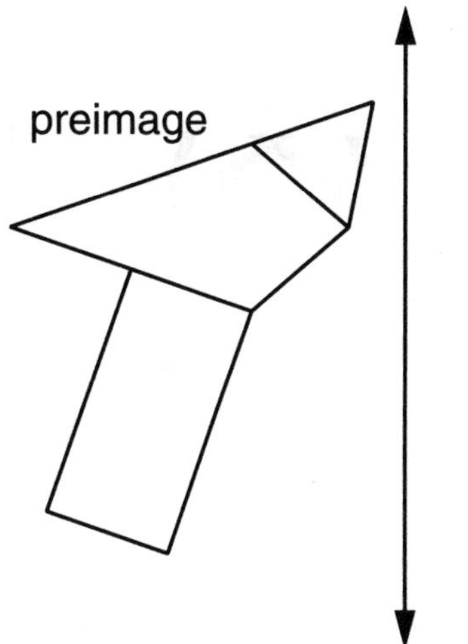

5.

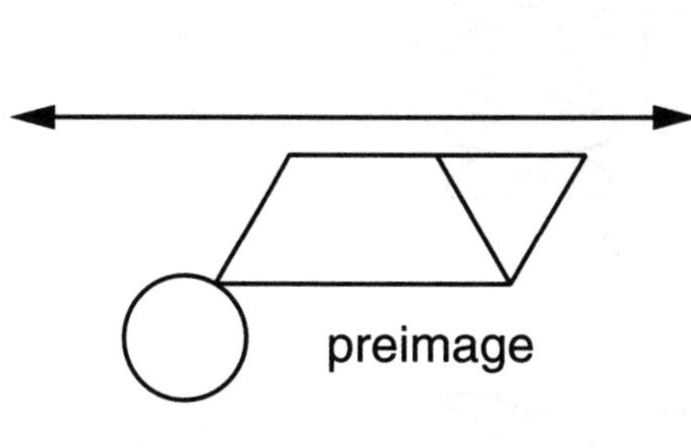

6.

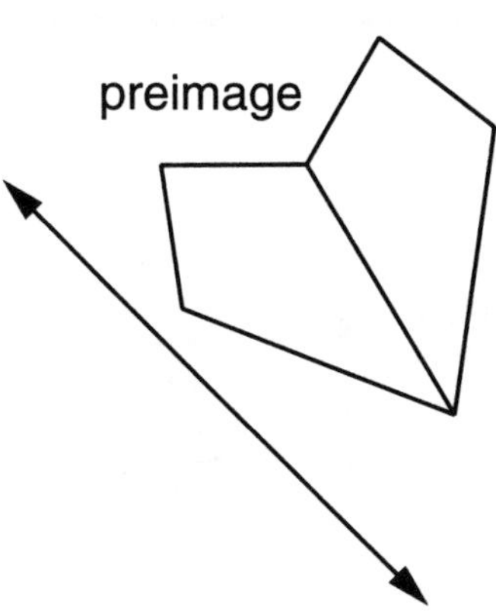

7. Create one of your own.

preimage

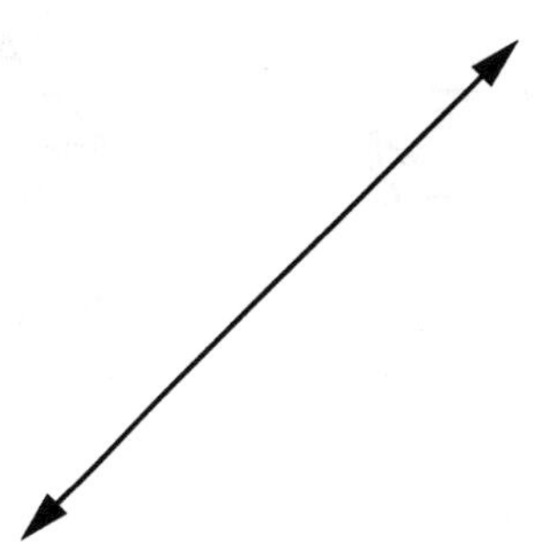

Name Date Time

Paper-Folding Puzzles

For each design, circle the pieces that could be unfolded to match it. For some problems, there is more than one correct answer.

The dashed lines represent folds. The pieces in Problems 3 and 4 have been folded two times.

1. 

A  B C 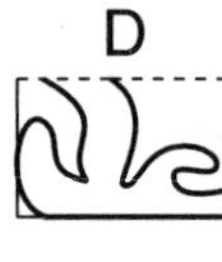 D E 

2. 

A B C 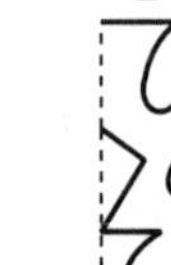 D E

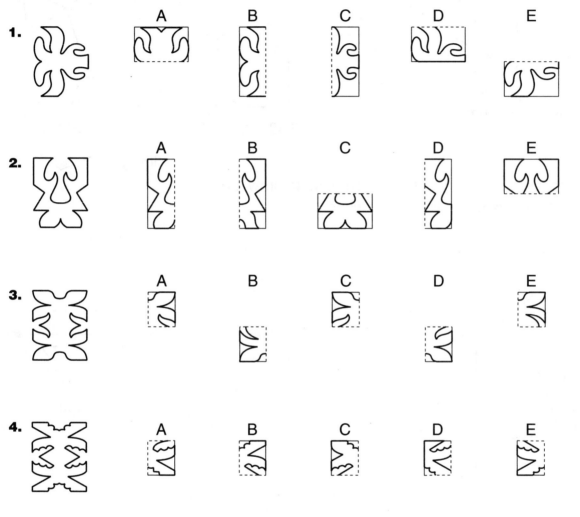

3. 

A  B C  D E

4. 

A B C D E

Try This

Match the folded piece to the correct unfolded design. Circle it.

5. 

A B C D E

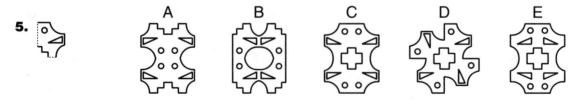

Name Date Time

Reflections

1. Use a transparent mirror to draw the reflected image of the head of the dog.

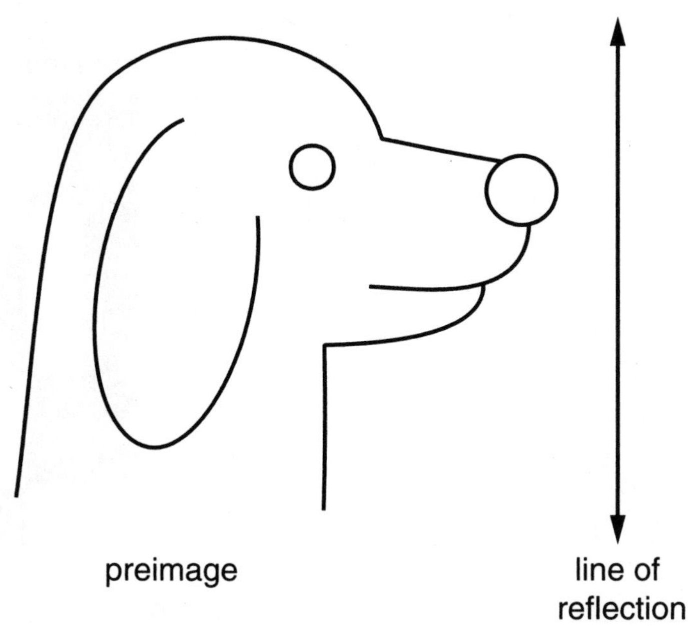

preimage | line of reflection | image

2. On the back of this page, describe how the two drawings in Problem 1 are alike and how they are different.

3. Draw a picture on the left side of the line. Ask your partner to use a transparent mirror to draw the reflected image of your picture.

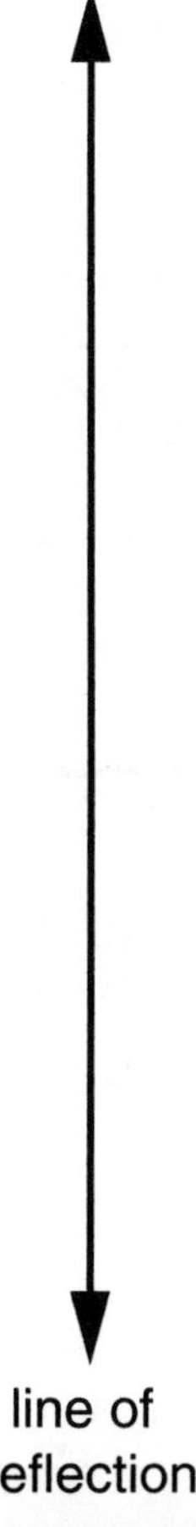

preimage | line of reflection | image

Name Date Time

STUDY LINK 10•3

Reflections

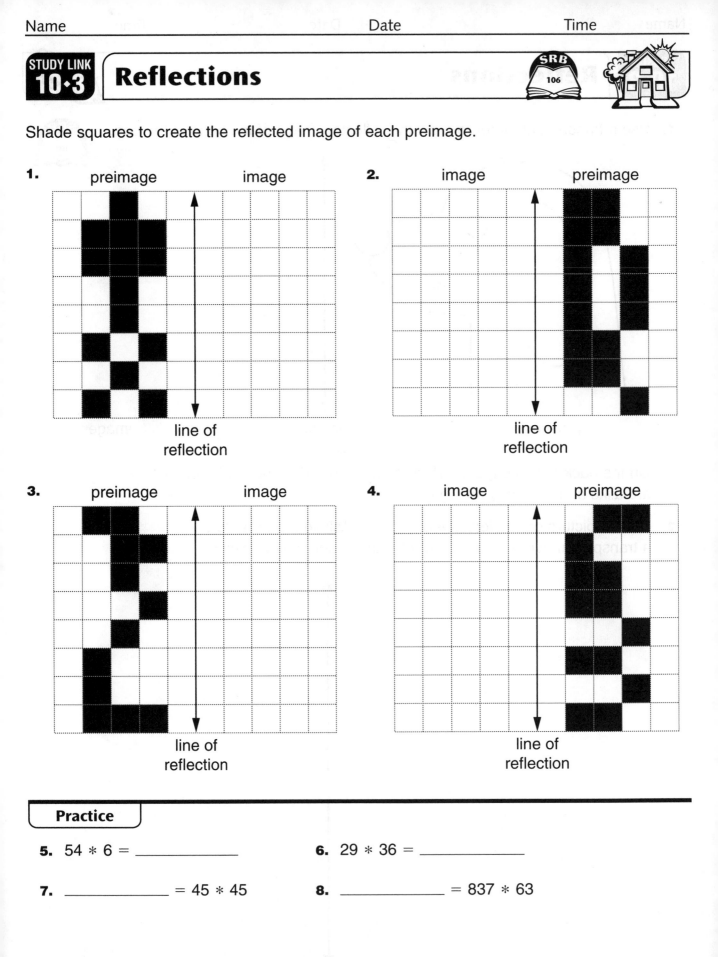

Shade squares to create the reflected image of each preimage.

1.

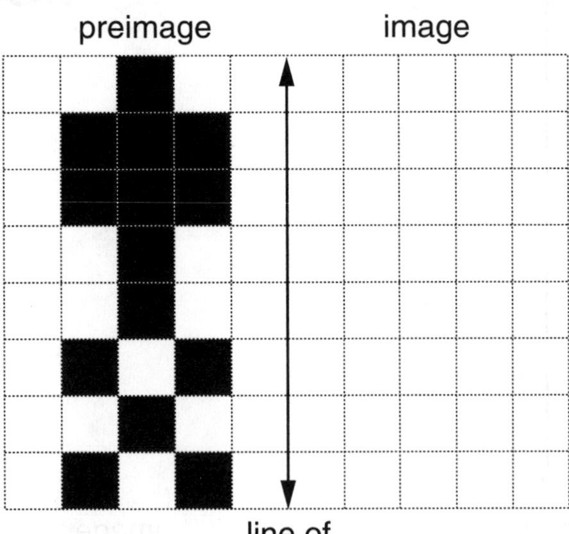

2.

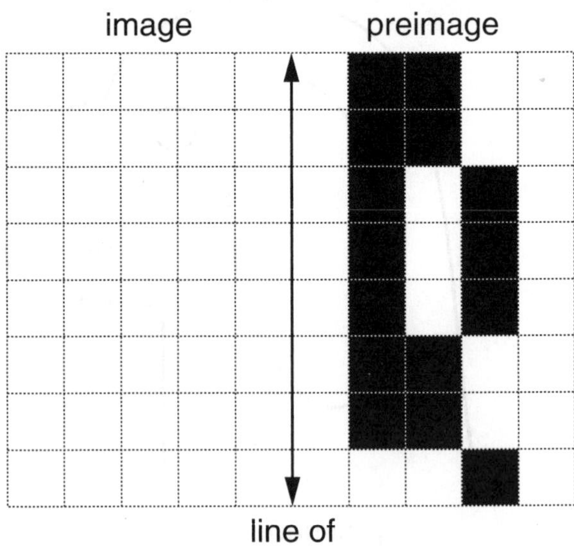

3.

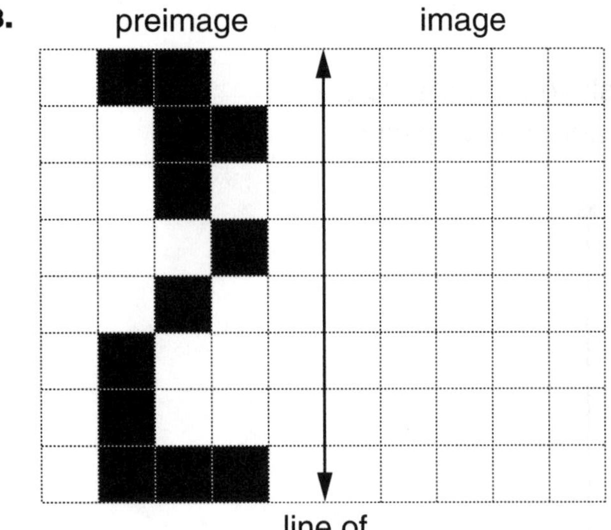

4.

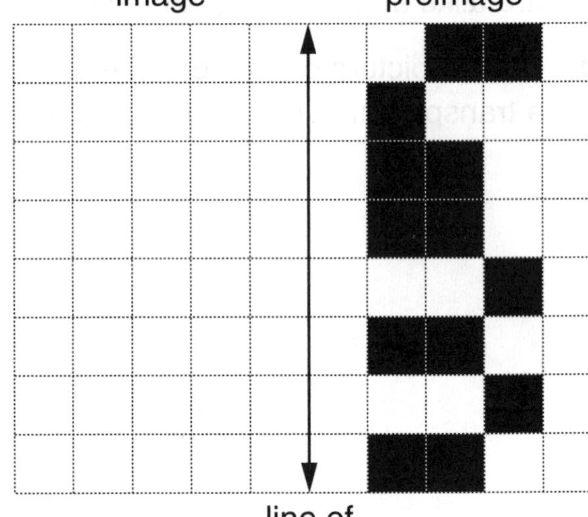

Practice

5. 54 * 6 = ____________

6. 29 * 36 = ____________

7. ____________ = 45 * 45

8. ____________ = 837 * 63

Name Date Time

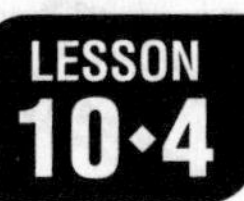

Half-Pictures

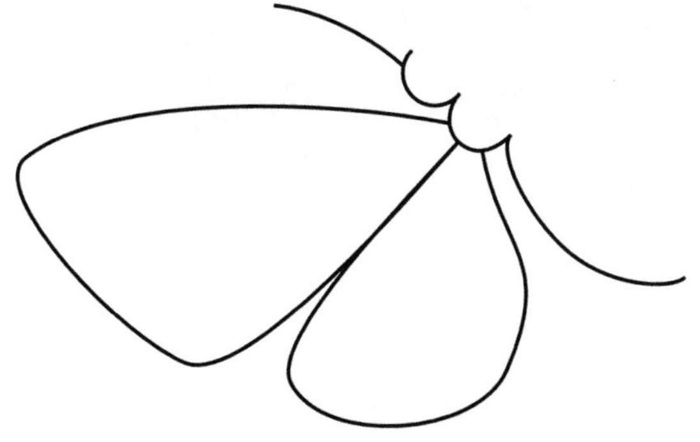

Name Date Time

Symmetric Pictures

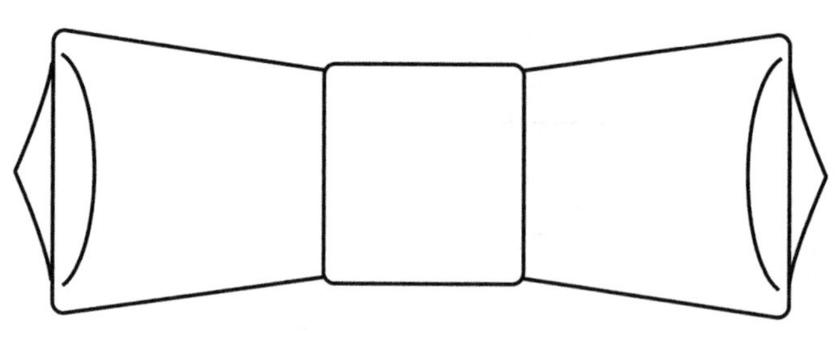

Name Date Time

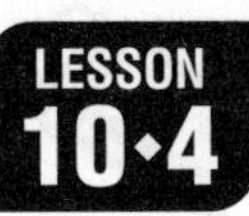

Polygons A–E

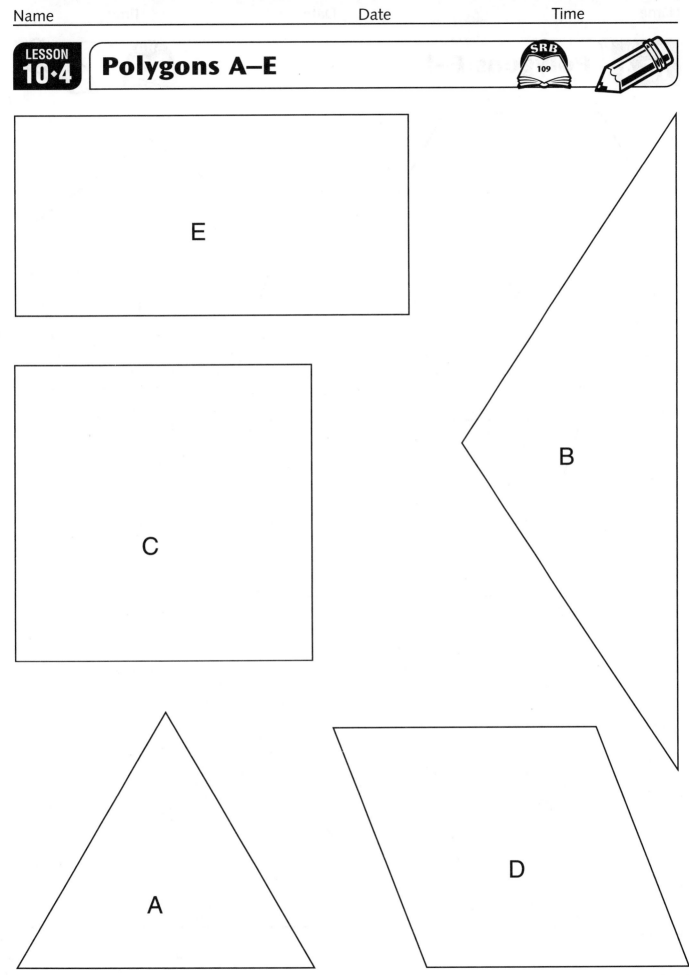

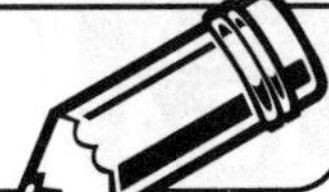

E

B

C

A

D

Name Date Time

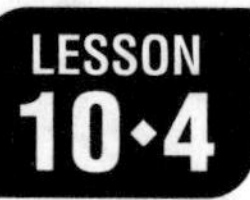

Polygons F–J

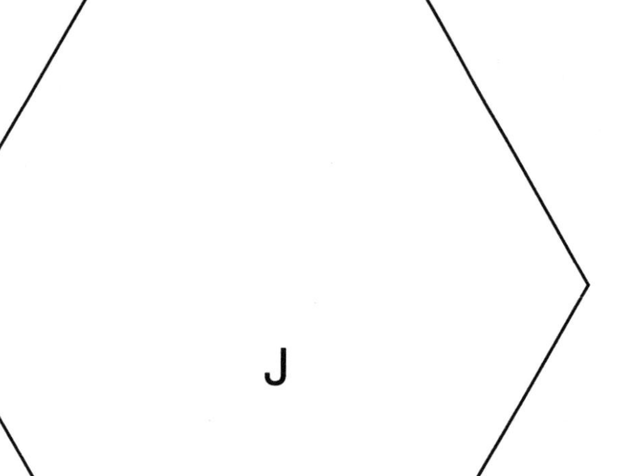

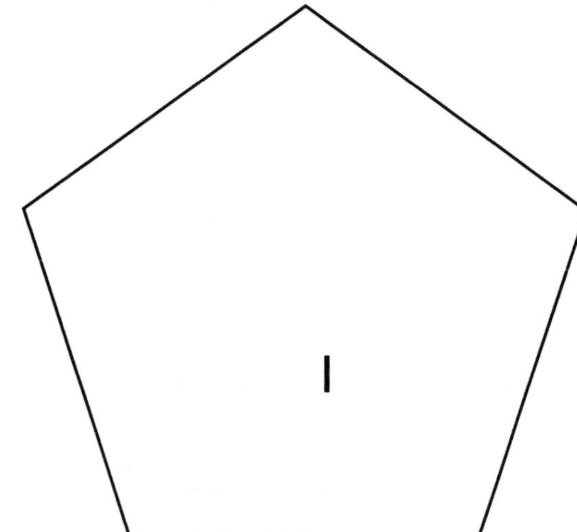

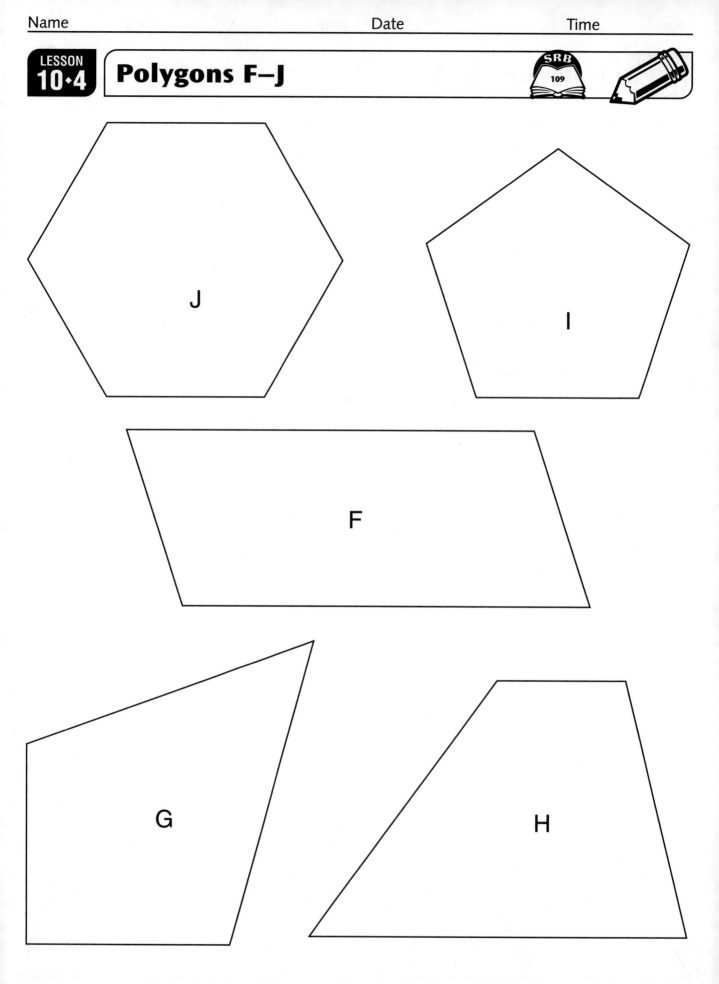

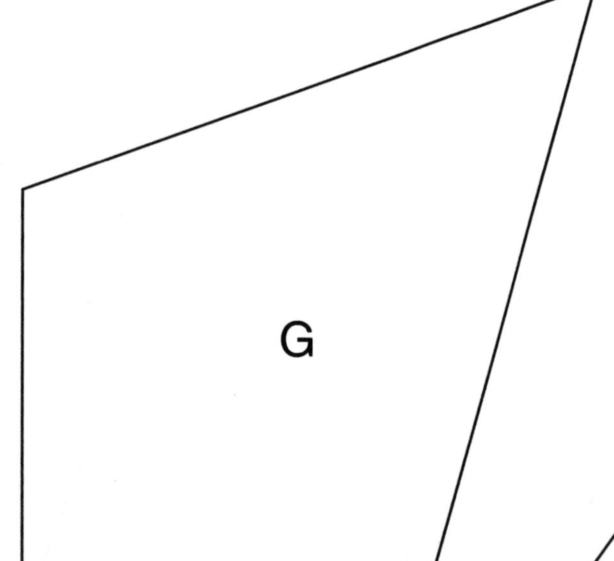

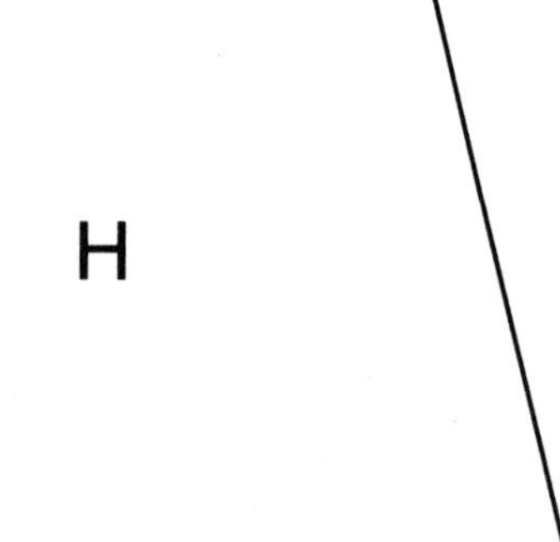

Name Date Time

Line Symmetry in the Alphabet

1. Print the 26 capital letters of the alphabet below.

___ ___ ___ ___ ___ ___ ___ ___ ___ ___ ___ ___ ___

___ ___ ___ ___ ___ ___ ___ ___ ___ ___ ___ ___ ___

2. The capital letter A has a vertical line of symmetry. 

The capital letter B has a horizontal line of symmetry. 

Use the letters of the alphabet to complete the Venn diagram.

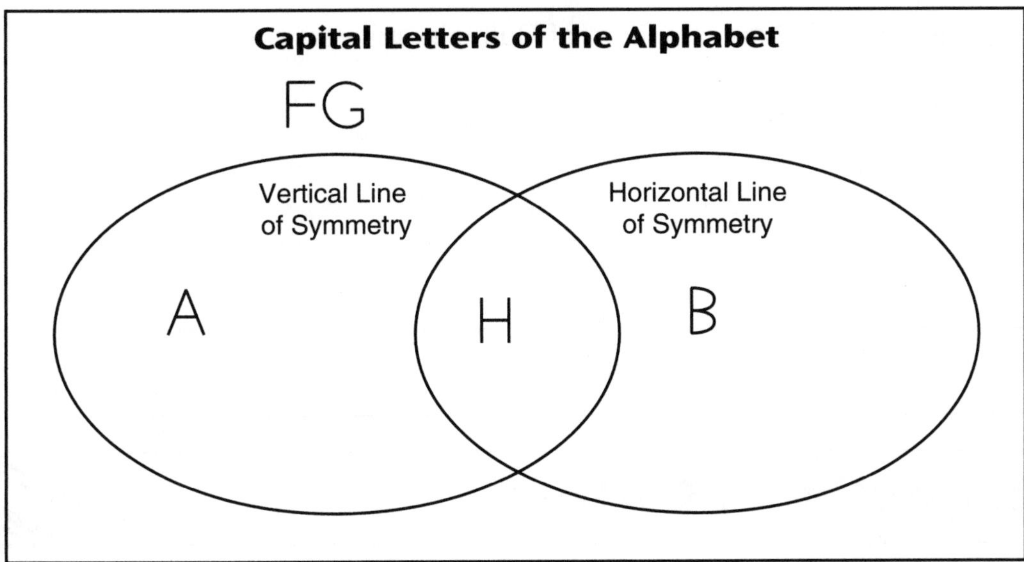

3. The word BED has a horizontal line of symmetry. 

The word HIT has a vertical line of symmetry. 

Use capital letters to list words that have horizontal or vertical line symmetry.

horizontal		vertical	
________	________	________	________
________	________	________	________

Practice

4. 86 ÷ 9 = ________

5. ________ = 68 / 4

6. 6)742 = ________

7. ________ = 855 / 7

Name Date Time

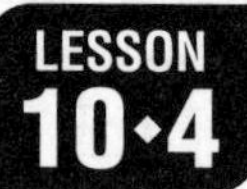

Interpreting a Cartoon

1. What answer does Ruthie's brother expect? ______

2. Explain and draw pictures to show why both of Ruthie's answers are correct.

Name Date Time

Interpreting a Cartoon

1. What answer does Ruthie's brother expect? ______

2. Explain and draw pictures to show why both of Ruthie's answers are correct.

Name Date Time

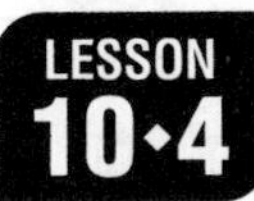

Line Symmetry

Use pattern blocks to create shapes with the given number of lines of symmetry.
Use your Geometry Template to record the shapes and draw the lines of symmetry.

1. 1 yellow hexagon, 2 orange squares
2 lines of symmetry

2. 1 orange square, 4 green triangles
0 lines of symmetry

3. 2 red trapezoids
6 lines of symmetry

4. 5 orange squares
1 line of symmetry

Try This

5. 5 red trapezoids
1 line of symmetry
Show two different ways.

6. On the back of this page, make up a problem of your own. Give it to a partner to solve.

Name Date Time

STUDY LINK 10•5

Geometric Patterns

1. Continue each pattern. Then tell if you continued the pattern by using a reflection, rotation, or translation of the original design.

a. ______________________

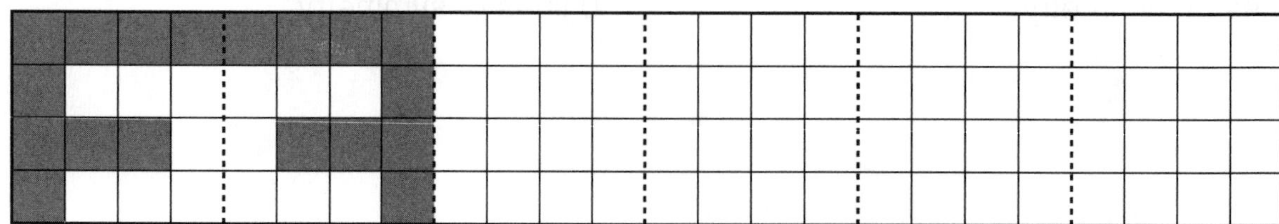

b. ______________________

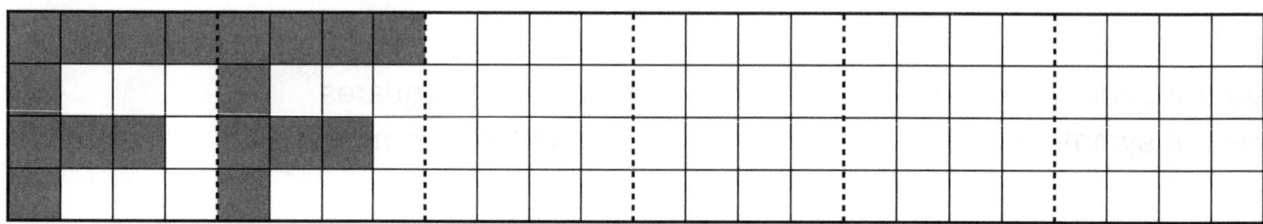

c. ______________________

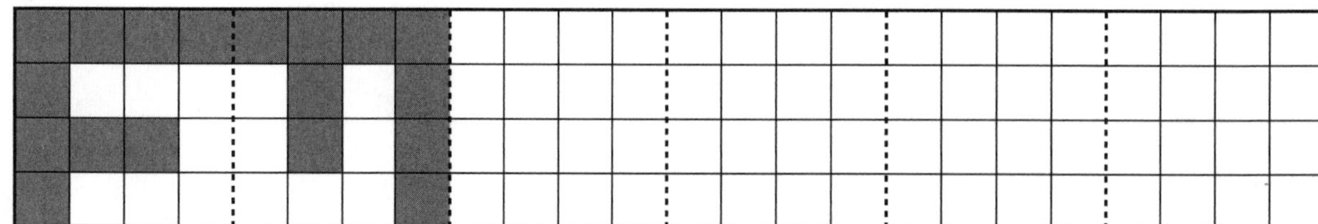

2. Make up your own pattern.

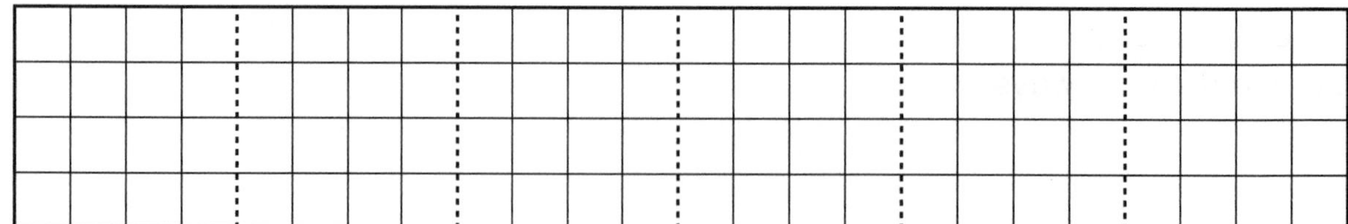

Practice

3. 50% of $25.00 = ______________

4. 25% of $10.00 = ______________

5. ______________ = 40% of $150.00

6. ______________ = 20% of $250.00

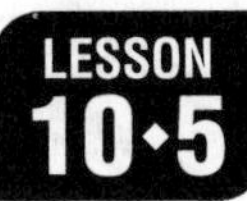

Making Frieze Patterns

1. Use an index card as a template for making frieze patterns. SRB 108

   a. Trim your index card to make a 3-inch by 3-inch square.

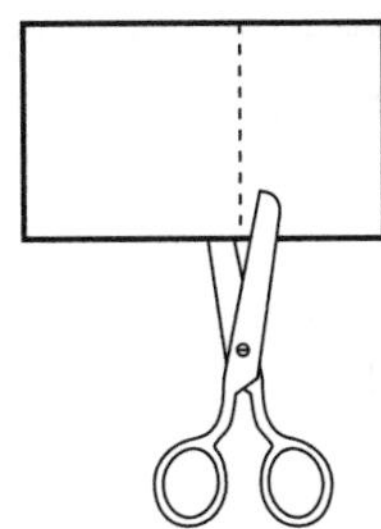

   b. Draw a simple design in the middle of the square.

   c. Cut out your design. If you need to cut through the edge of the index card, then use tape to repair the cut.

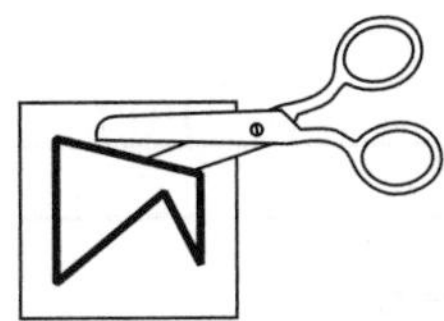

2. Make a frieze pattern with your template.

   a. Draw a long line on a large sheet of paper.

   b. Put your template at the left end of the line.

   c. Trace the shape of the design you cut out. Make a mark on the line at the right edge of the template.

   d. Move your template to the right along the line. Line up the left side of the template with the mark you made on the line.

   e. Repeat Steps c and d. To make more complicated patterns, give your template a turn or a flip every time you move it.

Name Date Time

Positive and Negative Numbers

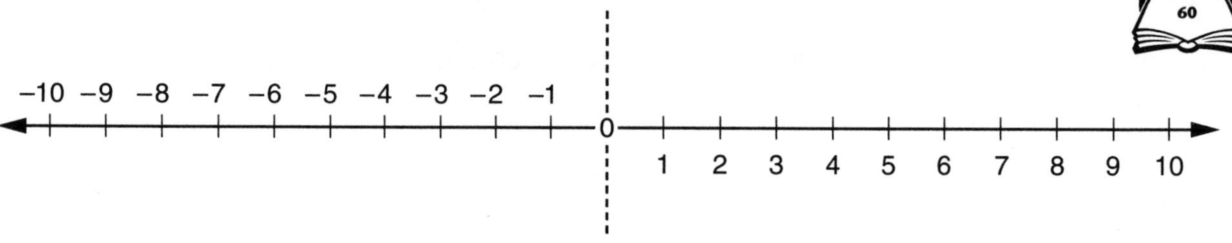

Place your transparent mirror on the dashed line that passes through 0 on the number line above. Look through the mirror. What do you see?

What negative number image do you see . . .

above 1? __________ above 2? __________ above 8? __________

Name Date Time

Positive and Negative Numbers

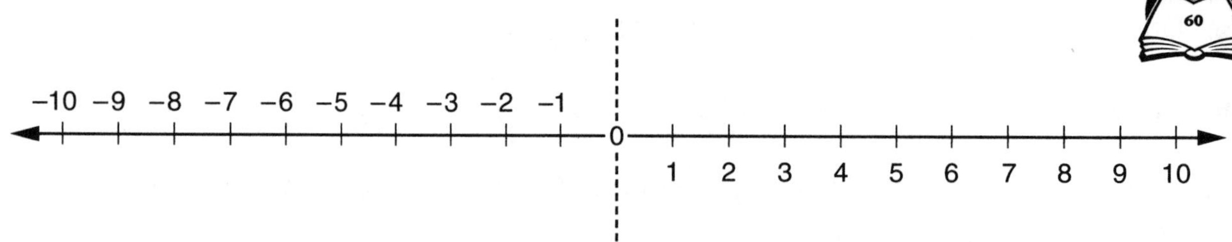

Place your transparent mirror on the dashed line that passes through 0 on the number line above. Look through the mirror. What do you see?

What negative number image do you see . . .

above 1? __________ above 2? __________ above 8? __________

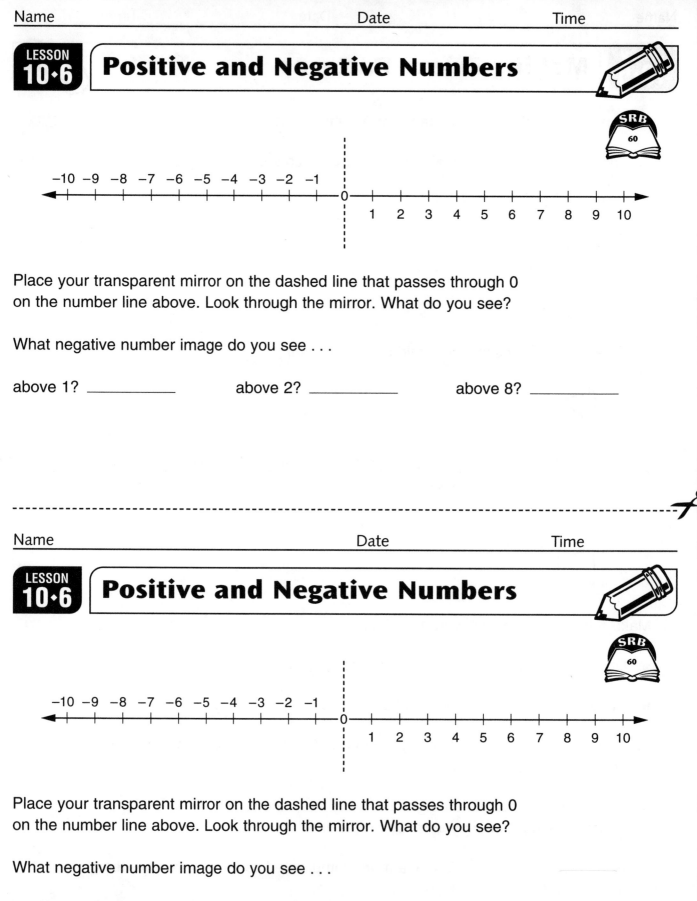

Name Date Time

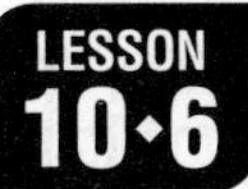

Ledger

Transaction	Start	Change	End/Start of Next Transaction

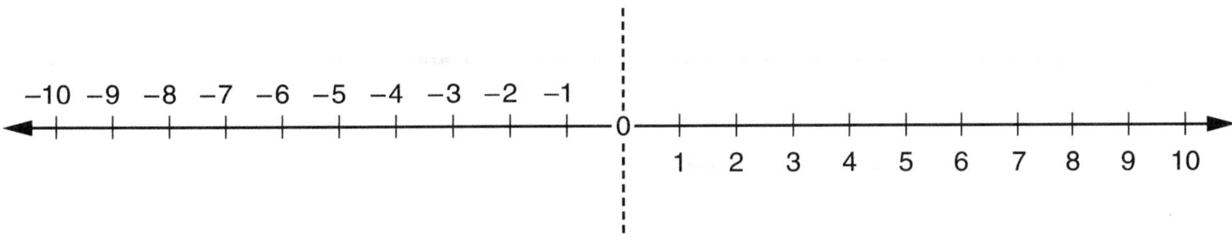

Name Date Time

STUDY LINK **10•6**

Positive and Negative Numbers

Write < or > to make a true number sentence.

1. 3 ______ 14 **2.** −7 ______ 7 **3.** 19 ______ 20 **4.** −8 ______ −10

List the numbers in order from least to greatest.

5. 5, −8, $\frac{1}{2}$, $-\frac{1}{4}$, 1.7, −3.4

______ ______ ______ ______ ______ ______

least **greatest**

6. −43, 22, $\frac{14}{7}$, 5, −3, 0

______ ______ ______ ______ ______ ______

least **greatest**

7. Name four positive numbers less than 2. ______ ______ ______ ______

8. Name four negative numbers greater than −3. ______ ______ ______ ______

Use the number line to help you solve Problems 9–11.

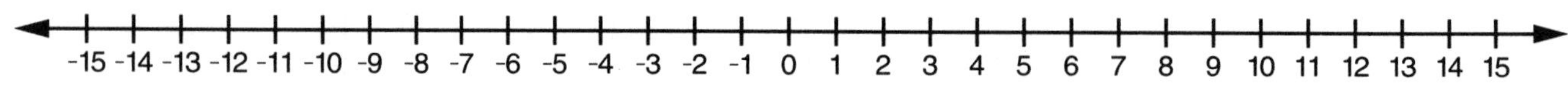

9. **a.** 4 + 9 = ______ **b.** 4 + (−9) = ______ **c.** (−4) + (−9) = ______

10. **a.** 5 + 3 = ______ **b.** (−5) + 3 = ______ **c.** (−5) + (−3) = ______

11. **a.** ______ = 2 + 13 **b.** ______ = (−2) + 13 **c.** ______ = (−2) + (−13)

Practice

12. 1.02 + 12.88 = ______ **13.** 7.26 − 1.94 = ______

14. ______ + 5.84 = 8.75 **15.** 3.38 − ______ = 2.62

Name Date Time

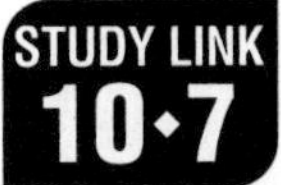

Unit 11: Family Letter

3-D Shapes, Weight, Volume, and Capacity

Our next unit introduces several new topics, as well as reviewing some of the work with geometric solids from previous grades and some of the main ideas your child has been studying this past year.

We begin with a lesson on weight, focusing on grams and ounces. Students handle and weigh a variety of objects, trying to develop "weight sense" so that they can estimate weights effectively. The class participates in creating a Gram & Ounce Museum by displaying everyday objects labeled with their weights.

As part of a review of the properties of 3-dimensional shapes (prisms, pyramids, cylinders, and cones), your child will construct models of geometric solids using straws and paper patterns. They will use these models as they discuss vocabulary such as *face, edge,* and *vertex* and compare features of geometric solids.

By experimenting with cubes, the class will develop and apply a formula for finding the volumes of rectangular prisms (solids that look like boxes).

We will consider familiar units of capacity (cups, pints, quarts, gallons) and the relationships among them.

Your child will also explore subtraction of positive and negative numbers by playing a variation of the *Credits/Debits Game* introduced in Unit 10.

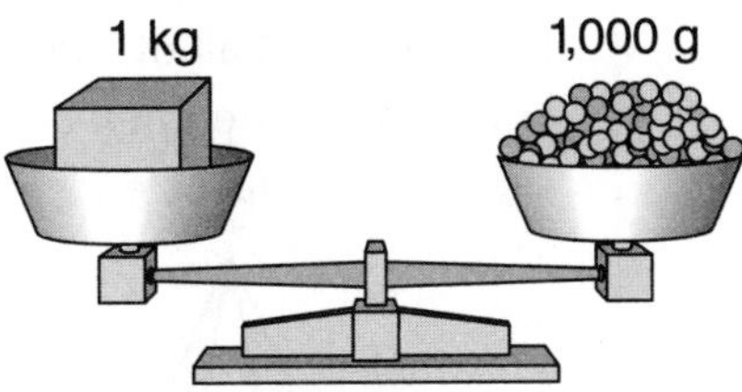

In Lesson 11-1, a pan balance is used to measure weight in grams.

Please keep this Family Letter for reference as your child works through Unit 11.

Vocabulary

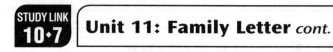

Important terms in Unit 11:

capacity (1) The amount of space occupied by a 3-dimensional shape. Same as *volume.* (2) Less formally, the amount a container can hold. Capacity is often measured in units such as quarts, gallons, cups, or liters. (3) The maximum *weight* a scale can measure.

cone A 3-dimensional shape that has a circular base, a *curved surface,* and one vertex, which is called the apex. The points on the curved surface of a cone are on straight lines connecting the apex and the circumference of the base.

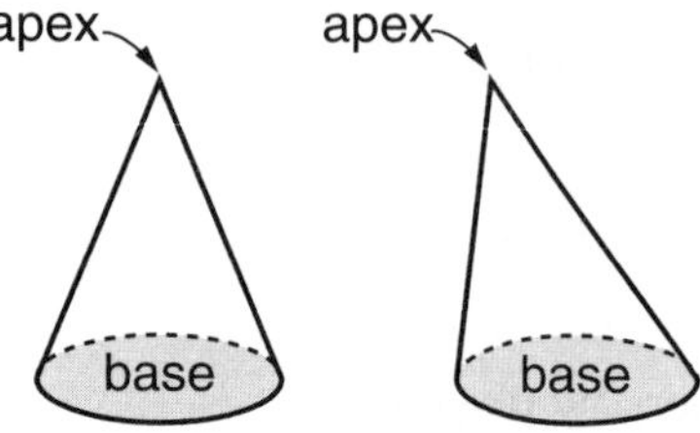

cubic unit A unit used in measuring *volume,* such as a cubic centimeter or a cubic foot.

curved surface A 2-dimensional surface that is rounded rather than flat. Spheres, *cylinders,* and *cones* each have one curved surface.

cylinder A 3-dimensional shape that has two circular or elliptical bases that are parallel and congruent and are connected by a *curved surface.* A can is shaped like a cylinder.

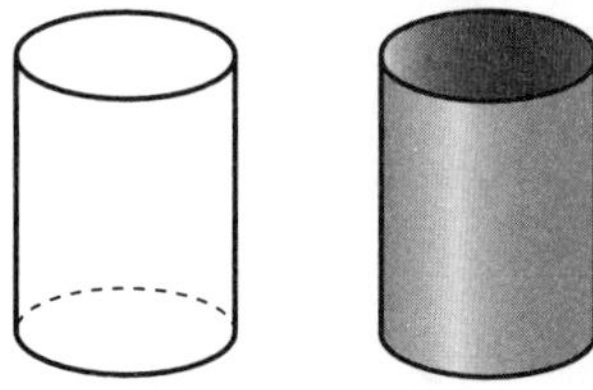

dimension A measure along one direction of an object, typically length, width, or height. For example, the dimensions of a box might be 24 cm by 20 cm by 10 cm.

formula A general rule for finding the value of something. A formula is often written using letters, called variables, that stand for the quantities involved.

geometric solid The surface or surfaces that make up a 3-dimensional shape, such as a *prism, cylinder, cone,* or sphere. Despite its name, a geometric solid is hollow; it does not contain the points in its interior.

prism A 3-dimensional shape with two parallel and congruent polygonal regions for bases and lateral faces formed by all the line segments with endpoints on corresponding edges of the bases. The lateral faces are all parallelograms.

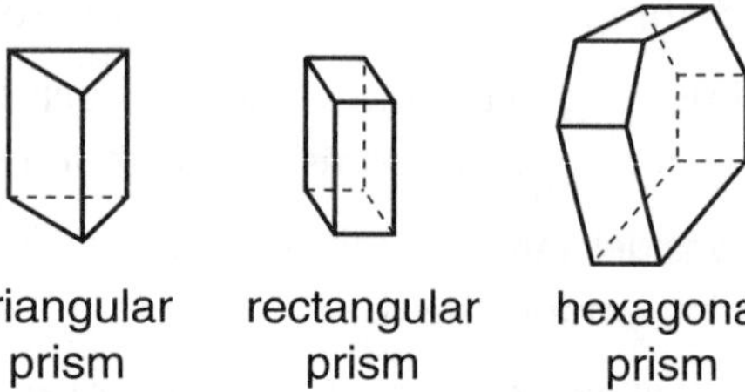

pyramid A 3-dimensional shape with a polygonal region for a base, a point (apex) not in the plane of the base, and all of the line segments with one endpoint at the apex and the other on an edge of the base. All faces except the base are triangular.

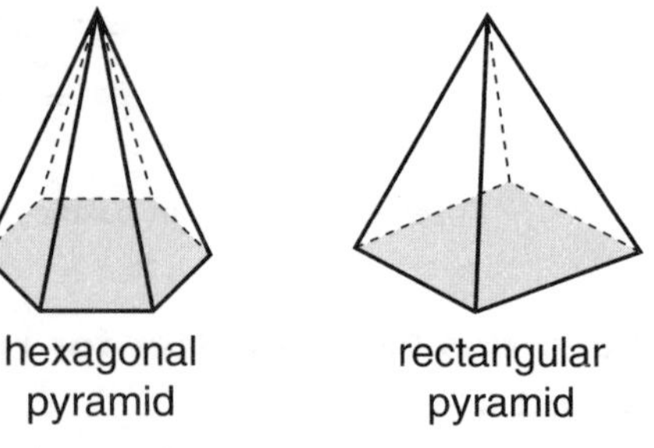

3-dimensional (3-D) shape A shape whose points are not all in a single plane. Examples include *prisms, pyramids,* and spheres, all of which have length, width, and height.

volume The amount of space occupied by a 3-dimensional shape. Same as *capacity.* The amount a container can hold. Volume is often measured in cubic units, such as cm^3, cubic inches, or cubic feet.

weight A measure of the force of gravity on an object. Weight is measured in metric units such as grams, kilograms, and milligrams and in U.S. customary units such as pounds and ounces.

Do-Anytime Activities

To work with your child on the concepts taught in this unit, try these interesting and rewarding activities:

1. Have your child compile a list of the world's heaviest objects or things. For example, which animal has the heaviest baby? What is the world's heaviest human-made structure? What is the greatest amount of weight ever hoisted by a person?
2. Have your child compile a portfolio of 3-dimensional shapes. Images can be taken from newspapers, magazines, photographs, and so on.
3. Encourage your child to create his or her own mnemonics and/or sayings for converting between units of capacity and weight. One such example is the old English saying "A pint's a pound the world around." (1 pint = 16 oz = 1 lb)

Building Skills through Games

In Unit 11, your child will play the following games. For detailed instructions, see the *Student Reference Book.*

Chances Are See *Student Reference Book,* page 236.
This game is for 2 players and requires one deck of *Chances Are* Event Cards and one deck of *Chances Are* Probability Cards. The game develops skill in using probability terms to describe the likelihood of events.

Credits/Debits Game See *Student Reference Book,* page 238.
This is a game for 2 players. Game materials include 1 complete deck of number cards and a recording sheet. The *Credits/Debits Game* helps students practice addition of positive and negative integers.

***Credits/Debits Game* (Advanced Version)** See *Student Reference Book,* page 239.
This game is similar to the *Credits/Debits Game* and helps students practice addition and subtraction of positive and negative integers.

As You Help Your Child with Homework

As your child brings assignments home, you may want to go over the instructions together, clarifying them as necessary. The answers listed below will guide you through this unit's Study Links.

Study Link 11•1

1. 59 **2.** 96,640

3. Bagel and pumpkin; or taco and gingerbread man

4. Pasta, Chocolate bar, Hamburger, Ice cream sundae

6. −\$50 **7.** −\$75 **8.** \$0

9. \$30

Study Link 11•2

1. **a.** square pyramid **b.** cone
c. sphere **d.** cylinder
e. rectangular prism **f.** triangular prism

2.

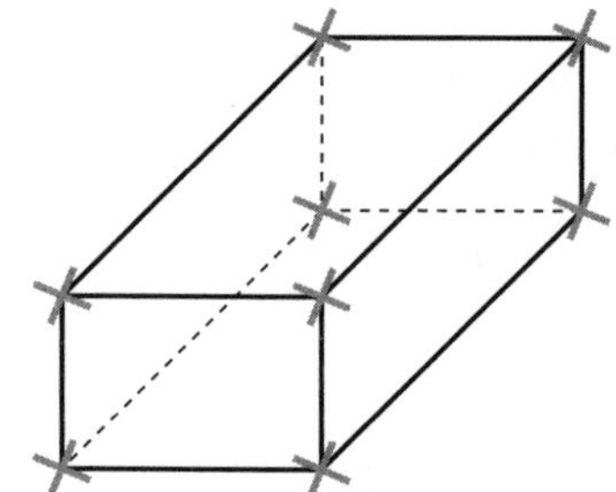

3. 6 **4.** 7,000; 63,560; and 91

5. 24; 120; 600

Study Link 11•3

1. cone **2.** square pyramid

3. hexagonal prism **4.** octahedron

6. \$10 **7.** −\$70

8. −\$15 **9.** −\$100

10. −\$55 **11.** −\$400

Study Link 11•4

4. 24 **5.** 17 R1, or $17\frac{1}{5}$

6. 29 **7.** 89 R2, or $89\frac{2}{4}$

Study Link 11•5

1. **a.** 39 **b.** 30

2. **a.** (3 ∗ 3) ∗ 6 = 54; 54
b. (2 ∗ 5) ∗ 9.7 = 97; 97

3. **a.** 150 **b.** 150

4. −49 **5.** −40 **6.** 29 **7.** 73

Study Link 11•6

1. −110 **2.** −8 **3.** −8

4. 15 **5.** 14 **6.** −19

7. −70 **8.** 18

11. $<$ **12.** $<$ **13.** $>$

14. $>$ **15.** $>$ **16.** $>$

17. −14, −2.5, −0.7, $\frac{30}{6}$, 5.6, 8

18. −7, $-\frac{24}{6}$, $-\frac{3}{5}$, 0.02, 0.46, 4

19. 2,652 **20.** 44,114 **21.** 158

22. 106 R4, or $106\frac{4}{7}$

Study Link 11•7

Answers vary for Problems 1–4.

5. 4 **6.** 48 **7.** 2

8. 3 **9.** 3 **10.** 10

11. 4 **12.** −4 **13.** −40

14. −120

Name Date Time

The World's Largest Foods

Food	Weight	Date	Location
Apple	3 pounds 11 ounces	October 1997	Linton, England
Bagel	714 pounds	July 1998	Mattoon, Illinois
Bowl of pasta	7,355 pounds	February 2004	Hartford, New York
Chocolate bar	5,026 pounds	March 2000	Turin, Italy
Garlic	2 pounds 10 ounces	1985	Eureka, California
Gingerbread man	372.13 pounds	November 2003	Vancouver, Canada
Hamburger	6,040 pounds	September 1999	Sac, Montana
Ice cream sundae	22.59 tons	July 1988	Alberta, Canada
Pumpkin	1,337 pounds	October 2002	Topsfield, Massachusetts
Taco	1,654 pounds	March 2003	Mexicali, Mexico

Source: www.guinnessworldrecords.com

Use the information in the table to solve the following problems.

1. The largest apple weighed ________ ounces.

2. A typical hamburger weighs about 4 ounces. The largest hamburger weighed ________ ounces.

3. Which 2 foods together weigh about a ton? ________________ and ________________

4. A kilogram is a little more than 2 pounds. Which 4 foods each weigh more than 1,000 kilograms?

____

5. On the back of this page, use data from the table to write and solve your own problem.

Practice

6. −\$75 + \$25 = ________

7. ________ = −\$45 + (−\$30)

8. ________ = −\$60 + \$60

9. \$55 + (−\$25) = ________

Name ______________________ Date ______________________ Time ______________________

Solids

1. The pictures below show objects that are shaped approximately like geometric solids. Identify each object as one of the following: **cylinder, cone, sphere, triangular prism, square pyramid,** or **rectangular prism.**

a.	**b.**	**c.**
Type: ______________	 Type: ______________	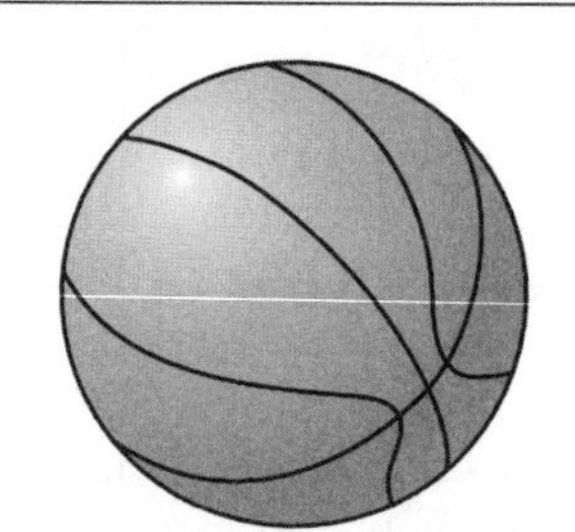 Type: ______________
d.  Type: ______________	**e.**  Type: ______________	**f.** 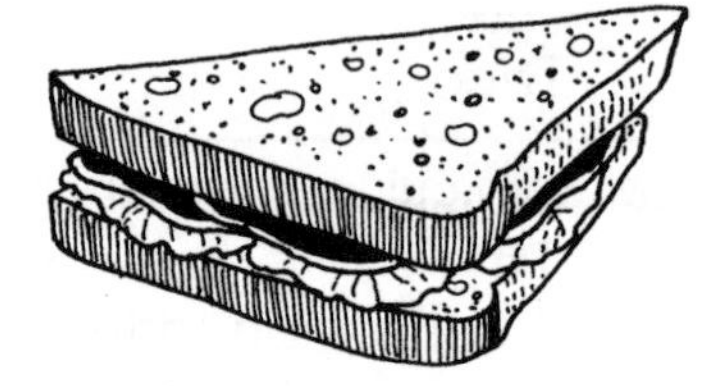 Type: ______________

2. Mark *X*s on the vertices of the rectangular prism.

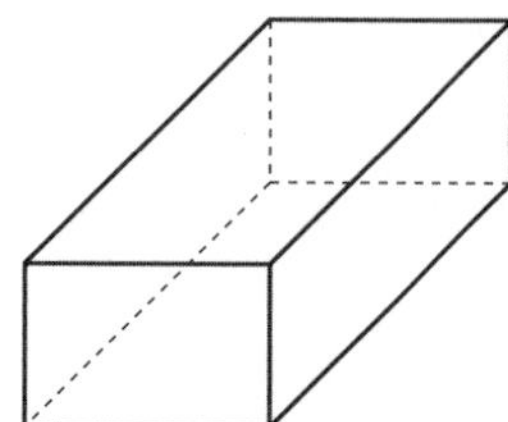

3. How many edges does the tetrahedron have? __________ edges

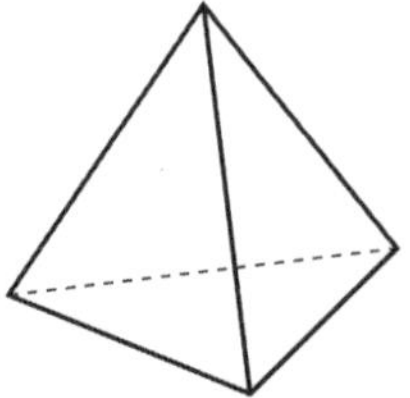

Practice

4. Circle the numbers that are multiples of 7. 132 7,000 63 560 834 91

5. Circle the numbers that are multiples of 12. 24 120 38 600 100 75

Name Date Time

STUDY LINK 11•3

Geometry Riddles

Answer the following riddles.

SRB 101–103

1. I am a geometric solid.
I have two surfaces.
One of my surfaces is formed by a circle.
The other surface is curved.

What am I? ______________

2. I am a geometric solid.
I have one square base.
I have four triangular faces.
Some Egyptian pharaohs were buried in tombs shaped like me.

What am I? ______________

3. I am a polyhedron.
I am a prism.
My two bases are hexagons.
My other faces are rectangles.

What am I? ______________

4. I am a polyhedron.
All of my faces are the same.
All of my faces are equilateral triangles.
I have eight faces.

What am I? ______________

Try This

5. Write your own geometry riddle.

____

____

____

____

____

____

____

Practice

6. −\$20 + \$30 = ______________

7. ______________ = −\$35 + (−\$35)

8. ______________ = \$10 + (−\$25)

9. \$0 + (−\$100) = ______________

10. −\$15 + (−\$40) = ______________

11. ______________ = −\$300 + (−\$100)

Name Date Time

Volume

Cut out the pattern below and tape it together to form an open box.

1. Find and record two items in your home that have volumes equal to about $\frac{1}{2}$ of the volume of the open box.

_______________ _______________

2. Find and record two items in your home that have about the same volume as the open box.

_______________ _______________

3. Find and record two items in your home that have volumes equal to about 2 times the volume of the open box.

_______________ _______________

Practice

4. $96 \div 4 =$ _______________

5. $86 / 5 =$ _______________

6. $\frac{232}{8} =$ _______________

7. $4\overline{)358} =$ _______________

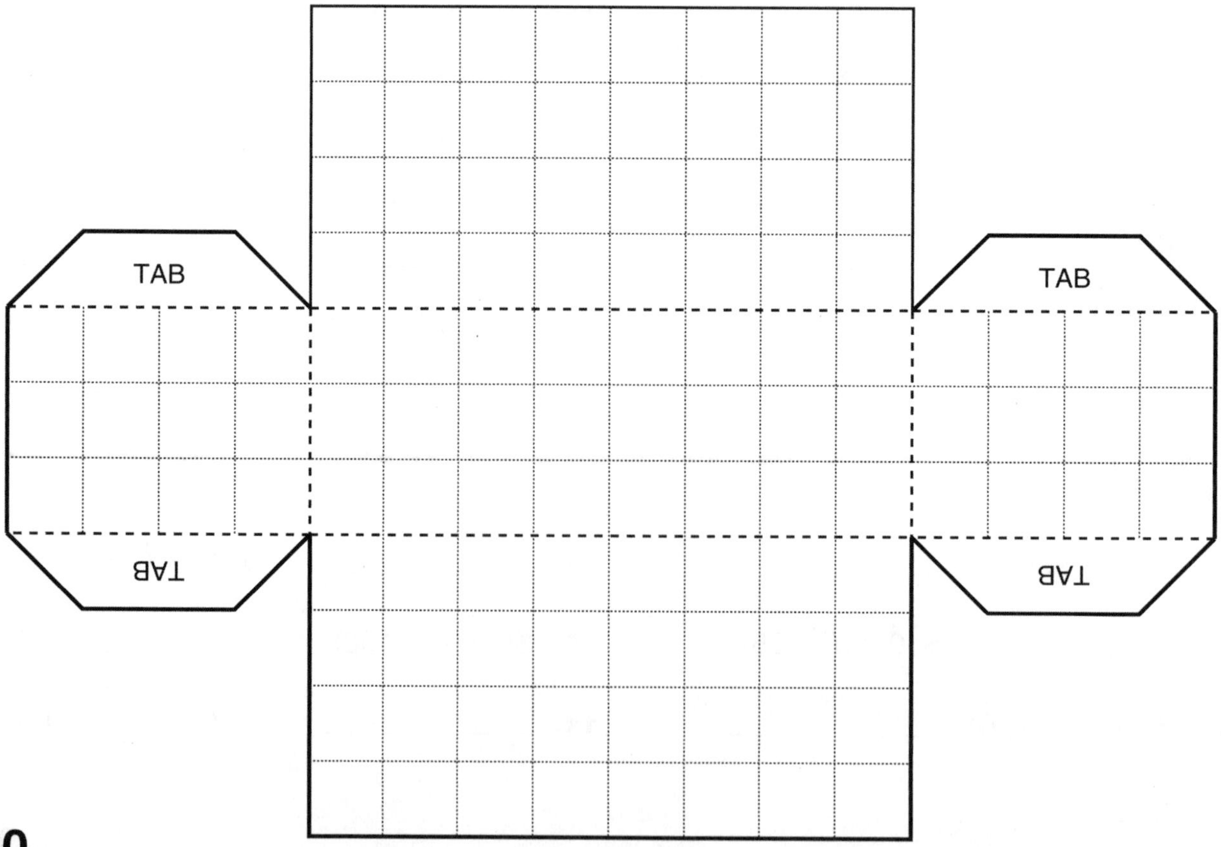

TAB

TAB

TAB

TAB

Name Date Time

Volume

1. Find the volume of each stack of centimeter cubes.

a.

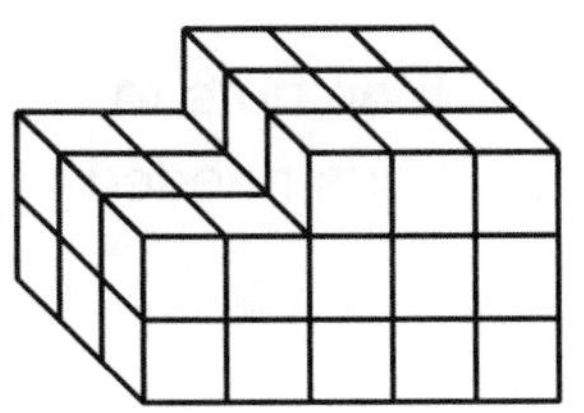

Volume = ________ cm^3

b.

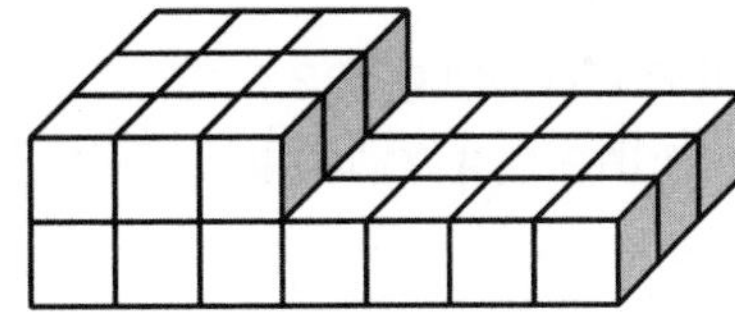

Volume = ________ cm^3

2. Calculate the volume of each rectangular prism.

a.

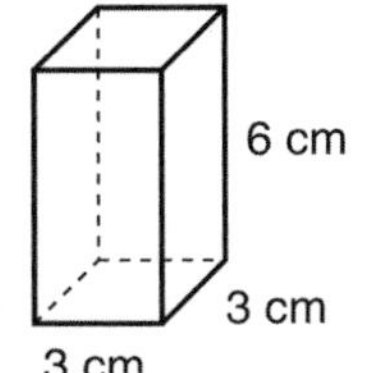

Number model: ____________________

Volume = ________ cm^3

b.

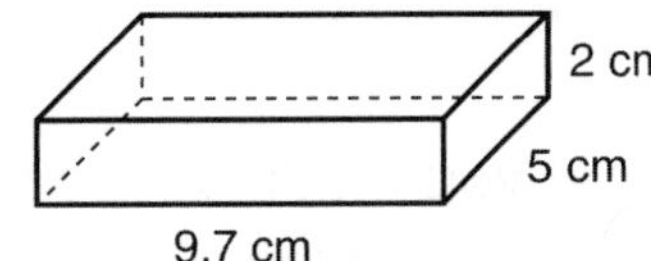

Number model: ____________________

Volume = ________ cm^3

3. What is the total number of cubes needed to completely fill each box?

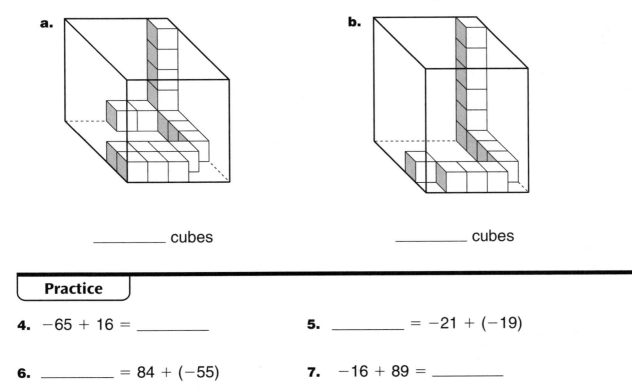

a.

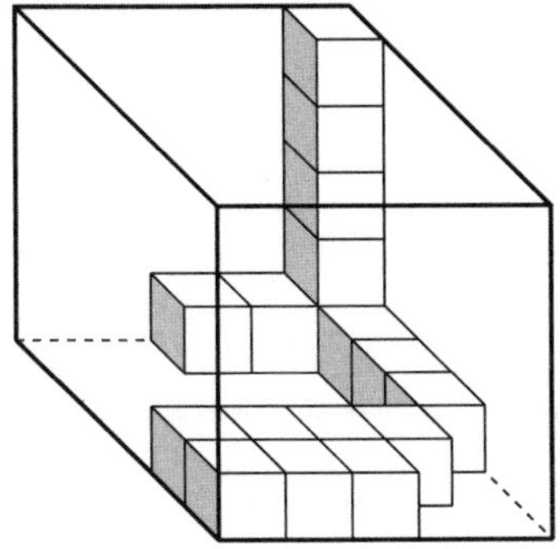

________ cubes

b.

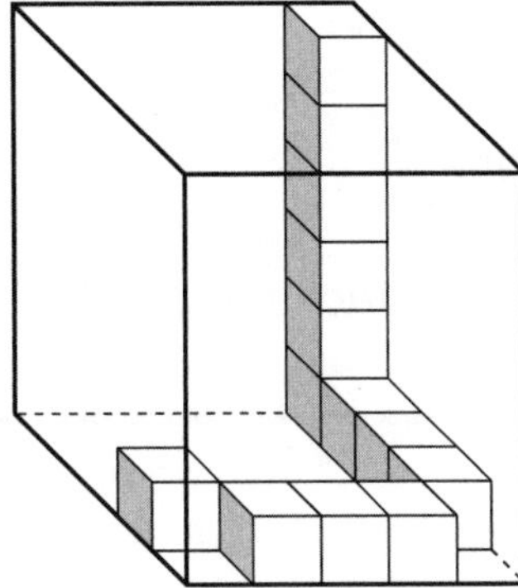

________ cubes

Practice

4. $-65 + 16 =$ ________

5. ________ $= -21 + (-19)$

6. ________ $= 84 + (-55)$

7. $-16 + 89 =$ ________

Name Date Time

LESSON 11•5 Hidden Cubes

1. The stacks of cubes shown below are called *soma cubes* and were first designed in 1936 by Piet Hein, a Danish poet and scientist.

Use interlocking cubes to build the stacks shown below. Use a small stick-on note to label each stack with the appropriate letter. Then record the number of cubes needed to build each stack.

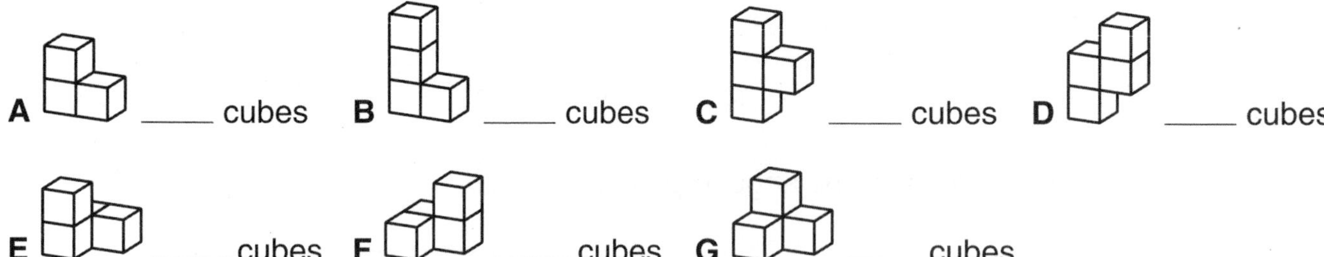

A _____ cubes **B** _____ cubes **C** _____ cubes **D** _____ cubes

E _____ cubes **F** _____ cubes **G** _____ cubes

Use the cube stacks that you made above to build each of the figures below. The figures do not have any hidden holes. Record the number of cubes needed to build each figure and the cube stacks that you used.

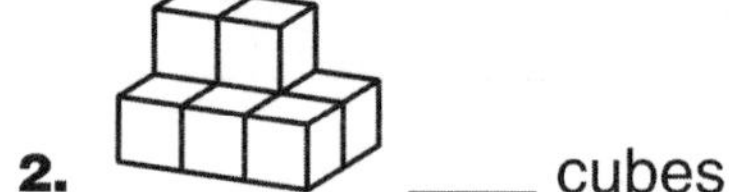

2. _____ cubes

I used the following cube stacks to build the figure: ______________________

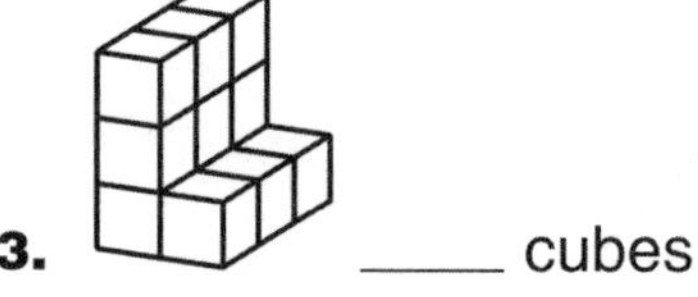

3. _____ cubes

I used the following cube stacks to build the figure: ______________________

Try This

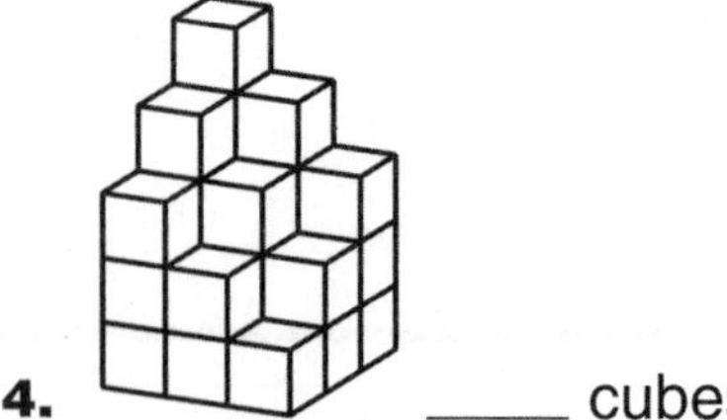

4. _____ cubes

I used the following cube stacks to build the figure: ______________________

Name ______________________ Date ______________ Time ______________

STUDY LINK **11•6**

Positive and Negative Numbers

SRB 6 60

Add or subtract.

1. $-40 + (-70) =$ ______

2. $12 - 20 =$ ______

3. ______ $= -14 - (-6)$

4. ______ $= 10 - (-5)$

5. $15 + (-1) =$ ______

6. $-12 - 7 =$ ______

7. ______ $= 60 + (-130)$

8. ______ $= -2 - (-20)$

9. Write two subtraction problems with an answer of -8.

______ $-$ ______ $= -8$ ______ $-$ ______ $= -8$

10. Write two addition problems with an answer of -30.

______ $+$ ______ $= -30$ ______ $+$ ______ $= -30$

Write $<$ or $>$ to make a true number sentence.

11. $0 - 7$ ______ -6

12. -11 ______ $-13 - (-5)$

13. $7 + (-2)$ ______ -8

14. $18 + (-8)$ ______ -18

15. $26 - (-14)$ ______ $27 + (-16)$

16. $9 - (-11)$ ______ $0 + (-20)$

List the numbers in order from least to greatest.

17. $\frac{30}{6}$, 8, -14, -0.7, 5.6, -2.5

______ ______ ______ ______ ______ ______

least greatest

18. 0.02, $-\frac{3}{5}$, -7, 4, 0.46, $-\frac{24}{6}$

______ ______ ______ ______ ______ ______

least greatest

Practice

19. ______ $= 34 * 78$

20. ______ $= 46 * 959$

21. $632 \div 4 =$ ______

22. $746 / 7 =$ ______

Name Date Time

Capacity

Find at least one container that holds each of the amounts listed below.
Describe each container and record all the capacity measurements on the label.

1. Less than 1 Pint

Container	Capacity Measurements on Label
bottle of hot chili sesame oil	5 fl oz, 148 mL

2. 1 Pint

Container	Capacity Measurements on Label
bottle of cooking oil	16 fl oz, 473 mL

3. 1 Quart

Container	Capacity Measurements on Label

4. More than 1 Quart

Container	Capacity Measurements on Label

Complete.

5. 2 quarts = ________ pints

6. 3 gallons = ________ cups

7. ________ pints = 4 cups

8. ________ quarts = 12 cups

9. 6 pints = ________ quarts

10. ________ quarts = $2\frac{1}{2}$ gallons

Practice

11. $-3 + 7 =$ ________

12. ________ $= 3 + (-7)$

13. ________ $= 40 + (-80)$

14. $-60 + (-60) =$ ________

Name Date Time

Unit 12: Family Letter

Rates

For the next two or three weeks, your child will be studying rates. Rates are among the most common applications of mathematics in daily life.

A rate is a comparison involving two different units. Familiar examples come from working (dollars per hour), driving (miles per hour), eating (calories per serving), reading (pages per day), and so on.

Our exploration of rates will begin with students collecting data on the rate at which their classmates blink their eyes. The class will try to answer the question "Does a person's eye-blinking rate depend on what the person is doing?"

During this unit, students will collect many examples of rates and might display them in a Rates All Around Museum. Then they will use these examples to make up rate problems, such as the following:

1. If cereal costs $2.98 per box, how much will 4 boxes cost?
2. If a car's gas mileage is about 20 miles per gallon, how far can the car travel on a full tank of gas (16 gallons)?
3. If I make $6.25 per hour, how long must I work to earn enough to buy shoes that cost $35?

Then the class will work together to develop strategies for solving rate problems.

The unit emphasizes the importance of mathematics to educated consumers. Your child will learn about unit-pricing labels on supermarket shelves and how to use these labels to decide which of two items is the better buy. Your child will see that comparing prices is only *part* of being an educated consumer. Other factors to consider include quality, the need for the product, and, perhaps, the product's effect on the environment.

Nutrition Facts	
Serving Size 1 link (45 g)	
Servings per Container 10	
Amount per Serving	
Calories 150	Calories from Fat 120
	% Daily Value
Total Fat 13 g	**20%**
Total Carbohydrate 1 g	**<1%**
Protein 7 g	

This unit provides a great opportunity for your child to help with the family shopping. Have your child help you decide whether the largest size is really the best buy. Is an item that is on sale necessarily a better buy than a similar product that is not on sale?

Finally, students will look back on their experiences in the yearlong World Tour project and 50-facts test routine and share them with one another.

Please keep this Family Letter for reference as your child works through Unit 12.

Vocabulary

Important terms in Unit 12:

comparison shopping Comparing prices and collecting other information needed to make good decisions about which of several competing products or services to buy.

consumer A person who acquires products or uses services.

per *For each,* as in ten chairs per row or six tickets per family.

rate A comparison by division of two quantities with different units. For example, a speed such as 55 miles per hour is a rate that compares distance with time.

rate table A way of displaying *rate* information as in the miles per gallon table below.

Miles	35	70	105	140	175	210
Gallons	1	2	3	4	5	6

unit price The price *per* item or unit of measure. For example, if a 5-ounce package of something costs \$2.50, then \$0.50 per ounce is the unit price.

unit rate A *rate* with 1 in the denominator. For example, 600 calories per 3 servings or $\frac{600 \text{ calories}}{3 \text{ servings}}$ is not a unit rate, but 200 calories per serving $\left(\frac{200 \text{ calories}}{1 \text{ serving}}\right)$ is a unit rate.

Do-Anytime Activities

To work with your child on concepts taught in this unit, try these interesting and rewarding activities:

1. Have your child examine the Nutrition Facts labels on various cans and packages of food. The labels list the number of servings in the container and the number of calories per serving. Have your child use this information to calculate the total number of calories in the full container or package. *For example:*

   A can of soup has 2.5 servings.
   There are 80 calories per serving.
   So the full can has $2.5 * 80 = 200$ calories.

2. Have your child point out rates in everyday situations. *For example:*

   store price rates: cost per dozen, cost per 6-pack, cost per ounce
   rent payments: dollars per month or dollars per year
   fuel efficiency: miles per gallon
   wages: dollars per hour
   sleep: hours per night
   telephone rates: cents per minute
   copy machine rates: copies per minute

3. Use supermarket visits to compare prices for different brands of an item and for different sizes of the same item. Have your child calculate unit prices and discuss best buys.

Building Skills through Games

In this unit, your child will play the following games. For more detailed instructions, see the *Student Reference Book.*

***Credits/Debits Game* (Advanced Version)** See *Student Reference Book,* page 239.
This game for 2 players simulates bookkeeping for a small business. A deck of number cards represents "credits" and "debits." Transactions are entered by the players on recording sheets. The game offers practice in addition and subtraction of positive and negative integers.

Fraction Top-It See *Student Reference Book,* page 247.
This game is for 2 to 4 players and requires one set of 32 Fraction Cards. The game develops skills in comparing fractions.

Name That Number See *Student Reference Book,* page 254.
This game is for 2 or 3 players and requires 1 complete deck of number cards. The game develops skills in representing numbers in different ways.

As You Help Your Child with Homework

As your child brings assignments home, you may want to go over the instructions together, clarifying them as necessary. The answers listed below will guide you through this unit's Study Links.

Study Link 12•1

2. $\frac{3}{5}$ **3.** $\frac{1}{8}$

4. 1 **5.** $\frac{5}{6}$

Study Link 12•2

1. $315

2. $12

3. 14 hours

4. a. 364 minutes per week

b. 156 minutes

5. 9,096 **6.** 54,810

7. 81 R4 **8.** 13

Study Link 12•3

1. 2,100 feet

2. a. 3,500 pounds

b. 420 gallons

3. 25 feet per second

4. a. 375 gallons

b. 1,500 quarts

5. a. 480 feet

b. 754 minutes, or $12\frac{1}{2}$ hours

6. 1,593 **7.** 55,080

8. 180 R4 **9.** 67

Study Link 12•4

1. 8 cents

2. $0.69

3. $0.35

4. Answers vary.

5. 1, 12; 2, 6; 3, 4

6. 1, 50; 2, 25; 5, 10

Study Link 12•5

1. $0.63

2. $0.37

3. $0.15

4. $0.35

5. $1.02

6. Sample answer: The 8-ounce cup is the better buy. The 8-ounce cup costs 9 cents per ounce, and the 6-ounce cup costs 10 cents per ounce.

7. Answers vary.

8. 1, 2, 3, 6, 7, 14, 21, 42

9. 1, 23

Study Link 12•6

1. 1,245 miles

2. About 9 times

3. a. About 69%

b. About 49%

4. $\frac{8}{54}$, or $\frac{4}{27}$

5. a. China

b. 6

c. 9

d. $9\frac{1}{2}$

Name Date Time

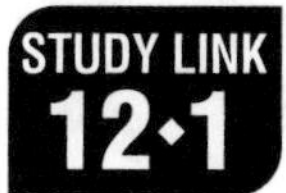

Examples of Rates

1. Look for examples of rates in newspapers, in magazines, and on labels.

Study the two examples below, and then list some of the examples you find. If possible, bring your samples to class.

Example: *Label on a can of corn says "Servings Per Container $3\frac{1}{2}$"*

Nutrition Facts
Serving Size 110 g
Servings Per Container 3 1/2
Amount Per Serving

Example: *Lightbulbs come in packages of 4 bulbs. The package doesn't say so, but there are always 4 bulbs in each package.*

Example: ______________________________

Example: ______________________________

Example: ______________________________

Practice

2. $\frac{4}{5} - \frac{1}{5} =$ __________

3. __________ $= \frac{7}{8} - \frac{3}{4}$

4. __________ $= \frac{1}{9} + \frac{8}{9}$

5. $\frac{1}{3} + \frac{3}{6} =$ __________

Name Date Time

Median and Mean

Anthony's first 4 test scores for his weekly 20-word spelling tests were 80%, 90%, 100%, and 75%.

1. What is Anthony's *median* score? ______%

2. What score must Anthony get on his next test to maintain his median score? ______% Explain your answer.

____

____

3. Anthony would like to raise his *mean* score to 90% or higher. If he takes one more spelling test, can he do it? ______ Explain your answer.

____

____

Name Date Time

LESSON 12•1

Median and Mean

Anthony's first 4 test scores for his weekly 20-word spelling tests were 80%, 90%, 100%, and 75%.

SRB 73 75

1. What is Anthony's *median* score? ______%

2. What score must Anthony get on his next test to maintain his median score? ______% Explain your answer.

____

____

3. Anthony would like to raise his *mean* score to 90% or higher. If he takes one more spelling test, can he do it? ______ Explain your answer.

____

____

Name Date Time

STUDY LINK 12·2

Rates

Solve the problems.

1. Hotels R Us charges $45 per night for a single room. At that rate, how much does a single room cost *per week?* $________

2. The Morales family spends about $84 each week for food. On average, how much do they spend *per day?* $________

3. Sharon practices playing the piano the same amount of time each day. She practiced a total of 4 hours on Monday and Tuesday combined. At that rate, how many hours would she practice *in a week?* ________ hours

Hours							
Days	1	2	3	4	5	6	7

Try This

4. People in the United States spend an average of 6 hours and 4 minutes each week reading newspapers.

   a. That's how many minutes *per week?* ________ minutes per week

   b. At that rate, how much time does an average person spend reading newspapers in a *3-day period?* ________ minutes

Minutes							
Days	1	2	3	4	5	6	7

Practice

5. ________ = 24 ∗ 379

6. 870 ∗ 63 = ________

7. 652 ÷ 8 = ________

8. 546 ÷ 42 = ________

Name Date Time

Mammal Rates

1. A mole can dig a tunnel 300 feet long in one night. How far could a mole dig in one week? About ________ feet

2. An elephant may eat 500 pounds of hay and drink 60 gallons of water in one day.

a. About how many pounds of hay could an elephant eat per week? About ________ pounds

b. About how many gallons of water could an elephant drink per week? About ________ gallons

3. The bottle-nosed whale can dive to a depth of 3,000 feet in 2 minutes. About how many feet is that per second? About ________ feet per second

4. A good milking cow will give up to 1,500 gallons of milk in a year.

a. About how many gallons is that in 3 months? About ________ gallons

b. About how many *quarts* is that in 3 months? About ________ quarts

Try This

5. Sloths spend up to 80 percent of their lives sleeping. Not only is a sloth extremely sleepy, but it is also very slow. A sloth travels on the ground at a speed of about 7 feet per minute. In the trees, its speed is about 15 feet per minute.

a. After one hour, how much farther would a sloth have traveled in the trees than on the ground (if it didn't stop to sleep)? About ________ feet

b. About how long would it take a sloth to travel 1 mile on the ground? (*Hint:* There are 5,280 feet in a mile.) About ________ minutes,

or ________ hours

Practice

6. 59 ∗ 27 = ________

7. ________ = 648 ∗ 85

8. 904 ÷ 5 = ________

9. ________ = 536 / 8

Name Date Time

Mammal 100-Yard Dash

It could not happen, of course, but suppose that you, an elephant, and a cheetah were to race a distance of 100 yards, or 300 feet. Which of you would win? Which would come in second? Third?

1. My Prediction: First _______________ Second _______________ Third _______________

2. On the diagram below, show the winner crossing the finish line. Estimate where you think the second-place and third-place mammals would be when the fastest mammal wins. Write "C" for the cheetah, "E" for the elephant, and "Me" for yourself.

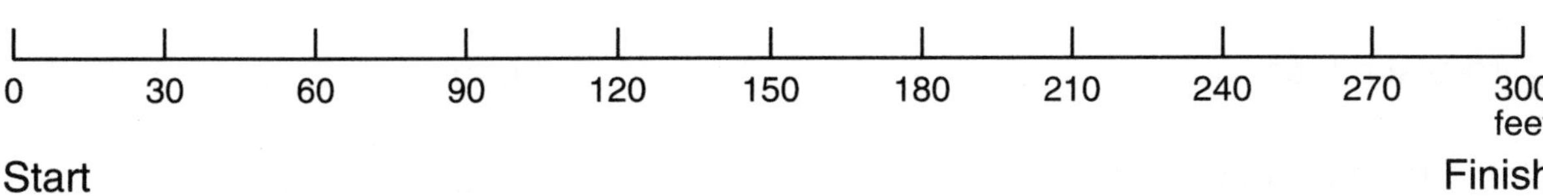

3. What information would help you predict the winner?

____

____

4. Complete the table below by using the "last race results" to find each mammal's top sprint speed in feet per second.

Mammal	Last Race Results	Top Sprint Speed (approximate)
Fourth Grader	84 yards in 12 seconds	_______ ft/sec
Cheetah	2,448 inches in 2 seconds	_______ ft/sec
Elephant	36 yards in 3 seconds	_______ ft/sec

Name Date Time

Mammal 100-Yard Dash *continued*

5. According to the ft/sec rates, how would the 300-foot race among an elephant, a cheetah, and a fourth grader turn out?

First ______________ Second ______________ Third ______________

6. About how long would it take for the winner of the race to run 300 feet? About ____________ seconds

7. By the time the winner crosses the finish line, how far would the other mammals have run?

Second-place mammal About ____________ feet

Third-place mammal About ____________ feet

8. Would it be a close race? ____________

9. On the diagram below, show which mammal will win the race and where the other two mammals will be when the winner crosses the finish line.

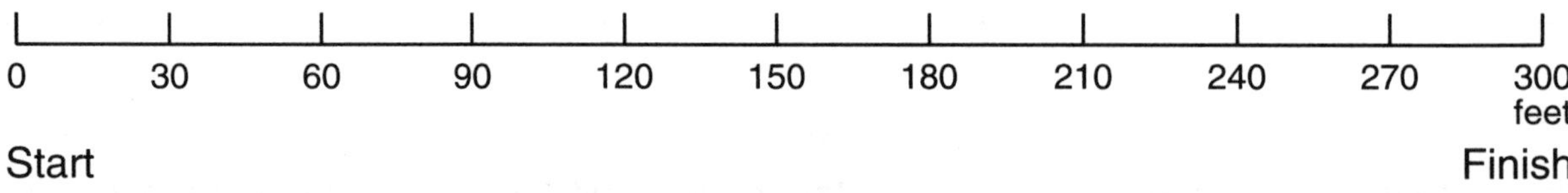

10. About how many times faster is the first-place mammal than

a. the second-place mammal? ____________

b. the third-place mammal? ____________

11. The top sprint speed for a squirrel is 18 feet per second. Does this mean that you could catch a squirrel by running after it? Explain.

____

____

____

Name Date Time

Unit Prices

Solve the unit price problems below. Complete the tables if it is helpful to do so.

1. A 12-oz bag of pretzels costs 96 cents. The unit price is ______________ per ounce.

Dollars				0.96
Ounces	1	3	9	12

2. A package of 3 rolls of paper towels costs \$2.07. The unit price is ______________ per roll.

Dollars			2.07
Rolls	1	2	3

3. A 4-liter bottle of water costs \$1.40. The unit price is ______________ per liter.

Dollars				1.40
Liters	1	2	3	4

4. Choose 4 items from newspaper ads. In the table below, record the name, price, and quantity of each item. Leave the Unit Price column blank.

Item	Quantity	Price	Unit Price
Golden Sun Raisins	*24 ounces*	*\$2.99*	

Practice

Name the factor pairs for each number.

5. 12 ______________ **6.** 50 ______________

Stock-Up Sale

Party Town is having a summer stock-up sale. The ad below shows the original price of each item and the sale price if you buy a certain number of items. Use bills and coins to help you find the stock-up price per item.

1.

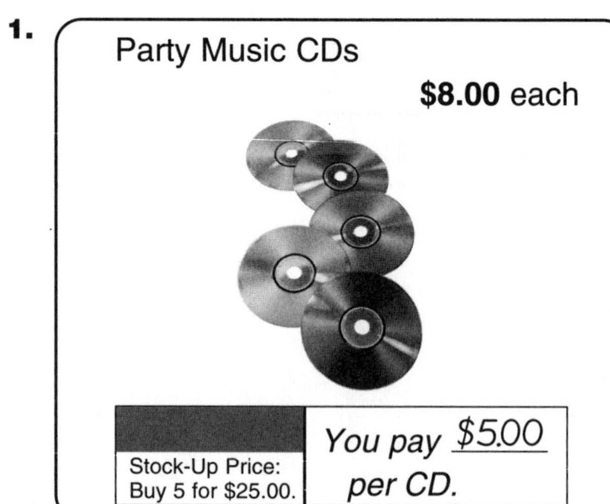

Party Music CDs
$8.00 each
Stock-Up Price: Buy 5 for $25.00.
You pay $5.00 *per CD.*

2.

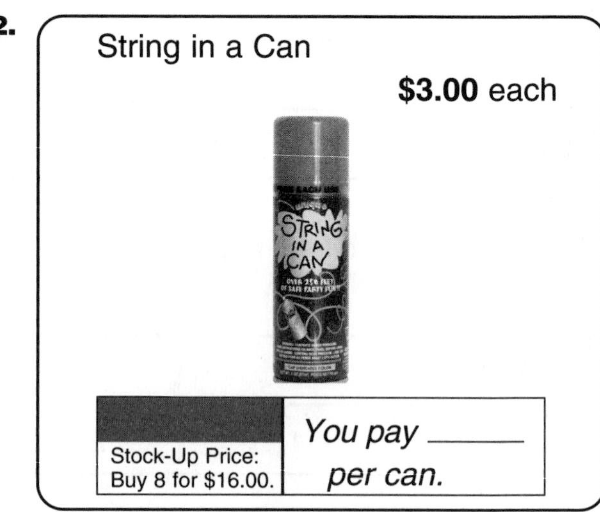

String in a Can
$3.00 each
String in a Can
Stock-Up Price: Buy 8 for $16.00.
You pay ______ *per can.*

3.

Mylar Balloon
$1.99 each
You're the Best!
Stock-Up Price: Buy 12 for $14.40.
You pay ______ *per balloon.*

4.

5.

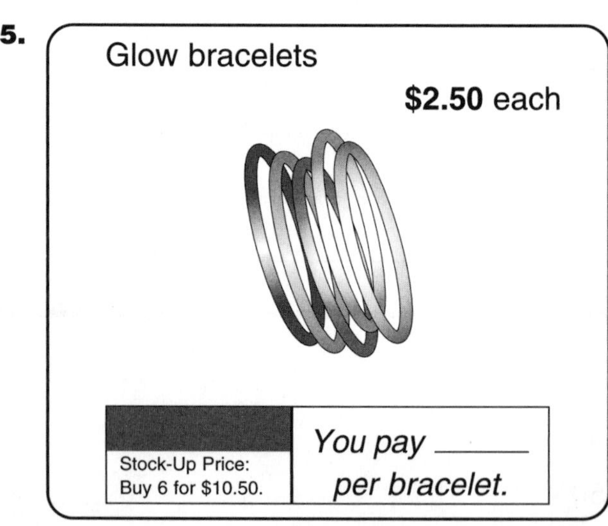

Glow bracelets
$2.50 each
Stock-Up Price: Buy 6 for $10.50.
You pay ______ *per bracelet.*

6.

Party Hats
$9.99 for a package of 45
Stock-Up Price: Buy 4 packages for $19.96.
You pay ______ *per package.*

Name Date Time

Unit Pricing

SRB 47

1. A package of 3 muffins costs $1.89.
What is the price *per muffin?* ________

2. A 5-pound bag of rice costs $1.85.
What is the price *per pound?* ________

3. Chewy worms are sold at $2.40 per pound.
What is the price *per ounce?* ________

4. A 6-pack of bagels costs $2.11.
What is the price *per bagel?* ________

5. A 2-pound bag of frozen corn costs $2.03.
What is the price *per pound?* ________

6. A store sells yogurt in two sizes: The 8-ounce cup costs 72 cents, and the 6-ounce cup costs 60 cents. Which is the better buy? Explain your answer.

____

____

____

____

7. Make up your own "better buy" problem. Then solve it.

____

____

____

____

____

Practice

Name all the factors.

8. 42 ________________________

9. 23 ________________________

Name Date Time

Which is the Better Buy?

For each problem, draw pictures and use bills and coins to decide which product is the better buy.

1. A 12-oz bottle of sports drink costs $0.75.
   A six-pack of 12-oz sports drink costs $3.60.

   Which is the better buy? ______________________
   Explain how you know.

2. One pencil costs $0.10. A box of 12 pencils costs $1.80.

   Which is the better buy? ______________________
   Explain how you know.

3. A cup of yogurt costs $0.90. A four-pack of yogurt costs $3.00.

   Which is the better buy? ______________________
   Explain how you know.

4. Write and solve your own "better buy" problem.

   ____

   ____

   ____

Name Date Time

LESSON 12•5 Measuring Air Pressure with a Barometer

Some people think that air does not weigh anything. But it does—you can prove this by doing a simple experiment. Weigh a deflated soccer ball or basketball. Next, pump it full of air. Weigh it again. The ball will weigh more after you have pumped air into it. This shows that the air you pumped in does have weight.

In 1643, Evangelista Torricelli, a student of Galileo, invented an instrument for measuring air pressure—how much the weight of air pushes on a surface. He made a glass tube about $3\frac{1}{2}$ feet long, closed it at one end, and filled it with mercury. Then he turned the tube upside down and put it into an open container that held more mercury. When he did that, the mercury in the tube fell a few inches and then stopped.

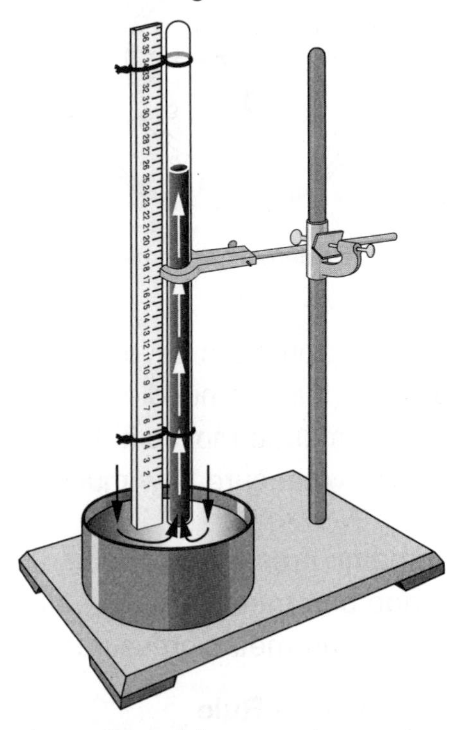

An early model mercury barometer

You may wonder why some of the mercury remained in the tube. Why didn't *all* the mercury flow out of the tube and mix with the mercury in the container? The reason is that the air above the open container pushes down on the mercury. This, in turn, supports the mercury in the tube. The greater the air pressure, the higher the level of the mercury in the tube.

The instrument Torricelli invented is called a mercury barometer. The height of the mercury in the tube depends on the barometric pressure. When a weather forecaster reports that the barometric pressure is 30.25, this means that the mercury in the tube has reached a level of 30.25 inches.

Barometers are used to predict the weather. In fact, Torricelli's barometer came to be known as the "weather glass." When the weather pattern is changing, the barometric pressure also changes. When the barometer readings fall steadily or suddenly, a storm is probably on its way. The faster the barometer readings fall and the lower the reading, the more severe the storm is likely to be. When the barometer readings rise, you can expect fair weather.

Name Date Time

Measuring Air Pressure with a Barometer *cont.*

Aneroid barometer

Mercury barometers are awkward to carry from one place to another. A more convenient type of barometer is the aneroid barometer. This is the sort of barometer you may have in your school or at home. *Aneroid* means "without liquid." The units on an aneroid barometer have the same meaning as the units on a mercury barometer. If your aneroid barometer reads 29.85, a mercury barometer would show 29.85 inches of mercury in the tube.

Aneroid barometers have two needles. One needle moves when the barometric pressure changes. (It is the needle pointing to 30 in the picture.) The other needle stays in place unless someone moves it. If you move the smaller needle to today's reading, later you will be able to measure how much the barometric pressure has changed.

Barometric pressure is affected by elevation—how high the land is above sea level. The average barometric pressure at sea level is about 30 inches. At higher elevations, the average barometric pressure will be less.

The Elevation Rule

- ◆ For every 100 feet you climb, the barometer reading will drop about 0.1 inch.
- ◆ For every 1,000 feet you climb, the reading will drop about 1 inch.

Denver, Colorado, is about 5,000 feet above sea level; the average barometric pressure in Denver is about 25 inches.

Here is a map of the island of Hawaii. The numbers on the map give barometer readings for the cities shown—all taken under similar weather conditions. All readings were also taken at the same time. They vary because the cities are at different heights, or elevations, above sea level.

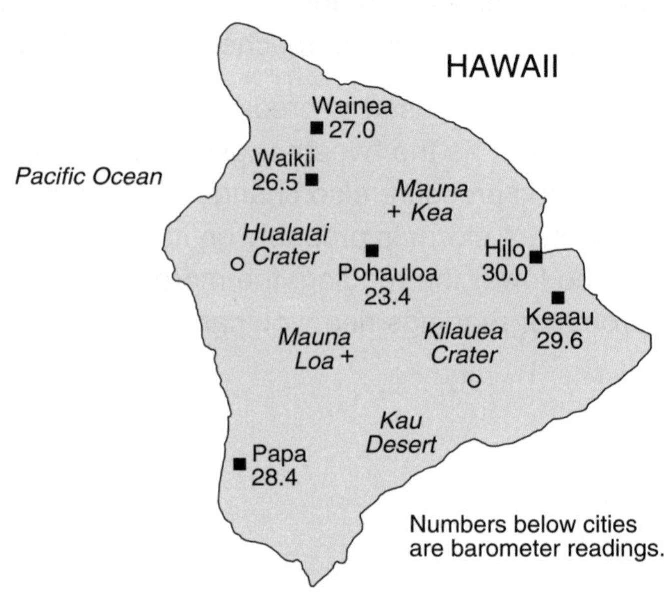

Name Date Time

LESSON 12•5

The Barometer and Elevation

Refer to the map of Hawaii and the Elevation Rule on *Math Masters,* page 350 to answer the following questions.

1. Hilo is the largest city on the island of Hawaii. It is at sea level. This means that its elevation is 0 feet above sea level. What is the barometer reading in Hilo? About ______________ inches

2. Compare Keaau to Wainea.

a. What is the barometer reading in Keaau? About ______________ inches

b. What is the barometer reading in Wainea? About ______________ inches

c. Which is higher above sea level: Keaau or Wainea? ______________________

3. Compare Waikii to Hilo.

a. What is the barometer reading in Waikii? About ______________ inches

b. How much less is the barometer reading in Waikii than in Hilo? ______________ inches less

c. What is the elevation of Waikii? About ______________ feet above sea level

4. The barometer reading at the top of Kilauea Crater is 1.7 inches less than at the top of Hualalai Crater.

a. Which crater has a higher elevation? ______________________

b. About how much higher is it? About ______________ feet

5. The Kau Desert is about 2,500 feet above sea level. What should the barometer reading be there? About ______________ inches

6. The highest mountains on Hawaii are Mauna Loa and Mauna Kea. Their heights are nearly the same. If the barometer reads 16.4 inches at the top of these mountains, what is their elevation? About ______________ feet above sea level

Name Date Time

Country Statistics

1. China has the longest border in the world—13,759 miles. Russia has the second longest border in the world—12,514 miles. How much shorter is Russia's border than China's border? _______ miles

2. The area of Russia is about 1,818,629 square miles. The area of Spain, including offshore islands, is about 194,897 square miles. About how many times larger is Russia than Spain? _______ times larger

3. Students in China attend school about 251 days per year. Students in the United States attend school about 180 days per year.

   a. About what percent of the year do Chinese students spend in school? _______%

   b. About what percent of the year do American students spend in school? _______%

4. English is officially spoken in 54 countries. Portuguese is officially spoken in 8 countries. Portuguese is spoken in about what fraction of the number of English-speaking countries? _______

5. The table to the right shows the countries in the world with the most neighboring countries.

Country	Number of Neighbors
Brazil	10
China	15
Dem. Rep. of Congo	9
Germany	9
Russia	14
Sudan	9

Use the data in the table to answer the following questions.

a. Which country has the maximum number of neighbors? _______

b. What is the range? _______

c. What is the mode? _______

d. What is the median? _______

Name Date Time

LESSON 12•6

Interpreting the Remainder

Draw a picture to illustrate the problem. Then solve the problem.

1. The roller coaster holds 24 people per ride. There are 65 people waiting in line. How many times does the roller coaster need to run before everyone in line gets a turn to ride?

Number model: ______________________ Picture:

Answer: ________ times

What did you do about the remainder? Circle the answer.

Ignored it.

Reported it as a fraction or decimal.

Rounded the answer up.

Why?

____

____

2. Cedric's teacher is ordering pizza for an end-of-year party. He has $35.00 to spend. A large cheese pizza costs $8.00. How many pizzas can he order?

Number model: ______________________ Picture:

Answer: ________ pizzas

What did you do about the remainder? Circle the answer.

Ignored it.

Reported it as a fraction or decimal.

Rounded the answer up.

Why?

____

____

Name Date Time

Family Letter

Congratulations!

By completing *Fourth Grade Everyday Mathematics,* your child has accomplished a great deal. Thank you for all of your support.

This Family Letter is a resource to use throughout your child's vacation. It includes an extended list of Do-Anytime Activities, directions for games that can be played at home, a list of mathematics-related books to check out over vacation, and a sneak preview of what your child will be learning in *Fifth Grade Everyday Mathematics.* Enjoy the vacation!

Do-Anytime Activities

Mathematics means more when it is rooted in real-life situations. To help your child review many of the concepts he or she has learned in fourth grade, we suggest the following activities for you and your child to do together over vacation. These activities will help your child build on the skills he or she has learned this year and help prepare him or her for *Fifth Grade Everyday Mathematics.*

1. Have your child practice any multiplication and division facts that he or she has not yet mastered. Include some quick drills.
2. Provide items for your child to measure. Have your child use personal references, as well as U.S. customary and metric measuring tools.
3. Use newspapers and magazines as sources of numbers, graphs, and tables that your child may read and discuss.
4. Have your child practice multidigit multiplication and division using the algorithms that he or she is most comfortable with.
5. Ask your child to look at advertisements and find the sale prices of items using the original prices and rates of discount or find rates of discount using original prices and sale prices. Have your child use a calculator and calculate unit prices to determine best or better buys.
6. Continue the World Tour by reading about other countries.

Name Date Time

Family Letter *cont.*

Building Skills through Games

The following section lists rules for games that can be played at home. You will need a deck of number cards, which can be made from index cards or by modifying a regular deck of cards as follows:

A regular deck of playing cards includes 54 cards (52 regular cards plus 2 jokers). Use a permanent marker to mark some of the cards:

- Mark each of the four aces with the number 1.
- Mark each of the four queens with the number 0.
- Mark the four jacks and four kings with the numbers 11 through 18.
- Mark the two jokers with the numbers 19 and 20.

Beat the Calculator

Materials number cards 1–10 (4 of each); calculator

Players 3

Directions

1. One player is the "Caller," one is the "Calculator," and one is the "Brain."
2. Shuffle the deck of cards and place it facedown.
3. The Caller draws two cards from the number deck and asks for their product.
4. The Calculator solves the problem with a calculator. The Brain solves it without a calculator. The Caller decides who got the answer first.
5. The Caller continues to draw two cards at a time from the number deck and asks for their product.
6. Players trade roles every 10 turns or so.

Example: The Caller draws a 10 and 7 and calls out "10 times 7." The Brain and the Calculator solve the problem.

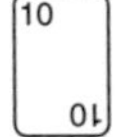

The Caller decides who got the answer first.

Variation 1: To practice extended multiplication facts, have the Caller draw two cards from the number deck and attach a 0 to either one of the factors or to both factors before asking for the product.

Example: If the Caller turns over a 4 and a 6, he or she may make up any one of the following problems:

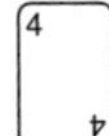

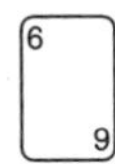

$4 * 60$ $40 * 6$ $40 * 60$

Variation 2: Use a full set of number cards: 4 each of the numbers 1–10, and 1 each of the numbers 11–20.

Name Date Time

Building Skills through Games

Name That Number

Materials 1 complete deck of number cards

Players 2 or 3

Object of the game To collect the most cards

Directions

1. Shuffle the cards and deal five cards to each player. Place the remaining cards number-side down. Turn over the top card and place it beside the deck. This is the **target number** for the round.
2. Players try to match the target number by adding, subtracting, multiplying, or dividing the numbers on as many of their cards as possible. A card may be used only once.
3. Players write their solutions on a sheet of paper or a slate. When players have written their best solutions:
   - They set aside the cards they used to name the target number.
   - Replace them by drawing new cards from the top of the deck.
   - Put the old target number on the bottom of the deck.
   - Turn over a new target number, and play another hand.
4. Play continues until there are not enough cards left to replace all of the players' cards. The player who sets aside more cards wins the game.

Example: Target number: 16 A player's cards:

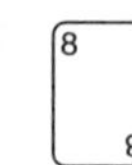
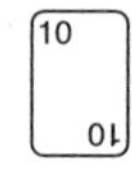

Some possible solutions:

10 + 8 − 2 = 16 (*three cards used*)

7 ∗ 2 + 10 − 8 = 16 (*four cards used*)

8 / 2 + 10 + 7 − 5 = 16 (*all five cards used*)

The player sets aside the cards used to make a solution and draws the same number of cards from the top of the deck.

Name Date Time

Vacation Reading with a Mathematical Twist

Books can contribute to children's learning by presenting mathematics in a combination of real-world and imaginary contexts. The titles listed below were recommended by teachers who use *Everyday Mathematics* in their classrooms. They are organized by mathematical topic. Visit your local library and check out these mathematics-related books with your child.

Geometry

A Cloak for the Dreamer by Aileen Friedman

The Greedy Triangle by Marilyn Burns

Measurement

The Magic School Bus Inside the Earth by Joanna Cole

The Hundred Penny Box by Sharon Bell Mathis

Numeration

Alexander, Who Used to be Rich Last Sunday by Judith Viorst

If You Made a Million by David M. Schwartz

Fraction Action by Loreen Leedy

How Much Is a Million? by David M. Schwartz

Operations

Anno's Mysterious Multiplying Jar by Masaichiro Anno

The King's Chessboard by David Birch

One Hundred Hungry Ants by Elinor J. Pinczes

A Remainder of One by Elinor J. Pinczes

Patterns, Functions, and Sequences

Eight Hands Round by Ann Whitford Paul

Visual Magic by David Thomas

Reference Frames

The Magic School Bus: Inside the Human Body by Joanna Cole

Pigs on a Blanket by Amy Axelrod

Looking Ahead: Fifth Grade Everyday Mathematics

Next year your child will . . .

- ◆ Develop skills with decimals and percents
- ◆ Continue to practice multiplication and division skills, including operations with decimals
- ◆ Investigate methods for solving problems using mathematics in everyday situations
- ◆ Work with number lines, times, dates, and rates
- ◆ Collect, organize, describe, and interpret numerical data
- ◆ Further explore the properties, relationships, and measurement of 2- and 3-dimensional objects
- ◆ Read, write, and use whole numbers, fractions, decimals, percents, negative numbers, and exponential notation
- ◆ Explore scientific notation

Again, thank you for all of your support this year. Have fun continuing your child's mathematical experiences throughout the vacation!

Project Masters

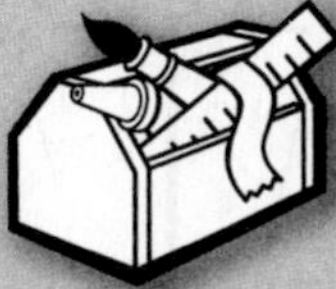

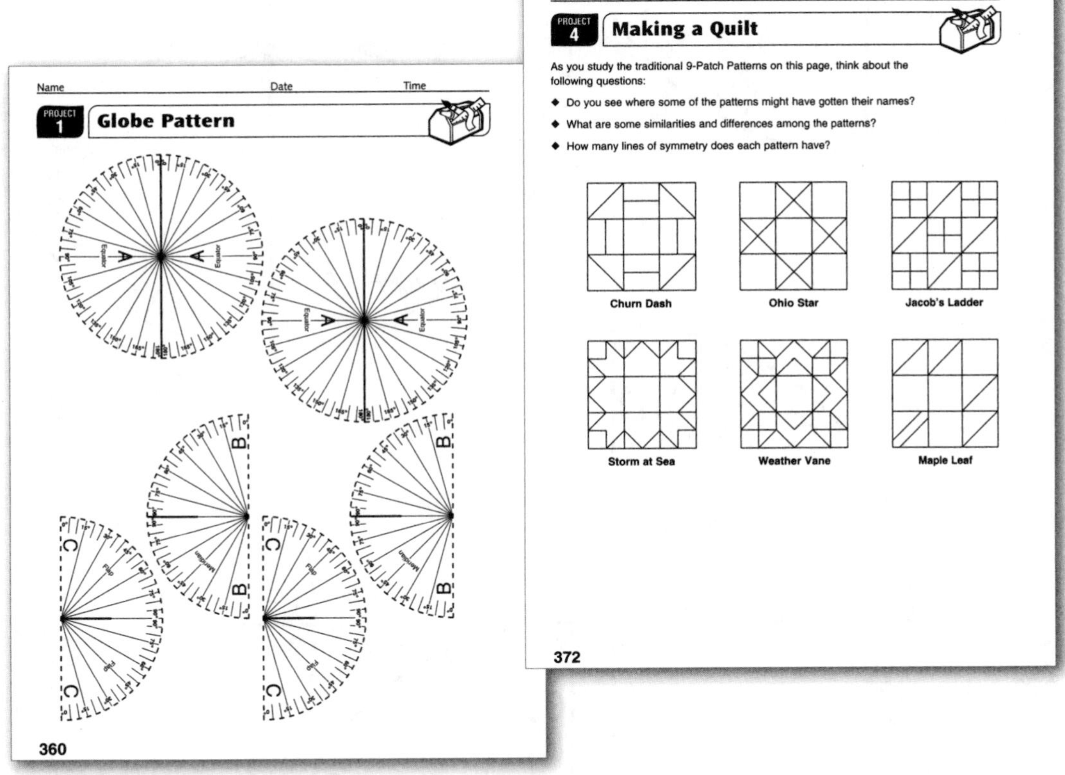

Name Date Time

Globe Pattern

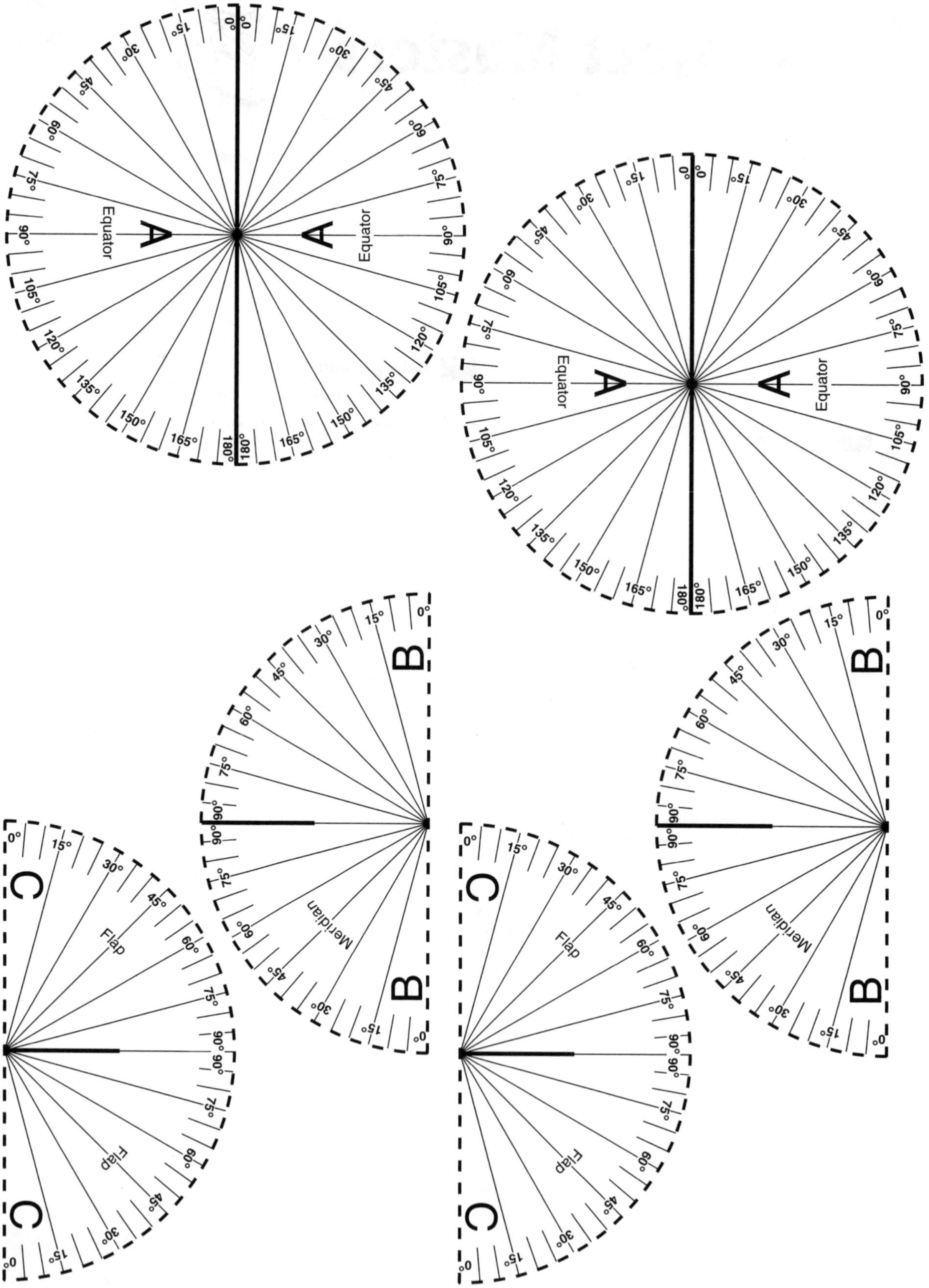

Name Date Time

How to Make a Cutaway Globe

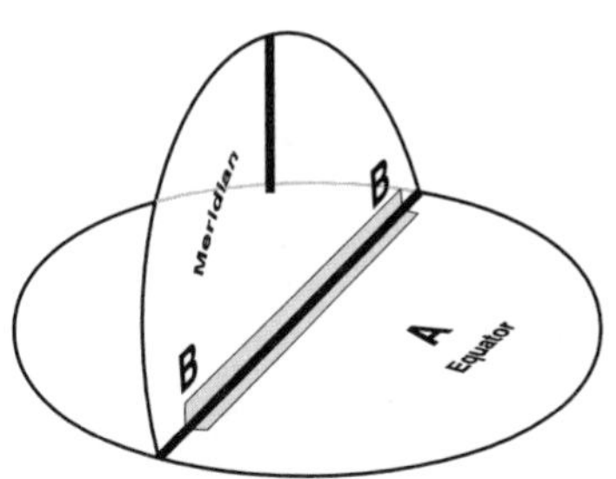

Figure 1

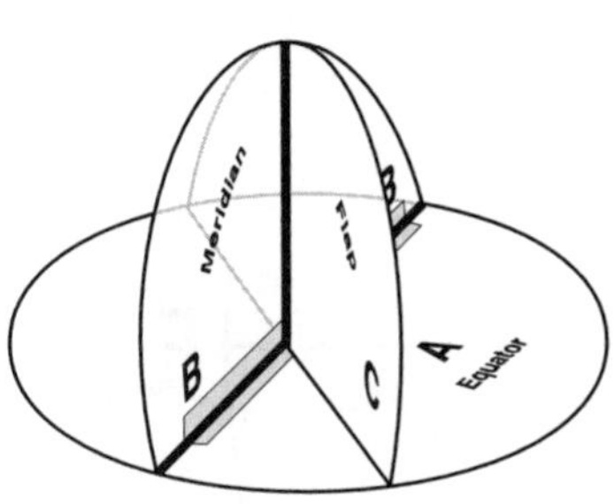

Figure 2

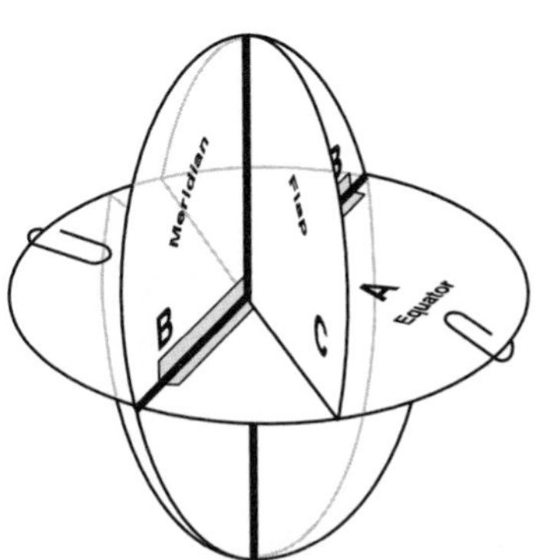

Figure 3

Directions:

Step 1: Carefully cut out one of the circles A along the dashed lines.

Step 2: Cut out one of the semicircles B; cut the thin slit on the semicircle.

Step 3: Lay semicircle B on circle A so that the base of the semicircle aligns with the 0° to 180° diameter shown on circle A. Tape the pieces together on both sides of the semicircle. Adjust the semicircle so that it stands straight up. See Figure 1.

Step 4: Cut out one of the semicircles C and cut along the slit. Fold the semicircle in half at the 90° line. Fold it back and forth several times at the same place until you have made a good crease.

Step 5: Slide the slit of semicircle C through the slit of semicircle B. See Figure 2.

Step 6: Repeat Steps 1–5 to make a second hemisphere.

Step 7: Put the two hemispheres together with paper clips to make a full globe. Put the 0° labels on circles A together. See Figure 3.

Name Date Time

A Paper Compass

N

0° 15° 30° 45° 60° 75°

W 270° 90° E

105° 120° 135° 150° 165° 180° 195° 210° 225° 240° 255° 285° 300° 315° 330° 345°

S

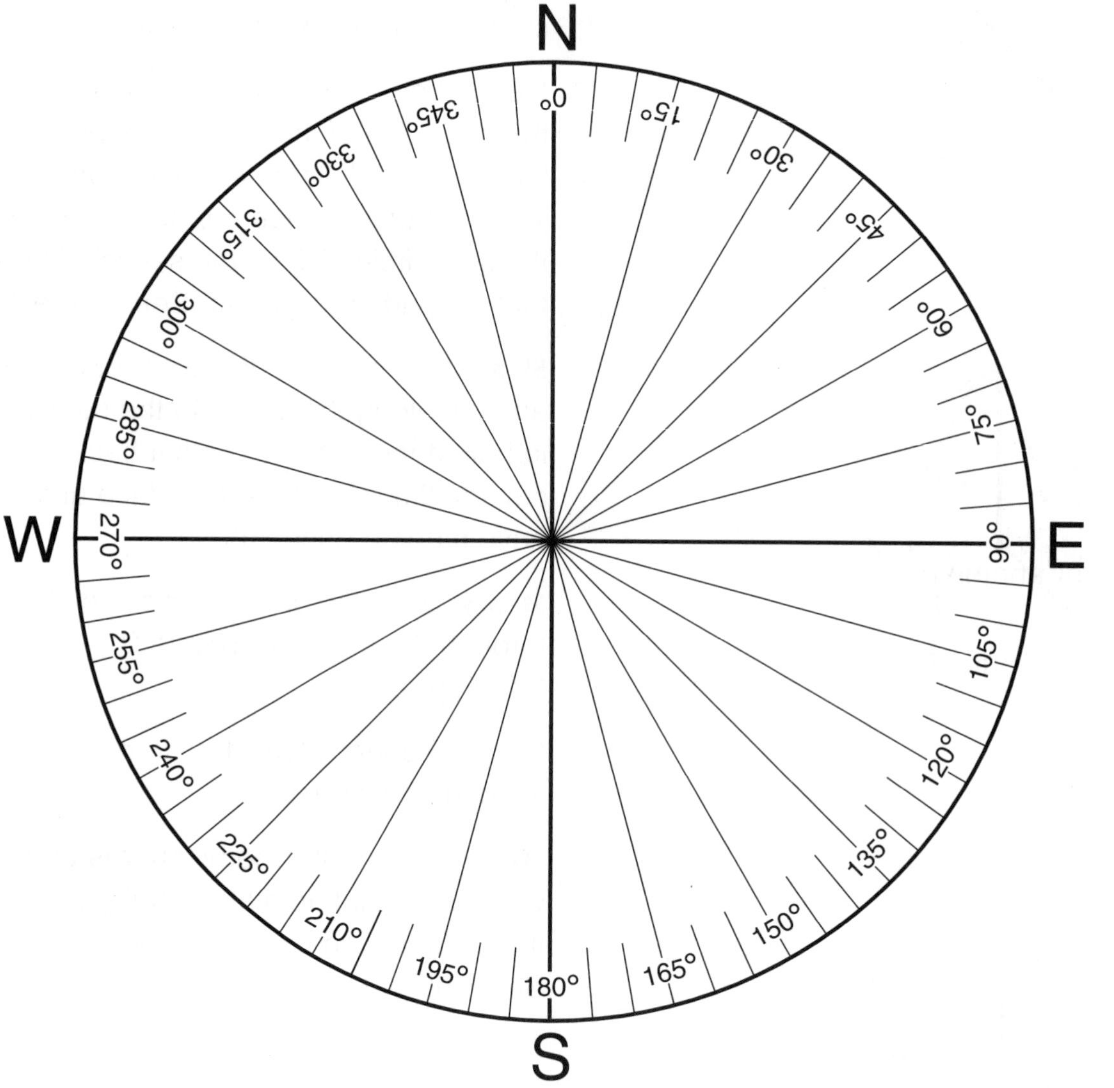

Name Date Time

PROJECT 2 Making a Compass

In ancient times, sailors had only the sun, moon, and stars to aid them in navigation. The most important navigational instrument was the **compass.** The compass was invented more than 1,000 years ago. The first compass was a small bar of magnetized iron that floated on a reed in a bowl of water. The magnet in the iron would make the reed point to the magnetically charged North Pole. Using a compass, sailors could tell in which direction they were traveling.

You, too, can make a floating compass.

1. Magnetize a steel sewing needle by stroking it with one pole of a strong bar magnet. Slowly stroke the needle from end to end **in one direction only.** Be sure to lift your hand up in the air before coming down for another stroke.

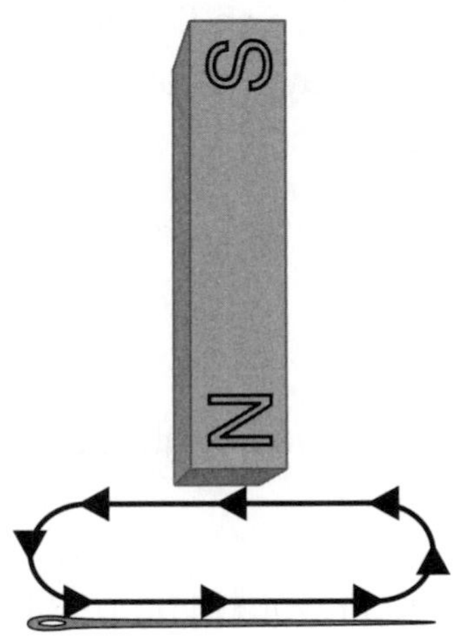

2. Slice a round ($\frac{1}{2}$-inch-thick) piece from a cork stopper. Cut a groove across the center of the top of the cork. Put the needle in the groove.

3. Place the cork into a glass, china, or aluminum dish filled with water. Add a teaspoon of detergent to the water. The detergent will lower the surface tension of the water and prevent the cork from moving to one side of the dish and staying there.

The needle will behave like a compass needle. It will assume a North-South position because of Earth's magnetic field.

Source: Science for the Elementary School. New York: Macmillan, 1993.

Name Date Time

PROJECT 3 A Carnival Game

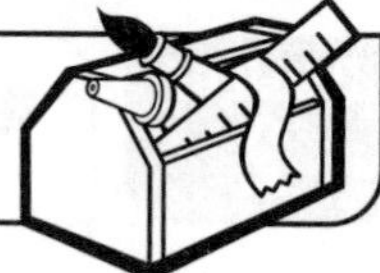

The class "quilt" of colored grids is placed on the floor and used as a target mat. The player stands about five feet from the mat and tosses a centimeter cube onto the mat. If the cube does not land on the mat, the player gets another turn. If the cube lands on more than one color, the color that is covered by most of the cube is used. The player may win a money prize, depending upon the color on which the cube lands. For each play, the player must buy a ticket for 10 cents.

Test your skill! Try your luck!
10¢ per toss
PRIZES
yellow... 50¢ blue.... 10¢
red..... 30¢ white... 0¢
green.. 20¢

1. Suppose that you bought 50 tickets.

   a. How much would you pay for 50 tickets? __________

   Suppose that your 50 tosses landed on the colors you recorded in the table at the bottom of page 215 of *Math Journal 2.*

   b. How much prize money would you have won? __________

   c. Would you win or lose money on the game? __________

   How much? __________

2. Suppose that the class decided to use the game to raise money to buy computer software. Pretend that students sold 1,000 tickets and that the cubes landed on the colors as shown on the board or on *Math Masters,* page 238.

   a. How much would the class collect on the sale of tickets? __________

   b. How much prize money would the class pay? __________

   c. How much money would the class raise? __________

Name Date Time

A Carnival Game *continued*

3. Work with your group to make up your own version of the carnival game.

a. Record how much you would charge for a ticket and what the prizes would be for each color.

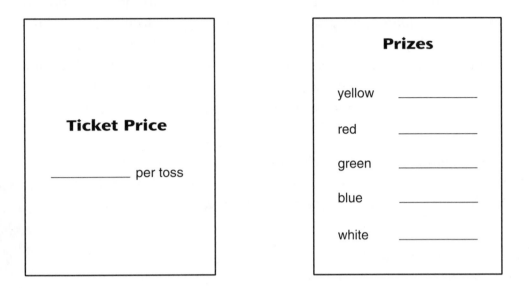

Ticket Price

__________ per toss

Prizes

yellow	__________
red	__________
green	__________
blue	__________
white	__________

b. Use the results for 1,000 cube drops shown on the board or on *Math Masters,* page 242 to answer the following questions:

Would the class have won or lost money? __________

How much? __________

4. Suppose that the class ran your game on Parents' Night.

a. How many tickets do you estimate the class would sell? __________

b. How much money would the class get from ticket sales? __________

c. About how much money should you expect to pay in prizes? __________

d. About how much money should the class expect to earn? __________

Name Date Time

Patchwork Quilts

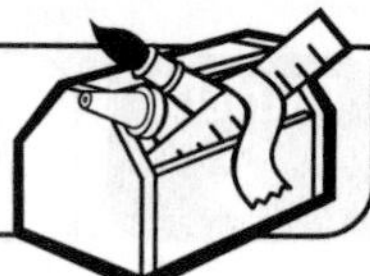

Throughout American history, women have worked together to make **patchwork quilts.** Because cloth was expensive and scarce, quilts were often made out of pieces of worn-out clothing or leftovers from another project. The quilters began by sewing together pieces of different colors, shapes, and textures to create a square pattern. Then they made more "patchwork" squares with the same pattern. When they had enough squares, they sewed them together to form the top of the quilt. Next they added a layer of wool fleece or cotton, called *batting,* and a cloth backing. They made a "sandwich" of the three layers—the backing on the bottom, the batting in the middle, and the patchwork on the top. They stretched the "sandwich" on a wooden frame and sewed the three layers together with tiny stitches.

The quilt was put together at a party, called a **quilting bee.** While cutting and sewing, the women would tell stories and share what went on in their lives. When the quilt was finished, the men joined the women for supper and dancing.

Buggy Wheel

Many patchwork patterns have become traditions. Their names and designs have come from the everyday lives of the people who created them. For example, the "Buggy Wheel" pattern was probably inspired by a trip in a buggy. Along with walking and riding horses, buggies were a popular form of transportation in early America.

Does and Darts

Although early quilters may not have studied geometry in school, we can see geometry in many of their designs. Patchwork quilting involves the cutting of fabric into various geometric shapes and sewing them together into patterns. The pattern may be repeated over and over to form a quilt, or it may be rotated or reflected as the patches are assembled. Many patchwork patterns, such as the "Buggy Wheel" and "Does and Darts," are symmetric. Others, such as the "Crazy Quilt," seem to have been created at random.

Crazy Quilt

The beauty of a quilt lies in its uniqueness. No two patches need ever be the same because there are many possible arrangements of fabrics and colors.

Name ______ Date ______ Time ______

Symmetric Patterns

Each pattern to the right of the "Pinwheel" pattern below has been colored in a different way. Notice how each color arrangement changes the number of lines of symmetry.

Pinwheel Pattern

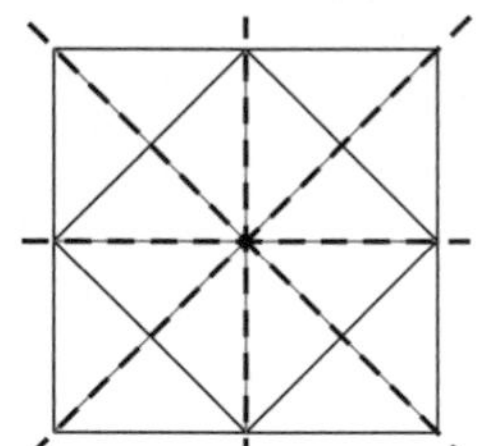

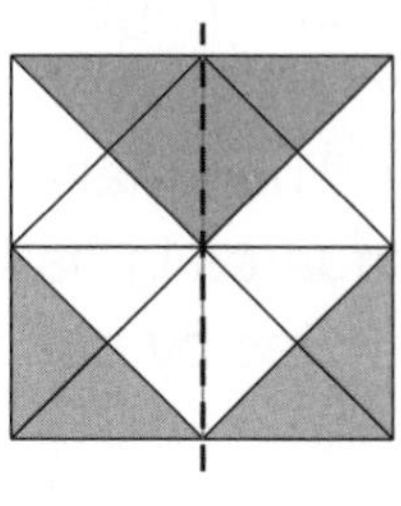

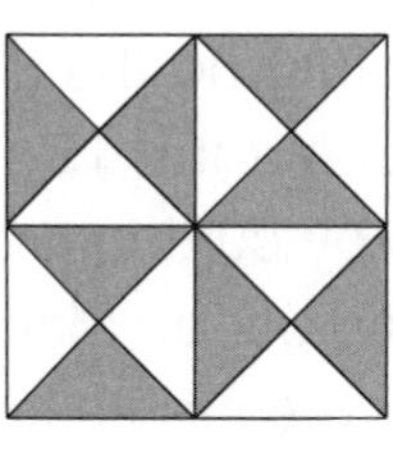

lines of symmetry: 4   2   1   0

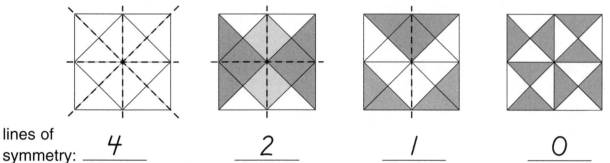

For each pattern below, draw all the lines of symmetry and record the number of lines of symmetry.

1. Bow-Tie Pattern

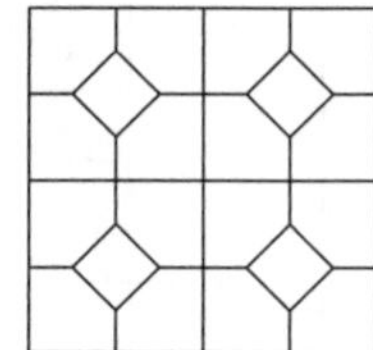

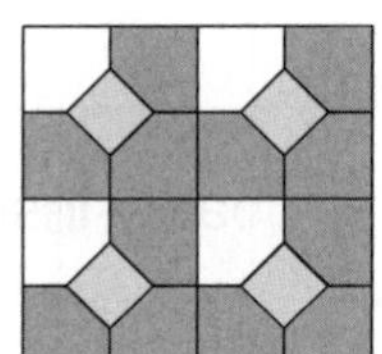

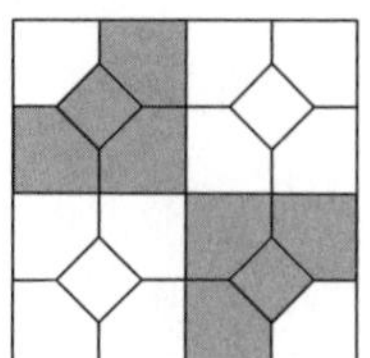

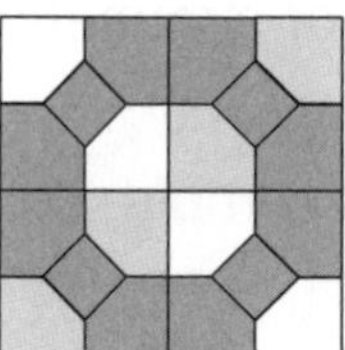

lines of symmetry: ______ ______ ______ ______

2. Ohio Star Pattern

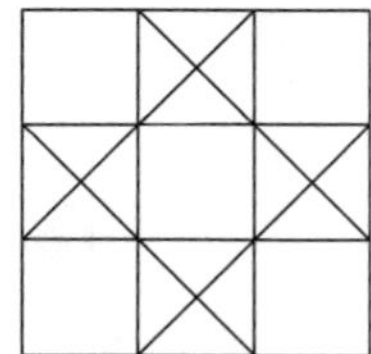

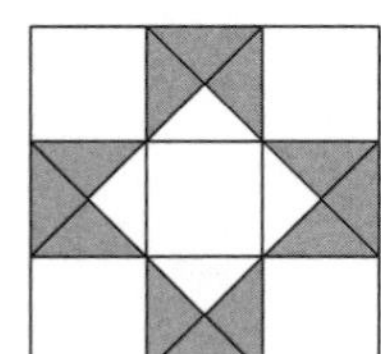

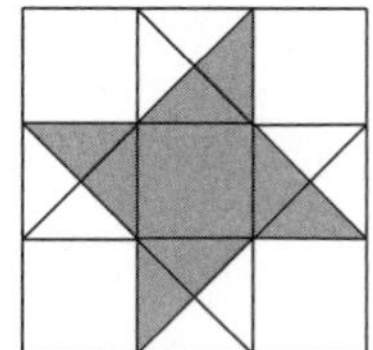

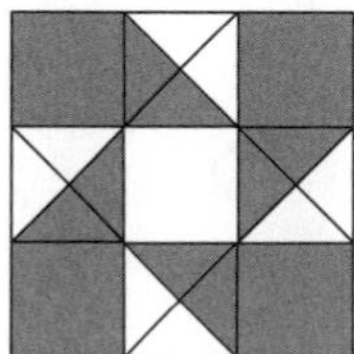

lines of symmetry: ______ ______ ______ ______

3. Pineapple Log Cabin Pattern

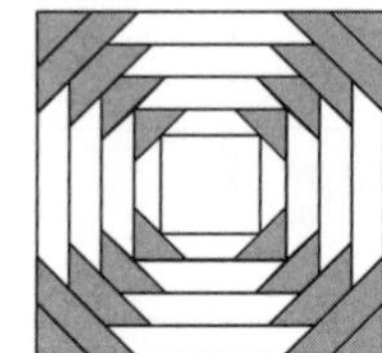

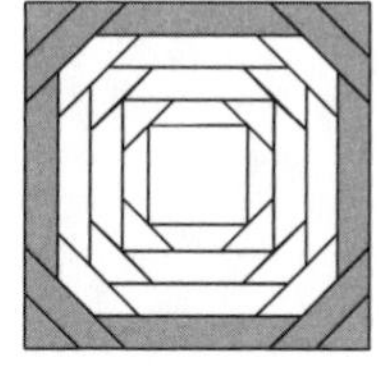

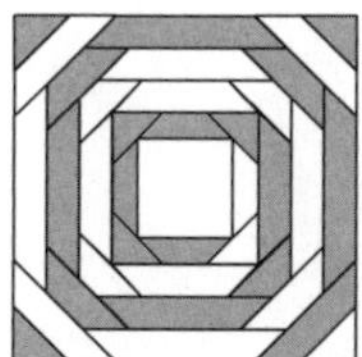

lines of symmetry: ______ ______ ______ ______

Name Date Time

Traditional 9-Patch Patterns

Some patterns, called **9-Patch Patterns,** look like they are made up of 9 squares. You can make your own 9-Patch Pattern on a 3-by-3 grid.

Take out *Math Masters,* pages 369 and 370. Color 6 squares on *Math Masters,* page 369 in one color and the other 6 in a different color. Cut out the 12 squares. Then make triangles by cutting 6 of the squares in half along a diagonal. Make rectangles by cutting the other 6 squares in half along a line through the middle.

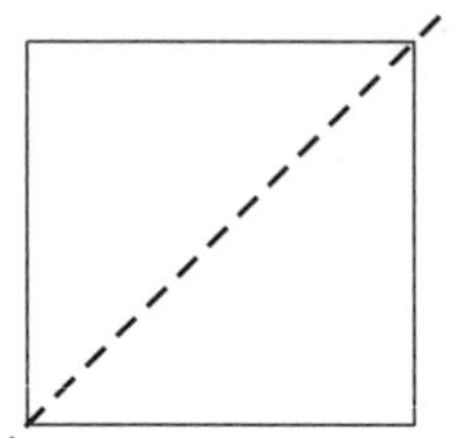

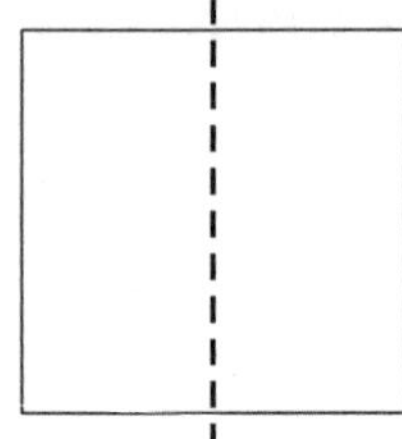

Now arrange some of the pieces on the grid on *Math Masters,* page 370 to make a pattern. Follow the directions below. When you have completed a pattern, draw and color it on one of the 3-by-3 grids below.

1. Make one or two patterns having 4 lines of symmetry.

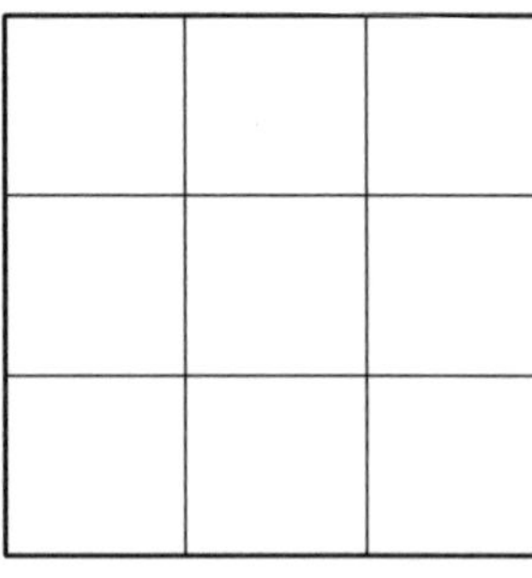

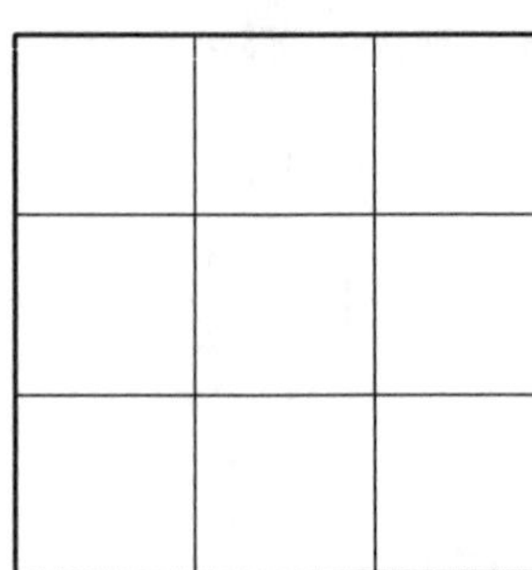

2. Make one or two patterns having 2 lines of symmetry.

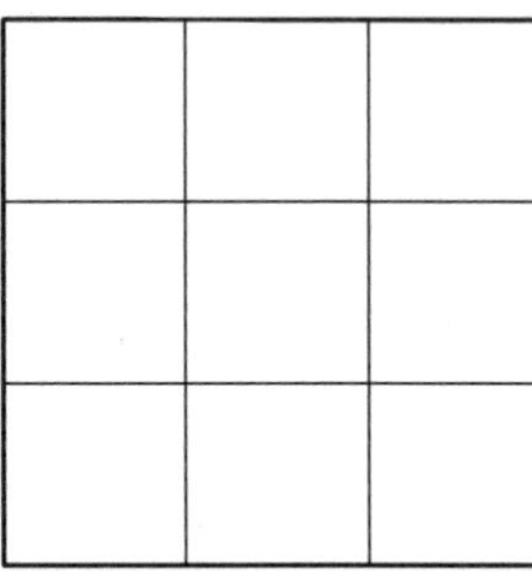

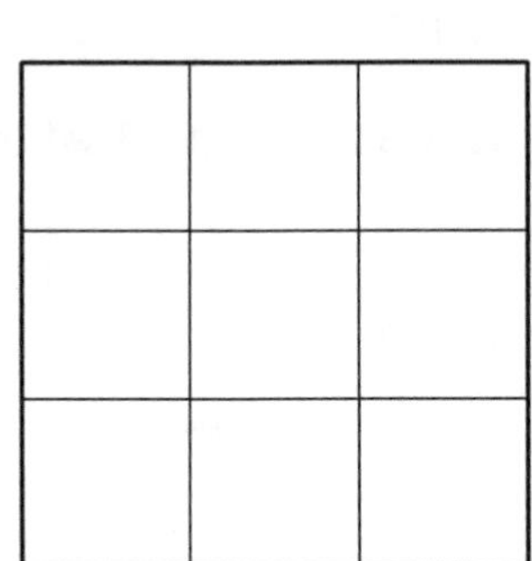

3. Make one or two patterns having no lines of symmetry.

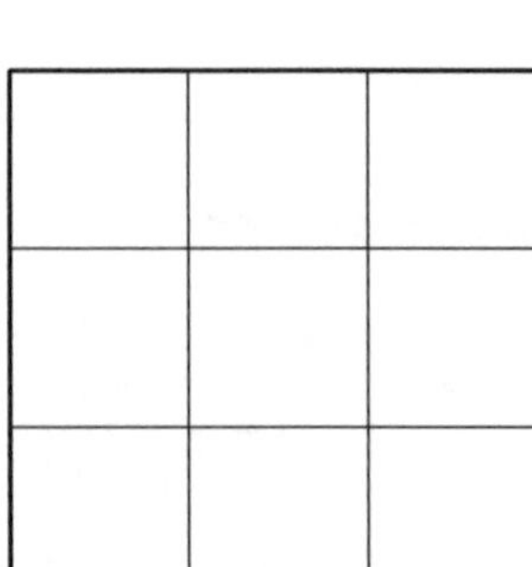

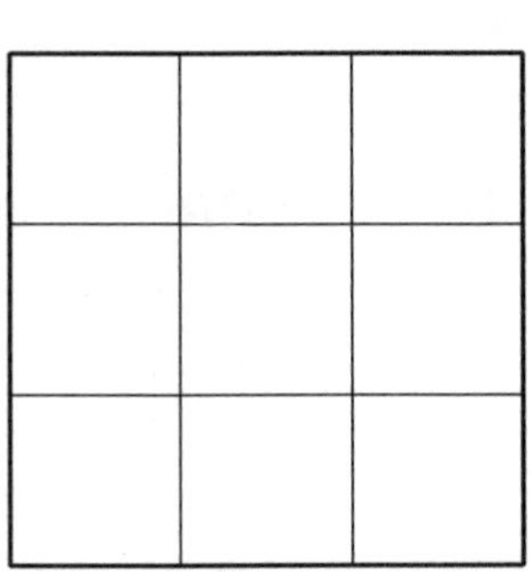

Name Date Time

9-Patch Pattern Pieces

Name Date Time

PROJECT 4

9-Patch Grid

Name Date Time

Rotating Patterns

Many traditional American quilts are made by rotating the square patterns as they are assembled into a quilt.

The first patchwork pattern below is a variation of the traditional "Grandmother's Fan" pattern. The patterns to the right of it show the pattern after it has been rotated clockwise a $\frac{1}{4}$, $\frac{1}{2}$, and $\frac{3}{4}$ turn.

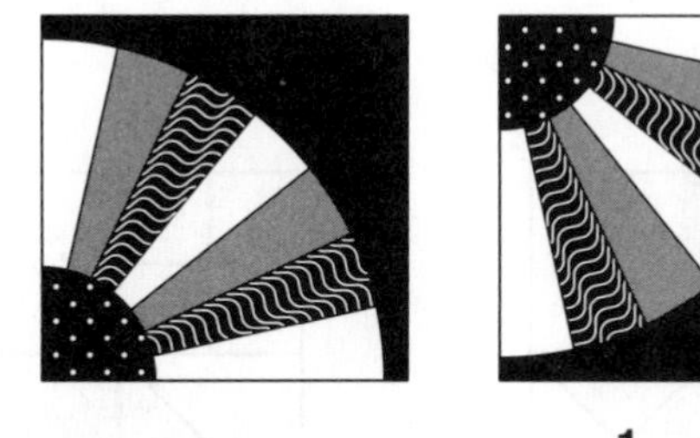

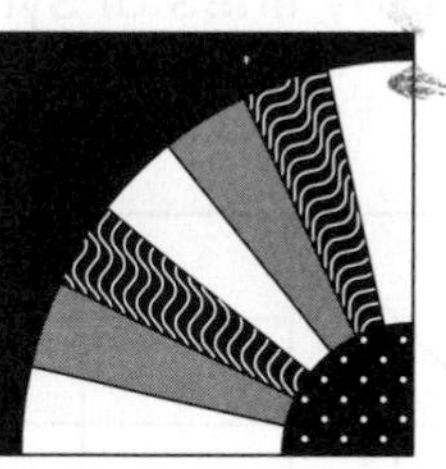

starting position **$\frac{1}{4}$ turn** **$\frac{1}{2}$ turn** **$\frac{3}{4}$ turn**

This is what part of the quilt might look like if some of the patterns are rotated:

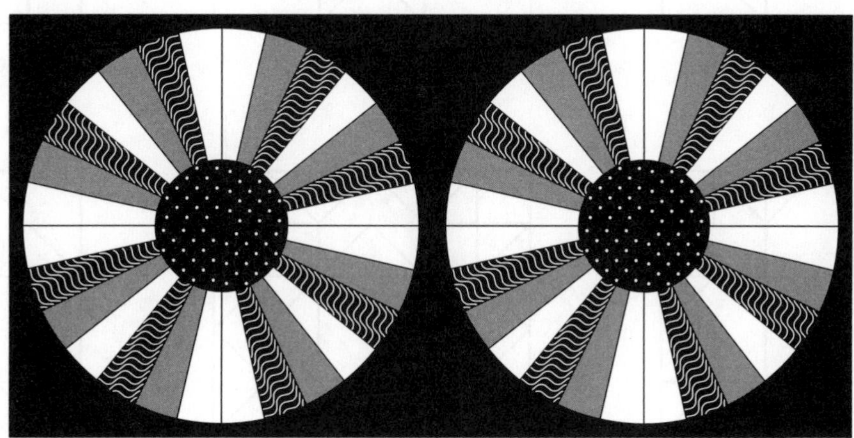

The "Wrench" pattern at the right, also known as the "Monkey Wrench," is a classic pattern that can be found in Amish and Mennonite quilts. Describe what it would look like if it were rotated a $\frac{1}{4}$, $\frac{1}{2}$, and $\frac{3}{4}$ turn.

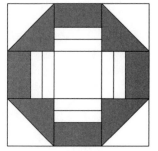

____

____

How many lines of symmetry does it have? ______________

Name Date Time

PROJECT 4

Making a Quilt

As you study the traditional 9-Patch Patterns on this page, think about the following questions:

- Do you see where some of the patterns might have gotten their names?
- What are some similarities and differences among the patterns?
- How many lines of symmetry does each pattern have?

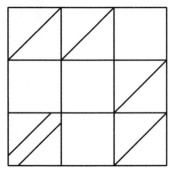

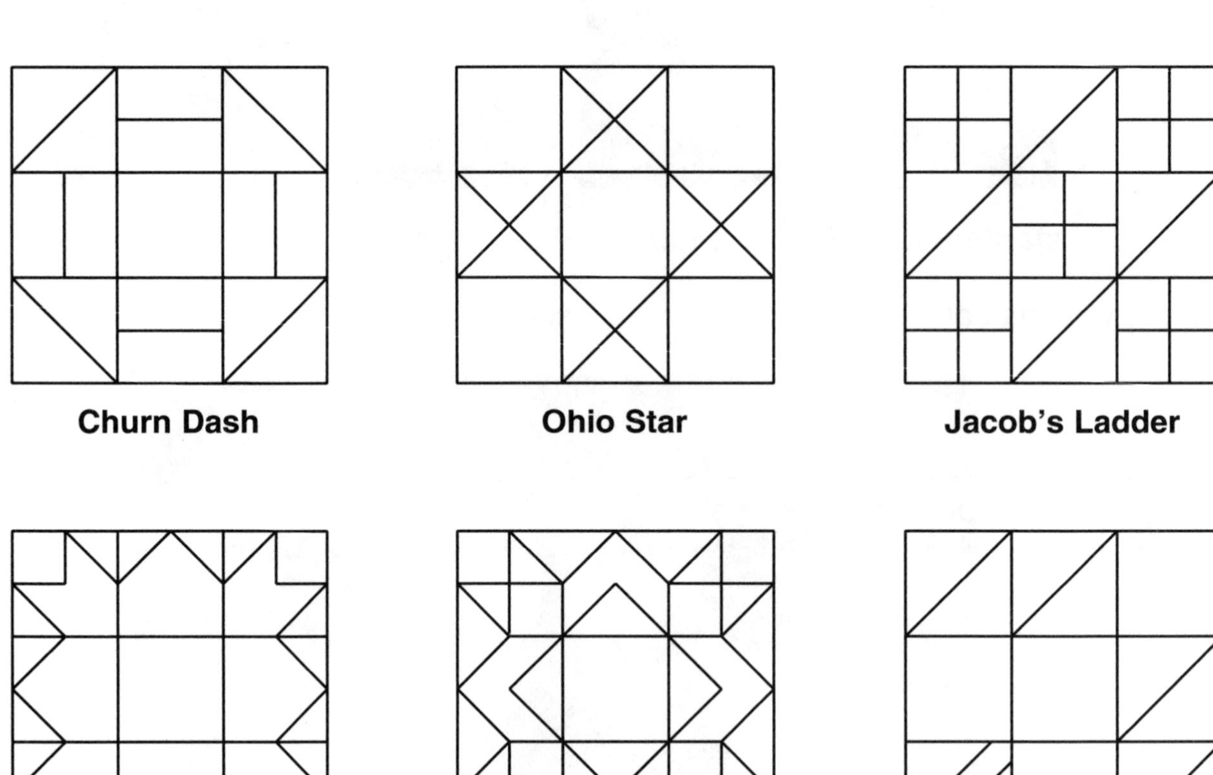

Name Date Time

Making a Quilt *continued*

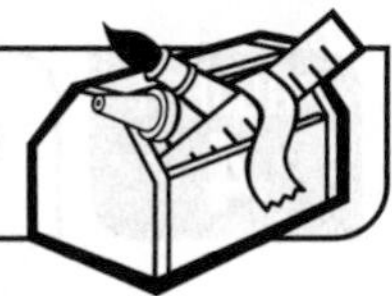

Work with two partners to make a quilt.

1. Each of you needs three copies of *Math Masters,* page 375. Cut out the 3-by-3 grid on each sheet. **Make sure you include the border with the dots.**

2. Cut out the quilting pattern shapes on *Math Masters,* page 374.

3. With your partners, choose one of the patterns on *Math Masters,* page 372. Decide on a way to color it. The colored pattern your group chooses **should not have more than two lines of symmetry.** Each group member should then copy this design onto three 3-by-3 grids. Use the pieces you cut out of *Math Masters,* page 374 to trace the pattern onto the 3-by-3 grids. Then color the pattern. Or you can trace the pieces onto colored paper, cut out the tracings, and paste them onto the 3-by-3 grids. Your group should end up with nine square "patches" that **look exactly alike.**

4. Punch holes through the dots along the border of the patches.

5. Lay all 9 square patches on the floor and arrange them so that some of the square patterns are rotated. When your group has agreed on an arrangement, line up the holes on the edges of the squares. Then fasten the pieces together by weaving yarn in and out of the holes. If you wish, make a ruffle for your quilt out of a strip of crepe paper. Pleat and glue the ruffle around the outer edges of the quilt.

Here is an example of a quilt with the "Maple Leaf" pattern:

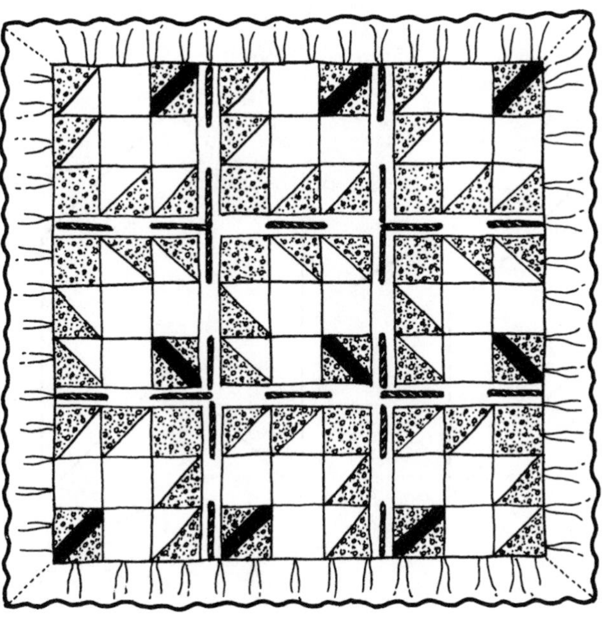

Name Date Time

Quilting Pattern Shapes

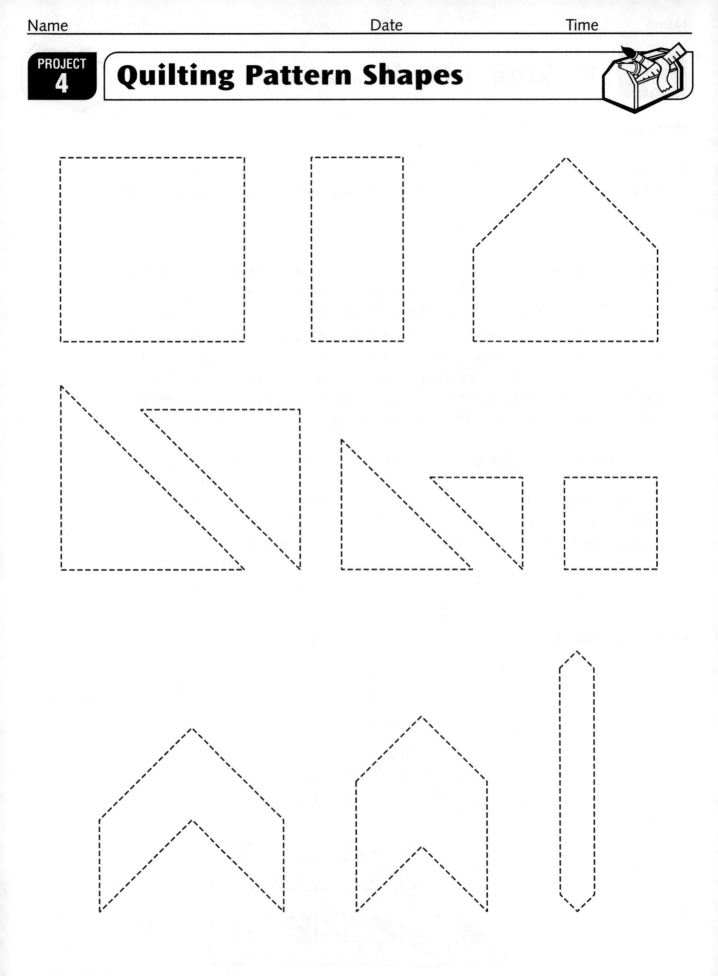

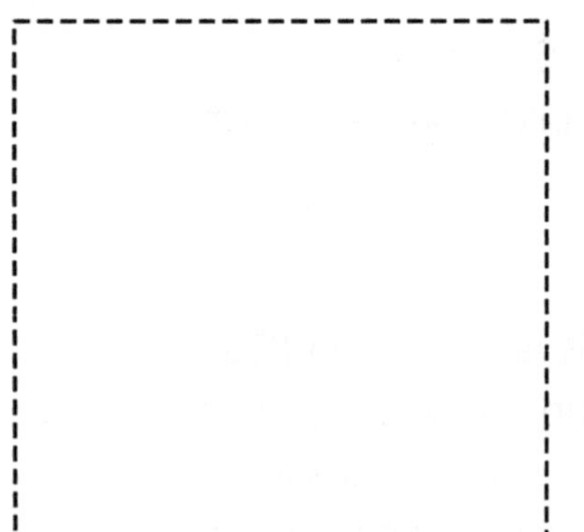

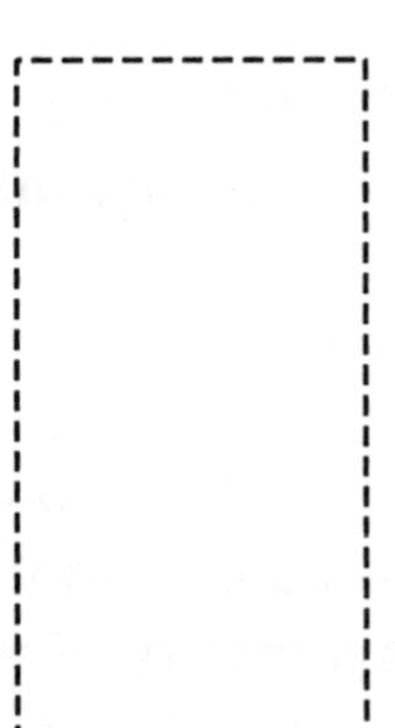

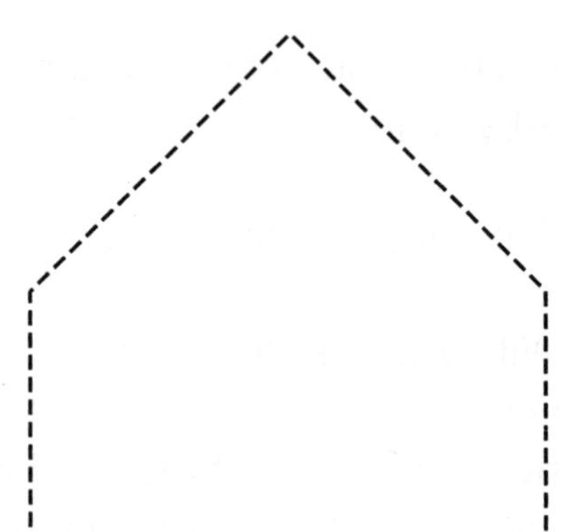

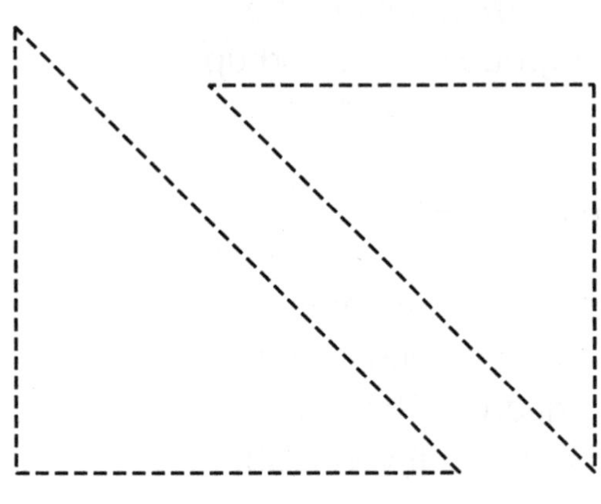

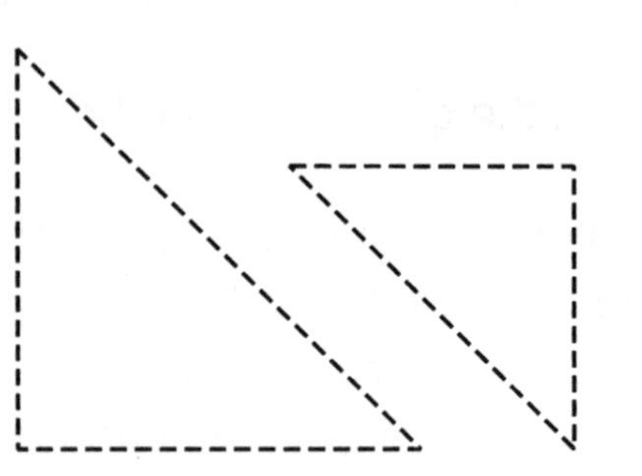

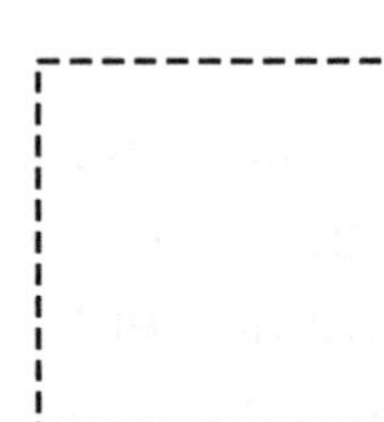

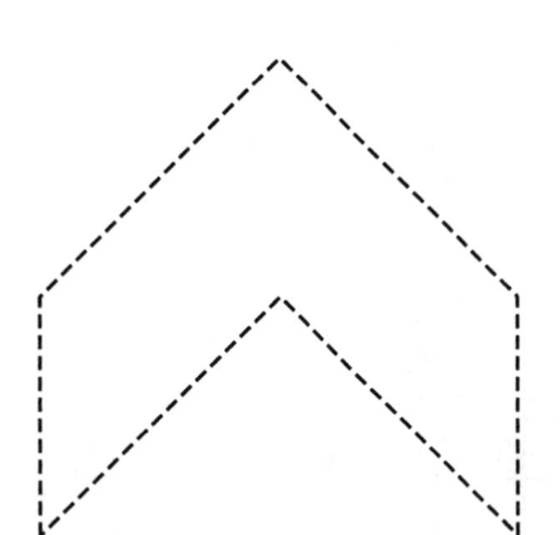

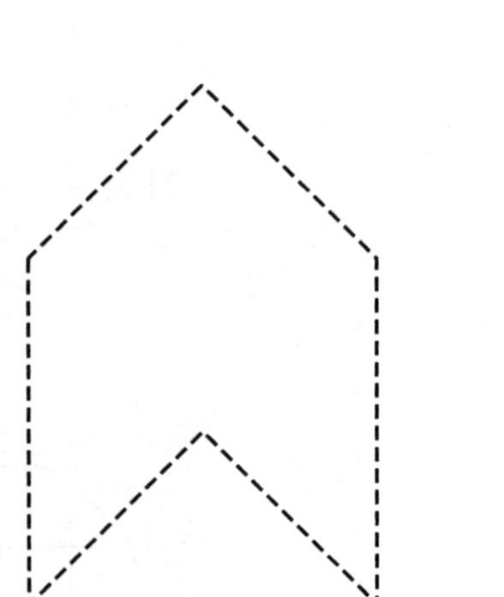

Name Date Time

9-Patch Grid with Border

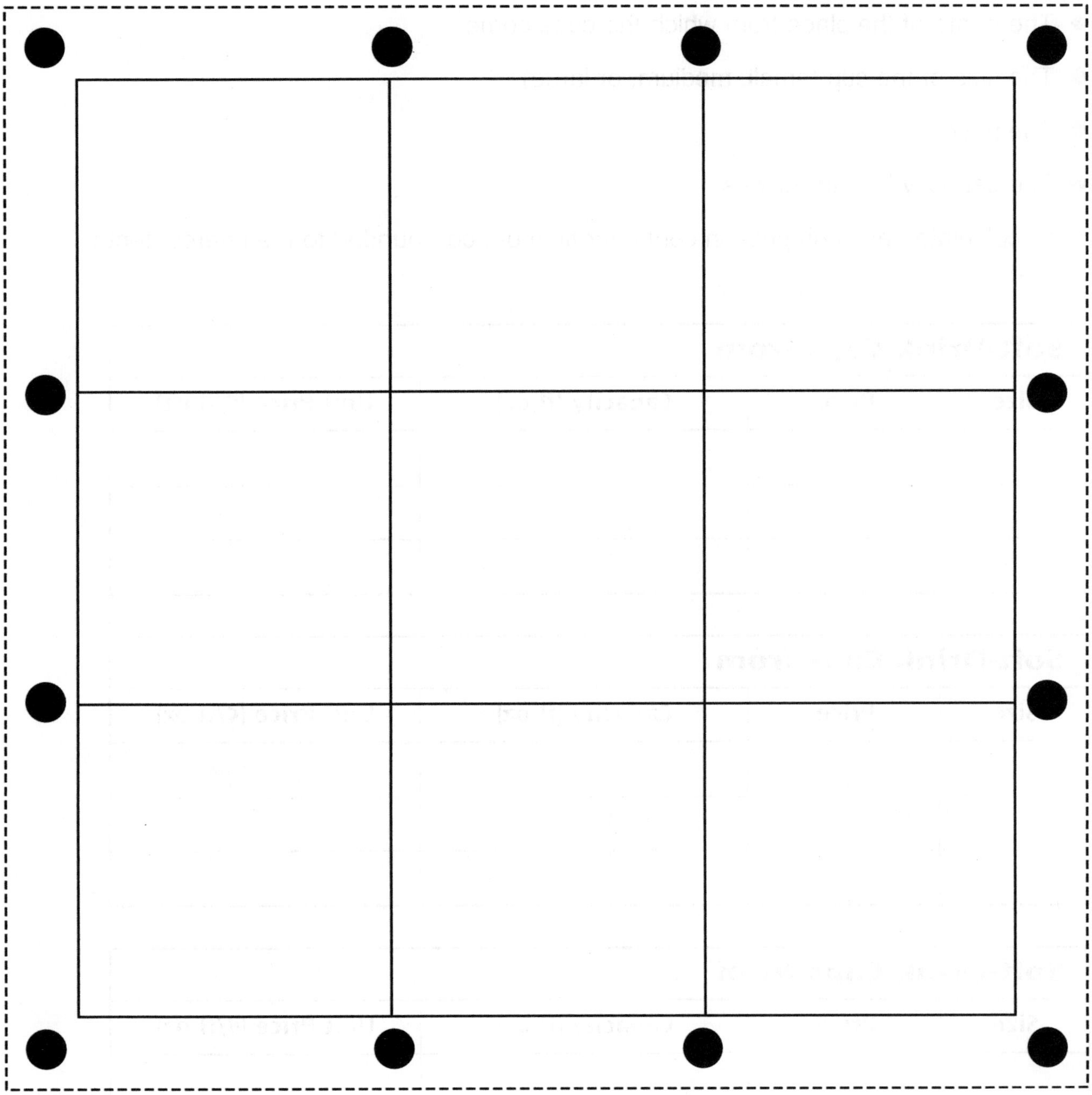

Name Date Time

Which Soft Drink Would You Buy?

For each set of soft-drink cups, record the following information:

- The name of the place from which the cups come
- The size of the cup (small, medium, or large)
- The price
- The capacity in fluid ounces

Then calculate each unit price in cents per fluid ounce, rounded to the nearest tenth of a cent.

Soft-Drink Cups from			
Size	**Price**	**Capacity (fl oz)**	**Unit Price (¢/fl oz)**

Soft-Drink Cups from			
Size	**Price**	**Capacity (fl oz)**	**Unit Price (¢/fl oz)**

Soft-Drink Cups from			
Size	**Price**	**Capacity (fl oz)**	**Unit Price (¢/fl oz)**

Name Date Time

PROJECT 5 Consumer Report: Best Soft-Drink Prices

Imagine that you have been assigned by *Kids' Consumer Reports* to investigate and report on the prices of soft drinks. Use the information your group recorded on *Math Masters,* page 376 to prepare a group report for the magazine. Your report might contain graphs, tables, and pictures. Try to answer some of the following questions in your report:

- ◆ Do small (or medium or large) cups at different places contain the same amount?
- ◆ Are prices similar for similar sizes? (For example, are the small-size drinks about the same price at different places?)
- ◆ Which places have the least expensive soft drinks? The most expensive soft drinks?
- ◆ Is the largest size always the best value?
- ◆ Which types of businesses offer better values? (For example, do restaurants generally offer better values than movie theaters?)
- ◆ What would you recommend to consumers? Do some places offer free refills? If so, how would this affect your recommendation?

Name Date Time

Blueprints

Sample Blueprint

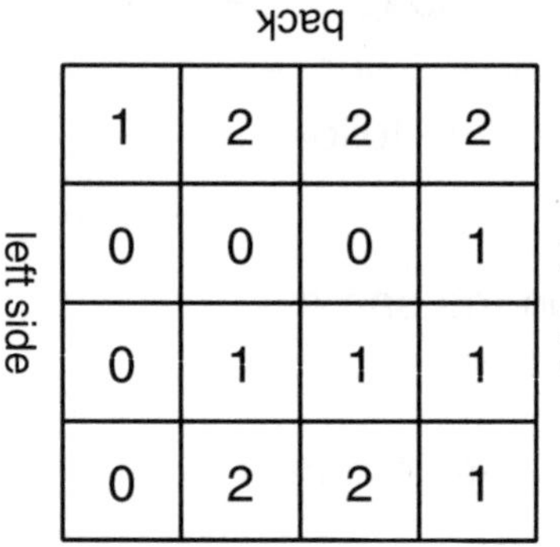

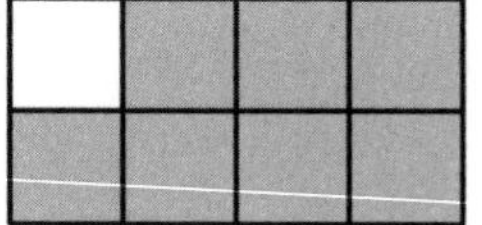
front view

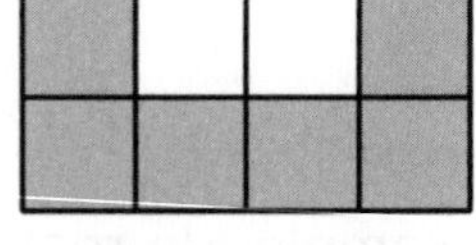
left-side view

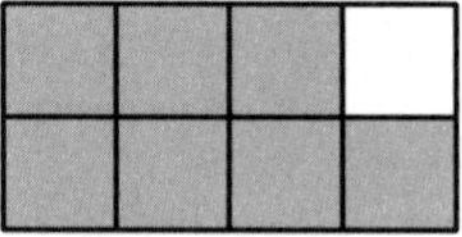
back view

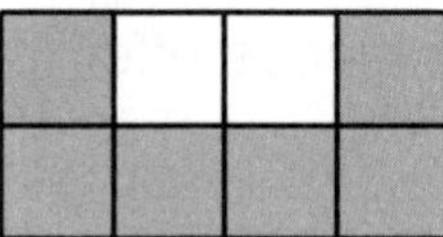
right-side view

Blueprint Mat

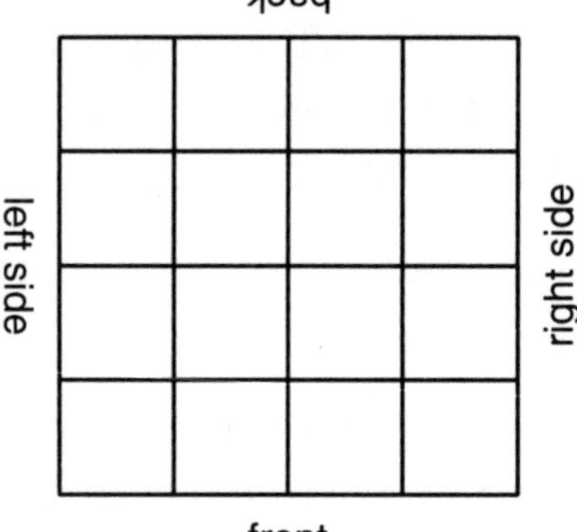

Group ______________

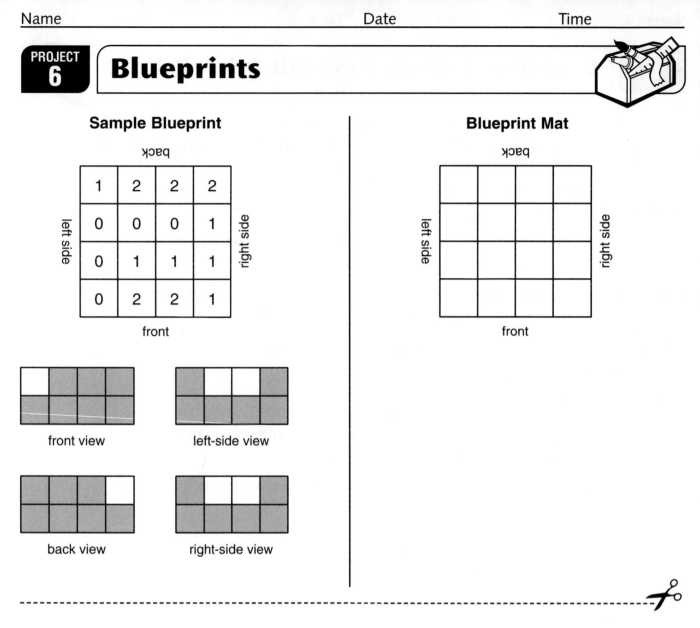

Cut the sheet apart along the dashed line. Build your own structure on the Blueprint Mat (upper right). Then record the front view and the left-side view in the grid squares below. Leave your structure so that other students can find it, using these views.

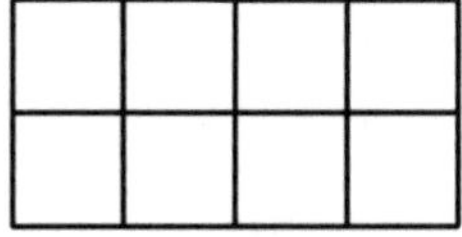
front view

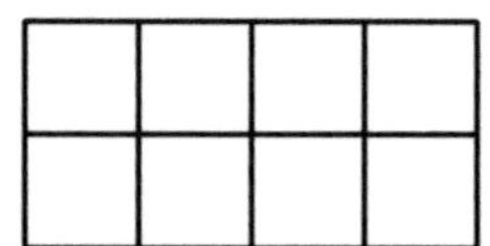
left-side view

If you make a mistake, use the grids below to draw the corrected views.

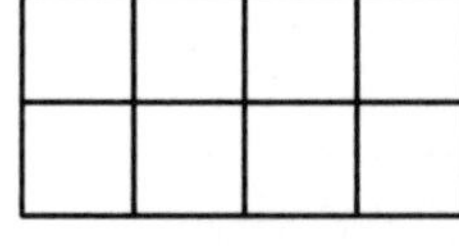
front view

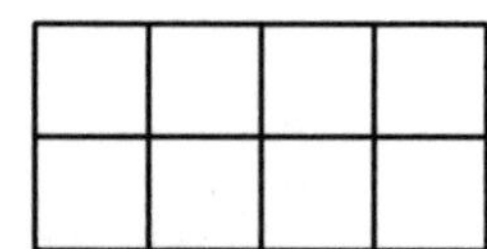
left-side view

Name Date Time

Building Structures

1. Use the blueprint at the right to build a structure on the Blueprint Mat (*Math Masters,* page 378). Use centimeter cubes.

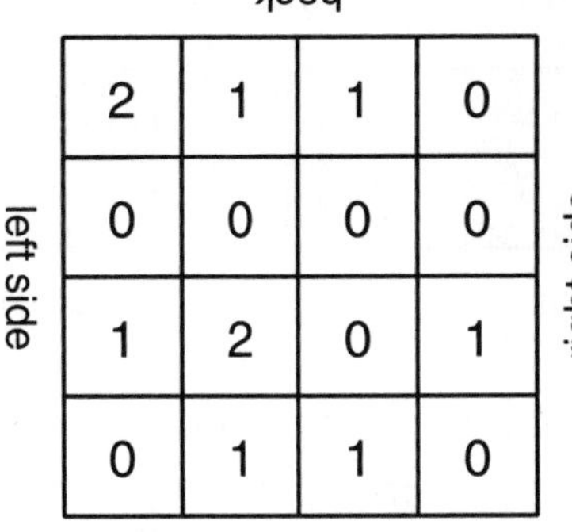

a. Compare your structure to the structure built by your partner. They *should* look the same.

b. Draw all 4 views of your structure by shading squares.

front view

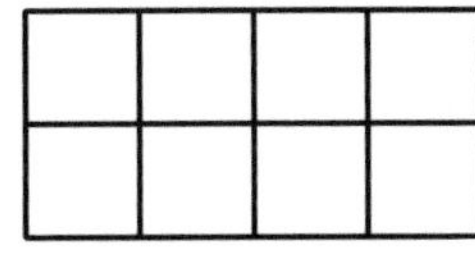

left-side view

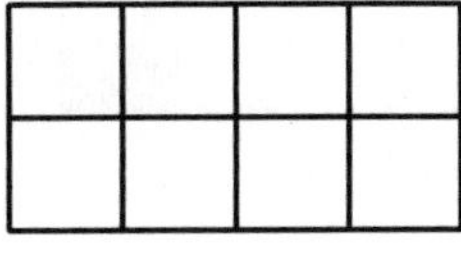

back view

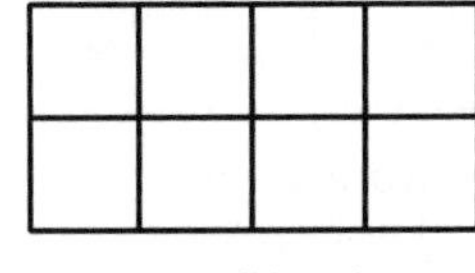

right-side view

c. Compare your views to those drawn by your partner. They *should* be the same.

2. Build any structure you wish on your Blueprint Mat. *Reminder:* Use no more than 2 centimeter cubes on a square.

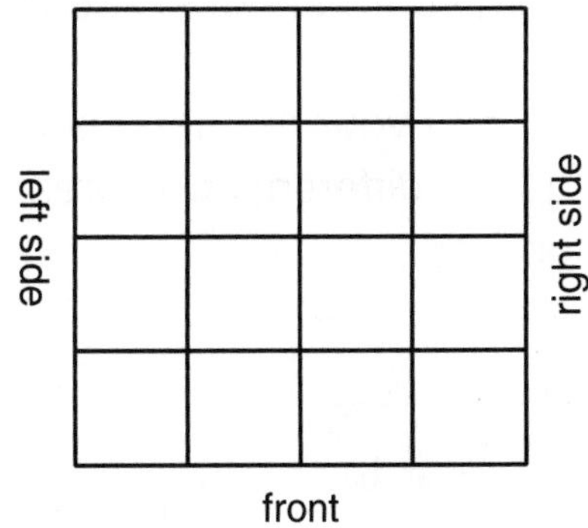

a. Record your structure on the blueprint at the right.

b. Draw all 4 views of your structure by shading the squares below. Ask your partner to check your work.

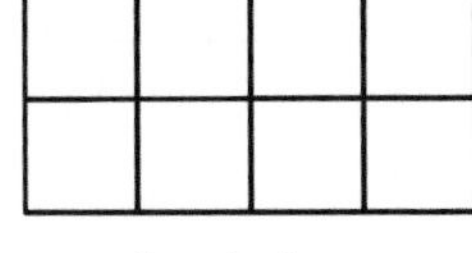

front view

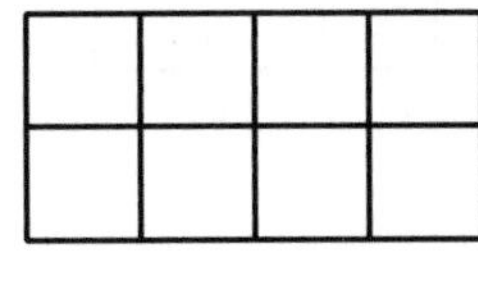

left-side view

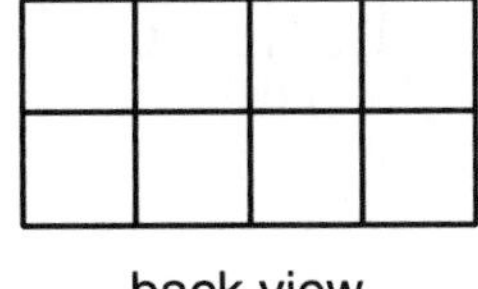

back view

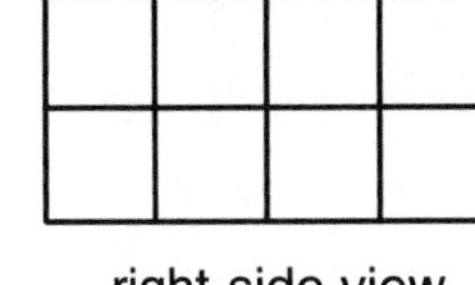

right-side view

c. Compare the views of opposite sides of your structure.

3. Here is the front view of a structure. Draw its back view.

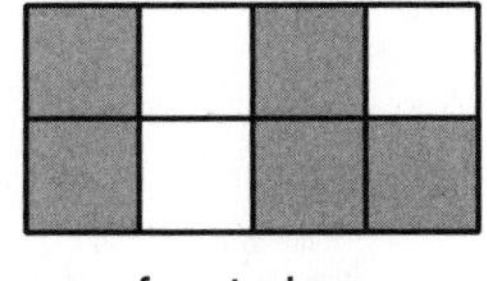

front view

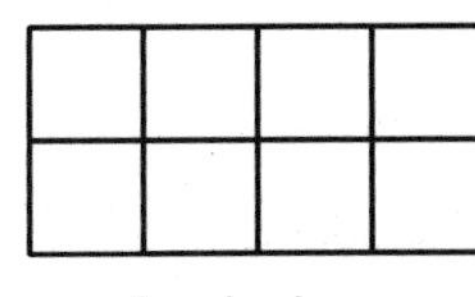

back view

Name Date Time

More Structures

1. Here are 2 views of a structure. Draw its other 2 views.

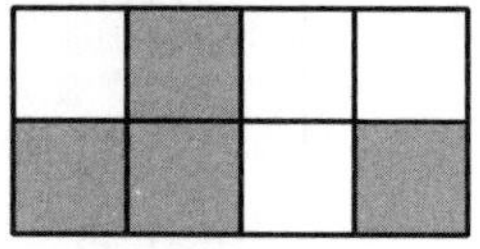

front view

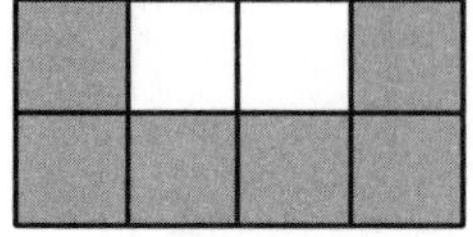

left-side view

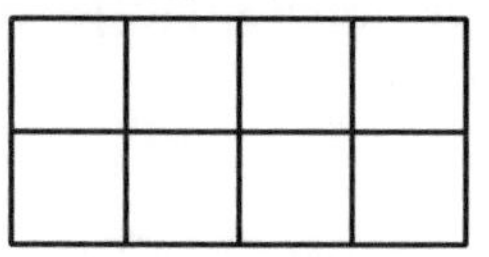

back view

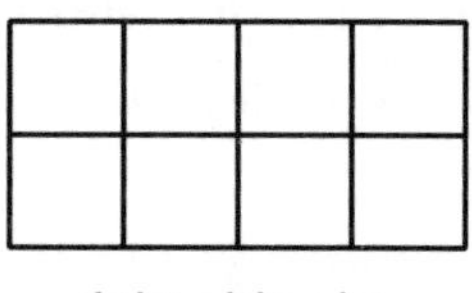

right-side view

2. Here is the front view, as well as the left-side view, of a structure.

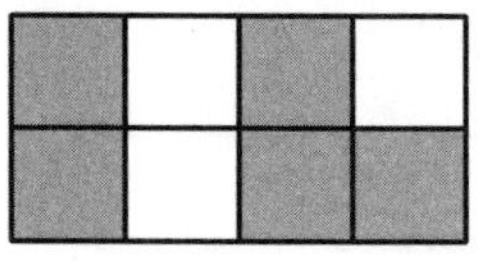

front view

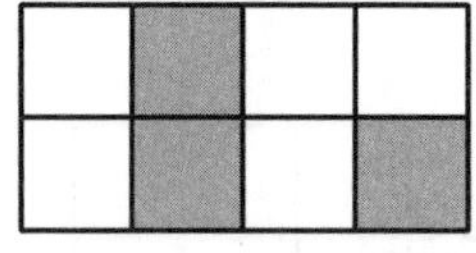

left-side view

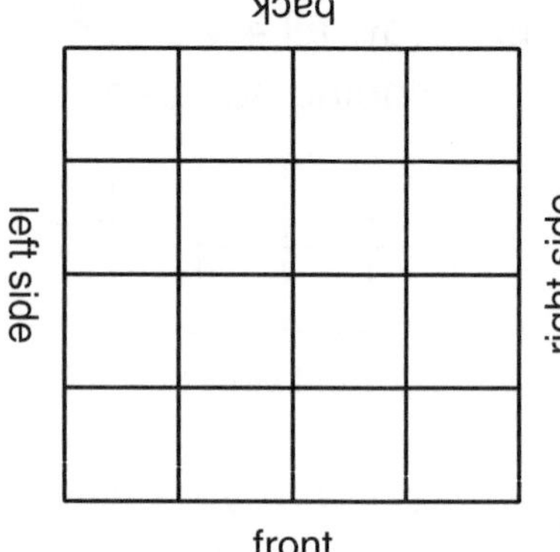

a. Build a structure that has these views. Record it on the blueprint at the right.

b. Compare your structure and blueprint with your partner's. Are they the same?

3. Work with your partner. Use the following front view and left-side view to build 3 different structures. Record each structure on one of the blueprints.

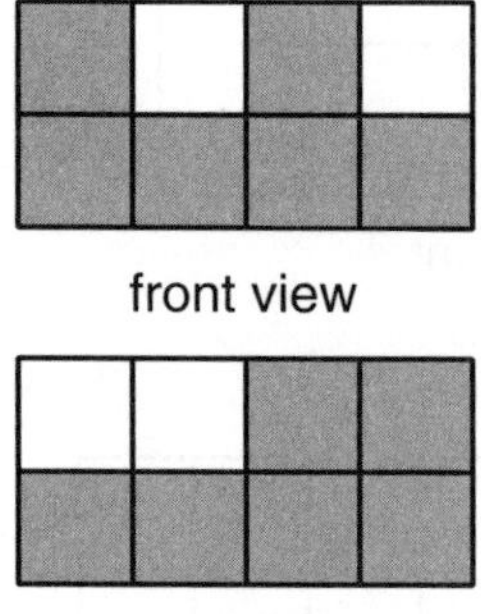

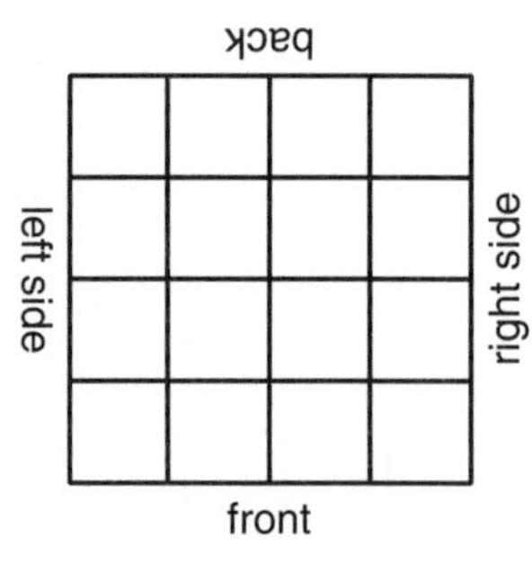

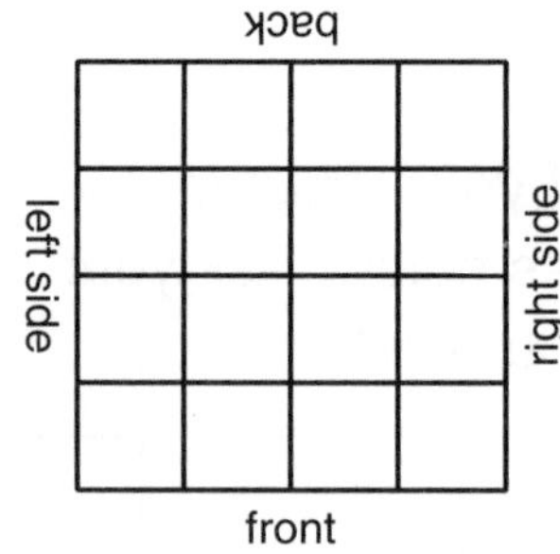

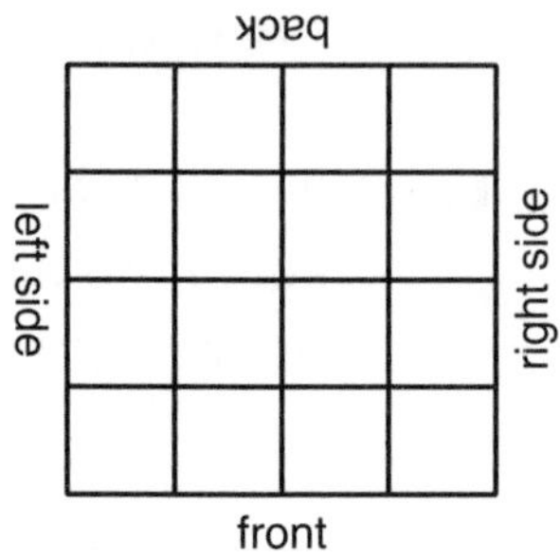

4. a. Is it possible to build 2 different structures from the same front and left-side views? _________

b. Is it possible to build 2 different structures from the same front, left-side, back, and right-side views? _________

Name Date Time

Numbers, Mayan Style

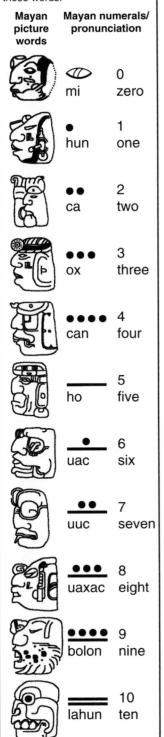

The ancient Maya used a writing system made of pictures. The Maya had words and numerals for numbers, just as we do. Below are the Mayan picture words and numerals for 0–10, and the pronunciation of those words.

Mayan picture words	Mayan numerals/ pronunciation	
	mi	0 zero
	• hun	1 one
	•• ca	2 two
	••• ox	3 three
	•••• can	4 four
	— ho	5 five
	uac	6 six
	uuc	7 seven
	uaxac	8 eight
	bolon	9 nine
	lahun	10 ten

The Maya are the native people who have lived for thousands of years in a 120,000-square-mile area of Central America stretching from the Valley of Mexico through Guatemala. Today there are about 6 million Maya in Central America.

The ancient Mayan civilization reached its height in A.D. 250 and flourished for more than 600 years. The Mayan people built large cities and tall limestone pyramids where they performed religious ceremonies. They traded cloth, cacao beans for making chocolate, and other items throughout Central America. Children, parents, grandparents, and even great-grandparents all lived together, and everyone helped with the housework and farming. The ancient Maya had no schools. Children learned everything by watching and helping adults.

The ancient Maya invented a number system using place value with dots and dashes to represent numbers, and a special symbol for zero. Their numbers read from top to bottom.

In our place-value system, we group numbers by tens and powers of ten. When we write a number like 2,457, we really mean (2 ∗ 1,000) + (4 ∗ 100) + (5 ∗ 10) + (7 ∗ 1). The Mayan place-value system works similarly with 20s and powers of 20. But while we use 10 different symbols to write all of our numbers (the digits 0–9), the ancient Maya used only three symbols.

Mayan Number Symbols

Symbol	Value
(shell)	0
•	1
—	5

Our Place-Value System	Mayan Place-Value System
10,000s (10 ∗ 10 ∗ 10 ∗ 10)	160,000s (20 ∗ 20 ∗ 20 ∗ 20)
1,000s (10 ∗ 10 ∗ 10)	8,000s (20 ∗ 20 ∗ 20)
100s (10 ∗ 10)	400s (20 ∗ 20)
10s	20s
1s	1s

To write the number 837 using the Mayan system, put a 2 in the 400s place, a 1 in the 20s place, and 17 in the 1s place:

2 ∗ 400 = 800
1 ∗ 20 = 20
17 ∗ 1 = + 17
837

Teaching Aid Masters

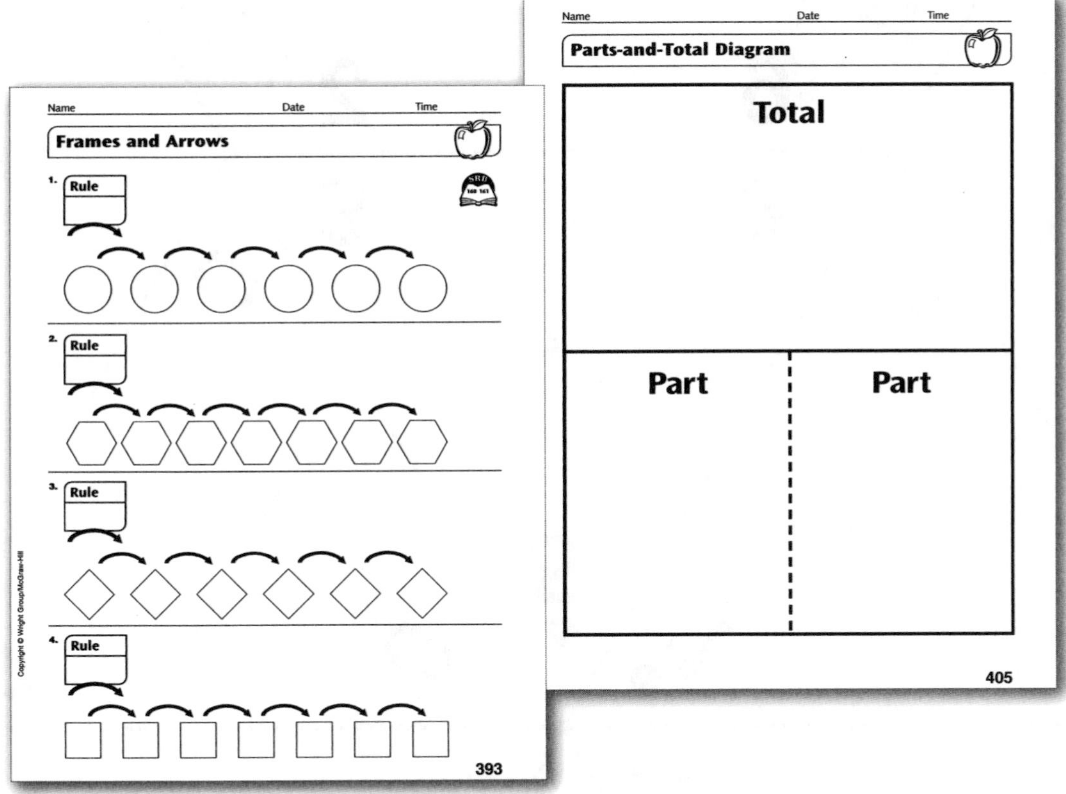

Name Date Time

Frames and Arrows

1. Rule

2. Rule

3. Rule

4. Rule

Copyright © Wright Group/McGraw-Hill

393

Name Date Time

Parts-and-Total Diagram

Total	
Part	Part

405

Name Date Time

+, − Fact Triangles 1

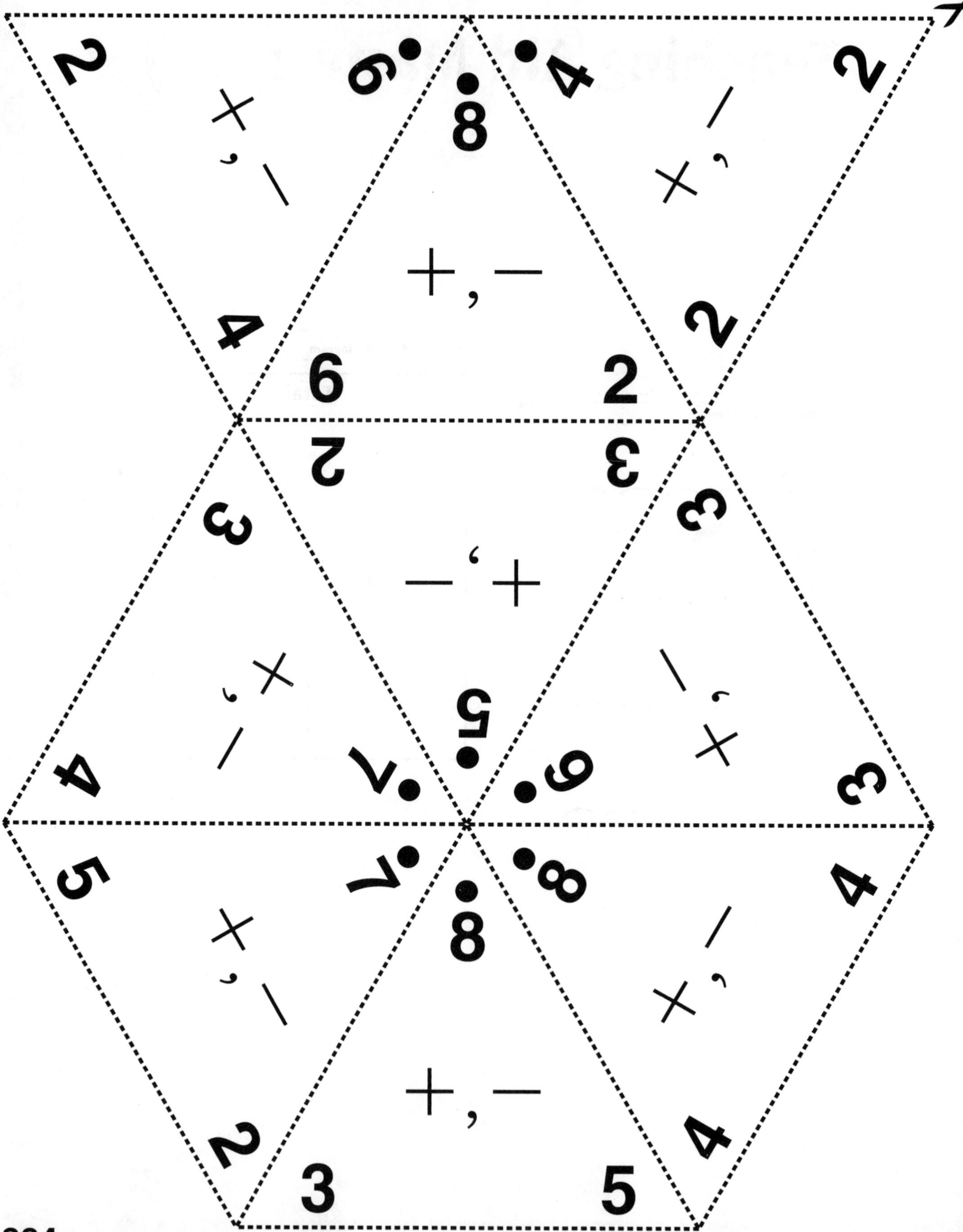

2 +, − 9•

8• +, − 4•

4 6 +, − 2 2

2 3 3 −, + 3

4 −, + 7• 5• 6• +, − 3

5 +, − 7• 8• +, − 8• 4

2 3 +, − 5 4

Name Date Time

+, − Fact Triangles 2

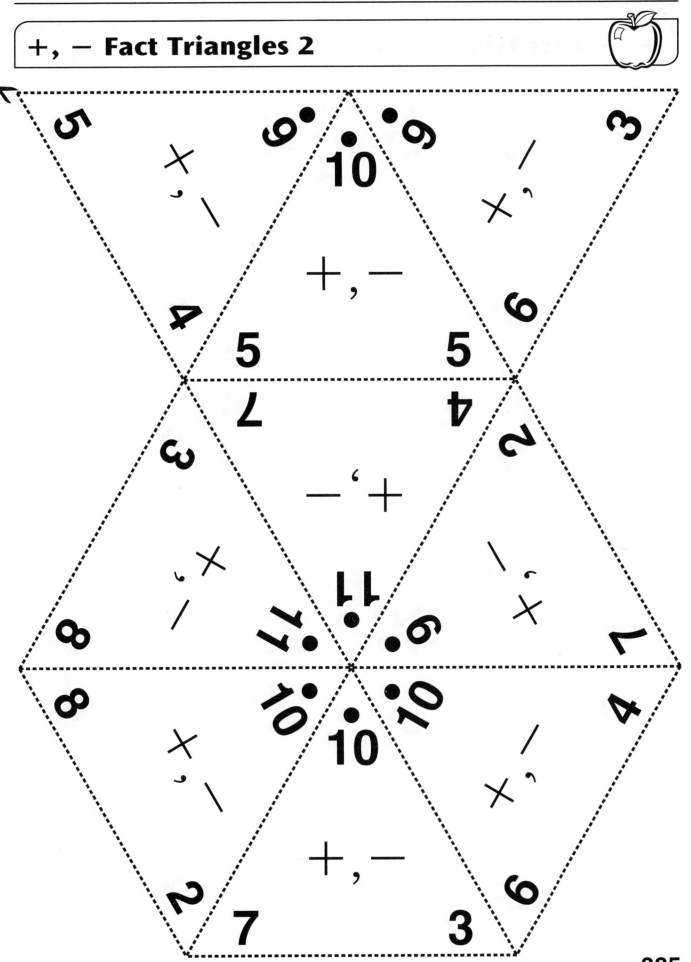

10 • 5 5 +, −

9 • 5 4 +, −

9 • 3 6 +, −

11 • 7 4 +, −

17 • 3 8 +, −

9 • 2 7 +, −

10 • 7 3 +, −

10 • 8 2 +, −

10 • 4 6 +, −

Name Date Time

+, − Fact Triangles 3

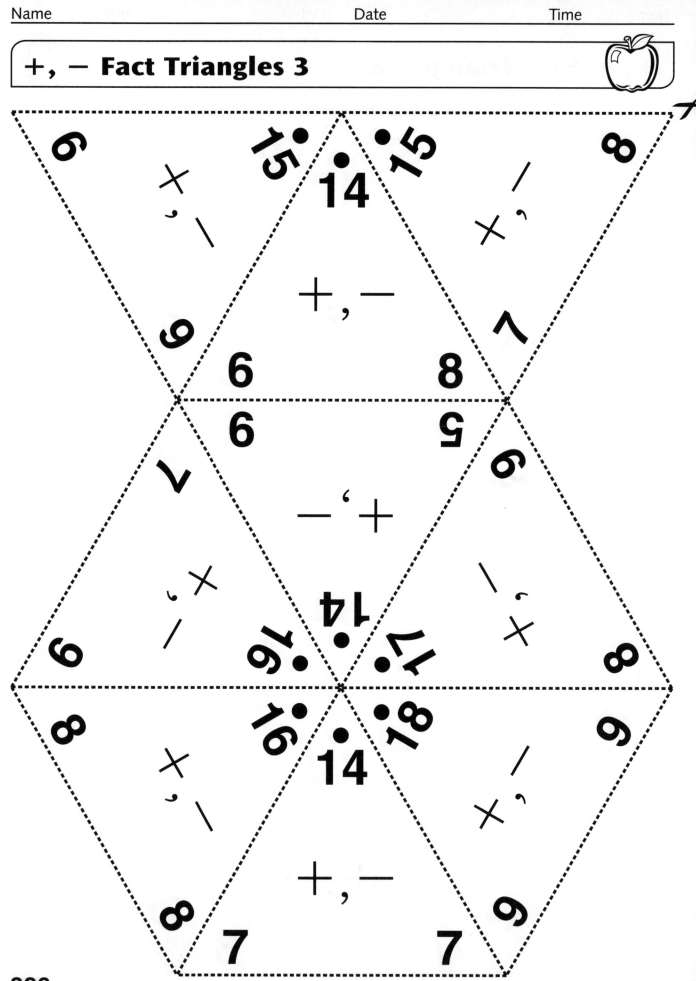

9 15 • +, − 9
• 14 +, − 6 8
• 15 8 +, − 7

6 5 +, − 7 • 14
9 +, − 16 •
• 17 +, − 8 9

8 16 • +, − 8
• 14 +, − 7 7
• 18 9 +, − 9

Name Date Time

+, − Fact Triangles 4

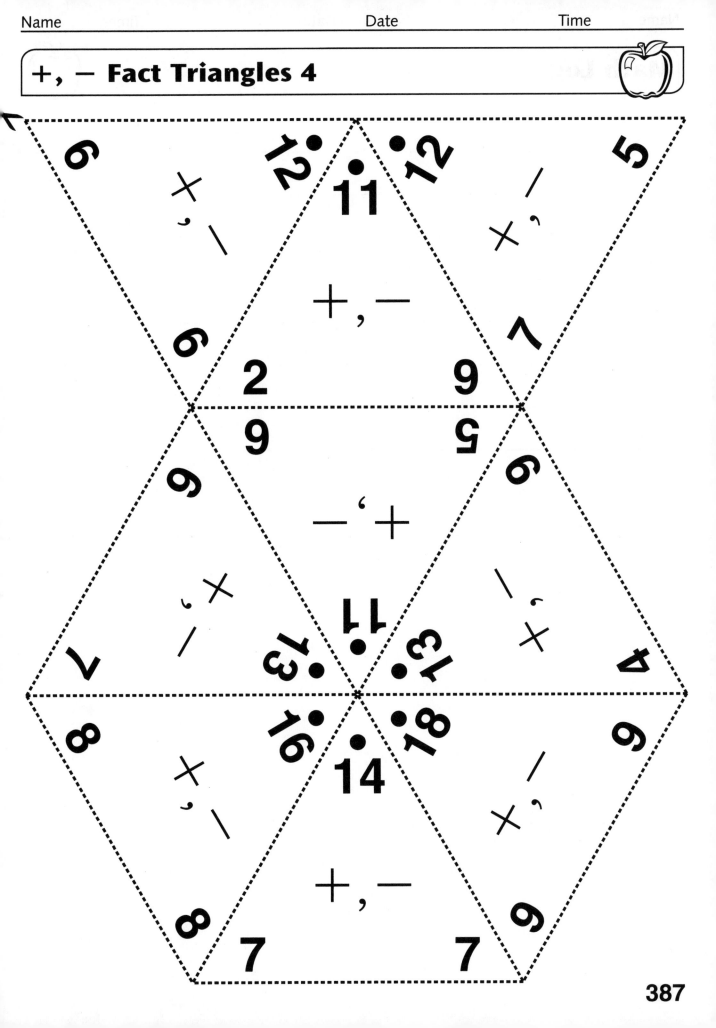

+, −

11

2 9

+, −

9 12

+, −

12 5

7

+, −

9 5

11

+, −

9 7

13

+, −

13 6

4

+, −

14

7 7

+, −

8 16

+, −

18 9

9

Name Date Time

Math Log

Name Date Time

Exit Slip

Name Date Time

Exit Slip

Name Date Time

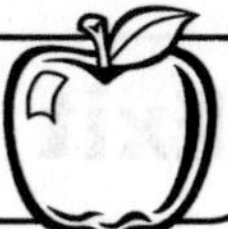

Venn Diagram

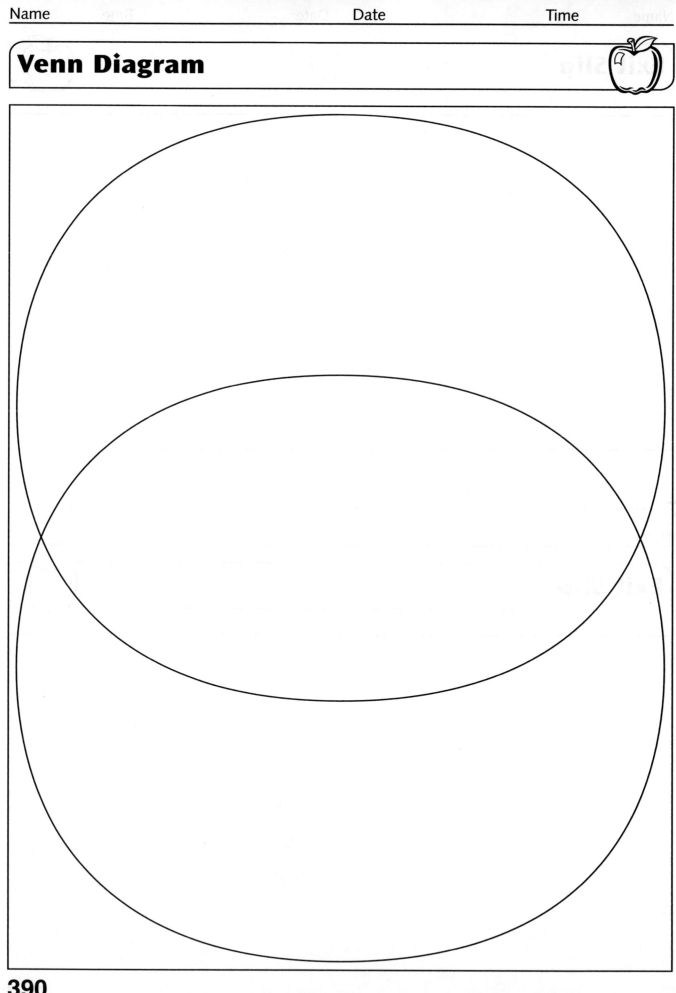

Name Date Time

Timed Test 1: Addition & Subtraction Facts

4 + 1 = ______	9 + 9 = ______	6 − 4 = ______	12 − 4 = ______
6 + 3 = ______	8 + 7 = ______	5 − 2 = ______	16 − 8 = ______
3 + 0 = ______	6 + 9 = ______	6 − 3 = ______	13 − 9 = ______
4 + 4 = ______	5 + 8 = ______	7 − 1 = ______	12 − 7 = ______
6 + 2 = ______	9 + 3 = ______	11 − 2 = ______	14 − 6 = ______
3 + 4 = ______	7 + 7 = ______	12 − 6 = ______	11 − 4 = ______
8 + 2 = ______	5 + 6 = ______	8 − 0 = ______	15 − 6 = ______
3 + 5 = ______	7 + 9 = ______	11 − 3 = ______	17 − 9 = ______
2 + 2 = ______	6 + 7 = ______	10 − 6 = ______	15 − 8 = ______
1 + 9 = ______	9 + 5 = ______	9 − 3 = ______	13 − 7 = ______
5 + 4 = ______	8 + 6 = ______	7 − 5 = ______	14 − 9 = ______
2 + 5 = ______	4 + 7 = ______	8 − 7 = ______	18 − 9 = ______
2 + 7 = ______	9 + 8 = ______	10 − 3 = ______	13 − 5 = ______

Name Date Time

Timed Test 2: Addition & Subtraction Facts

4 + 5 = ______

0 + 8 = ______

7 + 2 = ______

1 + 4 = ______

5 + 2 = ______

5 + 3 = ______

2 + 2 = ______

7 + 1 = ______

3 + 6 = ______

4 + 3 = ______

2 + 8 = ______

4 + 4 = ______

2 + 6 = ______

8 + 8 = ______

7 + 6 = ______

5 + 9 = ______

6 + 8 = ______

7 + 8 = ______

9 + 6 = ______

9 + 7 = ______

7 + 4 = ______

8 + 9 = ______

8 + 5 = ______

3 + 9 = ______

7 + 7 = ______

6 + 5 = ______

7 − 2 = ______

6 − 5 = ______

10 − 7 = ______

6 − 2 = ______

5 − 3 = ______

6 − 3 = ______

11 − 8 = ______

10 − 4 = ______

9 − 6 = ______

4 − 1 = ______

11 − 9 = ______

12 − 6 = ______

9 − 0 = ______

13 − 6 = ______

12 − 5 = ______

14 − 8 = ______

11 − 7 = ______

15 − 9 = ______

14 − 5 = ______

18 − 9 = ______

13 − 8 = ______

17 − 8 = ______

15 − 7 = ______

12 − 8 = ______

16 − 8 = ______

13 − 4 = ______

Name Date Time

Frames and Arrows

1. 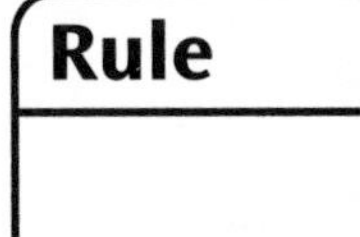

Rule

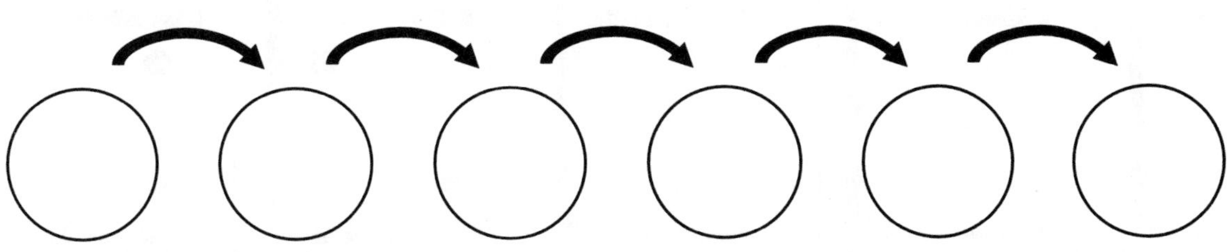

2. 

Rule

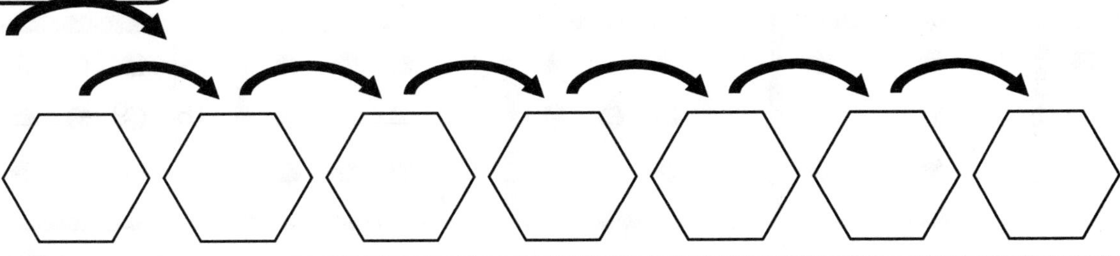

3. 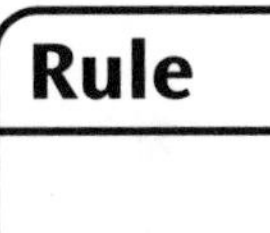

Rule

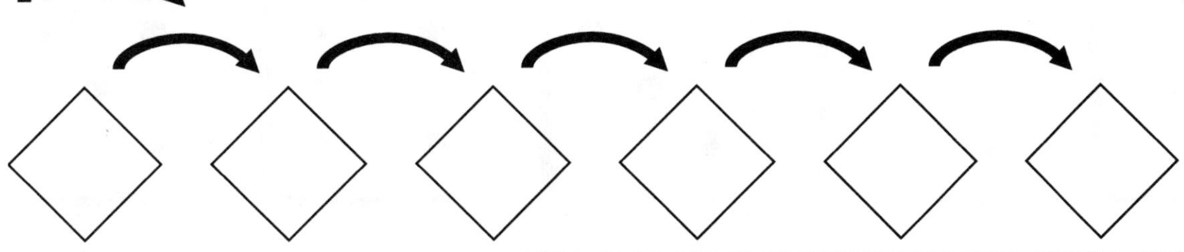

4. 

Rule

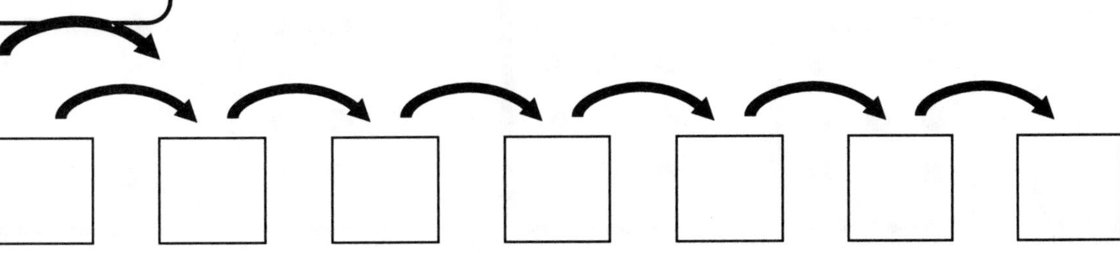

Name Date Time

Domino Cutouts

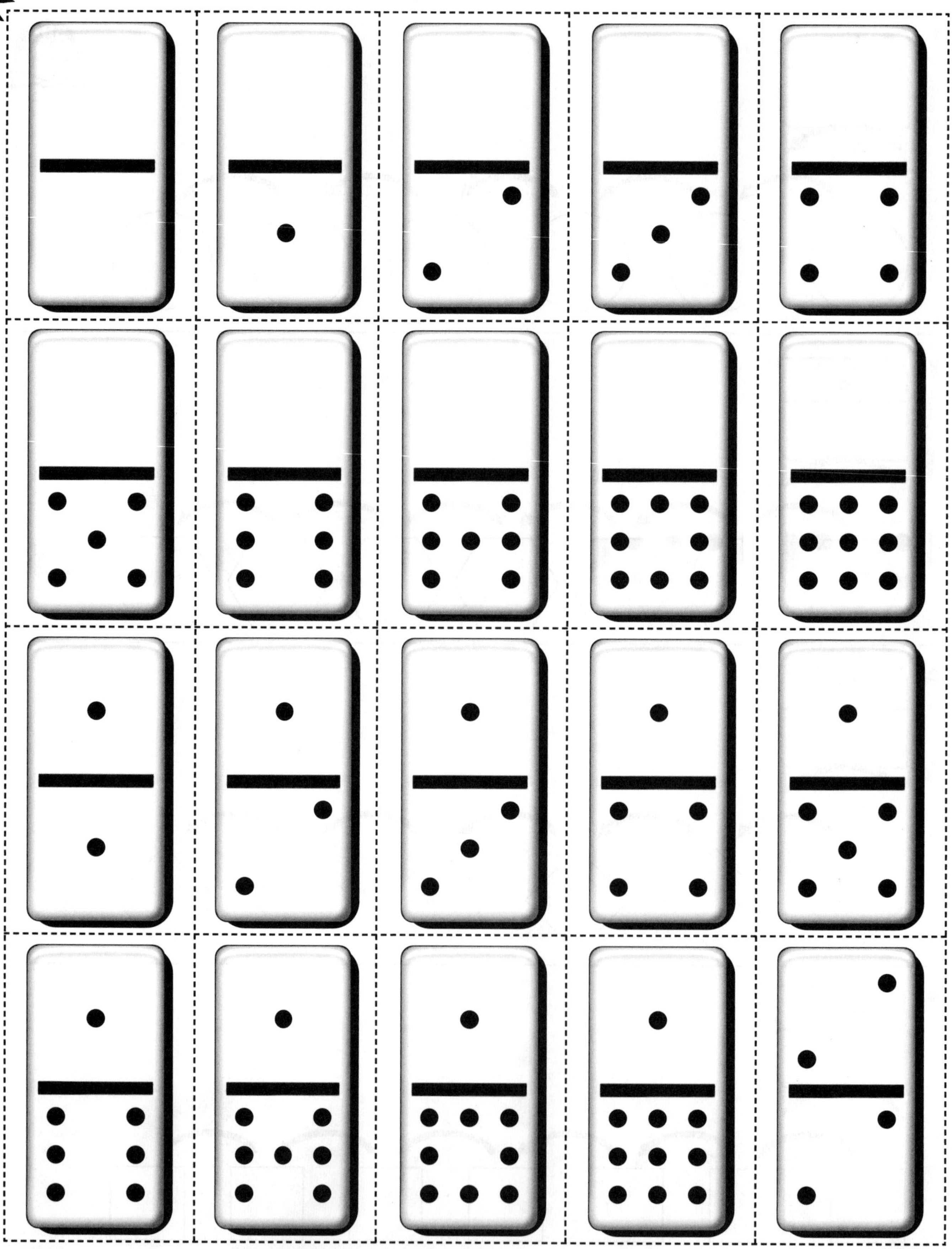

Name Date Time

Domino Cutouts *continued*

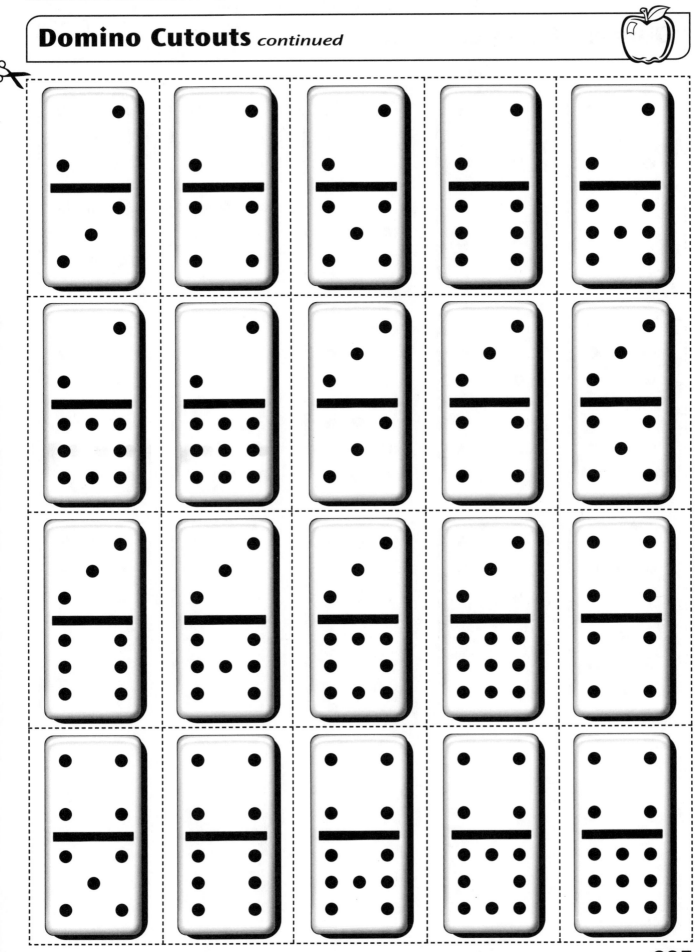

Name Date Time

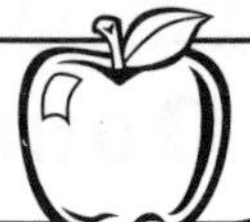

Domino Cutouts *continued*

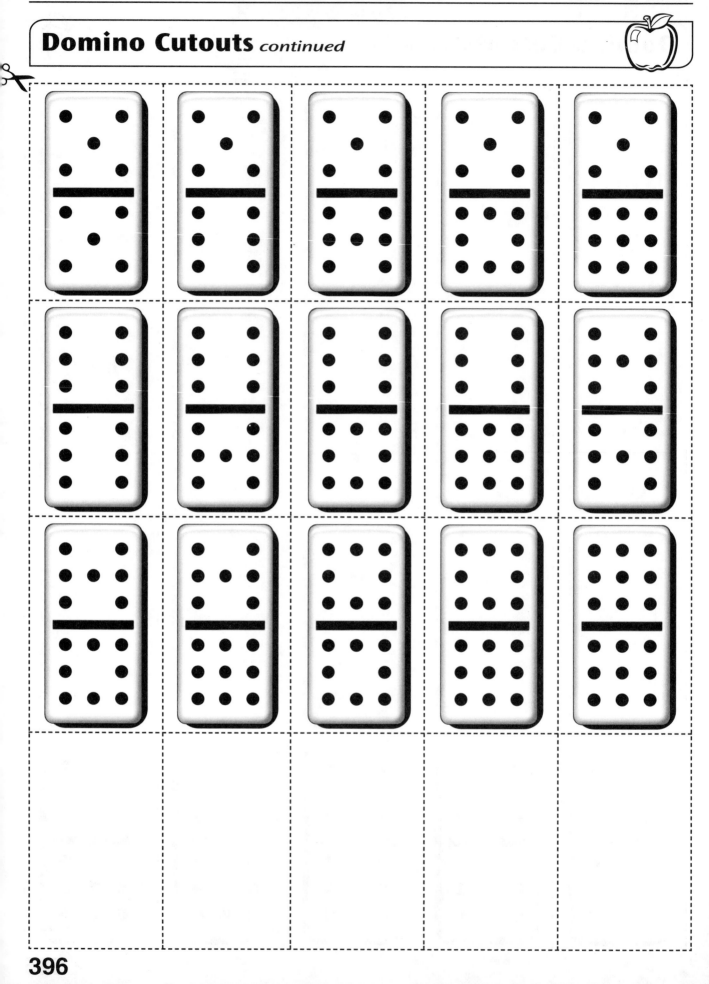

Name Date Time

Name-Collection Boxes

Name

Date

Name

Date

Name

Date

Name

Date

Name Date Time

Place-Value Chart

Number	Hundred Millions 100M	Ten Millions 10M	Millions M	Hundred Thousands 100K	Ten Thousands 10K	Thousands K	Hundreds H	Tens T	Ones O

Name Date Time

Compact Place-Value Flip Book

1. Cut each page along the dashed lines. Do NOT cut any of the solid lines.
2. Cut along the vertical dashed lines to separate the digits.
3. Assemble the pages in order.
4. Staple the assembled book. (Ask your teacher for help if you need it.)

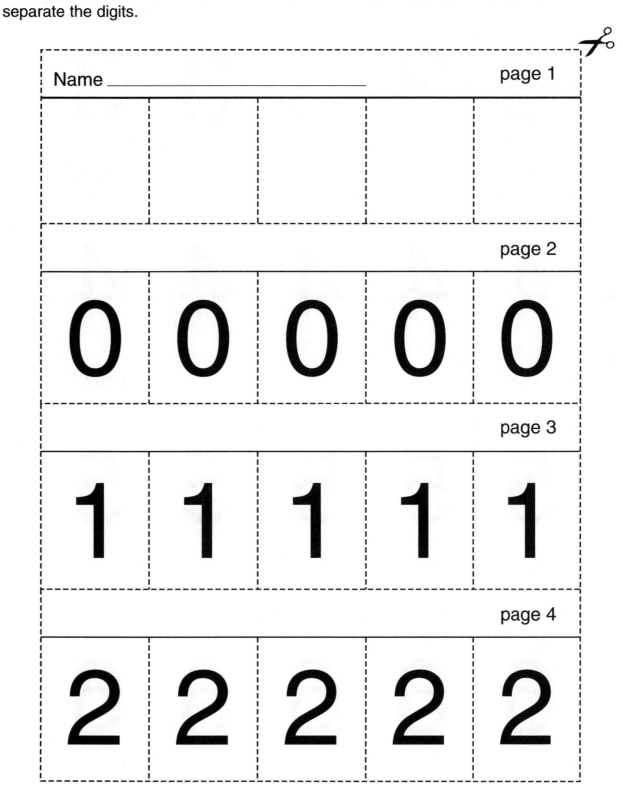

Name ______________________________ page 1

page 2

0	0	0	0	0

page 3

1	1	1	1	1

page 4

2	2	2	2	2

Name Date Time

Compact Place-Value Flip Book *continued*

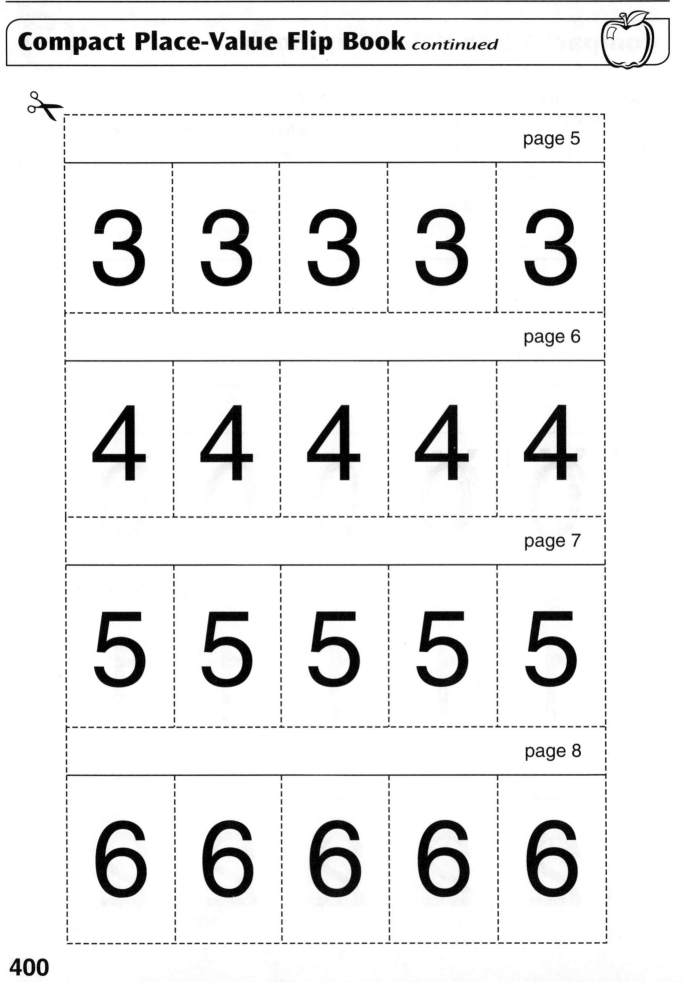

				page 5
3	3	3	3	3

				page 6
4	4	4	4	4

				page 7
5	5	5	5	5

				page 8
6	6	6	6	6

Name Date Time

Compact Place-Value Flip Book *continued*

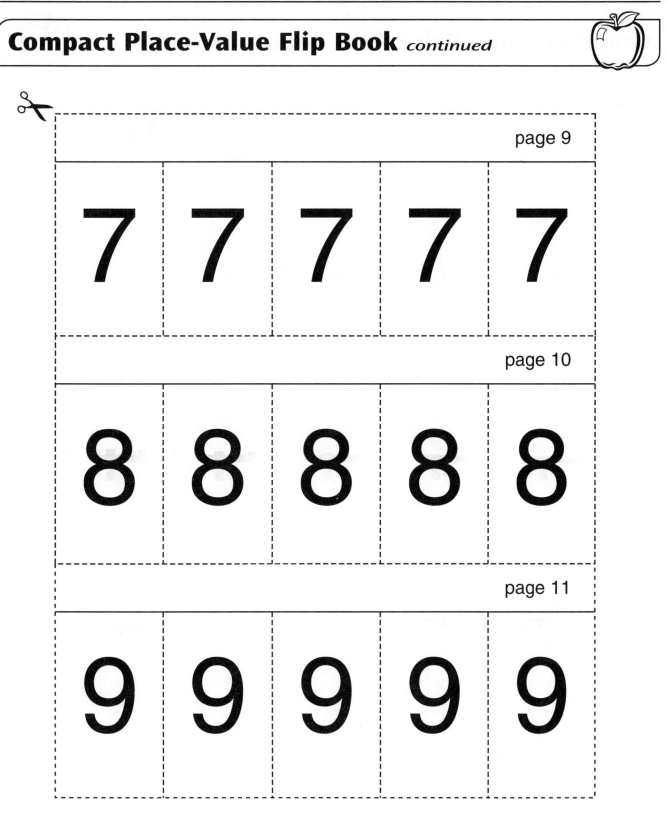

page 9

7	7	7	7	7

page 10

8	8	8	8	8

page 11

9	9	9	9	9

Name Date Time

Compact Place-Value Flip Book *continued*

page 12

•	•	•	•	•

page 13

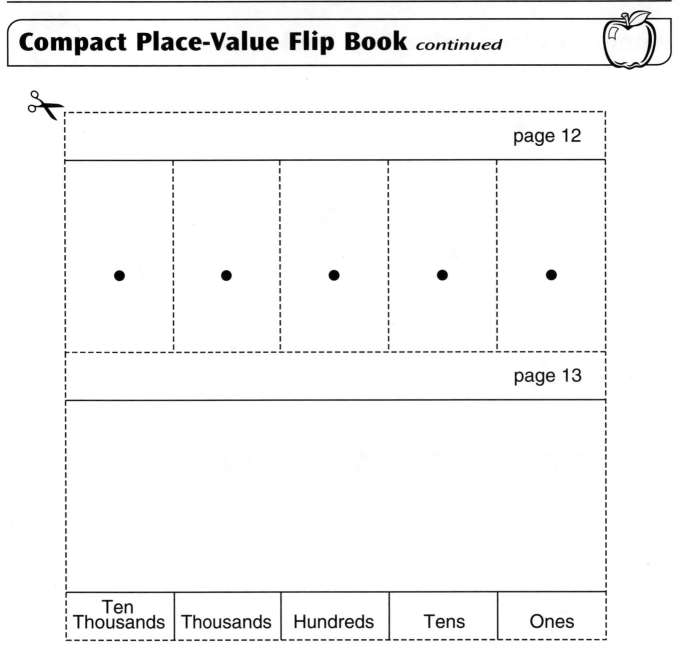

Ten Thousands	Thousands	Hundreds	Tens	Ones

Name Date Time

Grid Paper (1 cm)

Name Date Time

Computation Grids

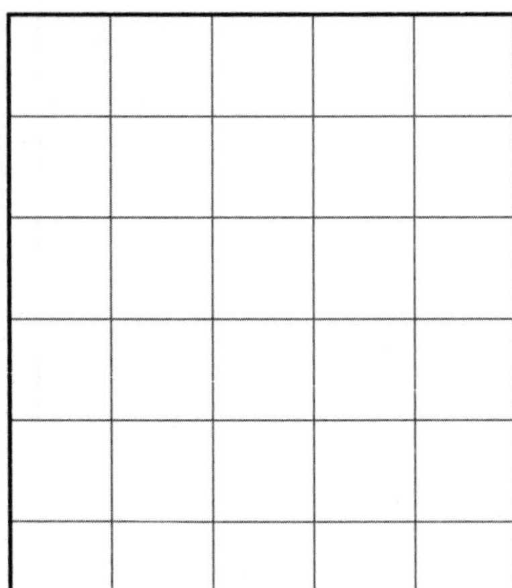

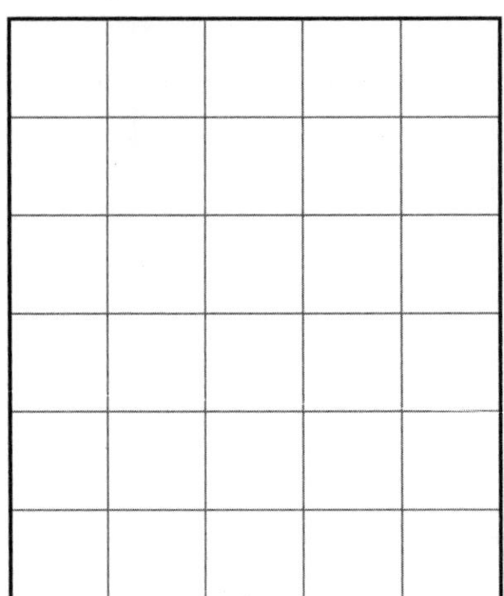

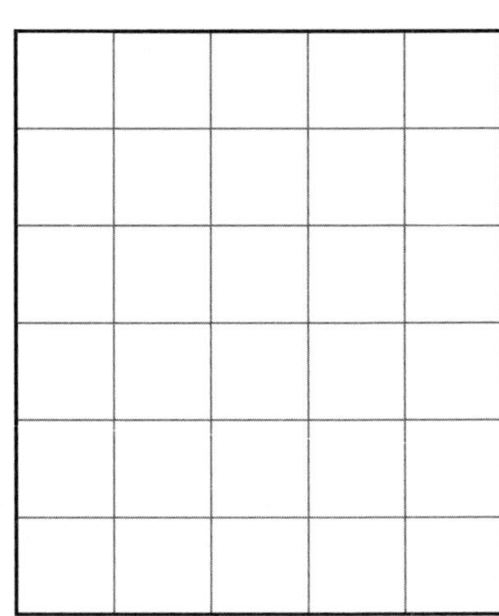

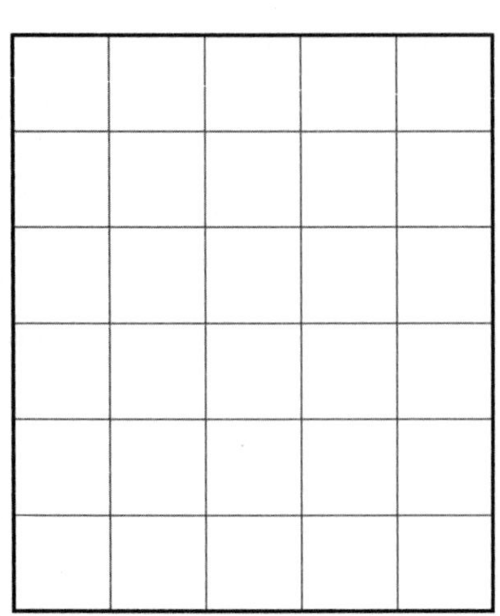

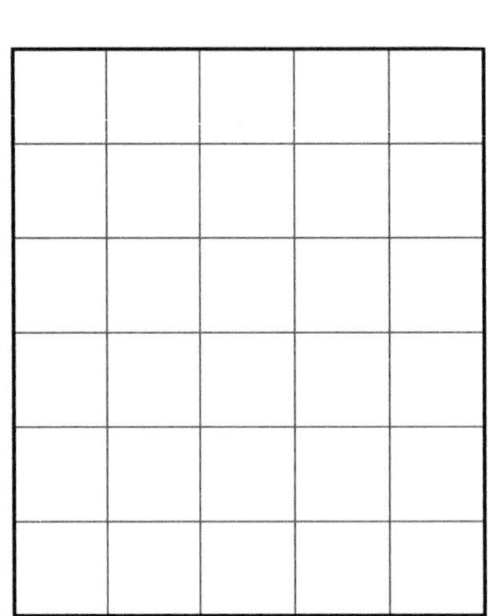

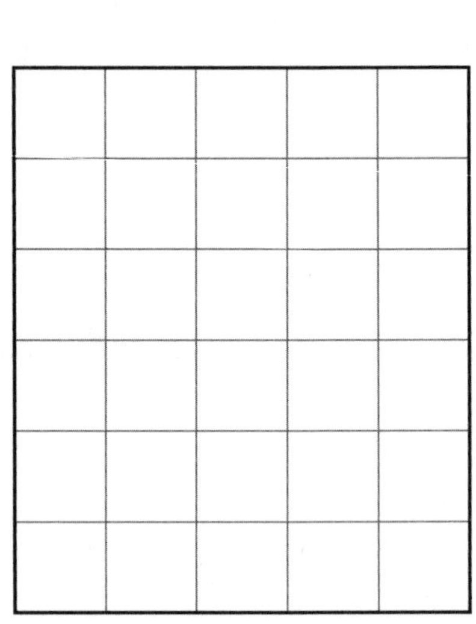

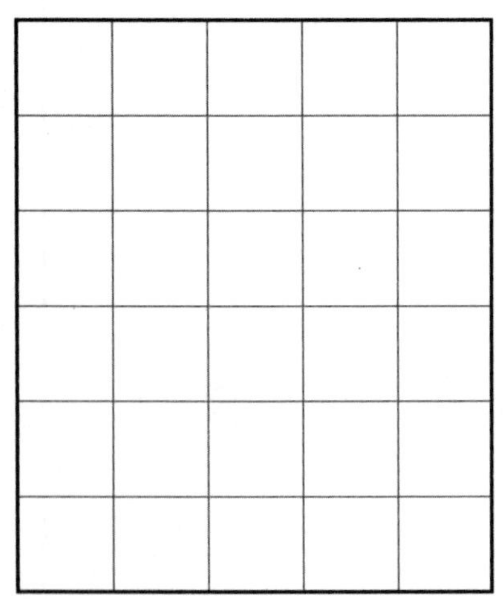

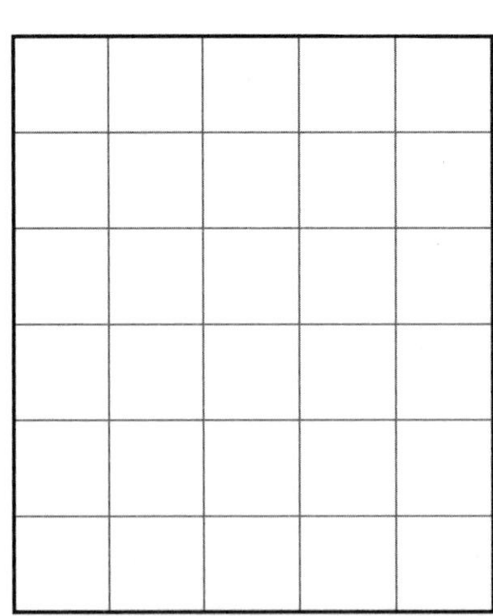

Name Date Time

Parts-and-Total Diagram

Total	
Part	Part

Name Date Time

Large Bar Graph

Name Date Time

"What's My Rule?"

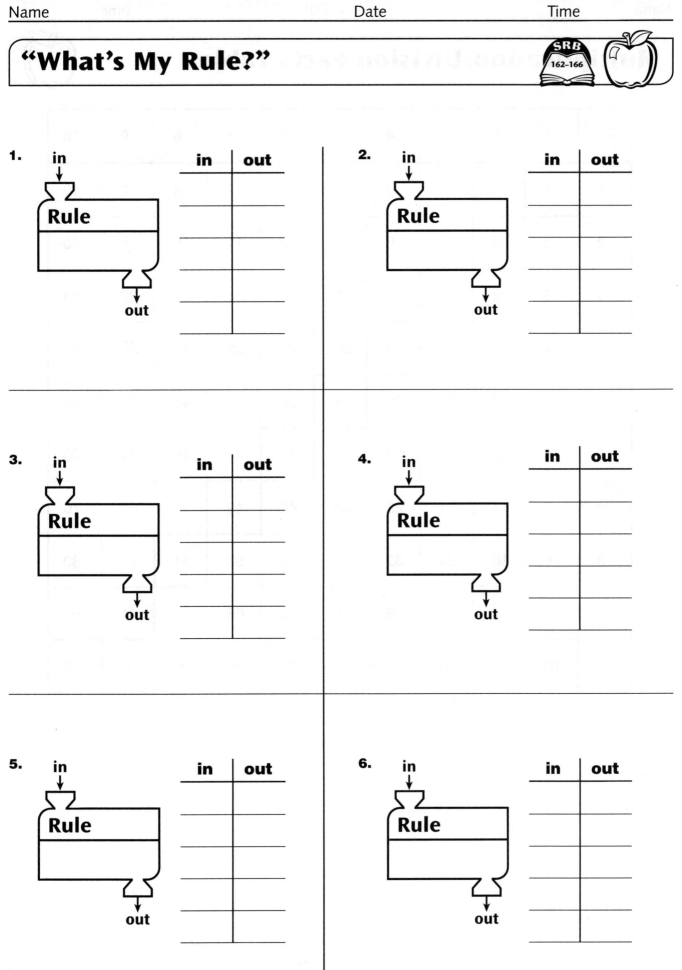

1.

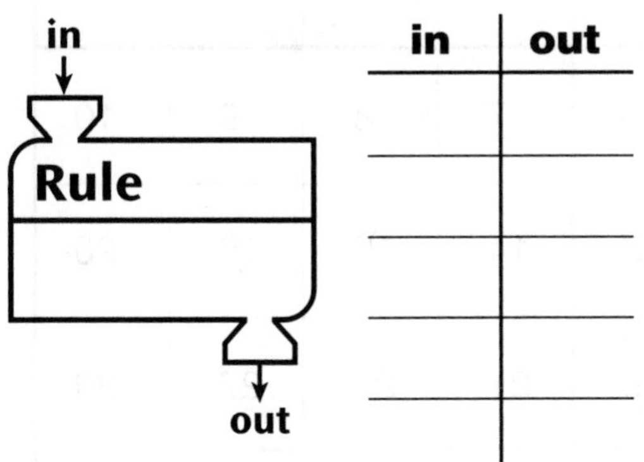

2.

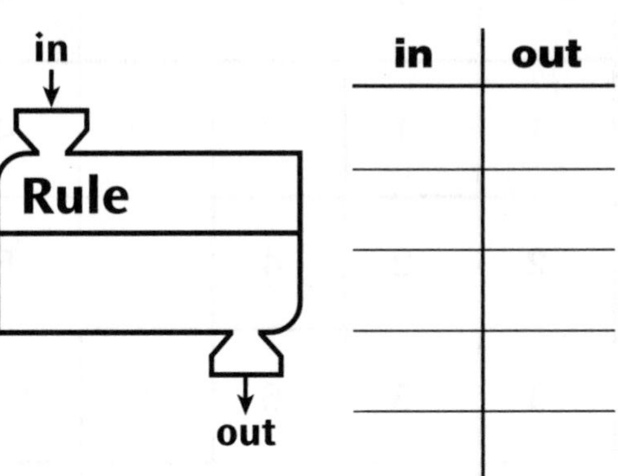

3. in

Rule

out

in	out

4.

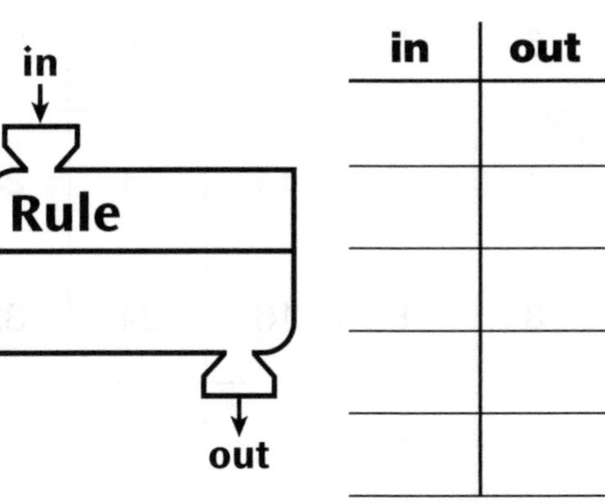

5. in

Rule

out

in	out

6.

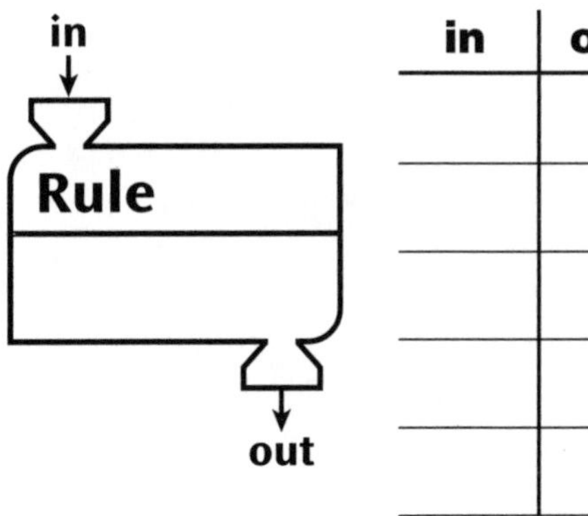

Name Date Time

Multiplication/Division Facts Table

*, /	1	2	3	4	5	6	7	8	9	10
1	1	2	3	4	5	6	7	8	9	10
2	2	4	6	8	10	12	14	16	18	20
3	3	6	9	12	15	18	21	24	27	30
4	4	8	12	16	20	24	28	32	36	40
5	5	10	15	20	25	30	35	40	45	50
6	6	12	18	24	30	36	42	48	54	60
7	7	14	21	28	35	42	49	56	63	70
8	8	16	24	32	40	48	56	64	72	80
9	9	18	27	36	45	54	63	72	81	90
10	10	20	30	40	50	60	70	80	90	100

Name Date Time

*, / Fact Triangle

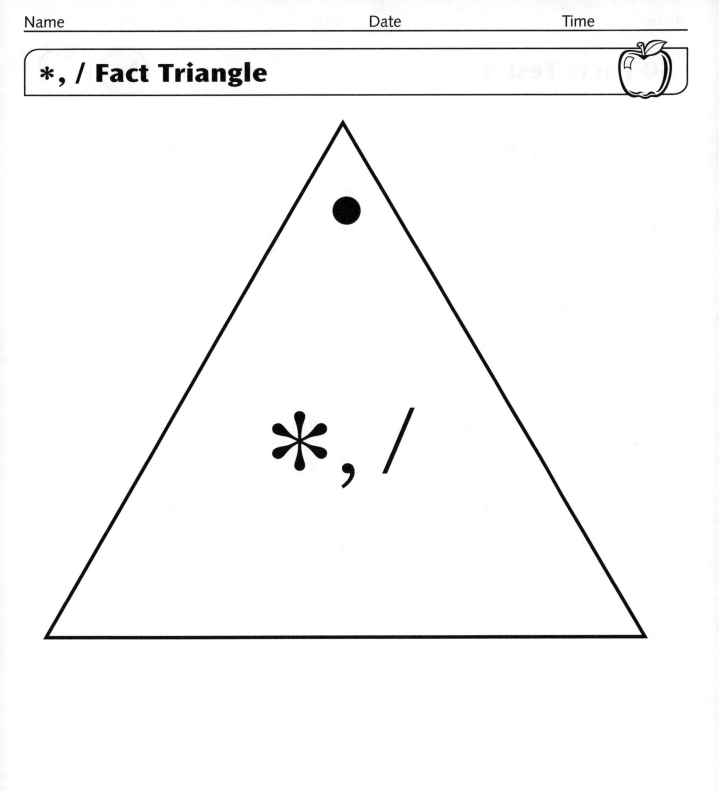

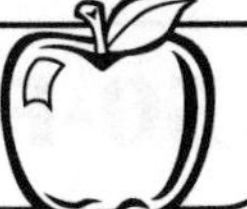

●

*, /

Name ____________ Date ____________ Time ____________

50-Facts Test 1

7 * 7 = ______

5 * 6 = ______

3 * 8 = ______

7 * 9 = ______

0 * 4 = ______

6 * 6 = ______

4 * 5 = ______

3 * 5 = ______

9 * 5 = ______

4 * 1 = ______

2 * 4 = ______

5 * 9 = ______

4 * 3 = ______

9 * 8 = ______

4 * 7 = ______

2 * 0 = ______

4 * 9 = ______

1 * 0 = ______

2 * 7 = ______

8 * 4 = ______

8 * 2 = ______

2 * 6 = ______

4 * 8 = ______

8 * 6 = ______

6 * 5 = ______

6 * 3 = ______

5 * 8 = ______

5 * 3 = ______

7 * 8 = ______

6 * 4 = ______

3 * 9 = ______

7 * 6 = ______

5 * 5 = ______

9 * 9 = ______

7 * 2 = ______

2 * 9 = ______

4 * 4 = ______

8 * 8 = ______

5 * 7 = ______

5 * 2 = ______

9 * 4 = ______

6 * 9 = ______

8 * 9 = ______

7 * 3 = ______

5 * 4 = ______

9 * 7 = ______

9 * 6 = ______

8 * 7 = ______

7 * 5 = ______

3 * 3 = ______

1-Minute Score: $\frac{\_\_\_\_}{50} = \frac{\_\_\_\_}{100} =$ ______%

3-Minute Score: $\frac{\_\_\_\_}{50} = \frac{\_\_\_\_}{100} =$ ______%

Name _______________ Date _______________ Time _______________

50-Facts Test 2

6 * 6 = ______	4 * 7 = ______	8 * 3 = ______	7 * 7 = ______
5 * 0 = ______	4 * 2 = ______	6 * 5 = ______	6 * 9 = ______
4 * 4 = ______	5 * 8 = ______	5 * 5 = ______	4 * 6 = ______
6 * 3 = ______	5 * 9 = ______	9 * 8 = ______	3 * 6 = ______
8 * 7 = ______	2 * 5 = ______	8 * 2 = ______	9 * 5 = ______
2 * 7 = ______	8 * 8 = ______	7 * 8 = ______	9 * 9 = ______
4 * 9 = ______	4 * 8 = ______	8 * 6 = ______	8 * 5 = ______
5 * 3 = ______	6 * 8 = ______	9 * 7 = ______	7 * 6 = ______
8 * 1 = ______	7 * 3 = ______	3 * 3 = ______	5 * 4 = ______
3 * 8 = ______	9 * 6 = ______	7 * 5 = ______	3 * 7 = ______
7 * 9 = ______	7 * 4 = ______	9 * 4 = ______	9 * 2 = ______
6 * 7 = ______	4 * 3 = ______	4 * 5 = ______	8 * 9 = ______
3 * 5 = ______	9 * 3 = ______		

1-Minute Score: $\frac{\_\_\_\_}{50} = \frac{\_\_\_\_}{100}$ = ______%

3-Minute Score: $\frac{\_\_\_\_}{50} = \frac{\_\_\_\_}{100}$ = ______%

Name ______ Date ______ Time ______

50-Facts Test 3

2 * 0 = ______	6 * 9 = ______	4 * 6 = ______	9 * 2 = ______
3 * 3 = ______	7 * 6 = ______	9 * 3 = ______	7 * 9 = ______
5 * 7 = ______	6 * 5 = ______	5 * 6 = ______	5 * 9 = ______
5 * 5 = ______	8 * 6 = ______	3 * 7 = ______	9 * 4 = ______
4 * 8 = ______	7 * 2 = ______	9 * 5 = ______	4 * 5 = ______
4 * 4 = ______	2 * 6 = ______	9 * 9 = ______	6 * 8 = ______
3 * 9 = ______	9 * 7 = ______	8 * 5 = ______	6 * 3 = ______
2 * 4 = ______	6 * 7 = ______	2 * 3 = ______	3 * 8 = ______
9 * 6 = ______	1 * 1 = ______	7 * 7 = ______	4 * 7 = ______
8 * 7 = ______	8 * 4 = ______	7 * 5 = ______	5 * 4 = ______
9 * 8 = ______	8 * 8 = ______	6 * 4 = ______	6 * 6 = ______
3 * 5 = ______	8 * 9 = ______	7 * 8 = ______	3 * 6 = ______
3 * 4 = ______	8 * 3 = ______		

1-Minute Score: $\frac{\_\_\_\_}{50} = \frac{\_\_\_\_}{100} = \_\_\_\_\%$

3-Minute Score: $\frac{\_\_\_\_}{50} = \frac{\_\_\_\_}{100} = \_\_\_\_\%$

Name Date Time

50-Facts Test 4

4 * 8 = ________

3 * 7 = ________

6 * 6 = ________

8 * 3 = ________

6 * 9 = ________

2 * 4 = ________

4 * 6 = ________

7 * 0 = ________

9 * 3 = ________

6 * 7 = ________

2 * 5 = ________

4 * 3 = ________

4 * 7 = ________

7 * 5 = ________

4 * 9 = ________

5 * 8 = ________

1 * 3 = ________

7 * 9 = ________

9 * 8 = ________

2 * 8 = ________

5 * 5 = ________

3 * 1 = ________

8 * 6 = ________

1 * 0 = ________

3 * 5 = ________

7 * 2 = ________

9 * 9 = ________

5 * 7 = ________

8 * 5 = ________

6 * 8 = ________

4 * 4 = ________

7 * 4 = ________

8 * 9 = ________

9 * 7 = ________

1 * 1 = ________

5 * 9 = ________

5 * 6 = ________

7 * 7 = ________

7 * 6 = ________

3 * 4 = ________

4 * 5 = ________

8 * 8 = ________

9 * 4 = ________

9 * 6 = ________

7 * 3 = ________

2 * 9 = ________

6 * 4 = ________

3 * 6 = ________

6 * 2 = ________

8 * 7 = ________

1-Minute Score: $\frac{\_\_\_\_}{50} = \frac{\_\_\_\_}{100}$ = ________%

3-Minute Score: $\frac{\_\_\_\_}{50} = \frac{\_\_\_\_}{100}$ = ________%

Name Date Time

My 50-Facts Test Scores

Write the date on the bottom line. Using a pencil, make a dot above each date to record your 1-minute score. Using a pen, make a dot above each date to record your 3-minute score. Connect the pencil dots. Then connect the pen dots.

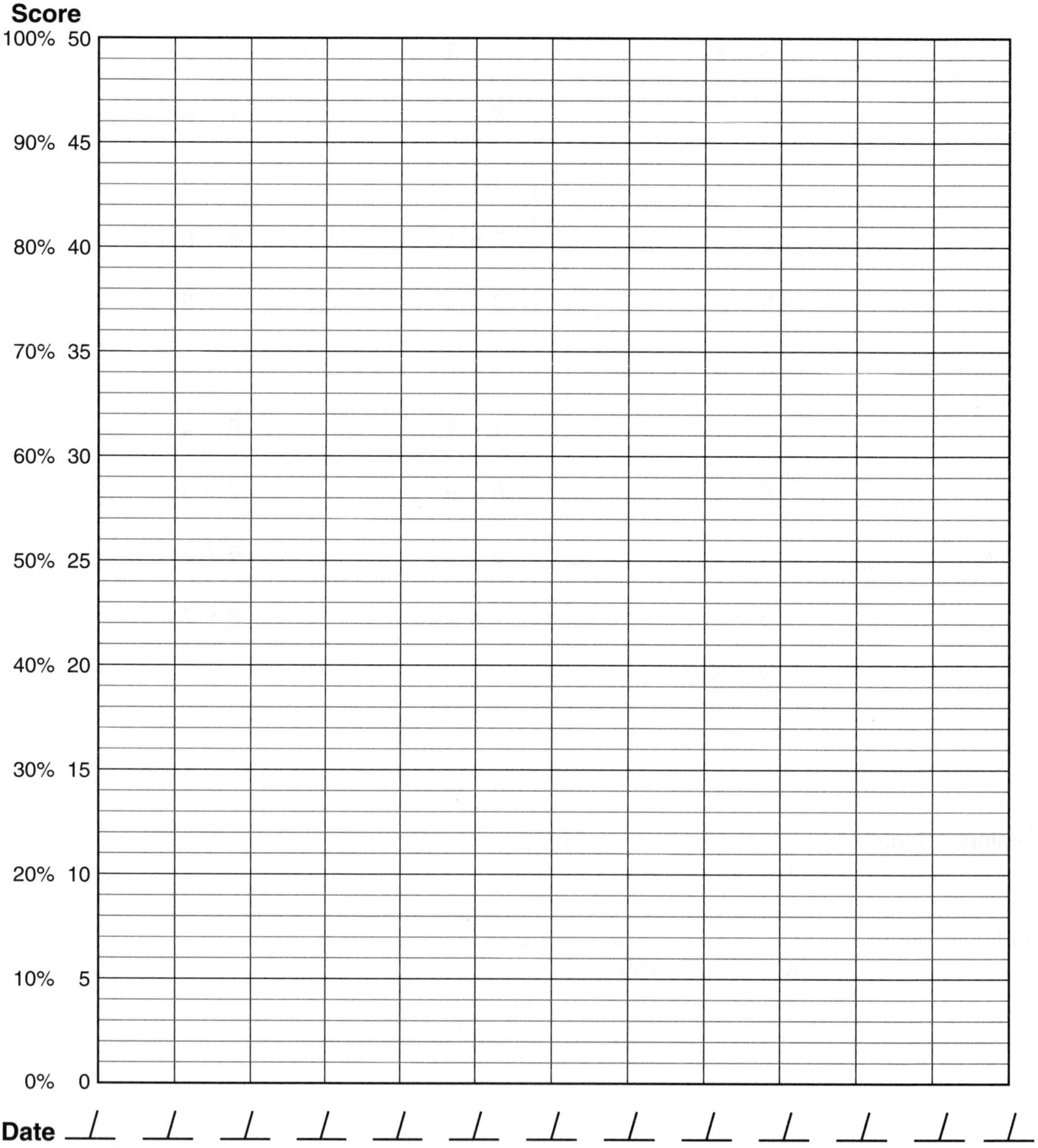

Score

100% 50

90% 45

80% 40

70% 35

60% 30

50% 25

40% 20

30% 15

20% 10

10% 5

0% 0

Date __/__ __/__ __/__ __/__ __/__ __/__ __/__ __/__ __/__ __/__ __/__ __/__ __/__

Name Date Time

My 50-Facts Test Scores *continued*

Tape this page to *Math Masters,* page 414 if that page is filled up.

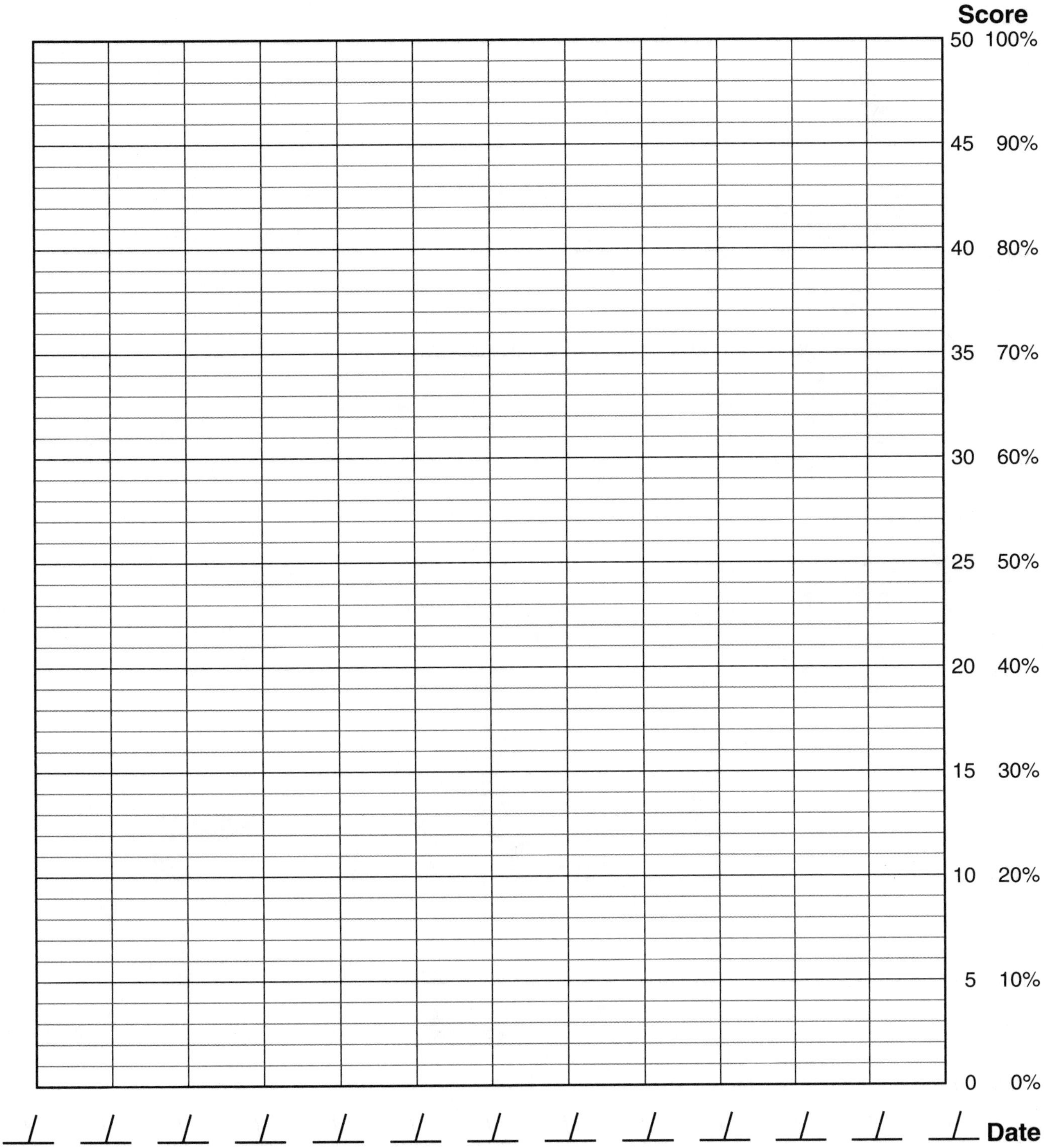

												Score	
												50	100%
												45	90%
												40	80%
												35	70%
												30	60%
												25	50%
												20	40%
												15	30%
												10	20%
												5	10%
												0	0%
__/__	__/__	__/__	__/__	__/__	__/__	__/__	__/__	__/__	__/__	__/__	__/__	__/__	**Date**

Name Date Time

Class 50-Facts Test Scores

Write the date on the bottom line. Make a dot above each date to record each student's 1-minute score. On the gridline above each date, mark "M" for the class median score and "A" for the class mean, or average, score.

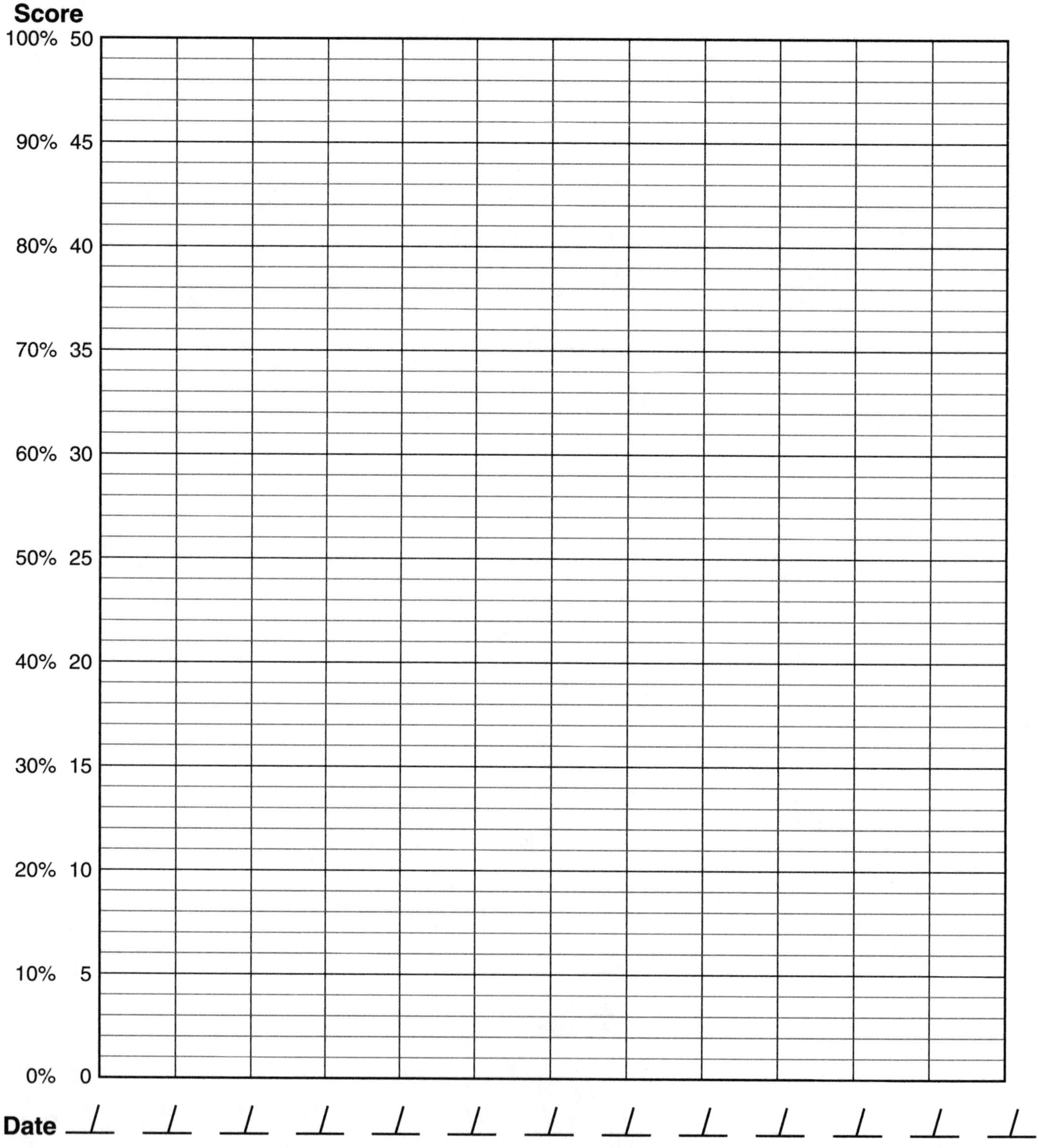

Score

Score	
100%	50
90%	45
80%	40
70%	35
60%	30
50%	25
40%	20
30%	15
20%	10
10%	5
0%	0

Date _/_ _/_ _/_ _/_ _/_ _/_ _/_ _/_ _/_ _/_ _/_ _/_ _/_

Name Date Time

Class 50-Facts Test Scores *continued*

Tape this page to *Math Masters,* page 416 if that page is filled up.

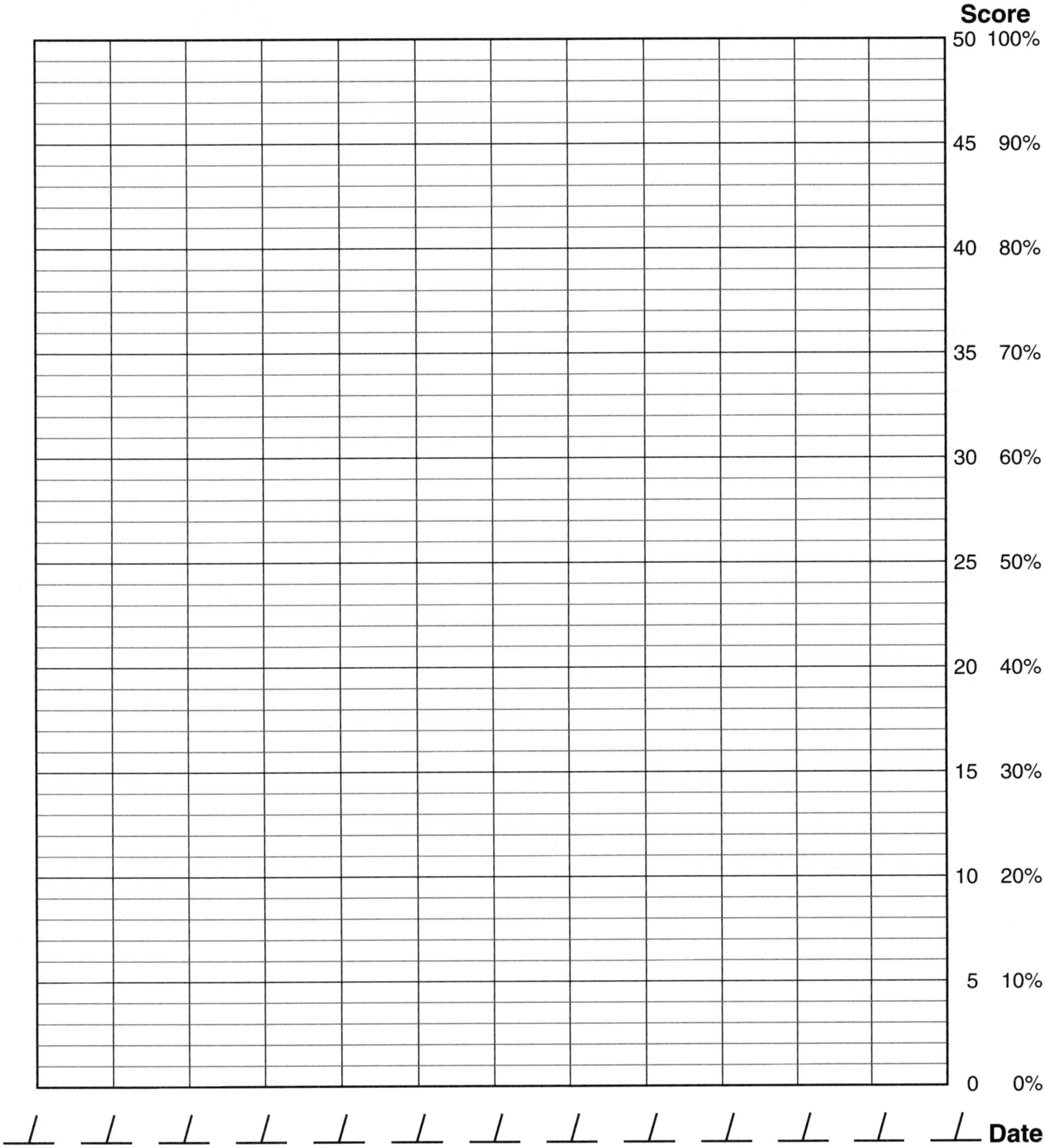

Score

50 100%

45 90%

40 80%

35 70%

30 60%

25 50%

20 40%

15 30%

10 20%

5 10%

0 0%

__/__ __/__ __/__ __/__ __/__ __/__ __/__ __/__ __/__ __/__ __/__ __/__ __/__ **Date**

Name Date Time

Fact Families

Complete each Fact Triangle. Write the fact family for each Fact Triangle.

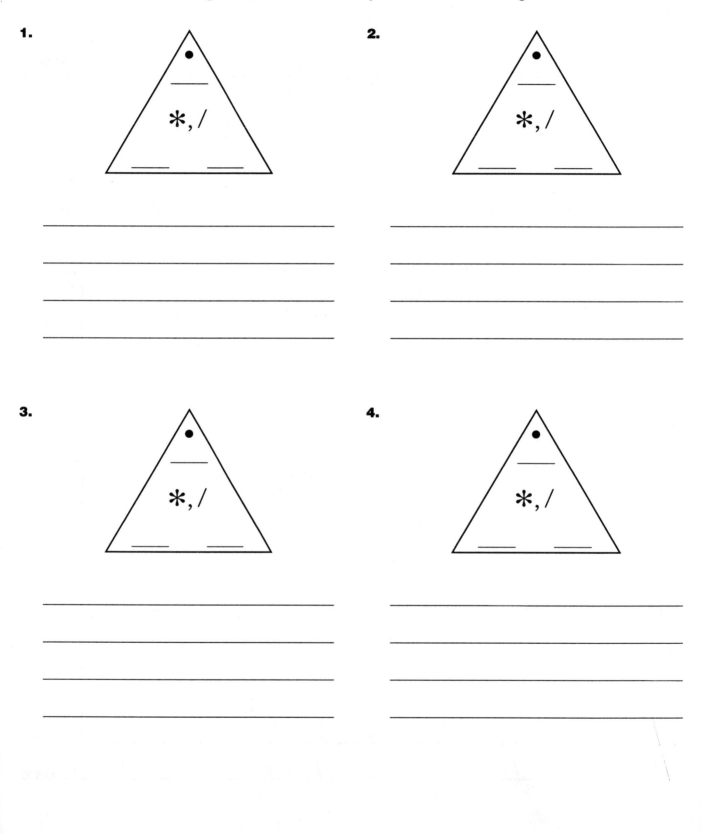

1.

2.

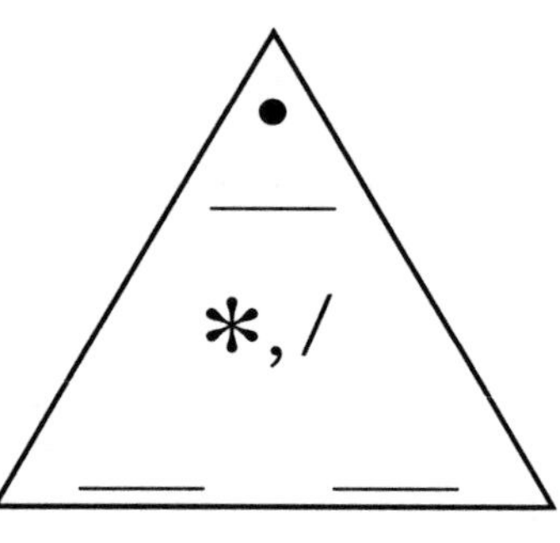

3.

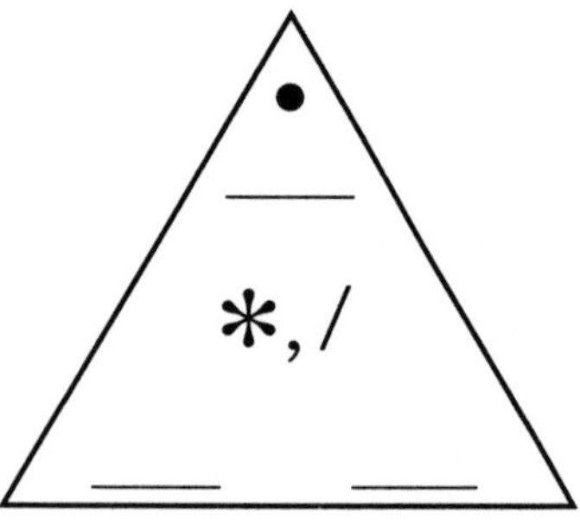

4.

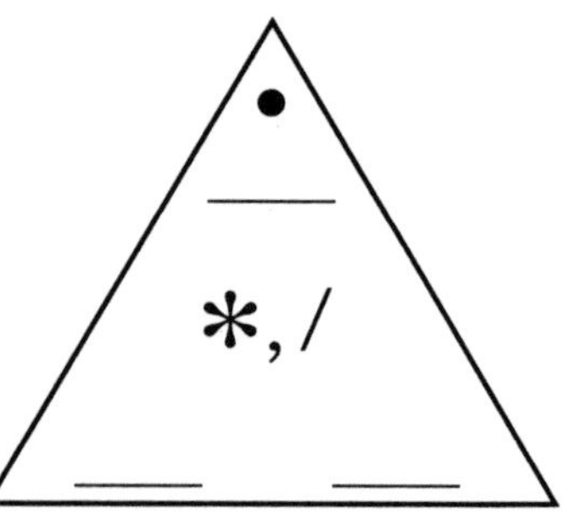

Name ______________________ Date ______________ Time ______________

My Country Notes

A. Facts about the country

________________________ is located in ________________________.
name of country | name of continent

1. It is bordered by ____
countries, bodies of water

____.

2. Population: ____________________ Area: ____________________ square miles

3. Languages spoken: ____

____

4. Monetary unit: ____

5. Exchange rate (optional): 1 ____________________ = ____________________

B. Facts about the capital of the country

________________________ Population: ________________________
name of capital

1. When it is noon in my hometown, it is ____________ in ________________________.
time (A.M. or P.M.?) | name of capital

2. In ________/________, the average high temperature in ________________________
month | month | name of capital

is about ____________ °F. The average low temperature is about ____________ °F.

3. What kinds of clothes should I pack for my visit to this capital? Why?

____

____

____

____

Name Date Time

My Country Notes *continued*

4. Turn to the Route Map found on journal pages 172 and 173. Draw a line from the last city you visited to the capital of this country.

5. If your class is using the Route Log, record the information on journal page 171 or *Math Masters,* page 421.

6. Can you find any facts on pages 302–305 in your *Student Reference Book* that apply to this country? For example, is one of the 10 tallest mountains in the world located in this country? List all the facts you can find.

____

____

____

____

____

C. My impressions about the country

Do you know anyone who has visited or lived in this country? If so, ask that person for an interview. Read about the country's customs and about interesting places to visit there. Use encyclopedias, travel books, the travel section of a newspaper, or library books. Try to get brochures from a travel agent. Then describe below some interesting things you have learned about this country.

____

____

____

____

____

____

____

____

Name Date Time

My Route Log

Date	Country	Capital	Air distance from last capital	Total distance traveled so far
	1 U.S.A.	Washington, D.C.		
	2 Egypt	Cairo		
	3			
	4			
	5			
	6			
	7			
	8			
	9			
	10			
	11			
	12			
	13			
	14			
	15			
	16			
	17			
	18			
	19			
	20			

Name Date Time

A Guide for Solving Number Stories

1. **Understand the problem.**
   - Read the problem. Can you retell it in your own words?
   - What do you want to find out?
   - What do you know?
   - Do you have all the information needed to solve the problem?

2. **Plan what to do.**
   - Is the problem like one that you have solved before?
   - Is there a pattern you can use?
   - Can you draw a picture or a diagram?
   - Can you write a number model or make a table?
   - Can you use counters, base-10 blocks, or some other tool?
   - Can you estimate the answer and check if you're right?

3. **Carry out the plan.**
   - After you decide what to do, do it. Be careful.
   - Make a written record of what you do.
   - Answer the question.

4. **Look back.**
   - Does your answer make sense?
   - Does your answer agree with your estimate?
   - Can you write a number model for the problem?
   - Can you solve the problem in another way?

Name Date Time

Situation Diagrams

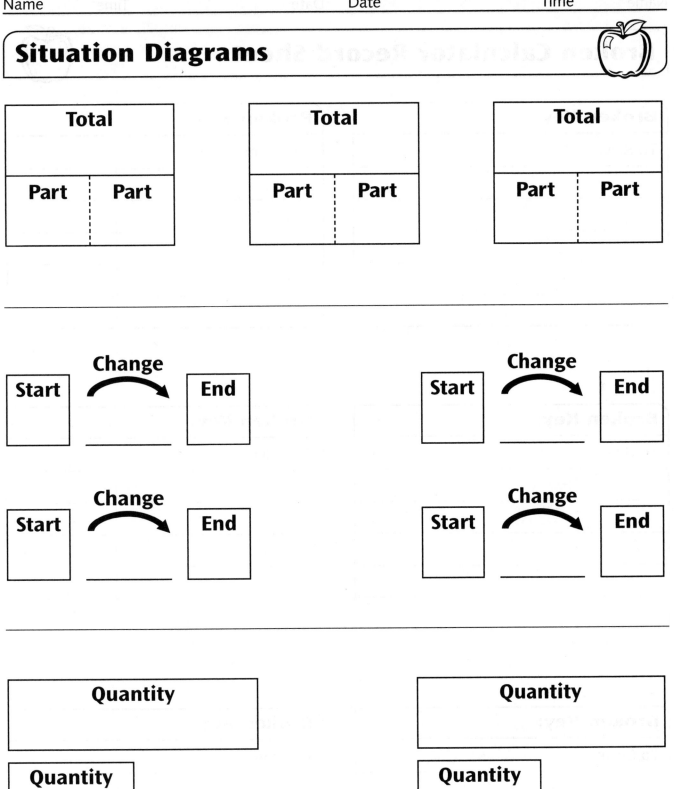

Total	
Part	Part

Total	
Part	Part

Total	
Part	Part

Start Change End

Start Change End

Start Change End

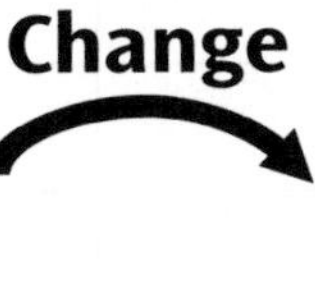

Start Change End

Quantity

Quantity

Difference

Quantity

Quantity

Difference

Name Date Time

Broken Calculator Record Sheet

Broken Key:	
To Solve:	

Broken Key:	
To Solve:	

Broken Key:	
To Solve:	

Broken Key:	
To Solve:	

Broken Key:	
To Solve:	

Broken Key:	
To Solve:	

Name Date Time

Broken Calculator

Broken Key:	
To Solve:	

Name Date Time

Base-10 Grids

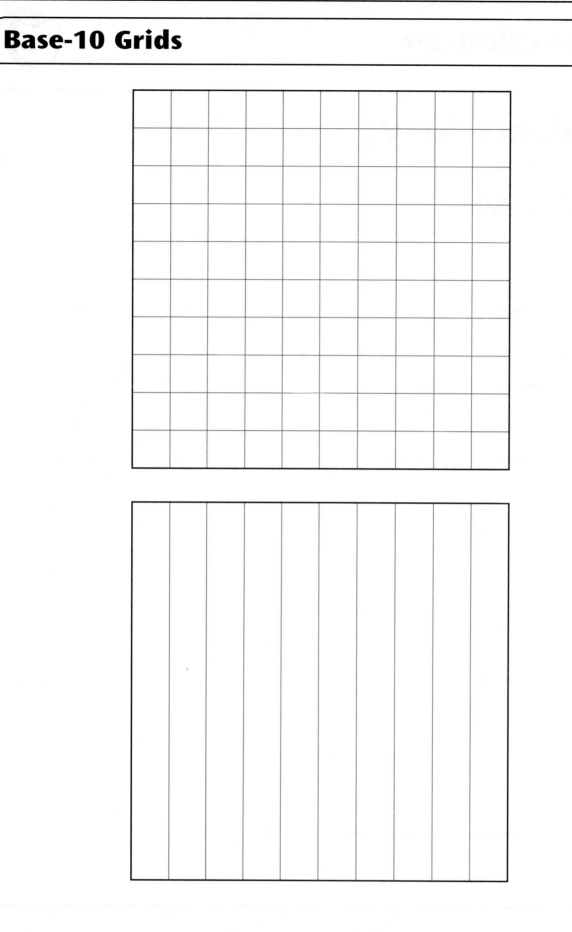

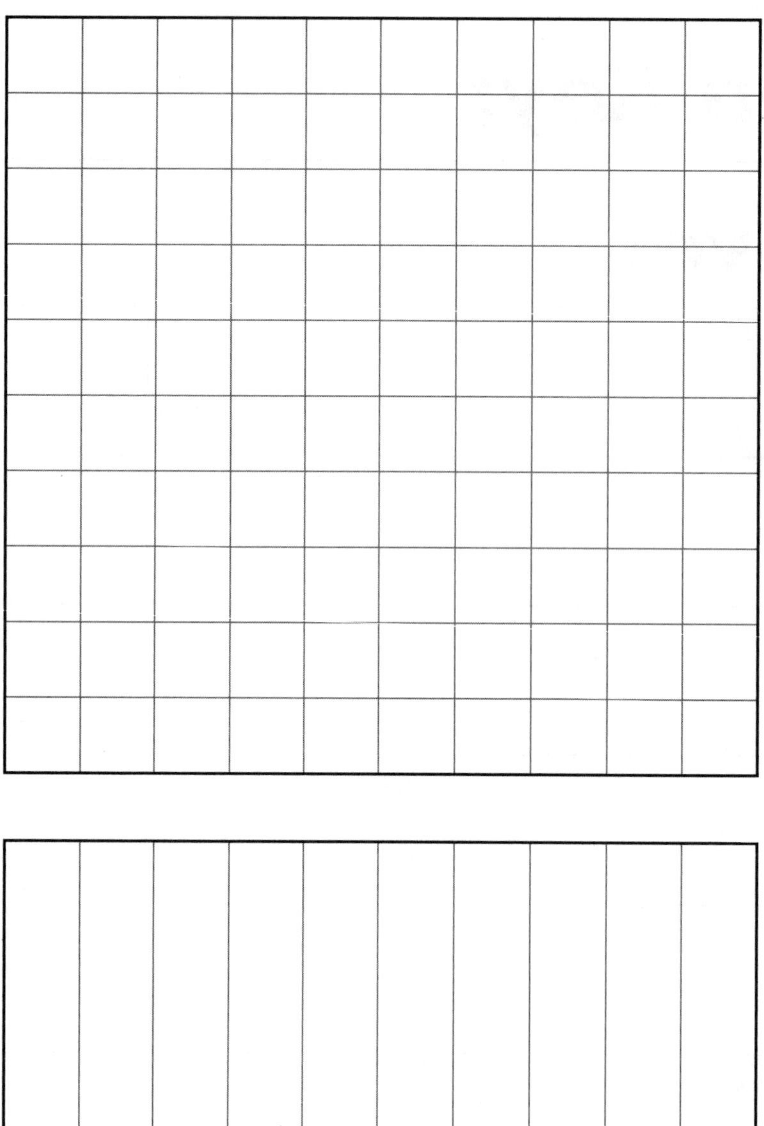

Name Date Time

Number Grid (Decimal Version)

									0
0.01	0.02	0.03	0.04	0.05	0.06	0.07	0.08	0.09	0.10
0.11	0.12	0.13	0.14	0.15	0.16	0.17	0.18	0.19	0.20
0.21	0.22	0.23	0.24	0.25	0.26	0.27	0.28	0.29	0.30
0.31	0.32	0.33	0.34	0.35	0.36	0.37	0.38	0.39	0.40
0.41	0.42	0.43	0.44	0.45	0.46	0.47	0.48	0.49	0.50
0.51	0.52	0.53	0.54	0.55	0.56	0.57	0.58	0.59	0.60
0.61	0.62	0.63	0.64	0.65	0.66	0.67	0.68	0.69	0.70
0.71	0.72	0.73	0.74	0.75	0.76	0.77	0.78	0.79	0.80
0.81	0.82	0.83	0.84	0.85	0.86	0.87	0.88	0.89	0.90
0.91	0.92	0.93	0.94	0.95	0.96	0.97	0.98	0.99	1.00

Name Date Time

$1 and $10 Bills

Name Date Time

A cm/mm Ruler

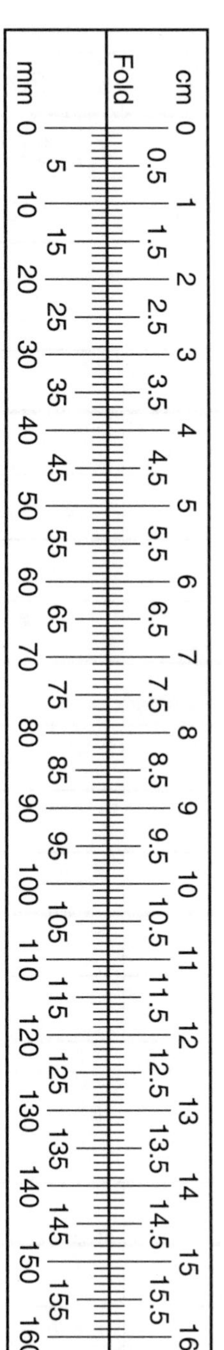

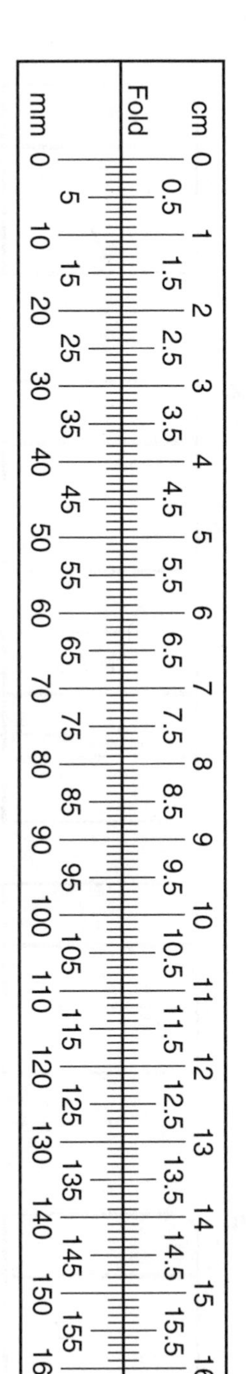

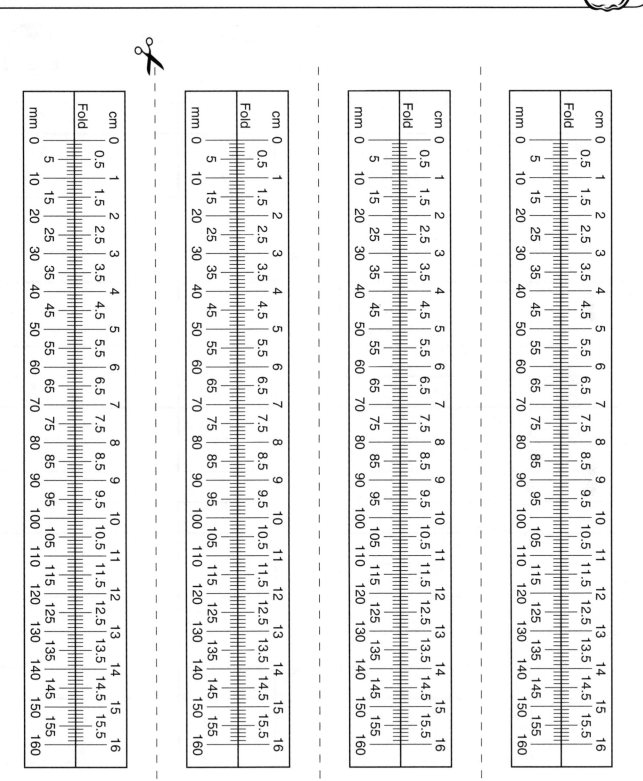

Name Date Time

Multiplication/Division Puzzles

Solve the multiplication/division puzzles mentally. Fill in the blank boxes.

Examples:

*,/	400	6,000
5	2,000	30,000
8	3,200	48,000

*,/	90	20
3	270	60
7	630	140

1.

*,/		

2.

*,/		

3.

*,/		

4.

*,/		

5.

*,/		

6.

*,/		

Make up and solve some puzzles of your own.

7.

*,/		

8.

*,/		

Name Date Time

Computation Grids

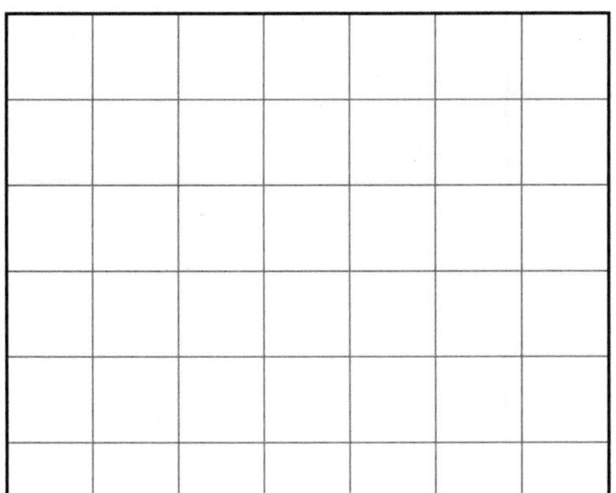

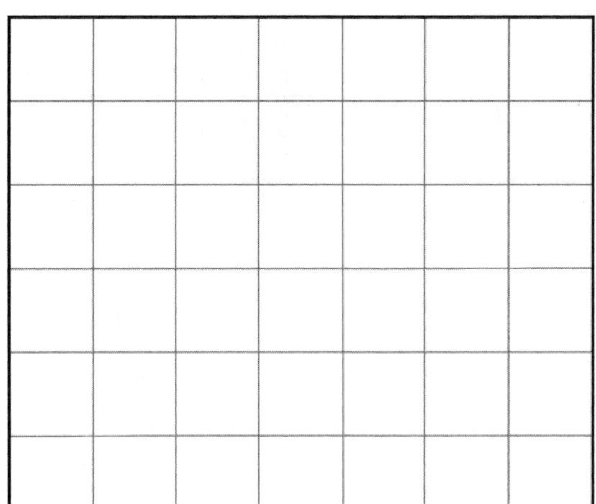

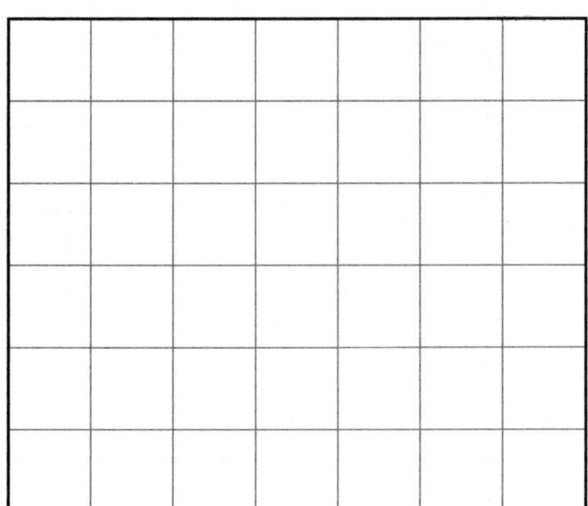

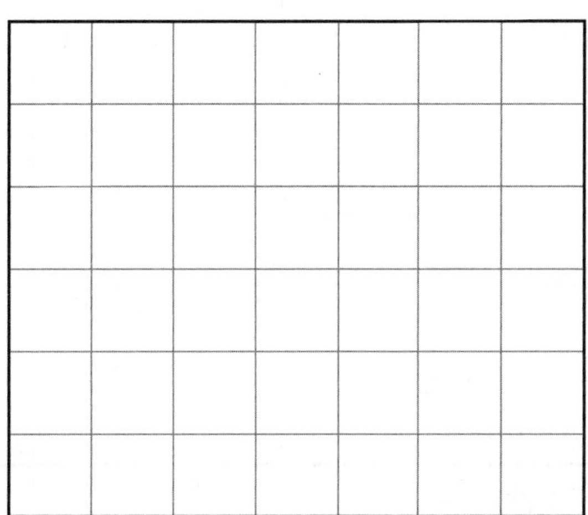

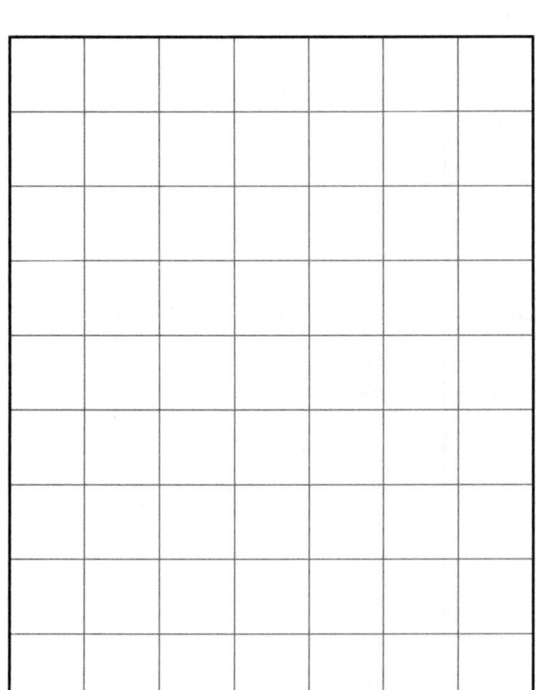

Name Date Time

Array Grid

GLUE OR PASTE EDGE OF PAGE 433 HERE

Start here.

Name Date Time

Array Grid *continued*

Name Date Time

Lattice Multiplication Computation Grids

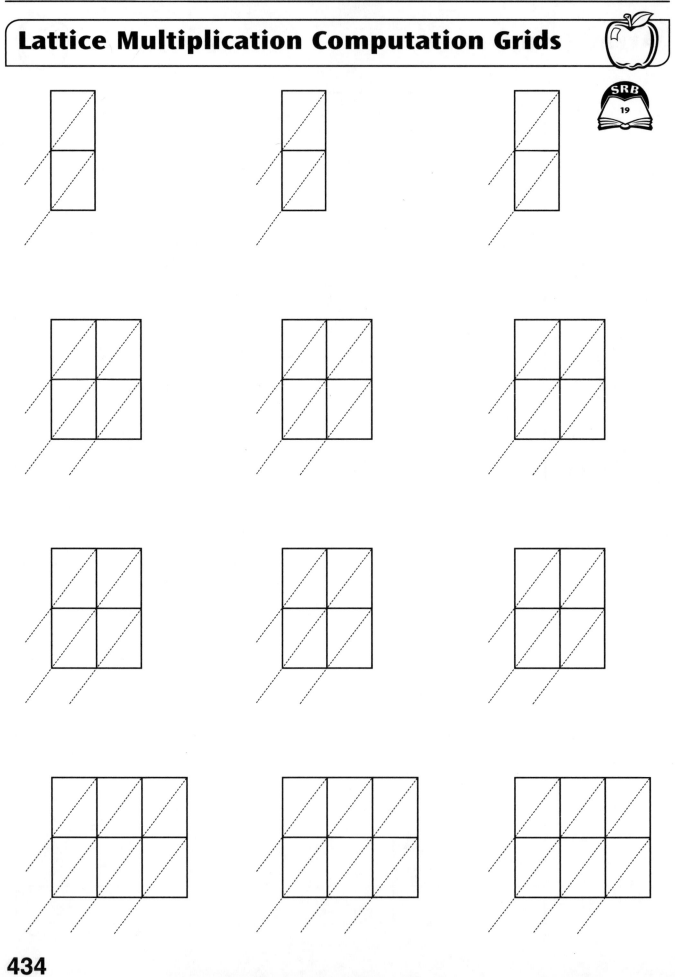

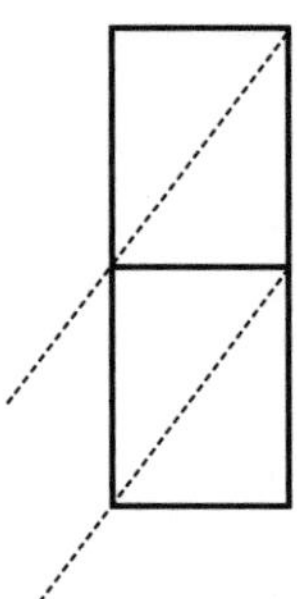

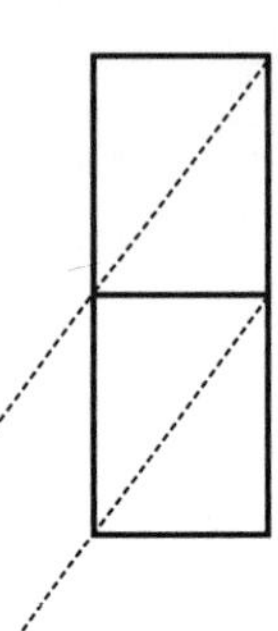

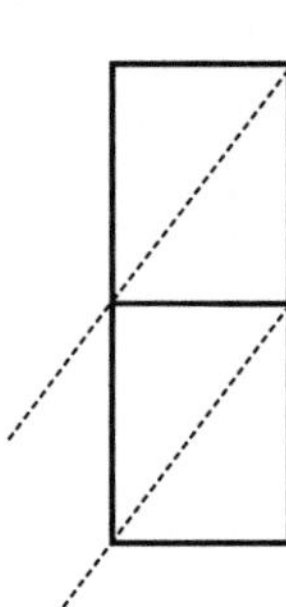

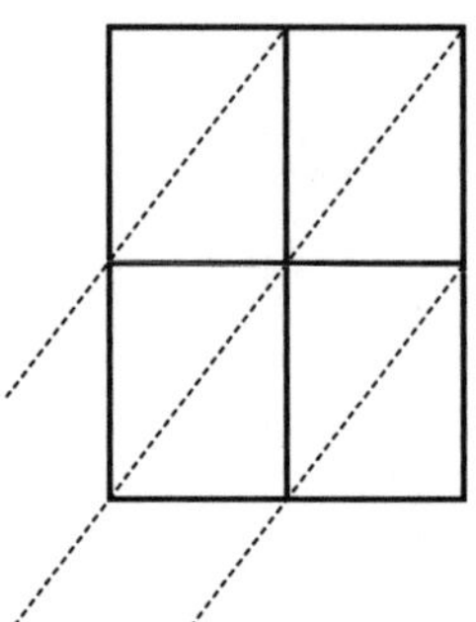

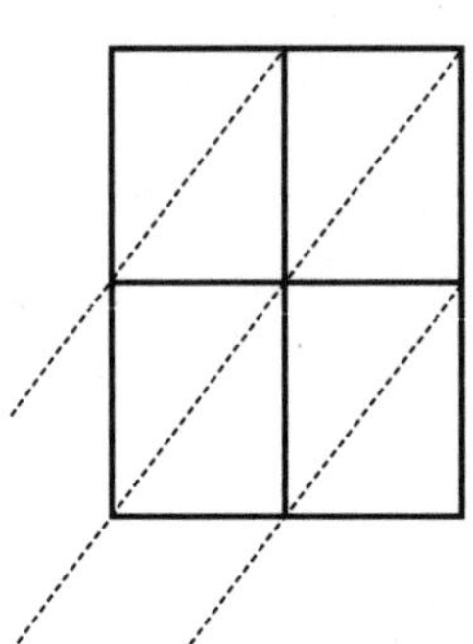

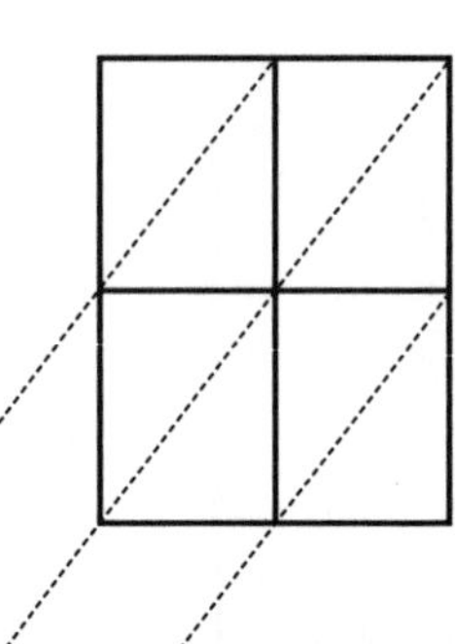

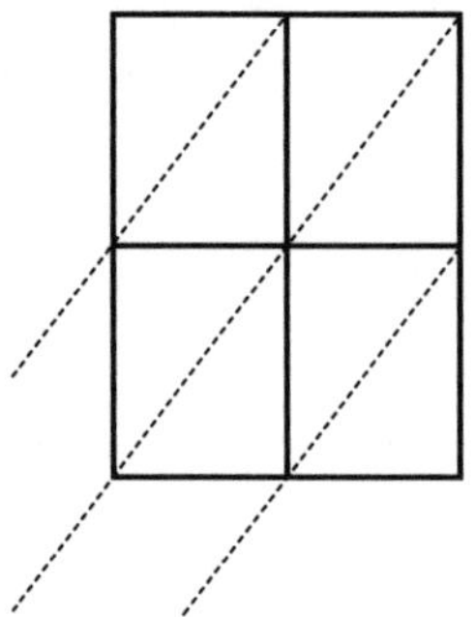

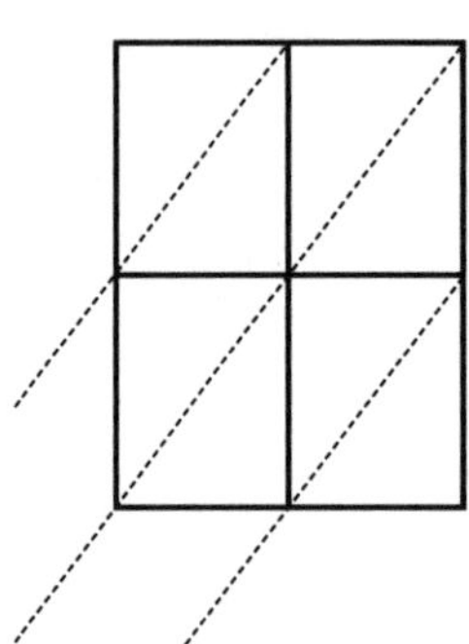

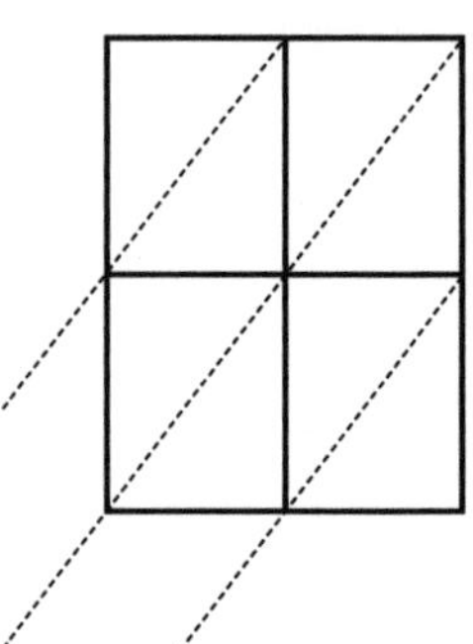

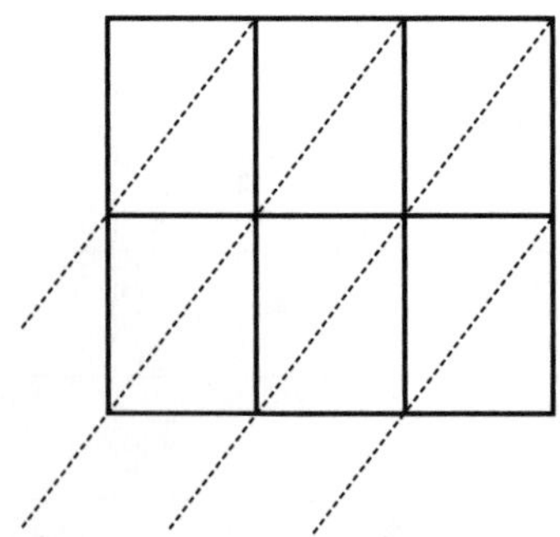

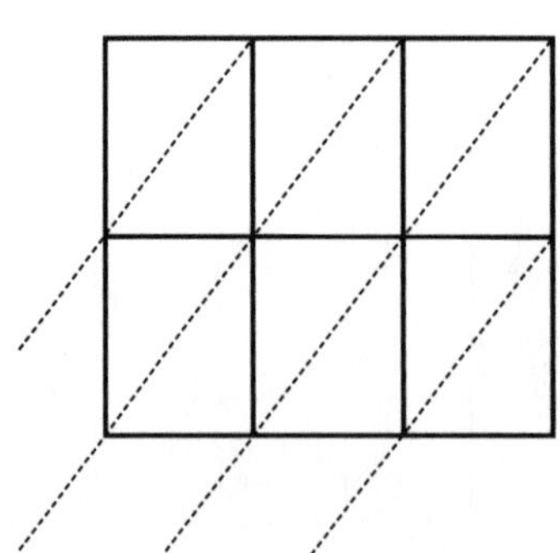

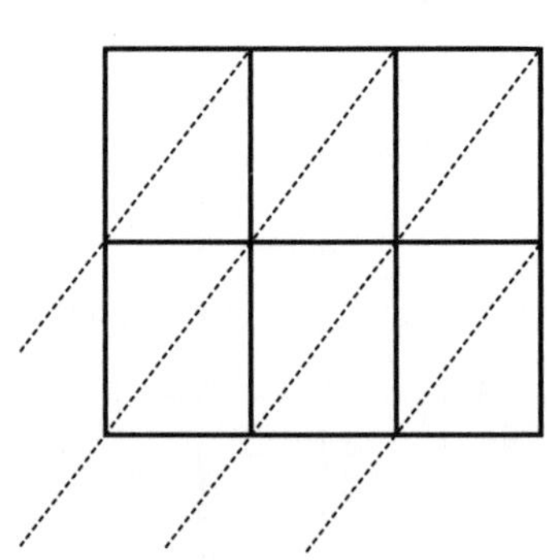

Name Date Time

Fact Lattice

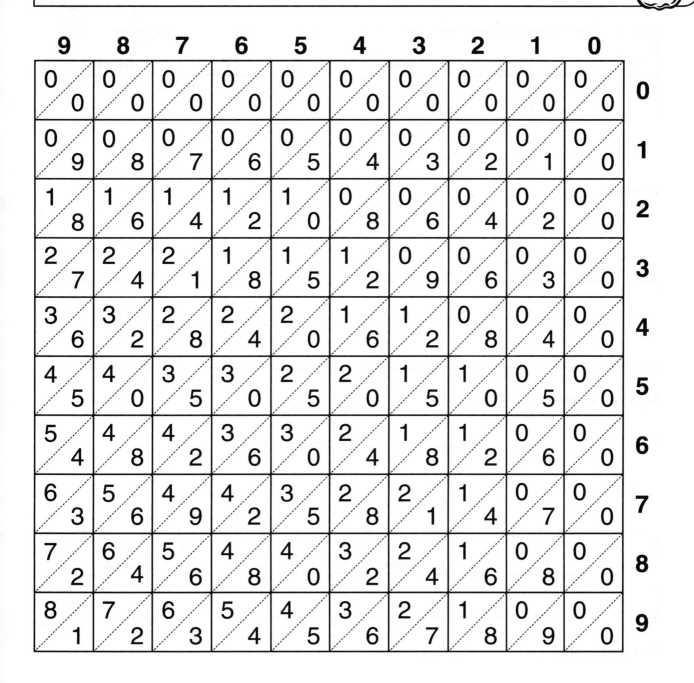

9	8	7	6	5	4	3	2	1	0	
0 / 0	0 / 0	0 / 0	0 / 0	0 / 0	0 / 0	0 / 0	0 / 0	0 / 0	0 / 0	**0**
0 / 9	0 / 8	0 / 7	0 / 6	0 / 5	0 / 4	0 / 3	0 / 2	0 / 1	0 / 0	**1**
1 / 8	1 / 6	1 / 4	1 / 2	1 / 0	0 / 8	0 / 6	0 / 4	0 / 2	0 / 0	**2**
2 / 7	2 / 4	2 / 1	1 / 8	1 / 5	1 / 2	0 / 9	0 / 6	0 / 3	0 / 0	**3**
3 / 6	3 / 2	2 / 8	2 / 4	2 / 0	1 / 6	1 / 2	0 / 8	0 / 4	0 / 0	**4**
4 / 5	4 / 0	3 / 5	3 / 0	2 / 5	2 / 0	1 / 5	1 / 0	0 / 5	0 / 0	**5**
5 / 4	4 / 8	4 / 2	3 / 6	3 / 0	2 / 4	1 / 8	1 / 2	0 / 6	0 / 0	**6**
6 / 3	5 / 6	4 / 9	4 / 2	3 / 5	2 / 8	2 / 1	1 / 4	0 / 7	0 / 0	**7**
7 / 2	6 / 4	5 / 6	4 / 8	4 / 0	3 / 2	2 / 4	1 / 6	0 / 8	0 / 0	**8**
8 / 1	7 / 2	6 / 3	5 / 4	4 / 5	3 / 6	2 / 7	1 / 8	0 / 9	0 / 0	**9**

Name Date Time

Multiplication/Division Diagrams

________	________ per ________	________ in all

Number model: ______________________

Answer: ______________________

________	________ per ________	________ in all

Number model: ______________________

Answer: ______________________

________	________ per ________	________ in all

Number model: ______________________

Answer: ______________________

Name Date Time

Dot Paper

Name Date Time

Easy Multiples

100 * ________ = ________

50 * ________ = ________

20 * ________ = ________

10 * ________ = ________

5 * ________ = ________

2 * ________ = ________

1 * ________ = ________

100 * ________ = ________

50 * ________ = ________

20 * ________ = ________

10 * ________ = ________

5 * ________ = ________

2 * ________ = ________

1 * ________ = ________

100 * ________ = ________

50 * ________ = ________

20 * ________ = ________

10 * ________ = ________

5 * ________ = ________

2 * ________ = ________

1 * ________ = ________

100 * ________ = ________

50 * ________ = ________

20 * ________ = ________

10 * ________ = ________

5 * ________ = ________

2 * ________ = ________

1 * ________ = ________

Name Date Time

Full-Circle Protractor

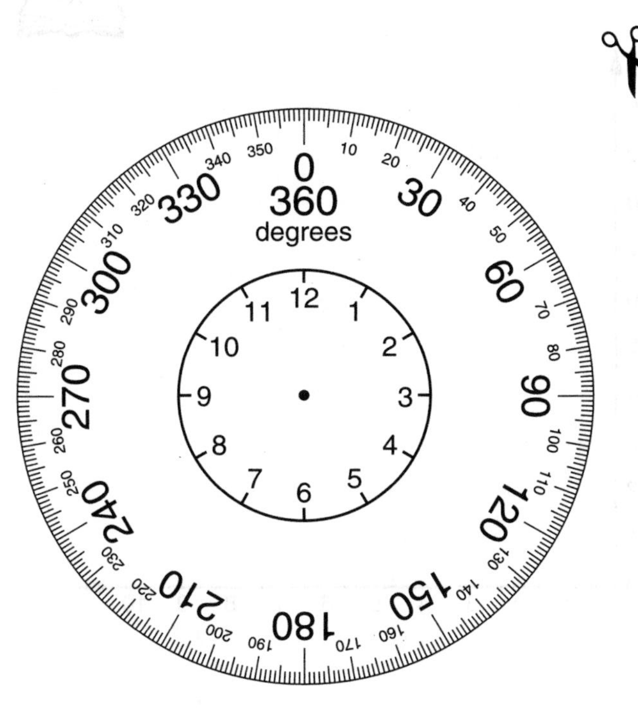

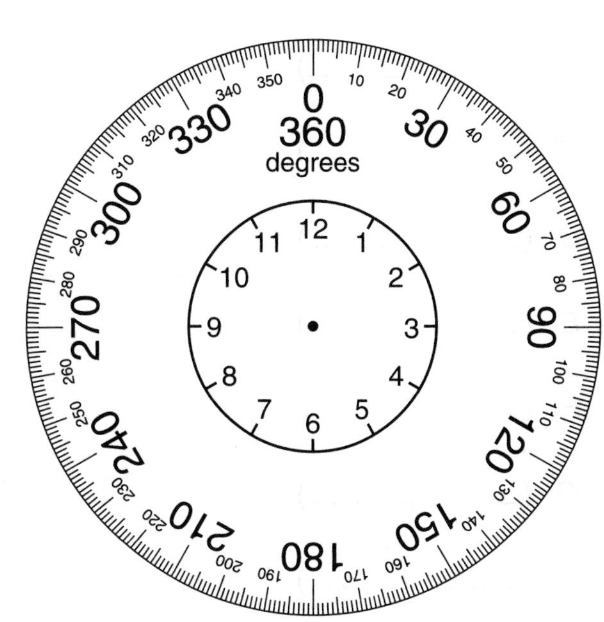

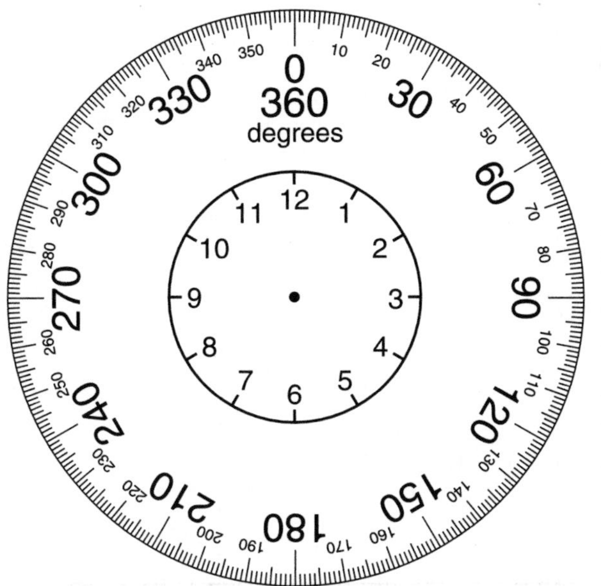

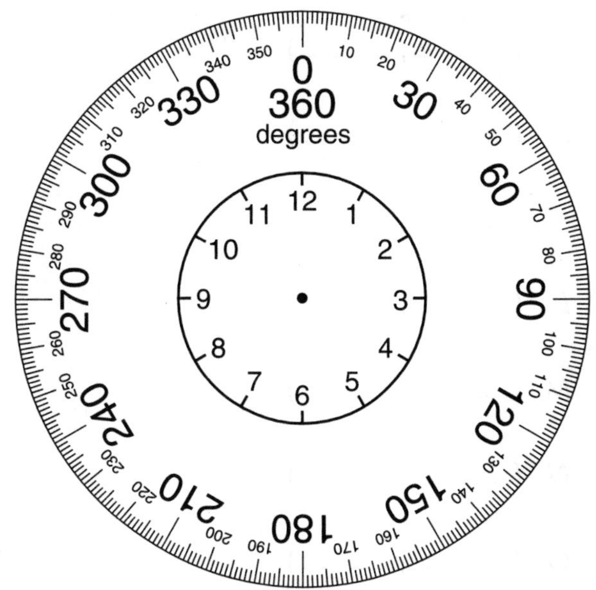

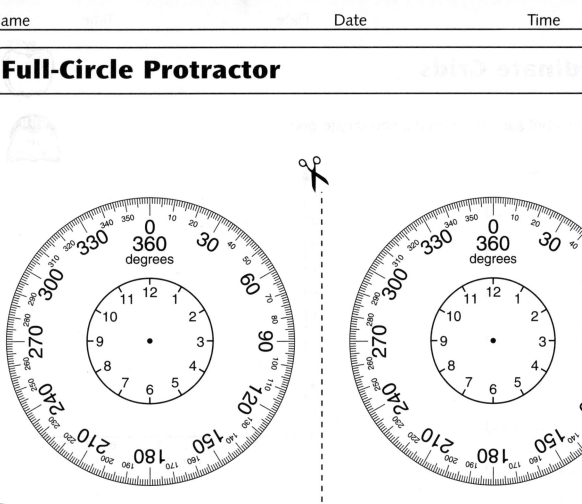

Name Date Time

Coordinate Grids

1. Plot and label each point on the coordinate grid.

A (_____,_____)

B (_____,_____)

C (_____,_____)

D (_____,_____)

E (_____,_____)

F (_____,_____)

G (_____,_____)

H (_____,_____)

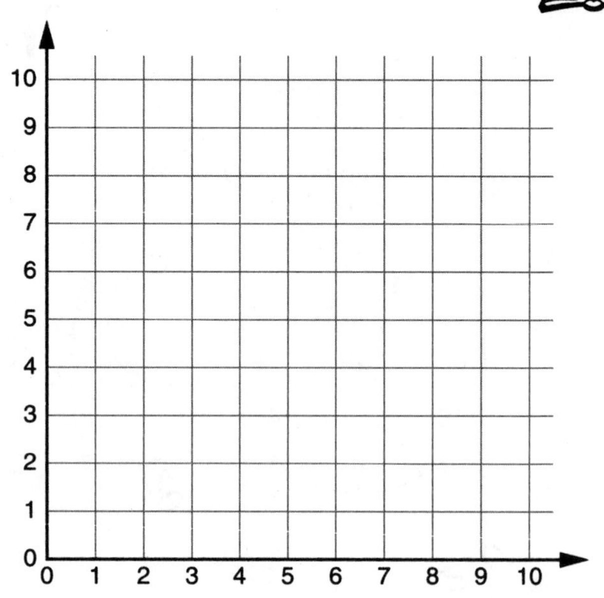

2. Write the ordered number pair for each point plotted on the coordinate grid.

I (_____,_____)

J (_____,_____)

K (_____,_____)

L (_____,_____)

M (_____,_____)

N (_____,_____)

O (_____,_____)

P (_____,_____)

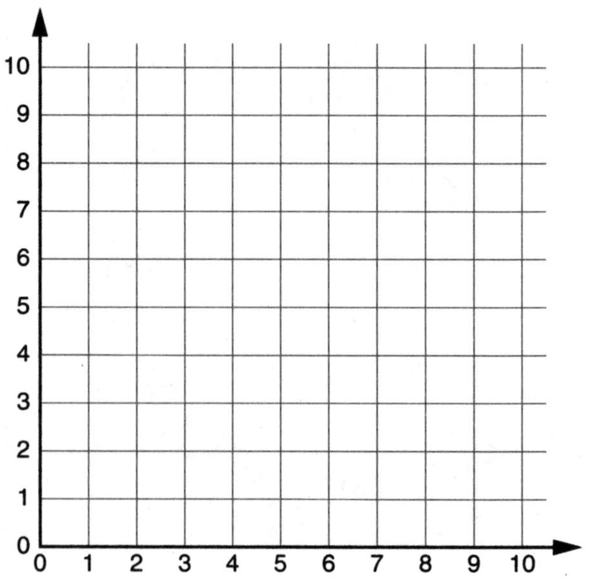

Name Date Time

Tangram Puzzle

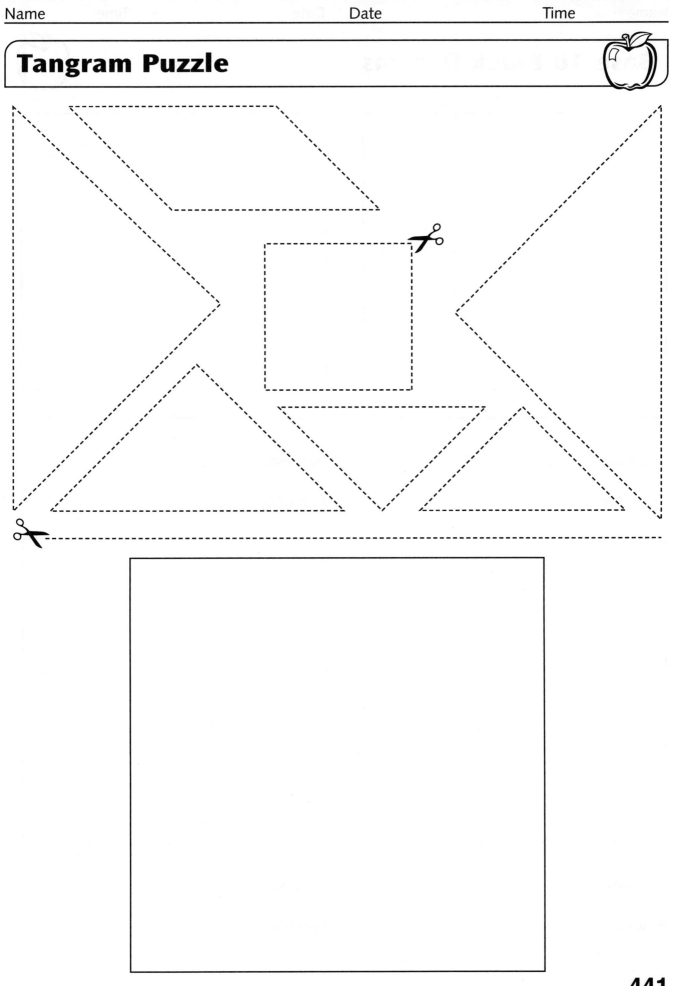

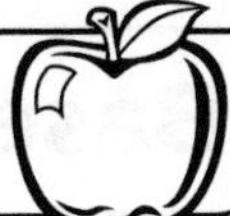

Name Date Time

Base-10 Block Designs

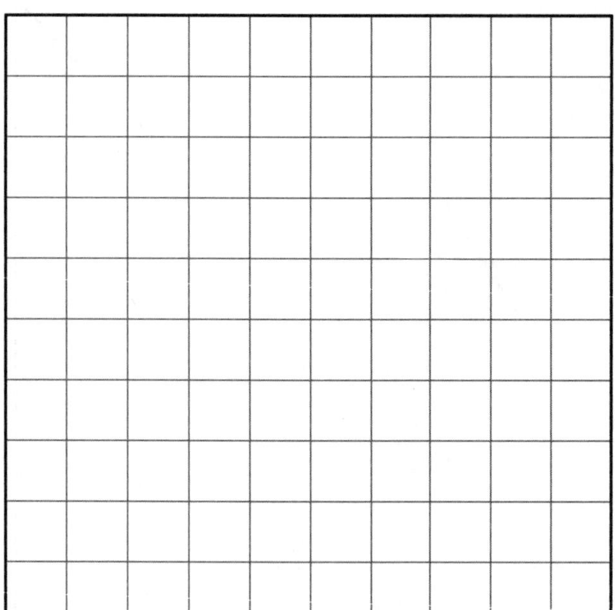

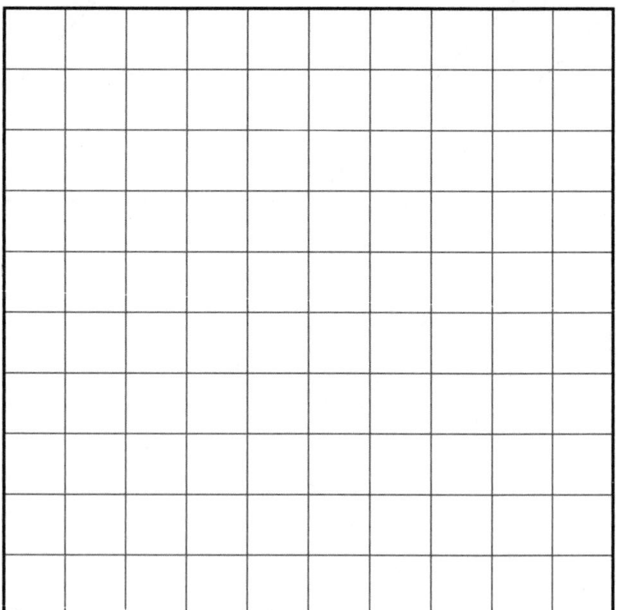

Decimal: ____________

Fraction: ____________

Decimal: ____________

Fraction: ____________

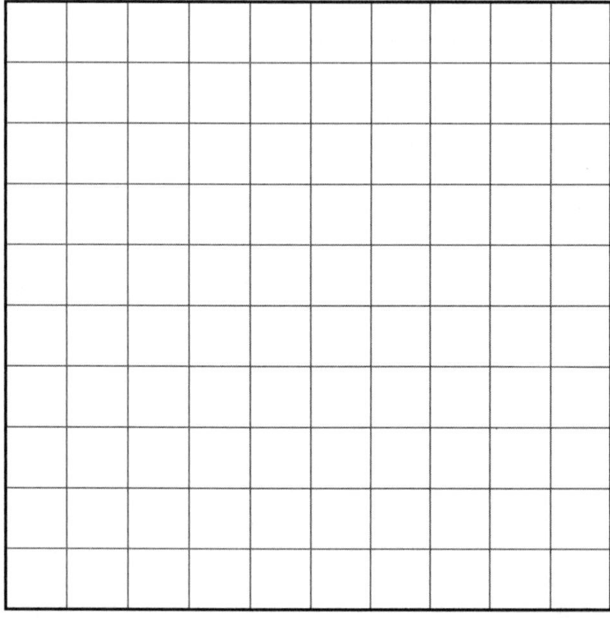

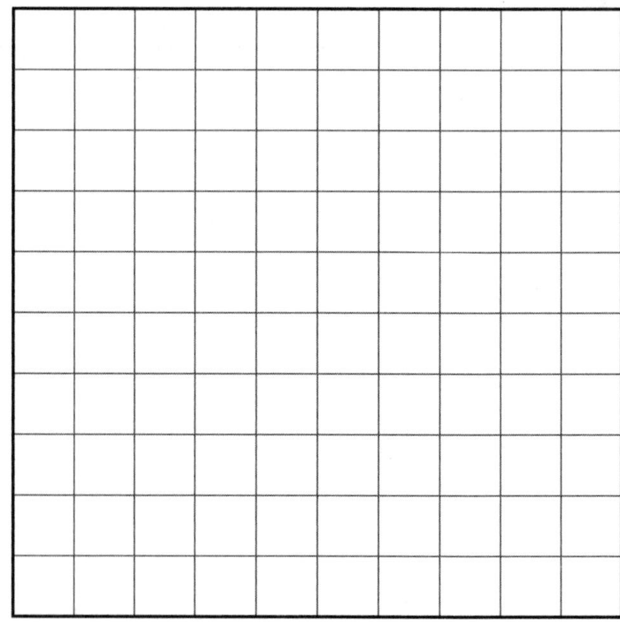

Decimal: ____________

Fraction: ____________

Decimal: ____________

Fraction: ____________

Name Date Time

Grid Paper ($\frac{1}{4}$ in.)

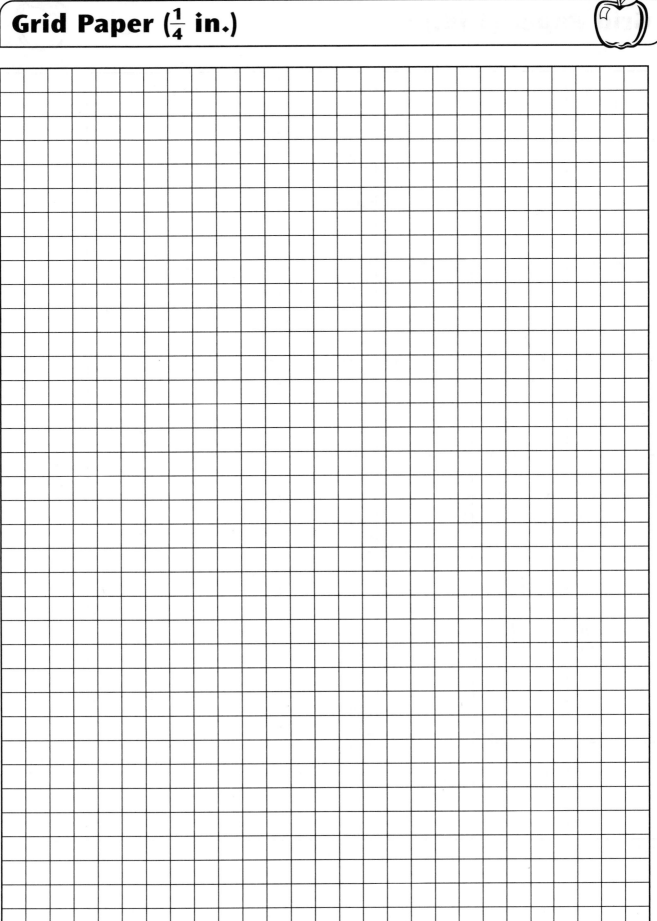

Name Date Time

Grid Paper (1 in.)

Name Date Time

Fractions, Decimals, and Percents

Fill in the missing numbers. If the grid is not shaded, then shade the grid.

100%
large square

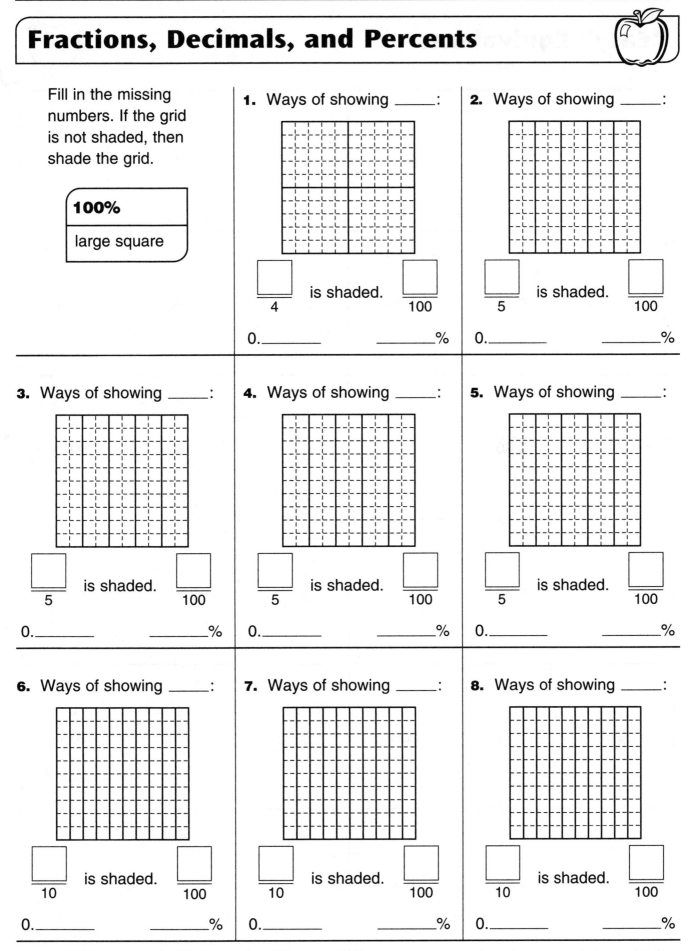

1. Ways of showing ____:

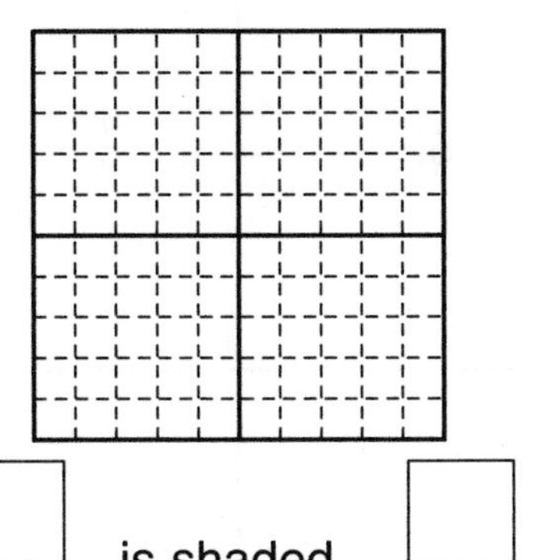

$\frac{\square}{4}$ is shaded. $\frac{\square}{100}$

0.____ ____%

2. Ways of showing ____:

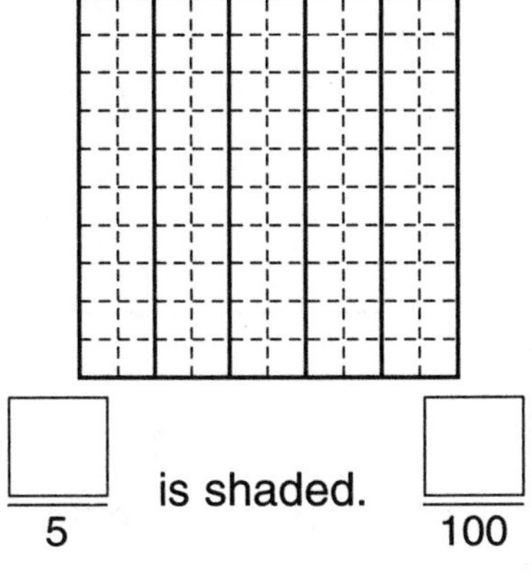

$\frac{\square}{5}$ is shaded. $\frac{\square}{100}$

0.____ ____%

3. Ways of showing ____:

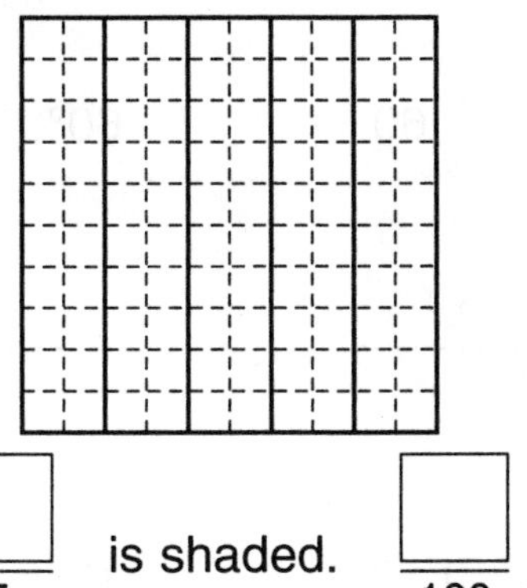

$\frac{\square}{5}$ is shaded. $\frac{\square}{100}$

0.____ ____%

4. Ways of showing ____:

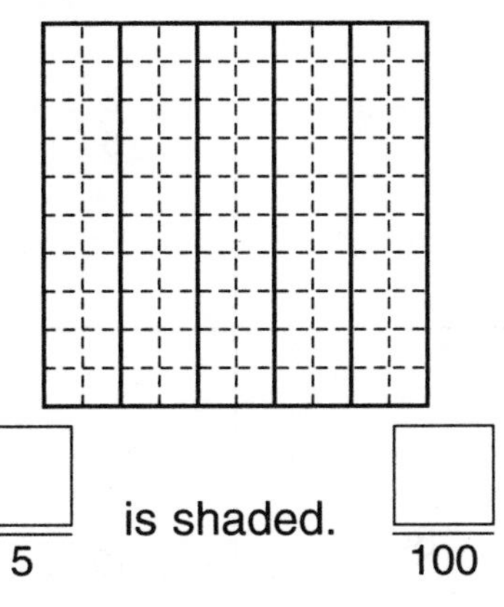

$\frac{\square}{5}$ is shaded. $\frac{\square}{100}$

0.____ ____%

5. Ways of showing ____:

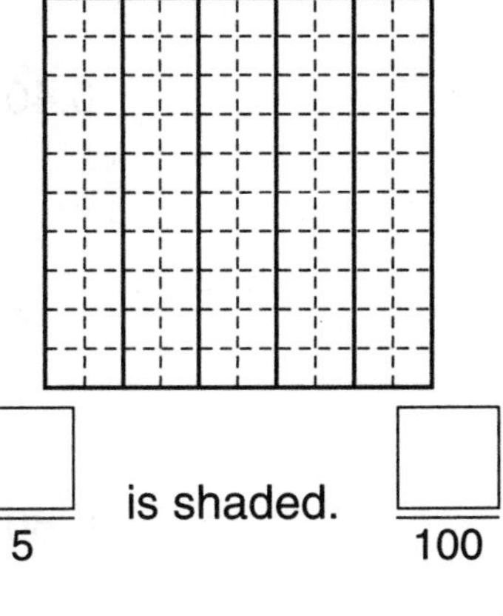

$\frac{\square}{5}$ is shaded. $\frac{\square}{100}$

0.____ ____%

6. Ways of showing ____:

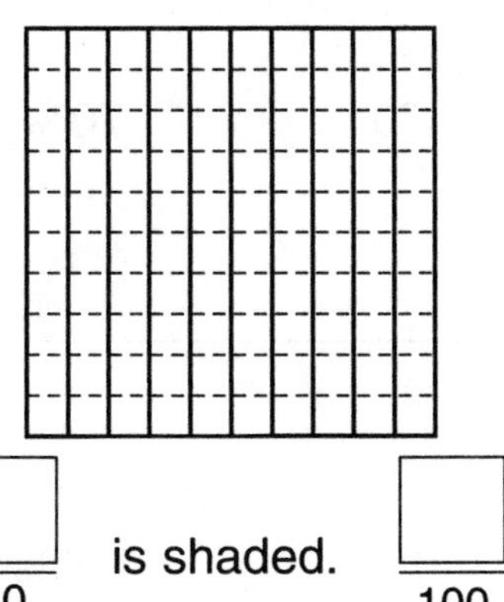

$\frac{\square}{10}$ is shaded. $\frac{\square}{100}$

0.____ ____%

7. Ways of showing ____:

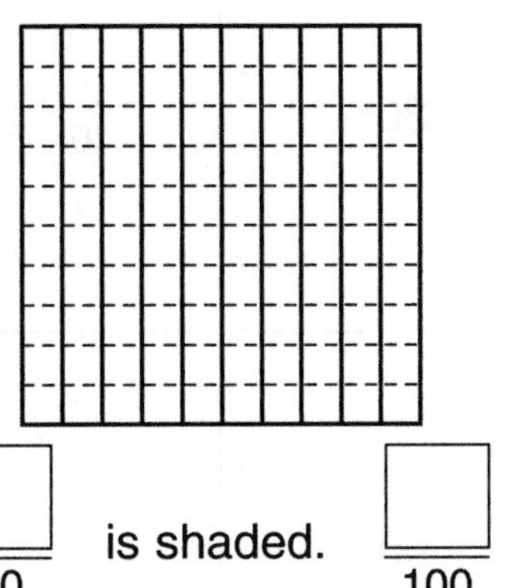

$\frac{\square}{10}$ is shaded. $\frac{\square}{100}$

0.____ ____%

8. Ways of showing ____:

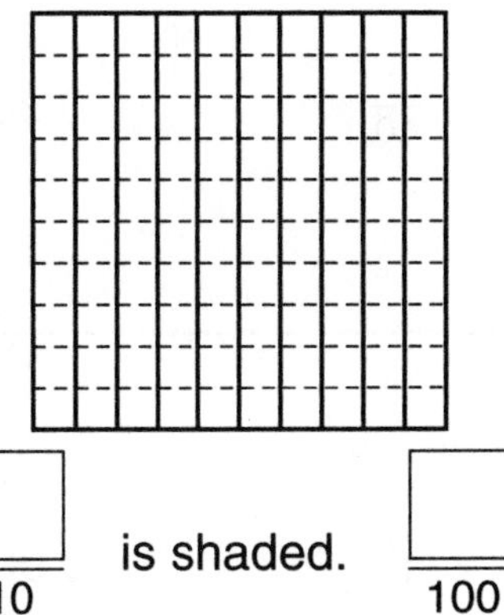

$\frac{\square}{10}$ is shaded. $\frac{\square}{100}$

0.____ ____%

Name Date Time

"Easy" Equivalents

$\frac{1}{2}$	0.50	50%	$\frac{1}{4}$	0.25	25%
$\frac{3}{4}$	0.75	75%	$\frac{1}{5}$	0.20	20%
$\frac{2}{5}$	0.40	40%	$\frac{3}{5}$	0.60	60%
$\frac{4}{5}$	0.80	80%	$\frac{1}{10}$	0.10	10%
$\frac{3}{10}$	0.30	30%	$\frac{7}{10}$	0.70	70%
$\frac{9}{10}$	0.90	90%	$\frac{2}{2}$	1	100%

Name Date Time

Isometric Dot Paper

Name Date Time

Ounces and Grams

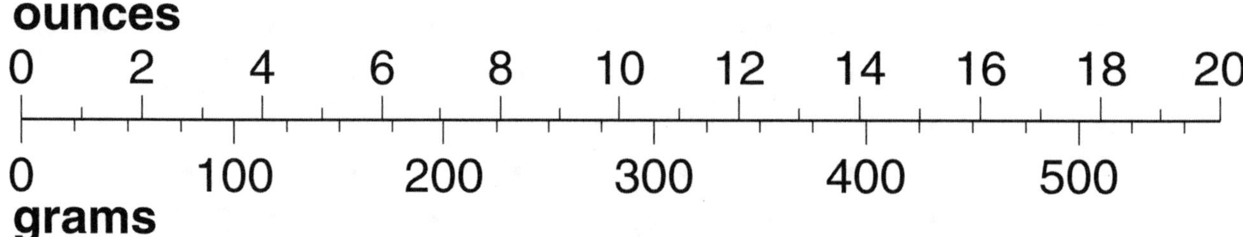

Name Date Time

Square Pyramid Template

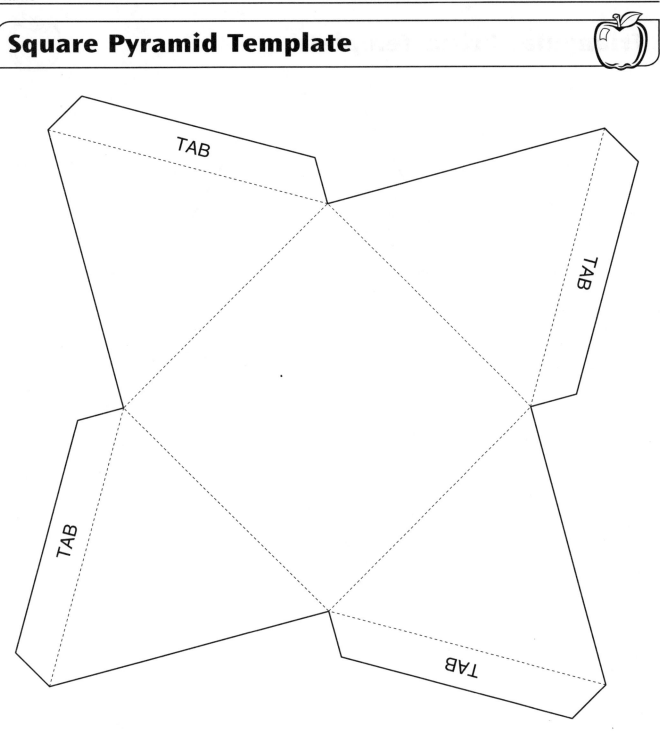

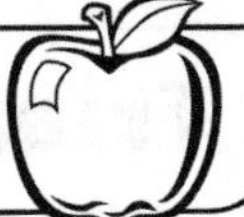

TAB

TAB

TAB

TAB

Name Date Time

Triangular Prism Template

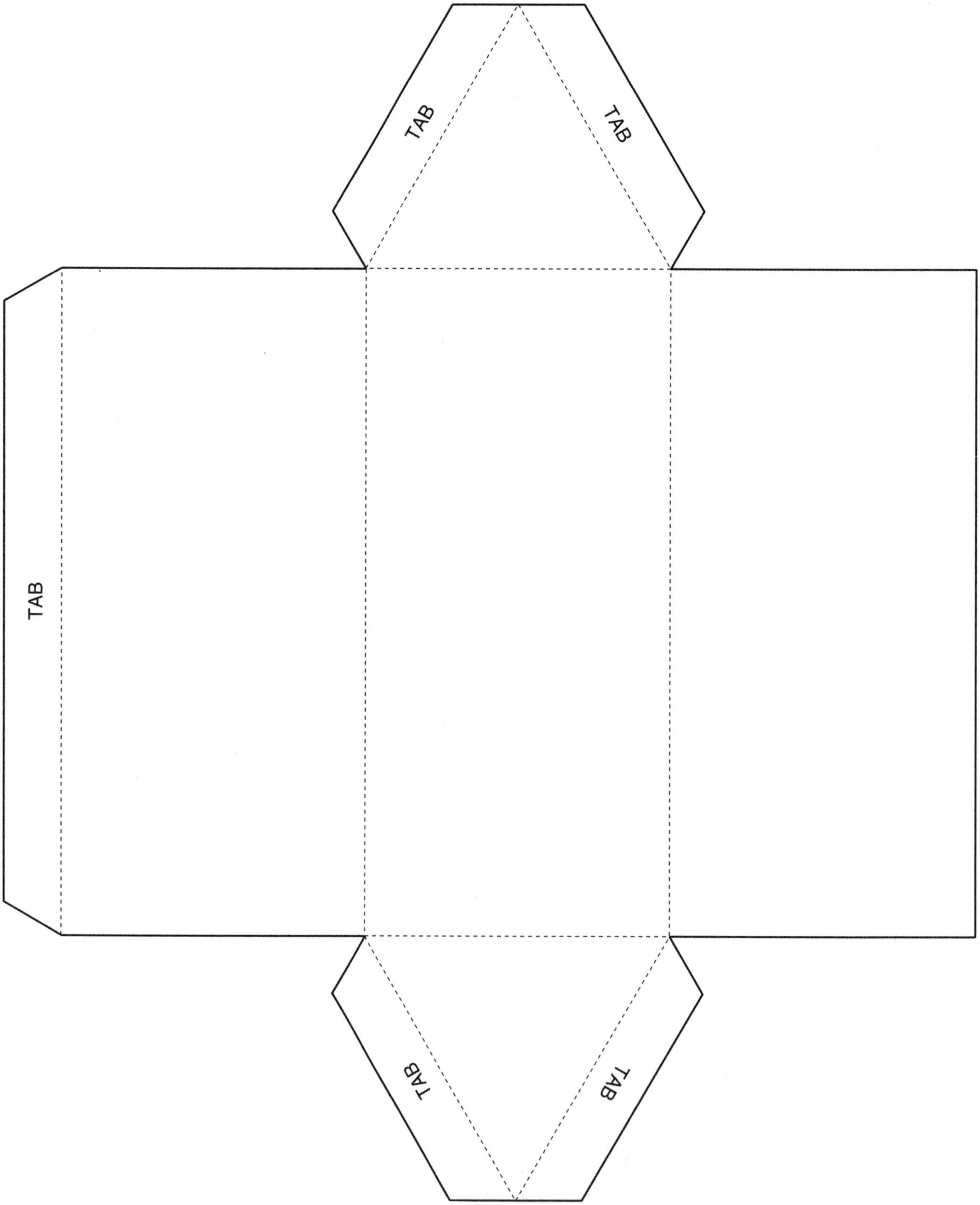

TAB

TAB

TAB

TAB

TAB

Name Date Time

Cone Template

TAB

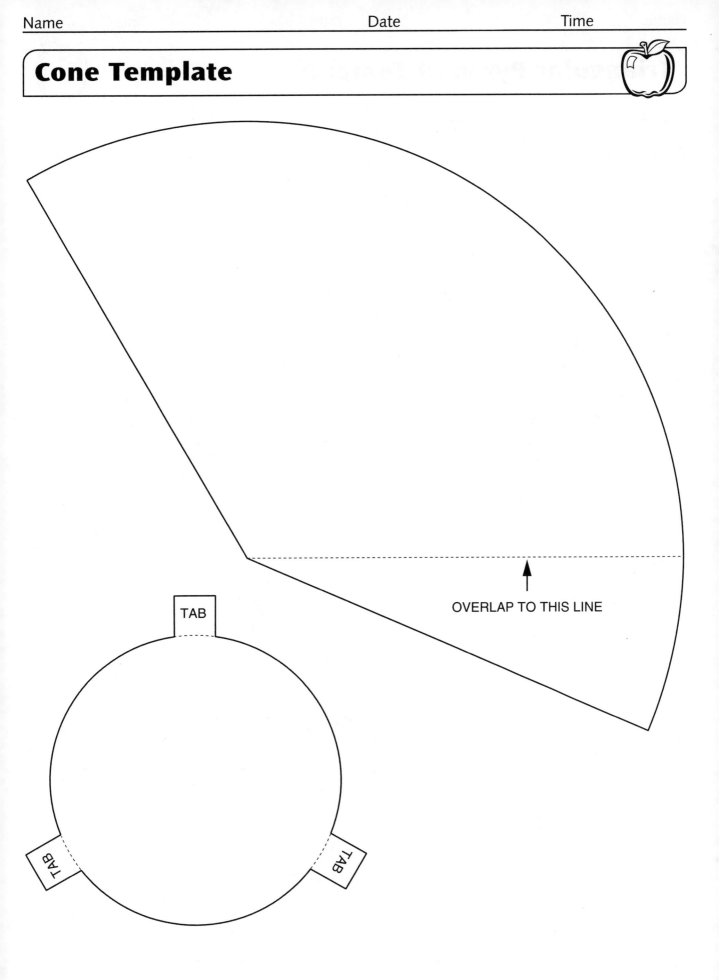

OVERLAP TO THIS LINE

TAB

TAB

Name Date Time

Triangular Pyramid Template

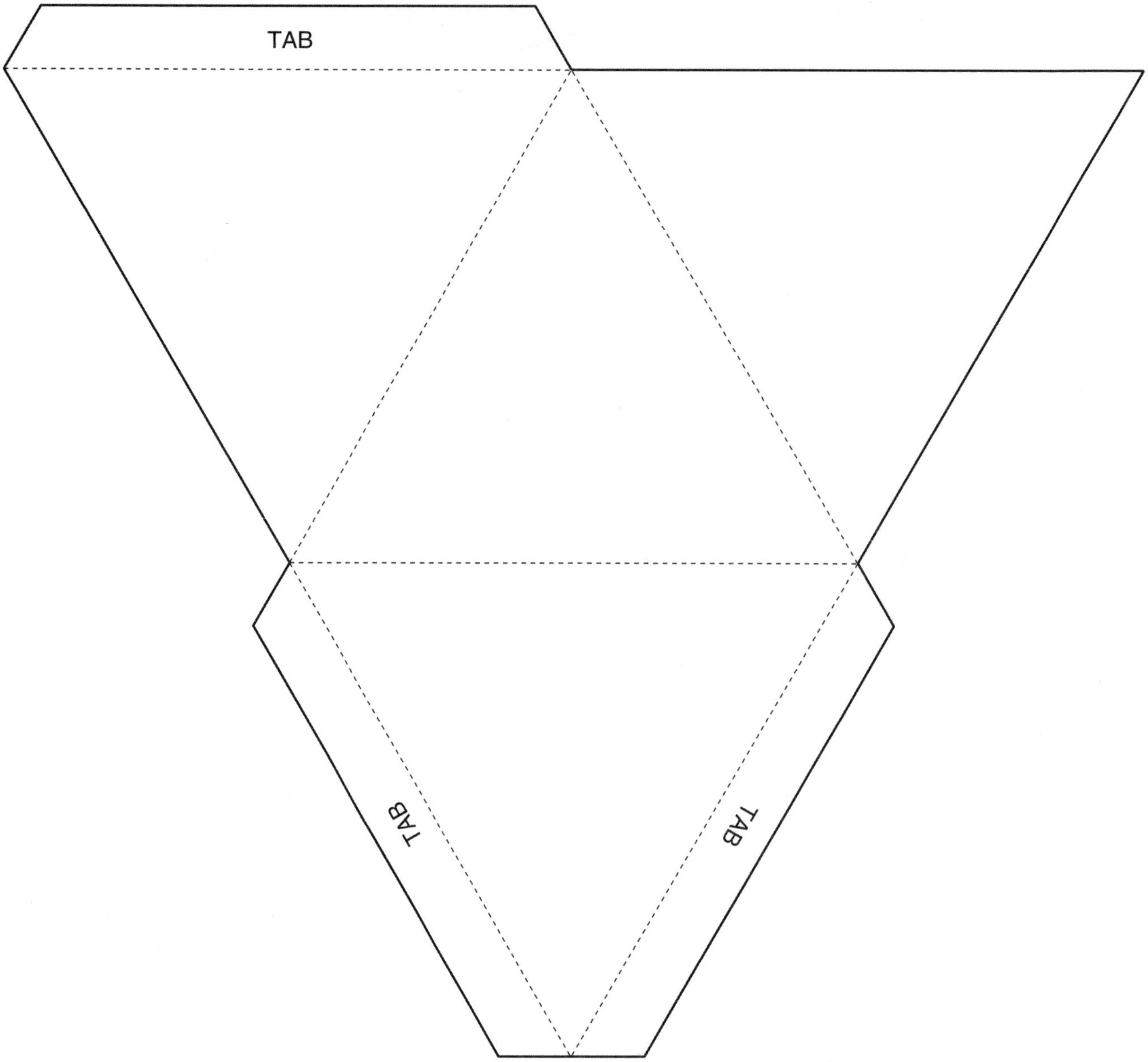

TAB

TAB

TAB

Name Date Time

Cube Template

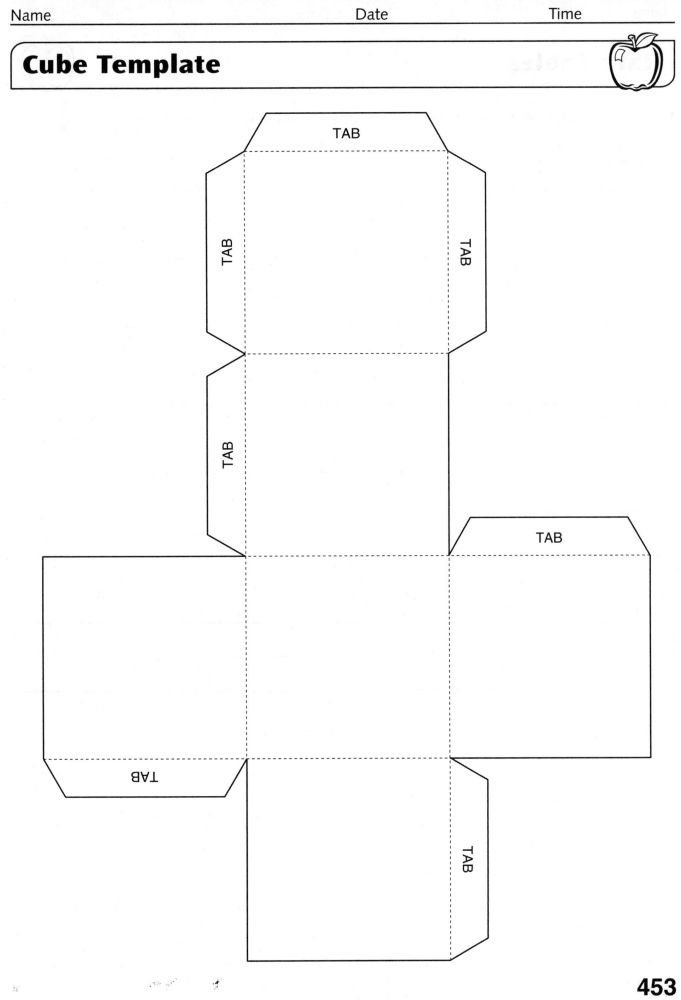

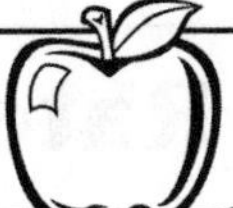

TAB

TAB

TAB

TAB

TAB

TAB

TAB

Name Date Time

Rate Tables

For each problem, fill in the rate table. Then answer the question below the table.

1. ______________________________

____

______________________________? ________ ________ (unit)

2. ______________________________

____

______________________________? ________ ________ (unit)

3. ______________________________

____

______________________________? ________ ________ (unit)

Game Masters

Name Date Time

Angle Tangle Record Sheet

Round	Angle	Estimated measure	Actual measure	Score
1		____°	____°	
2		____°	____°	
3		____°	____°	
4		____°	____°	
5		____°	____°	
			Total Score	

457

Name Date Time

Multiplication Wrestling Record Sheet

Round 1 Cards: ____ ____ ____ ____
Numbers formed: ____ * ____
Teams: (____ + ____) * (____ + ____)
Products: ____ * ____ = ____
____ * ____ = ____
____ * ____ = ____
____ * ____ = ____
Total (add 4 products): ____

Round 2 Cards: ____ ____ ____ ____
Numbers formed: ____ * ____
Teams: (____ + ____) * (____ + ____)
Products: ____ * ____ = ____
____ * ____ = ____
____ * ____ = ____
____ * ____ = ____
Total (add 4 products): ____

Round 3 Cards: ____ ____ ____ ____
Numbers formed: ____ * ____
Teams: (____ + ____) * (____ + ____)
Products: ____ * ____ = ____
____ * ____ = ____
____ * ____ = ____
____ * ____ = ____
Total (add 4 products): ____

488

Name Date Time

Alleyway Game Mat

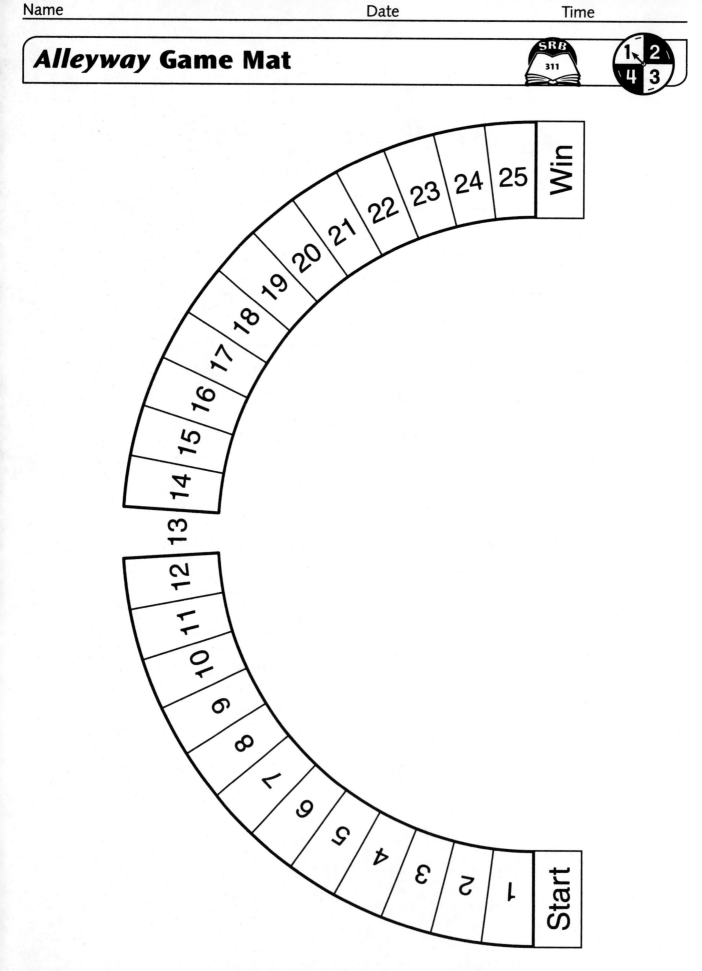

Start
1
2
3
4
5
6
7
8
9
10
11
12
13
14
15
16
17
18
19
20
21
22
23
24
25
Win

Name Date Time

Angle Tangle Record Sheet

Round	Angle	Estimated measure	Actual measure	Score
1		____°	____°	
2		____°	____°	
3		____°	____°	
4		____°	____°	
5		____°	____°	
			Total Score	

Name Date Time

Base-10 Exchange (Hundredths)

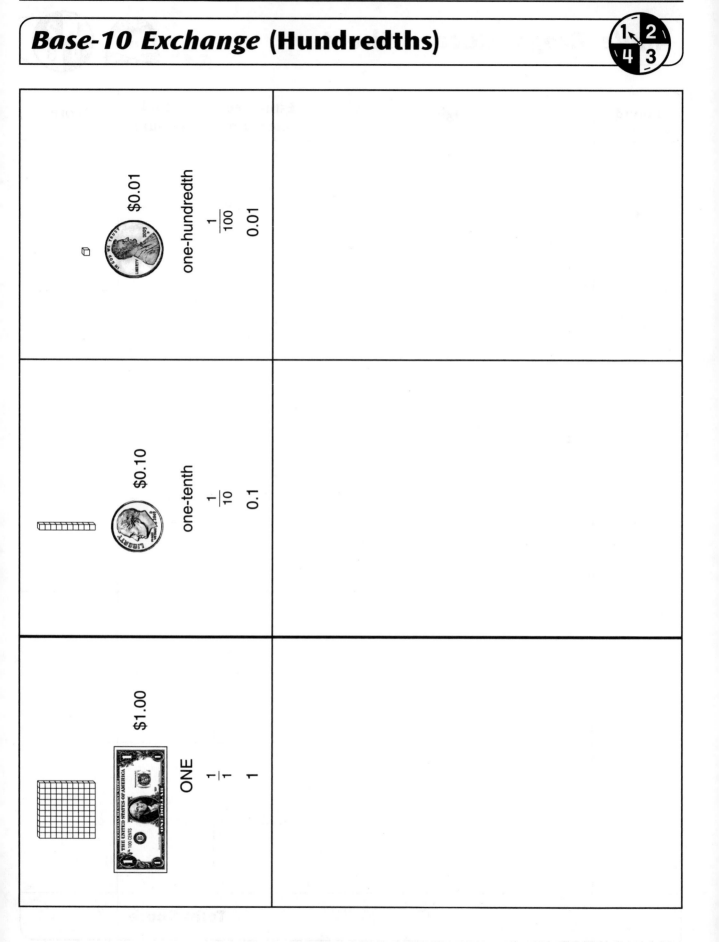

$1.00	$0.10	$0.01
ONE	one-tenth	one-hundredth
$\frac{1}{1}$	$\frac{1}{10}$	$\frac{1}{100}$
1	0.1	0.01

Name Date Time

Base-10 Exchange (Thousandths)

one-thousandth $\frac{1}{1,000}$ 0.001	
one-hundredth $\frac{1}{100}$ 0.01	
one-tenth $\frac{1}{10}$ 0.1	
ONE $\frac{1}{1}$ 1	

Name Date Time

Baseball Multiplication Game Mat

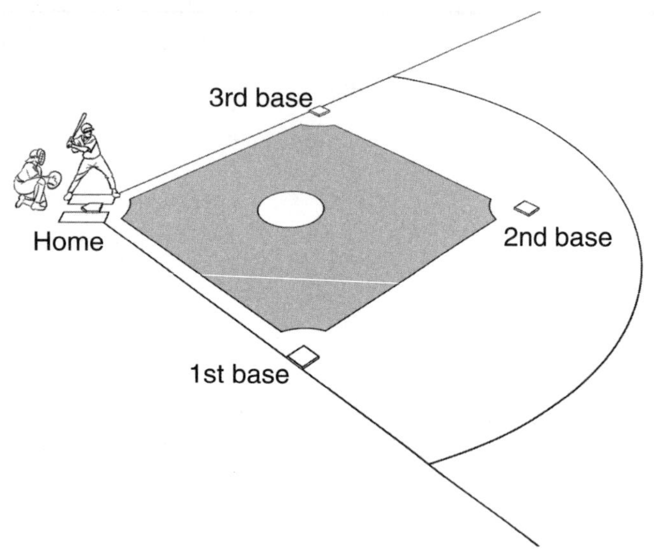

Hitting Table 1-to-6 Facts	
1 to 9	Out
10 to 19	Single (1 base)
20 to 29	Double (2 bases)
30 to 35	Triple (3 bases)
36	Home Run (4 bases)

Inning		1	2	3	Total
Team 1	Outs				
	Runs				
Team 2	Outs				
	Runs				

Inning		1	2	3	Total
Team 1	Outs				
	Runs				
Team 2	Outs				
	Runs				

Inning		1	2	3	Total
Team 1	Outs				
	Runs				
Team 2	Outs				
	Runs				

Name Date Time

Beat the Calculator Gameboard

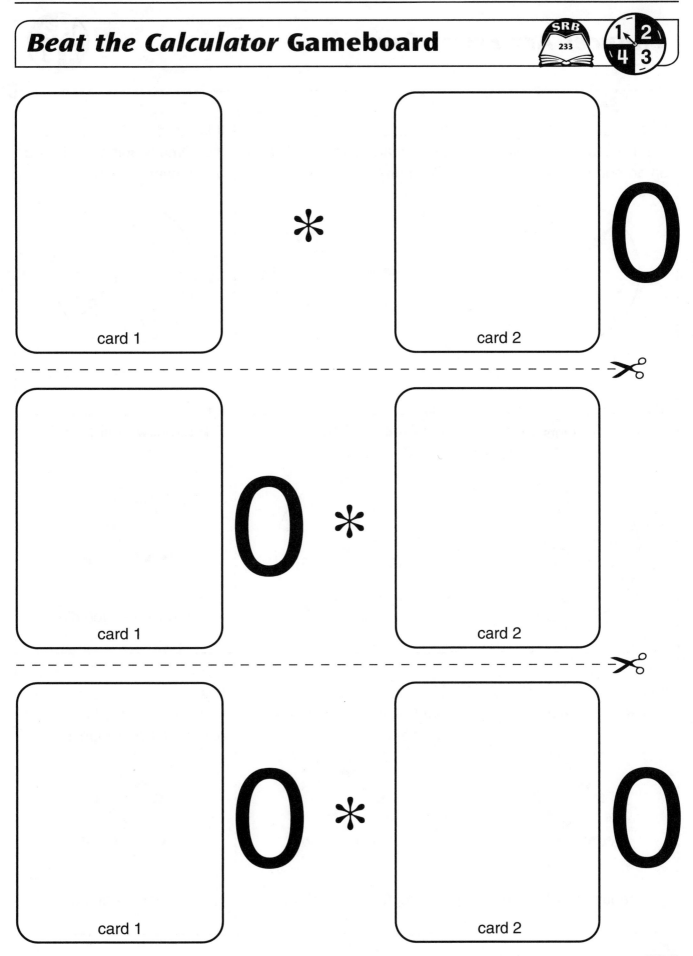

SRB 233

card 1 * card 2 0

card 1 0 * card 2

card 1 0 * card 2 0

Name Date Time

Chances Are Event Cards

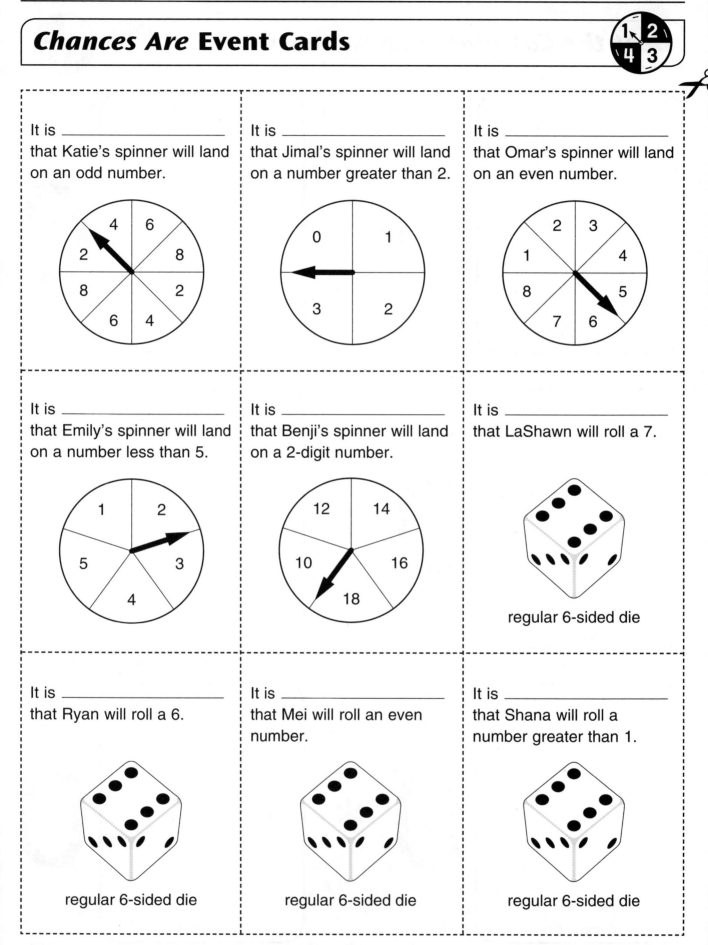

It is ________________
that Katie's spinner will land on an odd number.

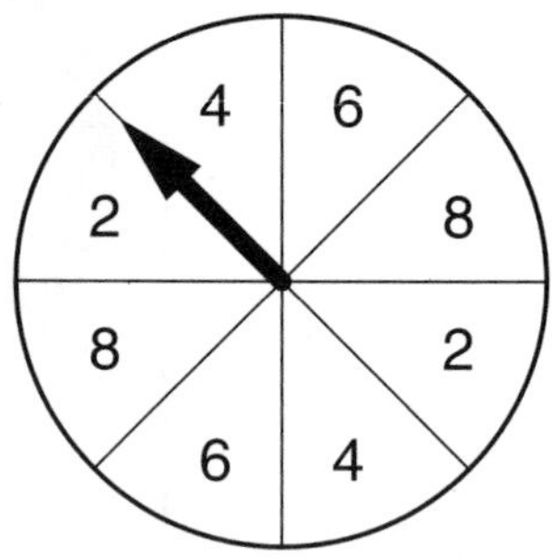

It is ________________
that Jimal's spinner will land on a number greater than 2.

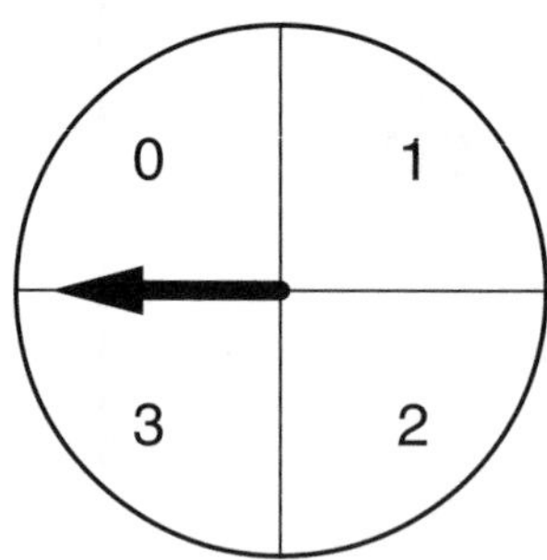

It is ________________
that Omar's spinner will land on an even number.

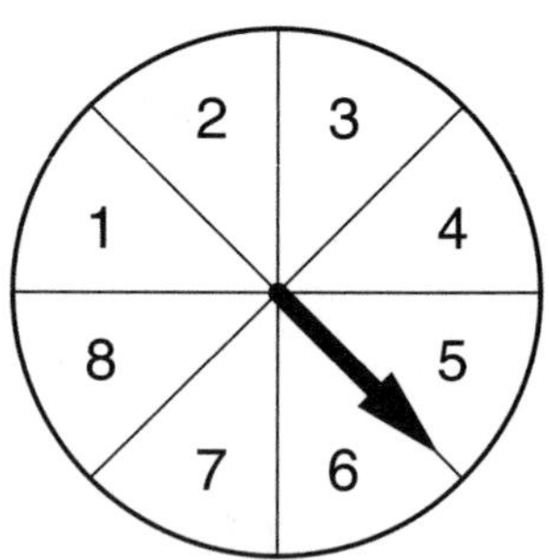

It is ________________
that Emily's spinner will land on a number less than 5.

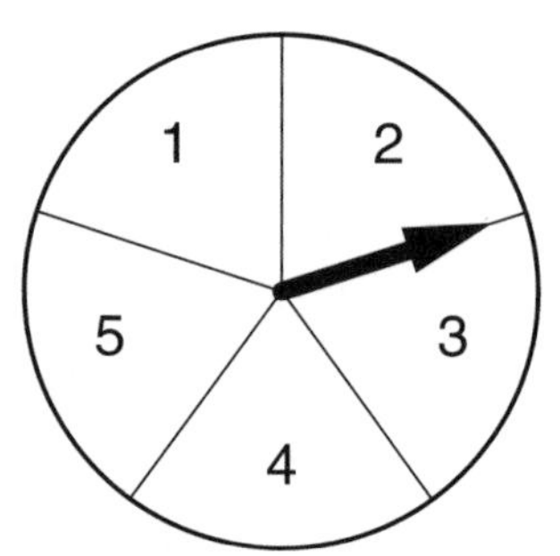

It is ________________
that Benji's spinner will land on a 2-digit number.

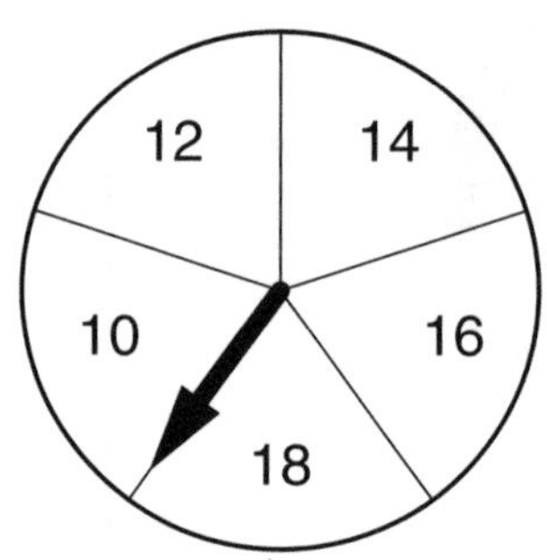

It is ________________
that LaShawn will roll a 7.

regular 6-sided die

It is ________________
that Ryan will roll a 6.

regular 6-sided die

It is ________________
that Mei will roll an even number.

regular 6-sided die

It is ________________
that Shana will roll a number greater than 1.

regular 6-sided die

Name _______________ Date _______________ Time _______________

Chances Are Event Cards *continued*

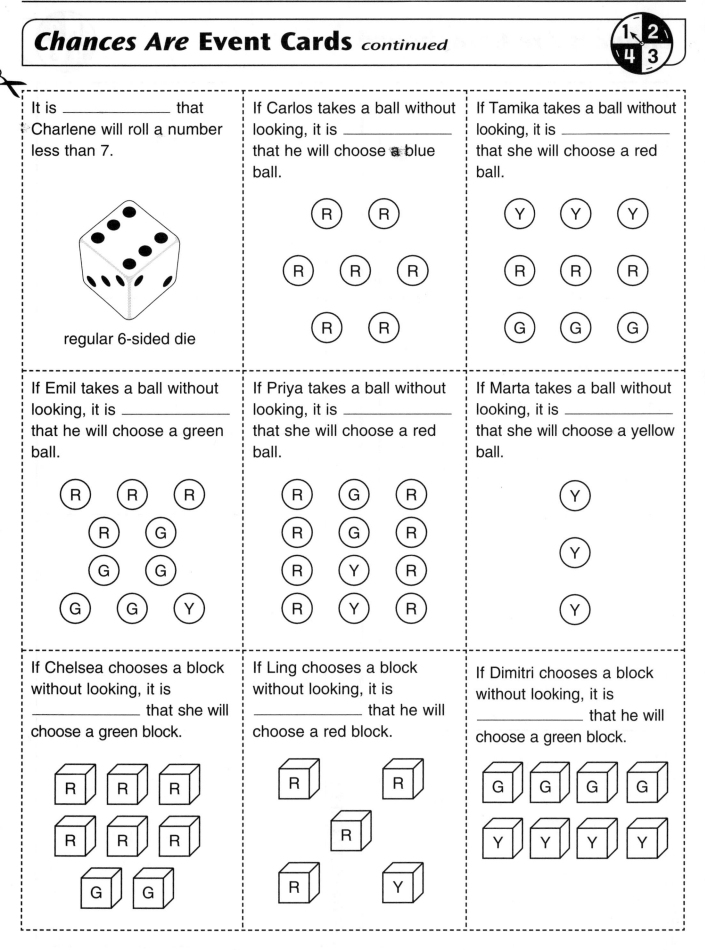

It is ______________ that Charlene will roll a number less than 7.

regular 6-sided die

If Carlos takes a ball without looking, it is ______________ that he will choose a blue ball.

If Tamika takes a ball without looking, it is ______________ that she will choose a red ball.

If Emil takes a ball without looking, it is ______________ that he will choose a green ball.

If Priya takes a ball without looking, it is ______________ that she will choose a red ball.

If Marta takes a ball without looking, it is ______________ that she will choose a yellow ball.

If Chelsea chooses a block without looking, it is ______________ that she will choose a green block.

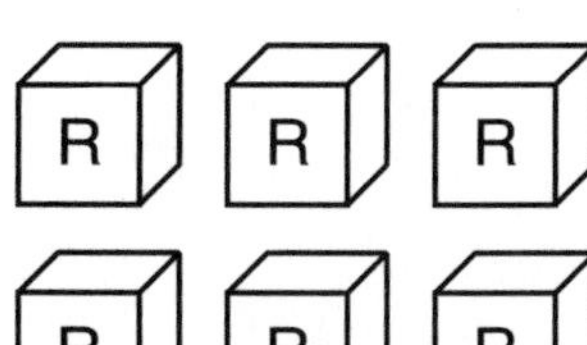

If Ling chooses a block without looking, it is ______________ that he will choose a red block.

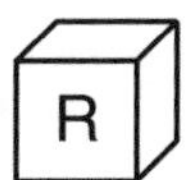

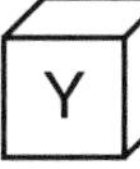

If Dimitri chooses a block without looking, it is ______________ that he will choose a green block.

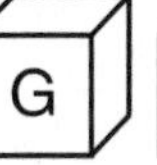

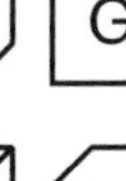

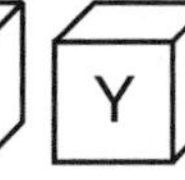

Name Date Time

Chances Are Gameboard

EVENT CARDS

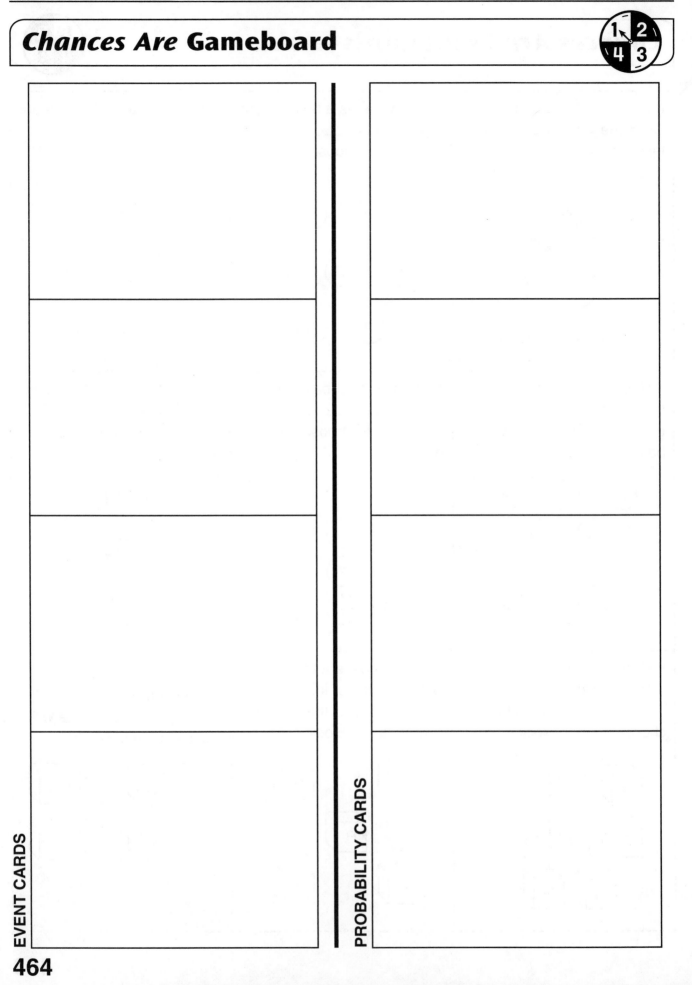

PROBABILITY CARDS

Name Date Time

Chances Are Probability Cards

Impossible No chance Can't happen No way	Impossible No chance Can't happen No way	Impossible No chance Can't happen No way
Unlikely Less than half Slight chance Not much	Unlikely Less than half Slight chance Not much	Unlikely Less than half Slight chance Not much
Unlikely Less than half Slight chance Not much	50-50 About half Even chance	50-50 About half Even chance

Name Date Time

Chances Are Probability Cards *continued*

50-50 About half Even chance	50-50 About half Even chance	Likely More than half Good chance Probably
Likely More than half Good chance Probably	Likely More than half Good chance Probably	Likely More than half Good chance Probably
Certain Sure thing Positive Absolutely	Certain Sure thing Positive Absolutely	Certain Sure thing Positive Absolutely

Name Date Time

Coin Cards

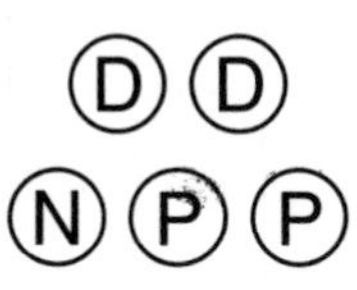

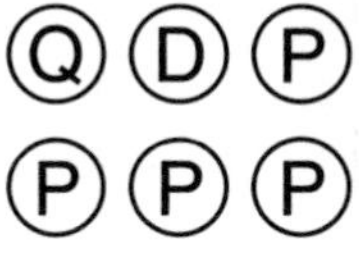

Q Q D
D P

Q Q Q
P P P

Q Q Q
N P
P P

Q Q Q
D N P

Q Q Q
D D P

Q Q Q
D D N

Q Q Q Q
D P P

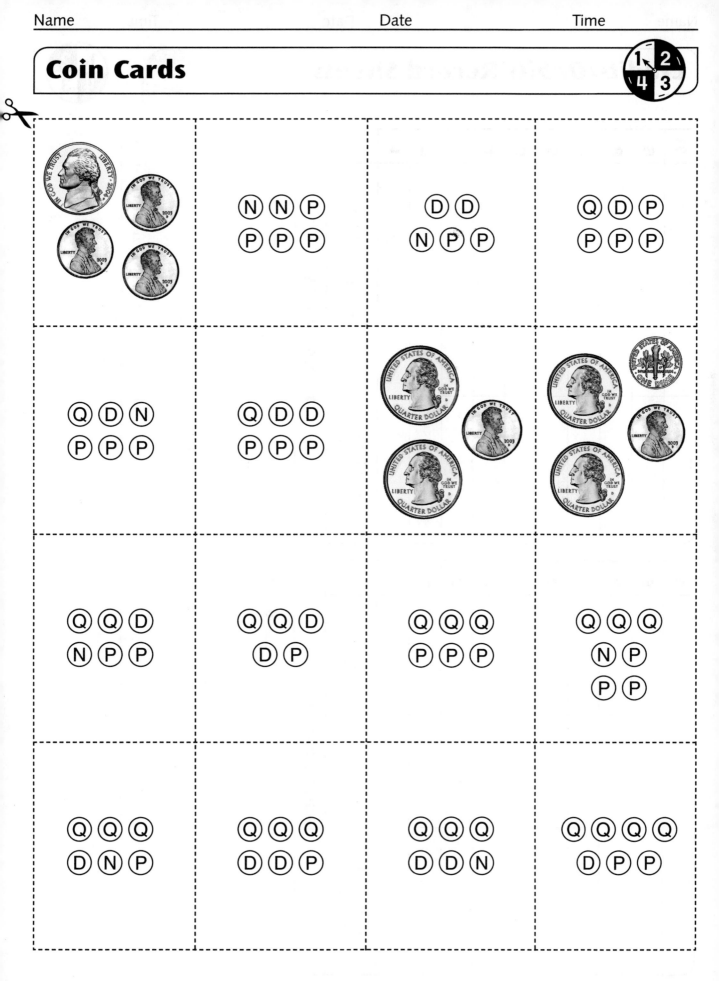

Name Date Time

Credits/Debits Record Sheets

–22 –21 –20 –19 –18 –17 –16 –15 –14 –13 –12 –11 –10 –9 –8 –7 –6 –5 –4 –3 –2 –1 0 1 2 3 4 5 6 7 8 9 10 11 12 13 14 15 16 17 18 19 20 21 22

Game 1

Record Sheet			
	Start	**Change**	**End, and next start**
1	+\$10		
2			
3			
4			
5			
6			
7			
8			
9			
10			

Game 2

Record Sheet			
	Start	**Change**	**End, and next start**
1	+\$10		
2			
3			
4			
5			
6			
7			
8			
9			
10			

Name Date Time

Credits/Debits Game (Advanced Version) Record Sheets

SRB 239

Game 1

	Start	Change		End, and next start
		Addition or Subtraction	Credit or Debit	
1				
2				
3				
4				
5				
6				
7				
8				
9				
10				

Game 2

	Start	Change		End, and next start
		Addition or Subtraction	Credit or Debit	
1				
2				
3				
4				
5				
6				
7				
8				
9				
10				

Name Date Time

Division Arrays Record Sheet

Your score is the number of counters per row. If there are 0 leftover counters, your score is double the number of counters per row.

Round	Rows	Counters per Row	Counters in All	Leftover Counters	Score
Sample	*3*	*5*	*15*	*0*	*10*
1					
2					
3					
4					
5					
				Total Score	

Name Date Time

Division Arrays Record Sheet

Your score is the number of counters per row. If there are 0 leftover counters, your score is double the number of counters per row.

Round	Rows	Counters per Row	Counters in All	Leftover Counters	Score
Sample	*3*	*5*	*15*	*0*	*10*
1					
2					
3					
4					
5					
				Total Score	

Name Date Time

Division Dash Record Sheet

	Division Problem	Quotient	Score
Sample	49 ÷ 4	12 R1	12
1			
2			
3			
4			
5			

Name Date Time

Division Dash Record Sheet

	Division Problem	Quotient	Score
Sample	49 ÷ 4	12 R1	12
1			
2			
3			
4			
5			

Name Date Time

Fishing for Digits Record Sheet

	Beginning Number	X						
1	New Number							
	New Number							
2	New Number							
	New Number							
3	New Number							
	New Number							
4	New Number							
	New Number							
5	New Number							
	Final Number							

Name Date Time

Fishing for Digits Record Sheet

	Beginning Number	X						
1	New Number							
	New Number							
2	New Number							
	New Number							
3	New Number							
	New Number							
4	New Number							
	New Number							
5	New Number							
	Final Number							

Name Date Time

Fraction Match Cards

$\frac{0}{2}$ $\frac{0}{2}$ $\frac{0}{2}$	$\frac{1}{2}$ $\frac{1}{2}$ $\frac{1}{2}$	$\frac{2}{2}$ $\frac{2}{2}$ $\frac{2}{2}$	$\frac{0}{3}$ $\frac{0}{3}$ $\frac{0}{3}$
$\frac{1}{3}$ $\frac{1}{3}$ $\frac{1}{3}$	$\frac{2}{3}$ $\frac{2}{3}$ $\frac{2}{3}$	$\frac{3}{3}$ $\frac{3}{3}$ $\frac{3}{3}$	$\frac{0}{4}$ $\frac{0}{4}$ $\frac{0}{4}$
$\frac{1}{4}$ $\frac{1}{4}$ $\frac{1}{4}$	$\frac{2}{4}$ $\frac{2}{4}$ $\frac{2}{4}$	$\frac{3}{4}$ $\frac{3}{4}$ $\frac{3}{4}$	$\frac{4}{4}$ $\frac{4}{4}$ $\frac{4}{4}$
$\frac{0}{5}$ $\frac{0}{5}$ $\frac{0}{5}$	$\frac{1}{5}$ $\frac{1}{5}$ $\frac{1}{5}$	$\frac{2}{5}$ $\frac{2}{5}$ $\frac{2}{5}$	$\frac{3}{5}$ $\frac{3}{5}$ $\frac{3}{5}$

Name Date Time

Fraction Match Cards *continued*

$\frac{4}{5}$ $\frac{4}{5}$ $\frac{4}{5}$	$\frac{5}{5}$ $\frac{5}{5}$ $\frac{5}{5}$	$\frac{0}{6}$ $\frac{0}{6}$ $\frac{0}{6}$	$\frac{1}{6}$ $\frac{1}{6}$ $\frac{1}{6}$
$\frac{2}{6}$ $\frac{2}{6}$ $\frac{2}{6}$	$\frac{3}{6}$ $\frac{3}{6}$ $\frac{3}{6}$	$\frac{4}{6}$ $\frac{4}{6}$ $\frac{4}{6}$	$\frac{5}{6}$ $\frac{5}{6}$ $\frac{5}{6}$
$\frac{6}{6}$ $\frac{6}{6}$ $\frac{6}{6}$	$\frac{0}{8}$ $\frac{0}{8}$ $\frac{0}{8}$	$\frac{2}{8}$ $\frac{2}{8}$ $\frac{2}{8}$	$\frac{4}{8}$ $\frac{4}{8}$ $\frac{4}{8}$
$\frac{6}{8}$ $\frac{6}{8}$ $\frac{6}{8}$	$\frac{8}{8}$ $\frac{8}{8}$ $\frac{8}{8}$	$\frac{0}{9}$ $\frac{0}{9}$ $\frac{0}{9}$	$\frac{3}{9}$ $\frac{3}{9}$ $\frac{3}{9}$

Name Date Time

Fraction Match Cards *continued*

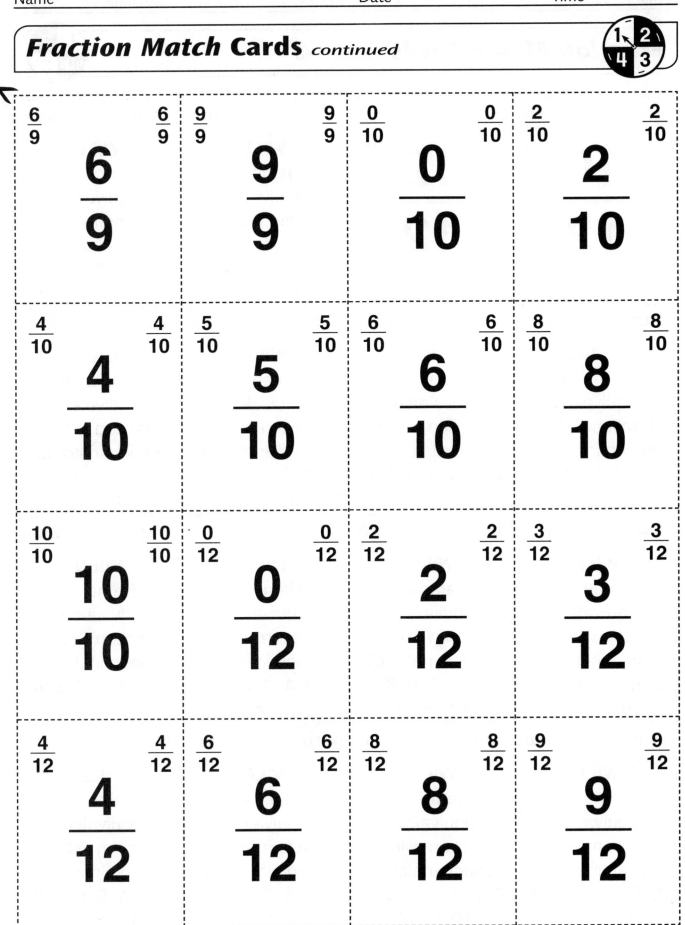

$\frac{6}{9}$ $\frac{6}{9}$ $\frac{6}{9}$	$\frac{9}{9}$ $\frac{9}{9}$ $\frac{9}{9}$	$\frac{0}{10}$ $\frac{0}{10}$ $\frac{0}{10}$	$\frac{2}{10}$ $\frac{2}{10}$ $\frac{2}{10}$
$\frac{4}{10}$ $\frac{4}{10}$ $\frac{4}{10}$	$\frac{5}{10}$ $\frac{5}{10}$ $\frac{5}{10}$	$\frac{6}{10}$ $\frac{6}{10}$ $\frac{6}{10}$	$\frac{8}{10}$ $\frac{8}{10}$ $\frac{8}{10}$
$\frac{10}{10}$ $\frac{10}{10}$ $\frac{10}{10}$	$\frac{0}{12}$ $\frac{0}{12}$ $\frac{0}{12}$	$\frac{2}{12}$ $\frac{2}{12}$ $\frac{2}{12}$	$\frac{3}{12}$ $\frac{3}{12}$ $\frac{3}{12}$
$\frac{4}{12}$ $\frac{4}{12}$ $\frac{4}{12}$	$\frac{6}{12}$ $\frac{6}{12}$ $\frac{6}{12}$	$\frac{8}{12}$ $\frac{8}{12}$ $\frac{8}{12}$	$\frac{9}{12}$ $\frac{9}{12}$ $\frac{9}{12}$

Name Date Time

Fraction Match Cards *continued*

$\frac{10}{12}$ $\frac{10}{12}$ $$\frac{10}{12}$$	$\frac{12}{12}$ $\frac{12}{12}$ $$\frac{12}{12}$$	WILD WILD **WILD** Name an equivalent fraction with a denominator of 2, 3, 4, 5, 6, 8, 9, 10, or 12.	WILD WILD **WILD** Name an equivalent fraction with a denominator of 2, 3, 4, 5, 6, 8, 9, 10, or 12.
WILD WILD **WILD** Name an equivalent fraction with a denominator of 2, 3, 4, 5, 6, 8, 9, 10, or 12.	WILD WILD **WILD** Name an equivalent fraction with a denominator of 2, 3, 4, 5, 6, 8, 9, 10, or 12.	WILD WILD **WILD** Name an equivalent fraction with a denominator of 2, 3, 4, 5, 6, 8, 9, 10, or 12.	WILD WILD **WILD** Name an equivalent fraction with a denominator of 2, 3, 4, 5, 6, 8, 9, 10, or 12.
WILD WILD **WILD** Name an equivalent fraction with a denominator of 2, 3, 4, 5, 6, 8, 9, 10, or 12.	WILD WILD **WILD** Name an equivalent fraction with a denominator of 2, 3, 4, 5, 6, 8, 9, 10, or 12.	WILD WILD **WILD** Name an equivalent fraction with a denominator of 2, 3, 4, 5, 6, 8, 9, 10, or 12.	WILD WILD **WILD** Name an equivalent fraction with a denominator of 2, 3, 4, 5, 6, 8, 9, 10, or 12.
WILD WILD **WILD** Name an equivalent fraction with a denominator of 2, 3, 4, 5, 6, 8, 9, 10, or 12.	WILD WILD **WILD** Name an equivalent fraction with a denominator of 2, 3, 4, 5, 6, 8, 9, 10, or 12.	WILD WILD **WILD** Name an equivalent fraction with a denominator of 2, 3, 4, 5, 6, 8, 9, 10, or 12.	WILD WILD **WILD** Name an equivalent fraction with a denominator of 2, 3, 4, 5, 6, 8, 9, 10, or 12.

Name Date Time

Fraction Of Fraction Cards

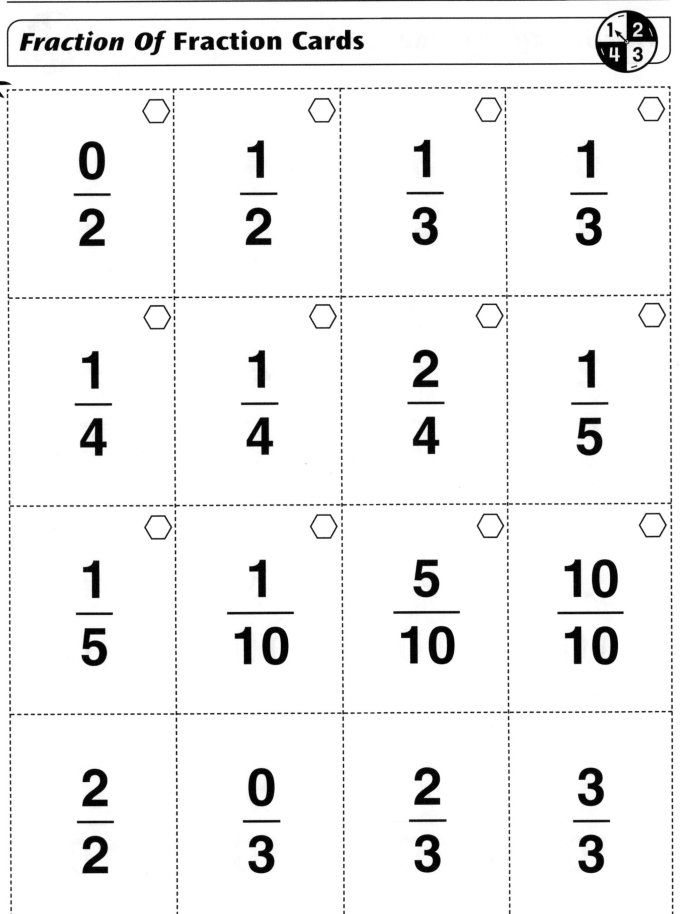

$\frac{0}{2}$	$\frac{1}{2}$	$\frac{1}{3}$	$\frac{1}{3}$
$\frac{1}{4}$	$\frac{1}{4}$	$\frac{2}{4}$	$\frac{1}{5}$
$\frac{1}{5}$	$\frac{1}{10}$	$\frac{5}{10}$	$\frac{10}{10}$
$\frac{2}{2}$	$\frac{0}{3}$	$\frac{2}{3}$	$\frac{3}{3}$

Name Date Time

Fraction Of Fraction Cards *continued*

$\frac{0}{4}$	$\frac{3}{4}$	$\frac{4}{4}$	$\frac{0}{5}$
$\frac{2}{5}$	$\frac{3}{5}$	$\frac{4}{5}$	$\frac{5}{5}$
$\frac{0}{10}$	$\frac{2}{10}$	$\frac{3}{10}$	$\frac{4}{10}$
$\frac{6}{10}$	$\frac{7}{10}$	$\frac{8}{10}$	$\frac{9}{10}$

Name Date Time

Fraction Of Gameboard and Record Sheet

Fraction card

of

WHOLE
(Choose 1 of these sets.)

Set card

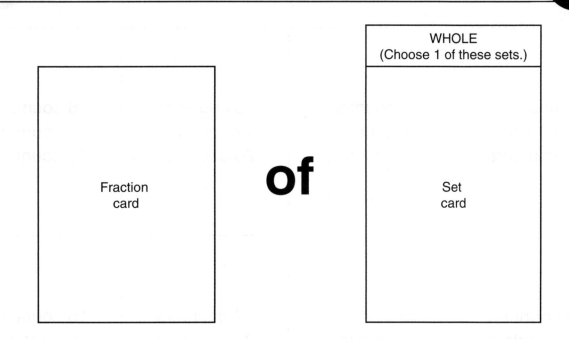

Round	"Fraction-of" Problem	Points
Sample	$\frac{1}{5}$ of 25	5
1		
2		
3		
4		
5		
6		
7		
8		
	Total Score	

Name Date Time

Fraction Of Set Cards

3 counters 20 counters 15 counters	4 counters 21 counters 30 counters	5 counters 12 counters 20 counters	6 counters 28 counters 40 counters
8 counters 27 counters 20 counters	10 counters 32 counters 24 counters	12 counters 30 counters 25 counters	15 counters 36 counters 20 counters
18 counters 36 counters 10 counters	20 counters 4 counters 3 counters	21 counters 30 counters 24 counters	25 counters 6 counters 40 counters
28 counters 35 counters 30 counters	30 counters 32 counters 15 counters	36 counters 20 counters 24 counters	40 counters 18 counters 25 counters

Name Date Time

Fraction/Percent Concentration

10%	20%	25%	30%
40%	50%	60%	70%
75%	80%	90%	100%
$\frac{1}{2}$	$\frac{1}{4}$	$\frac{3}{4}$	$\frac{1}{5}$
$\frac{2}{5}$	$\frac{3}{5}$	$\frac{4}{5}$	$\frac{1}{10}$
$\frac{3}{10}$	$\frac{7}{10}$	$\frac{9}{10}$	$\frac{2}{2}$

Name Date Time

Fraction/Percent Concentration *continued*

0.10	0.20	0.25	0.30
0.40	0.50	0.60	0.70
0.80	0.75	0.90	1

0.10	0.20	0.25	0.30
0.40	0.50	0.60	0.70
0.80	0.75	0.90	1

Name Date Time

Grab Bag Cards

Lina has a bag of ribbons. She has 2 red, 2 blue, x pink, and y green ribbons.

What are the chances she will pick a green ribbon without looking?

Mario has a bag of art pencils. He has 3 purple, 1 white, x violet, and y yellow pencils.

What are the chances he will pick a yellow pencil without looking?

Kenji has a bag of marbles. He has 6 striped, 1 clear, x solid, and y swirl marbles.

What are the chances he will pick a swirl marble without looking?

There are 2 red, 2 white, x black, and y brown beans in a bag.

Without looking, what are the chances of picking a brown bean?

There are 3 clear, 3 blue, x white, and y orange beads in a bag.

Without looking, what are the chances of picking an orange bead?

There are 5 lemon, 2 strawberry, x cherry, and y grape lollipops in a bag.

Without looking, what are the chances of picking a grape lollipop?

A bag of markers has 1 yellow, 2 green, x pink, and y blue markers.

Without looking, Kendra picks a blue marker and then returns it to the bag.

Without looking, what is the probability that Kendra will pick a blue marker again?

A bag of erasers has 3 pink, 3 white, x blue, and y red erasers.

Without looking, Cyrus picks a red eraser and returns it to the bag.

Without looking, what is the probability that Cyrus will pick a red eraser again?

A bag of buttons has 2 green, 3 gray, x black, and y white.

Without looking, Amir picks a white button and returns it to the bag.

Without looking, what is the probability that Amir will pick a white button again?

Name Date Time

Grab Bag Cards *continued*

Rosa has a bag of 2 red, 6 green, x white, and y blue centimeter cubes.

If she picks one out of the bag without looking, what is the probability that it will be a blue centimeter cube?

Ingrid has a bag of 3 red, 5 green, x blue, and y yellow flag stickers.

If she picks one out of the bag without looking, what is the probability that it will be a yellow flag sticker?

Boris has a bag of 1 red, 5 black, x orange, and y green toy cars.

If he picks one out of the bag without looking, what is the probability that it will be a green car?

Jesse has a bag of painted blocks: 2 with flowers, 3 with leaves, x with animals, and y with dots.

Without looking, what is the probability he will pull a block with dots from the bag?

Victor has a bag of family photos: 3 of his parents, 4 of his brothers, x of his cousins, and y of his grandma.

Without looking, what is the probability he will pull a picture of his grandma from the bag?

Simone has a bag of playing cards: 1 diamond, 4 hearts, x spades, and y clubs.

Without looking, what is the probability she will pull a club from the bag?

There are 1 green, 2 blue, x red, and y yellow paper clips in a bag.

Without looking, what are the chances of picking a yellow paper clip?

There are 3 orange, 2 blue, x green, and y pink dice in a bag.

Without looking, what are the chances of picking a pink die?

There are 2 green, 2 purple, x gold, and y silver crayons in a bag.

Without looking, what are the chances of picking a silver crayon?

Name Date Time

Grab Bag Record Sheet

Round	Number of Items Shown on Card		x	y	Total Number of Items in Bag	Probability of Event Occurring	Score
Sample	2	2	1	6 + 4 = 10	15	$\frac{10}{15}$	30
1							
2							
3							
4							
5							
						Total Score	

Name Date Time

Grab Bag Record Sheet

Round	Number of Items Shown on Card		x	y	Total Number of Items in Bag	Probability of Event Occurring	Score
Sample	2	2	1	6 + 4 = 10	15	$\frac{10}{15}$	30
1							
2							
3							
4							
5							
						Total Score	

Name Date Time

Grid Search Grids

Use Grids 1 and 2 to play a game.

SRB 250 251

My Pieces
(Grid 1)

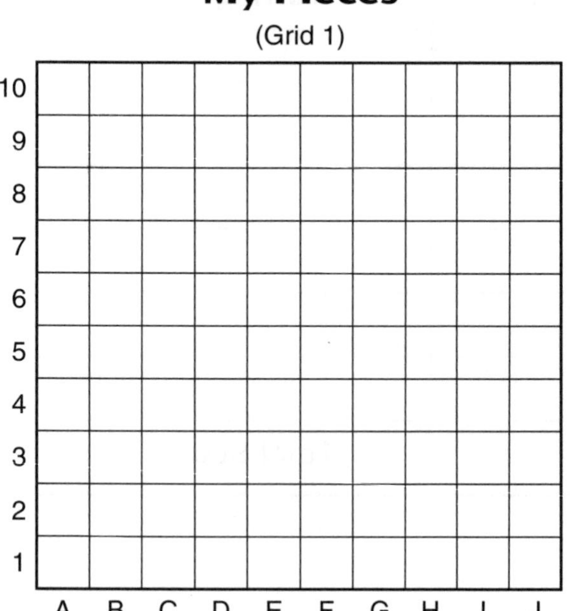

Opponent's Pieces
(Grid 2)

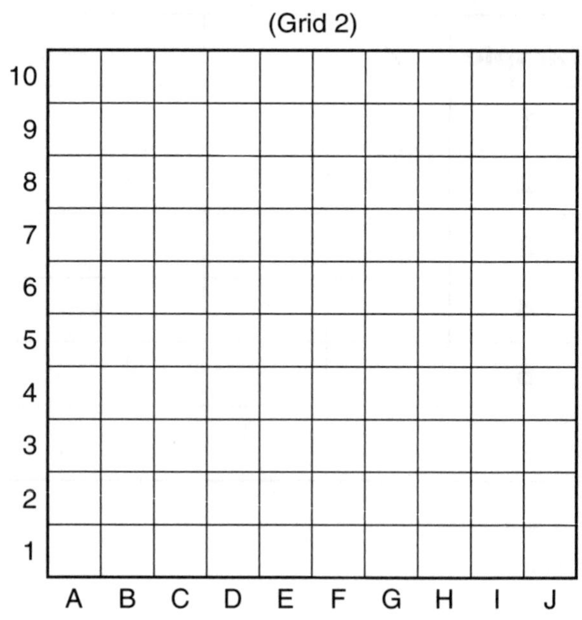

Use Grids 1 and 2 to play another game.

My Pieces
(Grid 1)

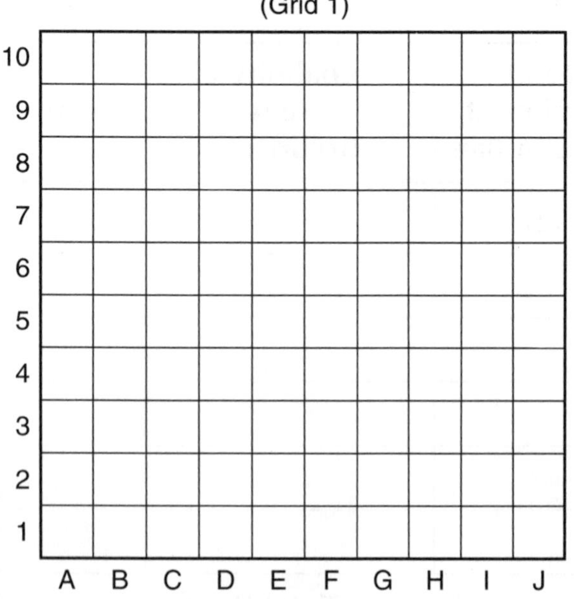

Opponent's Pieces
(Grid 2)

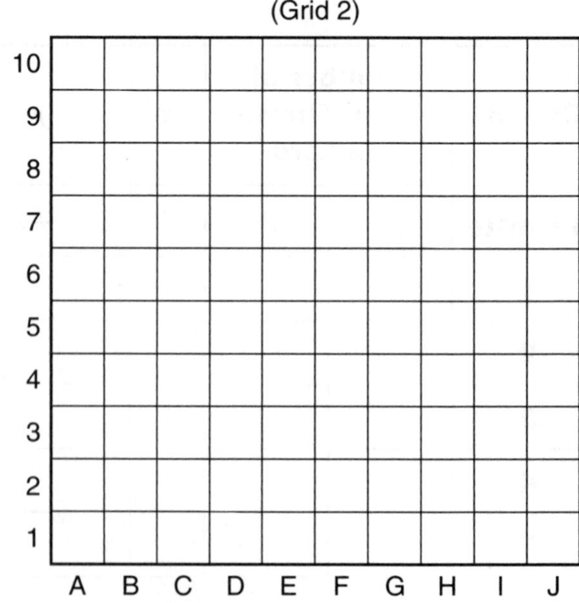

Name Date Time

High-Number Toss Record Sheet

Hundred Millions	Ten Millions	Millions	,	Hundred Thousands	Ten Thousands	Thousands	,	Hundreds	Tens	Ones

Round	Player 1	>, <, =	Player 2
Sample	1 3 2 , 6 132,000,000	>	3 5 6 , 4 3,560,000
1	___ ___ ___ , ___ __________		___ ___ ___ , ___ __________
2	___ ___ ___ , ___ __________		___ ___ ___ , ___ __________
3	___ ___ ___ , ___ __________		___ ___ ___ , ___ __________
4	___ ___ ___ , ___ __________		___ ___ ___ , ___ __________
5	___ ___ ___ , ___ __________		___ ___ ___ , ___ __________

Name _______________ Date _______________ Time _______________

Multiplication Wrestling Record Sheet

Round 1 Cards: ________ ________ ________ ________

Numbers formed: ________ * ________

Teams: (________ + ________) * (________ + ________)

Products: ________ * ________ = ________

________ * ________ = ________

________ * ________ = ________

________ * ________ = ________

Total (add 4 products): ________

Round 2 Cards: ________ ________ ________ ________

Numbers formed: ________ * ________

Teams: (________ + ________) * (________ + ________)

Products: ________ * ________ = ________

________ * ________ = ________

________ * ________ = ________

________ * ________ = ________

Total (add 4 products): ________

Round 3 Cards: ________ ________ ________ ________

Numbers formed: ________ * ________

Teams: (________ + ________) * (________ + ________)

Products: ________ * ________ = ________

________ * ________ = ________

________ * ________ = ________

________ * ________ = ________

Total (add 4 products): ________

Name _______________ Date _______________ Time _______________

Name That Number Record Sheet

Round 1

Target Number: ________ My Cards: ______ ______ ______ ______ ______ ______

My best solution (number sentence): ______________________________

Number of cards used: __________

Round 2

Target Number: ________ My Cards: ______ ______ ______ ______ ______ ______

My best solution (number sentence): ______________________________

Number of cards used: __________

Name _______________ Date _______________ Time _______________

Name That Number Record Sheet

Round 1

Target Number: ________ My Cards: ______ ______ ______ ______ ______ ______

My best solution (number sentence): ______________________________

Number of cards used: __________

Round 2

Target Number: ________ My Cards: ______ ______ ______ ______ ______ ______

My best solution (number sentence): ______________________________

Number of cards used: __________

Name Date Time

Number Top-It Mat (2-Place Decimals)

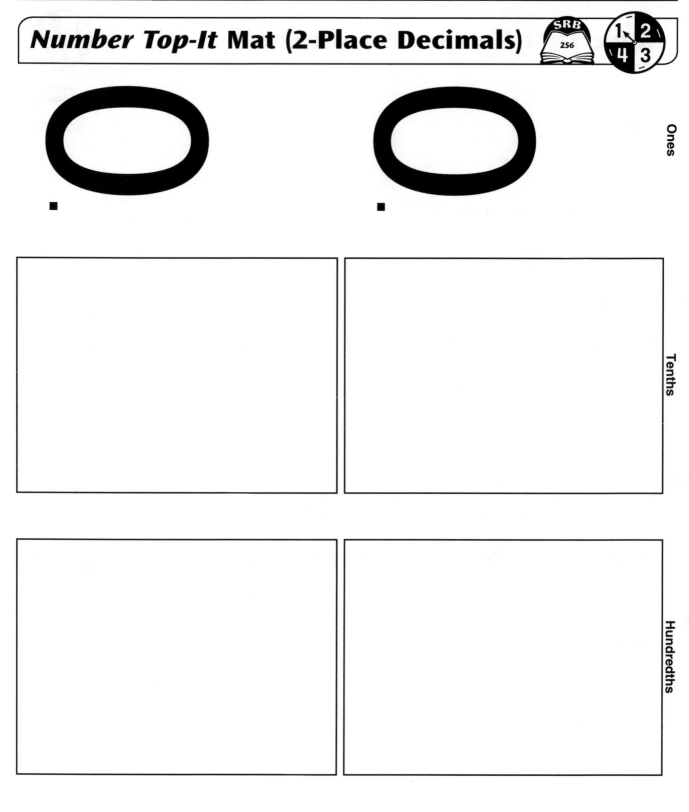

Ones

Tenths

Hundredths

Name Date Time

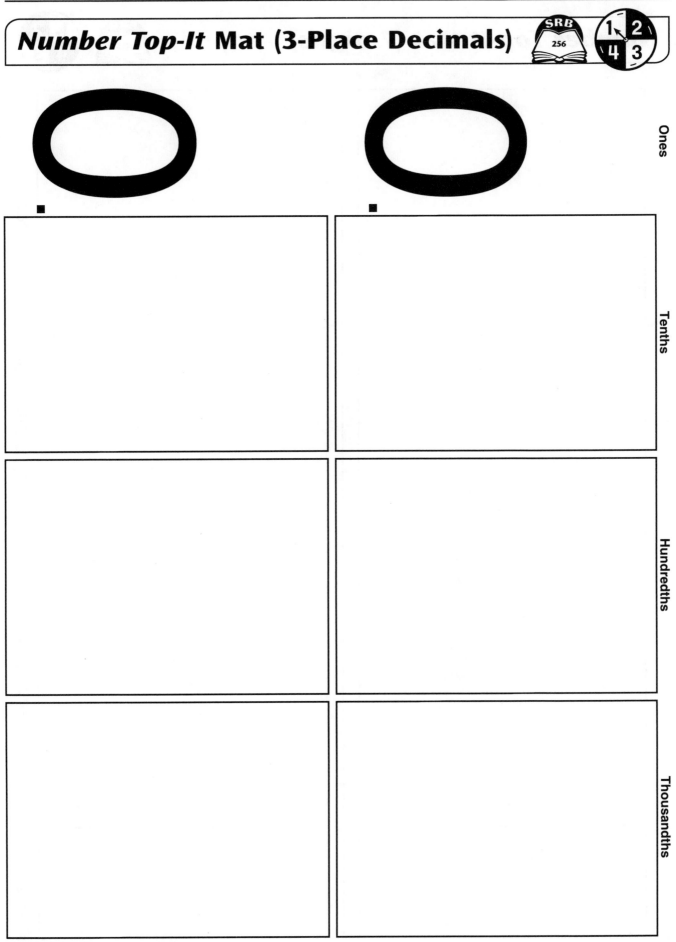

Number Top-It Mat (3-Place Decimals)

0 . 0 .

Ones

Tenths

Hundredths

Thousandths

Name Date Time

Number Top-It Mat (7-digits)

Millions

,

,

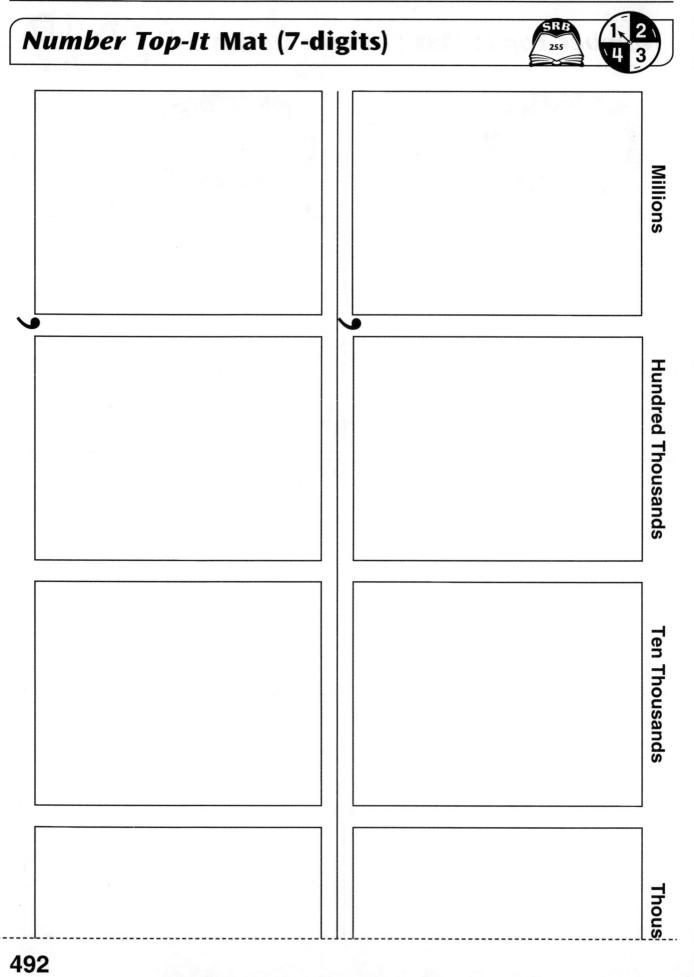

Hundred Thousands

Ten Thousands

Thous

Name Date Time

Number Top-It Mat (7-digits) *continued*

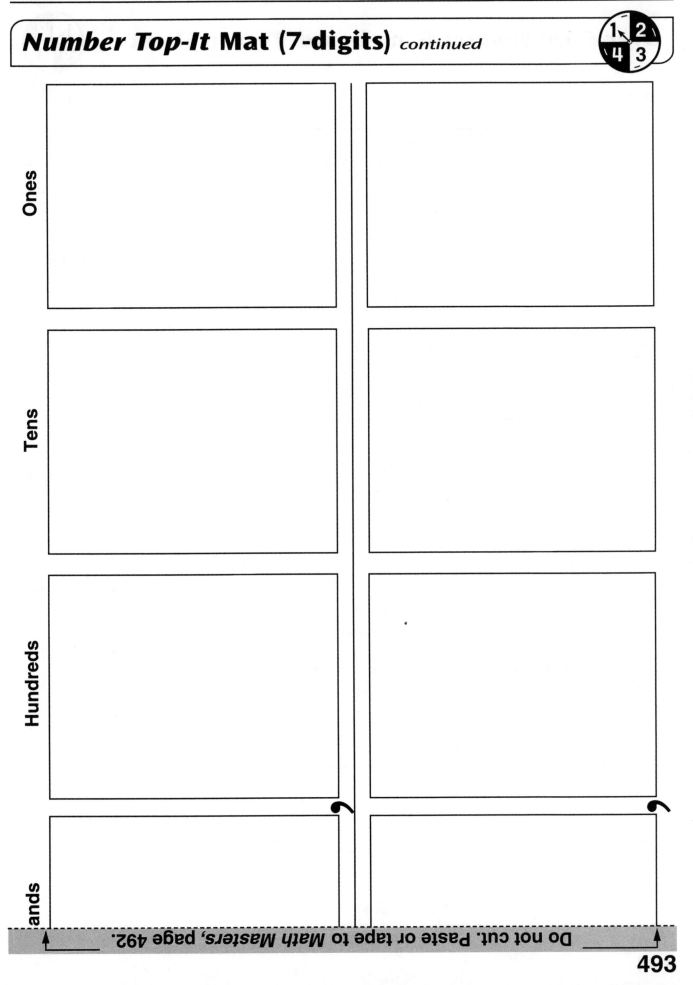

Ones

Tens

Hundreds

ands

Do not cut. Paste or tape to *Math Masters*, page 492.

Name Date Time

Over & Up Squares Gameboard/Record Sheet

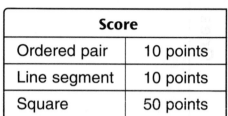

Player 1: ______________________________

Round	Over *x*-coordinate	,	Up *y*-coordinate	Score
1		,		
2		,		
3		,		
4		,		
5		,		
6		,		
7		,		
8		,		
9		,		
10		,		
			Total Score	

Score	
Ordered pair	10 points
Line segment	10 points
Square	50 points

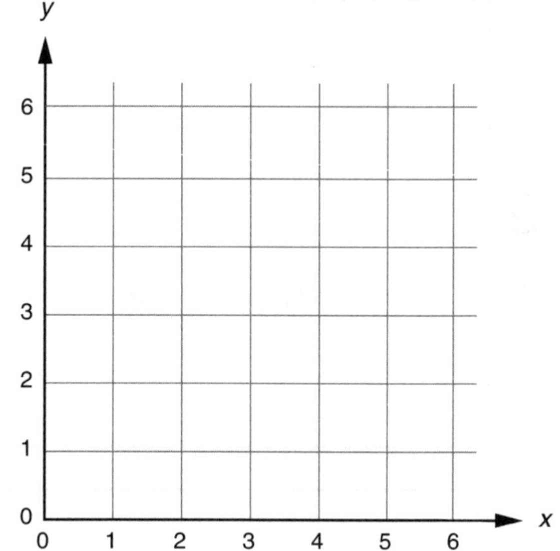

Player 2: ______________________________

Round	Over *x*-coordinate	,	Up *y*-coordinate	Score
1		,		
2		,		
3		,		
4		,		
5		,		
6		,		
7		,		
8		,		
9		,		
10		,		
			Total Score	

Name Date Time

Patolli Game Mat

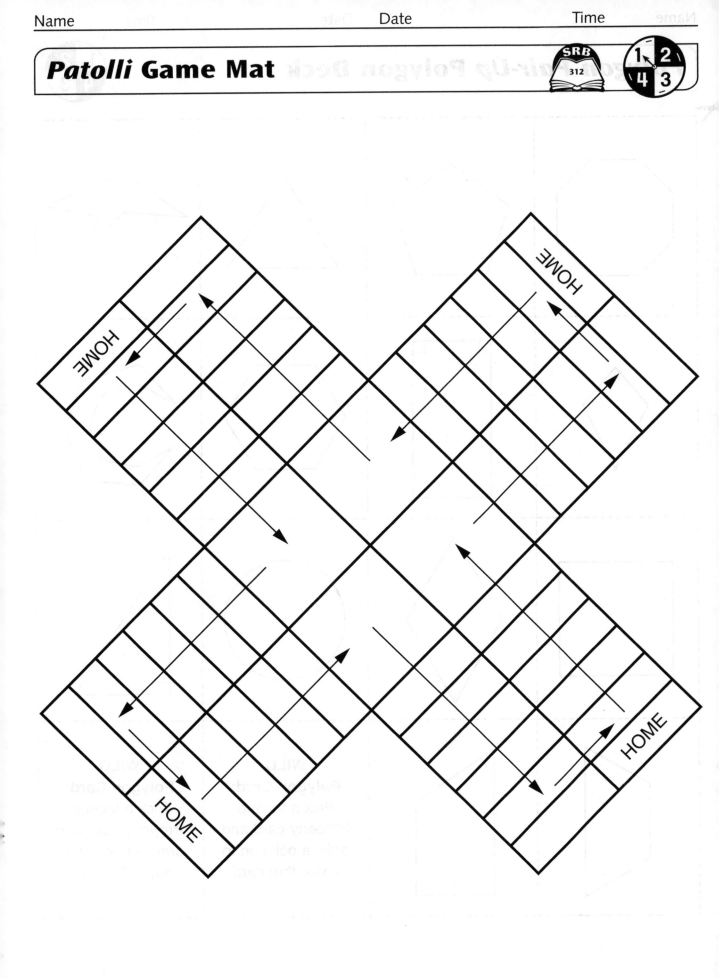

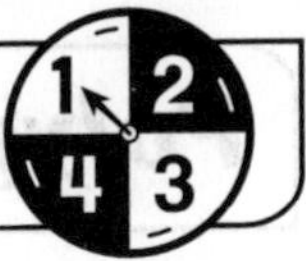

HOME

HOME

HOME

HOME

Name Date Time

Polygon Pair-Up Polygon Deck

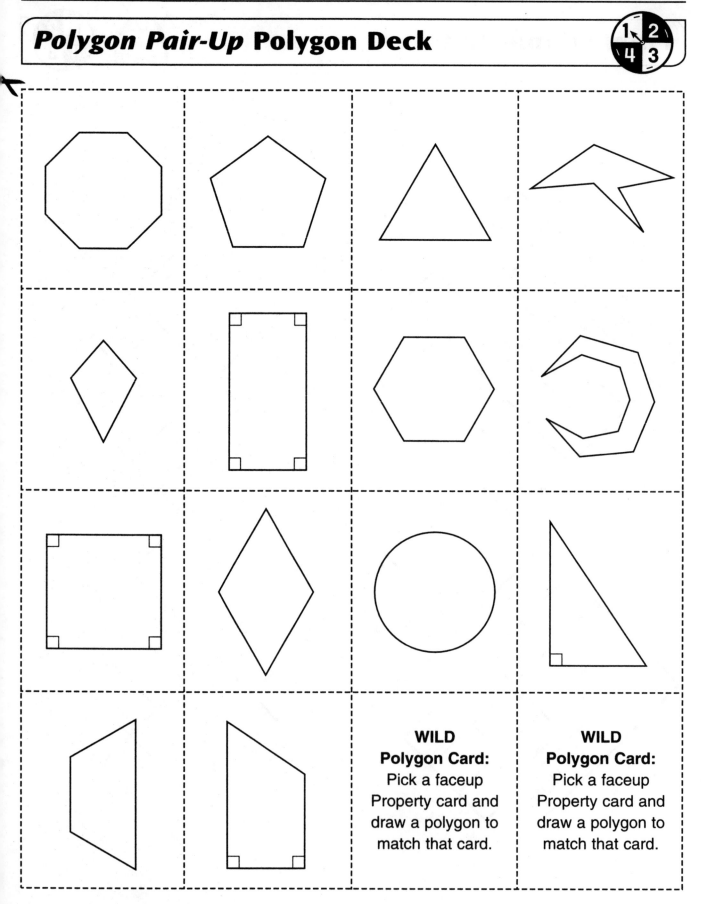

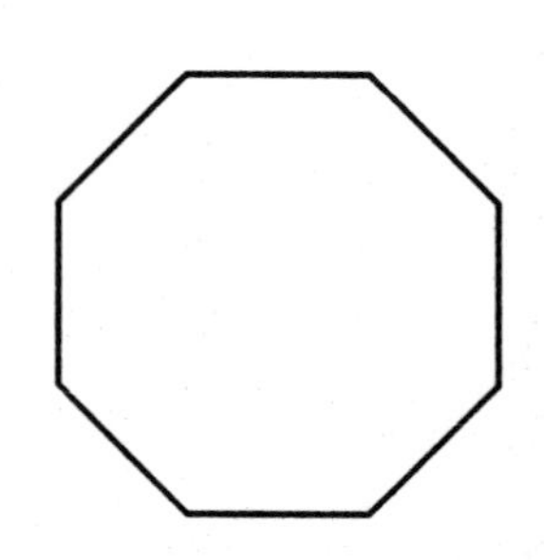

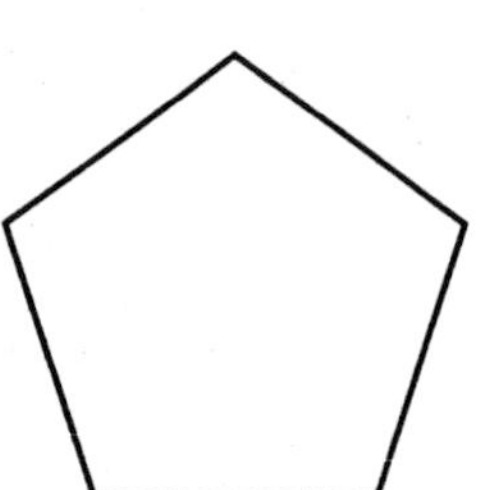

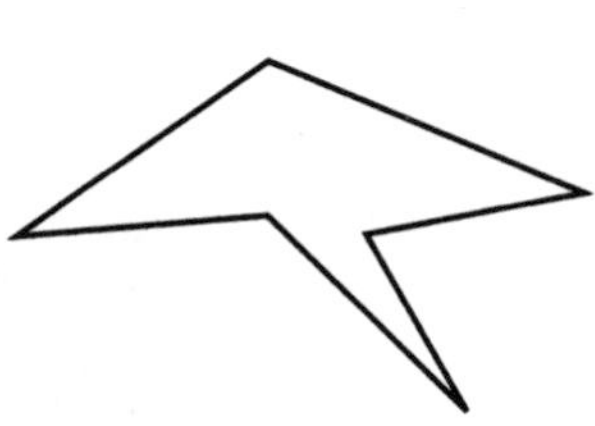

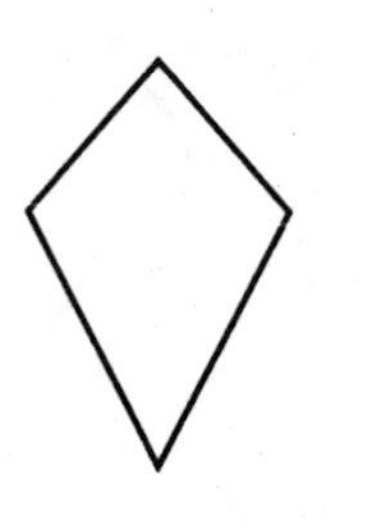

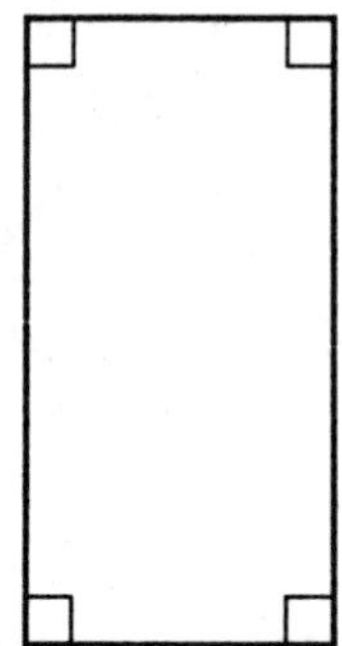

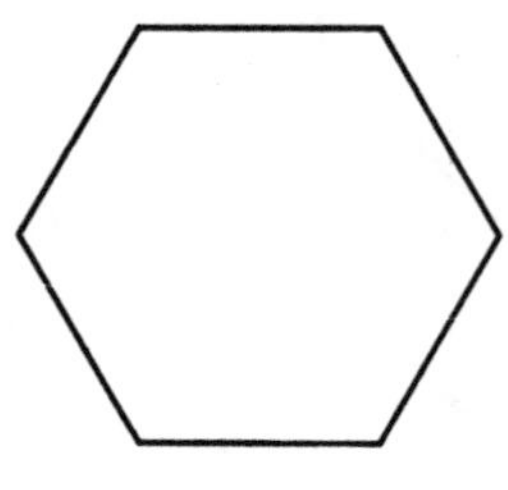

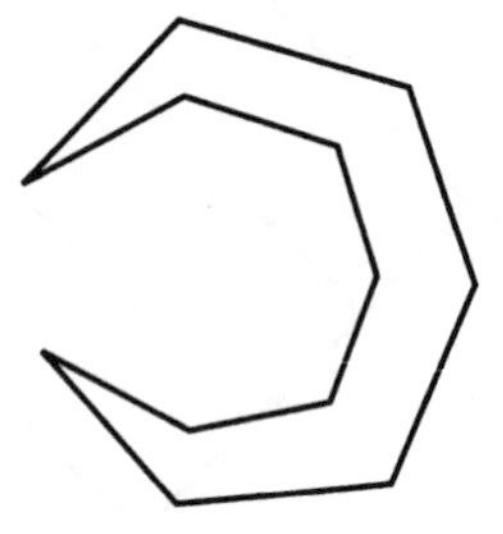

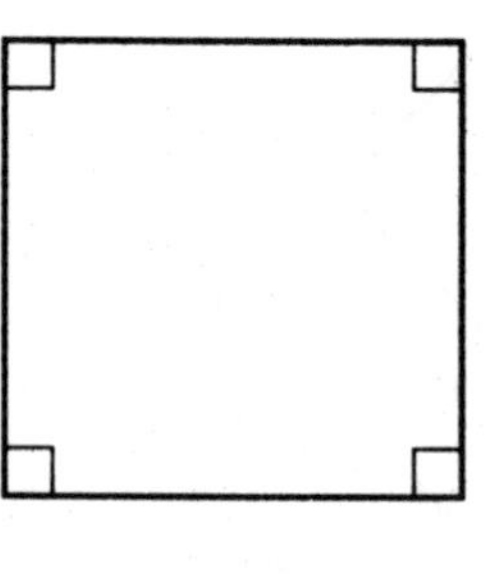

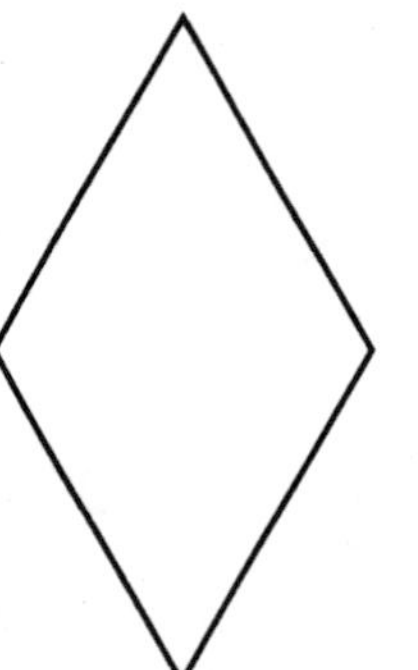

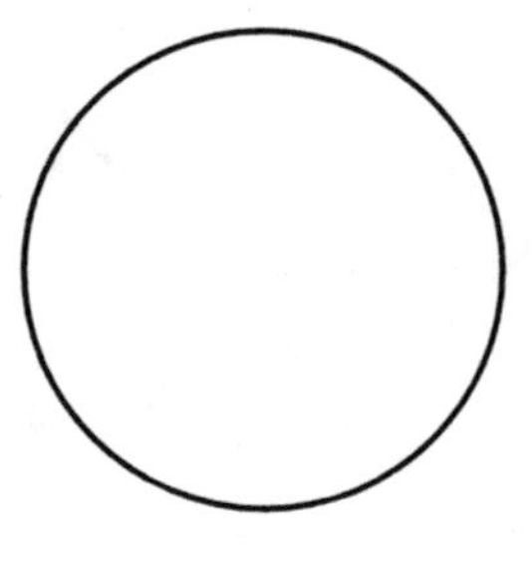

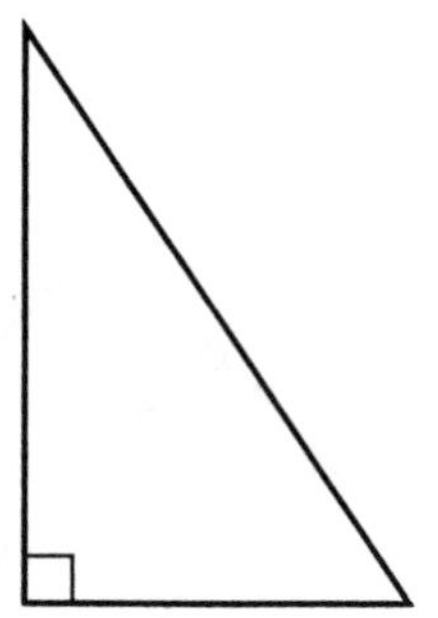

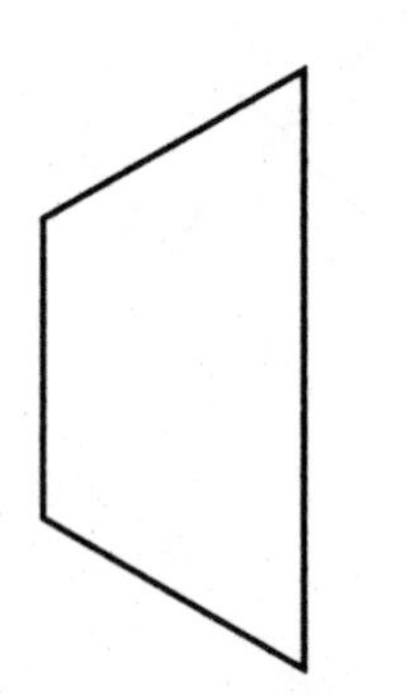

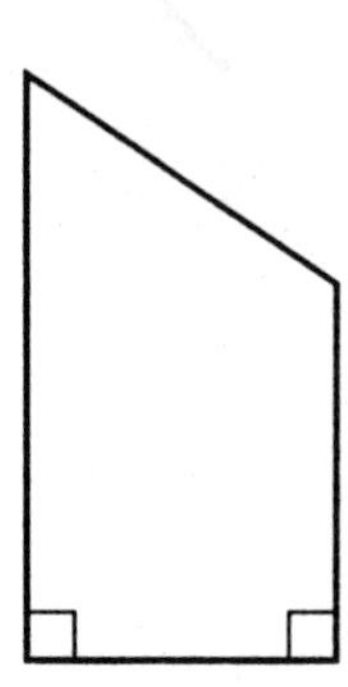

WILD
Polygon Card:
Pick a faceup Property card and draw a polygon to match that card.

WILD
Polygon Card:
Pick a faceup Property card and draw a polygon to match that card.

Name Date Time

Polygon Pair-Up Property Deck

All sides are the same length.	All opposite sides are parallel.	All angles are right angles.	There are more than 4 sides.
There are 4 sides of equal length.	There is only 1 right angle.	There are 2 pairs of parallel sides.	This shape is NOT a polygon.
There are only 3 vertices.	There is only 1 pair of parallel sides.	There are only 4 sides.	This polygon is concave.
There are 4 equal sides and 4 equal angles.	Pairs of sides next to each other have the same length. There are no parallel sides.	**WILD Property Card:** Pick a faceup Polygon card and name a property to match that card.	**WILD Property Card:** Pick a faceup Polygon card and name a property to match that card.

Name Date Time

Rugs and Fences Area and Perimeter Deck

A Find the area of the polygon.	**A** Find the area of the polygon.	**A** Find the area of the polygon.	**A** Find the area of the polygon.
P Find the perimeter of the polygon.	**P** Find the perimeter of the polygon.	**P** Find the perimeter of the polygon.	**P** Find the perimeter of the polygon.
A or P Opponent's Choice	**A or P** Opponent's Choice	**A or P** Opponent's Choice	**A or P** Opponent's Choice
A or P Player's Choice	**A or P** Player's Choice	**A or P** Player's Choice	**A or P** Player's Choice

Name Date Time

Rugs and Fences Polygon Deck A

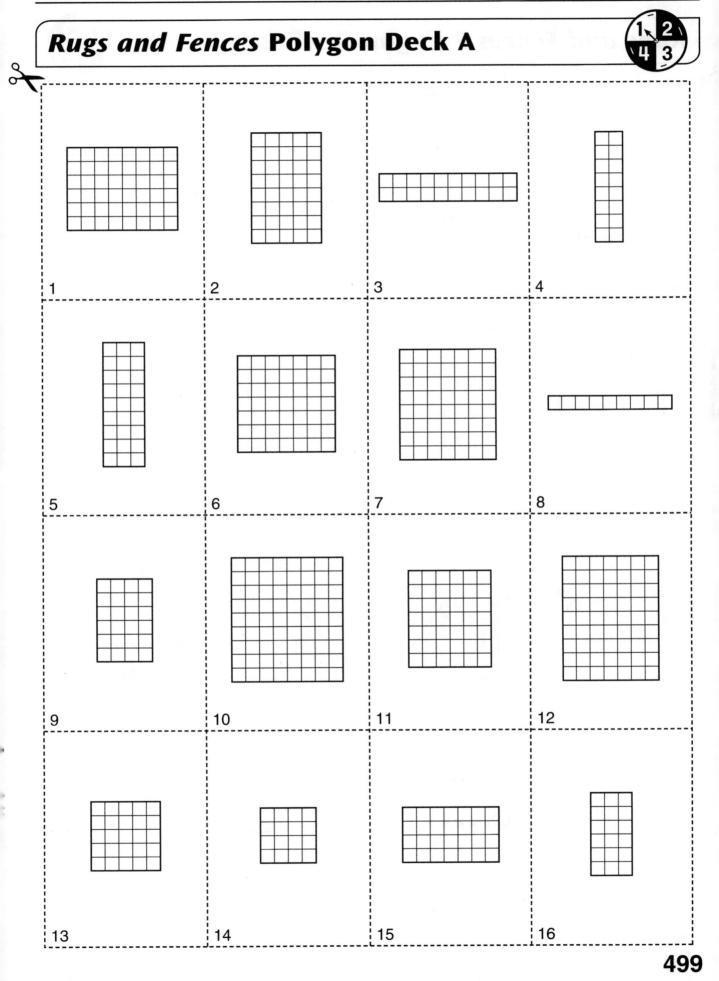

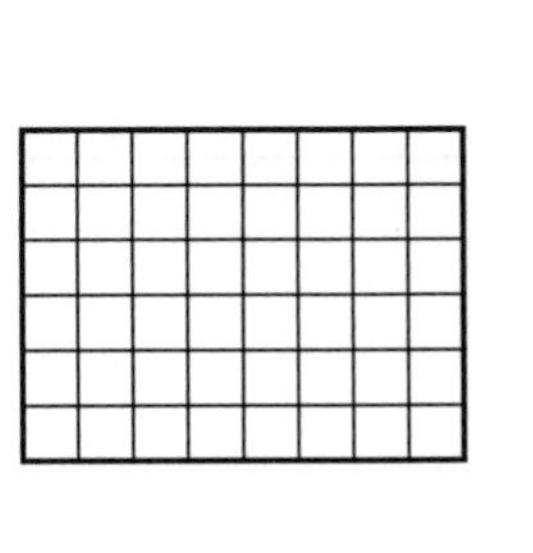

1

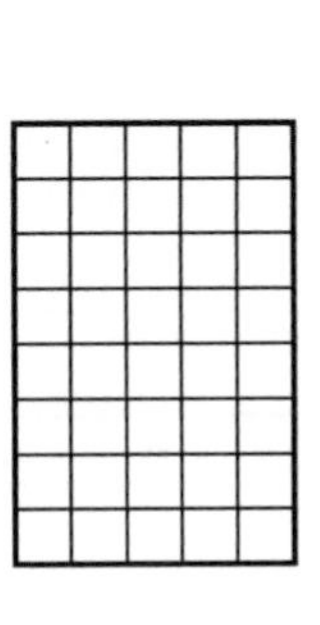

2

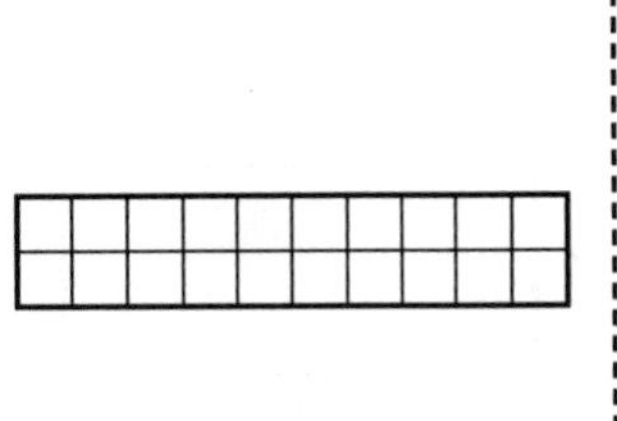

3

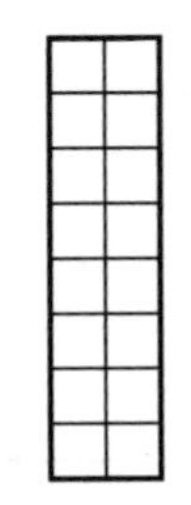

4

5

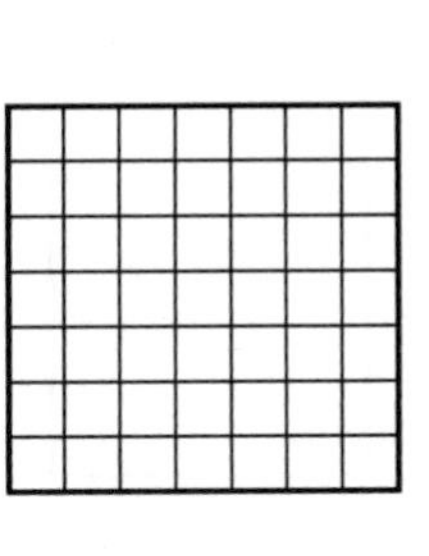

6

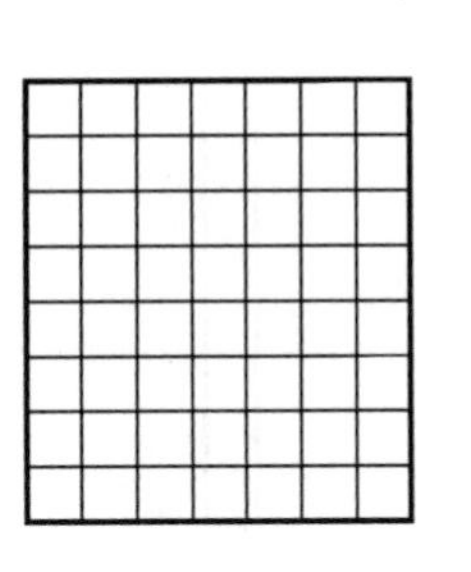

7

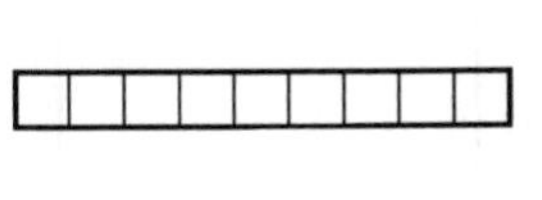

8

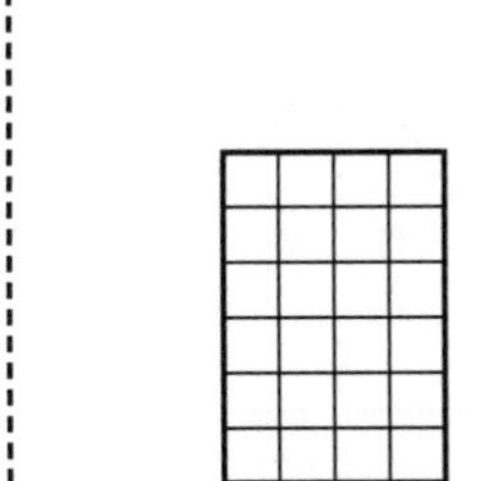

9

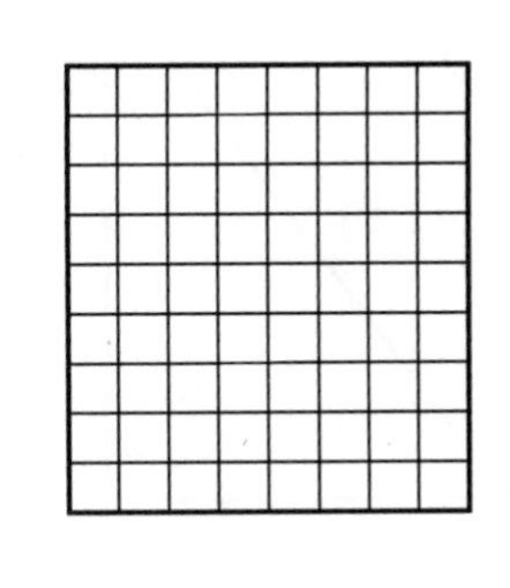

10

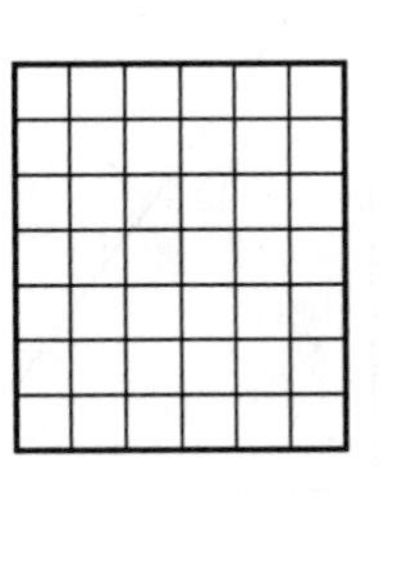

11

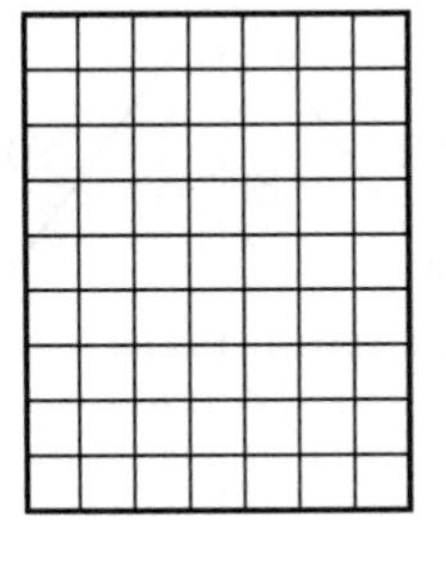

12

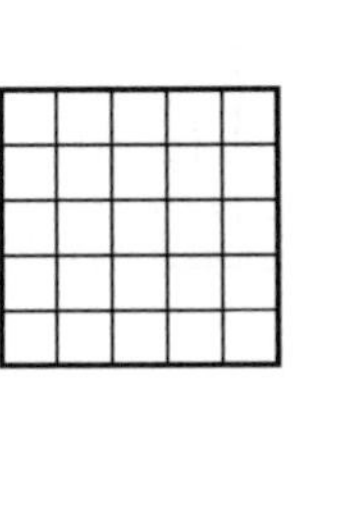

13

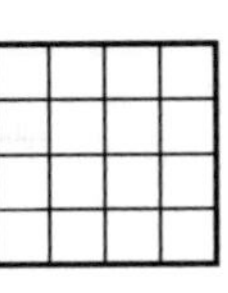

14

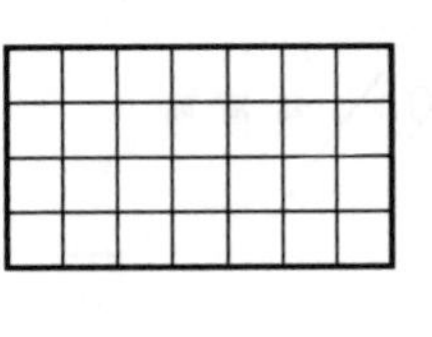

15

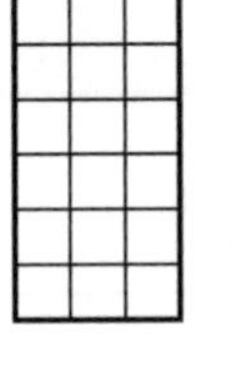

16

Name Date Time

Rugs and Fences Polygon Deck B

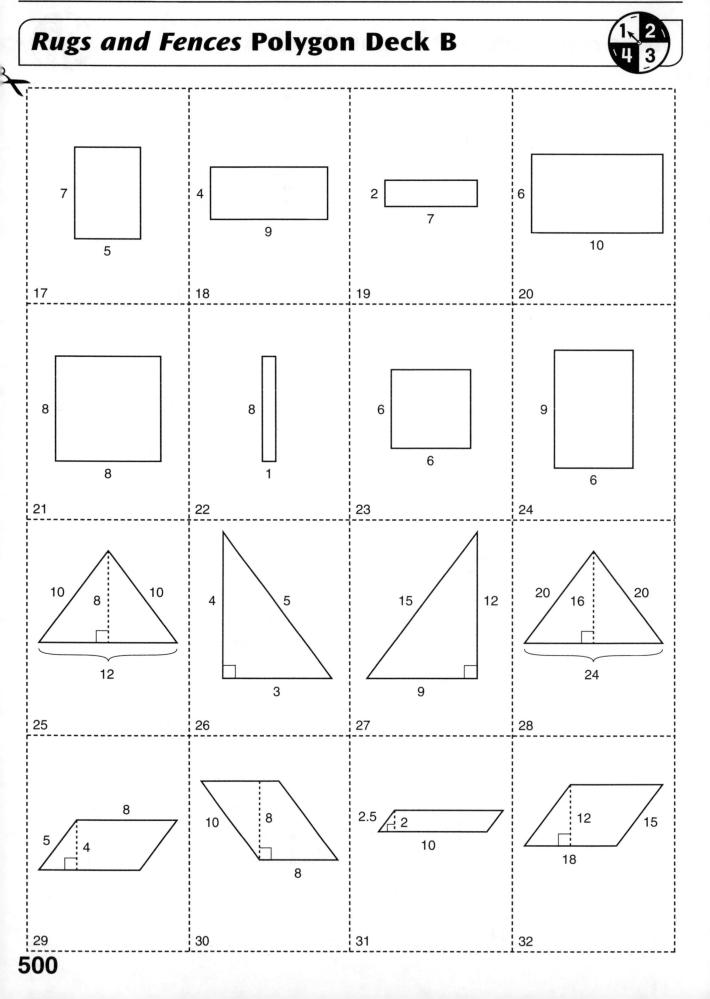

7, 5 — 17	4, 9 — 18	2, 7 — 19	6, 10 — 20
8, 8 — 21	8, 1 — 22	6, 6 — 23	9, 6 — 24
10, 10, 8, 12 — 25	4, 5, 3 — 26	15, 12, 9 — 27	20, 20, 16, 24 — 28
8, 5, 4 — 29	10, 8, 8 — 30	2.5, 2, 10 — 31	12, 15, 18 — 32

Name Date Time

Rugs and Fences Polygon Deck C

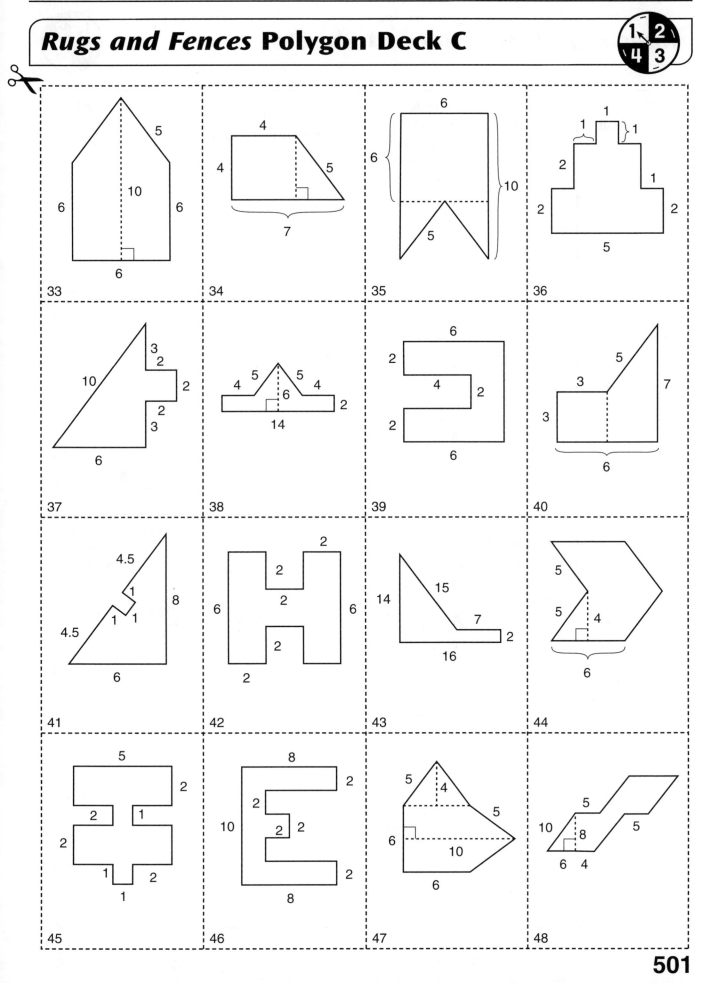

33

34

35

36

37

38

39

40

41

42

43

44

45

46

47

48

Name Date Time

Rugs and Fences Record Sheets

Round	Record the card number	Circle A (area) or P (perimeter)	Write a number model	Record your score
Sample	3	A or (P)	10 + 10 + 2 + 2 = 24	24
1		A or P		
2		A or P		
3		A or P		
4		A or P		
5		A or P		
6		A or P		
7		A or P		
8		A or P		
			Total Score	

Round	Record the card number	Circle A (area) or P (perimeter)	Write a number model	Record your score
Sample	3	A or (P)	10 + 10 + 2 + 2 = 24	24
1		A or P		
2		A or P		
3		A or P		
4		A or P		
5		A or P		
6		A or P		
7		A or P		
8		A or P		
			Total Score	

Name Date Time

Seega Game Mat

Player 1

Player 2

Name Date Time

Subtraction Target Practice Record Sheet

Turn	2-Digit Number	Subtraction
1		
2		
3		
4		
5		

Name Date Time

Subtraction Target Practice Record Sheet

Turn	2-Digit Number	Subtraction
1		
2		
3		
4		
5		

Name Date Time

Sz'kwa Game Mat

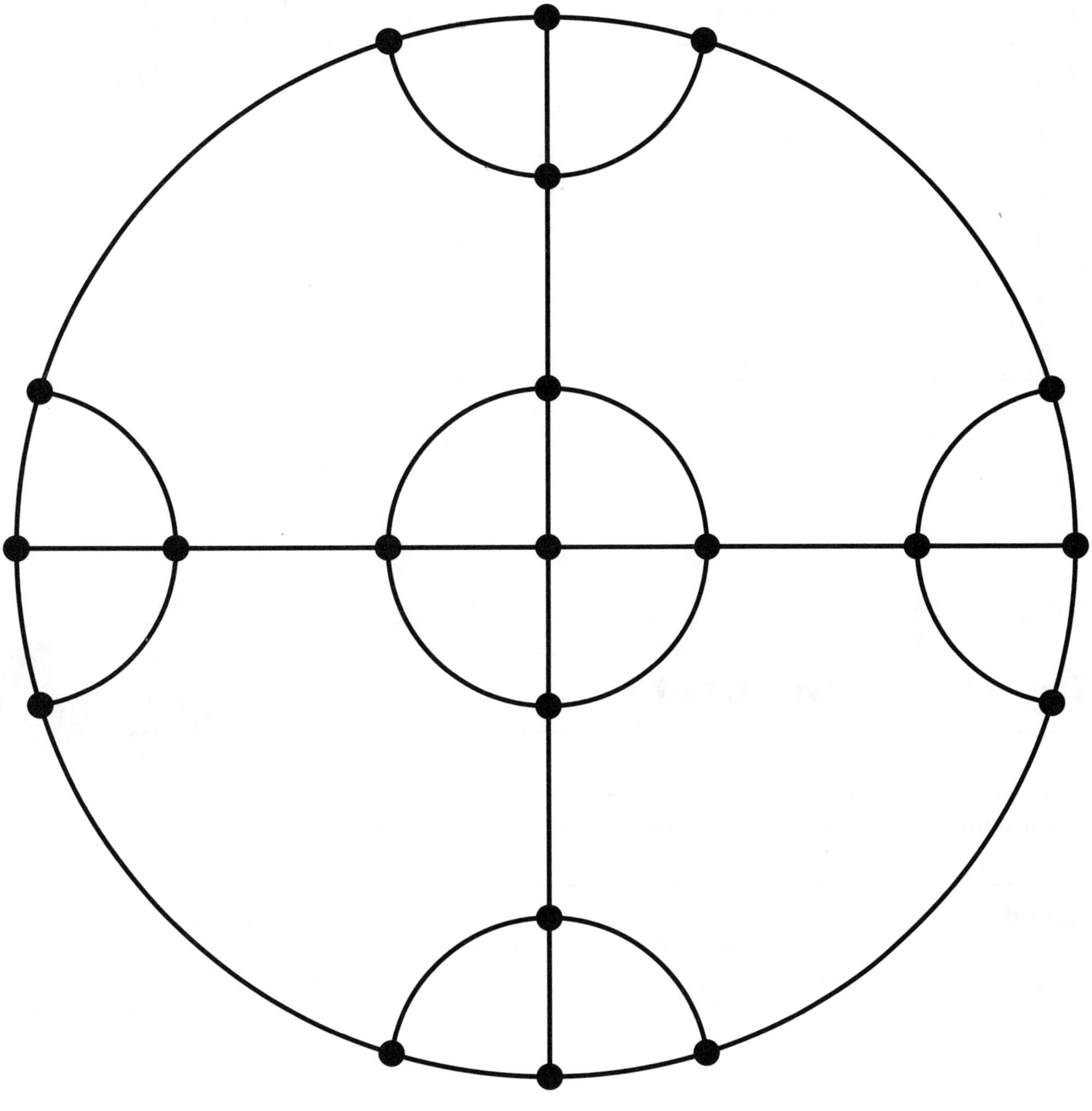

Name Date Time

Top-It Record Sheet

Play a round of *Top-It.* Record your number sentence and your opponent's number sentence. Write >, <, or = to compare the number sentences.

Round	Player 1	>, <, =	Player 2
Sample	4 + 6 = 10	<	8 + 3 = 11
1			
2			
3			
4			
5			

Name Date Time

Top-It Record Sheet

Play a round of *Top-It.* Record your number sentence and your opponent's number sentence. Write >, <, or = to compare the number sentences.

Round	Player 1	>, <, =	Player 2
Sample	4 + 6 = 10	<	8 + 3 = 11
1			
2			
3			
4			
5